Data Networks

Routing, Security, and Performance Optimization

Tony Kenyon

Digital Press
An imprint of Elsevier Science
Amsterdam • Boston • London • New York • Oxford • Paris • San Diego
San Francisco • Singapore • Sydney • Tokyo

Digital Press is an imprint of Elsevier Science.

 Recognizing the importance of preserving what has been written, Elsevier Science prints its books on acid-free paper whenever possible.

Library of Congress Cataloging-in-Publication Data

Kenyon, Tony, 1960–
    Data networks : routing, security, and performance optimization / Tony Kenyon.
      p. cm.
    Includes bibliographical references and index.
    ISBN 1-55558-271-0 (pbk. : alk. paper)
      1. Routers (Computer networks) 2. Computer networks—Security measures. 3. High performance computing. I. Title.

    TK5105.543 .K46 2002
    004.6--dc21
                                              2002019364

British Library Cataloguing-in-Publication Data

A catalogue record for this book is available from the British Library.

The publisher offers special discounts on bulk orders of this book.

For information, please contact:

Manager of Special Sales
Elsevier Science
225 Wildwood Avenue
Woburn, MA 01801-2041
Tel: 781-904-2500
Fax: 781-904-2620

For information on all Digital Press publications available, contact our World Wide Web home page at: http://www.digitalpress.com or http://www.bh.com/digitalpress

10 9 8 7 6 5 4 3 2 1

Printed in the United States of America

This book is dedicated to my wife Amita,
And to our beautiful son Jai.
Hardly an Indian love poem, but I'm sure
She understands.

Contents

Preface   **xi**

Acknowledgments   **xv**

1   A Review of the Basics   **1**

    1.1   Network design and performance   1
    1.2   An overview of the design process   3
    1.3   Building block 1: The framework   15
    1.4   Building block 2: Applications   20
    1.5   Building block 3: Protocols   24
    1.6   Building block 4: Hardware   37
    1.7   Building block 5: Physical connectivity   50
    1.8   Summary   54
           References   55

2   Addressing, Naming, and Configuration   **57**

    2.1   The IP addressing model   59
    2.2   Address mapping and configuration techniques   82
    2.3   Name-to-address mapping   105
    2.4   Directory services   122
    2.5   Design techniques for optimizing addressing   131
    2.6   Summary   150
           References   151

3   Routing Technology   **155**

    3.1   Internetwork architecture and topology   156
    3.2   Routing algorithms   161
    3.3   Routing design issues   165

3.4   Routing protocols   177
3.5   Router addressing issues   219
3.6   Route redistribution   222
3.7   Router architecture   223
3.8   Summary   235
        References   236

4   Multicast Network Design   239

4.1   Multicast application and routing concepts   240
4.2   Group registration with IGMP   256
4.3   Multicast routing with DVMRP   264
4.4   Multicast routing with MOSPF   272
4.5   Multicast routing with PIM   275
4.6   Multicast routing with CBT   281
4.7   Interoperability and interdomain routing   282
4.8   Multicast support protocols   289
4.9   Service and management issues   294
4.10   Summary   299
        References   300

5   Designing Secure Networks   305

5.1   The driving forces and issues behind security   306
5.2   Developing the security policy   316
5.3   Security technology and solutions   319
5.4   VPN architectures   353
5.5   IP Security architecture (IPSec)   356
5.6   Designing VPNs   380
5.7   Summary   386
        References   387

6   Designing Reliable Networks   391

6.1   Planning for failure   393
6.2   Network resilience   416
6.3   Fault-tolerant, high-availability, and clustering systems 432
6.4   Component-level availability   456
6.5   Example resilient network design   464
6.6   Summary   469
        References   470

7   Network Optimization   471

    7.1   Optimizing network bandwidth   472
    7.2   System-level traffic engineering   487
    7.3   Load-splitting and load-sharing techniques   502
    7.4   Optimizing applications   519
    7.5   Optimizing protocols   536
    7.6   Optimizing storage   542
    7.7   Summary   547
           References   548

8   Quality of Service   551

    8.1   Quality-of-service models   553
    8.2   Traffic engineering with policy and QoS constraints   571
    8.3   LAN and WAN media QoS features   587
    8.4   Integrated Services (IS)   598
    8.5   Differentiated Services (DS)   617
    8.6   Integrating QoS   623
    8.7   Summary   627
           References   630

9   Network Management   633

    9.1   Network management technologies   634
    9.2   Network troubleshooting tools   679
    9.3   Policy-based management   699
    9.4   Summary   707
           References   708

Appendix A: Mathematical Review   713

Appendix B: DNS Top Level Domain Codes   719

Appendix C: IP Protocol Numbers   721

Appendix D: UDP and TCP Port Numbers   727

Appendix E: Multicast and Broadcast Addresses   753

Appendix F: EtherType Assignments   767

Appendix G: Example MTTR Procedures   773

Index   775

Preface

In the developed parts of the world virtually all information-based organizations are underpinned by some form of communications infrastructure, and for many companies the communications network is intimately bound with core business operations. For large, multinational companies the annual cost of running such an infrastructure may run into millions of dollars, and the unexpected cost of service outages may be equally as large. Good network design and attention to detail are fundamental to providing cost-effective and reliable data networks. It is surprising, therefore, that there are very few books that deal with the subject of network design from the ground up, combining the theoretical, practical, and financial issues associated with real design networks.

Designing modern enterprise networks is now so complex that it cannot be achieved without the use of specialist software tools, and, as with any large problem, it is also beneficial to break down the problem into manageable components. There is, fortunately, a natural split in the design process between the delivery of the physical topology (be it a local or wide area network) and the routing and higher-layer services. This split mirrors what we find in the field today. There seem to be two broad classes of network designer: those who know much about routing and little about topology analysis, and vice versa. Unfortunately, knowledge of both is critical in planning and implementing an efficient data network. Network design must be approached holistically, from the ground up; otherwise, the result is typically a suboptimal network, with substantial reengineering costs due to inappropriate assumptions made during the design phase.

Since this is such a huge topic, I have divided my treatment into two books. In this book we discover how to deliver an optimized logical topology—covering the addressing, routing, and security issues required for delivering enterprise services, and how such networks should be tuned for performance, availability, and maintainability. The first book

(*High-Performance Data Network Design*) deals with the design techniques required to deliver an optimized physical topology. The book covers the design process from initiation, capacity planning, backbone and access design, and performance modeling, to the various LAN, MAN, and WAN switching technologies required to deliver a basic network infrastructure.

My objective in starting this project was to unite a number of apparently disparate areas of network design and to provide a balance of theoretical and practical information that practicing engineers would find useful in their day-to-day job. Since network design often receives very fragmented coverage, this book is an attempt to bring together those pieces so that they may be seen in context. In particular, the key issues in designing network addressing schemes are discussed, including how to design using the latest routing protocols, how to optimize performance using the latest technologies, how to build fault-tolerant and resilient networks within budget, how to assess and quantify risk in order to deploy security technologies appropriate for each network, how to deploy Virtual Private Networks (VPNs), understanding the latest developments in Quality of Service (QoS), and, finally, how to manage and maintain networks.

I started this project in an environment where the goalposts are far from static. The speed of change in information technology is simply staggering: Within the last 20 years we have seen a massive shift from large, centralized, host-centric networks to a situation where most of today's computing power reside on desktops. With processing power growing exponentially, and memory prices declining every year, we are now witnessing another paradigm shift toward an era of mobile personal computing. We have seen the emergence of distributed architectures, multimedia, and the explosive growth of the Internet and the World Wide Web (WWW), each forcing the development of new protocols and new applications. Network security has become a real force for change in recent years, with massive growth in the firewall market and completely new models of secure networking, such as the Public Key Infrastructure (PKI) and VPNs. Businesses are now demanding quality-of-service guarantees and information privacy, and there is increasing emphasis on Service-Level Agreements (SLAs). With overall improvements in the communications infrastructure we have also seen a significant increase in voice communications, new applications for packetized Voice over IP (VoIP), and the unification of both text and audio messaging systems. Finally, there are radical changes afoot in the field of user interfaces, including the take-up of voice recognition, text to audio translation, and the use of biometrics.

In all areas of technology the boundaries are blurring between local and wide area networks, data and voice, wired and wireless. All of these technologies are now being provisioned via a new breed of highly integrated hybrid devices with built-in routing, switching, bandwidth management, and security services. In a very short space of time every home will have Internet access via smart, integrated digital terminals. There has already been a massive shift in the adoption of mobile wireless computing and Internet access via a new generation of data-aware mobile phones. Over the next few years we will see the adoption of Java-enabled telephony, with high-resolution color displays capable of running more powerful applications. This, together with the use of more intuitive user interfaces and voice recognition, will truly mobilize the face of personal computing. We can only guess what changes the next two decades will bring.

About this book

This book is written for practicing engineers and project managers involved in planning, designing, and maintaining data networks. It is also appropriate for undergraduate students who have taken basic courses in data communications. The content reflects much of my experience in the industry, having worked for several leading network manufacturers in the areas of network design, network security, network modeling, and simulation.

This book represents the second of two complementary books on network design and optimization. This book covers addressing and naming schemes, routing protocols and router design, security techniques, virtual private networks, network optimization, designing high-availability and fault-tolerant networks, quality of service, and the management and maintenance of networks. The book deals with network design systematically, assuming that the core LAN, MAN or WAN infrastructure is in place, as described in the first book.

Since this book is concerned primarily with large-scale network design, it focuses heavily on the IP protocol suite, rather than attempting exhaustive coverage of other protocol stacks. Because my primary focus is on the design and performance characteristics of data networks, the approach taken throughout this book is to document technologies in sufficient depth only where they are relevant; for exhaustive information the book cites numerous good references, including *TCP/IP Explained*, by Phil Miller, from Digital Press.

Although the book does include occasional material where numerical techniques are presented, it is not heavily mathematical. The book also makes occasional use of programming code, although the reader may skip these sections. Unfortunately, the use of design algorithms and numerical modeling is an important part of network design. Where appropriate, suitable references are provided.

Conventions used in this book

Throughout the book I use the following format conventions:

- References are provided at the end of each chapter. Referrals within the text appear in square brackets [1].

- Items in angle brackets indicate that the contents of the brackets are to be replaced by appropriate keywords or data: <netID><hostID>.

- Numbers appear in decimal format unless otherwise indicated. The prefix 0x is used to indicate hexadecimal numbers (0x6e4d).

Acknowledgments

As anybody involved in such a large undertaking will attest, attempting to write such a book without feedback is a recipe for insanity. Therefore, I must thank a number of individuals for their time and constructive input on this project. For painstakingly reviewing the content and making numerous suggestions I have Brian Hill of Xyplex to thank. For reviews and helpful suggestions on security and routing topics I must thank my colleagues Philip Miller, Andrew Namboka, and Bob Brace of Nokia Internet Communications; Alex Challis of Asita Technologies; and Derin Mellor. For editing and compiling the final version of this text, I thank Dr. Paul Fortier and Gurukumar Anantharama Sarma of the University of Massachusetts, Dartmouth. I thank Pam Chester and the folks at Digital Press for affording me the opportunity to bring this project to life. Finally, I must thank my wife Amita and my son Jai for their patience and support.

This book does not reflect the policy or the position of any organization I have worked for. No financial support, resources, or direction was obtained from these organizations, and the ideas and opinions presented here (rightly or wrongly) are strictly personal. I apologize for any errors I have made that may offend or mislead. Please forward any constructive input to my e-mail address or to Digital Press.

About the Author

Tony Kenyon is the Chief Technical Officer of Advisor Technologies Ltd. (ATL), based in Berkshire, United Kingdom. ATL develops enterprise security management solutions for multivendor networks. He was formerly Technical Director for Europe, the Middle East, and Africa at Nokia Internet Communications and has worked in the data communications industry since 1983. Tony has designed several international communications networks and has developed a number of modeling tools, including an award-winning graphical object-oriented network design suite. For comments to the author he can be reached at tonyk@nildram.co.uk.

A Review of the Basics

Designing an efficient, cost-effective network that meets or exceeds the requirements is no easy matter. Today's equipment and technologies are becoming increasingly diverse and have the alarming property of becoming "old technology" almost as soon as they are installed. Mistakes can be, and often are, expensive. This chapter provides some basic definitions and introduces the concepts of a design process, the intention of which is to ensure that the design develops in a structured way, with all relevant data exposed during the process so that there are no late surprises. It resembles Chapter 1 of *High-Performance Network Design: Design Techniques and Tools* [1], and has been included for the sake of completeness. This chapter also introduces the basic hardware and software building blocks used in the construction of modern network designs.

1.1   Network design and performance

No two people agree exactly on what network design is. Network design is a generic and often subjective term that covers a whole range of skills and tasks, from the logical design elements (such as network protocols, addressing, subnetting), down to the physical design elements (such as physical topology, traffic modeling, circuit infrastructure). This book attempts to provide a holistic approach to network design by covering all the essential elements from the ground up. Whatever be your particular perspective at this point in time, by the end of this book you will get an appreciation of the subject as a whole.

1.1.1   Elements of good network design

The acid test of a good network design is whether it actually works. The fact is that many organizations today rely on networks that either perform suboptimally or cost more than they should, possibly due to poor design or implementation. These networks can soldier on for years, soaking up more and more resources and money, until somebody takes a serious look at what is going on and decides that things can be improved. The accumulated costs can be frightening in a badly designed international network, and it is still not unusual for a preferred supplier to be thrown out of an account after installation, simply because the proposed design just does not work or the equipment doesn't do what it was supposed to. Life is still full of surprises in the networking world, and every new technology appears to bring with it a new set of implementation issues.

A good network design should have the following characteristics:

- It should deliver the services requested by its users.
- It should deliver acceptable throughput and response times.
- It should be within budget and should maximize cost efficiencies.
- It should be reliable.
- It should be expandable without requiring a major redesign.
- It should be manageable and maintainable by support staff.
- It should be well documented.

Above all, a network must meet the application and business expectations of the users; otherwise, it has simply failed to deliver. With today's increasing shortage of skilled engineers it is also vital that even a well-designed network is modular, consistent, and well documented. The downside of ignoring these issues is that time and money are often wasted debugging problems, things are bolted onto the network in a nonstandard way (generating more problems), and eventually the business may have to outsource all management of the network as it becomes just too painful to administer. The golden rule, therefore, is: Keep it simple.

1.1.2   Network performance

Your job as a network designer, is to understand the complexities of performance analysis and then use that knowledge to build a network that satisfies its users.

In an environment where there is little technical competence it may be important to first educate the users about what they can reasonably expect from the network before moving ahead too quickly; this might at times involve stating the obvious. It is still not uncommon to hear statements such as "the new network is rubbish, there is absolutely no improvement in our database tool." For users who were previously using standalone applications and directly connected printers, installing a fast new network is generally not going to speed things up, and this can often lead to major misconceptions.

With any network design we must focus on what typically concerns the organization most: the performance of the applications and services accessed by its workers and its clients. For network users the most important performance characteristics are those they can directly experience, such as response time and delay. However, there are many other aspects of performance that are important for optimizing bandwidth and running costs—factors that may directly impact profitability of productivity for the business or organization as a whole.

Characterizing performance, particularly on a large heterogeneous internetwork, is a complicated task that requires expertise, since there are many complex interdependencies between systems, protocols, queues, and application software.

1.2   An overview of the design process

1.2.1   The life cycle of a design

Network designs are predominantly living entities; they rarely stay the same. Even from inception to initial implementation, a design will often change—typically because of improvements in the quality of the data about the users, applications, and traffic flows, or design changes concerning the equipment selected and delivery technologies used. The point at which a network is installed often marks the start of a new phase of design rather than the end of the process. Consequently, it is useful to think of network design as a cyclic process, as illustrated in Figure 1.1.

Before the design process can begin, a clear set of requirements should be established to capture what the organization and its users expect from the network and the services to be offered. The requirements should also clearly identify what the budget is and any other constraints that impact the design. The network design process then naturally follows a set sequence:

- Information gathering

- Planning

- Implementation

- Acceptance

- Expansion and modification

Just as with any living organism, networks have a limited life span. Over time networks become increasingly unreliable, inflexible, and unable to cope with the pressures placed on them. Advances in network technology and increases in overall traffic levels render most technology obsolete within a few short years. The lifetime of a network may be extended with the aid of transplants to vital organs (upgrading routers, links, etc.); however, there generally comes a point where the network design itself requires a major overhaul, often resulting in total replacement (at which point the cycle starts over).

Some networks are destined to age much faster than others. Since networks are becoming increasingly inseparable from the organizations they are built for, a dynamic organization can put severe strain on a design, forcing radical changes over a much shorter time than a more stable organization. Massive growth, mergers, acquisitions, downsizing, or radical new ways of working can all result in a design that is obsolete or inadequate much faster than anticipated. Networks may even be dismantled and replaced for purely political reasons; it is not unusual for one company to take over another and have the absorbed network completely scrapped (this could simply be

Figure 1.1
Network design process.

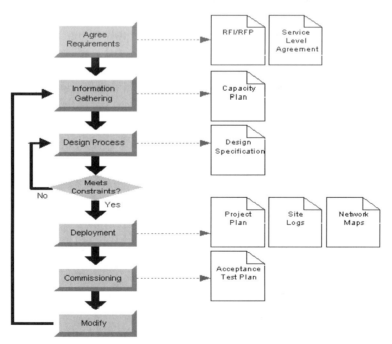

because the new decision maker does not like the installed technology, or it could be for strategic reasons). As companies expand and diverge, merge with other companies, and change their product focus and distribution methods, so too must the network.

1.2.2   Establishing requirements

To design and implement any new network or enhance an existing network, there must be two things: a requirement and a budget. At the early stages both elements may be quite loosely defined; without both in place and a willingness to expend effort in developing both, there is little point in proceeding. Large organizations that are very technology aware often have a rolling process of requirements and budgetary planning; to these organizations this comes as second nature and is fundamental to their business. Organizations that are less technically competent may have only the desire to improve matters and a willingness to spend money on it. Even so, in both cases the aims are the same—they just differ in the level of granularity. The job of the network designer is to cooperate with others in translating these wishes into a set of specific requirements, so that expenditure can be justified and appropriate technical choices can be made.

Engaging end users

Network engineering staff members often spend very little quality time with end users. The two groups may only interact when there is a serious problem, and then the engineer often feels outnumbered in a sea of angry users who are not the slightest bit interested in why the ISP router is down—they just expect service. On the other hand, users may have waited for hours to see any sign of progress, while business is being lost, commissions are being eroded, and angry customers are ringing in with complaints. Users often expect miracles; engineers often need them.

The design phase of any new network project is, however, a time for engaging user groups. It is important that the real users of the network and its services be involved from the start. Users are best placed to give feedback on how the applications should perform, what the current problem areas are, and what they like and don't like. Without user input you risk making fundamental errors with your design assumptions; by involving users throughout the transition you will achieve a much better buy-in (you really don't want to install a completely new infrastructure to find out that the users hate it). Having said this, user expectations need to be managed and prioritized. It is important that expectations are clearly defined, understood, and realistic. Before undertaking a design there should be a clear set of objectives visible to all interested parties.

Translating the requirements

Most reasonable-sized networks today are subject to a fairly formal process of specification. Requirements should ideally be specified from the top down. We start with the business objectives, and then refine these objectives by tighter specifications of what the business expects, what users expect, and any constraints that will be imposed on the designer. As part of the requirements specification process, it will become apparent that the requirement itself will be expressed in very different ways at different levels within the customer organization. At the board level, the requirement may simply be to increase adoption of client/server technology over the next three years to gain competitive advantage and achieve best practice.

While this may be the ultimate truth for a senior executive, it means very little to an engineer. The finance director may have his or her own requirement: to sustain a 35 percent return on investment while minimizing capital expenditure within this fiscal year.

We may have lost a few more engineers by this point. Joking aside, these are genuine requirements and must be translated and formulated into a set of specific requirements, aligned with the application strategy, user expansion plans, site geography, and available technology. The trick is to do all this without losing sight of the original business reasons for making the changes.

All too often the requirements come from the ground up. The network has been falling apart for several years, aided by an army of maintenance engineers performing artificial resuscitation on a daily basis, until new traffic levels and the loss of two key engineers finally bring the matter home. This is not a good start for a network design project, since the pressure is on to fix things quickly and there is unlikely to be a sensible budget in place (since clearly no planning has taken place). My advice here is to place a temporary bandage over the network while going through a full requirement and design process in parallel; otherwise, you could be throwing good money after bad.

Phasing the requirements

There is always a danger of overspecifying requirements too early, to the point where the requirements are simply unachievable. This is a particular problem if the authors of the requirements have very little knowledge of the networking technology. For example, a customer might express a requirement as follows: It is mandatory that all routers supplied should be supported and upgraded for the next ten years to incorporate new standards-based features and protocols.

Now, if you were investing serious money on this project, this might seem perfectly reasonable, but to most suppliers it appears impossible, or at least highly unattractive, for a number of reasons. Hence, requirements specification is generally a multistage process, starting with a fairly loose sense of direction and then progressively tightening the requirements as ideas firm up. It soon becomes apparent what is reasonable and what is achievable, as follows:

- Request for Information—An initial Request for Information (RFI) document is often generated first. This document defines what the business is trying to achieve and may have some specific questions on the potential technologies available. The aim of this document is to solicit responses from all likely candidates so that an initial short list can be created of those best able to provide a complete solution and those interested in proceeding. Potential suppliers may include a mixture of equipment vendors, consortia, and systems integrators. It is unlikely at this stage that any serious design work will be achieved. General architectural models may be produced; an overview of product availability is provided, together with information on the supplier's stability and suitability for the project.

- Request for Proposals—Once an initial short list of interested parties has been drawn up, the customer may issue a Request for Proposals (RFP) document to those suppliers. The recipients are expected to provide an initial outline design with budgetary costs and are expected to have addressed a number of questions posed by the customer. From the responses received a number of techniques are used to decide the final candidate list, including price, how many of the mandatory requirements are met, scalability, level of integration, and project management. The final short list is then drawn up based on the best responses, and those suppliers on the short list will be invited to present their proposals and to clarify any open issues with the customer directly.

- Detailed Requirements Specification—Once a [...] perhaps one other are selected, a more rigorous [...] cation, which will include a more expansive an[...] questions, may be produced. In response to th[...] are expected to provide a comprehensive desi[...] mitted costs and draft equipment lists. There [...]

between suppliers and the customer, including product demonstrations closely aligned with project functionality. Beyond this phase the customer will have selected the final supplier.

Once a final supplier is chosen, this supplier will be invited to finalize design and to produce final equipment lists and finished schematics for every location. There may be some adjustment of pricing based on functionality. For large networks the supplier is normally responsible for the entire project plan, specifying exactly how and when various components will be installed and tested.

Note that this is far from an exact science. Different organizations will approach the process in various ways. Some may require a long, drawn-out process with many intermediate phases (typically, government organizations); others will feel sufficiently comfortable to issue a detailed requirements specification to a small number of suppliers at the outset, and then go straight to final design with a chosen supplier.

Designing the requirements

The process of developing and gauging responses to requirements specifications is typically done either within the customer organization or between the customer and some third party (e.g., a consultancy group or in some cases even a potential supplier). In practice only large, well-funded organizations (e.g., large financial institutions, large retail organizations, or national service providers) tend to employ their own full-time design experts, who are capable of fulfilling this role. For those organizations that do not have the necessary skills in-house but have financial resources, there are many highly skilled consultancy groups able to take on the task as a contract project. For organizations that have neither the skills nor sufficient budget for external consultancy, often the answer is to pick the safest vendor (usually the largest) and use the vendor's internal design skills as part of the sales offering. Vendors will often provide a cut-price design service in order to win the business. In the latter scenario the customer is really at the mercy of the supplier, and it usually pays to get at least some independent advice during the process as a final sanity check, especially if you are not dealing one of the major suppliers. If the network design is suboptimal, the customer will end up paying for it over and over again.

Requirements should be structured in such a way that associated topics are grouped by function (e.g., network management, routing, cabling, etc.). Individual requirements should be concise, unambiguous, and measurable. All requirements should have a reference number. Once you have a complete set of requirements, go through each item and prioritize, according to following criteria:

- [M]—Mandatory: Must have. Failure to meet the requirement will eliminate the supplier from participating further.

- [H]—Highly desirable: Important but not absolutely essential. Would be very advantageous.

- [D]—Desirable: Not essential but would be nice to have.

- [N]—Note: Not a requirement, but information that the supplier should take note of and acknowledge.

Take care to ensure that all mandatory requirements are actually achievable; otherwise, you run the risk that no one will meet the basic requirement. In the short-list stage it is likely that the responses to the highly desirable questions will strongly influence who the preferred supplier will be (assuming that the responders meet all mandatory requirements and all responses are within budget). From a vendor perspective it is often instructive to pay particular attention to any requirements that appear implementation specific; they often indicate that a competitor has been overly helpful in the drafting of the document or that there is strong product bias, either with the customer or with the authors of the document. Customers should be aware that vendors, if allowed access, may use this process to disable the competition (hopefully with greater subtlety).

Assessing the requirements

In practice, the assessment phase is often part scientific and part instinctive. Aside from cases where the customer is required by law to choose the cheapest solution that meets all mandatory requirements, the process is normally a combination of assessing the true costs of deployment, some form of weighted evaluation matrix, and the much less quantifiable element of whether the customer feels comfortable with the supplier. For obvious reasons we cannot deal with the latter here; comfortable means different things in different parts of the world.

The true cost of the network needs to be fully explored in detail. Items for consideration include support and maintenance, depreciation, commissioning costs, project management fees, hardware and software upgrade costs, circuit bandwidth charges, ongoing consultancy charges, whether current prices are fixed against future changes in the price list, and so on. It is important to remember that this is not a one-off purchase; significant network costs are due annually, so when comparing solutions this needs to

Supplier ID: KWPK Micronetworks Associates

Ref	Pri	Description	Status	Mfail	Weight	Mult	Score
1.1	M	Supplier must have approvals for shipping to Europe and USA	FULL	0	100	1.0	**100**
2.1	M	Routers must support RIP, OSPF and BGPv4	FULL	0	100	1.0	**100**
2.1	H	Router must support OSPF unnumbered links	FULL	0	10	1.0	**10**
2.2.1	M	Router must support Ethernet, ATM and Token Ring interfaces	PART	1	100	0.5	**50**
2.2.2	H	Router must support Load balancing over serial links	NONE	0	10	0.0	**0**
3.1	M	PPP and HDLC are required for wide area encapsulation	PART	1	100	0.5	**50**
3.2	M	Modem dialback to be supported for secure remote configuration	FULL	0	100	1.0	**100**
3.2	H	Support for software update mechanisms across the network	FULL	0	10	1.0	**10**
4.1	D	Statistics mainained on routing and spanning tree convergences	FULL	0	1	1.0	**1**
4.2	D	An audit trail must be supported	FULL	0	1	1.0	**1**
5.1	M	Management system must support multi-users plus access levels	FULL	0	100	1.0	**100**
		TOTAL SCORES		2	632	9	**522**
		RANK					**17**

Figure 1.2   *Sample requirements analysis.*

be done for a period of at least three, and ideally five, years. What may initially be the cheapest solution may be far from it when calculated over the lifetime of the network. We dealt with cost modeling in detail in Chapter 4 of reference [1].

In assessing the specific requirements you should create a weighted matrix (e.g., using a spreadsheet) to clarify the responses and provide a quantitative view of the various responses. A simple weighting scheme is shown in Figure 1.2. The supplier with the lowest rank and the highest score will be most compliant. Note that this example is purely for illustration. Superior statistical analysis techniques are widely available and recommended.

In the unfortunate event that all suppliers fail to meet all of the mandatory requirements you may have to consider whether the requirements were really achievable or whether to reissue the document to a wider set of potential suppliers. Either way, with this approach you will be able to measure the best responses systematically.

1.2.3   Information gathering

Once you are clear about the business and user requirements, you must initiate research to characterize the behavior of the users and applications and where they are to be located. Clearly, this information is vital for understanding traffic flows over the network and will ultimately impact cost. It is important, therefore, that you attempt to be as comprehensive and accurate as possible during this phase, since poor-quality data could lead to poor choices being made later on. Ideally we want to build a database of information, such as the following:

- Where are users to be located; how many per location; which services will they access, and how often?

- How many sites are involved in the new network, and where are they?

- Are there any constraints regarding how traffic can flow between sites (e.g., security, political, or cost related)?

- Where are the main servers and services located? Do they need to be centralized, distributed, or mixed?

- How much traffic is likely over the key backbone and wide area links?

- What protocols are required to support the applications and services. Should they be routed, bridged, or switched? Is there any requirement for gateway-style translation?

- Is there any legacy equipment (routers, hubs, etc.) that must be retained and integrated into the new design?

- Are there any proprietary protocols or legacy services that must be integrated (e.g., SNA or old Wang hosts)?

- Are there any specific availability requirements for the network or its systems (e.g., backup links between key sites, mirrored server sites, online trading floors, etc.)?

- Are there any specific security requirements for the network or its systems?

- What changes in user, application, or service populations are predicted over the next three to five years, and how is the network expected to meet these demands?

- What are the budgetary constraints, by location?

Depending upon whether this is a new design or a modified existing design, you will face different challenges when attempting to collate some of this information, as follows:

- Greenfield site—Installing a brand new network without the constraints of existing infrastructure is often seen as the ideal scenario, but it does have its drawbacks. On the plus side you have no existing hardware or cabling to deal with, often you can install and test the equipment without having to work around real users, and you can ensure that everything is really working as it should before real users come online. On the minus side you may find it hard to determine what the real network loads and stresses are, since often you will have no existing data to work with and no feedback on any existing systems. In order to get these data you are going to have to talk to the potential suppliers, get detailed specifications of the applications and the underlying protocols, and perform some form of simulation or pilot network to gauge the real performance issues and how they will scale.

■ Existing site—With an existing site you will have different problems to deal with. Often your access to the site may be limited to unsociable hours, and any testing on a live network may be heavily restricted. You could be limited for space or power supplies for the new equipment, and installing or reusing cabling may be a nightmare, especially if the existing cabling is either substandard or not clearly documented. On the positive side you may already be aware of the potential bottlenecks, and perhaps some of the services are already in place and so can be investigated by putting traffic analyzers onto the network.

The list presented here is far from exhaustive, since the relevance of these data will vary by project. However, by starting to capture information concerning issues presented here it will quickly become clear which information is most important and the level of detail required. In Chapter 2 of reference [1] we worked through a process of systematically refining and presenting this information to create a formal database called the capacity plan.

1.2.4   Planning

By this stage you should have established what the requirements are, and there should be a database of all relevant information concerning users, services, hosts, and how those entities interwork. The process typically starts with a rough conceptual design, often using a whiteboard. At this point the designer must remain open to making changes later on, since firm decisions made at this stage generally result in a design that is far from optimal. The conceptual design is repeatedly analyzed and refined until it begins to make sense. It may be appropriate to consider a number of local and wide area technologies, different equipment vendors, and possibly different application vendors. Choices in any of these areas can completely change the direction of the design.

Technology choices may be directed by pragmatic issues, such as the geographic relationships between sites, services, and users or the region of the world where the network is to be deployed (e.g., a developing country may have only a single service provider offering low-bandwidth leased lines). Such factors often simplify the design, and, although the results are not optimal, such compromises are common in large-scale international network design.

Through an iterative process involving brainstorming sessions, design reviews, and possibly the use of modeling tools, a detailed design will eventually emerge that meets all (or at least most) of the performance and cost constraints and delivers the expected service levels outlined by the requirements specification. This is unceremoniously referred to as the final design (although in practice this tends to be the first draft of the real final design).

The design specification

A network design is just a bunch of ideas in somebody's head unless there is detailed documentation describing that design. The network design specification not only communicates that design, but it also acts as a benchmark for changes made to the design. If there were good reasons for the design choices made in the final design, then there must be equally good reasons for changing that design, so all modifications to the design specification need to be documented together with appropriate justification.

Changes are often made at the commissioning stage that are not reflected back into the design specifications. Failure to record the change history can have serious consequences for the maintenance staff later on. Strong project management can help, and all key personnel in the organization should be regularly updated with current network diagrams and configuration data, and these data should be archived and easily retrievable. Above all, an accurate network design specification must be maintained. The penalty for not maintaining knowledge is at best the cost of retraining all key staff and at worst the job of redesigning the entire network so that the new staff can make sense of it (and this does occasionally happen).

The early stage conceptual design might be fine to get things moving, but ultimately you need detailed documentation to support the design, and it needs to be in a format that can readily be archived and distributed electronically. The design should ideally be presented as a top-down series of schematics, with accompanying documentation explaining the overall design concepts and individual configuration aspects that are significant. Documentation should include the following:

- Cable plans for all floor and riser cabling, including patch panel and equipment cabinet layouts and locations, rack space, power requirements, and so on.

- Configuration scripts for all core-networking components (routers, bridges, switches, gateways, etc.).

- Network addressing models and location of address allocation systems (e.g., DHCP servers).

- Resilience and high-availability features, the reasons why they are implemented, a description of how they work, and what the effects of failover are predicted to be.

- Any security features that have been implemented (if so there should be a separate policy document explaining the security policy).

- A clear description of how the network should be modified and enhanced in the future should be available. Several of the future changes may already have been anticipated at the design phase and should be addressed in the initial design documentation.

Armed with a network design specification, we can now begin to implement the technology.

1.2.5 Implementation

Successful implementation of the design depends upon many factors. At the outset it is vital that there is a clear project plan identifying all key activities, who will perform them, and when they will take place. From the business perspective, and for many other pragmatic reasons, any new technology should be introduced in a phased approach, as follows:

- Educate: Start with a demonstration and presentation to senior representatives of the users. Explain what will happen and when. Ensure that access to floor areas and sites is cleared with the appropriate management team.

- Pilot test: Install a pilot installation for a small group of users, who must be prepared for possible bugs and glitches. For some projects this may be a luxury, but on large projects this is essential to avoid nasty surprises.

- Acceptance: Perform a comprehensive acceptance test to prove that the network performs as intended, and ensure that all outstanding items are resolved. The acceptance test should be used as a benchmark for any subsequent fine-tuning or optimization activities.

- Deployment: Install the production network. As the network goes live, ensure that you have plenty of support around and make sure that you can invoke fallback plans in the event of critical problems.

Feedback must be taken at each level and either resolved by making explicit changes or by explaining what the limitations are and agreeing on possible future enhancements. It is important not to move between phases without getting consent from all interested parties. A clear head is required for the final deployment stage; on a large network installation, particularly when replacing existing infrastructure, there often comes a point of no return, and nerves may be stretched to the limit. There are no prizes for delivering a malfunctioning network regardless of how much effort has been put in to it.

1.3   Building block 1: The framework

The framework for internetworking is based on a set of standards. Most of today's internetwork technology is based on the work of standards bodies, such as the IAB/IETF, IEEE, ANSI, and the ITU; however, the model most often used for positioning this technology is the Open Systems Interconnection (OSI) reference model, developed by the International Organization for Standardization (ISO). Although occasionally problematic, this model is still one of the best ways to represent protocols, applications, and internetworking hardware in context. The OSI model presents an abstract seven-layer architecture and should not be confused with the OSI protocol suite; in real-world internetwork designs the TCP/IP protocol suite dominates the market.

1.3.1   Standards organizations

Today's large-scale, heterogeneous, multivendor internetworks would not exist without standards; there would be chaos. Over the past few decades there are several key organizations that have provided forums for discussion groups and contributed to internetworking standards through the development of formal specifications. Some of the most important organizations include the following:

- International Organization for Standardization (ISO)—ISO is a voluntary body, responsible for a wide range of standards, including many that are relevant to networking. Their best-known contribution is the development of the ISO OSI reference model and the OSI protocol suite.

- Internet Advisory Board (IAB)—IAB is a group of internetwork researchers who discuss Internet-related issues and set Internet policies through decisions and task forces. The IAB coordinates a huge number of Request for Comments (RFC) documents, which are broadly divided into informational, experimental, proposed, drafts, and full standards. Some of the best-known standards include protocols in the TCP/IP suite (e.g., TCP, IP, ICMP, ARP, RIP, OSPF, and SNMP).

- Institute of Electrical and Electronics Engineers (IEEE)—IEEE is a professional organization that defines networking and other standards. It is made up of representatives primarily from the user and equipment manufacturing communities. The IEEE is perhaps best known for the widely used LAN standards, such as IEEE 802.3 and IEEE 802.5.

- American National Standards Institute (ANSI)—ANSI (a member of the ISO) is the coordinating body for voluntary standards groups within the United States. ANSI has developed several communications standards, including the Fiber Distributed Data Interface (FDDI). ANSI attempts to adopt ISO standards, but its specifications may differ to reflect North American requirements.

- Electronic Industries Association (EIA)—EIA is hardware oriented and specifies electrical transmission standards, including those used in networking. The EIA developed the widely used EIA/TIA-232 standard (formerly referred to as RS-232 and first issued in 1962).

- International Telecommunications Union, Telecommunication Standardization Sector (ITU-T)—The ITU-T was formerly called the International Telephone and Telegraph Consultative Committee (CCITT). The ITU-T is now an international organization, made up mainly of the major carriers, that develops communication standards (perhaps the best known is X.25). See reference [2].

- European Computer Manufacturers Association (ECMA)—ECMA is not a trade association as the name might imply; it is a noncommercial organization dedicated to the development of standards applicable to computer and communications technology. ECMA was formed in 1961 and now includes all European computer manufacturers. It works closely with ISO and the ITU-T.

- National Bureau of Standards (NBS)—NBS is another very active international standards committee. The NBS has been active in the upper layers of the OSI standards, including the specification of the Government OSI stack, GOSIP. The NBS also produces the Federal Information Processing Standards (FIPS).

1.3.2   **ISO OSI reference model**

The OSI reference model emerged from early work done by the ISO standards group. The ISO OSI model comprises seven layers, as shown in Figure 1.3. This architecture was originally intended as the benchmark for the international standardization of computer network protocols. The ISO OSI model is said to be an open systems architecture, because it enables interworking between different systems over well-defined interfaces and protocols. The systems do not have to be from the same vendor, nor do they have to run on the same operating system.

Each OSI layer represents a discrete function (such as point-to-point connectivity, end-to-end connectivity, data presentation, etc.). The layering is somewhat arbitrary, although there is general agreement on the demarcation of functions (note, however, that several protocol stacks, such as IBM's SNA, do not fit this model well at all). Layers do not necessarily equate to a single protocol. In practice, layers may comprise a number of protocols; for example, the Data Link Layer is usually subdivided into the MAC and LLC sublayers, with different MAC protocols used to handle different media types. A brief summary of the key functions of each layer is as follows:

- Application Layer—provides a set of services that act as the interface between the user application (such as file transfer, remote terminal access, or e-mail) and the communications protocol stack. The Application Layer communicates with a peer application protocol that resides on a remote system. In true OSI-speak the user application sits above Layer 7. However, it is commonplace in the TCP/IP world to see user applications sitting inside this layer, since many IP-based applications (Telnet, FTP, SMTP, etc.) have session, presentation, and application services integrated directly into the user application code.

Figure 1.3
The ISO OSI
seven-layer
reference model.

Layer 7	Application
Layer 6	Presentation
Layer 5	Session
Layer 4	Transport
Layer 3	Network
Layer 2	Data Link
Layer 1	Physical

■ Presentation Layer—concerned mainly with data manipulation rather than communications functions. This layer determines how data are to be represented and formatted. For example, ASCII to EBC DIC translation might take place here, as well as perhaps data compression. When data are being transmitted, they pass from the Application Layer to the Presentation Layer, and the Presentation Layer reformats and/or compresses these data before passing them on to the Session Layer. When data are received, they pass from the Session Layer to the Presentation Layer, where they may be reformatted and perhaps uncompressed before passing up to the Application Layer.

■ Session Layer—manages the process-to-process communication sessions between hosts. It's responsible for establishing and terminating connections between cooperating applications.

■ Transport Layer—performs end-to-end error detection and correction. This layer guarantees that the receiving application receives the data exactly as these data were sent. Examples include OSI transport classes 0–4, TCP, and Novell SPX.

■ Network Layer—manages network connections. It takes care of data packet routing between source and destination computers as well as network congestion. Examples include OSI IP, X.25 PLP, DoD IP, and Novell IPX.

■ Data Link Layer—provides reliable data delivery across the physical network. It doesn't assume that the underlying physical network is necessarily reliable. Examples of Data Link protocols include LLC 1–3, MAC (Token Ring, Ethernet), HDLC, LAPB, LAPD, LAPF, and PPP.

■ Physical Layer—responsible for transmitting and receiving bits over a physical communication channel (e.g., Ethernet). This layer has knowledge of voltage levels and of the pin connections to the physical hardware media.

Layers are used to abstract and isolate groups of related functions, so that development and flexibility is promoted through the use of well-defined interfaces (i.e., using the divide-and-conquer analogy). Each layer is insulated from the addressing details used by the layer below, so, for example, the Network Layer should never see the MAC header in frames passed upward (all MAC details should be stripped away before passing up to Layer 3, and so on through the stack). For performance or functionality reasons some of these rules are ignored (clearly it is much faster to simply pass pointers to a single packet buffer when one moves up or down the stack rather than perform multiple copies). In practice the seven-layer model is most widely used to position other (i.e., non-OSI) protocol suites in an attempt to understand what services they provide. For the purpose of this book, the most important protocol suite for internetwork design (especially large internetwork design) is TCP/IP.

1.3.3   Addressing

Addressing is an important concept in network design. In the context of network design we are primarily interested in Layer 2 (Data Link or MAC addresses) and Layer 3 (Network) addresses, although addresses higher up the stack are becoming more relevant for issues such as quality of service provisioning and network security. Layers 1 through 4 can be described as follows:

- Layer 1—Strictly speaking there are no physical addresses in the OSI model. However, most users associate physical addresses with the term Medium Access Control (MAC) address. Technically the MAC layer is a sublayer of the OSI Data Link Layer (Layer 2), but since these addresses are typically burned into network interface cards and other networking hardware, it is reasonable to informally refer to the MAC address as the hardware address (OSI purists can debate this ad infinitum). MAC addresses assume a flat address space, with a universally unique address for each network device. Addresses are assigned by the original manufacturer of the data communications equipment. MAC addresses have two main parts: a manufacturing (MFG) code and an organizationally unique identifier (OUI).

  - The MFG code is assigned to each vendor by the IEEE. The vendor assigns a unique identifier to each board it produces. Users generally have no control over these addresses because MAC addresses are burned into devices at the time of manufacture. Some manufacturers do configure MAC addresses dynamically; for example, DEC routing protocols use dynamic MAC addresses, and hub manufacturers may use dynamic indexing from a fixed base address for multiple interface chassis.

  - Some vendors have been assigned their own universal addresses that contain an OUI. For instance, IBM has an identifier of 0x10005A, so, for example, all IBM token-ring cards that use IBM token-ring chip sets have the first six digits of their addresses begin with 0x10005A. Other identifiers are 0x000143 for IEEE 802 and 0x1000D4 for DEC. IEEE universal addresses, whether for token-ring or 802.3 stations, are all allocated out of the same common pool, but uniqueness is guaranteed.

- Layer 2—Data Link addresses are called LSAPs in OSI terminology (Link Layer Service Access Points), although this is simply a Layer 2 abstraction and we are generally more concerned with the hardware address of a device (MAC address). As indicated previously, LSAPs are, strictly speaking, associated with the upper sublayer of the Data Link Layer (i.e., above the MAC layer). LSAPs are typically used to identify different protocol suites running over a common link layer (e.g., at a receiving station on an Ethernet network, TCP/IP, Novell IPX or OSI could be differentiated using unique LSAPs, where the frame type being used is IEEE 802.3 rather than EtherType).

- Layer 3—Network addresses are called NSAPs in OSI terminology (Network Service Access Points). Network addresses are usually assigned by the network administrator (either statically or via a dynamic allocation protocol such as DHCP) as part of the overall network design hierarchy. Protocols such as IP, OSI, IPX, and Apple-Talk all use Layer 3 addressing. By assigning different network addresses, a network administrator creates subnetworks, which act as discrete traffic partitions and enable better control over routing information. In practice, network addresses are usually assigned statically for important resources, such as routers, Web, file, and database servers, whereas user devices are assigned addresses dynamically for ease of administration.

- Layer 4—Transport addresses are referred to in the OSI world as Transport Service Access Points (TSAPs). In the IP world they are called ports. These addresses have only local significance for hosts but are important in network design, since they are a way of uniquely identifying applications running over the network. By using port numbers, firewalls and routers can deny or allow specific applications, and special bandwidth preferences can be set up to meet different quality of service requirements.

Above Layer 4 there are additional service access points corresponding to each layer in the OSI stack (SSAPs, PSAPS, or equivalents). These addresses are generally of interest only to end systems, security systems, high-level switches, and gateway devices.

1.4   Building block 2: Applications

Networked applications such as word processing, spreadsheet, database, e-mail, and Web browsing are now routinely deployed on a massive scale in order to enable entire organizations to work together and share resources.

However, the way in which application architecture imposes itself on a network can have a profound influence on the traffic flows imposed over that network, and the network designer should understand the basic application models commonly deployed today. In a home office or even a home network, all applications are typically installed and run in isolation on the user's workstation. On a network, particularly a medium-sized to large network, applications may be centralized, fully or partially distributed, to improve productivity and decrease overall costs.

1.4.1 Computing models

Applications architectures have evolved significantly over the past decade, and understanding how various application models will impact the network is vital in order to accurately characterize traffic flows. The key application models are presented in the following text and are illustrated in Figure 1.4.

- Centralized Model. Network application models were initially quite simple. Before the explosion of desktop computing, the application typically ran on shared central computers (usually a large mainframe).

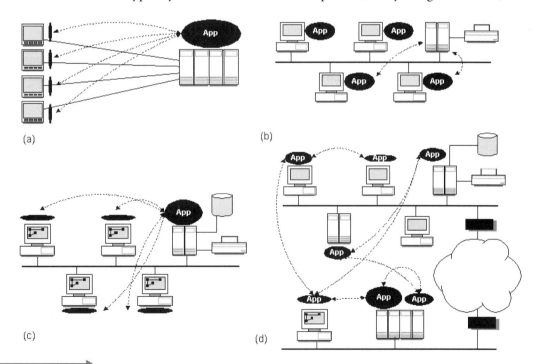

Figure 1.4   *(a) Centralized model, (b) decentralized model, (c) client/server model, (d) distributed model.*

Remote users logged in to the mainframe via a virtual terminal protocol (either block or character oriented). The traffic between the user and the mainframe effectively comprised keystrokes or blocks of display updates, and data were predominantly text.

- Decentralized Model. With the rise in desktop computing we saw for the first time a move toward distributed computing, with discrete applications running on user workstations, and these workstations were networked together to share common resources such as printers and file servers. The advantage of decentralization was increased power and performance to the desktop; the disadvantage was cost and maintenance. Imagine, for example, trying to ensure that your 3,000-member workforce has the latest patch for the word processing application.

- Client/Server Model. The next major shift in application architecture was to combine the best of the centralized and decentralized approaches to form a hybrid architecture, where a centralized server running the application cooperated with high-performance thin client software. In this way data integrity and consistency could be managed centrally, while high-bandwidth features, such as graphical interface handling, could be devolved locally.

- Distributed Model. It seemed only natural to evolve this architecture one step further, so that many cooperating entities could be involved in the provision of an application without any knowledge of the location of each entity; this is the so-called distributed object model. There are now a number of middleware stacks that support application distribution (including DCOM, CORBA, and EJB).

We discuss the client/server and the distributed model in more detail.

Client/server model

In the client/server model the application is divided into two functions: a front-end client, which presents information to the user and collects information from the user, and a back-end server, which stores, retrieves, and manipulates data and generally handles the bulk of the computing tasks for the client. Typically the server part of the application runs on a more powerful platform than does the client (e.g., a minicomputer or mainframe) and also acts as a central data repository for many client computers (thereby promoting consistency and making the system easy to manage). The client/server architecture increases workgroup productivity by combining the best features of standalone workstations with the best features of minicomputers and mainframes. The model makes the best use of high-end server hardware and reduces the load on client PCs.

In terms of operation the server is a program that runs on a network-attached computer, and provides a service to one or more clients. The server receives requests from clients over the network, performs the necessary processing to service those requests, and returns results to the clients. A request could even be to download part of the application. The client is the program (typically running on a user PC or workstation) that sends requests to a server and waits for a response (e.g., a database query). A single server instance can service several client requests concurrently. For this reason, designing and implementing servers tends to be more difficult than implementing clients. For a client and server to communicate and share workload, an interprocess communication (IPC) facility is required (such as the TCP socket interface).

The client/server architecture contrasts with the classical centralized architecture adopted by early mainframe installations. In a centralized environment, the clients are little more than dumb terminals that act as simple data entry and display devices. The terminal process does very little actual work; the user typically fills in the fields of a text-based form and these data are simply forwarded to the central computer for processing. All processing and screen formatting are performed by the central computer; the terminal simply displays the preformatted data as they arrive. However, in a client/server environment the client has much more control over the final visual presentation to the user. Instead of the data being preformatted at the server, data are sent back in raw format, and the client application must determine how best to translate and display these data. This model enables changes to be made at the client interface without having to change the server code. A good example of a client/server application is the X Windows protocol.

Distributed model

Common Object Request Broker Architecture (CORBA) and Enterprise Java Beans (EJB) are examples of new software architectures that enable applications to be fully distributed and isolated from the plumbing aspects of the network infrastructure. The architecture of these platforms enables components of an application to communicate transparently regardless of location—with entities running on the same machine, different machines, or indeed different networks. For applications such as e-commerce this represents a powerful and highly flexible way to distribute performance and features. These architectures can present interesting challenges for a network planner, both in terms of the traffic dynamics and in areas such as security. Distributed applications are being deployed on a large scale for Internet e-commerce, health care, and financial applications and represent the new wave of truly distributed computing.

CORBA is the de facto set of APIs and middleware services for developing distributed applications at present; the specifications for CORBA are defined by the Object Management Group (OMG) [9]. Applications can access distributed objects by using an API called the Object Request Broker (ORB). The ORB transparently forwards object requests from clients to the appropriate server objects and returns the results. Distributed objects can be organized in a client/server or peer-to-peer relationship, often dynamically changing depending upon the context of the transaction. The Internet Inter-ORB Protocol (IIOP) is a high-level communications protocol used by CORBA objects to support remote method invocation (i.e., it enables cooperating entities to communicate transparently and activate remote functions over protocols such as TCP/IP). IIOP afterwards gets the nearest CORBA to network plumbing and is analogous to the HTTP protocol (the communications protocol used to transport Web traffic). For example, by using the CORBA/IIOP protocol, a Java applet running in a client machine could communicate transparently with a servlet running in the Web server (it need know nothing about the location of the servlet). However, IIOP is more scalable and efficient than HTTP, since IIOP can reuse a single connection for multiple requests; hence, the applet and the servlet can exchange method calls in both directions, using a single connection. Once IIOP communication is established, object activations and method calls on those objects may occur using either a direct IIOP connection or IIOP over HTTP. Note that it is the client ORB that decides whether to use a direct IIOP connection or revert to IIOP over HTTP. The client will use the best quality of service available. It tries to establish a direct IIOP connection first and, if that doesn't work, it uses IIOP over HTTP.

1.5   Building block 3: Protocols

This section discusses some of the key software components used as building blocks for constructing internetwork designs. The most common protocols running over networks today include Novell NetWare, AppleTalk, DECnet Phase V, IBM SNA/LU6.2/NetBIOS, and OSI. However, over the past decade (especially in the backbone environment), network implementers have largely united around a common protocol stack, based on TCP/IP. This book, therefore, focuses mainly on the application of IP-based protocols and services. Specific implementation details of the IP protocol suite are discussed in many classic texts, so we will only briefly review them here. The interested reader is strongly urged to read the related TCP/IP references provided at the end of this chapter, specifically [3–6].

1.5.1 A review of the IP protocol suite

Today, IP has become universally accepted as the protocol of choice for internetworking. Back in the early 1980s the protocol debate was not so clear-cut. Xerox Network Systems (XNS) was seen by many as a superior solution, IBM had a whole raft of protocols built around SNA, and the ISO OSI protocol stack appeared as the strategic choice for a number of large organizations and equipment vendors (including Digital Equipment Corporation [DEC]). In the LAN environment proprietary protocols such as Novel's IPX NetWare suite offered better functionality and higher performance than TCP/IP, and AppleTalk was used to support Apple's user-friendly desktop machines. From humble beginnings, IP's widespread adoption is widely attributed to a number of factors, including the following:

- Initial funding from the U.S. Department of Defense (DoD)

- Rapid free development of services and support by many academic institutions

- The development and public domain (PD) distribution of Berkeley UNIX (Free BSD), which included TCP/IP

- Free use of the Advanced Research Projects Agency Network (ARPA-NET), as an experimental WAN created by the U.S. DoD in 1969. The ARPANET adopted IP as its standard and has now evolved into the Internet

IP continues to be successful because it is essentially simple to implement and understand, and no single vendor controls its specifications. Stable specifications and implementations have been available for many years, and practically every serious business application has been ported to run over the IP protocol suite. IP is still considered by many to be somewhat crude and is not without its limitations, including the well-known address space limitations (described in RFC 1296 and RFC 1347), lack of security, and its limited service support for upper-layer protocols and applications. However, it is here and it works. The approach so far has been to fix problems and add functionality as and when required. This has led in recent years to initiatives such as IP version 6 (which takes care of the addressing problem) and IPSec (which takes care of the security problem).

1.5.2   The IP and the OSI model

The IP stack comprises a suite of protocols used to connect more computers in the world today than any other. The IP protocol suite actually predates the ISO OSI model and so does not map neatly onto the OSI seven layers, at least not above Layer 4. The OSI model was driven by a large standards body with very ambitious aims and consequently took considerable time and effort to produce; in many areas it was too isolated from the practicalities of real-world implementation. In contrast, IP was originally driven by the needs of the U.S. government and subsequently by a large community dominated by vendors and users. Working implementations appeared early on, giving developers useful feedback on what was possible and what was practical. Most of the advances in IP have been made by individuals and small dynamic working groups, through the publication of Requests For Comments (RFCs). The process of creating and adopting an RFC has proved far quicker than the equivalent procedure in the ISO. IP development is, therefore, considerably streamlined and based on the ability to provide real implementations and demonstrable interoperability. It is not burdened by the academic and perhaps more stringent requirements suffered by OSI.

In several areas OSI protocols are significantly richer in functionality, more efficient, and generally better thought out than their TCP/IP counterparts. Unfortunately, they are also much more complex, difficult to implement, and demand more resources (and were introduced at a time when networking resources were particularly scarce). OSI failed to get a significant install base and has failed to attract either vendors or customers to adopt them in the same way that IP has. It is instructive to use the OSI seven-layer model as a frame of reference when discussing IP. Figure 1.5 shows how IP and its services map onto the layered architecture of OSI. Essentially, IP protocols and services start above Layer 2 and typically sit on top of a media service (such as FDDI, Ethernet, or a wide area stack such as Frame Relay).

Figure 1.5
TCP/IP model in context.

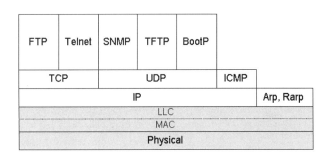

The following list summarizes five of the layers:

- Application Layer—The Application Layer consists of services to assist applications that peer over the network. As described previously, in the IP world user applications typically have OSI session, presentation, and application services built in, so it is hard to differentiate between user application and services above the Transport Layer. For this reason it is commonplace to see TCP/IP stack models with user applications placed at Layers 5 through 7. Example applications include the file-transfer utilities (FTP and TFTP), electronic mail (SMTP), remote virtual terminals (Telnet), and smaller utilities such as the finger program.

- Transport Layer—The Transport Layer provides end-to-end data delivery. The OSI model's Session and Transport Layers fit into this layer of the TCP/IP architecture. The concept of OSI's session connection is comparable to TCP/IP's socket mechanism. A TCP/IP socket is an end point of communications composed of a computer's address and a specific port on that computer. OSI's Transport Layer has an equivalent in TCP/IP's TCP. TCP provides for reliable data delivery and guarantees that packets of data will arrive in the order they were sent, with no duplicates and with no data corruption.

- Network Layer—The Network Layer defines the datagram and handles the routing of datagrams. The datagram is the packet of data manipulated by the IP protocol. A datagram contains the source address, destination address, and data, as well as other control fields. This layer's function is equivalent to that of the OSI's Network Layer. IP is responsible for encapsulating the underlying network from the upper layers. It also handles the addressing and delivery of datagrams.

- Data Link and Physical Layer—TCP/IP does not define the underlying network media and physical connectivity; what is running below Layer 3 is largely transparent. IP makes use of existing standards provided by such organizations as the EIA and Institute of Electrical and Electronics Engineers (IEEE), which define standards such as 802.3, Token Ring, RS232, and other electronic interfaces used in data communications.

The movement of an IP datagram through the various layers of a TCP/IP stack is shown in Figure 1.6.

When a message is sent by an application, it is passed to the Transport Layer (in this example TCP), where the transport header is added (which includes socket information to indicate source and destination transport

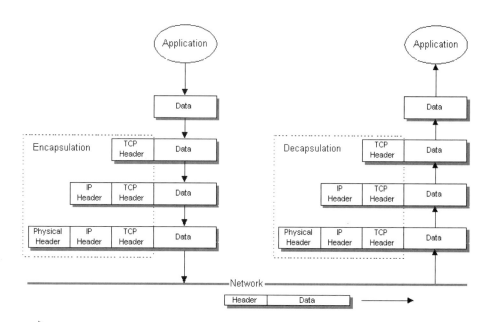

Figure 1.6   *Packet flow through the TCP/IP layers.*

addresses). Once transport processing is complete, the message is passed to the Network Layer (IP), where the Internet header is added (which includes source and destination IP addresses). The message is eventually passed down to the Physical Layer, where a MAC header is added (which includes source and destination MAC addresses). The message can then be transmitted to a peer system as a frame of bytes, comprising both data and protocol headers. When a frame is received by the peer system, the process is reversed, and the peer application eventually receives the intended data.

1.5.3   The Data Link Layer

The Data Link Layer is not strictly part of the TCP/IP protocol suite; however, since it underpins the IP layer, it is important to understand some of the key elements involved. As illustrated in Figure 1.5, the Data Link Layer is divided into two sublayers: the Medium Access Control (MAC) layer lies below a Logical Link Control (LLC) layer.

MAC sublayer

The MAC sublayer addresses the requirement for upper-layer insulation from various media types. For example, in an IEEE 802.3/Ethernet LAN environment, features such as error detection, framing, collision handling, and binary backoff are handled at this level. Source and destination station addresses (sometimes called physical addresses) are also contained within the MAC header. Many of the standards for local area networking at this level are standardized by the IEEE rather than the IETF.

LLC sublayer

The LLC sublayer defines services that enable multiple higher-level protocols such as IP, IPX, XNS, or NetBIOS to share a common data link. There are three classes of LLC, depending upon the quality of service required, as follows:

- LLC Type 1—offers a simple best-effort datagram service. There is no error control, no sequencing, no flow control, or buffering. LLC 1 merely provides source and destination LSAPs for multiplexing and demultiplexing higher-layer protocols.

- LLC Type 2—offers a connection-oriented service and is a superset of LLC 1. LLC 2 features sequence numbering and acknowledgments, buffering, and separate data and control frames. LLC 2 is based on HDLC, designed to run over less reliable point-to-point links.

- LLC Type 3—offers a semireliable service with fewer overheads than LLC 2.

LLC Type 1 is the most common implementation in the LAN environment, since higher-level protocols such as TCP are expected to provide guaranteed services, and the physical medium is generally highly reliable. LLC Type 2 is commonly used to support applications that do not offer complete reliability at the Transport Layer, such as older IBM-style services (it is even possible to run X.25 over LANs via LLC Type 2). LLC Type 3 is primarily used on Token Bus for process control applications.

LLC defines three one-byte fields: the Destination Service Access Point (DSAP), the Source Service Access Point (SSAP), and the Control (CTL) field. The two SAP fields are used to identify the next higher-layer protocol above LLC for peer devices. The CTL field is used to indicate the frame type, and can be either Unnumbered Information (UI), Exchange Identification (XID), or test frames. Note that with LLC Type 2 the CTL field may be one or two bytes long, depending upon whether sequence numbers are required. For further information on the Data Link Layer the interested reader is referred to reference [7].

1.5.4   The Internet Layer

The Internet Layer corresponds to Layer 3 on the OSI model. It defines the datagram and handles the routing of those datagrams. IP is the most important protocol of the TCP/IP protocol suite, because it's used by all other TCP/IP protocols and all data must flow through it. IP is also considered the building block of the Internet. Some of the key components are described in the following text.

Internet Protocol (IP)

IP is a connectionless Network Layer protocol, which means that no end-to-end connection or state is required before data are transmitted (and there are no sequence and acknowledgment numbers to maintain). This is in contrast to a connection-oriented protocol that exchanges control information between hosts to establish a reliable connection before data are transmitted. IP does not guarantee reliable data delivery; packets could arrive at their destination out of order, duplicated, or not at all. IP relies on higher-level protocols, such as TCP, to provide reliability and connection control.

The basic format of the IPv4 datagram is illustrated in Figure 1.7(a). Each datagram, or packet of data, has a source and destination address. Routing of data is done at the datagram level. As a datagram is routed from one network to another, it may be necessary to break the packet into smaller pieces. This process is called fragmentation, and it's also the responsibility of the IP layer. Fragmentation is required on some internetworks because the many hardware components that make up the network have different maxi-

Figure 1.7
(a) IP version 4,
(b) IP version 6
message formats.

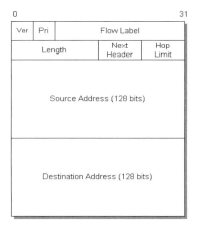

(a)   (b)

mum packet sizes. IP must also reassemble the packets on the receiving side so that the destination host receives the packet as it was sent.

A new version of IP is currently being introduced (IP version 6, or IPv6). This version extends the addressing fields of IP and also changes the way Type of Service (ToS) is implemented to assist with Quality of Service (QoS) requirements (see Figure 1-7[b]). For complete details the interested reader is referred to references [4, 6].

Address Resolution Protocol (ARP)

Because of the layering of the protocol stack, Physical Layer entities are insulated from Network Layer entities. This means that physical network hardware (such as the Ethernet adapter card in your PC) does not understand how to reach another network-attached system using the remote system's IP addresses, at least not without assistance. In Figure 1.6 the transmitting station on the left does not know initially how to reach the station on the right, since it only has a destination IP address to work with (i.e., there is no destination MAC address in the message because at this stage that is unresolved).

The Address Resolution Protocol (ARP) is used to create a dynamic map of the IP addresses associated with specific physical addresses used by network hardware. ARP operates by broadcasting a message onto the local network, asking for the owner of a certain IP address to respond with its hardware (MAC) address. If the host with the designated IP address is listening, it returns a message to the source, listing its physical MAC address. All other systems that receive the broadcast ignore it. Once the correct addressing details are received, they can be stored locally in an ARP cache, so that future messages can be sent without having to requery the network. Note that ARP operates within a broadcast domain, since broadcasts are not forwarded by routers (at least not by default). For complete details the interested reader is referred to references [4, 6].

Internet Control Message Protocol (ICMP)

The Internet Control Message Protocol (ICMP) is a low-level diagnostic protocol used primarily by the network to report failures or assist in resolving failures. ICMP runs over IP and is an integral part of IP operations. ICMP must, therefore, be implemented by every IP-enabled system. ICMP is widely used to perform flow control, error reporting, routing manipulation, and other key maintenance functions. Network engineers make extensive use of the ping utility, which uses ICMP's echo feature to probe remote IP systems for reachability and response times. A successful response from ping indicates that network routing is operational between the two nodes and that the remote node is alive. For complete details the interested reader is referred to references [4, 6].

1.5.5   The Transport Layer

IP is responsible for getting datagrams from system to system. The Transport Layer is responsible for delivering those data to the appropriate program or process on the destination computer. The two most important protocols in the Transport Layer related to IP are User Datagram Protocol (UDP) and Transmission Control Protocol (TCP). UDP provides unreliable connectionless datagram delivery; TCP provides a reliable connection-oriented delivery service with end-to-end error detection and correction. To facilitate the delivery of data to the appropriate program on the host computer, the concept of a port is used. In TCP version 4 a port is a 16-bit number that identifies an endpoint for communication within a program. An IP address and port combination taken together uniquely identify a network connection into a process (the socket paradigm developed by the University of California at Berkeley makes more intuitive the use of IP addresses and ports).

Services built on top of UDP or TCP typically listen on well-known ports. These are special reserved ports, which are publicly known and enable clients to access common services on servers without having to interrogate some form of directory service beforehand. For example, clients wishing to connect to a server using the Telnet service simply use the destination port 23.

User Datagram Protocol (UDP)

The User Datagram Protocol (UDP) allows data to be transferred over the network with a minimum of overhead. UDP provides unreliable data delivery; data may be lost, duplicated, or arrive out of order. UDP is, therefore, suitable for applications that either do not require a connection state or cannot guarantee it (such as SNMP). UDP is also very efficient for transaction-oriented applications, when error-handling code resides within the application. It may also be used for applications such as IP multicasting. Figure 1.8 shows the simple format of a UDP header. The header contains a 16-bit

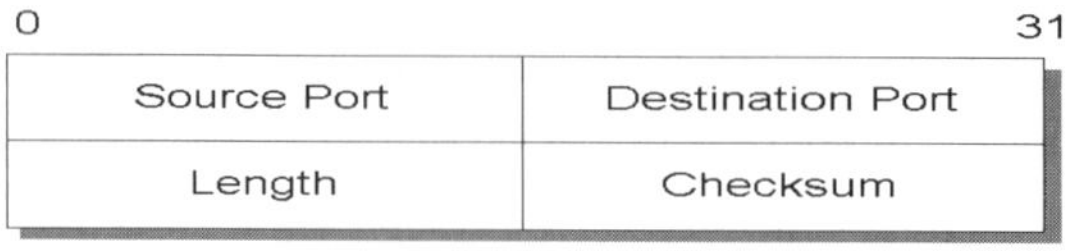

Figure 1.8
*UDP header
format.*

0	31
Source Port	Destination Port
Length	Checksum

source and destination port. For complete details the interested reader is referred to references [4, 6].

Transmission Control Protocol (TCP)

Transmission Control Protocol (TCP) is a reliable, byte-oriented, connection-oriented transport protocol, which enables data to be delivered in the order they were sent and intact. TCP is connection oriented, because the two entities communicating must first perform a handshake before data transmission can begin, and the connection state is maintained until explicitly terminated or timed out. The handshake phase is used by the transmitter to establish whether or not the receiver is able to accept data. The flag fields, illustrated in Figure 1.9, are key to connection establishment and release. A connection is initiated with a SYN (S) bit set, responded to with the SYN and ACK (A) bits set, and completed with an ACK bit; hence, the term three-way handshake. Connection release is achieved in the same way, except that the FIN (F) bit is used instead of SYN.

Figure 1.9 shows the format of a TCP header. The header contains a 16-bit source and destination port (as in UDP); however, the header also includes sequence and acknowledgment fields (to ensure that packet ordering and dropped packets are identified). Reliable delivery is implemented through a combination of positive acknowledgments (acks) and retransmission timeouts. TCP also includes a checksum with each packet transmitted. On reception, a checksum is generated and compared with the checksum sent in the packet header. If the checksums do not match, the receiver does not acknowledge the packet, and the transmitter automati-

Figure 1.9
TCP message format.

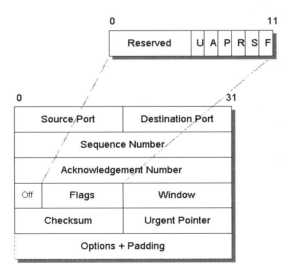

cally retransmits the packet. TCP is an end-to-end protocol; therefore, the sender relies on feedback from the receiver to implement congestion control and flow control. For complete details the interested reader is referred to references [4, 6].

1.5.6   TCP/IP applications

As we have seen, TCP and UDP support different types of service, and most applications are implemented to use only one or the other (some may sit directly on IP). TCP is used where a reliable stream delivery is required, especially if an application needs to run efficiently over long-haul circuits. UDP is best for datagram services, such as simple best-effort polling applications (SNMP) or multicast distribution from a news or trading system. If you need more reliability with UDP, then this must be built into the application running over UDP. UDP is also useful for applications requiring efficiency over fast networks with low latency. Many network applications are now supported over these transport systems. Some applications (such as Telnet and FTP) have existed since the start of Internet technology. Others (such as X Windows and SNMP) are relatively new. The following is a brief description of the more widely used applications.

- Telnet is a widely used virtual terminal protocol, which allows users on a local host to remotely access another host as if they were locally attached. Telnet runs over TCP and is typically invoked by the command-line interface of the host operating system. For example, on the command line the user could type telnet mitch and receive a login prompt from the computer called mitch (alternatively the user could type telnet 193.125.66.2 for example if the IP address of the remote host is known). Implementations of Telnet are available on many operating systems, and interoperability is normally taken for granted. For instance, a Telnet client may be running on a DEC VAX/VMS and a Telnet server on BSD UNIX.

- File Transfer Protocol (FTP) runs over TCP and is widely used. The basic operation and appearance are similar to Telnet, but with additional commands to move around directories and send or receive files. The user must be identified to the server with a user ID and a password before any data transfer can proceed.

- Trivial File Transfer Protocol (TFTP) is a file transfer application implemented over the Internet UDP layer. It is a disk-to-disk data transfer, as opposed to, for example, the VM SENDFILE command, a function that is considered in the TCP/IP world as a mailing function, where you send out data to a mailbox (or reader in the case of VM). TFTP can only read/write a file to/from a server and, therefore, is primarily used to transfer files among personal computers. TFTP allows files to be sent and received but does not provide any password protection (or user authentication) or directory capability. TFTP was designed to be small enough to reside in ROM and is widely used in conjunction with BOOTP to download operating code and configuration data required to boot a diskless workstation or thin client.

- Remote Execution Protocol (REXEC) is a protocol that allows users to issue remote commands to a destination host implementing the REXEC server. The server performs an automatic login on a local machine to run the command. It is important to note that the command issued cannot be an interactive one; it can only be a batch process with a string output. For remote login to interactive facilities, Telnet should be used.

- Remote Procedure Call (RPC) is an API for developing distributed applications, allowing them to call subroutines that are executed at a remote host. It is, therefore, an easy and popular paradigm for implementing the client/server model of distributed computing. A request is sent to a remote system (RPC server) to execute a designated procedure, using arguments supplied, and the result returned to the caller (RPC client). There are many variations and subtleties, resulting in a variety of different RPC protocols.

- Remote shell ("r" series commands) is a family of remote UNIX commands, which includes the remote copy command, rcp; the remote shell command, rsh; the remote who command, rwho; and others. These commands are designed to work between trusted UNIX hosts, since little consideration is given to security. They are, however, convenient and easy to use. For example, to execute the cc myprog.c command on a remote computer called target, you would type rsh target cc myprog.c. To copy the myprog.c file to target, you would type rcp myprog.c target. To log in to target, you would type rlogin target.

- Network File System (NFS) was developed by SUN Microsystems and uses Remote Procedure Calls (RPCs) to provide a distributed file system. The NFS client enables all applications and commands to use the NFS mounted disk as if it were a local disk. NFS runs over UDP and is useful for mounting UNIX file systems on multiple computers; it allows authorized users to readily access files located on remote systems. This enables thin clients or diskless workstations to access a server's hard disk as if the disk were local, and a single instance of a database on a mainframe may be used (mounted) by other mainframes. NFS can be problematic in internetworks, since it can add significant load to a network and is inefficient over slow WAN links.

- Simple Mail Transfer Protocol (SMTP) provides a store-and-forward service for electronic mail messages (see [8] for details of these messages). Mail is sent from the local mail application (e.g., a Netscape mail client) to an SMTP server application running on a mail server (e.g., Microsoft Exchange mail server). The server stores the mail until successfully transmitted. In an Internet environment, mail is typically handled by a number of intermediate relay agents, starting at the Internet Service Provider (ISP).

- Domain Name System (DNS) provides a dynamic mapping service between host names and network addresses and is used extensively on the Internet.

- Simple Network Management Protocol (SNMP) is the de facto network management protocol for TCP/IP-based internetworks. SNMP typically runs over UDP and is used to communicate management information between a network management system (NMS) and network management agents running on remote network devices. The NMS may modify (set) or request (get) information from the Management Information Base (MIB) stored on each network device. Network devices can send alerts (traps) asynchronously to inform management applications about anomalous or serious events. SNMP is covered in detail in Chapter 9.

- The X Windows system is a popular windowing system developed by Project Athena at the Massachusetts Institute of Technology (MIT) and is implemented on a number of workstations. The X Windows system uses the X Windows protocol on TCP to display graphical windows on a workstation bitmapped display. X Windows provides a powerful environment for designing the client user interface. It provides simultaneous views of local or remote processes and allows the application to run independently of terminal technology. For example, X Windows can run on OS/2, Windows, DOS, and X Windows terminals.

For further information on TCP/IP and its applications refer to [4, 6]. For detailed internal protocol information about TCP/IP and key applications refer to [5].

Figure 1.10
Network devices in context.

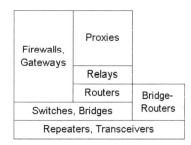

1.6   Building block 4: Hardware

In this section we briefly explore some of the key hardware devices you will encounter when designing networks. In order to place these devices in context, it is useful to position them using the ISO OSI seven-layer model, as shown in Figure 1.10.

Since the mid-1980s, we have seen a gradual shift in the presentation of networked devices from largely discrete units (such as standalone bridges, standalone repeaters, etc.) to highly integrated devices with many hybrid functions (such as multimedia hubs with repeater, bridge, and multiprotocol router interface cards). This is largely the result of functionality becoming a commodity, a general trend toward increased miniaturization, and the need to improve functionality to remain competitive. As these tools have matured and improved in performance there has also been a shift in network design from the use of simple bridged and repeated networks to more sophisticated router-switch networks capable of optimizing traffic flows with much greater accuracy and granularity. Scalability, convergence, and traffic optimization are now key driving forces behind today's large-scale network designs. We will now examine some of these devices in more detail.

Figure 1.11 is a somewhat simplified network design illustrating where you would typically expect to find these devices in a real network today. It shows discrete devices, although it is common to see much of the functionality integrated into a single device. The Head Office site uses a firewall to prevent unauthorized internal access and offers a Demilitarized Zone (DMZ) for shared hosts at lower security levels. A gateway is used to convert IBM SNA into TCP/IP protocol for wide area transport. Campus 1 has a number of LANs, segregated either via repeaters (LAN extension) or bridges and routers. Line drivers (LD) are used to extend the campus to a remote office in Building 9. Building 5 is a multistory building with Layer 2 and Layer 3 switches to provide Virtual LAN (VLAN) traffic domains.

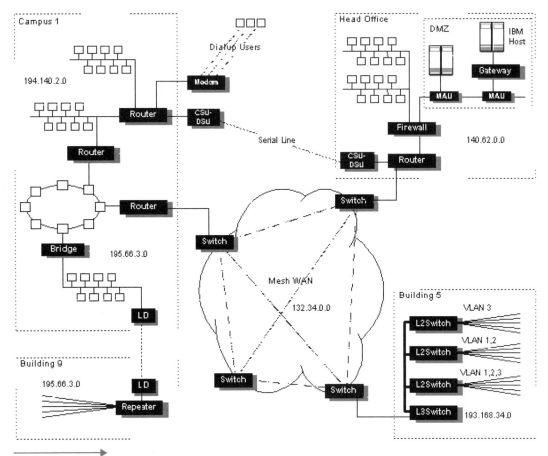

Figure 1.11   *Simplified network design illustrating the typical locations for key hardware devices.*

Note that the Layer 3 switch includes wide area support for access to the meshed WAN.

1.6.1   Media Attachment Units (MAUs)

MAUs, or transceivers, provide the means of encoding data (framed bits) into purely electrical or light signals ready for transmission onto the physical media, typically a piece of cable. An MAU is also responsible for decoding electrical or light signals and converting them back into data for receiving stations. Note that MAU should not be confused with the Token Ring concentrator Multiple Access Unit. All devices attached to a network will typically have either a built-in transceiver interface (such as an onboard 10 Base T interface provided on a PC network adapter) or will provide a standard AUI interface, which can be mated to a discrete transceiver via a drop cable. MAUs come in various guises, depending on the media technology to be used to carry data and the media access control (MAC) technology used to frame the data (e.g., Token Ring, Ethernet, FDDI, etc.). MAUs may be small, single-port discrete units or multiport LAN-in-a-box units. MAUs provide a physical connection to LAN. They may also include features that protect against misuse of the LAN (e.g., Ethernet Jabber Protect) and diagnostic tests (SQE on Ethernet).

1.6.2 Repeaters

Repeaters are used to extend LAN segments, either due to the standard distance limitations on the length of a segment or to expand a network because the number of devices attached to a segment is at the recommended limit (e.g., four repeater hops for CSMA/CD). There are various types of repeater, ranging from single-port unmanaged units to multiport devices with full network management support. Repeaters may present a range of interfaces and physical connectors; typical examples are as follows:

- AUI via D type connectors
- 10 Base 2, via BNC connectors
- 10/100 Base T, via multiple RJ45, or bulk RS266 connectors
- 10/100 Base F, via SC, ST (bayonet), SMA (screw), or RJ45 fiber connectors
- Token Ring STP, via IBM connectors

A repeater must regenerate incoming frames to its other port(s) as a frame is received. A typical dumb repeater copies any incoming frames on any port to all other ports, so there is no traffic management capability. The standards documentation also specifies maximum acceptable delays (called bit-budget delays) between the receipt and retransmission of bits in a frame. If these delay thresholds are exceeded, then the device is considered noncompliant and may cause problems in networks where repeaters are chained off in sequence. One special type of repeater, a buffered repeater, not often seen nowadays, is really a hybrid between a bridge and a repeater. This device stores incoming frames temporarily in a memory buffer, prior to regeneration on its other port(s). In this scenario the bit-budget delays do not apply. Furthermore, buffered repeaters can be used in the same way as bridges to segment two or more networks where multiple nonbuffered repeaters are used in series. Buffered repeaters also inhibit the regeneration of error frames and collision frames between segments. Repeaters are a commodity item and are widely available from electrical retailers. They are simple, reliable, and easy to install but are otherwise of little interest from the network designer's perspective.

1.6.3   Line drivers, modems, and CSU/DSUs

Line drivers

Line drivers (sometimes referred to as limited distance modems—LDMs) are used to extend physical circuits over longer distances. Line drivers are typically used in designs where point-to-point links between two devices would exceed the maximum distance supported by the underlying media and protocols. They are a form of signal amplifier.

Modems

Modulator/Demodulators (modems) are typically used between a CPU and a telephone line. This device modulates an outgoing binary bit stream onto the analog carrier, and demodulates an incoming binary bit stream from an analog carrier. Modem standards are defined by the International Telecommunications Union (ITU) and include the following:

- V.32—Up to 9,600 bps for use over dial-up or leased lines

- V.32 bis—Up to 14,400 bps for use over dial-up or leased lines

- V.42—Error control procedures

- V.42 bis—A data compression technique for use with V.42

- V.34—28,800 bps for use over dial-up line V.42. When used with V.42 bis compression, it can theoretically reach 115,200 bps.

- V.34-1996—Provides two additional data transmission rates of 31.2 and 33.6 Kbps

CSU/DSUs

The terms Channel Service Unit (CSU) and Data Service Unit (DSU) are often used synonymously, although they perform different functions. CSU and DSU functionality is often combined in a single device called a Digital Data Set (DDS). A DSU is a low-speed device used to terminate digital circuits, providing protocol translation and signal formatting. There are several categories of DSU, as follows:

- Fixed-rate DSUs at 19.2 Kbps and below (subrate) or at fixed rates of 56 Kbps

- Multirate DSUs operating at variable speeds up to 56 Kbps

- Switched 56-Kbps DSUs, operating with switched 56-Kbps digital services

- T1/E1 DSUs and switched T1/E1 DSUs

A CSU terminates digital circuits at higher speeds but provides additional features such as filtering, line equalization and conditioning, signal regeneration, circuit testing, and error control protocol conversion (e.g., B8ZS). Some combined CSU/DSUs can also support Extended Super Frame (ESF) monitoring and testing, together with the ability to multiplex traffic from multiple interfaces into a single point-to-point or multidrop circuit. Standard CSUs offer a T1/E1 circuit interface. Many combined CSU/DSUs can now offer T3/E3 support via the High-Speed Serial Interface (HSSI). Some combined CSU/DSUs support SMDS via the Data Exchange Interface (DXI) and include many functions beyond the scope of a traditional DDS (including segmentation, protocol conversion, etc.).

1.6.4 Bridges

Bridges provide Layer 2 Data Link Layer functionality and are protocol independent of Layer 3 protocols and higher. They can, therefore, transparently connect multiple 802.x-compliant networks (either locally or remotely). The Data Link Layer uses physical addressing schemes and is responsible for line discipline, topology reporting, error notification, flow control, and ordered delivery of data frames. Since bridges operate at the Data Link Layer, they do not examine protocol information that occurs at the upper layers. This means that there is minimal processing overhead relative to devices such as routers or gateways, and bridges may forward different types of protocol traffic (e.g., DECnet, IP, or Novell IPX) between two or more networks. The IEEE committee defines four key standards for bridges, as follows:

- Transparent Bridging (TB)

- Spanning Tree Algorithm (STA)

- Source Routing Bridging (SRB)

- Source Routing Transparent Bridging (SRT)

Transparent Bridging is synonymous with the Ethernet world, and Source Routing is synonymous with Token Ring. There is a de facto standard called Adaptive Source Routing, or Translation Bridging. This allows mixed Translation and Source Routing environments to coexist effectively via an internal kludge using address-mapping tables. Note that Source Routing bridges are not considered completely transparent [1].

Bridges offer filtering and forwarding capabilities based on Layer 2 fields, which are used to create discrete traffic domains to optimize backbone efficiency. Bridges may have filters configured to accept and forward only frames of a certain type or frames that originate from a particular subnet. This filtering capability is extremely useful for controlling traffic flows. Filters may be static (configured by the system or user) or dynamic (learned). In general, bridges offer at least some traffic management capability by associating node MAC addresses with particular interfaces and forwarding (at the Data Link level) semi-intelligently. Bridges are also typically responsible for preserving topology integrity by stopping the formation of network loops using protocols such as Spanning Tree, or proprietary variations [1].

1.6.5   Switches

The increasing power of desktop PCs and the growth of client/server and multimedia applications have driven the need for higher-bandwidth, shared-access LANs. Consequently, network designers are replacing older repeaters and bridges in their wiring closets with intelligent LAN switches to increase network performance and protect their existing wiring investments. Switches are basically high-speed bridges, usually with significant hardware assist to ensure low latency and high throughput. Switches can be functionally divided into two main categories: LAN switches (Layer 2/multilayer devices that provide Layer 2 and Layer 3 switching capabilities) and ATM switches. LAN switches can reduce congestion in existing shared-media hubs while using new backbone technologies, such as Fast Ethernet and ATM. Gigabit Ethernet and ATM switches and routers offer greater backbone bandwidth required by high-throughput data services.

1.6.6   Routers

WAN operations were historically performed by hosts. However, in the early 1980s these tasks started to migrate into dedicated Layer 3 devices called routers. The first routers were single protocol only, and did not offer any concurrent bridge operations. As both memory and CPU power increased and became much less expensive, more functionality was added until we arrive at the situation today, with routers being the ubiquitous general-purpose, multiprotocol network tool. Routers form discrete broadcast domains and are used to connect different networks. Routers forward traffic based on the destination Network Layer address rather than the MAC address. Routers can provide transparent connectivity over mixed technol-

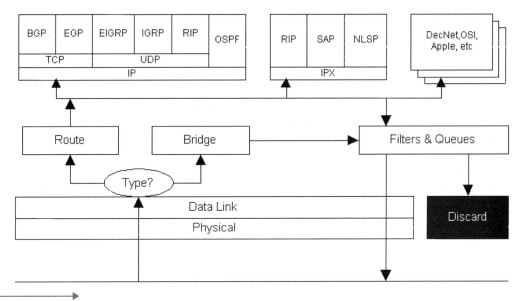

Figure 1.12   *Architecture of a multiprotocol bridge router.*

ogy subnetworks and are commonly used to extend LANs (both locally and remotely). Routers typically communicate with one another, learning neighbors, routes, costs and addresses, and selecting the best path routes for individual packets.

Multiprotocol bridge routers have become the preferred tool used to create large scalable internetworks. They offer all the benefits of protocol transparency traditionally provided by bridges, together with effective bandwidth utilization and the security advantages of routers. Router networks are functionally more robust than those provided by bridges; they do not suffer issues such as LLC timeouts, susceptibility to broadcast storms, and poor congestion control. Routers are much more scalable and can support very large internetworks in terms of both load and addressing; they do, however, require more skilled support and maintenance staff. The basic operation of a multiprotocol bridge router is as follows:

- Incoming packets are examined and then passed to the appropriate protocol handlers or discarded.

- If the packet is not routable, and bridging is enabled, then a bridge handler deals with the packet just like a typical MAC bridge.

- If the packet is routable and a suitable routing protocol is configured, then the packet is passed to the correct handler. Note that if the handler is not enabled, the packet will typically be dealt with as a bridged packet.

■ Filtering may occur at the point of receipt or transmission.

The conceptual architecture of hybrid multiprotocol bridge routers is illustrated in Figure 1.12. It is important to understand that this hybrid integrated product provides more functionality than a discrete bridge and router pair, either in parallel or in series. In fact, it performs a unique function that cannot be emulated with discrete devices. In Figure 1.13 we can see that the closest we can get to emulate the operation of the integrated device is via two bridges and a router. However, the configuration shown on the right still fails to provide the same functionality and will drop bridged packets at the router interface if they are nonroutable, so protocols such as DEC LAT will be passed through both bridges but are blocked at the router. The single-protocol router will always discard nontransparent protocols.

In Figure 1.14 we see an alternate way to emulate this functionality. On the surface this also looks promising; however, now we immediately run the risk of having duplicate packets circulating around the network. The bridge on the far right will blindly copy all nonlocal traffic regardless of whether or not the single protocol router (running in parallel) is already dealing with some of the traffic. As a result, the top and bottom networks are in effect joined, as if we were running multiple IP addresses on the same physical LAN. This will potentially confuse the router, since it will see packets of identical network source addresses on both interfaces. Strictly speaking, this

Figure 1.13
Integrated bridge router and discrete bridge routers in parallel.

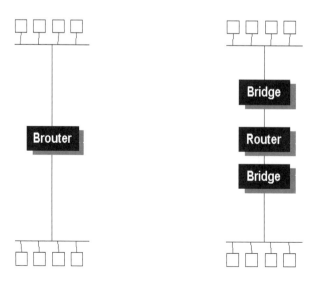

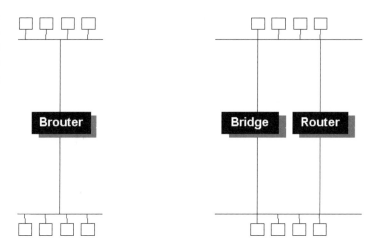

Figure 1.14
Integrated bridge router and discrete bridge and routers in parallel.

configuration is not legal. Of course, one could consider setting up some fancy filtering scheme on the bridge to discard all routable packets, but frankly this would be a management nightmare and is strongly discouraged.

Hybrid integrated devices exhibit behavior that is often quite unique. Here, all of the routing and bridging decisions are handled internally, and the device always handles forwarding or routing decisions consistently, which greatly simplifies the design rules. We discuss the use of routers in network design in Chapter 3. In Chapter 5 we discuss the emergence of a new breed of hybrid device called the router firewall.

1.6.7   Gateways

The term gateway is used as a generic term in networking; the only thing that defines it is that there is some functional or protocol conversion or translation implied. In this broad sense we will also include devices such as transport relays, since, as far as we are concerned, these are all gateways. Examples of gateways include the following:

- DEC LAT to TCP/IP translation
- IBM cluster controller to TCP/IP transport gateways
- OSI TP Class 4 to TP Class 0 translation
- OSI TP4 to TCP translation
- Telnet to OSI virtual terminal protocol translation
- ICL OSLAN to TCP/IP translation
- OSI X.400 EMAIL gateways

You should be aware that many of the older IP standards documents (RFCs) use the term gateway to mean a router, which can lead to further confusion. In this book router means router, and gateway means some form of protocol translator.

1.6.8   Firewalls

Firewalls are hybrid security devices that are built using packet-filter routers, application proxies, or stateful packet forwarding systems. Their primary purpose is to intercept traffic flows and police the content of these flows, allowing only sessions that comply with policy rules through the firewall. Firewalls are widely deployed at perimeter interfaces to enable organizations to interface with untrusted wide area networks (such as the Internet). They are increasingly being deployed within internal networks to police traffic between groups of users.

1.6.9   End systems and intermediate systems

The terms end system and intermediate system are frequently used in networking texts. We define these terms as follows:

- An End System (ES) is most often characterized as a personal computer sitting on a user's desk. This is not a useful definition, since the PC may have no network connection, in which case it is a standalone system. End systems are, therefore, required to a have network connectivity as a basic requirement. This also requires that they also have a network address, so that they can be made reachable from other end systems and intermediate systems. In practice, end systems comprise a range of devices, including servers, personal computers, laptops, PDAs, WAP phones, terminal servers, print servers, intelligent disk arrays, and so forth. The key difference between an end system and an intermediate system is that the end system does not relay or forward packets (e.g., it does not run a full routing protocol). An end system merely terminates or originates packet flows.

- Intermediate System (IS) is a general term, defined in standards documentation as any device capable of acting as a packet relay (e.g., a router). In earlier IETF standards the term gateway is frequently used in the context of intermediate system. Those new to reading RFCs may be forgiven for the confusion this inevitably causes between the term router and real gateways. Note also that intermediate systems frequently operate as end systems in practice. For example, a router could initiate a Telnet connection to log in to another router for diagnostic purposes. In this event both routers could be said to be operating in end system mode for that session context. As another example, an IPSec VPN gateway can operate in transport or tunnel mode. In transport mode the gateway is acting as an end system; in tunnel mode the gateway is acting as an intermediate system.

In an internetwork environment end systems communicate over a backbone of intermediate systems. Although they do not actively participate in routing, end systems require basic reachability information in order to talk to a router. This is achieved by running a router discovery protocol (such as a limited form of RIP) or via static hard-coded entries. Note that it is important not to confuse the physical appearance of a device with its logical function; it is not unusual, for example, to equip a high-performance workstation with full routing capability.

1.6.10   Comparing bridges, switches, and routers

It is useful to briefly summarize the various issues and benefits of using these three complementary technologies in a network design.

Bridge benefits

The key advantages of using bridges in designs are as follows (note that most of these features also apply to switches):

- Bridges are largely plug-and-play devices that require relatively little expertise to install and maintain.

- Bridges enable you to automatically isolate traffic domains, which can bring instant benefits to overall network performance. Local network traffic is contained within learned interfaces.

- Bridges extend LANs and eliminate local node limitations on cable segments.

- Bridges are in the main transparent to higher-layer protocols and therefore are truly multiprotocol. This allows them to forward packets of protocols that are not routable.

- Bridges are generally transparent to end systems. Routers require end systems to be aware of the router's addresses, either by static configuration or by running a limited routing protocol.

- Bridges typically have better price/performance than routers. Since bridges have much less work to do on a packet basis, they can operate at higher speed, with much lower latency, and can be constructed using cheaper components. Router performance has, however, improved significantly in recent years.

Bridge issues

Bridge issues include the following:

- Layer 2 incompatibilities make some MAC-to-MAC implementations quite complicated.

- Interworking issues across end-to-end WAN links may require both bridges to be from the same vendor.

- Manageability becomes an issue in large networks.

- Learning table sizes can get large and overflow on very large networks, making traffic management ineffective.

- Bridges can reconfigure to get around topology changes, but the process is typically much slower than for routers.

- Different implementations of STA do not interwork and can cause stability problems. Underpowered Spanning Tree bridges in particular (i.e., those capable of dropping packets under load) can cause serious stability problems if STP packets are being lost. Spanning Tree configurations can also be expensive for resilient WAN configurations, and there are no standards for load sharing over multiple paths with separate bridges.

- Transparent bridges use only a subset of network topology at any one time, since only a single path can exist at any time between two points in a bridged internetwork. Routers, however, can use the best path that exists between source and destination and can readily switch paths as better ones become available.

- Bridges offer little protection against broadcast storms. In forwarding broadcast packets, bridges are only carrying out their normal function, but in doing so they can impact internetwork performance and function. This is a particular problem with remote bridges, where broadcasts have to traverse interbridge serial links.

- Bridges must drop packets that are too large for their attached networks. Routers, because they support the Network Layer, have the capability of fragmenting packets to accommodate networks with a smaller MTU.

- Bridges have no capability to provide congestion feedback to other bridges or to end nodes. This can lead to the need to discard packets, with consequent impact on end-system performance. Routers provide congestion feedback using the capabilities of the Network Layer protocol.

- Bridges cannot distinguish applications or higher-layer protocols. They cannot, therefore, prioritize application traffic or offer QoS guarantees.

Router benefits

Because routers use Layer 3 addresses, which are typically hierarchical, routers can use techniques such as address summarization to build networks that maintain performance and efficiency as they grow in size. Routers can use redundant paths and determine optimal routes even in a dynamically changing network. Routers are necessary to ensure scalability as the network grows and expands. They provide the following capabilities, which are vital in network designs:

- Broadcast and multicast control

- Broadcast segmentation

- Security

- Quality of Service (QOS)

- Multimedia support

Since routers operate at Layer 3, they can enforce a hierarchical addressing structure. Therefore, a routed network can tie a logical addressing structure to a physical infrastructure—for example, through IP subnets for each segment. Traffic flow in a bridged or switched (flat) network is, therefore, inherently different from traffic flow in a routed (hierarchical) network. Hierarchical networks offer more efficient traffic flows than flat networks because they can use the network hierarchy to determine optimal paths and contain broadcast domains. Routers offer several advantages over bridges and switches, as follows:

- Scalability—routed networks can be much larger than bridged networks, and the traffic engineering capabilities are much more efficient.

- The Data Link Layer packet header has very little useful information to determine optimal routing; routers offer real least-cost routing. Routers are much more sensitive to protocols and traffic conditions.

- Topological reconfiguration is much faster in routers during failure conditions. For example, OSPF can reconverge around a link failure in several seconds.

- Routers contain broadcasts and so prevent the possibility of broadcast storms.

- Routing is much better suited for uniting dissimilar networks.

Router issues

Router issues include the following:

- IP network multicasting may introduce broadcast storm–like problems.

- Network headers are more complex to parse than a Data Link Layer header (checksums, variable-length fields, and options); hence, more CPU and latency are required. Packet latency is generally an order of magnitude higher for routers than for bridges.

- Single-protocol routers lack flexibility in multivendor environments. Routers must encapsulate if bridging is not supported.

- Routers are generally not quite so plug-and-play as bridges.

- In campus environments high-speed switches are generally preferred to routers for better performance, lower cost per port, and ease of use.

1.7   Building block 5: Physical connectivity

In this final section, we briefly discuss ways in which all of the previous elements can be physically interconnected. Over the decades this infrastructure has evolved from the centralized mainframe architecture, with terminals attached via RS.232 or RS.422 (or some proprietary means) through to a wide armory of local and wide area connectivity options.

1.7.1   Connectivity

Today there are many ways to interconnect network elements, each with its own particular strengths and weaknesses. The following list is far from exhaustive:

- Low-speed, direct-attached, serial lines (RS.232, RS.422, etc.)

- Dial-up serial lines (analog and digital)

- Local Area Networks (Ethernet, Token Ring, AppleTalk, ATM)

- Metropolitan Area Networks (FDDI, SMDS, ATM, SONET/SDH)

- Wide Area Networks (Frame Relay, ATM, ISDN, X.25, leased lines, satellite links)

- Wireless LANs and WANs (802.11, Bluetooth, GSM, GPRS, UMTS)

There are marked differences among many of these technologies; some of the key differentiators are as follows:

- Packet, cell, or circuit switching

- Wired or wireless

- Distances supported

- Performance

- Bandwidth

- Quality of Service (QoS)

- Availability

To the uninitiated the choice can be bewildering, and even more perplexing is the fact that many countries have different standards, different charging models, and different service availabilities. In Figure 1.15, we see that a variety of packet-switched (ps), circuit-switched (cs), and point-to-point (pp) technologies are available, each applicable for the LAN, MAN, WAN, or all environments. Although most of these technologies have a range of bandwidth offerings, the choice has continued to expand vertically and horizontally over the past 40 years, beginning with simple leased circuits back in the 1960s.

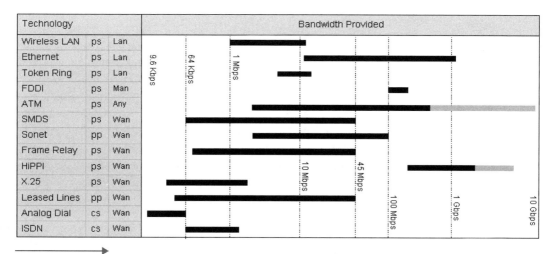

Figure 1.15 *Sample media and bandwidth choices available today.*

Switching

One of the key differentiators between data network connectivity is whether the technology is circuit or packet switched.

Circuit switching

Circuit switching has its history firmly rooted in voice networks. In the telephone network Pulse Code Modulation (PCM) is used to transmit digital information by sampling voice at 8,000 times per second (corresponding to 125 μs per sample), where each sample is encoded as an 8-bit number (note that this is where the magical 64-Kbps circuit multiplier originates: 8 × 8,000 = 64,000 bps). Unlike packet switching, this digital information does not require a protocol header and addressing information to be routed. In order to transfer data between two locations a call is made to the destination node. This call reserves a discrete set of physical resources (circuits or channels) across the network; only when these resources have been allocated can data be transferred. Routing is therefore implicit in the physical path. Although the circuit is dedicated, on large trunk connections traffic can be interleaved with other users' traffic through strict timing control (called multiplexing). Once the data transfer is complete, the call may be disconnected. Note that this model supports permanent calls if required, and either packetized data or digitized voice can be carried over circuit-switched networks. Examples of circuit-switching technologies include voice calls, analog dial-up circuits, and ISDN.

Packet switching

Packet switching covers packet, frame, or cell switching (the main difference being that cells have fixed length, and both packets and frames are variable). In packet-switched networks each packet is an autonomous unit (called a datagram), with source and destination address information placed in a header preceding each packet. When data are transferred between two nodes, each packet traverses the network following logical paths created by intermediate nodes (such as routers or switches). Packets are normally interleaved with traffic from other sources, although there is no strict timing required, and packets may travel autonomously down different routes to reach their destinations. Examples of packet-switching technologies include X.25, Frame Relay, ATM, and SMDS.

There are fundamental differences in the way the circuit- and packet-switched networks behave under load. In essence, with circuit switching, network resources are either utilized or they are not. While a circuit and associated switch ports are in use, the subscriber has exclusive access to that resource; the circuit is effectively dedicated. In heavy subscription periods it is, therefore, possible that all resources will be allocated (referred to as a period of oversubscription). In this event new subscribers are blocked from making new calls until circuits are freed up, even though in practice many circuits could be underutilized (i.e., any spare bandwidth is locked up). A circuit-switched network, therefore, needs to have sufficient circuit and switching equipment capacity to cope with heavy use periods in order to keep customers satisfied. This can lead to substantial resource waste and cost inefficiencies during average/low use periods, leading to a practice referred to as overprovisioning.

By contrast, with a packet-switched network, traffic is generally competing for shared circuit resources. As more users subscribe to the network, circuit utilization increases and performance gradually degrades. As resources approach saturation, packets are simply discarded (either because they cannot be serviced or because they are aged out of queues); new users are not explicitly blocked. Overall the network can be better optimized through traffic-engineering techniques, enabling service providers to provision the network more cost effectively. To enable different service classes to be supported, soft policy control can be imposed over the whole network (in which case best-effort packets could be discarded prior to saturation to alleviate congestion problems).

Note that these two switching techniques arc applicable to both wired and wireless network solutions. We will discuss these issues in more depth later in the book.

1.7.2 Bandwidth

Providing connectivity, whether packet or circuit switched, is only half of the problem. To satisfy traffic requirements we also need to provide an appropriate level of bandwidth. The technologies we have introduced so far operate at different speeds, and the methods used to access the physical media, the quality of the media, the distances traveled, and the protocols used to transfer data all have a part to play in determining the effective rate at which data can be transferred. Figure 1.15 illustrates a selection of the key local, metropolitan, and wide area networking technologies available today and their respective bandwidth ranges. The unique operational characteristics of these technologies often mean that different design techniques must be used in each case. The various design implications are discussed in detail later in the book.

1.8   Summary

This chapter discussed the building blocks for internetworking design and the key components of the software and protocols running over such networks. We can summarize these as follows:

- Network design is an iterative process of continuous refinement. A good network design is logical and consistent and should deliver acceptable performance and cost metrics.

- IP is the dominant protocol suite today. Its role is now central to all Internet application delivery. IP protocols and services are independent of the underlying network hardware. Each host on an IP network should have a unique IP address, which universally identifies the device. IPv4 addresses are becoming depleted. A new version of IP, IPv6, is being introduced to provide scalability for the next-generation Internet.

- Networks can be constructed from a wide variety of local and wide area media interconnected using devices such as repeaters, bridges, switches, routers, and gateways. All of these devices have different uses depending upon the scale of the network and the protocols in operation. The boundary between devices such as switches, routers, and bridges is becoming blurred. Current trends indicate that further integration and greater performance are likely as these technologies mature.

- LAN switches are best used to provide simple connectivity for local workgroups, server clusters, and LAN backbone applications. Bridges can be used for similar applications, but they are dying out, largely replaced by higher-speed switches (unless they are required for specific applications such as bridging between different media technologies). Switches and bridges are useful on sites where there is limited technical and management support available and are best suited for environments where it is undesirable or impractical to configure end systems for operation with routers. Bridges and switches may also be the only option where some of the protocols in use are nonroutable (e.g., DEC LAT or IBM SNA).

- Hybrid multiprotocol routers have largely replaced conventional bridges and routers in the marketplace; this is because they combine the functions and hence the benefits of dedicated bridges and routers. Subject to costs, they are suitable as standard all-purpose intermediate nodes for most internetwork requirements. Routers provide superior traffic management by enforcing hierarchical addressing and least-cost routing to optimize expensive wide area bandwidth.

References

[1]   T. Kenyon, *High-Performance Network Design: Design Techniques and Tools* (Woburn, MA: Digital Press, 2001).

[2]   www.itu.ch, the International Telecommunications Union (ITU) home page

[3]   U. Black, *TCP/IP and Related Protocols,* (New York: McGraw-Hill, 1992).

[4]   D. E. Comer, *Internetworking with TCP/IP,* Vol. I: *Principles, Protocols, and Architecture* (Englewood Cliffs, NJ: Prentice Hall, 1991).

[5]   D. E. Comer, *Internetworking with TCP/IP,* Vol. II: *Design, Implementation, and Internals,* (Englewood Cliffs, NJ: Prentice Hall, 1991).

[6]   P. Miller, *TCP/IP Explained,* (Woburn, MA: Digital Press, 1997).

[7]   W. Stallings, *Data and Computer Communications,* (Englewood Cliffs, NJ: Prentice Hall, 1997).

[8]   D. Crocker, Standard for the Format of ARPA Internet Text Messages, RFC 822, August 13, 1982.

2

Addressing, Naming, and Configuration

This chapter discusses some of the key issues involved in the design of network addressing models, the allocation of network addresses and names, and some of the techniques used to support a device configuration in medium- to large-scale internetworks. Since we are largely concerned with sizable networks, we will focus primarily on the IP address model, although we will briefly touch upon other addressing schemes that you may encounter. Network addressing is closely associated with routing design; hence, this chapter makes cross-references, as appropriate, to Chapter 3. The following topics are covered here:

- An overview of the IP addressing schemes in IP versions 4 and 6 and the function of unicast, multicast, and broadcast addresses. IP address and Autonomous System Number (ASN) registration, private addressing schemes, and Network Address Translation (NAT) are also discussed.

- Dynamic address and configuration services such as RARP, DHCP, and BOOTP.

- Name-to-address mapping and directory services—DNS, WINS, X.500, LDAP.

- Commonly used design techniques for efficient addressing models, static and Variable Length Subnetting (VLSN), route summarization, Supernetting/Classless InterDomain Routing (CIDR).

Figure 2.1 illustrates some of the basic components of the overall IP architecture required for naming, addressing, and configuration services. As we can see in Figure 2.1, several layers of abstraction are introduced as we move up the stack. Address allocation and configuration are typically performed by DHCP or BOOTP. Address resolution (IP to MAC and vice versa) is performed by ARP and RARP. Unreachability is indicated via ICMP. Dynamic name services are provided via DNS. Directory services are

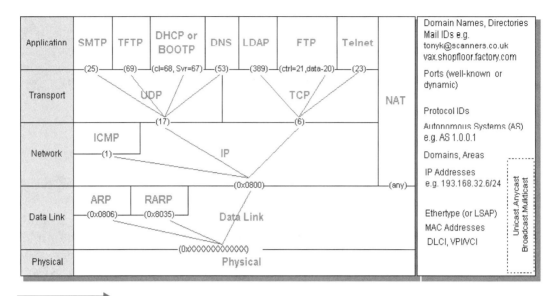

Figure 2.1   *Conceptual model showing the key protocols and context for addressing, naming, and configuration operations in an IP internetwork environment.*

provided by LDAP. Electronic mail is provided via SMTP. Address translation services at both the protocol and application layers are performed by NAT.

One of the problems of many large internetworks is that either they have evolved organically, or very little planning has taken place with respect to network address allocation. While at first this may seem a secondary issue for the network designer, a poorly thought out addressing model can result in severely degraded network performance and often limit scalability, as we will see shortly. A savvy designer can optimize valuable network bandwidth by using hierarchical addressing techniques coupled with modern hierarchical routing protocols such as OSPF.

Another key scalability issue for large-scale internetworks is the ability to manage address allocation and device configuration. On a network of 3,000 workstations it is clearly undesirable to hand-configure each device locally, especially if you have to do this more than once. Furthermore, there is an increasing trend toward mobile networking, so a static model is inappropriate. A means of dynamic configuration is required, and we will examine some common methodologies. On larger internetworks it is also likely that a naming service will be offered to provide a form of yellow pages directory service. In fact, with the scaling up of internetworks and the emergence of tools such as firewalls and dynamic dial-up VPNs, there is a growing need to configure and manage policies for features such as authentication, service quality, configuration data, and bandwidth. This huge mass of data is now beginning to be centralized and coordinated via directory services and protocols such as the Lightweight Directory Access Protocol (LDAP—described in section 2.5). We start by examining the underlying addressing model offered by IP.

2.1   The IP addressing model

TCP/IP implements a universal addressing scheme. Every device on an IP network, and every IP network itself, has a unique address that identifies it. This addressing scheme enables communication for millions of devices over public networks such as the Internet, as well as private intranets.

2.1.1   Implementation

We start by reviewing the provisions made within the IP protocol itself for Network Layer addressing. This is complicated by the fact that two versions of the IP protocol (IP version 4 and IP version 6) are likely to coexist on public and private networks for some time, for reasons we will discuss later in this chapter. Figure 2.2 illustrates the relative size of the address fields for IPv4 and IPv6. IPv4 provides 32 bits each for both the source and destination address fields. While this may seem huge, with 4,294,960,000 possible addresses available to each field (i.e., 2^{32}), we will discuss why the hierarchical model chosen for IPv4 has led to serious problems with address depletion. IPv6 provides 128 bits per address and implements a new addressing model designed to overcome some of the more obvious problems with IPv4. This addressing scheme makes it possible for devices such as IP routers to deliver messages between hosts in different parts of the world. With IPv4 each host has a unique address composed of a 32-bit (4-byte) number, and this is broken down into two parts: <netID><hostID>.

Since binary is not especially user friendly, IPv4 addresses are typically represented in dotted decimal notation, where each of the four bytes is represented in decimal form 0 to 255 (e.g., 140.55.3.2). This makes IP addresses easier for people to use and recall. All devices on an IP network must have an address; otherwise, they are not logically part of the network.

The netID is administered by the Internet Network Information Center (NIC). This part of the address is unique throughout the Internet.

Figure 2.2
IP header formats showing the space allocated for source and destination IP addresses.
(a) The IPv4 header length is a minimum of 20 bytes, supporting 32-bit addresses.
(b) The IPv6 header length is a minimum of 40 bytes, supporting 128-bit addresses.

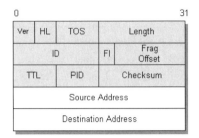

(a)

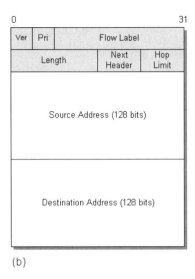

(b)

The hostID refers to an individual end system, unique within a network or subnetwork, which is typically administered locally by a systems administrator or a network design team.

The standards for IP addresses are described in [1], and specifically IPv4 and IPv6 are described in [2, 3]. IPv4 uses a system of hierarchical address classes, as described in the following text. IPv6 is discussed in section 2.1.7.

2.1.2 IP version 4 address classes

Because a host's IP address must uniquely identify not only the device itself but also the network to which the device is attached, the IP address requires at least two components: the network identifier (netID) and a host identifier (hostID). The division of the address space is, in fact, slightly more sophisticated to allow for different sized networks and is currently arranged to offer three classes of network—A, B, and C—together with a special class, D, for multicasting and a reserved class, E.

Of the five IP address classes, only the first three are relevant to the majority of users. Classes A, B, and C are for general-purpose unicast use; class D is used by special multicast applications and routing protocols such as OSPF and RIP II. In order to differentiate address classes quickly, the most significant bits of the netID field (the classID) are used, as illustrated in Figure 2.3. The class ID is a variable-length bit field, used to differentiate between different IPv4 address classes.

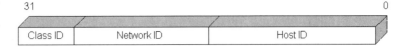

Figure 2.3
*General IPv4
address format.*

Figure 2.4 illustrates how the current IPv4 address space is broken down into the five address classes. Classes are differentiated by the most significant bits of the first byte. Classes A, B, and C each comprise a network part and a host part, which varies to accommodate different sized networks and different host population sizes. Class D is used for multicast applications and routing protocols such as OSPF and RIPv2. Associated with each of the three unicast address classes is a mask, or prefix. This is a bit mask, which is used by hosts and routers to determine how much of the netID is treated as significant for forwarding decisions. Note that IPv6 uses a completely different model, as described in section 2.1.7. The classes can be summarized as follows:

■ Class A addresses have the high-order bit set to 0. There are 7 bits available for network addresses. The remaining 24 bits are used for host addresses. The default mask is 255.0.0.0; the default prefix is /8.

■ Class B addresses have the high-order bits set to 10. There are 14 bits available for network addresses. The remaining 16 bits are used for host addresses. The default mask is 255.255.0.0; the default prefix is /16.

■ Class C addresses have the high-order bits set to 20. There are 21 bits available for network addresses. The remaining 8 bits are used for

Figure 2.4
*Classes A through
E: IP version 4
address formats.*

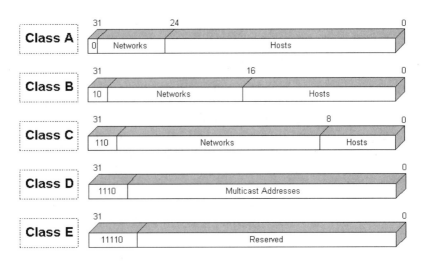

host addresses. The default mask is 255.255.255.0; the default prefix is /24.

■ Class D addresses have the high-order bits set to 210. There are 28 bits available for multicast addresses. These addresses are effectively group addresses, used by applications that need to send the same IP packet to many destinations concurrently. This can be a very efficient way to distribute such information, since the alternative would be to duplicate all of the information for every destination—for example, a financial application might use multicasts to distribute share prices to a group of subscribers. OSPF uses IP multicasts for delivering routing messages to other OSPF routers. See section 2.1.4 for further information.

Class E addresses have the high-order bits set to 220. The remaining 27 bits are reserved for experimental use only (not for use on public networks).

Masks and prefixes

As mentioned previously, each of the three classes of unicast IP addresses has a fixed contiguous series of bits called the network mask associated with it. In fact, we refer to this as the natural mask, when the number of bits used exactly matches the number of bits allocated to the netID, as illustrated in Figure 2.4. The natural mask indicates exactly how much of the address is allocated to the netID, the remainder being the hostID. For example, the class A address 10.0.0.0 has a natural mask of 255.0.0.0, indicating that only the first 8 bits are used by the netID; the remaining 24 bits are available for hosts. In fact, it is possible to vary the length of the mask (forming unnatural masks) to facilitate address optimization through operations such as subnetting or supernetting. These advanced topics are described later in this section.

The mask is important for any device that transmits or forwards packets, since by ANDing this mask with a destination address we can readily determine if a packet should be sent directly to the local network or forwarded to another network. For example, assume a host using the IP address 195.66.3.6 wishes to communicate with another host at 195.66.5.3. By ANDing these two addresses with the host's own natural mask, 255.255.255.0, we can see that they are not part of the same network, and, therefore, the host must forward packets for this destination to its nearest router (as described in Chapter 3).

```
200002 01000010 0000002 0000020 = 195.66.3.6    // Class C address
200002 01000010 00000101 0000002 = 195.66.5.3   // Class C address
```

```
2222 2222 2222 XXXXXXXX   255.255.255.0    // Natural Network Mask
---------------------------------         logical_AND
200002 01000010 0000021 XXXXXXXX = 195.66.7.X // Different IP prefix!
```

In recent years a shorthand method of representing masks has emerged, called the address prefix. The prefix indicates the number of contiguous bits used by the mask (note that a mask can be noncontiguous, but this makes no sense for a prefix). Using our example class A address 10.0.0.0, the appropriate natural prefix for this address is /8, so we can use the shorthand form 10.0.0.0/8 to indicate both the address and the size of the mask.

Address ranges

Classes A, B, and C are used for a range of large to small IP networks, respectively, where the netID portion of the address competes for space with the hostID portion (since there is only a fixed number of bits). Very few organizations have class A addresses, and they are now practically impossible to get hold of. Class B addresses are used for large organizations, but even they are in rationed supply. When you connect into an ISP nowadays, you will most likely get a class C address, or a number of class C addresses. Table 2.1 illustrates the ranges available. Note that the class A address 127.0.0.0 is reserved as the local loopback address. Max Networks is calculated as $2^{(netIDbits)} - 1$ (we subtract the prefix bits). Max Hosts is calculated as $2^{(hostIDbits)} - 2$. We subtract 2 from this number because all 1s are usually reserved for broadcasting and all 0s is reserved for historical reasons (it was originally used as a broadcast address in early implementations of IP).Nodes with the same address class and prefix can communicate directly. Nodes with a different address class, or the same address class and a different prefix, would normally communicate via an intermediate device (i.e., a Layer 3 switch, router, proxy, or possibly NAT). It is possible to have hosts configured with multiple IP addresses of different classes on the same physical interface.

Table 2.1   *Classes A through E: Address Ranges and Configuration Data*

Class	Prefix	Address Range From	To	Max Networks	Max Hosts	Type
A	0	1.0.0.0	126.0.0.0	126	16,777,124	Unicast
B	10	128.1.0.0	191.255.0.0	16,383	65,534	Unicast
C	110	192.0.1.0	223.255.255.0	2,097,151	254	Unicast
D	1110	224.0.0.0	239.255.255.255	na	na	Multicast
E	11110	240.0.0.0	tbd	tbd	tbd	Reserved

Special and reserved addresses

There are several network addresses that are reserved for special purposes, as follows:

- Source network and host address bits set to 0—Generally there are two cases: either all bits set to 0 or just the network portion set to 0 together with a valid host address. In both cases this equates to This Host This Network and should be seen only in the source IP address field. A typical use of this option would be when a host is initializing, and wants to communicate over a network but does not yet know the network IP address and so solicits help. For example, BOOTP is a good example of this use; a reply from a BOOTP server contains the fully qualified network address, which the sender will then record for subsequent use. BOOTP is described later in this chapter.

- Destination address broadcasts—There are several forms of special IP destination broadcasts, as summarized in section 2.1.3.

- Loopback address—The special class A network 127.0.0.0 is reserved as a special loop-back network address for devices implementing an IP stack. It should never appear outside a host. This network address is typically used for testing and debugging communication software, since it can act as a target sink point inside the host system. For example, a client/server application could easily be tested inside a single host by referencing ports on this IP address, without packets ever leaving the host itself.

2.1.3   Broadcast addresses

A broadcast is a special group destination address, where everybody is expected to be a member of that group by default. In the IP world, as with many other technologies, broadcasts are very common, and in the IP addressing model there are several forms of special IP destination broadcasts to be aware of, including the following:

- Limited broadcast—If all bits of the destination IP address field are set to 1, then this means all networks or all hosts and is effectively a limited broadcast to all nodes on the local network segment (i.e., routers should not forward any such messages).

- Directed broadcast—If the network number is a valid netID but the host number bits are all set to 1, then this is called a directed broadcast—for example, 140.56.255.255. This would be sent to all hosts on the class B network 140.56.0.0. This form of broadcast would be forwarded to all subnetworks of this address if subnetting were employed (assuming that all routers in the distribution path have routing protocols that are subnet aware, as described in Chapter 3).

- Subnet broadcast—The above rules also apply at the subnet level. If subnetting is implemented, then the subnet address containing all 1s must be reserved for broadcast use. For example, a class C network, 193.160.30.0, could have a subnet mask 255.255.255.192 (prefix /26), where the first two bits of the host address are reserved for subnet addresses. The subnet broadcast in this case is, therefore, 193.160.30.192 (i.e., both bits set).

- HostID zero—HostIDs of all 0s should never appear in destination address fields, (i.e., <netID>.0 or <netID>.<subnetID>.0).

Note that when creating subnetworks you must remember that not all permutations of the subnet bits are valid subnetwork addresses. In the example using a /26 prefix given above we would create four subnets: 192, 128, 64, and 0 (using bit permutations 2, 10, 01, and 00). As stated, we cannot use 2 since this is a subnetwork broadcast. It is also not recommended to use all zero (00) subnet addresses, since some older (before BSD 4.3) IP implementations used 0.0.0.0 for limited broadcasts. Having said that, it is now a fairly common practice to use the all-zero subnet address.

Broadcast forwarding

Routers must discard limited broadcasts unless explicitly configured to relay them. Sometimes broadcasts are required to be flooded through the entire internetwork (e.g., if a device is advertising a global service or issuing a BOOTP request for configuration data). Some routers support a technique by which these broadcasts are forwarded over a Spanning Tree of the network, rather than all branches. (Reference [4] indicates that the Spanning Tree of a graph ensures complete reachability without duplicated traffic.) Another form of broadcast assistance is accommodated with a relay mechanism (often called a helper address [4]). Typically you would manually configure helper addresses on a router, or a series of routers in a path, to relay broadcasts that would otherwise be discarded. Note that enterprise and access routers may support this functionality for several protocol stacks in addition to IP. For example, you could permit retransmission of Novell service announcement (SAP) broadcasts using helper addresses, thereby notifying clients on remote network segments about NetWare services available locally.

Performance issues

Reference [4] discusses how broadcast replication can seriously affect scalability in NonBroadcast MultiAccess (NBMA) networks such as Frame Relay and ATM. On multiaccess LANs, such as Ethernet, the issues are more subtle. IP broadcasts are mapped to the MAC broadcast address 0xFFFFFFFF. This is an address that all network interface cards (NICs) and network-attached devices must listen to, and if necessary respond to. Receipt of a broadcast results in an interrupt, since the receiving node must process all broadcasts to assess whether the packet is relevant or should be discarded. The higher the broadcast rate, the more interrupts, sapping valuable CPU time. Unless broadcast levels are controlled, network bandwidth and system resources can be seriously degraded. Routers typically offer various broadcast-limiting functions that reduce network traffic and minimize the probability and scope of broadcast storms. It is notable that IPv6 has done away with the concept of the broadcast altogether, as described in section 2.1.7. This should facilitate tighter control of traffic over internetworks in the future.

2.1.4   Multicast group addresses

The final 28 bits of a class D address are unstructured (there is no associated bit mask) and range in value from 224.0.0.0 through 239.255.255.255. The multicast group address is basically an aggregation of the high-order 4 bits (210) and the multicast group ID (although multicast group addresses are represented by the dotted-decimal notation, this is primarily for ease of use; there is no class prefix). A group of hosts that listens and responds to a particular IP multicast group address is referred to as a host group, and a host group can be physically located on multiple networks. Hosts typically join or leave a group dynamically, although some implementations may allow static configuration (further information on IP multicast protocol operations is provided in Chapter 4). Well-known multicast group addresses (i.e., the equivalent of a well-known port) are assigned by the Internet Assigned Numbers Authority (IANA): There are two kinds of host group, as follows:

- Permanent—The multicast group address is permanently assigned by IANA. A permanent group exists even if it has no members. Hosts can join or leave a group at will.

- Transient—Any multicast group that is not permanent is transient and can be dynamically assigned as and when required. Unlike permanent groups, transient groups cease to exist when they have no members.

An application can retrieve a permanent host group address from the domain name system using the domain mcast.net, or retrieve the permanent group from an address by using a pointer query in the domain 224.in-addr.arpa (see section 2.3.2 for the operation of the in-addr.arpa domain). The current list of IP addresses assigned to permanent host groups is specified in [5]. Table 2.2 provides a list of important multicast group addresses.

Address mapping to Ethernet

The IANA owns a block of Ethernet addresses in the range 00:00:5e:00:00:00 through 00:00:5e:ff:ff:ff. Half of this block is allocated for multicast addresses. Since the first byte of an Ethernet address must be set to 0x01 to signify a multicast, the actual addresses that map to IP multicast addresses are in the range 01:00:5e:00:00:00 through 01:00:5e:7f:ff:ff. The least significant 23 bits of the Ethernet address are, therefore, available for mapping to IP multicast group IDs. The mapping places the low-order 23 bits of the multicast group ID into these 23 bits of the Ethernet address. For example, an OSPF Hello message (see Chapter 3) uses the multicast destination address 224.0.0.5, which maps onto the Ethernet MAC address 01005e000005. Figure 2.5 shows an example of how mapping works at the bit level.

Since the five high-order bits of the multicast address are ignored in this mapping, the resulting address is not unique; in fact, 32 different multicast group IDs map to each Ethernet address. Because the mapping is not unique, the interface card is likely to receive some multicast frames that the host is really not interested in, so the device driver or IP stack must filter out unwanted frames.

Table 2.2   *Examples of Well-known Multicast Group Addresses*

Address	Description
224.0.0.0	Reserved Base Address
224.0.0.1	All Systems on this subnet
224.0.0.2	All routers on this subnet
224.0.0.5	All OSPF Routers
224.0.0.6	OSPF Designated Routers
224.0.0.9	All RIP2 Routers

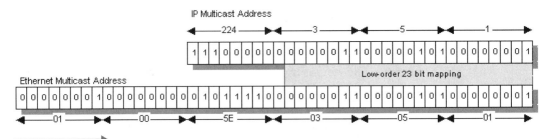

Figure 2.5   *Multicast addresses mapping between an IPv4 address and Ethernet. In this example the class D multicast 224.3.5.1 is mapped onto the MAC address 0x01005e030501.*

Multicasting on a multiaccess network is quite straightforward. The sending process inserts a destination IP multicast address into the IP packet header, and a media device driver maps this to the corresponding multicast MAC address before transmission. The media device driver also handles multicast reception. The receiving process must notify its own IP protocols and services to establish whether they want to receive packets destined for a given multicast address; if so, then it must deliver a copy to all processes belonging to that group (multiple processes on a given host can belong to the same multicast group). In a routed environment the situation is more complicated; the processes and protocols required for group registration and multicast delivery are dealt with in Chapter 4.

2.1.5   The official IP address space

In order to guarantee any-to-any communication over public networks such as the Internet, all participating systems must use IP addresses that have been officially allocated (often called legal addresses). If you are setting up an entirely private network and do not intend to communicate with systems over the Internet, then you are free to choose your own network numbers. However, if circumstances change, you run the risk of redesign of your network or having to use address translation devices (see section 2.1.6 for the recommended way to design private addressing schemes).

Obtaining registered addresses

IP addresses belong to what is referred to as the IP Address Space, and are administered by the Internet Assigned Numbers Authority (IANA—see [6]). The IANA is the overall authority for administration of IP addresses, Domain Name System (DNS) names, Autonomous System Numbers (ASNs), and Top-Level Domains (TLDs). When discussing IP addresses, you will come across the terms assigned and allocated. The terms have the following meanings:

- Assigned—The number of network numbers in use. The class C figures are somewhat inaccurate, because the figures do not include many class C networks in Europe, which were allocated to [7] and subsequently assigned but are still recorded as allocated.

- Allocated—This includes all of the assigned networks and, additionally, those networks that have either been reserved by IANA or have been allocated to regional registries by IANA and will subsequently be assigned by those registries.

There is a hierarchy of assignment authority, with authority delegated down from the IANA itself. Below the IANA are the Regional Registries (RRs); below them lie the subregistries (Local Internet Registries [IRs], Internet Service Providers [ISPs], etc.). Requests are normally made to the higher authority unless a particular organization is large enough to require a direct dialog with the IANA (requirements for a class A network, for example, are handled on an individual case basis). There are three regional registries that handle worldwide IP address assignments, as follows:

- APNIC (Asia-Pacific Network Information Center)—Handles IP address allocation for Asia-Pacific. Contact [8] for registration.

- ARIN (American Registry for Internet Numbers)—Handles IP address allocation for North and South America, the Caribbean, and sub-Saharan Africa. Contact [9] for registration.

- RIPE NCC (Réseau IP Européens)—Handles IP address allocation for Europe and surrounding areas. Contact [7] for registration.

To obtain an official IP address and have your host name officially recognized, you must register with the appropriate authority. Depending on your needs, you will most likely be allocated a class C network identifier. Class B addresses are now only available to large organizations, and class A network space is effectively used up (remember that there are only 126 possible class A networks). When you register, you'll also need to choose a domain name. For the interested reader, reference [10] describes the rules and guidelines governing the distribution of the official IP address space.

IP address depletion

When the IP protocols were first devised, it was reasonable to assume that a 32-bit address space would satisfy all future demands. Unfortunately, this is now known not to be the case; over the past decade the number of networks on the Internet has been roughly doubling annually, and the distribution host space within the address classes varies enormously. The class A portion of the number space represents 50 percent of the total IP host addresses; class B is 25 percent of the total; and class C is approximately 12 percent of the total. By 1993, 38 percent of class A addresses, 45 percent of class B addresses, and only 2 percent of class C addresses were already allocated. Many new network addresses assigned in the late 1980s were actually class B, and it became apparent in 1990 that if this trend continued, the last class B network number would be assigned during 1994. Since class C networks were rarely being used, this made no sense at all. By 1996, all class A addresses were either allocated or assigned, as were 62 percent of class B addresses and 36 percent of class C addresses. The result is that the amount of address space currently available for new networks is quite limited and requires careful control. Because of these limitations, many organizations have been using privately assigned (unregistered) IP addresses, either because they were not expecting to use the Internet or because they did not want the constraints of building a network around a small number of registered addresses.

The reasons for IP address depletion are in part due to the inefficiency of the IPv4 addressing scheme, and the way in which addresses have been allocated to users, as follows:

- Address model inefficiency—There is a substantial difference between the number of host addresses allocated and those actually needed. Although the natural byte-aligned divisions of the IP address classes are simple and relatively user friendly, with hindsight it is not the most efficient scheme. The host space in class B networks is invariably too huge to be fully populated by the majority of organizations, and class C networks are simply too small to be useful in many cases.

- Demand for class B—Many users realized that a class B address was future proof (accommodating up to 65,534 hosts). Since it makes sense to use the largest address space available, even designers of small networks chose class B addresses. Since many class B networks were also being assigned to small networks (well below 65,534 hosts), these networks effectively locked out huge areas of the address space.

- Inflexibility and hidden costs for class C—Many users regard class C addresses (with a maximum of 254 hosts) as extremely limiting. Clearly, one could use multiple class C networks; however, this could be much more expensive in real terms, since routers are required to communicate between each network and more sophisticated designs are required.

A network of 5,000 hosts could be supported by a single class B network (65,534 hosts) or 20 class C networks ($2 \times 254 = 5,080$). While the class B address copes with this requirement comfortably, it is only 7.6 percent efficient (5,000/65,534), locking up 92.4 percent of perfectly good address space. On the other hand, our class C approach is 98 percent efficient but requires special techniques such as supernetting (described in section 2.5.4) to deal with the fact that we now have 20 routing advertisements to cope with.

IP address allocation guidelines

As a result of these problems, several measures have been put in place to avoid complete depletion as the number of new networks requiring Internet access rises. Since 1990, the number of assigned class B networks has been increasing at a much lower rate than the total number of assigned networks, due largely to the introduction of tighter address allocation policies by IANA. In 1993, much stronger constraints were introduced in the address allocation guidelines outlined in RFC 1466 (made obsolete by [10]). In late 1996, these policies were refined further and are briefly summarized as follows:

- The IANA and the IR retain sole responsibility for the assignment of class A network numbers. The upper half of the class A address space (network numbers 64 through 127) is reserved indefinitely to allow for the possibility of using it for transition to a new numbering scheme. The lower half of the class C address space (network numbers 192.0.0 through 207.255.255) is divided into eight blocks, which are allocated to regional authorities, as shown in Table 2.3. The upper half of the class C address space (208.0.0 through 223.255.255) remains unassigned and unallocated. In Table 2.3 others are to be used where flexibility outside the constraints of regional boundaries is required. Multiregional incorporates the class C networks that were already assigned before this scheme was adopted. The 192 networks were assigned by the InterNIC, and the 193 networks were previously allocated to RIPE in Europe.

- One of the key factors in determining how much address space is appropriate for an organization is the expected utilization rate of the network. This is expressed as the number of hosts attached to the network divided by the total number of hosts possible on the network. In addition, the estimated number of hosts should be projected over a reasonable time frame—that is, one in which the requesting enterprise has a high level of confidence. The minimum utilization rate is set by the IANA. Depending upon the type or number of addresses requested, details of the network design and intended numbering plan may also be required.

- In effect, the traditional concept of IP assignment by address class has been abandoned. To maximize use of address space, IP addresses are now assigned in classless blocks (i.e., by prefix length). Consequently, an organization that would previously have been assigned a class B will now be assigned a /16 prefix, regardless of the actual address class.

- The use of static IP address assignments (e.g., one address per customer) for dial-up users is strongly discouraged.

- CIDR addresses (discussed in section 2.5.4) are allocated to ISPs in blocks, and fragmentation of blocks is discouraged. ISPs are recommended to treat address assignments as loans; if a customer terminates the ISP contract, it is recommended that the address be returned and the customer should renumber (presumably from a new ISP's address space). The ISP should allow sufficient time for the renumbering process to be completed before the IP addresses are reused. This recommendation could prove interesting for large organizations unhappy with their ISP, since the burden of renumbering could be significant.

Many of the guidelines are rightly concerned with controlling the rate of address allocation based on quantifiable measurements—that is, predicted and achieved consumption rates provided by the ISP or requesting organization. There is also more emphasis on documented evidence, such as

Table 2.3   *Class C Address Allocation*

| Address Range | | Allocation |
From	To	
192.0.0	193.255.255	Multi-Regional
194.0.0	195.255.255	Europe
196.0.0	197.255.255	Others
198.0.0	199.255.255	North America
200.0.0	201.255.255	Central & South America
202.0.0	203.255.255	Pacific Rim
204.0.0	205.255.255	Others
206.0.0	207.255.255	Others

accounting and historical address allocation data and future deployment plans. The complete guidelines can be found in [10]. In particular, the move toward prefix-based allocation will become apparent in the following sections; this is not a permanent solution to the overall IP address space constraints but will help in the interim. A long-term solution is available with IPv6, as discussed in section 2.1.7.

2.1.6   Private intranet addressing

Another approach to conservation of the IP address space is described in [11] and is generally referred to as private IP addressing. Private addressing relaxes the rule that IP addresses must be globally unique, by reserving part of the official IP address space for networks that are used exclusively within a single organization and that do not need to communicate publicly (e.g., over the Internet). A large organization may feel, for example, that a set of class C addresses or a subnetted class B address may be too clumsy or inflexible to deal with and may choose its own addressing scheme. In this event you are strongly advised not to choose just any address at random. The only application where unregistered addresses are appropriate is for lab-testing equipment in isolation (where you may, in fact, need to replicate legal addressing to simulate a customer network).

Registered private addresses

It turns out that there are three official IP address blocks that have been reserved by IANA for private use [11]. The fact that addresses will not be unique is irrelevant, since by definition all users of these addresses must be running their networks in isolation. The following chart lists these addresses.

From	To	Prefix	Class
10.0.0.0	10.255.255.255	/8	A
172.16.0.0	172.31.255.255	/12	B
192.168.0.0	192.168.255.255	/16	C

The first block is a single class A network number, while the second block is a group of 16 contiguous class B network numbers, and the third block is a group of 256 contiguous class C network numbers. Any organization can use any of these addresses privately. You are, therefore free, for example, to build a huge class A network, so long as its address is 10.x.x.x/8. The advantage of this scheme (at least from the Internet's point of view) is that if you should accidentally connect into the Internet via an ISP, then your traffic should be discarded. Since ISPs are aware of these addresses, they should filter any traffic originating from these addresses to avoid any duplicate addressing issues.

Migrating to public network access

If access to public networks is subsequently required by an organization, regardless of whether it has chosen an illegal or an RFC 1918–compliant addressing scheme, then the choices are as follows:

- Obtain registered addresses and reconfigure all network attached devices (as described in section 2.1.5).

- Use application gateways or application proxies, which are legally addressed on their public interfaces.

- Use Network Address Translation (NAT) to convert legal to private addresses dynamically at the public-private edge.

It is not hard to obtain legal addresses, but the implications for a large enterprise in terms of redesign and reconfiguration could be daunting. A business may not sanction the need to take the network offline while this work is done, and a less aggressive migration path may have to be found. Application proxies are widely available for most of the common IP-based services (such as FTP, HTTP, and SMTP). Proxies have the added bonus of providing a good security barrier, as described in Chapter 5. The downside is that they are not transparent and require all users to be relayed through them, leading to potentially serious throughput and latency problems. Since proxies are also application specific, they can limit flexibility; it is difficult to find good proxies for protocols other than TCP. Perhaps the most popular and convenient solution to this problem is Network Address Translation (NAT), discussed in section 2.5.2. NAT is a generic solution and completely transparent to users. NAT's flexibility means that access to public networks can be granted immediately, while remedial work to rework the network can take place in parallel. Furthermore, for increased performance NAT can be deployed in load-sharing clusters, as described in Chapter 6.

2.1.7   IP next generation (IPng)

Because of the well-publicized limitations of IPv4, in 1992 the IETF issued a call for proposals for a new version of IP, commonly referred to as IP Next Generation (IPng). IPng emerged in final form in late 1994 as IPv6 (the more observant will have noted the absence of IPv5; in fact, IPv5 exists

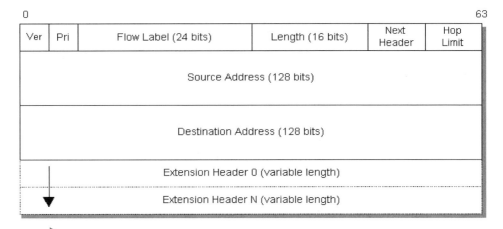

0   63

Ver	Pri	Flow Label (24 bits)	Length (16 bits)	Next Header	Hop Limit

Source Address (128 bits)

Destination Address (128 bits)

Extension Header 0 (variable length)

Extension Header N (variable length)

Figure 2.6 *IPv6 message format. Only the version field (Ver) remains intact from the IPv4 format.*

today as the so-called stream protocol used in some routers). The designers of IPv6 paid particular attention to the following areas: addressing, performance, class of service, and security enhancements (outlined as major requirements in [12]). These features are discussed below and in subsequent chapters. For full details of IPv6 and the addressing architecture the interested reader is referred to [3, 13].

Message format

The IPv6 header is a radical departure from the IPv4 header format, as illustrated in Figure 2.6. The minimum header size is now 40 bytes (as opposed to 20 bytes with IPv4). The most significant change is the expansion of the address space to support 128-bit (16-byte) source and destination addresses (discussed in section 2.1.1). IPv6 also integrates strong security features via the IP Security Architecture (IPSec), as described in Chapter 5.

As indicated, the IPv6 header can be supplemented by a series of extension headers of variable length. The following extension headers are currently defined [3], listed in the order they would appear in the packet (if included):

- Hop-by-hop options header—for special operations that require hop-by-hop processing.

- Routing header—provides extended routing (such as IPv4 source routing).

- Fragment header—contains fragmentation and reassembly information.

- Authentication header (AH)—provides packet authentication and integrity for network security.

- Encapsulating Security Payload (ESP) header—provides privacy.

- Destination options header—provides additional data to be examined by the destination node.

The AH and ESP headers are an integral part of IPSec, and are discussed in more detail in Chapter 5. We now briefly review some of the more important aspects of this new format.

Field definitions

- Ver—The IP version number. Set to 6.

- Priority—Enables the source to specify the desired transmit and delivery priority on a per-packet basis. Packets can be assigned one of eight priority levels. This field also identifies traffic that is congestion controlled at source.

- Flow label—Enables the source to label packets for special handling by intermediate devices.

- Length—The payload length in bytes (i.e., all data following the mandatory 40-byte IP header).

- Next header—Signifies the type of header following the IPv6 header—either an extension header or a higher-layer protocol, such as TCP, UDP, OSP.

- Hop limit—The number of hops remaining valid for this packet. Set by the source and decremented by intermediate devices. The packet is discarded if a decrement operation results in zero.

- Source address—The address of the source node. Described further in the following sections.

- Destination address—The address of the destination node. Described further in the following sections.

- Extension headers—Special options headers. Described further in the following sections.

Addressing model

IPv6 supports three modes of addressing: unicast, anycast, and multicast, as follows:

- Unicast addresses operate as expected, in that they target individual host interfaces. There are several variations of unicast, including an IPv4-compatibility mode (intended to provide a smooth migration path). Unicast addresses may be assigned to multiple physical interfaces if the implementation treats the interface group as a single interface at the Internet layer (useful for load sharing over multiple physical interfaces).

- Anycast addressing is a refinement of unicast that streamlines routing. It identifies a set of interfaces (typically belonging to different nodes). A packet sent to an anycast address is delivered to one of the interfaces identified by that address (the nearest one, according to the routing metric employed).

- Multicast addresses operate as expected; they allow messages to be sent to a predefined group of interfaces with a single multicast address.

The IPv6 address model approaches host addressing in a manner subtly different from IPv4. IPv6 addresses are assigned to interfaces, not nodes. A node can have several interfaces and any of the unicast addresses assigned to an interface can be used as an identifier for the node. There are no broadcast addresses in IPv6; these are superseded by multicast addresses. In IPv6, all zeros and all ones are legal values for any field, unless specifically excluded. Specifically, prefixes may contain zero-valued fields or end in zeros. There are two special addresses to note, as follows:

- The unspecified address—The special address 0:0:0:0:0:0:0:0 must never be assigned to any node. It indicates the absence of an address. One example of its use is in the source address field of any IPv6 datagrams sent by an initializing host before it has learned its own address. The unspecified address must not be used as the destination address of IPv6 datagrams or in IPv6 routing headers.

- The loopback address—The special unicast address 0:0:0:0:0:0:0:1 may be used by a node to send an IPv6 datagram to itself. It may never be assigned to any interface. The loopback address must not be used as the source address in IPv6 datagrams that are sent outside of a single node. An IPv6 datagram with a destination address of loopback must never be sent outside of a single node. Note that [14] states that the IPv4-compatible IPv6 address ::127.0.0.1 should also be treated as a loopback address for migration purposes.

Address format

The address field in IPv6 is 128 bits (16 bytes) wide, as illustrated in Figure 2.2. This is four times wider than the IPv4 address space, and so unfortunately requires a new syntax. The preferred form for writing IPv6 addresses is H:H:H:H:H:H, where H is a hexadecimal 16-bit piece of the address. For example:

> FF0E:0:0:A0B9:0:23
> FEDC:BA98:7654:3210:FEDC:BA98:7654:3210
> 1080:0:0:0:8:800:200C:417A

It is not necessary to write the leading zeros in an individual field, but there must be at least one numeral in every field. Having said that, in IPv6 it is common for addresses to contain long strings of zeros. Reference [13], therefore, specifies the use of the special shorthand indicator ::, which can be used once in the address to compress arbitrary length strings of zeros. For example:

Address	*Shorthand*	*Type*
1080:0:0:0:8:800:200C:417A	1080::8:800:200C:417A	unicast
FF01:0:0:0:0:0:0:43	FF01::43	multicast
0:0:0:0:0:0:0:1	::1	loopback
0:0:0:0:0:0:0:0	::	unspecified

In mixed IPv4 and IPv6 environments it may also be beneficial to use the form H:H:H:H:H:H:D.D.D.D, where H is a 16-bit hexadecimal value and D is an 8-bit decimal value corresponding to the standard IPv4 representation. For example:

> 0:0:0:0:0:0:193.128.68.1
> 0:0:0:0:0:FFFF:12.100.50.77

Clearly, in an IPv6 environment the importance of name services (described in section 2.3) will be brought to the fore! For the interested reader [14] provides useful material on IPv6 addressing formats with several examples.

Address type representation

As with IPv4, the leading bits in the address field determine the address type. In IPv6 this is called the Format Prefix (FP). The initial allocation of these prefixes is shown in the following chart.

Allocation	Prefix (binary)	Fraction of Address Space
Reserved	0000 0000	1/256
Unassigned	0000 0001	1/256
Reserved for NSAP Allocation	0000 001	1/128
Reserved for IPX Allocation	0000 010	1/128
Unassigned	0000 02	1/128
Unassigned	0000	1 1/32
Unassigned	0001	1/16
Unassigned	001	1/8
Provider-Based Unicast Address	010	1/8
Unassigned	02	1/8
Reserved for Geographic-Based Unicast Addresses	100	1/8
Unassigned	101	1/8
Unassigned	20	1/8
Unassigned	210	1/16
Unassigned	22 0	1/32
Unassigned	22 10	1/64
Unassigned	22 20	1/128
Unassigned	22 210 0	1/512
Link Local Use Addresses	22 210 10	1/1024
Site Local Use Addresses	22 210 2	1/1024
Multicast Addresses	22 22	1/256

Unicast addresses are distinguished from multicast addresses by the high-order octet: a value of 0xFF (binary 2222) identifies a multicast address; any other value identifies a unicast address. Anycast and unicast addresses use the same FP and the same address space. Note that the unspecified address, the loopback address, and IPv6 addresses with embedded IPv4 addresses are assigned out of the 0000 0000 FP space. For full details of the IPv6 addressing model the interested reader is referred to [13].

Performance

IPv6 has the potential to improve performance in three ways, as follows:

- Fewer header fields. Although the IPv6 header is twice the size of the IPv4 header (see Figure 2.2), it contains fewer fields (8, as opposed to 12 in IPv4), reducing the processing overhead on routers.

- Fixed-length headers. IPv4 supports variable-length options in the header; this complicates packet processing in routers and end systems. IPv6 has a fixed 40-byte header.

- No fragmentation. IPv6 determines the MTU requirements of inter-mediate networks at source by using an algorithm to discover the lowest MTU supported over the transmission path. This negates the requirement for fragmentation and reassembly at the expense of the discovery process (especially useful in long-haul networks over mixed media types).

On the downside, addresses are significantly larger, so any address manipulation operations will spend more time parsing. Routing table entries will also be significantly larger, so routing protocols need to carry more payload, and memory requirements on routing systems generally will increase.

Migration to IPv6

IPv6 is designed to ease the task of migrating from IPv4, but nobody seri-ously expects the process to be without a great deal of pain and cost. Fea-tures such as IPv4-compatible addressing and IPv6-over-IPv4 tunneling at least make coexistence possible, but there are several major obstacles to overcome, including the following:

- The memory requirements for intermediate devices and devices that manipulate and store address–based data (e.g., routers, switches, and firewalls) are increased by a factor of four (worst case) for network addresses. These devices will also need to support both IPv4 and IPv6 devices in the interim.

- During the transition phase IPv6 hosts are likely to have both a 32-bit IPv4 address and a 128-bit IPv6 address. This causes extra prob-lems for applications such as the Domain Name System (DNS), which will have to respond to queries from IPv6 hosts with both addresses. The implications for DNS resources and performance are significant.

■ The installed base of TCP/IPv4 applications, tools, and services is huge and have for years assumed 32-bit IP addresses. The ability to manipulate and store larger addresses is almost certainly going to require some element of redesign, as are the user interfaces. In the interim these applications will be unable to communicate with IPv6 hosts without some form of intermediate gateway.

The transition to a pure IPv6 network will be gradual, although there is mounting pressure to deploy migration services now. IP addresses are becoming increasingly scarce, as organizations expand and demand for Internet access increases daily. All of the major router vendors have already implemented, or are planning to implement, IPv6 in their operating systems in preparation for the road ahead. The interested reader is referred to [15].

2.1.8   Autonomous System Numbers (ASNs)

At the top of the IP address hierarchy is a layer of abstraction called the Autonomous System (AS). An AS is essentially a group of LANs and WANs interconnected via routers, under common administrative control (i.e., having a single routing policy). ASs are identified by a globally unique Autonomous System Number (ASN). This number is used in both the exchange of exterior routing information (between neighboring ASs) and as an identifier of the AS itself. ASNs are, therefore, configured on routers and routing protocols and are entirely transparent to users. They are primarily an administrative addressing layer used to constrain and route traffic. Furthermore, ASNs are applicable only to routing nodes that run exterior gateway routing protocols such as BGP and IDRP. End systems are not configured as AS members.

ASNs are 16 bits wide, and, therefore, a total of 65,535 ASNs are possible. ASNs are ultimately administered by the IANA. The IANA has reserved the block of ASNs between 64,512 and 65,535 for private use (these ASNs are not to be advertised publicly). This leaves only 6,452 ASNs for user allocation, so this address space requires careful monitoring and strict control over registration if it is not to be depleted. In March 1996 approximately 5,100 ASNs had been allocated, with approximately 600 actively routed over the Internet [16]. Commercial organizations must register for an official ASN; it is not recommended that you choose your own, particularly if you intend to attach your network to a public network such as the Internet. The basic criteria for deciding whether an ASN is required are summarized as follows:

- Exchange of external routing information—An ASN is required for exchanging external routing information with other ASs through an exterior routing protocol such as BGP. Note that the exchange of external routing information alone does not constitute the need for an AS.

- Many prefixes, one AS—As a general rule, one should try to place as many prefixes as possible within a given AS, provided all of them conform to the same routing policy. So, for example, a single-homed site with a single prefix should use the ASN of the provider and does not require one of its own. The same is true for a single-homed site with multiple prefixes. A multihomed site attached to different service providers and different ASs does, however, require its own ASN.

- Unique routing policy—An ASN is required when you have a routing policy that differs from that of your border gateway peers.

For ease of use ASNs are generally represented using the familiar dotted-decimal notation, although the ASN number space is entirely flat, with no prefix or class bits to worry about. For example, 1.0.0.1 is a valid ASN number. Note that ASNs are also configured on routers running hierarchical interior routing protocols (such as OSPF and Dual-IS-IS). In this case, however, ASNs are used as routing tags, and in practice are not seen by exterior routing protocols. You could, therefore, use your own ASN internal to your network; the key issue is not to configure a private ASN on your BGP-enabled interfaces pointing out to a public network. For further detail on routing operations refer to Chapter 3. For full details on registration and use guidelines refer to [16]. For an up-to-date list of assigned ASNs refer to [17].

2.2   Address mapping and configuration techniques

In large internetworks automating address allocation and device configuration is a must. Long gone are the days when network administrators hand-crafted every single host; today's internetworks are simply too large and too dynamic to make this either practical or economical. For example, a workstation typically needs the following items resolved at boot time:

- IP address and subnet mask (a basic requirement for any form of IP communication)

- Host name, domain name, DNS server name (covered in section 2.3)

- Default gateway (i.e., the nearest router)

- Primary and secondary DNS server

- Primary and secondary WINS server address (for Microsoft networks)

- Boot image (if the workstation has no local persistent storage capability)

At the very least a workstation needs an IP address and subnet mask, together with knowledge of how to reach the nearest router; otherwise, communication over an IP network is not practical. Today there are several protocols and services that are widely used to assist with address allocation, booting, and device configuration. These include ARP, RARP, Proxy ARP, BOOTP, and DHCP. Another important protocol used to indicate errors with their operations is ICMP. We will discuss these protocols in turn.

2.2.1 Address Resolution Protocol (ARP)

Address resolution is fundamental to the operation of IP networks and enables IP to be insulated from various types of hardware and networking media. The configuration of address resolution software can significantly affect network and application performance, and it is worth understanding some of the subtleties that could impact the network design. The key components of this functionality include a simple request-response protocol, a number of application-oriented implementations (including ARP, RARP, Proxy ARP, and Gratuitous ARP), and a database known as the ARP cache.

The Address Resolution Protocol (ARP) is used to resolve addressing queries where the IP address is known but the corresponding hardware address is not (e.g., we may know that a server on the local LAN can be reached at IP address 193.167.56.1, but we do not know what the MAC address of that server is). Without both pieces of relevant information we cannot sensibly place a frame on the wire. ARP is transparent to the end user and is not IP or media specific (variations exist with other protocol stacks such as AppleTalk's AARP).

When using ARP the host uses a lookup table (called the ARP cache) to maintain a list of associated IP and hardware addresses. This cache may contain static entries (typically hard-coded by the administrator and loaded at boot time) together with dynamically discovered associations. For example, under DOS we can view the ARP cache by typing the command:

```
arp -a
```

To add a static entry we could, for example, type:

```
arp -s 158.34.3.3 00-aa-00-61-c7-0a
```

ARP is also typically implemented on devices such as routers. For example, on a Cisco router we could examine the ARP cache using the show arp command, as follows:

```
c3550#sh arp
Protocol Address      Age (min)  Hardware Addr  Type Interface
Internet 1.1.1.1       -     0010.7b1f.4a61 ARPA Ethernet0/0
Internet 1.1.1.5      28     00a0.c903.6077 ARPA Ethernet0/0
Internet 32.97.105.46  153     0000.0caa.2350 ARPA Ethernet0/1
Internet 1.1.1.6      4     00a0.c903.6064 ARPA Ethernet0/0
Internet 171.68.225.9   145     0000.0caa.2350 ARPA Ethernet0/1
Internet 209.17.176.120 142     0000.0caa.2350 ARPA Ethernet0/1
Internet 204.71.200.74  91     0000.0caa.2350 ARPA Ethernet0/1
Internet 128.32.18.166  156     0000.0caa.2350 ARPA Ethernet0/1
Internet 152.163.241.223  161     0000.0caa.2350 ARPA Ethernet0/1
Internet 38.15.254.206  144     0000.0caa.2350 ARPA Ethernet0/1
Internet 206.79.171.51  153     0000.0caa.2350 ARPA Ethernet0/1
```

When a station wishes to transmit a frame, it will first examine the ARP cache to recover the destination MAC address, using the destination IP address from the frame. If the MAC address cannot be resolved using the ARP cache, the source node will first queue the frame and then issue an ARP request, with the destination MAC address set to the broadcast address (0xFFFFFFFFFFFF, which could, therefore, be forwarded over bridges and switches). Within the ARP header the source and destination IP addresses are set using the known data, and the source hardware address is set to the source node's own MAC address. All nodes within the broadcast domain receive the frame and unpack the ARP header to see if the query is relevant. The node with the matching source IP address fills in the missing hardware information and returns an ARP reply as a unicast frame. Upon receipt the source node will update the local ARP cache with this new binding (setting an aging timer for this entry to allow for possible topology or address binding changes). Since we now have complete addressing information, the queued frame can now be transmitted. This whole process normally takes a few milliseconds and so is transparent to the user. All subsequent transmissions for this destination node can now be translated locally using the cache. However, if the source and destination nodes are on different subnets (either side of a router perhaps), then one of two actions may take place, as follows:

- If the source and destination nodes are using natural masks, or understand subnetting, then the source will know that the destination IP address must be reached via the router. In this case the source will typically forward the packet directly to the default (or nearest) router. The router is responsible for forwarding the packet to its ultimate destination. If the MAC address of the router is unknown, then the source must issue an ARP request for the router itself. Thus, the packet will traverse the network with a consistent source and destination IP address, but the MAC addresses will be modified to reflect each data link hop.

- If subnetting is used but the two nodes do not understand subnetting, then the router must run Proxy ARP to fool the nodes into believing that they are communicating directly (as explained later in the section).

ARP runs directly over the MAC layer and is identified by EtherType (0x0806). An example ARP request is shown in the following Ethernet packet trace. In this example the source node (193.128.2.34) is looking for the MAC address associated with IP address 193.128.2.33.

```
File:IPXDIRSV.ENC  Type:SNIFFER_ENC Mode:•••••• Records:4021
=============================================================
Frame  : 52        Len   : 60        Error  : None
T Elapsed: 01:27:34:333   T Delta : 00:00:00:000
---------------------------[mac]---------------------
Dest Mac : ffffffffffff   Sourc Mac: Xyplex12a36a   Type    : ARP
---------------------------[arp]---------------------
HW Type : 10Mb Ethernet  Protocol : IP       Opcode   : ARP REQuest
HW AddLen: 6  Bytes     PR AddLen: 4  Bytes
SrHW Addr: 08008712a36a
SrPR Addr: 193 128 2 34
DeHW Addr: ffffffffffff
DePR Addr: 193 128 2 33
===============================[data:  0]====[pad: 18]=====================
002A 00 00 00 00 2 4F 4B D1 00 00 00 00 00 00 00 00  .....OK.........
003A 00 00
```
Note that the destination MAC address is broadcast in both the frame header and data field (since it is unknown). The corresponding ARP response from node 193.128.2.33 would be as follows:
```
File:IPXDIRSV.ENC  Type:SNIFFER_ENC Mode:•••••• Records:4021
=============================================================
Frame  : 53        Len   : 60        Error  : None
T Elapsed: 01:27:34:333   T Delta : 00:00:00:000
---------------------------[mac]---------------------
Dest Mac : Xyplex12a36a  Sourc Mac: Xyplex12a362   Type    : ARP
---------------------------[arp]---------------------
HW Type : 10Mb Ethernet  Protocol : IP       Opcode   : ARP RESPonse
HW AddLen: 6  Bytes     PR AddLen: 4  Bytes
SrHW Addr: 08008712a362
SrPR Addr: 193 128 2 33
```

```
DeHW Addr: 08008712a36a
DePR Addr: 193 128 2 34
==============================[data:  0]====[pad: 18]=========================
002A 00 00 00 00 2 4F 4B D1 00 00 00 00 00 00 00 00  .....OK.........
003A 00 00
```

Note that the response is unicast, since all addresses have been resolved by this stage.

Issues with ARP on mixed-media LANs

In [4] several popular LAN media types are discussed, and it was described how these could be integrated transparently via bridging. Current hardware types supported by ARP include those shown in the following chart:

ID	Protocol	ID	Protocol
1	Ethernet (10 Mb)	12	LocalNET (IBM PCNet or SYTEK LocalNET)
2	Experimental Ethernet (3 Mb)	13	Ultra link
3	Amateur Radio AX.25	14	SMDS
4	Proteon ProNET Token Ring	15	Frame Relay
5	Chaos	16	ATM
6	IEEE 802 Network	17	HDLC
7	Arcnet	18	Fibre Channel
8	Hyperchannel	19	ATM
9	Lanstar	20	Serial Line
10	Autonet Short Address	21	ATM
11	LocalTalk		

One of the key differences between media types such as Ethernet and Token Ring/FDDI is bit ordering on the wire. Token Ring and FDDI use the noncanonical format (most significant bit first), whereas Ethernet uses the canonical form (least significant bit first). Converting the source and destination MAC addresses in the header is trivial, but since ARP frames also carry addressing information inside their payload, these fields need to be consistent on either side of a bridge, and the standards are not helpful in this respect. Another problem you may encounter is minor incompatibilities between Token Ring and Ethernet ARP implementations. For example, at least one bridge manufacturer I have come across fails to convert the hardware ID in the ARP packet when translating ARP frames from Token Ring to Ethernet. Some implementations of ARP are quite relaxed in dealing with this, but other implementations may reject an ARP frame where the hardware ID specified in the ARP source fields does not match the interface type over which the frame is received. In short, you need to check with the equipment manufacturer to establish what facilities are available to cope with these problems.

Issues with ARP on NBMAs

Since we have already stated that ARP uses broadcasts, this implies that we cannot use ARP over media types that do not support broadcasts (i.e., Non-broadcast MultiAccess networks [NBMA] such as X.25 and Frame Relay). In fact, on NBMA networks you will need to configure static ARP entries at the edge devices. Since these connections are more likely to be PVCs, this should not present too much of a problem. If the network topology changes frequently or SVCs are used, then other techniques should be considered (e.g., ATMarp, as described in [4]). Alternatively, INARP could be used to resolve DLCIs to IP addresses for Frame Relay networks.

Issues with ARP table size

On a large, bridged network there can be thousands of directly attached stations, and each station will cache address bindings for any device it communicates with. The ARP table has finite size (usually determined by the OS) and if the number of entries is exceeded, this can lead to a situation where ARP requests are continually rebroadcasted and responded to unnecessarily. The level of traffic can seriously degrade performance, and in rare cases can cause a broadcast storm. You should, if possible, tune the size of your ARP caches in line with the worst-case number of active nodes on the network within the aging timer period.

Issues with ARP synchronization

Most ARP implementations, particularly those on end systems, do not allow the aging timer for the ARP cache to be modified. The default timer is typically 5 minutes, but it may also be as long as 20 to 60 minutes. This timer ensures that the ARP cache will be flushed of any entries that have not been refreshed within the allotted time period. This means that the cache is kept in sync with the current network topology, and it also ensures that the cache does not continue to grow indefinitely. In general, frequently active flows are rewarded. Less active flows are penalized, since any requests for addresses that have been flushed require a new ARP request to be broadcasted and resolved. Note that if you set this aging timer too low, this could potentially result in a great deal of unnecessary traffic. As the ARP timer approaches zero, more and more stations must issue ARP broadcast requests for addresses flushed from their local cache. In theory, with an ARP timer of zero all stations must issue ARP requests for every frame transmitted.

If a station is reconfigured (e.g., by swapping out a line card) or uses some form of dynamic addressing (e.g., hot-swapping technology), then current ARP entries may be invalid. This may result in lost connectivity (typically for the duration of the aging timer). This could be a trivial annoyance or a more serious problem (especially if the device undergoing the change is a router or server). One way to resolve this problem is to flush all entries in the ARP cache or explicitly delete the out-of-date entry (e.g., using the arp –d command under DOS). We could then issue a broadcast ping (e.g., ping 140.42.255.255) to rebuild the table. For example, if a station loses connectivity to its default router, flushing the ARP table and issuing a broadcast ping should enable the station to locate its backup router (if configured). Broadcast pings can be more or less specific, as discussed in section 2.1.3. If flushing the ARP cache is not practical, then we can either wait for the entries to flush naturally or consider lowering the aging timer, subject to the caveat mentioned previously.

2.2.2 Proxy ARP

Proxy ARP is a variation of ARP, which enables older devices to communicate in a subnetted environment. It is sometimes referred to as promiscuous ARP, or ARP hack. Typical applications are as follows:

- Subnetting, where devices do not understand subnets.
- Multiple LAN segments share a common subnet number, and the segments are not bridged.
- To provide IP address mapping for dial-in users.

Old terminal servers may not understand subnetting and may rely on natural IP masks only. In a subnetted environment, where routers are used, this can mean that communication across routers for such devices is not possible. Consider the example shown in Figure 2.7, where node-T does not understand subnetting (note the prefix is /16 even though all other nodes attached to the 140.16.0.0 class B network are using a subnetted /24 prefix). Router-1 has been configured with a /24 prefix on all interfaces and so is able to route requests from one subnet to the other; however, in this case, when node-T attempts to send traffic to node-S1, it firmly believes that node-S1 is a local host (i.e., directly reachable). It will, therefore, not

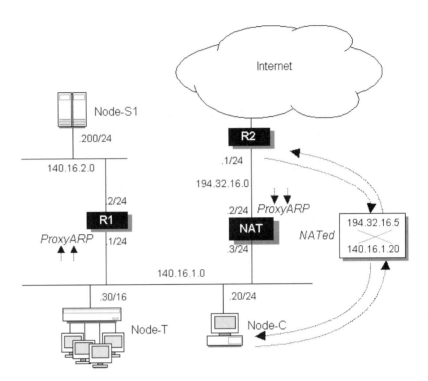

Figure 2.7
Examples of Proxy ARP applications.

forward this traffic to the Router-1 (its default router), so we have a problem. On the left in Figure 2.7, we have a terminal server that does not understand subnetting. To reach node-S1 Proxy ARP must be enabled on Router-1; otherwise, node-T will issue ARP requests for node-S1 in vain. On the right we have a gateway performing NAT. If Router-2 does not have host-specific static routes configured, then it too will ARP in vain. Proxy ARP is run on the NAT gateway's external interface, and NATed addresses are mapped to the gateway's own MAC address.

We can resolve this by running Proxy ARP on the 140.16.1.1 interface of Router-1. When node-T attempts communication with node-S1, it will first broadcast an ARP request, requesting the source MAC address for node-S1. Since this is a limited broadcast, the router will not forward it, so node-S1 will never see this packet. However, since the router can now listen for ARP request, it will service any ARP requests for devices known to be remote (since it is also subnet aware). In this case, instead of supplying node-S1's source MAC address, it supplies its own source MAC address for the .1 interface. On receipt of the ARP reply, node-T caches the IP address of node-S1 together with the source MAC address of Router-1 in its ARP table and starts sending traffic. Note that node-T believes it is having a

direct conversation with node-S, whereas in reality it is forwarding traffic to
the router. Remember that the source and destination IP addresses in this
case are the real client and server IP addresses—the trickery is achieved via
the IP address to MAC address mapping.

Figure 2.7 also illustrates another scenario for using Proxy ARP. To the
right of the diagram we see a NAT gateway which, for security reasons, is
translating node-C's source IP address before forwarding it to the wide area
router for access to the Internet. In this example assume that node-C's
NATed address is 194.32.16.55/24. Unless Router-2 has a host-specific
static route configured, incoming traffic for node-C will trigger Router-2 to
send out an ARP request to discover node-C's MAC address. Since node-C
is on the other side of the gateway, it will never respond. To resolve this we
could map the 194.32.16.55 address to the gateway's MAC address on the
external .2 interface and also run Proxy ARP on that interface. This way the
gateway responds by proxy, and the router forwards traffic to the gateway,
which then performs reverse address translation and forwards packets to
node-C. NAT is explained in more depth in section 2.5.2.

Issues with Proxy ARP

You should be careful to enable Proxy ARP only where necessary (note that
some routers enable Proxy ARP by default). A router running Proxy ARP
between subnets may result in some confusion and possible IP addressing
problems (e.g., ARP caches on various hosts may display multiple IP
address entries, each associated with the same MAC addresses).

2.2.3 RARP

During the boot process some network devices know their hardware
addresses but not their IP addresses (e.g., diskless workstations). Reverse
ARP (RARP) can be used by such a device to dynamically retrieve its IP
address, based solely on knowledge of its hardware address. RARP is documented in [18]. Note that RARP uses the same frame structure as ARP but
is identified by a different EtherType (0x8035). RARP requires one or
more RARP servers to maintain a database of mappings from hardware
address to IP addresses and respond to requests for mapping information
from clients. For example, a diskless workstation could issue a RARP
request (using the destination MAC broadcast address 0xFFFFFFFFFFFF)
so that any RARP servers listening on the local subnet can respond. A
RARP server simply examines the source hardware address in the RARP
request and returns the relevant IP address if available. Note that extensions
to RARP for dynamic address mapping services (Dynamic RARP, or

DRARP) are documented in [19]; but since RARP is limited to providing addressing information, it has been largely superseded by more sophisticated protocols such as BOOTP and DHCP. These protocols are now more commonly used (especially DHCP), since they also facilitate the transfer of configuration data and boot images.

2.2.4 Gratuitous ARP

There are occasions where it is necessary for devices to use ARP for broadcasting unsolicited address mappings; this feature is generally referred to as Gratuitous ARP. In a scenario where the binding of IP addresses to MAC addresses is dynamic, such as when a client PC boots up and requests an IP address from a DHCP server, it is advantageous to inform the network about this new address binding immediately (e.g., a Windows NT client will issue a Gratuitous ARP immediately after DHCP is successfully run). A Gratuitous ARP frame is broadcasted using the same format as the standard ARP request (EtherType 0x0806); however, both the source and destination IP address fields in the ARP payload will be set to the station's recently acquired IP address. The source hardware address field is set to the station's MAC address, with the destination hardware address set to 00-00-00-00-00-00. In this way all devices that are listening can precharge their ARP caches so that multiple ARP requests from devices subsequently wishing to communicate with this node are avoided. Therefore, this feature saves both time and bandwidth.

In a scenario where the IP address binding may change more frequently while a system is active, this can cause connectivity problems because the default ARP cache aging timers are too slow to react to such events. For example, two gateways, G1 and G2, with addresses 140.1.1.1 and 140.1.1.2, could be configured in a high-availability configuration running the Virtual Redundant Router Protocol (VRRP). In this case G1 is configured as master, with G2 backing up its IP address. In the stable state all end systems have physical MAC addresses of G1 in their caches, associated with IP address 140.1.1.1. However, if G1 dies, then G2 takes ownership of address 140.1.1.1 but somehow needs to announce that its own MAC address is now associated with 140.1.1.1. By sending an unsolicited ARP broadcast, advertising this change of mapping, any devices that are listening have the opportunity to update their ARP cache entries immediately, rather than suffer interim connectivity problems until those ARP entries age out (note that since ARP frames are not acknowledged, the implementation may issue more than one broadcast to be sure that all interested parties see the announcements).

2.2.5   Bootstrap Protocol (BOOTP)

BOOTP was developed to enable remote booting of diskless hosts over a network and has been widely deployed to automate device configuration. BOOTP protocol and operations are documented in [20], with extensions in [21]. BOOTP enables a device with a minimal IP stack and little local configuration information to download boot code (and possibly configuration data) from a BOOTP server. The download protocol is not defined by BOOTP but is typically the Trivial File Transfer Protocol (TFTP—see [22]). Since BOOTP relies on limited broadcasts, both the client and server must be on the same subnet, or a router must be available that supports BOOTP forwarding or relaying, as described in Chapter 3 and [21]. BOOTP has been somewhat overshadowed by Dynamic Host Configuration Protocol (DHCP) in the enterprise, but for legacy environments several enhancements to BOOTP enable it to interoperate with the DHCP (see section 2.2.4).

Message format

BOOTP runs directly over UDP, although TCP operation is possible; the BOOTP server process uses port 67; the BOOTP client process uses port 68. UDP uses a simple checksum to check data integrity (a 16-bit one's complement of the one's complement sum of a pseudo-IP header, UDP header, and the data field [23]). The format of a BOOTP message is shown in Figure 2.8.

Field definitions

- Code—1 Indicates a request; 2 indicates a reply.

- Hwtype—The type of hardware,. Refer to [5] for a complete list. For example, Ethernet = 1, IEEE 802 = 6.

- Length—Hardware address length in bytes. For example, Ethernet and Token Ring both use 6.

- Hops—The client sets this to 0. It is incremented by a router, which relays the request to another server and is used to identify loops. Reference [20] suggests that a value of 3 indicates a loop.

- Transaction ID—A random number used to match this boot request with the response it generates.

- Seconds—Set by the client. It is the elapsed time since the client started its address acquisition or renewal process.

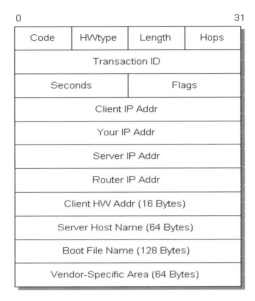

Figure 2.8
BOOTP message format.

- Flags field—The most significant bit is used as a broadcast flag. All other bits must be zero and are reserved for future use. Normally, BOOTP servers attempt to deliver BOOTREPLY messages directly to a client using unicast delivery. The destination address in the IP header is set to the BOOTP Your IP Address and the MAC address is set to the BOOTP client hardware address. If a host is unable to receive a unicast IP datagram until it knows its IP address, then this broadcast bit must be set to indicate to the server that the BOOTRE-PLY must be sent as an IP and MAC broadcast. Otherwise, this bit must be zero. This field is defined in [21].

- Client IP addr—Set by the client. Either its known IP address, or 0.0.0.0.

- Your IP addr—Set by the server if the client IP address field is 0.0.0.0.

- Server IP addr—Set by the server.

- Router IP addr—This is the address of a BOOTP relay agent to be used by the client. It is set by the forwarding agent when BOOTP forwarding is being used (see Chapter 3).

- Client hardware addr—Set by the client and used by the server to identify which registered client is booting.

- Server host name—Optional server host name terminated by 0x00.

- Boot file name—The client either leaves this null or specifies a generic name or the boot file to be used. The string is null terminated (0x00). The server returns the fully qualified file name of a boot file suitable for the client.

- Vendor-specific area—Optional information. Clients should set the first four bytes with a magic cookie. If a vendor-specific magic cookie is not used, the client should use 99.130.83.99 followed by an end tag (255) with the remaining bytes set to zero. The vendor-specific area can also contain vendor extensions; these are options that can be passed to the client at boot time along with its IP address. BOOTP shares many of the same options as DHCP; see [24] for full details.

Operations

Once the client has determined its own hardware address (usually this is held locally in ROM or on the NIC), the BOOTP process proceeds as follows:

- The client sends a BOOTP request (UDP source port 68, destination port 67) to the server, stating its hardware address. The client will use 0.0.0.0 for its own IP address and a limited broadcast 255.255.255.255 for the destination (server) address.

- The server receives the request and looks for the associated IP address in its database (usually a BOOTP configuration file). The server fills in the remaining fields in the request message and returns a BOOTP response to the client (UDP source port 67, destination port 68), using one of the following methods:

  - If the client IP address was included in the BOOTP request, then the server returns the datagram directly to the client. If the ARP cache on the server has not already cached the client IP and hardware address, then ARP will be used to resolve these addresses.
  - If the client uses 0.0.0.0 as its address in the BOOTP request, then the server cannot use ARP to resolve this mapping, since the client knows only its hardware address. In this case the server must either have a mechanism for directly updating its own ARP cache, or it must send a limited broadcast response.
  - Once the client has processed the response, it has enough IP configuration data to download a boot file if required (typically via the TFTP protocol). The client can then execute the full boot process. In the case of a diskless device this process will often

replace the minimal IP stack (loaded from ROM) with a full IP stack, downloaded using the boot file.

BOOTP can be used for centralized configuration of multiple clients. However, this requires a static table to be configured, with mapping entries for every client that requires service. This is clearly inflexible and a potential maintenance problem on large networks. This approach can be considered partly secure, however, since a client can be allocated an IP address by the BOOTP server only if it has the associated MAC address. One of the things you may have picked up from this discussion is that BOOTP uses limited broadcasts, and clearly these are nonroutable by their very nature. So how does BOOTP operate in internetwork environments? Chapter 3 describes a feature supported on many routers called BOOTP forwarding.

Issues with BOOTP over IEEE 802.5 Token Ring networks

BOOTP was originally introduced for Ethernet use, and its operations needed to be modified for Token Ring LANs because of the use of non-transparent bridging [4]. On Token Ring LANs the client should send its broadcast BOOTREQUEST with an All Routes Explorer RIF. This will enable servers and relay agents to cache the return route if required. For those server or relay agents that cannot cache the return route (e.g., because they are stateless), the BOOTREPLY message should be sent to the client's hardware address (extracted from the BOOTP message) with a Spanning Tree Rooted RIF. The bridge route will be recorded by the client and server (or BOOTP relay agent) via ARP. For further information on this topic refer to [21].

2.2.6 Dynamic Host Configuration Protocol (DHCP)

The Dynamic Host Configuration Protocol (DHCP) is based mainly on BOOTP with several extensions. DHCP was introduced by Microsoft via the Windows 95 and NT operating systems and is now a key component of many large enterprises. DHCP comprises two main features, as follows:

- Address assignment mechanisms—for the assignment of permanent or temporary client network addresses, from either static or dynamic address lists held on the server.

- Client/server protocol—a protocol that downloads host-specific configuration data from a DHCP server to a client. For example, the default gateway or WINS server address.

Address allocation can be achieved by one of the following methods:

- Automatic—where DHCP assigns a permanent address to a host.

- Dynamic—where DHCP leases an IP address to a client for a limited period of time. This allows efficient and automatic reuse of addresses that are no longer in use.

- Manual—where addresses are statically mapped (usually by the network administrator). This method is typically used for devices such as routers, firewalls, or permanent servers.

It may be appropriate to run multiple DHCP servers on your network, each controlling a pool of addresses. If there are multiple servers, then a DHCP client will select the most appropriate response from those servers that answer the request. A DHCP server provides permanent storage of configuration parameters associated with clients. It stores a <key><value> entry for each client, the key being a unique identifier (e.g., a combination of IP subnet number and hardware address), and the value being the configuration parameters previously allocated to the client. This means that a DHCP client will tend to be allocated the same IP address by the server on successive occasions, provided the address pool is not oversubscribed.

Message format

DHCP messages use the same UDP ports as BOOTP—port 67 (server) and port 68 (client)—and DHCP devices can interwork with BOOTP

Figure 2.9
DHCP message format.

0			31
Code	HWtype	Length	Hops
Transaction ID			
Seconds		Flags	
Client IP Addr			
Your IP Addr			
Server IP Addr			
Router IP Addr			
Client HW Addr (16 Bytes)			
Server Host Name (64 Bytes)			
Boot File Name (128 Bytes)			
Vendor-Specific Area (64 Bytes)			

devices, as described in section 2.2.4. The format of a DHCP message is shown in Figure 2.9. Note that all field definitions are as per BOOTP, with the exception of those defined explicitly here. The interested reader is referred to [24, 25] for further details.

Operations

This section briefly describes the DHCP client/server interaction for activities such as address allocation, configuration, and lease renewal.

Allocating a new network address

Assume that the DHCP server has a block of addresses from which it can satisfy new requests. Each server also maintains a database of allocated addresses and leases in permanent local storage. Remember that there may be multiple servers available on the network.

Field definitions (otherwise as per BOOTP)

- Client hardware address—Set by the client. DHCP defines a client identifier option, which is used for client identification. If this option is not used, the client is identified by its MAC address.

- Boot file name—The client either leaves this null or specifies a generic name, such as router, indicating the type of boot file to be used. In a DHCPDISCOVER request this is set to null. The server returns a fully qualified directory path name in a DHCPOFFER request. The value is terminated by 0x00.

- Options—The first four bytes contain the magic cookie (99.130.83.99). The remainder comprises tagged parameters called options. A DHCP client must be prepared to receive DHCP messages with an options field of at least 312 bytes. Several options have been defined. One particular option—the DHCP message type option—must be included in every DHCP message. This option defines the type of the DHCP message. DHCP messages fall into one of the following categories:

  - DHCPDISCOVER—broadcasted by a client to find available DHCP servers.
  - DHCPOFFER—a response from a server to a DHCPDISCOVER, offering IP address and other parameters.
  - DHCPREQUEST—sent from a client to servers. This either requests the parameters offered by one of the servers and declines all other offers, verifies a previously allocated address after a sys-

tem or network change (e.g., a reboot), or requests the extension
of a lease on a particular address.

- DHCPACK—an acknowledgment from server to client with
  parameters, including IP address.

- DHCPNACK—a negative acknowledgment from server to client,
  indicating that the client's lease has expired or that a requested IP
  address is incorrect.

- DHCPDECLINE—sent from client to server indicating that the
  offered address is already in use.

- DHCPRELEASE—sent from client to server canceling a lease
  and relinquishing the network address.

- DHCPINFORM—sent by a client that already has an IP address
  (e.g., manually configured), requesting further configuration
  parameters from the DHCP server.

Additional options may be allowed, required, or not allowed, depending
on the DHCP message type. Refer to [24].

The DHCP client/server interaction, illustrated in Figure 2.10, proceeds
as follows:

- The client broadcasts a DHCPDISCOVER message on its local subnet. The DHCPDISCOVER message may include options such as
  the offered address and lease duration. If multiple servers are available, each server may respond with a DHCPOFFER message, which
  includes an offered network address (your IP address) together with
  other configuration options. The servers may mark the address as
  offered to prevent the same address from being offered elsewhere in
  the interim.

- The client receives one or more DHCPOFFER messages. The client
  chooses one based on the configuration parameters offered and
  broadcasts a DHCPREQUEST message, which includes the server
  identifier option, to indicate which message it has selected, as well as
  the requested IP address option taken from Your IP Address in the
  selected offer. In the event that no offers are received, if the client has
  cached its previous network address, the client may attempt to reuse
  that address if its lease is still valid.

- The servers receive the DHCPREQUEST broadcast from the client.
  Those servers not selected by the DHCPREQUEST message use the
  message as notification that the client has declined that server's offer.
  The selected server saves the binding for the client to persistent storage (e.g., hard disk) and responds with a DHCPACK message con-

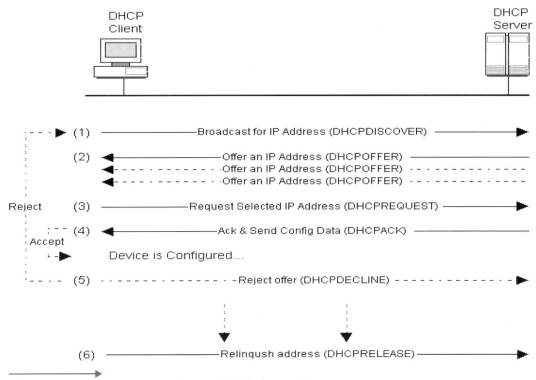

Figure 2.10   *Interaction between DHCP client and server.*

taining appropriate configuration parameters. The combination of client hardware and assigned network address constitutes a unique identifier for the client's lease and is used by both the client and server to uniquely identify a lease. The selected network address is inserted into the Your IP Address field in the DHCPACK message.

- The client receives the DHCPACK message with configuration parameters. The client performs a final check on the parameters (e.g., using ARP for allocated network addresses) and notes the duration of the lease and the lease identification cookie specified in the DHC-PACK message. At this point, the client is configured. If the client detects a problem with the parameters in the message (e.g., the address is already in use on the network), then the client sends a DHCPDECLINE message to the server and restarts the configuration process. The client should wait a minimum of ten seconds before restarting to avoid excessive network traffic in the event of looping. On receipt of a DHCPDECLINE, the server must mark the offered address as unavailable (and possibly inform the system administrator that there is a configuration problem). If the client receives a DHCP-NAK message, the client restarts the process.

- At any time the client may choose to relinquish its lease on a network address by sending a DHCPRELEASE message to the server. The client identifies the lease to be relinquished by including both its network address and its hardware address.

Responses from the DHCP server to the DHCP client may be broadcast or unicast, depending on whether the client is able to receive a unicast message before the TCP/IP stack is fully configured; this varies between implementations.

Lease renewal

DHCP defines a process to control lease expiration and renewal for clients that have already been configured, but have not been active for some time. This process is as follows:

- When a server sends the DHCPACK message to a client, it includes the lease time for the allocated address as one of the options in the message, together with two timer values, T1 and T2. The client is entitled to use the address for the duration of the lease time. Once the configuration is applied, the client also starts its own T1 and T2 timers, where T1 must be less than T2, and T2 must be less than the lease time. Reference [24] states that T1 defaults to ($0.5 \times$ lease time) and T2 defaults to ($0.875 \times$ lease time).

- When timer T1 expires, the client unicasts a DHCPREQUEST message back to the originating server, requesting an extension to the lease period. The server typically responds with a DHCPACK message indicating the new lease time. Timers T1 and T2 are reset at the client accordingly. The server also resets its record of the lease time. If a DHCPACK is not received before timer T2 expires, the client broadcasts a DHCPREQUEST message to attempt to extend its lease. This request can be confirmed with a DHCPACK message from any DHCP server on the network.

- In normal circumstances, an active client would continually renew its lease in this way indefinitely without letting the lease expire. However, if the client does not receive a DHCPACK message after its lease has expired, it must stop using the address. The client may then restart the process by issuing a DHCPDISCOVER broadcast.

A host should use DHCP to reacquire or verify its current IP address and network configuration whenever the local network parameters have changed—for example, at system boot time or after a disconnection from the local network, since the local network configuration can change without the host's or user's knowledge. If a client has multiple IP interfaces, each of them must be configured by DHCP separately. For further information, please refer to [24, 25].

Issues with DHCP

DHCP relieves the network administrator of great deal of manual configuration work. The ability for a device to be moved from network to network and to automatically obtain valid configuration parameters can be of great benefit to mobile users. Since IP addresses are allocated only when clients are actually active, it is possible (by using shorter lease times, as well as the fact that mobile clients do not generally require more than one address) to optimize the address space used by an organization. However, the following points should be considered when DHCP is being implemented:

- DHCP runs over UDP and lacks built-in security. In normal operation, an unauthorized client could connect to a network and obtain a valid IP address and configuration. To prevent this, it is possible to preallocate IP addresses to particular MAC addresses (similar to BOOTP), but this increases the administration workload and removes the benefit of recycling of addresses. Unauthorized DHCP servers could also transmit false and potentially disruptive information to clients (possibly initiating a denial of service attack—see Chapter 5).

- With automatic or dynamic address allocation it is generally not possible to predetermine the IP address of a client. In this case, if static DNS servers are also used, the DNS servers are unlikely to hold valid host-name-to-IP-address mappings for the clients. If having client entries in the DNS is important, you may use DHCP to manually assign IP addresses to those clients and then administer the client mappings in the DNS accordingly.

- Using DHCP may have some impact on your installation if you are using security implementations that map user IDs to IP addresses (sometimes called source IP address–based security schemes). This is likely to cause problems if you use the dynamic allocation or leasing capability.

- Devices that use large ARP cache aging timers may experience or cause problems if DHCP reissues IP addresses to different hosts before the previous ARP entries either age out or are manually flushed. For example, if a router maintained old entries in its ARP cache, then it could be temporarily forwarding packets using the wrong MAC address.

There is a relatively new enhancement (proposed as an IETF draft) for DHCP to improve resilience, called DHCP Safe Failover Protocol. In the situation where we have a primary and backup DHCP server, all DHCP requests are sent to both servers. The primary server updates the backup with lease information. The backup takes over when primary fails. Backup servers use a dedicated pool of addresses allocated by the primary to prevent duplicate IP addresses from being assigned. Servers synchronize when the primary is up. For further information, see [4].

2.2.7 Using BOOTP and DHCP concurrently

The format of DHCP messages is, for the most part, identical to the format of BOOTP messages (in fact, on network analyzer traces, DHCP messages are often interpreted as BOOTP). This enables BOOTP and DHCP clients to interoperate in certain circumstances. All DHCP messages must include a DHCP message type (51) in the options field. Any message without this option is, therefore, assumed to be a BOOTP message. DHCP servers will ordinarily discard any BOOTP message, unless configured by a system administrator to handle both BOOTP and DHCP clients. If BOOTP clients are supported, a DHCP server will respond to BOOTPREQUEST messages with BOOTPREPLY, instead of a DHCPOFFER. A DHCP server may offer static addresses or automatic addresses to a BOOTP client. Note that if an automatic address is offered to a BOOTP client, then it must have an infinite lease time, since the client has no concept of a lease mechanism. DHCP messages may be forwarded by routers configured as BOOTP relay agents. For further information on interoperability, refer to [26].

2.2.8 Internet Control Message Protocol (ICMP)

The Internet Control Message Protocol (ICMP) is important for addressing and router operations, since it typically informs a sender when destination addresses or port numbers are either unavailable or unresolvable. ICMP is essentially a diagnostic protocol that runs directly over IP. ICMP must be implemented by every IP module and uses IP datagrams to send messages that perform flow control, error reporting, routing manipulation, and other key functions. Network engineers make extensive use of the ubiquitous ping utility (described in Chapter 9), which uses ICMP's Echo facility to test reachability and response times for any device with an IP address. A response from ping means that network routing is operational between the two nodes and that the remote node is alive. ICMP allows routers and hosts to communicate between themselves for control purposes. It provides feedback about problems in the communication environment but does not make IP reliable.

ICMPv4

ICMP messages have a common header, including the type and code fields, plus 64 bits of the original data datagram if applicable. IPv4 ICMP functions are as follows (type fields are in parentheses):

- Echo Request (8), Echo Reply (0)—allows return of information to verify paths.

- Destination Unreachable (3)—indicates whether the net, host, protocol, or port is unreachable; whether fragmentation is needed; or whether the source route failed.

- Source Quench (4)—is sent when the gateway discards a datagram due to a number of conditions, such as insufficient buffer space for incoming packets. The gateway may send source quench to a host that is transmitting too aggressively. There is no guarantee that the host or application will back off or even understand what to do in such circumstances.

- Redirect (5)—sent when the gateway recognizes a shorter path or if a remote path becomes unavailable.

- Router Discovery (9), Router Solicit (10)—The ICMP Router Discovery Protocol (IRDP) uses router advertisement and router solicitation messages to dynamically discover the addresses of routers on directly attached subnets. We cover IRDP specifically in Chapter 3.

- Time Exceeded (2)—generally indicates that TTL of a packet was exceeded in transit (or if fragment reassembly time was exceeded).

- Parameter Problem (12)—indicates header parameter problems such that it cannot complete processing of the datagram. This may include incorrect arguments in an option.

- Timestamp Request (13), Timestamp Reply (14)—returns the time the sender last touched the message before sending it, the time the echoer first touched it on receipt, and the transmit time when the echoer last touched the message on sending it.

- Information Request (16), Information Reply (16)—returns the number of the network it is on (obsolete).

- Address Mask Request (17), Address Mask Reply (18)—broadcasted by a host to discover the subnet mask for the network specified. Typically responded to by a router.

For protocol-specific details of ICMP the interested reader is referred to [27, 28].

ICMPv6

A new version of ICMP that will operate with IPv6 is specified in [29]. The new protocol is called ICMPv6. Each ICMPv6 message is preceded by an IPv6 header, and zero or more IPv6 extension headers. The ICMPv6 header is identified by an IPv6 Next Header value of 58. The following functions are currently specified:

- Destination Unreachable (1)—Generated by a router or by the IPv6 layer in the originating node in response to a packet that cannot be delivered to its destination address for reasons other than congestion.

- Packet Too Big (2)—must be sent by a router in response to a packet that it cannot forward because the packet is larger than the MTU of the outgoing link.

- Time Exceeded (3)—If a router receives a packet with a hop limit of zero, or a router decrements a packet's hop limit to zero, it must discard the packet and send an ICMPv6 Time Exceeded message with Code 0 to the source of the packet. This indicates either a routing loop or too small an initial hop limit value.

- Parameter Problem (4)—If an IPv6 node processing a packet finds a problem with a field in the IPv6 header or extension headers such that it cannot complete processing the packet, it must discard the packet and should send an ICMPv6 Parameter Problem message to the packet's source, indicating the type and location of the problem.

- Echo Request (128)—Every node must implement an ICMPv6 Echo responder function that receives Echo Requests and sends corresponding Echo Replies. A node should also implement an application-layer interface for sending Echo Requests and receiving Echo Replies, for diagnostic purposes.

- Echo Reply (129)—As per Echo Request.

ICMP protocol packet exchanges can be authenticated using the IP Authentication Header [30]. For further information on ICMPv6, the interested reader is directed to [29]. The implications of ICMP for routers are explained in Chapter 3. Further information on diagnostic tools that exploit ICMP is provided in Chapter 9.

ICMP redirects

ICMP Redirects (Type 5 in IPv4) are of particular importance for routers, since they are often used to redirect a source to a better next-hop router if problems are detected upstream. For example, if there are two LAN-attached routers, R1 and R2, and a host has a default route to R1, if R1 loses the upstream path it can send an ICMP Redirect to the host, informing it that there is a better path via R2 (this is to stop the host from sending traffic to R1 and relying on R1 to forward the traffic over the LAN to R2). Routers generally send ICMP Redirects when the following conditions are met:

- The OS supports ICMP Redirects and is configured to send them.

- The router's receiving interface for a packet must be the same interface on which the packet is currently being forwarded (i.e., in our example R1's LAN interface is receiving host traffic and then having to forward this traffic back out of the same interface to R2).

- The network or subnet address of the routed packet's IP source address must be consistent with the next-hop IP address.

- The packet is not source routed.

Note that ICMP Redirects may be disabled in some circumstances—for instance, when using the HSRP protocol in high-availability cluster configuration [4]. You should check the vendor documentation for your particular platform.

2.3   Name-to-address mapping

Most people have difficulty remembering numbers, so a user-friendly scheme is often required for real networks, where names are used to refer to computer systems, networking devices, and services. In essence there are two basic ways to use names on a network, as follows:

- By static mapping tables associating addresses with names, such as the /etc/hosts file under UNIX.

- By using a dynamic name resolution system, such as the Domain Name Service (DNS).

Another key advantage of mapping names to addresses is that there is another layer of abstraction between users and resources. This enables hosts and network devices to be swapped out or modified without affecting users or services. For example, a file server is installed called BigDisk, and is mapped to 192.162.35.5. Subsequently this host is reassigned to other duties (perhaps because a host supporting a disk array is subsequently installed). The new host could be located on a different subnet and simply mapped to the name BigDisk without the user ever knowing.

In this section we discuss naming techniques and services used to complement the network design. Note that advanced applications such as load balancing and performance optimization of these services are covered in reference [4].

2.3.1   Static name service: The hosts file

The simplest method of mapping names to addresses can be achieved using a simple text lookup file, held locally on each device. On many operating systems this file is referred to as the hosts file. Under UNIX, for example, this function is typically implemented as /etc/hosts. In /etc/hosts each line of the file has the IP address (in dotted-decimal notation) on the left and the associated text name, and possible aliases, on the right. Note that the semicolon (;) is used for comments. For example:

```
; hosts file
;
IP address        name              alias
;
127.0.0.0         Lookback          me myself
140.45.4.6        HomeServer        mainman bigcheese
140.45.5.1        AccessRouter1     Wanman
192.168.76.1      MainRouter        fatboy slim
193.145.8.2       Big.name.com      fiction
```

Using this example, a user might, for example, Telnet to 140.45.4.6, HomeServer, mainman, or bigcheese with the same result. This approach is very simple, and can be relatively easy to deploy on small networks (e.g., a LAN with less than 100 hosts). In order to ensure a consistent naming system the hosts file simply needs to be copied to all other hosts on the network. In fact, this method was used on the original ARPANET; the Network Information Center (NIC) administered a single file (hosts.txt), which was retrieved using FTP by all attached hosts. The problem is that this method simply does not scale. Other problems include the following:

■ Hierarchy—The first problem with this scheme is the lack of hierarchy. As with any large problem, it is often necessary to break it down into manageable pieces, and here we have an essentially flat name space.

- Uniqueness—While the network administrator can guarantee unique names in the hosts file, there is no way to stop local users adding host names themselves, resulting in the possibility of name collisions (multiple hosts with the same name). Duplicated names will result in connectivity problems and are also difficult to troubleshoot.

- Maintenance—Moves and changes need to be reflected in all files. On a large network there is no easy way to synchronize host files across the network. The network administrator could keep a master file and ensure synchronization either through batch downloads or by insisting that users download this file regularly, but this is neither dynamic nor reliable and may not be secure or even practical in a large network. Maintenance can become a major headache.

- Security—There is no inherent way to protect against either accidental misconfigurations or malicious misconfigurations. There is plenty of scope for denial-of-service attacks or host intrusion.

- Load—As the network grows, the service demands placed on the central host system can become intolerable. The load placed on the network also becomes a major problem.

To overcome these problems a hierarchical distributed database is required, together with dynamic name synchronization and name query mechanisms. In November 1983 such a system was proposed in RFC 882 and RFC 883 (now both obsolete); this system is called the Domain Name Service (DNS).

2.3.2   Domain Name System (DNS)

The Domain Name System (DNS) comprises a client/server protocol together with a distributed database that holds name-to-IP-address mappings. The DNS is accessed by IP applications to dynamically discover address-name bindings and e-mail routing information. To promote scalability and better performance, the administration of parts of the database is devolved locally. Each site (e.g., campus, company, or department) typically maintains its own database for the local domain and runs a server program that other DNS servers can query over an IP network. The DNS is a large topic, and a complete discussion is outside the scope of this book. Here we will briefly review its operation and discuss the pertinent issues for network design and performance analysis. For more detailed information, the interested reader is referred to [28, 31–34]. DNS extensions to support IPv6 are specified in [35].

Before we discuss DNS operations we first need to understand the structure and implementation of domain names.

Domain names

The DNS structure contains a hierarchy of names, not unlike the UNIX file system in organization. The highest level, or root, of the DNS is unnamed (null). Each node in the tree represents a domain, which is a segment of the overall name database. Domains are broken up into subdomains (note that domains are an entirely separate concept from networks: domains are a higher administrative abstraction that can span many networks and subnetworks, transparent to the end user). Immediately below the root node are a number of Top-Level Domains (TLDs), as illustrated in Figure 2.11. TLDs are designed for the following applications:

- COM—a worldwide generic domain used by commercial organizations. This domain has grown very large due to explosive demand from businesses for the .COM label.

- EDU—a worldwide generic domain used by educational organizations. Many universities, colleges, schools, and educational service organizations have registered here, although outside the United States such organizations are often registered under the country code.

- NET—a worldwide generic domain used by major network providers and network support centers.

- INT—a worldwide generic domain used by international organizations.

- GOV—a domain used by government organizations in the United States.

- MIL—used by the U.S. military.

- ORG—a worldwide generic domain used by nonprofit organizations that do not fit into any other category.

- <CountryCode>—used for geographical-based domains (two-character domains based on country codes).

- ARPA—a special domain, originally used for ARPANET migration but now used for name-to-address resolution via the subdomain in-addr.

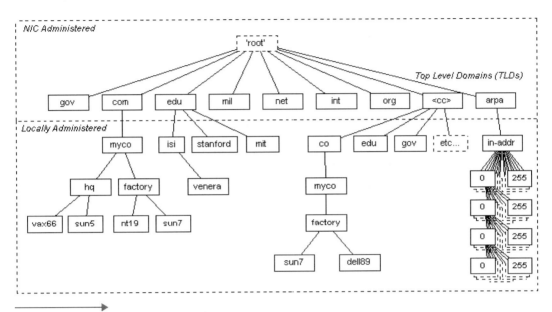

Figure 2.11 *Domain hierarchy.*

The <CountryCode> top-level node can be used to enforce a geographic naming model and is reserved for country codes (originally this was supposed to be the international telephone dial code, but this has been superseded by a two-letter abbreviation, as defined in ISO 3166). Most U.S. organizations have elected to use the flat organizational approach (illustrated in Figure 2.11 under myco.com), while many non-U.S. organizations use the geographic approach (attaching via the country code node). For example, a server in the United Kingdom with IP address 167.142.10.2 could be referenced by the domain name dell89.factory.myco.co.uk. Within a particular domain it is sufficient to use only enough detail to uniquely identify the device in that domain; the higher-level domain information is automatically appended by the software responsible for sending the DNS request. Note that in Figure 2.11 there are seven generic Top-Level domains (TLDs), together with the Country Code (CC) domain and a special ARPA TLD. In some countries, such as the United Kingdom, .COM is abbreviated to .CO, and .EDU is referenced as .AC.

Domain name format

Domain names comprise a series of dot-delimited labels, in reverse order. Every node within the tree must have a unique domain name, but the same label can be used at different points in the tree (e.g., twin.uni.edu and twin.mother.uni.edu are both unique). Although the root node is unnamed, Fully Qualified Domain Names (FQDNs) should end with a dot (.) to signify the root, (e.g., solaris.mydomain.com.). In practice this is rarely done, since it is universally assumed that DNS implementations automatically append the dot. Note that within the tree hierarchy domain names cannot be distinguished from object names (i.e., there is no obvious way to tell if obviouslyahost.cs.noname.edu. is really a host or a subdomain).

To simplify implementations, the total length of a domain name (including label bytes and label length bytes) is restricted to 255 bytes or less. Within DNS Resource Records (RR), each label is represented as a one-byte length field, followed by the specified number of bytes. Since the root node uses a null label, all domain names are terminated by a length byte of zero. The most significant two bits of every length field must be 00; hence, the remaining six bits limit the label length to 63 bytes or less. DNS supports a feature called message compression [34] to conserve space, based on the fact that there is often repetition in name lists. When the most significant two bits of the length byte are 2, the length is interpreted as a two-byte sequence, denoting an offset from the beginning of the message (i.e., the Type field).

Domain name registration

Domain names are administered by the IANA (see [6]). Most TLDs have been delegated to individual country managers, whose codes are assigned from ISO 3166-1. These are referred to as country-code Top-Level Domains (ccTLDs). In addition, there are a small number of generic Top-Level Domains (gTLDs), which do not have a geographic or country designation. Responsibility for procedures and policies for the assignment of Second-Level Domain Names (SLDs) and lower-level hierarchies of names has been delegated to TLD managers. Country-code domains are each organized by a manager for that country. Reference [36] provides information about the structure of the names in the DNS and on the administration of domains. A list of current TLD assignments and names of the delegated managers can be found in [37].

DNS components

DNS runs over UDP or TCP, using port 53 in both cases (UDP is the norm; TCP is used for database transfers). DNS is a client/server application and comprises the following components:

- The Domain Name Space (described earlier)

- The distributed database, stored as Resource Records (RR)

- Name servers

- Name resolvers

Instead of using static mapping files, DNS relies upon the dynamic interaction of two software components: a name resolver and a name server. DNS also implements a distributed database comprising a set of Resource Records (RR) held on each node in a hierarchical tree structure. Note that on many host systems the utility nslookup is available for debugging and checking the status of DNS.

The Domain Name Space (DNS) and Resource Records (RR)

Conceptually, each node and leaf of the domain name space tree names a set of information, and a DNS query attempts to extract specific information from a particular set. A query describes the domain name of interest and specifies the type of resource information required. To implement the DNS distributed database, data structures called Resource Records (RR) are defined for each node in the tree. RRs are divided into classes—for example, IN = Internet, CH = Chaos—with the Internet class being by far the most popular. Many RR types are experimental, and the complete list is defined in [34]. Important examples include the following:

Mnemonic	Description
A	Address
PTR	Pointer
MX	Mail Exchanger
NS	Name Server
SOA	Start of Authority
HINFO	Host Information
CNAME	Canonical Name
TXT	Text
WKS	Well-Known Services

Several Internet class RRs are shown in the following example:

```
ISI.EDU.                    IN    MX    10 VENERA.ISI.EDU.
                            IN    MX    10 VAXA.ISI.EDU.
VENERA.ISI.EDU.             IN    A     128.9.0.32
                            IN    A     10.1.0.52
```

```
VAXA.ISI.EDU.              IN    A      10.2.0.27
                          IN    A      128.9.0.33
USC-ISIC.ARPA             IN    CNAME  C.ISI.EDU
C.ISI.EDU                 IN    A      10.0.0.52
52.0.0.10.IN-ADDR.ARPA    IN    PTR    c.ISI.EDU
```

For further information, refer to [33]. Note that a new resource record type called AAAA has been defined for IPv6 addresses [35].

Name servers

Name servers are server programs that hold information about the domain tree's structure and set information. A name server may cache structure or set information about any part of the domain tree, but in general a particular name server has complete information about a subset of the domain space and has pointers to other name servers for additional information from any part of the domain tree. There are two modes of operation for name servers: primary and secondary. The primary domain name server is required to hold a master database of all names and IP addresses for all hosts in that domain. The secondary domain name server has a copy of this database and maintains synchronization with the primary server by copying this database at regular intervals. The secondary server will also respond to DNS requests from hosts, just as the primary server does. The use of multiple servers provides redundancy, and name resolvers should be configured with both the primary and backup addresses. There are two other variations of name servers in common use: A caching server is used to cache frequently used resolutions but does not hold the full database (it is aware of the location of the primary and secondary servers and uses them to resolve queries). A slave server operates similarly to a caching server but can only operate with recursion, using the list of servers specified in its database.

When a request to translate a name to its associated IP address is received by the name server, it performs a database lookup. If the address is not found, it must contact another name server (referred to as an authoritative server). Since each name server cannot possibly know how to contact every other server, each name server must at least know how to contact the root name servers. The root servers know the name and address of each authoritative name server for all the second-level domains.

Within the domain tree hierarchy, name servers control the parts of the tree for which they have complete (referred to as authoritative) information. Authoritative information is organized into units called zones. A zone is a subtree of the DNS comprising a group of connected domain names that are administered separately (as illustrated in Figure 2.12). A name server is said to have authority for one zone or multiple zones. Zones can be auto-

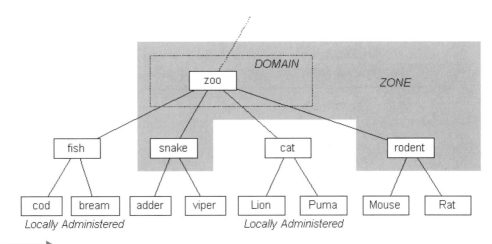

Figure 2.12   *Zone relationship with a domain. The zone extends down to all subdomains that are not self-administered.*

matically distributed to the name servers that provide redundant service for the information in a zone. Each zone typically maintains a separate DNS database. Whenever a new system is installed in a zone, the DNS administrator for that zone must allocate a name and an IP address for the new system and add these details into the name server's database. The DNS requires that each zone be supported by at least two servers (the primary and secondary servers). The primary loads all the information for the zone from persistent storage (e.g., hard disk). When a new host is added to a zone, the administrator adds the appropriate name and addressing information to a file located on the primary name server. The primary name server is then notified to reread its configuration files. Secondary servers query the primary on a regular basis (typically every three hours). If updates to the database are detected, secondary servers retrieve data using what is called a zone transfer.

Name Resolvers

Name resolvers are software programs that query name servers for information in response to client requests. A resolver will typically be a system routine that is directly accessible to user programs; hence, no protocol is necessary between the resolver and the user program. Resolvers must be able to access at least one name server and use that name server's information to answer a query directly or pursue the query using referrals to other name servers. A name resolver is typically installed on an end-user device. End systems that do not implement a name resolver but simply issue DNS queries are called stub resolvers. Here the name resolver is integrated with the name server platform; the stub needs only to maintain a list of name server addresses that will perform the recursive requests on its behalf. In all cases the name server performs the translation by accessing a dynamic database of names and IP addresses.

Operations

In any system that has a distributed database, where many systems have only partial information, a name server may frequently be presented with a query that can be answered only through cooperation with some other server. The two general approaches to dealing with this problem are as follows:

- Iterative—in which the initial name server refers the client to another server if the information requested is not known. The client is responsible for pursuing the query and may iterate many times until successful.

- Recursive—in which the initial name server pursues the query on behalf of the client with other servers until the result is passed back to the client. DNS queries contain a bit called Recursion Desired (RD). Name servers should perform recursion only if this bit is set in the request.

Both approaches have advantages and disadvantages. The DNS requires implementation of the simplest approach (iterative) by default but allows the recursive approach as an option. In fact, recursion is the most common mode, since it results in lower load on the client system (since it does not require a resolver and operates as a stub).

Query operation

In Figure 2.13, network devices either implement a resolver (R) or a name server plus a resolver (N+R). Each name server has its own portion of the database to administer and typically implements local cache to improve performance. Most DNS queries are serviced by the local DNS name server within the subdomain. Unresolved queries are redirected to the root name server. In this example a request for a .COM company is unknown locally and so is redirected to the root server, which in turn queries the .COM TLD server. Since the .COM server has the information cached locally, the response is sent back to the root server and forwarded to the originator.

DNS basically operates as follows:

- Clients query their local name server for address resolution.

- Name servers respond directly if they are authoritative for the domain in question. If not, then they may examine the local cache. The cache is updated dynamically and queried before firing out requests to other name servers. The cache returns references if found.

- Name resolution beyond the local name server is top down. If the local server cannot resolve the name, it starts with the root name server, which then recursively queries DNS servers, starting with the TLDs, until it finds a server that can resolve the name.

- Once the local server has the resolved IP address, it responds to the client and caches these data so that future requests are dealt with locally. In practice the local name server will deal with the majority of queries if caching is available.

Secondary servers check the primary for changes in the zone serial number (updates are controlled by the refresh rate in SOA record for zone). Both Notify and Incremental Zone Transfers are used to reduce propagation delay and bandwidth utilization (see [33]).

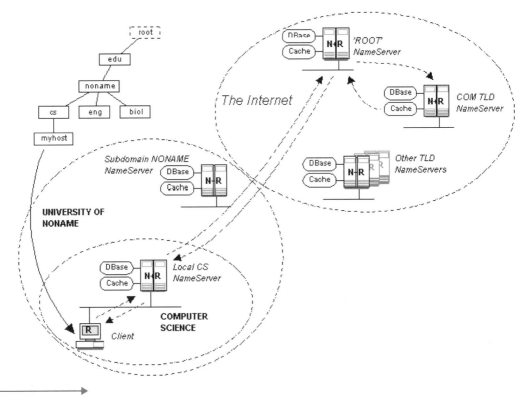

Figure 2.13   *DNS operation in a fictitious university campus.*

Mapping names to addresses

As well as resolving names to addresses, we need a way of resolving addresses to names. For example, this might be required to postfilter an event log file so that IP addresses within the file are automatically mapped onto their domain names for easier interpretation. Given the naming structure we have defined so far this would appear to be a difficult task, requiring a brute-force search of the entire domain space, since there is no correlation between the naming hierarchy and the IP addresses. However, the mechanism used to resolve this problem with IPv4 is quite simple: Below the arpa TLD is a special subdomain called in-addr. Nodes within the in-addr.arpa domain are named according to dotted-decimal notation rather than labels—the first level under in-addr comprising nodes 0–255, each with 0–255 subdomains and so forth. In this way all available IP addresses can be represented, and data associated with each node are the domain label itself. Note that in this format the IP address, when represented in domain name format, will appear backwards, since the name is read leaf to root. Reference [38] describes some of the shortcomings of DNS, in particular the in-addr implementation, and proposes that addresses should be queried directly for corresponding domain names using two new ICMP types: Domain Name Request and Domain Name Reply. This work remains experimental, and the interested reader should refer to [38].

With IPv6 a special domain is defined to provide address-to-name mapping, rooted at ip6.int. An IPv6 address is represented as a name in the ip6.int domain by a sequence of nibbles (half-bytes) separated by dots with the suffix .ip6.int. The sequence is encoded in reverse order—that is, the low-order nibble is encoded first, followed by the next low-order nibble and so on. Each nibble is represented by a hexadecimal digit. For example, the inverse lookup domain name corresponding to the address

```
4321:0:1:2:3:4:567:89ab
```

would be:

```
b.a.9.8.7.6.5.0.4.0.0.0.3.0.0.0.2.0.0.0.1.0.0.0.0.0.0.
1.2.3.4.IP6.INT.
```

Not a pretty sight! For further details refer to [34].

Inverse query operation

The in-addr.arpa domain is restricted to recovering information associated with addresses. Inverse DNS queries are used to dynamically map a domain name to some arbitrary data, via a kind of exhaustive search, restricted in scope to the name server that received the query. Inverse queries are not guaranteed to be successful, since the local server will drop the query if it cannot service the request using its own local database or cache (this limitation avoids the potential for DNS meltdown).

Caching

Name servers usually employ a local cache for storing recently used names as well as a record of where the mapping information for that name was obtained. Caching is fundamental to the efficient operation of the DNS in two ways: by reducing latency in turning around mapping information and by reducing traffic on the network. The process is quite simple: When a resolver asks the name server to resolve a name, the server first checks to see if it has authority for the name. If so, then the server already controls the associated binding in its database and can respond directly. If not, then the server checks its cache (if implemented) to see whether the name has already been resolved and cached. If so, then the server responds using the cached information for this and all subsequent queries, and this does not result in additional queries to other servers. Some DNS implementations (e.g., BIND version 4.9.3) go one step further, by supporting a feature called negative caching. This is the ability to cache responses from a name server that indicate that the information requested does not exist in a particular domain (hence, subsequent queries in that domain would be fruitless). The interested reader is referred to [39].

Since binding information may change over time, it is important that the name server flushes these cached data regularly to maintain network synchronization, so a Time to Live (TTL) value is associated with cached entries. Whenever an authority responds to a request, it includes a TTL value in the response that specifies how long it guarantees the binding to remain valid.

Implementing DNS

If you have a small LAN with no Internet access, then you can get away with using static mapping files or perhaps an alternative naming system such as Sun's Network Information Service (NIS). If you are connecting to the Internet, then you must use the DNS. There are two basic ways to configure DNS. You could either use your ISP's DNS server (most ISPs support this capability; alternatively, you could set up a DNS server on your own network). The choice between the two approaches is influenced by the need for local control and your ability to configure and maintain these services on site, as follows:

- ISP Maintained Primary and Secondary DNS Service—For a small network it is advisable to let your ISP maintain DNS services. In this case the ISP will supply you with the IP addresses of the primary and secondary DNS servers, which you must then configure on all end system TCP/IP stacks (either manually or via a DHCP server). You must inform your ISP as to which names you wish to advertise to enable outside users to connect to services on your network. In addition, if you want to receive e-mail from the Internet, you must have a Mail Exchange (MX) record for your domain in your ISP's DNS database. This record identifies a machine that accepts e-mail for your domain and has three parts: your domain name, the name of the machine that will accept mail for the domain, and a preference value. You can have multiple MX records for your domain; the preference value lets you build some fault tolerance into your mail setup. If you plan to use your ISP's DNS server, you'll also need to have the ISP set up some A records, which associate IP addresses with computer names. Each of the computers mentioned in your MX records needs an (A) record to associate them with an IP address. You may also want to set up A records for each of your workstations if your users need to use FTP to download software from the Internet. This is because some FTP sites perform a lookup to get the DNS name of the machine from which they receive download requests. If the machine has no name, the sites deny the request. You'll also need A records for any public servers you maintain. For example, if you have a World Wide Web server, you'll need to have the ISP set up an A record linking the name www.mycompany.com to the IP address of your Web server.

- Locally Maintained Primary and Secondary DNS Service—If your ISP does not support name services or if you need to have a DNS server running on your local site (for security, control, or performance reasons), then you must have at least two name servers: a primary and a secondary. You will not be granted an official domain name unless there are at least two DNS servers on the Internet with information about your domain. The second server also provides fault tolerance in the event of a primary server failure. If you choose to administer the primary name server yourself, bear in mind that you'll have to maintain the DNS records.

- ISP Maintained Primary and Locally Maintained Secondary DNS Service—For many networks it may be appropriate to maintain the secondary DNS server on the local site and have this peer with the primary server maintained by the ISP. In this mode the ISP will still do all of the maintenance work, and your name server will periodically download the data about your domain from the primary server automatically. This configuration provides additional resilience in the event the ISP connection fails (e.g., if you had a backup Internet connection via another ISP, then your end systems would automatically fail over to the secondary server and service would be resumed).

If you plan to run your own name services, then perhaps the most popular software to implement is the BIND application, which often comes as a standard part of the UNIX operating system. The BIND source code is also freely available and so can be recompiled or ported to other platforms. The interested reader is directed to [31, 40].

Split DNS

Split DNS is essentially a security feature for implementing DNS where you have a public and private interface to your network (typically interfacing with a firewall). Essentially you configure two primary DNS servers for the domain. The external server hides the structure of the internal network and publishes a subset of the resources available (typically Web, mail, FTP, and other externally available servers). The internal clients point to the internal primary DNS server, which publishes all useful resources, including potentially sensitive servers behind the firewall. See Chapter 5 for more details.

Dynamic DNS

With DHCP a host may request not only an IP address but also a dynamic name. Clearly, dynamic names are inappropriate for some network devices (e.g., Web or mail servers and FTP servers), since these must by definition use well-known statically assigned names. However, given that the physical devices used to provide these services might change dynamically, it would be extremely useful to have static names associated with dynamic IP addresses. Several vendors have developed solutions for Dynamic DNS (DDNS), although the IETF is currently working on a standard for this feature.

Resilience

There is redundancy built into DNS in that secondary servers automatically back up primary servers. If the primary fails, then client software (the resolver) is responsible for switching over to a secondary server. Furthermore, Root and TLD servers are normally duplicated for resilience. At the time of writing there were nine root servers distributed internationally.

DNS performance

The organization of the domain system is based on several assumptions about the needs and use patterns of its user community. The DNS is designed to avoid many of the complicated problems found in general-purpose database systems. The assumptions are as follows:

- The size of the total database will initially be proportional to the number of hosts using the system, but it will eventually grow to be proportional to the number of users on those hosts, as mailboxes and other information are added to the domain system.

- Most of the data in the system will change very slowly (e.g., mailbox bindings, host addresses), but the system should be able to deal with subsets that change more rapidly (on the order of seconds or minutes).

- Access to information is more critical than instantaneous updates or guarantees of consistency. Hence, the update process allows updates to percolate out through the users of the domain system rather than guaranteeing that all copies are simultaneously updated.

In the interests of performance, implementations often integrate several functions. For example, a resolver on the same machine as a name server might share a database comprising the zones managed by the name server and the cache managed by the resolver.

Issues

There are many subtle issues with DNS performance; therefore, it is difficult to predict performance, since there are many scenarios and design options to consider, including the following:

- Since domain names are often repeated many times within DNS messages, DNS uses an optional form of message compression through special encoding (described earlier). So message size is not absolute but varies depending upon the amount of repetition.

- Primary DNS servers in very large domains should be implemented on dedicated machines to cope with the number of requests. Typically, DNS services are implemented under UNIX, via the standard name daemon (Berkeley Internet Name Domain, BIND, or, alternatively, named). DNS servers typically require high-performance disk I/O (preferably a RAID system) to keep up with dynamic DNS updates.

- Caching can improve performance and reduce network traffic substantially, and you should deploy large caches in strategic locations to get the best hit ratio. For example, if your network has many small branch offices connected to a central headquarter site, each branch location could have a separate domain. The primary DNS server for each remote site zone would typically be held at the central site, and, if possible, a secondary DNS server would be configured at each remote site. For Small-Office-Home-Office (SOHO) configurations all DNS requests would typically be handled via the central site. Caching timers should be configured so that cached data do not become hopelessly out-of-date, resulting in performance or connectivity problems. The time limit for cached data is usually set in seconds (say 86,400 seconds for a day, or 604,800 seconds for a week). A larger interval reduces network traffic, but remember that these data could be cached on thousands of name servers. Reference [39] states that a large proportion of DNS traffic on the Internet could be eliminated if all resolvers implemented negative caching.

- Even with extensive caching deployed, root name servers are particularly hard hit, and for resilience purposes there are several root servers deployed around the world (although less than a dozen at the time of writing). Clearly, these devices need to scale as the requirement for DNS access grows.

- The .COM domain has grown very large and there is concern about the administrative load and system performance if the current growth pattern is continued. Consideration is being taken to subdivide the .COM domain and to allow future commercial registrations only in the subdomains [41].

Relatively new DNS standards enhancements include Dynamic DNS updates [42], Incremental Zone Transfers [43], and Notify [44]. These features dramatically reduce propagation delays and WAN bandwidth utilization. They also integrate DHCP with DNS so that newly configured devices (via DHCP) trigger incremental DNS updates via the primary domain name server.

2.3.3   Windows Internet Names Service (WINS)

Windows Internet Names Service (WINS) is found on Microsoft operating systems. It assumes a flat name space and provides basic functions including the NetBIOS Names Service (NBNS) and Windows NT file and print services. WINS can coexist with DNS. WINS, unfortunately, has real scalability problems when used in large networks and is likely to disappear with Windows 2000, which uses a feature called Active Directory, which is dependent on DNS.

2.3.4 Network Information Service (NIS)

Network Information Service (NIS) is an implementation of name service functionality available from Sun, running on Sun platforms. NIS is generally deployed in small enterprises; it is recommended for access to the Internet DNS (via BIND), since DNS is the native name service for the Internet.

2.4   Directory services

2.4.1 Introduction to directories

Directory services emerged from pioneering work done in the early 1980s at the Xerox Palo Alto Research Center (PARC). The first real implementation was called Clearinghouse and was developed as part of a system architecture called Grapevine. Clearinghouse was used initially to enable users to roam around the network using a personalized desktop profile. As with many PARC inventions, this was a product ahead of its time. In essence, directories are specialized databases containing abstract content (i.e., a collection of objects). Directory services enable networked users or applications to locate resources or retrieve data using one or more attributes. The terms white pages and yellow pages are often used to describe how a directory is accessed (i.e., by name or by subject). For example, a directory of user information (e.g., a company's telephone directory) could be queried to find a person's job title, telephone number, and e-mail address by using his or her name and location as search attributes. A directory of network resources could be searched to find the location of the closest PostScript printer on the network, an ActiveX/CORBA/Java object, X.509 Certificate, or biometric data (for an authentication query).

Directories are increasingly being used to coordinate large-scale network activities, such as security policy management and configuration management data. For example, directories enable single sign-on services as part of an enterprisewide security infrastructure. The key aim of directory services is to provide fast access to a single repository of network data in a managed and authenticated manner. Historically, much of the data would have been spread around the network or held on different servers, often with overlapping or conflicting elements. Directory services reduce the information maintenance burden, improve consistency, eliminate duplication, and thereby improve scalability.

Directories and relational databases and networked file systems

A directory system is not the same as a networked file system directory. Directory systems are also not suitable repositories for storing file information, since they are not designed to hold large binary objects and do not have the granular read/write locking mechanisms required to protect file access.

Directories and name services

All directory services are accessed via a naming service. Names are used to identify unique objects within the directory. Objects are associated with one or more attributes (name-value pairs). The DNS is a very simple form of directory service that includes a name service. DNS takes a Fully Qualified Domain Name (FQDN) and returns an IP address, or vice versa. Other name services include the CORBA's naming service, Common Object Service (COS), and Sun's Network Information Service (NIS/NIS+).

Directories and Relational Databases Management Systems (RDBMS)

A directory has several characteristics that differentiate it from general-purpose relational databases. Unlike most relational databases, directories are designed to handle largely static data. Information flow is highly asymmetrical; directories are typically queried often but seldom updated. Since directories must, therefore, be able to support high volumes of read requests, they are optimized for read access (with write access often limited to system administrators or to the specific owner of the data to be written). Unlike RDBMS, directory services do not support a two-phase commit process and cannot handle transactions against multiple operations.

Another important difference between a directory and a general-purpose relational database is the way in which information may be accessed. Most RDBMS support the standard Structured Query Language (SQL). SQL enables powerful query and update functions to be generated—for example, a query could look as follows:

```
SELECT DISTINCT TXDAT.Period, TXDAT.Rate, TXDAT.Metric_ID,
TXDAT.DoW, TXDAT.From, TXDAT.To, TXDAT.RadMin,
TXDAT.RadMax, TXDAT.Zone, TXDAT.SubZone FROM TXDAT WHERE
(RateID Like "BTLL64K") AND (Type Like "Rate") AND (Zone
Like "LLoop")" AND (BitsSec =64000) ORDER BY Rate DESC
```

This relatively simple query retrieves the contents of ten fields from a table, where three of the fields meet specific criteria, and then sorts the output by the contents of one of those fields. However, a more advanced query could retrieve data from several tables where the defined search criteria are met and then update another table depending upon the results of that query (referred to as table joins). This level of flexibility and sophistication does not come without cost (usually expressed as program size, application complexity, and performance).

By contrast, since directories are not intended to provide as many features as general-purpose databases, both the client/server application architecture and the query protocol can be streamlined, providing applications with rapid and efficient access to data in large distributed environments. A directory can, therefore, be visualized as a limited-function database (in fact, some vendors implement a veneer of directory services over a standard relational database). This distinction may blur in the future as transaction-oriented features are added to directory services.

Client/server model

Directories are generally accessed using a client/server model. Directory clients issue requests, and the process that retrieves information is called the directory server (note that a server may act as a client for other server requests). The format and content of the messages exchanged between the client and server are defined by a directory access protocol (e.g., the Lightweight Directory Access Protocol (LDAP), discussed shortly). The data within directories may be held locally on a particular server, distributed across multiple servers, or replicated across multiple servers. The three dimensions of a directory (i.e., the scope of information, location of clients, and distribution of servers) are independent of each other. As users and applications increasingly begin to rely on common directories, it is important that these directories are robust, secure, and scalable. In practice directory services are, therefore, widely replicated to increase performance and availability. This infrastructure in turn promotes much tighter management and control and enables application developers to focus more on application functionality, instead of wasting time developing custom database subsystems and resolving data conflicts. Applications that have the ability to interact with directories are said to be directory enabled.

When not to use a directory

Directory systems are clearly invaluable in a networked environment; however, given the caveats already presented, there are circumstances where RDBMS or conventional file systems are better suited, as follows:

■ Directories are not appropriate for transactional work (where data are stored as part of a transaction).

- Directories are not good repositories for dynamic information (such as share prices, device status, etc.).

- Directories are not ideal where the relationships between data objects are complex (requiring table joins).

- Directories are not ideal where there is a major requirement for reporting. Conventional RDBMS typically include far superior report-generation tools.

Although the directory architecture does not impose limitations on content, in practice it tends to be restricted (by implementation) as to the type and scope of data it holds. A directory will often come with standard schema (data templates) geared around a particular type of application (telephone directory, resource repository, etc.). This schema may or may nor be extensible.

2.4.2   OSI directory service standard (X.500)

In 1988 the CCITT produced a comprehensive directory service specification called X.500. This was standardized in 1990 as ISO 9594, Data Communications Network Directory, Recommendations X.500–X.521. X.500 defines an authentication framework, powerful search capabilities, and a powerful naming/information model, which organizes objects into a hierarchal name space, capable of scaling to contain huge amounts of data. The query protocol used between the client and the server is called the Directory Access Protocol (DAP). DAP runs as an OSI Application Layer protocol (Layer 7) and therefore requires six additional layers of underlying protocol to function. DAP also mandates that the transport class be used, making it very inflexible.

Unfortunately, X.500 is big, nontrivial to implement, and contains functionality that is considered overkill for most small-scale embedded network platforms and desktop devices (especially when one considers that in 1988 most desktop PCs had very little CPU or memory by today's standards). It seemed appropriate, therefore, to develop a streamlined interface to an X.500 directory server. In 1991 the IETF produced two informational RFCs: the Directory Assistance Service (DAS) [45] and the DIXIE Protocol Specification [46]. DAS defines a way for a streamlined client to communicate with the X.500 directory server via a proxy. Since X.500 DAP implementations never really took off, a more direct approach was required, so DIXIE provides a more direct translation of the DAP. This work eventually led to the development of a lightweight DAP protocol in 1993 [47], which subsequently became Lightweight Directory Access Protocol (LDAP) [48].

Note that much of the early work on DIXIE and LDAP was carried out at the University of Michigan in cooperation with members of the IETF Directory Services working group. The University of Michigan provides reference implementations of LDAP and maintains related Web pages and mailing lists.

2.4.3   Lightweight Directory Access Protocol (LDAP)

As indicated, Lightweight Directory Access Protocol (LDAP) was developed as a more practical alternative to X.400 DAP. While X.500 has traditionally been deployed only in very large organizations that have the resources necessary to support it, LDAP is also appropriate for small organizations. Although LDAP still embodies many concepts introduced in X.500, and uses the same basic information and naming model, it uses a simplified functional model, streamlines many X.500 operations, and omits a number of esoteric functions. LDAP uses the LDAP Data Interchange Format (LDIF) to represent data in ASCII strings for exchange between LDAP servers [49, 50]. This may eventually be replaced by Directory Service Markup Language (DSML) (an XML-based markup language used to describe directory information). ASN.1/BER is used for representing binary data. At present LDAP normally runs over TCP/IP but does not mandate any particular transport layer (Novell has an LDAP interface to its IPX-based NDS). This enables LDAP to use security services such as SSL (TLS) and IPSec. LDAP also extends some of the services of X.500 and provides additional security features (e.g., Simple Authentication and Security Layer [SASL]).

LDAP defines a communication protocol between an LDAP client and an LDAP server; it does not define the directory service itself. The client initiates an LDAP session by calling an LDAP API function. The general interaction between an LDAP client and an LDAP server takes place in three phases, as follows:

- Binding—The client must establish a session with an LDAP server before any operations are possible. The client specifies the host name or IP address and TCP/IP port number of the LDAP server. The client may be required to provide a user name/password for authentication or may establish an anonymous session using default access rights. For additional security the session may be encrypted.

- Operations—Once connected, the client can perform operations on directory data (i.e., search, modify, add, delete, compare, or abandon). Note that in LDAPv3 an extension mechanism has been added, in order to allow implementers to define additional operations (e.g., digitally signing) [51].

- Unbinding—When the client is finished making requests, it closes the session with the server. This is also known as unbinding.

An X.500 directory server does not understand LDAP messages; an LDAP server either operates as a gateway (proxy) to an X.500 directory server or runs in standalone mode, providing local access to a directory service. If acting as a gateway, then the server must support the OSI and TCP/IP stacks, as well as the LDAP and DAP protocols. In standalone LDAP (SLDAP) mode the server need support only TCP and LDAP, but the server architecture is significantly more complex to accommodate access to a local directory. From the client's perspective the directory location is transparent; LDAP clients simply talk to LDAP servers [48, 51].

LDAP versions 2 and 3

Both LDAP version 2 and LDAP version 3 standards are currently defined for use by the IETF, as follows:

- LDAPv2 is currently a draft standard within the IETF. Reference [48] defines the LDAP protocol itself. Several other RFCs define related aspects of LDAPv2, such as attribute syntaxes [38], distinguished names, URL formats, and search filters. Since this specification is unlikely to change significantly, many vendors have already implemented products that support LDAPv2.

- LDAPv3 is a proposed standard [51]. Even though minor revisions of a proposed standard are likely, a number of vendors are implementing products that support LDAPv3 now. LDAPv3 extends LDAPv2 in several areas, as follows:

  - Referrals—a server that does not hold the requested data can refer the client to another server.
  - Security—extensible authentication using Simple Authentication and Security Layer (SASL) mechanism.
  - Internationalization—UTF-8 support for international characters.
  - Extensibility—new object types and operations may be dynamically defined with schema published in a standard manner.

LDAP has now become the de facto standard for accessing directory systems. LDAP reduces the complexity of clients so that directories can be made accessible even to thin clients (e.g., PDAs and WAP microbrowsers).

Throughout this book, the term LDAP refers to LDAPv3 unless specified otherwise.

LDAP information model

LDAP uses an information model similar to that of X.500. Objects are organized within a hierarchical tree structure referred to as the Directory Information tion Tree (DIT). The highest element in the tree is referred to as the Top-Level Domain (TLD). Below the TLD are the subdomains (referred to as Organizational Units [OUs] or branches). A branch without any child elements is called a leaf. Tree objects are referred to as entries (similar to a relational database row). Each entry is associated with an object class, which determines the associate attributes. The attribute comprises of a type and a value.

A schema is a set of rules used to define the data structure of entries. The schema defines what object classes are allowed in the directory, what attributes they must contain, what attributes are optional, and the syntax of each attribute. For example, a schema could define a person object class. The person schema might require a surname attribute (defined as a character string) and an optional telephone number attribute (defined as a number string, with spaces, hyphens, etc.). (See Figure 2.14.)

Replication

Replication is important for scalability in large enterprises by improving both performance and availability. The LDAP specifications do not cover replication or synchronization of multiple directories. In practice many vendors provide some form of proprietary replication model.

LDAP naming model

The LSAP naming model specifies how entries are referenced within the TID; this is based both on a hierarchical naming model and on X.500.

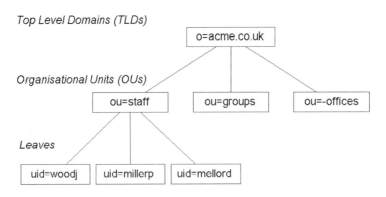

Figure 2.14
LDAP directory information tree hierarchy.

Each entry has a Distinguished Name (DN), determined by its position in the tree. A DN is made up of a number of components, each called a Relative Distinguished Name (RDN). X.500 naming is quite cumbersome—for example:

```
dn: uid=woodj, ou=Marketing, o=Acme Ltd, l=Berkhamsted, c=UK
```

where

- `dn`—Distinguished Name
- `c`—Country
- `l`—Location
- `o`—Organization (e.g., company name)
- `ou`—Organizational Unit (i.e., department or business unit)
- `uid`—User ID (i.e., normally the login ID)

Since there is already a perfectly good global naming system in operation (i.e., DNS FQDNs) the architects of LDAP decided that FQDNs should be used as the TLD within a distinguished name (with the assumption that anyone technically able to deploy LDAP would probably have a Web presence). Our example would, therefore, appear as follows:

```
dn: uid=woodj, ou=Marketing, o=acme.co.uk
```

The IETF has also proposed a draft standard [52] recommending that DNs should be constructed from an FQDN using a domain component (dc) attribute. For example:

```
dn: uid=woodj, ou=Marketing, dc=acme, dc=co, dc=uk
```

In practice both schemata are used at present.

LDAP URL

Note that if an LDAP-enabled Web browser is used on a client, directory information can be retrieved using an LDAP URL. This takes one of two forms:

```
ldap://<domain>:<port>/query_string
```

```
ldaps://<domain>:<port>/query_string
```

where the latter syntax is the secure format for LDAP queries. Default ports are 389 and 636, respectively. An example query might be:

```
ldap://10.0.0.1:389/uid=woodj, ou=Marketing, o=acme.co.uk
```

Referrals

LDAP supports referrals in LDAPv3 [51]. If an LDAP server does not have the required data, then a referral can be provided as a pointer to another server (or set of servers) in response to a query. This is similar to the way DNS servers can refer resolvers to other DNS servers if they do not hold the correct bindings. In LDAP the client code must always handle or ignore a referral (similar to DNS iterative mode).

Aliases

LDAP supports aliasing (a metaphor for the UNIX symbolic link). Aliases act as a shortcut to eliminate the need for a strict hierarchy when referencing objects. Since aliases are validated each time they are used, they may present performance overheads.

Security

Since LDAP is connection oriented, a client must first bind to a server to create an LDAP session before performing any operations. LDAP supports a flexible security model. At the basic level a simple authentication option provides authentication via a cleartext password. In practice, in a TCP/IP environment, SSL (TLS) is commonly used to secure the session (or variations such as WTLS for wireless applications). Many LDAP implementations also support Access Control Lists (ACLs). These can be used to control user or group access to directory elements (i.e., permissions for read/write/modify/delete). The IETF is currently working on specifications for syntax associated with the ACL attribute; therefore, implementations are currently using private formats.

LDAP implementations and APIs

Both Netscape and Microsoft Web browsers include LDAP client support as standard. Vendor implementations of LDAP servers include the following:

- Novell Directory Services (NDS)—NDS is based on X.500 but runs over IPX. Later versions of NetWare enable clients to query NDS via an LDAP interface [53].

- Microsoft's Active Directory Services (ADS)—Active Directory/ LDAP functions are incorporated into Windows 2000 [54].

- Netscape/iPlanet Directory Server—A powerful alliance currently dominating the directory service market. It includes Sun Microsystems, AOL/Netscape, and Innosoft [55].

- Open LDAP—code derived from the University of Michigan [56].

Although LDAP defines the communication protocol between the directory client and server, it does not define an Applications Programming Interface (API) for the client. Commercial LDAP packages include the following:

- Sun's JNDI

- Microsoft's ADSI

- Netscape's LDAP C SDK and LDAP Java SDK

- University of Michigan's OpenLDAP C API

Reference [57] defines a C language API to access a directory using LDAPv2. Note that this is an informational RFC; however, it has become a de facto standard. At the time of writing, RFC 1823 is being updated to support LDAPv3.

2.4.4   Directory-Enabled Networking (DEN)

The Directory-Enabled Network (DEN) initiative is a proposal to enable information about people, applications, network equipment, protocols, topology, security policy, and so on to be stored in a unified manner (i.e., an LDAP directory). DEN specifies an information model with a schema that defines the object classes and their related attributes. DEN is a relatively new specification; its first draft was published late in 1997 through the collaboration of Cisco and Microsoft. Many other vendors and organizations have since supported this initiative. The DEN specification defines LDAPv3 as the core protocol for accessing DEN information.

The availability of this information in a common repository, accessible through standard methods, enables vendors to better cooperate at the enterprise level through a consistent database. This greatly simplifies tasks such as provisioning and security policy, reduces overall maintenance, and promotes better network management and scalability. DEN is, therefore, a key component for building intelligent networks and has particular relevance for Policy Management Systems, as discussed in section 2.4.4. For further information about the DEN initiative the interested reader is referred to [54, 58, 59].

2.5   Design techniques for optimizing addressing

This section provides some general guidelines for implementing addressing models and also provides details on specialist techniques in common use in large-scale internetworks today.

2.5.1   General guidelines for addressing models

Addressing models for internetworks play a crucial role in improving efficiency, conserving bandwidth, ensuring scalability, improving general maintenance, and troubleshooting. When devising an addressing scheme there are several basic rules, as follows:

- Legal or private addressing—Based on the size of your network and the extent of communications over public networks, decide whether you want to implement a registered or private addressing model. If using a registered set of class C addresses, ensure that you get a large enough block of contiguous addresses to allow for future expansion. Some ISPs may be short of addresses in contiguous blocks, and you may have to select another ISP. Private addressing is much more flexible, but you must control external interfaces rigorously and install NAT or application gateways in front of any public interfaces.

- Impose structure—Before allocating addresses work out the overall structure of your network design. Focus on the main functional, topological, and geographical boundaries and work out where the key interfaces are. Your model should display a natural hierarchy that mirrors the inherent high-level structure and distribution characteristics of your organization. A structured model will be much more scalable than a flat or random model. If your network is large enough to warrant an ASN and meets the topology constraints imposed by IANA, use registered AS numbers.

- Delegate authority—Wherever possible, delegate authority for address allocation on a regional basis. Providing that the basic ground rules are documented, this will improve your ability to react to changes while maintaining consistency.

- Associate physical features—Allocate blocks of addresses to match this hierarchical model. Addresses should be allocated according to physical location rather than by group function. Groups move, expand, dissolve, and may become distributed, and this will be hard to track.

- Impose meaning and consistency—Try to impose some meaning and consistency into the addresses you allocate. For example, IP subnet 1 through N could be allocated according to floor levels or building numbers on a campus network. HostID 1 could be the default router on each subnet. In mixed-protocol environments it may be appropriate to map different addressing schemes accordingly. For example, in a private address IP network, the IPX network number 2021 could correspond to an IP network number 20.2.1.0. All of these features will greatly improve troubleshooting.

- Maximize efficiency—Optimize the address space allocated to you, using techniques such as variable-length subnet mask, classless inter-domain routing, and route summarization.

- Dynamic configuration—Where possible use dynamic means to allocate addresses and configuration data, preferably via DHCP or BOOTP. Static configurations do not scale.

- Build in security—Consider security as part of the design. On public interfaces try to hide or minimize the exposure of your internal network by using techniques such as NAT and Split DNS.

- Document the model—Any model should be clearly documented and readily available to all interested parties. Failure to do this will lead to inconsistency, duplicate addressing, and potentially serious wastes of time and resources firefighting unnecessary problems.

Often the network designer may be involved in renumbering an existing model, and there are special considerations to be aware of. For the interested reader, references [60, 61] provide a useful insight into this topic.

2.5.2   Network Address Translation (NAT)

Network Address Translation (NAT), defined in [62], was initially proposed as a short-term solution to the problem of IP address exhaustion, since NAT provides an immediate solution for attaching unregistered IP networks to public networks such as the Internet. NAT is also commonly used to secure internal network details from the outside world. NAT operates based on the observation that, typically, only a small proportion of the hosts in a private network are communicating externally. If each host is dynamically and transparently provided with a legal IP address only when external communication takes place, then only a small address pool is required. NAT is commonly used to enable networks that have private or illegal addresses to communicate with Internet services. Without address translation any traffic originating from the private intranet using illegal addresses would at best result in external traffic reaching the desired services but responses being routed to some other location (i.e., the real owner of those addresses, who would doubtless be unhappy to receive such traffic). Three modes of NAT are typically available, as follows:

- Static Address Translation (SAT)—A permanent one-to-one mapping of internal-to-external IP addresses. This may be configured for both incoming (static destination mode) and outgoing (static source mode) traffic. This is typically used for fixed services where you need the addresses to be persistent (such as HTTP or SMTP servers or router addresses). For example, you may need to maintain consistency with external services such as DNS or require fixed addresses for network management status polling. It may also be difficult to troubleshoot key services if their addresses are dynamically assigned. The downside is that you must maintain these static associations.

- Dynamic Address Translation (DAT)—A dynamic one-to-one mapping of internal-to-external IP addresses from a small pool of legal IP addresses. This is the simplest and most common mode for large-scale host address translation, where the addresses do not need to be consistent and low maintenance is required.

- Port Address Translation (PAT)—A dynamic many-to-one mapping of internal addresses to a single external legal IP address. Sometimes referred to as address overloading. Effectively many private addresses are multiplexed onto a single official source IP address using different UDP and TCP port numbers to identify internal hosts. This mode is especially useful if you have a very small pool of public addresses. Generally this mode allows outgoing connections only for security reasons (often referred to as hide mode); this topic is described further in Chapter 5.

Figure 2.15 illustrates the basic concepts of NAT on a public-private edge device. NAT dynamically translates the source IP address of an outgoing packet into an official IP address. For incoming packets destined for the private network it does the reverse, translating the official IP destination address into the corresponding private IP address before it can be forwarded. Clearly, this is a stateful process requiring the NAT module to establish and maintain data structures for flows. A timeout value is typically configured to enable NAT to free up IP associations so that addresses in the pool can be reused. The default idle timer is typically about 15 minutes. Connection-oriented protocols usually indicate very clearly when a session is about to be terminated (e.g., TCP uses the FIN bit in a three-way exchange to close a session). This knowledge can be used to preempt the timer and free up the address immediately if required. For statically mapped addresses NAT must be preconfigured by the administrator. Clearly, statically assigned NAT addresses must not overlap with addresses in the dynamic address pool. In Figure 2.15, we see that incoming packets on either interface may be matched against a rule base to see if they should be

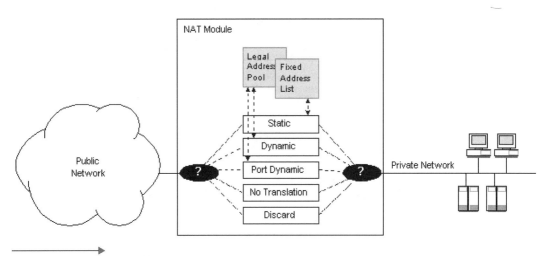

Figure 2.15   *NAT concepts.*

NATed. Typically, we NAT on packets traveling from the internal (private) network to the public network. If a source IP address requires NATing, then it may either be allocated statically (from a list of hard-coded addresses) or dynamically (from a small pool of legal addresses). Dynamic allocation may provide a unique IP address per source address or a single IP address using multiple ports to differentiate sessions.

Typically a NAT device is run at edge devices or as part of the ISP's router or firewall configuration on the customer's premises. The NAT addresses assigned at the WAN interfaces need to be officially registered addresses (described in section 2.1.5) if used for any external public or Internet access. If using NAT on a multiport router or firewall router, then NAT should be configured to comply with normal routing operations (i.e., the NAT IP addresses configured for different interfaces should appear to be from separate networks or subnets).

NAT issues

NAT is not always protocol transparent and must, therefore, be regarded as a useful tool rather than a panacea. Usually only TCP and UDP packets are translated by NAT. SNMP and the ICMP protocol (which runs over IP) may not be fully supported (check with your equipment vendor). In the latter case, if ICMP is not supported, then pinging a NATed address will not work, which can impair troubleshooting. NAT operations with applications such as multimedia, H.323, NetBIOS, DNS, SQLNET, and those that offer dynamic port negotiation are achievable but much more difficult.

Address translation means that applications that use embedded IP addresses may not operate correctly; if these addresses are internal (i.e., unregistered), then they must also be NATed or the application may simply not work. For example:

- ICMP messages often contain embedded IP addresses within their payloads.

- DNS queries may return addresses or send addresses within their payloads.

- FTP interactions may use an ASCII-encoded IP address as part of the PORT command.

- A public Web page may unfortunately specify hyperlinks as local IP addresses instead of DNS names. Since these addresses are advertised publicly but will not have been translated, any attempt to follow a link will lead to an entirely different device (i.e., the real owner of the public registered address). A final point is that, in general, if there are multiple NATs operating in a network, their translation mechanisms should be synchronized, or at least carefully configured, to avoid potential ambiguities.

Performance issues

As we have discussed, NAT performs address translation on the fly. This is a reasonable amount of work in itself, but a NAT device has more work to do, and you need to be aware of this for performance reasons, including the following:

- Checksum fixes—When NAT translates an IP address, the IP checksum is invalidated and must be recalculated (fortunately the checksum algorithm is a trivial one's complement integer addition of the IP header content, but this must be done per packet).

- Embedded addresses—For some applications there may be even more work to do; HTTP, FTP, and NetBIOS can pass important addresses in payload fields. For example, the FTP PORT command contains an IP address in ASCII format. This level of translation requires more work but is still relatively straightforward. Some protocols are harder or impossible to work with.

- IP fragmentation—This can cause latency problems if fragments need to be reassembled before NATing. For example, if the protocol uses embedded addressing (as described above), then reassembly may be necessary so that the data space can be examined.

As a result, NAT often introduces a significant performance hit on the host system, dependent upon the number of concurrent sessions and the volume of traffic. On edge devices this is offset by the speed of the WAN link; the slower the WAN interface, the less problematic this will be. On high-speed WAN interfaces (such as multimegabit ATM interfaces) or devices such as firewalls (which can concentrate thousands of concurrent sessions over multiple wide area feeds), NAT may become a real bottleneck. For this reason some sites may wrap CPU-intensive devices such as firewalls inside wire-speed switching equipment, where the NAT is performed on the switches themselves. Some NAT implementations may also be configured to provide simple session-based load distribution.

Security issues

One concern with NAT is that host addresses are hidden outside the local domain. While this is often desirable for security reasons (NAT is often supported on firewalls for this very reason, as described in Chapter 5), it also presents a problem for network management and diagnostic processes. Reference [61] suggests the possibility of developing a NAT MIB that could be queried by SNMP to find the active local-to-global address mappings. While this seems a viable approach, it also raises the issue of secure access to the MIB via a trusted SNMP application. Since SNMP is still largely deployed in an untrusted mode, this requires widespread adoption of secure forms of SNMP.

2.5.3   Subnetting

In section 2.1.2 we introduced the concepts of natural network masks. As we saw in section 2.1.5, one of the main problems with natural masks is that they are not granular enough, and this has led to serious inefficiencies in the allocation of IP addresses, since the vast majority of networks are not populated according to byte boundaries. Subnetting is a method of locally extending the natural mask by using bits from the hostID space contiguously (noncontiguous masks are possible but not recommended, since they can lead to some nasty debugging challenges). By moving the boundary that separates the hostID from the netID, effectively expanding the netID, multiple additional networks can be created from a single IP address, with a reduced number of hosts on each subnetwork. The designer can trade off how many hosts and networks are required on a per-site basis. The new subnet mask can be represented in dotted-decimal notation in much the same way as an IP address is represented:

<netID><subnetID><hostID>

Tables 2.4 and 2.5 illustrate the range of contiguous mask configurations for a class B and class C address, respectively. For example, if you were to subnet a class B network by stealing 4 bits from the hostID space, then the mask would be 255.255.240.0, providing $2^4 - 1$ networks (i.e., 15) and $2^{12} - 2$ hosts (i.e., 4,094). There is nothing to stop you from extending the mask over multiple bytes—for example, class A addresses could be subnetted using a /24 prefix, but this is usually not necessary

There are effectively two types of subnetting in common use today. They are essentially variations on the same theme, as follows:

- Bit-wise (static) subnets—where all subnets in the subnetted network use the same subnet mask. This is simple to implement and easy to maintain, but it implies some wasted address space for small networks, since the mask must match the largest requirement for subnets. For example, if we subnet a class B address to accommodate several regional groups within the organization and one of those groups requires 12 subnets, then our extended bit mask must be at least 4 bits long, even though some groups may require only one or two subnets.

- Variable-Length Subnet Masks (VLSM)—where the network is comprised of subnets that use different length subnet masks. Given the example just described, we could vary the length of the subnet mask according to the specific requirements of individual groups, and this is a much more efficient way of allocating address space. A well-thought-out design can accommodate localized expansion of the address space with minimum disruption to other parts of the network. Not all hosts and routers support variable-length subnetting.

Since VLSM is essentially a refinement of static subnetting, both schemes can be used together. Hosts that support only static subnetting do not prevent variable-length subnetting from being used, as long as the routers (and routing protocols) between subnets support VLSM. Such routers recognize subnet masks and route packets based on the most specific mask. On subnetted networks, where older end systems do not understand subnet masks, some routers provide support for proxy ARP (described in section 2.2.1). When deploying VLSM, it is important that you do not allow address spaces created by using different subnet masks to overlap. This would eventually result in duplicate addresses on the network as the network expands and these overlapping addresses get allocated multiple times.

Table 2.4   *IP class B subnet configuration. Subnet addresses that are OK to use are indicated in the final column. Addresses that have been excluded are either subnet broadcasts or host broadcast/my addresses.*

Bits Used		Mask (binary)				Mask (Decimal)	Prefix	Created		OK
Subnet	Host							Subnets	Hosts	
0	16	11111111	11111111	00000000	00000000	255.255.000.000	16	0	65,534	✕
1	15	11111111	11111111	10000000	00000000	255.255.128.000	17	1	32,766	✓
2	14	11111111	11111111	11000000	00000000	255.255.192.000	18	3	16,382	✓
3	13	11111111	11111111	11100000	00000000	255.255.224.000	19	7	8,190	✓
4	12	11111111	11111111	11110000	00000000	255.255.240.000	20	15	4,094	✓
5	11	11111111	11111111	11111000	00000000	255.255.248.000	21	31	2,046	✓
6	10	11111111	11111111	11111100	00000000	255.255.252.000	22	63	1,022	✓
7	9	11111111	11111111	11111110	00000000	255.255.254.000	23	127	510	✓
8	8	11111111	11111111	11111111	00000000	255.255.255.000	24	255	254	✓
9	7	11111111	11111111	11111111	10000000	255.255.255.128	25	511	126	✓
10	6	11111111	11111111	11111111	11000000	255.255.255.192	26	1,023	62	✓
11	5	11111111	11111111	11111111	11100000	255.255.255.224	27	2,047	30	✓
12	4	11111111	11111111	11111111	11110000	255.255.255.240	28	4,095	14	✓
13	3	11111111	11111111	11111111	11111000	255.255.255.248	29	8,191	6	✓
14	2	11111111	11111111	11111111	11111100	255.255.255.252	30	16,383	2	✓
15	1	11111111	11111111	11111111	11111110	255.255.255.254	31	32,767	0	✕
16	0	11111111	11111111	11111111	11111111	255.255.255.255	32	65,535	0	✕

Table 2.5   *IP class C subnet configuration. Subnet addresses that are OK to use are indicated in the final column. Addresses that have been excluded are either subnet broadcasts or host broadcast/my addresses.*

Bits Used		Mask (binary)				Mask (Decimal)	Prefix	Created		OK
Subnet	Host							Subnets	Hosts	
0	8	11111111	11111111	11111111	00000000	255.255.255.000	24	0	254	✕
1	7	11111111	11111111	11111111	10000000	255.255.255.128	25	1	126	✓
2	6	11111111	11111111	11111111	11000000	255.255.255.192	26	3	62	✓
3	5	11111111	11111111	11111111	11100000	255.255.255.224	27	7	30	✓
4	4	11111111	11111111	11111111	11110000	255.255.255.240	28	15	14	✓
5	3	11111111	11111111	11111111	11111000	255.255.255.248	29	31	6	✓
6	2	11111111	11111111	11111111	11111100	255.255.255.252	30	63	2	✓
7	1	11111111	11111111	11111111	11111110	255.255.255.254	31	127	0	✕
8	0	11111111	11111111	11111111	11111111	255.255.255.255	32	255	0	✕

Example 1—Subnetted class C

Assume we have a class C address, 193.168.54.0, natural mask 255.255.255.0. Assume also that we want to subnet this address to partition the network into at least four subnets, making the most efficient use of the address space. So how many bits do we need to provide four subnets? To answer this first consider how many bits we have to play with. Since the class C mask is already 24 bits long, we only have 8 bits remaining, and clearly with only 254 host addresses we need to be as economical as possible. So how many bits are required to give us four permutations? Clearly, one bit will only give us two possible subnetworks: 0 and 1. Not enough. Two bits will give us four possible subnetworks: 00, 01, 10, 2. So should two bits be enough? However, we cannot use all 1s, since these must be reserved for subnet broadcasts, and some older networks may also require all 0s to be reserved (as described in section 2.1.3). So to be safe we must use at least 3 bits, giving us eight possible subnetworks, of which at least one is unavailable. So our subnet mask should be 255.255.255.224 (binary 2222.2222.2100000.00000000), leaving us with 5 host bits ($2^5 - 2 = 30$ hosts) per subnet. The following chart illustrates this concept.

Binary	Decimal	Note
21	224	Subnet broadcast
20	192	Subnet 6
101	160	Subnet 5
100	128	Subnet 4
02	96	Subnet 3
010	64	Subnet 2
001	32	Subnet 1
000	0	Subnet 0—possibly old-style subnet broadcast

Note that routers that support Classless InterDomain Routing (CIDR) can make full use of all the 0s and 1s subnet addresses in this example. With CIDR there is no natural mask to consider and, therefore, no concept of subnets, so all bits in the network space are treated as a contiguous network address. CIDR is covered in section 2.5.4.

Example 2—Subnetted class B

Assume that the IP address of a workstation is 140.21.32.2. With a natural mask this would equate to network address 140.21 and host address 32.12. If, however, we subnet this class B network address by extending the natural mask by 5 bits (i.e., a prefix of /21 and a mask of 255.255.248.0), this gives us 31 new subnetworks plus the reserved address, 248, for subnet broadcasts. Since we have 2 bits left for the hostID, this gives us $2^2 - 2 = 2,046$ host addresses per subnet.

Example 3—VLSM with class B

Assume we have a class B address, 130.50.0.0, and an organization with seven functional workgroups as illustrated in Figure 2.16. This is typical of many large organizations. Let us assume that this network was installed several years ago, and addresses were allocated in a linear fashion; over time this scheme has become almost random, since several reconfigurations have left the network effectively at the mercy of the users. At the present time the network is bridged—effectively a single IP domain. If we analyze the

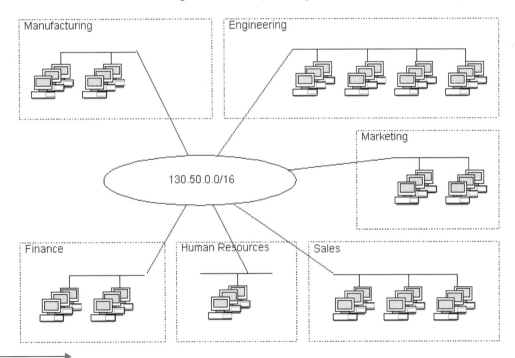

Figure 2.16   *A single class B network with 7 functional work groups.*

makeup of each functional group, we find that these groups are logically separated into smaller workgroups (typically teams within a functional group). The approximate number of hosts per work group is listed in the following chart.

Clearly, if our address allocation is linear/random and a natural class B mask is used, then there is no way to segment the traffic (at Layer 3) on this network without a major reconfiguration.

Functional Group	Workgroups	Hosts/Workgroup	Total Hosts
Finance	2	100	200
Human Resources	1	50	50
Manufacturing	2	800	1,600
Engineering	4	1,000	4,000
Marketing	2	200	400
Sales	3	90	270
TOTAL	14		6,520

Our first option is to impose some hierarchy on the network using static subnet masks. To provide up to 14 subnets we will need at least a 4-bit subnet mask—hence, 255.255.240.0. This would give us up to 4,094 hosts per subnet. This concept is illustrated in the following chart.

Functional Group	Subnet	Bits	Address
Finance	1	0001	16
	2	0010	32
Human Resources	3	002	48
Manufacturing	4	0100	64
	5	0101	80
Engineering	6	020	96
	7	021	22
	8	1000	128
	9	1001	144

Functional Group	Subnet	Bits	Address
Marketing	10	1010	160
	11	102	176
Sales	12	200	192
	13	201	208
	14	210	224
Broadcast	15	22	240

If we planned, for example, to install routers in this network at a later date, then we could still configure this addressing scheme now, but leave the natural network mask (255.255.0.0) in place. Once routers are installed, we could change the mask to 255.255.240.0 to enable routing between subnets. Furthermore, all of these networks can be summarized externally as one class B network if the natural mask is propagated over the external links.

This works fine, but we can already see that there are large disparities in the relative size and subnet requirements of these groups, and clearly a static mask is going to be very wasteful, especially if the network grows substantially in the future. What we need, ideally, is a more flexible way of handing out address space. We, therefore, examine the possibilities with Variable-Length Subnet Masks (VLSM). Let us assume that the network has expanded and we are now faced with the requirements shown in the following chart.

Functional Group	Workgroups	Hosts/Group	Total Hosts
Finance	2	200	400
Human Resources	1	150	150
Manufacturing	3	2,000	6,000
Engineering	5	2,500	12,500
Marketing	18	60	1,200
Sales	25	80	2,400
TOTAL	54		22,650

If we applied our static mask here, we would need at least a 6-bit mask (255.255.252.0) to provide 54 subnetworks. This would be grossly inefficient. What we need is a way of handling some of the larger subnets, such as engineering and manufacturing, as well as the smaller subnet populations, such as human resources and sales. Our largest subnet requirement is 25, requiring at least a 4-bit mask. Apart from marketing and sales, all other functional groups require less than 15 subnetworks. If we are to allow for future expansion, we could at the very least apply two separate masks according to size. For those groups requiring less than 15 subnets we can use a 4-bit mask (255.255.240.0), and for those networks requiring 15 or more subnets we could apply an 8-bit mask (255.255.255.0). This concept is illustrated in the following chart.

Functional Group	Mask	Bits	Address
Finance	4	0001xxxx	130.50.16.0
		0010xxxx	130.50.32
Human Resources	4	002xxxx	130.50.48
Manufacturing	4	0100xxxx	130.50.64
		0101xxxx	130.50.80
		020xxxx	130.50.96
Engineering	4	021xxxx	130.50.22
		1000xxxx	130.50.128
		1001xxxx	130.50.144
		1010xxxx	130.50.160
		102xxxx	130.50.160
Marketing	8	2000001	130.50.192.1 to 130.50.192.18 (18)
		||	
		2010010	
Sales	8	201002	130.50.192.19 to 130.50.192.43 (25)
		||	
		210102	

Note that this allocation scheme is not contiguous, nor is it depleted. There is an unused gap between marketing and sales to allow for expansion either way.

2.5.4   Supernetting or Classless InterDomain Routing (CIDR)

In section 2.1.5 we covered the issue of IP address space depletion. IPv6 will overcome this problem in time, but what can be done in the interim? One idea was to use a range of class C addresses instead of a single class B address. The problem there is that each network must be routed separately, because standard IP routing understands only classes A, B, and C network addresses (see Chapter 3). Within each of these types of network, subnetting (i.e., using a subnet mask larger than the natural network mask) can be used to provide better granularity of the address space within each network, but there is no way to specify that multiple class C networks are actually related. The result of this is referred to as the routing table explosion problem: A class B network of 3,000 hosts requires one routing table entry at each backbone router, whereas the same network, if addressed as a range of class C networks, would require 16 entries.

The solution to this problem is a scheme called Classless InterDomain Routing (CIDR). CIDR, also called supernetting, is described in [41, 63, 64]. Supernetting works by relaxing the normal rules of IP addressing, so that the IP address prefix can be shorter than the natural mask length (hence, the term classless). For example, the class C address 196.20.136.0 can be represented as a supernet using the format 196.20.0.0/16. This represents all networks starting with the prefix 196.20.

Supernetting is a powerful technique, which can be used to group contiguous blocks of routes together for route summarization. This process is more formally called aggregation. For example, to summarize a block of eight class C addresses with a single routing entry, the following representation would suffice: 196.20.136.0/21 (i.e., a mask of 255.255.248.0). This single routing entry would, from a backbone point of view, summarize the address block from 196.20.136.0 to 196.20.143.0 as a single network, as illustrated in the following code segment:

```
2000100 00010100 10001000 00000000 = 196.20.136.0 // Class C address
2222 2222 221XXX XXXXXXXX  255.255.248.0 // Supernet mask
-------------------------------- logical_AND
2000100 00010100 10001XXX XXXXXXXX = 196.20.136  // IP prefix
```

```
2000100 00010100 100022 00000000 = 196.20.143.0  // Class C address
2222 2222 221XXX XXXXXXXX 255.255.248.0  // Supernet mask
-------------------------------- logical_AND
2000100 00010100 10001XXX XXXXXXXX = 196.20.136  // Same IP prefix
```

The current Internet address allocation policies and guidelines for CIDR are described in [63]. They are summarized as follows:

- IP address assignment reflects the physical topology of the network and not the organizational topology; wherever organizational and administrative boundaries do not match the network topology, they should not be used for the assignment of IP addresses. In general, network topology will closely follow continental and national boundaries and, therefore, IP addresses should be assigned on this basis.

- There will be a relatively small group of networks that carry a large amount of traffic between routing domains and that will be interconnected in a nonhierarchical manner across national boundaries. These are referred to as Transit Routing Domains (TRDs). Each TRD will have a unique IP prefix. TRDs will not be organized in a hierarchical manner where there is no appropriate hierarchy. However, wherever a TRD is wholly within a continental boundary, its IP prefix should be an extension of the continental IP prefix.

- There will be many organizations that have attachments to other organizations that are for the private use of those two organizations and that do not carry traffic intended for other domains (transit traffic). Such private connections do not have a significant effect on the routing topology and can be ignored.

- Most routing domains will be single-homed (i.e., they will be attached to a single TRD). They should be assigned addresses that begin with that TRD's IP prefix. All of the addresses for all single-homed domains attached to a TRD can, therefore, be summarized into a single routing table entry for all domains outside that TRD. This implies that if an organization changes its Internet service provider, it should change all of its IP addresses. This is not the current practice, but the widespread implementation of CIDR is likely to make it much more common.

- There are a number of address assignment schemes that can be used for multi-homed domains, including the following:

  - The use of a single IP prefix for the domain. External routers must have an entry for the organization that lies partly or wholly outside the normal hierarchy. Where a domain is multihomed but all of the attached TRDs are topologically nearby, it would be appropriate for the domain's IP prefix to include those bits common to all of the attached TRDs. For example, if all of the TRDs were wholly within the United States, an IP prefix implying an exclusively North American domain would be appropriate.

- The use of one IP prefix for each attached TRD, with hosts in the domain having IP addresses containing the IP prefix of the most appropriate TRD. The organization appears to be a set of routing domains.

- Assigning an IP prefix from one of the attached TRDs. This TRD becomes a default TRD for the domain, but other domains can explicitly route by one of the alternative TRDs.

- The use of IP prefixes to refer to sets of multihomed domains having the TRD attachments. For example, there may be an IP prefix to refer to single-homed domains attached to network A, one to refer to single-homed domains attached to network B, and one to refer to dual-homed domains attached to networks A and B.

- Each of these has various advantages, disadvantages, and side effects. For example, the first approach tends to result in inbound traffic entering the target domain closer to the sending host than the second approach, and, therefore a larger proportion of the network costs are incurred by the receiving organization.

Because multihomed domains can vary significantly in character and none of the above schemes is suitable for all such domains, there is no single policy that is best; reference [63] does not specify any rules for choosing between them.

CIDR implementation

The implementation of CIDR in the Internet is primarily based on the BGPv4 protocol (see Chapter 3). The implementation strategy, described in [64] involves a staged process through the routing hierarchy beginning with backbone routers. Service providers are divided into four types, as follows:

- Type 1—Those that cannot employ any default interdomain routing.

- Type 2—Those that use default interdomain routing but require explicit routes for a substantial proportion of the assigned IP network numbers.

- Type 3—Those that use default interdomain routing supplemented with a small number of explicit routes.

- Type 4—Those that perform all interdomain routing using only default routes. The CIDR implementation involves an implementation beginning with the Type 1 network providers, then the Type 2, and finally the Type 3 providers. CIDR has already been widely deployed in the backbone, and over 9,000 class-based routes have been replaced by approximately 2,000 CIDR-based routes.

2.5.5   Hierarchical addressing and route summarization

An important technique, which optimizes routing resources and routing performance, is hierarchical addressing. This technique is available only to routing protocols that have the ability to support hierarchical models such as OSPF and IS-IS (described in Chapter 3). Hierarchical routing is a valuable technique used in building large networks. As networks grow their use of finite routing resources, such as memory, CPU, and bandwidth grow, and, therefore, a more efficient design will reduce the overall resource deterioration. In Chapter 3 we see that in flat routed designs (i.e., not flat in the sense of bridged networks) the OSPF routing table grows linearly with the number of IP segments O(n), but with hierarchical routing we can slow the growth to a logarithmic rate, O(log[n]). Clearly this is a major improvement.

Hierarchical routing partitions the internetwork by segmenting the network recursively into manageable chunks, each grouped by address and subnet mask to form a tree-like structure. At the very lowest level we are using flat routing within the partition, but in this case the routers require only minimal knowledge of other partitions in the network; they just need to know how to get there. Consider the network models illustrated in Figures 2.17 and 2.18. Here we have a simple three-layer hierarchy, with nine level 1 partitions, three level 2 partitions, and one level 3 partition. We start with a class A network, 12.0.0.0, using a classic 8-bit mask. We then subdivide the network into three partition—12.1.0.0, 12.2.0.0, 12.3.0.0—mask 255.255.0.0, and then further subdivide these partitions as shown.

When routers need to forward to destinations outside their immediate partitions, they rely on higher-level routing to complete the task. This approach significantly reduces routing table size. For example, suppose we have 25 segments in every level 1 partition, and we examine a router in the 12.1.1.0/24 partition, as follows:

- If flat routing is implemented, the routing table will have 9 × 25 = 225 entries.

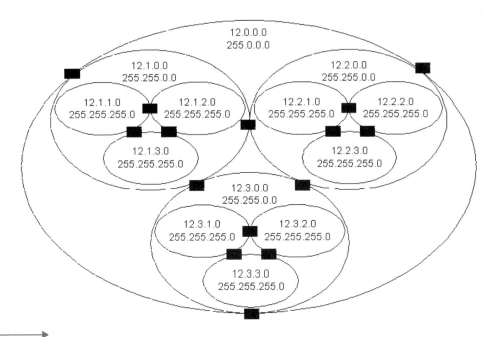

Figure 2.17   *Three-layer hierarchical routing scheme—bird's-eye view.*

- If we use a hierarchical scheme, each level 1 router will have only 25 + 4 = 29 entries (25 local level 1 entries, plus two level 2 entries, 12.1.2.0/16, 12.1.3.0/16, plus two level 3 entries, 12.2.0.0/8, 12.3.0.0/8).

Clearly, we can see the benefit in table size (87 percent), but this will also mean that convergence is speeded up, since the routing algorithm has to scan less routing entries when building its forwarding tables. The Internet employs a hierarchical routing hierarchy for these very reasons. However, there are some disadvantages, in that suboptimal paths may be chosen in a hierarchical scheme, resulting in longer paths than would be achieved with flat routing. Note that the preceding example illustrates the simplest form of

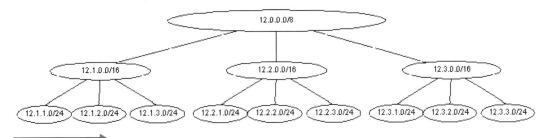

Figure 2.18   *Three-layer hierarchical routing scheme—tree view.*

route summarization, where subnet routes are collapsed into a single net-work route. Routing protocols that support VLSMs may support route summarization at any bit boundary (rather than just by natural mask). Some routing protocols summarize automatically; others may require manual con-figuration. Further information on this subject can be found in Chapter 3, where its association with specific routing protocols is covered in depth.

2.6   Summary

This chapter discussed the issues in designing an efficient addressing, nam-ing, and configuration model for your network. Specifically, the following topics were covered:

- Each device on a TCP/IP network must have a unique IP address that universally identifies it. IPv4 provides for several classes of address, but this rigid mechanism is wasteful. IPv6 provides a future-proof addressing scheme but is not widely implemented today.

- Decide at the outset if there will be a requirement for public network connectivity, such as the Internet. This will influence your decision on whether to choose a private or public IP addressing model. In either case choose the most appropriate class of IP address to cope with current demands and future growth. Make allowances for the fact that a number of IP addresses have special applications and can-not be used. If you opt for public access, make sure you use registered addresses via your ISP or nearest IANA authority.

- A number of organizations may have chosen to implement private addressing schemes to build their intranets. Subsequent changes in those organizations may now force them to provide public interfaces to resources such as the Internet. NAT has a valuable role in network renumbering; it can greatly reduce the amount of renumbering required or even negate it entirely. NAT offers static or dynamic address translation, enabling unregistered private networks to com-municate freely with the Internet. NAT, however, is not completely transparent and may not cope with some applications that rely upon embedded IP addresses. Performance overheads mean that NAT may become a bottleneck on large, busy networks.

- A hierarchical addressing scheme promotes more efficient routing and salability. Subnetting with Variable-Length Subnet Mask (VLSM) and supernetting with Classless InterDomain Routing (CIDR) are invaluable techniques for designing scalable networks.

- Depending on the size and mobility of stations on your network, you may want to make use of dynamic address allocation services to reduce the administrative burden. Dynamic addressing tools such as DHCP and BOOTP have their problems but are an invaluable aid to allocating addresses and configuration data in large networks. BOOTP has been somewhat overshadowed by DHCP in the enterprise, but for legacy environments several enhancements enable interoperability. The approach to automated configuration, address allocation, naming, and device booting has been somewhat fragmented to date. For large internetworks these activities need to be well integrated if network administrators are expected to cope with the increasing scale of modern data networks, the lack of skilled resources, and burdens placed on them. Work is underway within the IETF to provide a more holistic approach.

- IP version 6 is the best get-out-of-jail card for resolving the IP address space problem; however, the transition to IPv6 is likely to be painful and costly. There is a huge installed base of IPv4 devices and applications out there. Some of these applications will require redesigning, and this will take time. The migration phase will require the coexistence of IPv4 and IPv6 devices for several years, placing additional burdens on networking devices and services in the interim. Nevertheless, start making preparations for IPv6 now.

- Directory services are a key component in the development of intelligent networks through initiatives such as Directory-Enabled Networks (DEN). LDAP, based on OSI's X.500 DAP, is the de facto standard for client access to directory services.

References

[1] Internet Numbers, RFC 266, July 1990.

[2] Internet Protocol, RFC 791, September 1981.

[3] Internet Protocol, Version 6 (IPv6) Specification, RFC 2460, December 1998.

[4] T. Kenyon, *High-Performance Network Design: Design Techniques and Tools* (Woburn, MA: Digital Press, 2001).

[5] Assigned Numbers, RFC 1700, October 1994.

[6] www.iana.org, IANA home page.

[7] www.ripe.net, Reseau IP Européens (RIPE NCC) home page.

[8]   www.apnic.net, Asia-Pacific Network Information Center (APNIC) home page.

[9]   www.arin.net, American Registry for Internet Numbers (ARIN) home page.

[10]   Internet Registry IP Allocation Guidelines, RFC 2050, November 1996.

[11]   Address Allocation for Private Internets, RFC 1918, February 1996.

[12]   IPng Requirements of Large Corporate Networks, RFC 1678, August 1994.

[13]   IP Version 6 Addressing Architecture, RFC 1884, December 1995.

[14]   A Compact Representation of IPv6 Addresses, RFC 1924, April 1996.

[15]   Transition Mechanisms for IPv6 Hosts and Routers, RFC 1933, April 1996.

[16]   Guidelines for Creation, Selection, and Registration of an Autonomous System (AS), RFC 1930, March 1996.

[17]   ftp://ftp.isi.edu/in-notes/iana/assignments/as-numbers, latest IANA ASN assignments.

[18]   Reverse Address Resolution Protocol, RFC 903, June 1984.

[19]   Dynamic RARP Extensions for Automatic Network Address Acquisition, RFC 1931, April 1996.

[20]   Bootstrap Protocol, RFC 951, September 1985.

[21]   Clarifications and Extensions for the Bootstrap Protocol, RFC 1542, October 1993.

[22]   Bootstrap Loading Using TFTP, RFC 906, June 1984.

[23]   D. E. Comer and D. L. Stevens, *Internetworking with TCP/IP, Vol. II: Design, Implementation, and Internals* (Englewood Cliffs, NJ: Prentice Hall, 1991).

[24]   DHCP Options and BOOTP Vendor Extensions, RFC 2132, March 1997.

[25]   Dynamic Host Configuration Protocol, RFC 2131,March 1997.

[26]   Interoperation between DHCP and BOOTP, RFC 1534, October 1993.

[27] Internet Control Message Protocol, RFC 792, September 1981.

[28] P. Miller, *TCP/IP Explained* (Woburn, MA: Digital Press, 1997).

[29] Internet Control Message Protocol (ICMPv6) for the Internet Protocol Version 6 (IPv6) Specification, RFC 2463, December 1998.

[30] IP Authentication Header, RFC 2402, November 1998.

[31] P. Albitz and C. Liu, *DNS and BIND*. (O'Reilly & Associates, 1997).

[32] W. R. Stevens, *UNIX Network Programming*, vol I, 2d ed. (Englewood Cliffs, NJ: Prentice Hall, 1998).

[33] Domain Names—Concepts and Facilities, RFC 1034, November 1987.

[34] Domain Names—Implementation and Specification, RFC 1035, November 1987.

[35] DNS Extensions to Support IP Version 6, RFC 1886, December 1995.

[36] Domain Name System Structure and Delegation, RFC 1591, March 1994.

[37] www.iana.org/cctld.html, IANA Web page for registered Top-Level Domains.

[38] ICMP Domain Name Messages, RFC 1788, April 1995.

[39] Negative Caching of DNS Queries (DNS NCACHE), RFC 2308, March 1998.

[40] www.isc.org, The Internet Software Consortium's Web site; contains source for the BIND application.

[41] Classless Inter Domain Routing (CIDR): An Address Assignment and Aggregation Strategy, RFC 1519, September 1993.

[42] Dynamic Updates in the Domain Name System (DNS UPDATE), RFC 2136, April 1997.

[43] Incremental Zone Transfer in DNS, RFC 1995, August 1996.

[44] A Mechanism for Prompt Notification of Zone Changes (DNS NOTIFY), RFC 1996, August 1996.

[45] Directory Assistance Service, RFC 1202, February 1991.

[46] DIXIE Protocol Specification, RFC 1249, August 1991.

[47] X.500 Lightweight Directory Access Protocol, RFC 1487, July 1993 (obsoleted by RFC 1777).

[48] Lightweight Directory Access Protocol, RFC 1777, March 1995 (obsoletes RFC 1487).

[49] Universal Multiple-Octet Coded Character Set (UCS)—Architecture and Basic Multilingual Plane, ISO/IEC 10646-1, 1993.

[50] UTF-8: A Transformation Format of Unicode and ISO 10646, RFC 2044, October 1996.

[51] Lightweight Directory Access Protocol (v3), RFC 2251, December 1997.

[52] Naming Plan for Internet Directory-Enabled Applications, RFC 2377, September 1998.

[53] www.novell.com, Novell home page. See Novell Directory Services (NDS).

[54] www.microsoft.com, Microsoft home page. See Active Directory.

[55] www.iplanet.com, a powerful alliance offering directory services, including Sun Microsystems, AOL/Netscape, and Innosoft.

[56] www.openldap.org, LDAP code derived from the University of Michigan.

[57] The LDAP Application Program Interface, RFC 1823, August 1995.

[58] www.cisco.com, Cisco home page.

[59] www.universe.digex.net/~murchiso/den/, Information on the DEN initiative.

[60] Network Renumbering Overview, RFC 2071, January 1997.

[61] Router Renumbering Guide, RFC 2072, January 1997.

[62] The IP Network Address Translator (NAT), RFC 1631, May 1994.

[63] An Architecture for IP Address Allocation with CIDR, RFC 1518, September 1993.

[64] Exchanging Routing Information across Provider Boundaries in the CIDR Environment, RFC 1520, September 1993.

3

Routing Technology

During the early 1980s, many organizations started to build their operations around local area networks, with a few point-to-point wide area links to facilitate LAN interconnection. Wide area bridges were often used to provide packet forwarding, accomplished using either source routing or the Spanning-Tree protocol [1]. With the rise of the Internet as a business resource; the increased use of remote access, the World Wide Web, intranets and extranets; and new multimedia applications, the demands placed on backbones are now huge. In this chapter we investigate a smarter method of optimizing packet forwarding over expensive WAN links, using a device called the router. Routers are the glue that binds together internetworks into a single entity, albeit often a heterogeneous entity. Routers from many different vendors cooperate using sophisticated distributed algorithms in order to create a holistic view of the network in the form of routing tables. Compared to bridges, routing is much more sensitive to topology, bandwidth, performance, and availability, and therefore provides superior traffic engineering. Routers may also have to deal with heterogeneous media, providing scheduling support for differential services and possibly filtering or basic firewalling features. All of these features mean that a router-based network design is more robust and can be far better optimized than a flat network design.

In this chapter we are primarily concerned with the logical topology of the network rather than the physical topology. Layer 3 devices concern themselves only with logical interfaces, which are abstracted from the Physical Layer through path metrics. This chapter covers the basics of routing technology, end-system interaction, protocol operations, and addressing concepts required for designing IP networks. We will focus on the following issues:

- Internetwork architecture and topology
- Routing algorithms and protocols for interior, exterior, and end-system routing

- Route selection, network addressing, and route summarization
- Network scalability, convergence, and performance issues
- Router architecture and design issues

The vast majority of network traffic today is based on unicasts, and this chapter is primarily concerned with unicast routing, unless otherwise indicated. Chapter 4 covers the more specialized area of multicast routing. Many of the features and techniques discussed in the chapter are applicable to both forms of routing.

3.1   Internetwork architecture and topology

3.1.1   Architectural model

In previous chapters we illustrated that large problems are best approached by a divide-and-conquer strategy, and logical internetwork design is just another large problem. You will not be surprised to learn, therefore, that in general, most modern internetwork protocols support hierarchical models for partitioning networks into increasingly smaller, manageable, units.

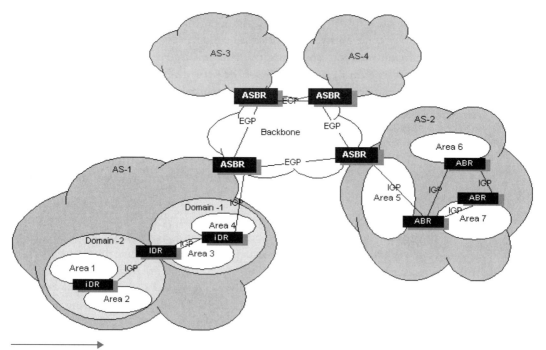

Figure 3.1   *Routing architecture.*

Figure 3.1 illustrates the key aspects of the generic internetwork architecture, and we will use this as the point of reference in subsequent discussions. Even though we are primarily focusing on IP, many of these concepts apply to other routing architectures, such as OSI, DECnet, and Novell's routing architecture. Figure 3.1 attempts to integrate some of the current thoughts on network hierarchy adopted by OSI and IETF standards. Currently, the highest level of administrative control is the Autonomous System (AS). At the AS level there are often business or political reasons for the differentiation (typically an AS is a large organization, multinational company, or a government body). Below the AS level there are further refinements of the infrastructure, and this partitioning is essentially driven by the need to provide scalability by traffic or routing management and control. In the OSI world ASs can be subdivided into one or more domains, which comprise one or more areas. Areas comprise one or more subnetworks. In the IETF world there is currently no support for domains, just areas. Intermediate Systems (IS) are used to interconnect all of these partitions, including Autonomous System Border Routers (ASBR), Area Border Routers (ABR), IntraDomain Routers (iDR), and InterDomain Routers (IDR).

3.1.2   Network hierarchy

The network is divided into several hierarchical traffic and administrative boundaries. At the highest level we have the concept of AS, communicating over a backbone. Autonomous systems are generally used for very large organizations and typically contain a group of networks and routers administered by a single authority, running one or more Interior Gateway Protocols (IGPs). It may be useful to reflect on the definitions of autonomous systems used in the standards. RFC 1267 [2] states: "The use of the term autonomous system here stresses the fact that, even when multiple IGPs and metrics are used, the administration of an AS appears to other ASs to have a single coherent interior routing plan and presents a consistent picture of what destinations are reachable through it. From the standpoint of exterior routing, an AS can be viewed as monolithic: reachability to destinations directly connected to the AS must be equivalent from all border gateways of the AS."

RFC 2386 [3] puts it more succinctly: "AS: A routing domain that has a common administrative authority and consistent internal routing policy. An AS may employ multiple intradomain routing protocols internally and interfaces to other ASs via a common interdomain routing protocol."

Each AS will require a registered AS Number (ASN) if connected into the Internet. Routing information is exchanged between ASs via an Exterior

Gateway Protocol (EGP) such as the Border Gateway Protocol (BGP). There are basically two classes of AS, as follows:

- Stub AS is an AS (sometimes called a single-homed AS) that reaches external networks via a single exit point.

- Multihomed AS is an AS with multiple exit points, which can be used to reach external networks. A multihomed AS can operate as a transit AS if it allows traffic originated and destined for other ASs to pass through it; otherwise, it is called a nontransit AS.

Next, we have the concept of routing domains. Again, it may be useful to reflect on the definition of a domain used in the IETF standards: A routing domain is a collection of routers that coordinate their routing knowledge using a single [instance of a] routing protocol.

By definition, a routing domain forms a single autonomous system, but an autonomous system can be composed of a collection of routing domains.

A routing domain can itself comprise one or more areas. Areas are logical collections of contiguous networks and nodes. As illustrated in Figure 3.1, OSI routing (i.e., IS-IS) standards use the term domain as a collection of areas, whereas in IETF parlance, OSPF supports only areas and has no concept of a domain. In much of the literature the term domain is used as a generic term. Each area runs a separate instance of a dynamic routing algorithm; therefore, each area has its own topological database. Within an area there may be several networks, divided into subnetworks. All of these entities are connected together via Intermediate Systems (IS), which are Layer 3 switches more commonly referred to as routers. Devices that do not forward packets but are attached to the network are called End Systems (ES). For example, servers and workstations with Network Interface Cards (NICs), or a network-attached storage device, can all be classified under as end systems.

3.1.3   Router hierarchy

The ability to design a hierarchical internetwork presupposes that the routing protocols and addressing models used are capable of enforcing hierarchy on the logical topology. In order to satisfy the architecture presented in section 3.1.1, it is possible to define four levels of routing, as follows:

- Level 0 Routing—routing traffic between end systems and routers on the same subnetwork

- Level 1 Routing (Interior Routing)—routing traffic between routers within the same area

■ Level 2 Routing (Border Routing)—routing traffic between different areas within the same AS

■ Level 3 Routing (Boundary Routing)—routing traffic between different ASs

In order to meet the requirements of the different levels of routing functionality, there are three generic classes of routing protocols, as follows:

■ End System to Intermediate System (ES-IS) routing protocols handle Layer 0 host to router communication (either via a simple static configuration such as a default route or a more dynamic approach, such as passive RIP or IDRP). For multicast routing a more specialized protocol called IGMP is employed.

■ Interior Gateway Protocols (IGPs) handle inter-Area (Layer 2) and/or intra-Area (Layer 1) routing. Examples of IGPs in this class include OSPF, EIGRP, ISIS, RIP, IGRP, and NLSP. Note that although RIP is an IGP, it does not support the concept of hierarchy and, therefore, performs purely Level 1 routing. For multicast routing a small number of specialized protocols are available, including DVMRP, PIM, and MOSPF.

■ Exterior Gateway Protocols (EGPs) handle policy routing at Layer 3 between ASs. Examples of EGPs include static routing and the protocols Exterior Gateway Protocol (EGP) and Border Gateway Protocol (BGP). For multicast routing this requirement is currently covered by a kludged combination of protocols, including MBGP, PIM, and MDSP.

Sophisticated unicast dynamic routing protocols (such as OSPF and IS-IS) require the creation of an explicit hierarchical topology through the establishment of a backbone and logical areas (or domains). The topology produced takes precedence over the topology created using the addressing model. When hierarchical routing is used, the network addressing scheme should comply with the logical hierarchy that is created (i.e., addressing should be consistent with the backbone and area boundaries). The topological information about a network depends on a router's role, as follows.

■ Router reachability—For topology information, a Level 1 router need only know the existence of the other Level 1 routers in its area and at least one Level 2 router in its area, plus the way in which these routers are interconnected. Similarly, a Level 2 router need only know the identity of the other Level 2 routers in its routing domain and how they are interconnected. In either case, we can abstract the topology into a graph consisting of nodes connected by edges. Each node is a router, and each edge is either a point-to-point link or a subnetwork.

- End-system reachability—In the case of a Level 1 router, it needs to know, for each end system in its area, the identity of the subnetwork that contains that end system. In the case of a Level 2 router, it needs to know, for each router, the area that contains that end system and a Level 2 router in that area. Although there are clear distinctions here, in reality devices may operate at several levels. Powerful workstations (generally assumed to be end systems) are quite capable of running a full routing stack, for example, and routers typically run multiple routing stacks and operate at different routing levels concurrently.

There are two recommended ways to assign addresses in a hierarchical network. The simplest way to achieve this is to give each area (including the backbone) a unique network address. An alternative is to assign address ranges to each area. Some older routing protocols (such as RIP) have no concept of a logical hierarchy and are, therefore, referred to as flat or nonhierarchical routing protocols. Typically there are no facilities within this class of protocol to create logical topologies, and the designer must rely upon the network addressing model alone to establish a logical routing topology.

3.1.4   Benefits of a hierarchical model

The combination of routing hierarchy and techniques such as route summarization offer several major design benefits, including the following:

- The amount of information exchanged and held by routers is greatly reduced, simplifying router operations at all levels, speeding up route calculations, and constraining local routing traffic. This typically leads to faster convergence.

- The scope of router misconfigurations is localized (with a nonhierarchical approach a single router problem can affect all routers in the network). This, therefore, promotes better availability, since there will be fewer network outages.

- Boundary interfaces between different levels of hierarchy are ideal locations for implementing traffic and security policy. Access control lists or basic firewalling are frequently configured on perimeter and border routers.

- Network expansion and upgrade operations are simplified. Protocol upgrades can be deployed separately within the various hierarchical domains; routers at one level need not know the protocol or topology of another.

All of these factors contribute to improving overall scalability and management. One downside of hierarchical networks is that route selection can be suboptimal for certain paths (since traffic between areas or domains is always forwarded through border routers, the paths chosen may not always be as short as those that would be selected if all routers had complete topological knowledge). Given the significant benefits achieved with hierarchical routing, this inefficiency is normally acceptable.

3.2 Routing algorithms

On any internetwork, packets may traverse many networks and router hops in order to reach their final destination, and many forwarding decisions must be made en route. For this purpose, a routing algorithm is required to determine the best path for each source-destination pair (s, d), and a routing protocol is required to enable intermediate systems to exchange topology and state information, so that a routing table can be formulated.

3.2.1 Distance-vector routing algorithms

Routing protocols that incorporate distance-vector algorithms are often called minimum hop. RIP is perhaps the best-known example in use today, although other examples include the original ARPANET routing protocol, AppleTalk RTMP, and Cisco's IGRP. Distance-vector provides a straightforward and effective routing mechanism, in that shortest path lengths are calculated by simply adding up hop counts between routers [1]. This relative simplicity leads to several significant drawbacks for modern internetwork design.

Protocols that implement distance-vector typically lack sensitivity to delays induced on a network. Distance-vector protocols do not generally support load balancing. Another issue is that convergence around routing failures tend to be very slow (often minutes), and even normal operation can cause routing loops. Overall these protocols scale badly—first in that they are typically constrained in diameter (i.e., the number of hops) of the network and second in that they generally broadcast entire routing tables at regular intervals, and so the protocol overhead grows linearly $O(N)$ with the number of networks. Cisco's proprietary adaptation of RIP, called IGRP, does offer workarounds for several of these problems; however, in general, this class of protocol is considered unsuitable for large internetworks

(Cisco's EIGRP uses a hybrid routing algorithm, which, although based on the distance-vector, results in convergence times similar to that of OSPF).

3.2.2 Link-state routing algorithms

Link-state algorithm is a term synonymous with Shortest Path First (SPF) and Dijkstra (a shortest path algorithm described in [1]). The term "link" in this context refers to an interface on the router. The term "state" means a description of that interface and of its relationship to its neighboring routers. For example, this might include the IP address of the interface, the mask, the type of network it is connected to, and a list of neighboring routers connected to that interface. The repository that holds all of these link states is called a link-state database.

In a link-state network each router knows the complete topology of its local domain, since all routers maintain a complete copy of the topology database. Link-state routing protocols use a much richer set of metrics than hop-based protocols and consequently are much better suited to Type of Service (TOS)–based routing. The other major benefit of this class of protocols is that once routing databases are synchronized, only link-state updates are propagated throughout the network, significantly reducing background routing traffic. The first link-state routing protocol was developed for use in the ARPANET back in the 1980s, and this work was the springboard for a new generation of link-state routing protocols such as OSPF and IS-IS.

3.2.3 Link-state versus distance-vector routing

The most important differences between the different routing algorithms from the network designer's perspective are scalability, bandwidth and protocol efficiency, stability, and convergence time. Scalability is a key factor in your choice of routing protocol. Distance-vector protocols have the reputation of scaling badly, largely because they tend to distribute the entire routing table at regular intervals. This can represent a significant overhead for low-speed WAN links and is amplified by the lack of hierarchy in many of these protocols. Distance-vector protocols also tend to use broadcasts (RIPv2 supports the option of multicast distribution). With these protocols regular broadcasts occur regardless of whether the routing table has changed.

Changes in LSAs cause each router within the area to recalculate the forwarding table. The fact that LSAs need to be flooded throughout the area in failure mode and the fact that all routers recalculate routing tables constrain

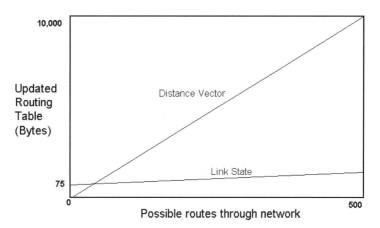

Figure 3.2
Scalability of link-state protocols versus distance-vector protocols as the number of routes increase.

the number of neighbors that can be in an area. Link-state protocols tend to be more CPU and RAM intensive, but their background bandwidth requirements are much less of an overhead than distance-vector traffic (although the startup requirements for link-state routers tends to be higher due to synchronization traffic). Figure 3.2 graphically illustrates the scalability issues for distance-vector protocols as compared with link-state protocols.

Distance-vector protocols typically use flooded updates that are sent to all routers. Link-state protocols such as OSPF also flood routing information but use bounded updates to their nearest neighbors (by setting the TTL to 1). When the network is stable, distance-vector protocols behave well but waste bandwidth because of the periodic transmission of complete routing table updates, even when no change has occurred. When a failure occurs in the network, distance-vector protocols do not add excessive load to the network, but they generally take a long time to reconverge and provide an alternate path or to flush a bad path from the network.

Link-state protocols do have some drawbacks. Each time there is a topology change, each link-state router must rerun the SPF algorithm locally to recalculate its forwarding database; while in this state no forwarding is taking place, so this must be achieved quickly. On a large network the processing and memory requirements can be significant, and an SPF tree must be created for each area supported on a router. Another issue with SPF protocols is that they are much more sensitive to changes in topology. While this is inherently a good thing, and precisely what you would want from a routing protocol, in some circumstances this is undesirable. On a network that has unstable links, this can lead to frequent reconvergences, and this affects users and network services directly. Some implementations, therefore, implement interface or path-dampening techniques, so that unstable links are taken offline and monitored (using some form of hysteresis or hold-down timer) until they are classed as stable.

Link-state protocols tend to support network hierarchy.

DUAL algorithm

Cisco's EIGRP routing protocol implements a hybrid distance-vector algorithm with a Diffusing Update Algorithm (DUAL), which exhibits some of the attractive properties of link-state protocols (such as very fast convergence and lower bandwidth consumption in a steady-state network). EIGRP uses a hello mechanism to determine neighbor reachability and sends updates only when topology changes occur. In failure conditions EIGRP looks for feasible successors by sending messages to its neighbors. To achieve rapid convergence, however, a significant amount of traffic can be generated during the search for feasible successors (i.e., updates, queries, and responses). This behavior constrains the number of neighbors that are possible and, therefore, affects scalability. For further information, the interested reader is referred to reference [4].

In multiprotocol environments (such as enterprise networks) it may be necessary either to run multiple protocols on the router simultaneously (so-called ships in the night mode) or use a routing protocol such as Cisco's EIGRP, which is capable of supporting several protocol types concurrently. Fortunately the networking industry is now focusing all efforts on the common IP protocol, and this is the protocol of choice for backbone networks. This means that several of these legacy protocols are already starting to die out. In this book we will focus primarily on the routing protocols that support IP traffic. For reference, the stack also includes the multicast routing protocols IGMP, MOSPF, PIM, and DVMRP, which are discussed in detail in Chapter 4.

Table 3.1 lists the classification of routing protocols. These protocols broadly fall into those using distance-vector (DV) algorithms, or link-state (SPF) algorithms. Cisco's EIGRP uses a hybrid algorithm based on distance-vector. ES-IS is the OSI standard for gateway discovery and offers similar functionality to ARP plus ICMP redirect. GGP is an old protocol design by the BBN for use on LS/11 gateways (it has some serious drawbacks). The hello protocol was also developed for LS/11 gateways and attempted to use available bandwidth by monitoring round-trip delay but was not especially successful.

Table 3.1   *Classification of Routing Protocols*

Routing Protocol	Description	Type	Rout Alg	Open Std	Encap	Metric	Mcast Distrib	Update Timer	VLSM
BGP	Border Gateway Protocol	EGP	PV	yes	ip		no	trig	
EGP	Exterior gateway Protocol	EGP	na	yes	ip		no		
EIGRP	Enhanced Integrated Gateway Routing Protocol	IGP	DV+	no	ip	chd	Y	trig	yes
GGP	Gateway to Gateway Protocol	IGP	DV	yes	ip		no		
Hello	Hello Protocol	IGP	DV	yes	ip	d	no		
IGRP	Interior Gateway Routing Protocol	IGP	DV	no	ip	chd	no	90sec	no
Int IS-IS	OSI Integrated IS-IS	IGP	SPF	yes	ip, osi	c	no	trig	yes
Novell NLSP	Netware Link State Protocol	IGP	SPF	no	ipx,ip		no	trig	
Novell RIP	Novell's implementation of RIP	IGP	DV	yes	ipx		no		
OSI ES-IS	OSI End System to Intermediate System	IGP	na	yes	osi		yes		
OSI IS-IS	OSI Intermediate System to Intermediate System	IGP	SPF	yes	osi	c	no	trig	yes
OSPF	Open Shortest Path First	IGP	SPF	yes	ip	c	yes	trig	yes
RIPv1	Routing Information Protocol Version 1	IGP	DV	yes	ip	h	no	30sec	no
RIPv2	Routing Information Protocol Version 2	IGP	DV	yes	ip	h	no	30sec	yes
RTMP	Apple Router Table Maintenance Protocol	IGP	DV	no	atalk		no	10sec	

Fundamental to the routing table is the concept of the best path. The table of best paths is computed using a distributed routing algorithm. Paths may be weighted according to a simple hop count or a more sophisticated metric (such as the real tariff or a function influenced by congestion, throughput, etc.). Hop-based paths are closely associated with a class of algorithms called distance-vector. Cost-based paths are generally associated with link-state algorithms. Exterior Gateway protocols such as BGP use a class of algorithm called path vector.

3.3   Routing design issues

3.3.1   Routing tables

A dynamic routing protocol typically creates a number of topology-related databases in memory, holding key information on neighbors, locally configured interfaces, statically configured information, and routing information acquired from peers. All of this information is used to construct a routing table—a list of routing entries that is consulted whenever a router makes a packet forwarding decision (actually, for performance reasons, there is often a separate forwarding table, derived from the routing table, which holds the shortlist of the active preferred routes, held in data structures that enable rapid traversal and retrieval).

3.3.2 Routing entry types

There are several types of routing table entries, including the following:

- Static routing entries are fixed table entries, usually configured by a network operator for special purposes, such as default routes, preferred routes, or host routes. Static routing is also commonly used for permanent paths such as point-to-point WAN links to remote sites or dial-up ISDN lines, where there is no alternate path and, therefore, no need for the overhead of a dynamic routing protocol. In recent years several router vendors have associated preference values with static routing entries.

- Dynamic routing entries are automatically generated by dynamic routing protocols, such as OSPF and EIGRP. The routing table is populated through a learning process, using direct knowledge of the local topology and information acquired from neighboring routers. Dynamic routing reflects the true state of the network by automatically responding to topology changes and reflecting those changes in the routing table.

- Direct interface routing entries are routes where the destination network or subnetwork is on a directly attached physical interface (i.e., there is no next hop).

- Default routes are a special form of static route. A default route identifies a default router to which all traffic should be forwarded if the destination address is unknown (i.e., not included in the routing database). While default routing has its advantages, it can lead to loss of control over certain types of traffic. For example, hosts may occasionally send packets to nonexisting hosts (so-called Martian Hosts). If a default route is configured, then, instead of being dropped, these packets will be forwarded over the default route.

3.3.3 Routing metrics

In order to determine best paths in a network topology, there must be some cost component that can be used to compare alternate choices. The fundamental cost element used in networks is the interface metric. There are three broad metric implementations, largely dependent upon the type of routing entry and the class of routing protocol used. These implementations are as follows:

- Hop count—A link metric may be a simple hop count—a metric most commonly associated with distance-vector protocols. Some distance-vector protocols allow hop counts to be configured, which enables differences in line speed, asymmetry, or geographic preferences to be imposed.

- Abstract value—Some interface metrics are integer values that may be customized. Often, these metrics automatically default to values calculated from interface line speeds but can be overridden, using arbitrary values, by the network designer. For example, OSPF offers a two-byte integer. This metric could be tuned to almost any scheme the designer creates. IS-IS offers a similar scheme.

- Combinatorial—Some routing protocols offer more sophisticated metrics based on a combination of metrics, such as available circuit bandwidth, monetary cost, reliability, congestion, latency, delay, jitter, Round-Trip Time (RTT), and so on. These protocols would need to include more sophisticated (possibly proprietary) feedback mechanisms on aspects of network utilization and to ensure that topology oscillation does not occur when performance changes rapidly.

3.3.4   Path selection

In a very simple network topology, there may be only one physical and logical path between a source and a destination. This makes route selection trivial and negates the need for any dynamic routing protocol (i.e., routes could be configured statically). In more complex topologies, dynamic routing protocols must figure out the best path at a particular time between a particular source and destination from a wide range of possibilities. Should the topology fail at any point, then the routing protocol must also respond to those changes by establishing new paths, if available. (See Figure 3.3.)

Single path or multipath

The advantages of multipath algorithms are clear; they can provide substantially greater throughput and also offer topological robustness. Multipath algorithms typically allow traffic to be multiplexed over several circuits (WAN or LAN) according to a range of criteria, as follows:

- Packet based—Traffic may be load balanced on a per-packet basis using round-robin techniques. Usually one packet or destination is distributed to each possible path in turn.

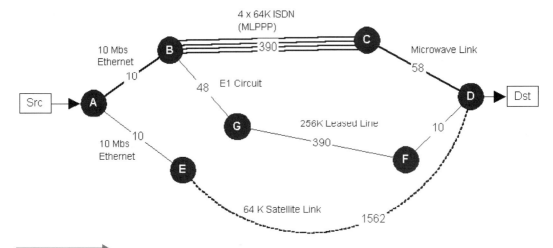

Figure 3.3   *Based on various path selection criteria and the routing algorithm chosen, any number of bad choices could be made in selecting the optimum path.*

- Session based—Traffic may be load shared on a session or flow basis, typically by using source-destination or destination hash function. This technique tends to preserve packet order.

The distribution algorithm may mandate equal end-to-end aggregate metrics (as with OSPF) or may perform fair load distribution over different speed links with different end-to-end aggregate metrics (as with EIGRP). Some topologies may also mandate that send and return paths are consistent (e.g., stateful firewall configurations).

Note that this form of load sharing should not be confused with lower-level, point-to-point load-sharing techniques, such as offered by Multi-Link PPP (MLPPP [1]). Such techniques are transparent to routing protocols and will reorder packets into a single stream before delivery to the routing layer. In Figure 3.3, for example, link B-C comprises four ISDN circuits aggregated via MLPPP. From the routing protocol perspective this simply appears as a single 256-K circuit.

Choosing the best paths

The problem for a router is how to decide what the best path is, especially when there are contradictory issues to consider [1]. A number of factors should be taken into account in order to determine the optimum path, including the following:

- Routing metrics (aggregate hops, abstract metric, combinatorial, etc.)

- Throughput, delay, congestion

- Link stability

- Real-world cost

As a general rule, routing protocols simply compare aggregate link metrics to select the best path from a group of possible paths. With increasing interest in service quality, performance optimization, and cost reduction, an approach more intelligent than automatic metrics is required, which considers more of the factors that make links attractive.

A routing protocol doesn't have quite a clear view. For example, the distance-vector protocol RIP would see no problem in selecting A-E-D; after all, it's only two hops from router A (in fact the optimum path here has the highest aggregate number of hops). OSPF does better, giving us the option of either A-G-F-D, A-B-C-D, or both (using equal cost multipath load sharing). With EIGRP we have even more options, and we would not necessarily have to modify any metrics. EIGRP can load balance over multiple hops of unequal cost, weighting traffic proportionally if necessary.

The point here is that the design choices are far from simple, and, by insulating the routing protocol from the real nature of the network, we blur its view of network to the point where the network designer must take an active part in the choices made. This has led to initiatives such as Multi-Protocol Label Switching (MPLS), which provides sufficient granularity to switch individual flows, each with its own service characteristics.

3.3.5 The IP forwarding decision

When an IP packet arrives at the interface of a router, a decision must be made whether to forward that packet and, if so, onto which interface(s). These decisions are made by the IP forwarding algorithm and lookups to tables such as the local Forwarding Table and ARP cache held on the device. Figure 3.4 illustrates the basic routing algorithm used by an IP device.

Forwarding algorithm

When an IP packet arrives at an interface on a router, the router will first decide if the packet is destined for itself (perhaps an SNMP poll or part of a telnet session into the management console) or for a remote network or subnetwork. To determine whether destinations are local or remote, the packet's destination IP address and associated mask are ANDed and compared with each of the receivers' local interfaces (each with their own IP addresses and ANDed network mask).

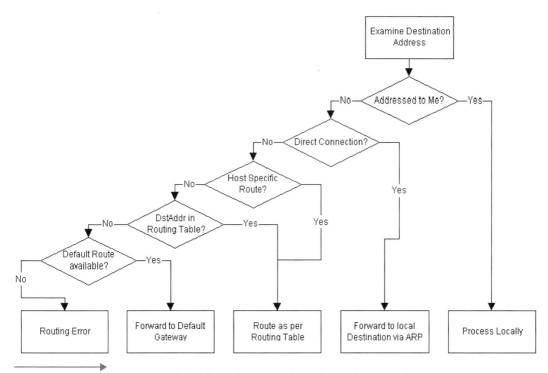

Figure 3.4 *Conceptual flowchart illustrating the IP forwarding algorithm.*

If the address-mask comparison fails, then the packet is determined to be for a remote network, in which case the router performs a longest prefix matched lookup in the forwarding table, and the packet is sent to the next-hop router. Routing tables are typically created by the use of dynamic routing protocols and/or users populating the tables with static routes.

If the address-mask comparison is successful for a particular interface, then the packet is forwarded directly to that interface.

In either case, ARP is required to resolve the Layer 2 address of the next-hop router. The appropriate Layer 2 address will be used to replace the MAC destination address before the frame is transmitted (i.e., the next-hop router MAC address or host address). The ARP cache is maintained dynamically by the router (or host), although, again, it may contain static entries configured by the user. Aside from static ARPs, each entry in the ARP cache will have a timer associated with it to flush out an entry and ensure that the cache is a true reflection of the network.

The prefix-based route lookup operation is particularly time consuming, especially with large table sizes. This is a concern for backbone routers, where forwarding tables are typically in excess of 50,000 route entries. We briefly review the concepts of route lookup next.

Route lookup

As described earlier, IP is datagram based, and whenever a packet is scheduled for forwarding, a router tries to match the packet's destination address in its forwarding table to determine the destination port (or interface). The forwarding table stores routing entries of the form:

<network address><mask><port>

The destination address is parsed from the received packet, and the router iterates through all of its forwarding table entries for matches. For each entry, the router masks the destination address with the mask associated with that entry. If a match is found, the port associated with the entry is appended to a set of candidate destination ports. The destination port ultimately chosen will be the candidate with the largest mask (referred to as the longest prefix match), since this is the most specific choice available (note that this assumes that contiguous masks are mandated, since noncontiguous masks would mean that there may be no better algorithm for route lookup than an iterative search of all entries). For example, a packet with destination address 146.30.225.5 arrives at a router. The router has the following entries in its forwarding table:

Entry	Distance Address	Prefix	Distance Port
1	130.42.3.0	/24	1
2	146.30.1.5	/16	6
3	146.30.225.0	/18	2
4	193.168.32.0	/24	11
5	146.0.0.0	/8	3
6	2.2.5.0	/8	16
7	146.30.230.0	/19	14

After a route lookup there are four address matches found in the forwarding table (entries 2, 3, 5, 7), and so the set of candidate destination ports for this packet is (2, 3, 6, 14). Since entry 7 has the longest prefix (19 bits), the destination port selected is port 14.

3.3.6   Convergence

When a topology change is detected in a routing network, it must be prop-agated to other routers and a new topology must be calculated. During this period it is possible for the behavior of the network to become unpredict-able; packets could be sent in routing loops or can disappear completely into black holes. The time taken for a community of routers to detect changes and reconfigure the topology correctly is called convergence time. Clearly, it is imperative that this value be kept low. Convergence time is influenced by several factors, some of which can be influenced directly by the designer, as follows:

- The speed with which local hardware failures are detected and flagged to higher-layer routing software

- Tunable parameters, such as hello timers, dead intervals, hold-down timers, cache-aging timers, and so on

- The size of the network (number of routers, link speeds, routing delays)

- Network topology

- Choice of routing protocol (link-state, distance-vector, hybrid)

In general, link-state routing protocols converge much faster than dis-tance-vector protocols (in the order of several seconds as opposed to min-utes). The notable exception is Cisco's EIGRP, which converges at rates comparable to OSPF and IS-IS.

3.3.7   End-system routing

Devices such as servers and workstations must be able to locate routers when they need to access devices external to the local network. The main problem here is how to get the end system to learn the whereabouts of its nearest router without imposing a full routing stack on the device. A subsid-iary problem is how to make those configuration data manageable on large networks with potentially thousands of hosts. The fancy name for this func-tionality is End System to Intermediate System routing (or ES-IS—in fact, OSI provides a protocol called ES-IS to do this very thing). There is cur-rently no uniformly agreed-upon method for end stations to locate routers in the IETF/IP world. In essence there are two main possibilities: static gateway configuration and dynamic router discovery. Note that the term gateway is used here just to add an extra layer of confusion. In many early

IETF standards the term "gateway" is synonymous with router. This terminology still persists in the client configuration.

Static gateway configuration

Gateway configuration involves the nomination of a primary (and possibly secondary) gateway. The simplest way to tell a station where its nearest router is to configure it explicitly by manually editing a file with the address and mask. For example, under Windows 98 you would simply edit network properties for the TCP/IP protocol service (see Figure 3.5). This means that no protocol is required, and whenever the station needs to send a packet to a remote destination it simply forwards that packet to the nominated router. The station can easily work out whether the packet is local or remote by comparing the destination address and mask with its own address and mask. If the station does not know the MAC address of the router then ARP is used as standard.

One drawback of this scheme is fault tolerance. If the primary gateway dies, then there is no way for the station to send packets remotely. To counter this, many implementations support the concept of a secondary gateway. The secondary gateway will be used in the event that the primary gateway cannot be reached (say the ARP cache entry times out, and all sub-

Figure 3.5
Default gateway configuration under Windows 98.

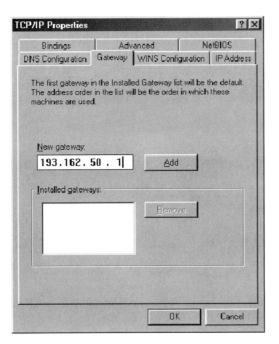

sequent ARP requests are never responded to). Another drawback is maintenance. While this scheme is fine for small networks, where change can be managed easily, on large, dynamic internetworks this is simply not scalable. To deal with large system configuration, many network designers enlist the use of DHCP. DHCP servers dynamically allocate default gateways from a pool; usually there is a default gateway assignable on a per-subnet basis.

Dynamic router discovery

When multiple routers are attached to a host's local segment, the host should ideally locate the router that offers the optimal path to a particular destination and should be aware of topology changes. This process of dynamically finding routers is called router discovery. The following are router discovery protocols:

- RIP

- OSPF

- End System to Intermediate System (ES-IS)

- Proxy Address Resolution Protocol (ARP)

- ICMP Router Discovery Protocol (IDRP)

3.3.8 Choosing a routing strategy

Choosing an interior gateway protocol

Choosing the IGP most appropriate for your network is almost never a purely technical decision. There are often commercial and even company-political issues to consider, especially in large organizations. Table 3.2 lists

Table 3.2 *Comparison of IGP Features*

Routing Protocol	Subnet Support	Multi Protocol	Metric	Load Sharing	Open Standard	Converg-ence	Routing Algorithm	Complexity
RIPv1	No	No	Hop	No	Yes	Slow	dv	Low
RIPv2	Yes	No	Hop	No	Yes	Slow	dv	Low
Cisco IGRP	No	No	Combined	Yes	No	Slow	dv	Low
Cisco EIGRP	Yes	Yes	Combined	Yes	No	Fast	dv+	Moderate
OSPF	Yes	No	Abstract	Yes	Yes	Fast	spf	High
IS-IS	Yes	Yes	Abstract	Yes	Yes	Fast	spf	High

Note that although dual IS-IS is multiprotocol it supports only OSI and IP packets. EIGRP uses a hybrid algorithm based on distance-vector techniques.

several of the key characteristics of IGPs. The following items are just some of the considerations you must make when choosing a routing protocol:

- Protocols to transport

- Network size and scalability

- Standards and interoperability

- Ease of deployment and maintenance

- Network management and debugging facilities

- Convergence time

- Router vendor

If your network is IP only, you have a range of protocols to choose from, including RIP, OSPF, IGRP, EIGRP, and IS-IS. If your network is multiprotocol, then you may need to run IGRP or EIGRP. For a pure OSI network you would most probably choose IS-IS.

In small networks, where there is very little skill on site and the application requirements are not stringent, RIP is a reasonable choice. It is very easy to set up and quite robust. Neither IS-IS nor OSPF is intuitive for novice engineers; both involve a degree of complexity and require at least some understanding of their theory and operational characteristics. EIGRP is meant to fuse the simplicity of distance-vector protocols such as RIP with the performance benefits of link-state protocols such as OSPF. Figure 3.6 provides a simple decision system for assessing which IGP is appropriate for your network.

RIP is suitable for a small network (say, up to a dozen routers) and is also commonly used as an ES-IS protocol to provide hosts with limited routing awareness (i.e., instead of a static default gateway configuration, described earlier in this chapter). If you require load balancing, then RIP cannot be used. If your network uses Variable-Length Subnet Masks (VLSM), then RIP and IGRP cannot be used since they do not carry mask data and must, therefore, assume either natural masks or use mask information associated with local interfaces. RIPv2 does support VLSM. For medium to large networks you would be strongly advised not to use a pure distance-vector protocol. These protocols scale very badly and are very inefficient in their use of bandwidth. Distance-vector protocols converge very slowly in comparison to link-state protocols such as OSPF and IS-IS. RIPv2 does scale a little better than RIPv1, but it is generally regarded as too little too late. RIP was never really intended for anything other than modest local network topologies.

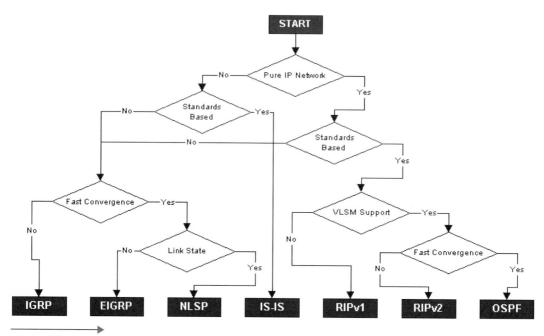

Figure 3.6   *Simple flowchart for possible IGP selection.*

OSPF, EIGRP, and, increasingly, IS-IS are the main contenders for large network design (each converges quickly, on the order of several seconds). OSPF is essentially state of the art, and is the prime interior protocol for large IP routed environments; OSPF is very widely deployed in a range of environments (corporate enterprise, regional backbone networks, health care, finance, and so on). IS-IS (particularly integrated IS-IS, which can route both OSI and IP protocols simultaneously) is also technically a very strong candidate for medium to large IP networks; however, it is not widely deployed at present (restricted mainly to backbone telco networks and government applications). With IS-IS you are likely to have to redistribute routes in and out of the IS-IS domain, and you may not wish to add another layer of complexity.

If you have a pure Cisco site, then you may have been persuaded to deploy EIGRP (although Cisco is nowadays equally happy to promote the benefits of OSPF). EIGRP is a hybrid distance-vector protocol that scales well. Although proprietary, since Cisco has by far the largest installed base of routers, including the Internet, one could argue that EIGRP is a de facto standard. EIGRP is a mature protocol and has the advantage of rich, multiprotocol features—a strong advantage in multiprotocol enterprise networks.

However, now that IP has become so pervasive the potential advantages of EIGRP over OSPF are becoming less clear. In multivendor environments EIGRP would have to be redistributed (e.g., into OSPF) to allow interoperability, and this is an extra layer of complexity you may want to avoid.

If you are running a large BAY (now part of Northern Telecom) network, you will almost certainly be running OSPF, since BAY was one of the chief proponents of OSPF when it was first made available (alongside pioneering companies such as Proteon). My personal preference for medium to large internetworks is OSPF, mainly because of its ability to converge very quickly and scale across a range of environments and also because it is an open standard and interoperates well in multivendor environments.

3.4 Routing protocols

3.4.1 Routing Information Protocol (RIP)

Background

RIP is formally defined in the XNS Internet Transport Protocols publication (1981) and in RFC 1058. Since its initial release there have been several improvements to RIP, culminating in a new standard called RIP version 2 (RIPv2), specified in RFC 2453. RIPv2 overcomes some of the more basic limitations of RIPv1, most significantly with the following features:

- The ability to carry subnet mask data with routing entries

- Support for authorization data for link security

- Optional support for sending routing updates using a multicast destination address (instead of broadcasting)

- Support for autonomous systems and IGP/EGP interactions through externally tagged information

These features are all welcome extensions to RIPv1, but they do nothing to deal with scalability limitations such as slow convergence and routing hop limitations.

Protocol stack

Transport

RIP runs directly over UDP and uses socket 520 for all RIP communication.

Figure 3.7
RIPv1 header
format.

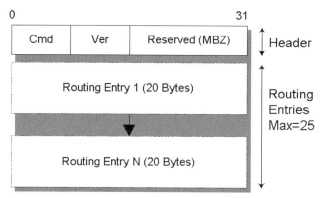

Packet formats

Common header format

Figure 3.7 illustrates the RIP packet header format for both RIPv1 and RIPv2 (specified in RFC 1058).

RIPv1 header definitions

- Cmd—The command field indicates either a request or a response. A request command asks another system to send all or part of its routing table. A response command can be a reply to a request or a regular unsolicited routing update. With unsolicited routing update response messages the host router will include the entire routing table.

- Vers—Specifies the RIP version implemented. This field is used to differentiate potentially incompatible implementations.

- Reserved—A 16-bit field of all zeros. Must be zero. Not used in RIPv1.

RIPv1 routing entries

RIPv1 routing entries (see Figure 3.8) do not carry subnet mask information and so cannot distinguish among various types of addresses (host address, subnet number, network number, or all zeros—default route).

RIPv1 routing entry definitions

- AFI—This is an address family identifier specifying the address family being used. With IP this address family is set to IP (value = 2), but other network address types are allowed (e.g., Novell IPX).

- Reserved—A 16-bit field of all zeros. Must be zero. Not used in RIPv1.

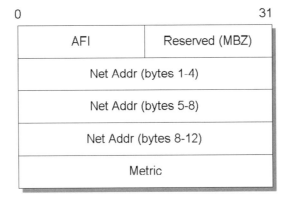

Figure 3.8
RIPv1 routing entry format.

- Net Addr—One of a series of network addresses. With IP only the first four bytes of each address field are used (leaving eight bytes effectively wasted).

- Metric—This is a distance-vector metric associated with each route entry and is implemented as a hop count. The hop count indicates how many hops must be traversed before the destination can be reached. The limit is 15.

An RIP router must, therefore, use the mask associated with an interface (if a direct route) or the default natural mask when interpreting routing updates. RIPv1 cannot, therefore, support Variable-Length Subnet Masks (VLSM), and this is a significant drawback in anything other than small internetworks. The maximum datagram size (i.e., the RIP portion of the packet) is 512 octets.

A typical RIPv1 router update is illustrated in Figure 3.9. A single RIP routing update can hold up to 25 route entries. The RIP routing update timer is generally set to 30 seconds, ensuring that each router will send a complete copy of its routing table to all neighbors every 30 seconds. The route invalid timer determines how much time must expire without a router having heard about a particular route before that route is considered invalid. When a route is marked invalid, neighbors are notified of this fact by setting the metric to 16 (infinity) in the next routing update. This notification must occur prior to expiration of the route flush timer.

RIPv2 routing entries

RIPv2 uses the same header format as RIPv1 but adds functionality to routing entries. Since RIPv1 has a lot of spare capacity in its packet structure, all

```
File:IPXDIRSV.ENC  Type:SNIFFER_ENC Mode:••••••• Records:402
======
306      Error  : None
T Elapsed: 01:27:19:913     T Delta : 00:00:00:527
---------------------------[mac]-------------------------------
Dest Mac : ffffffffffff       Sourc Mac: Xyplex12a362  Type  : IP
---------------------------[ip]--------------------------------
IP Ver  : 4        IP       HLen : 20 Bytes
TOS    : 0x00      Pkt Len : 292      Seg ID  : 0x008f
Flags   : FRAG:X.LAST   Frag Ptr : 0   (8 Octet) TTL   : 64
PID    : UDP ( 17)   Checksum : 0x7599 (Good)
Dest IP : 255.255.255.255 Source IP: 193.128.2.33
---------------------------[udp]-------------------------------
Dest Port: RIP [ 520]       Src Port : RIP [ 520]
Length  : 272          Checksum : 0x0000
---------------------------[rip]-------------------------------
Command : RESPonse     Version : 1      Reserved : 00
---------------------------[routes: 13]------------------------
Family: 2 {192. 0. 1. 0} Hops: 1  Family: 2 {192. 0. 2. 0} Hops: 1
Family: 2 {192. 0. 3. 0} Hops: 1  Family: 2 {193.128. 2. 64} Hops: 1
Family: 2 {193.128. 2. 96} Hops: 1  Family: 2 {193.128. 2.236} Hops: 1
Family: 2 {193.128. 2.237} Hops: 1  Family: 2 {193.128. 2.238} Hops: 1
Family: 2 {193.128. 9. 0} Hops: 1  Family: 2 {194. 0. 2. 0} Hops: 1
Family: 2 {195. 0. 0. 0} Hops: 1  Family: 2 {196. 0. 0. 0} Hops: 1
Family: 2 {197. 0. 0. 0} Hops: 1
==============================[data: 0]========================
```

Figure 3.9 *RIPv1 routing update message.*

of the RIPv2 changes are neatly packaged into the same RIP messages, as illustrated in Figure 3.10.

All fields are the same as RIPv1 with the following exceptions.

RIPv2 routing entry definitions

- Route tag—The RT field is an attribute assigned to a route that must be preserved and readvertised with a route. The intended use of the route tag is to provide a method of separating internal RIP routes from external routes (e.g., those imported from an exterior gateway protocol).

- IP address—A 32-bit IP address.

- Subnet mask—A 32-bit subnet mask. If this field is zero, then no subnet mask has been included for this entry.

- Next hop—The immediate next-hop IP address should be forwarded to the destination specified by this route entry. A value of 0.0.0.0 in this field indicates that routing should be via the originator of the

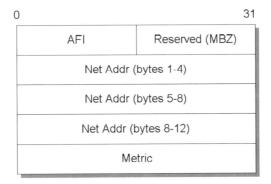

Figure 3.10
RIPv2 routing entry format.

RIP advertisement. The purpose of the next-hop field is to eliminate packets being routed through extra hops in the system. It is particularly useful when RIP is not being run on all of the routers on a network.

■ Metric—This is a distance-vector metric associated with each route entry and is implemented as a hop count. The hop count indicates how many hops must be traversed before the destination can be reached. The limit is 15.

Handling new subnet mask information

RIPv2 is likely to coexist in environments where RIPv1 is also running, so special attention needs to be paid on how routing information is interpreted and distributed. On an RIPv2-enabled interface the following rules apply:

■ Information internal to one network must never be advertised into another network.

■ Information about a more specific subnet may not be advertised where RIPv1 considers it a host route.

■ Supernet routes (where the network mask is less specific than the natural mask) must not be advertised where they could be misinterpreted by RIPv1 routers.

Authentication

RIPv1 has no security features; RIPv2 improves on this by implementing authentication support on a per message basis. It was thought that there was insufficient space in the RIP header for a useful authentication scheme (only two bytes spare), so the authentication scheme for RIPv2 uses a whole RIP entry, denoted by a special AFI value of 0xFFFF. This means that there are only 24 routing entries per advertisement if authentication is used. The

Figure 3.11
*RIPv2
authentication
format.*

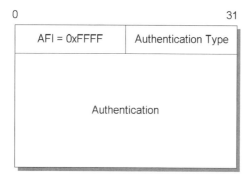

RIPv2 authentication entry format is illustrated in Figure 3.11. The only authentication type supported at present is a simple password (authentication type 2). The remaining 16 bytes contain the plaintext password. If the password is under 16 bytes, it must be left justified and padded to the right with null (0x00) characters. RFC 2082 describes enhancements to this scheme.

Addressing

RIPv1 uses broadcasts (both network and MAC) to advertise and request routes; all updates will have a MAC destination of 0xFFFFFFFFFFFF and an IP destination of 255.255.255.255. This makes RIPv1 traffic difficult to isolate without using network Layer 4 filters (e.g., on dial-up bridge links you may want to isolate some broadcast types, and with RIP you would have to access at least the UDP port fields). RIPv2 supports either broadcast or multicast operations. Multicasts can be easily filtered and also reduce unnecessary load on those hosts that are not listening to RIPv2 messages. The IP multicast address 224.0.0.9 can optionally be used by RIPv2 stacks for periodic routing updates. On NonBroadcast MultiAccess (NBMA) networks, unicast addressing may also be used; however, if a response addressed to the RIPv2 multicast address is received, it should be accepted and processed.

Operation

Routing algorithm

RIP uses a distance-vector algorithm to calculate optimal routes; more specifically it uses the Bellman-Ford Algorithm. Each router is responsible for building its own shortest path routing table, based on its own knowledge of directly attached interfaces and announcements from other routers. Each route has an associated distance (in hops) to a destination network. The metric takes no account of link speed or delay. The SPF algorithm is very effective (in some cases more efficient than Dijkstra); the distribution protocol is quite inefficient, and sometimes these two aspects are confused. One key aspect to appreciate here is that an RIP router is aware only of the next hop to a destination network; it has no higher-level map of the topology (as implemented in link-state protocols such as OSPF).

Each RIP router sends out regular announcements to all RIP-enabled interfaces every 30 seconds. These messages contain the entire routing table and are propagated to all neighbors on directly connected segments. Clearly, when a router first boots up, the only information it can announce is the distance to its own interfaces, at a cost of 1. Announcements are sent whenever an update timer elapses or whenever there is a detected change (via triggered updates). Once a router has integrated all routing information from its neighbors, it can rebuild a Spanning Tree based on which immediate neighbors offer the lowest metric to each destination. If a new destination is subsequently announced, this will be added into the routing table. If a destination is subsequently discovered with a lower metric, the current route entry is replaced. If a destination is announced that has the same next hop as the current route entry, but a lower metric, then the new metric will be used.

Routing tables

Each entry in an RIP routing table includes the following information: the destination network IP address, the next-hop router's IP address, and the cost to get there (i.e., the metric). The metric indicates the distance in number of hops to the destination—that is, how many routers the packet must traverse in order to reach the destination. Default routes are advertised as 0.0.0.0. Depending upon the implementation, other information may also be present in the routing table (such as timers associated with the route; the source of the routing information; and possibly an administrative distance, which is used to set preferences if two routes to the same destination are advertised from different IGPs). A typical RIP routing table would look as follows:

Network	Next Hop	Hops	Interface
181.4.0.0	181.4.5.2	—	e0
150.7.0.0	181.4.5.2	5	e0
192.168.30.0	181.7.3.1	3	e1
193.128.34.0	181.4.5.2	2	e4
195.6.6.0	164.23.2.5	16	s0

RIP selects the best route to a destination; there is no inherent support for load balancing. All routes are advertised regularly in routing updates as broadcasts. If a topology change occurs, it is reflected in the next routing update.

Timers

The main timers controlling RIP operation are as follows:

- Routing update timer—Default is 30 seconds (the basic route table update interval).

- Dead interval—Default is 120 seconds (triggered when a route metric goes to 16).

- Garbage collection timer—Default is 120 seconds (triggered after dead interval lapses).

- Hold-down timer—Default is 180 seconds (optional, depending upon implementation).

On some implementations the first three timers may be referred to as update, invalid, and flush, respectively, and the defaults may vary. For example, on a Cisco router these timers will be 30, 180, 240, and 180, respectively.

Passive and active RIP

A router or host will typically offer the choice of configuring RIP on specific interfaces, in either active or passive mode. Active mode means that full routing capability is enabled. Passive mode means that the interface is in listen-only mode and no RIP updates are sent out. For example, on a Cisco router we could define the first serial interface as passive using the following command:

```
Helsinki(config)#router rip
Helsinki(config-router)#passive interface serial 0
```

RIP issues and enhancements

RIP suffers from the classic issues associated with distance-vector routing protocols (i.e., routing loops and slow convergence). As such, RIP implementations typically include several enhancements—namely, triggered updates, hold-down timers, split horizon, and poison reverse. Check your vendor's implementation to see which of these features are supported.

Performance

RIP has several significant performance implications for any network. When planning any design, especially with low-speed WAN links, you must be aware of the following issues:

- Broadcast overheads
- Protocol inefficiency
- Convergence

Scalability

RIP specifies a maximum hop count of 15, so by definition we cannot build a backbone with RIP that is larger than 15 hops in diameter (or we could, but the farthest points of such a network would not be able to communicate). This generally limits the use of RIP to small local internetworks and end-system integration. Another problem with RPv1 is the lack of VLSM support. This can seriously deplete the available address space and limit the growth of your internetwork. RIPv2 does support VLSM.

Demand circuits

RIP may be required to operate in an environment with demand circuits. Demand circuits refer to those network segments whose monetary cost depends on factors such as connect time or use (typically expressed in terms of bytes or packets). Examples include ISDN dial circuits and X.25 SVCs. A generalized algorithm for demand circuits that can be applied to distance-vector routing protocols (such as IP RIP, NetWare RIP, or NetWare SAP) is documented in RFC 1582. A summary of the main features is as follows:

- Presumption of reachability—Once routing information is exchanged over dial-up links, those networks are assumed to be reachable even though a circuit's data-link connection may subsequently be closed, unless error conditions indicate otherwise.

- Triggered updates—Routing updates are sent only when there has been an update to the routing database, a change in the reachability of a next-hop router, or a specific request for a routing update has been received. Low-demand RIP adds support for triggered requests, triggered responses, and triggered acknowledgments.

- Acknowledgments and retransmissions—An acknowledgment and retransmission system is required to provide reliability. If a triggered request or response is not acknowledged after ten retransmissions, routes to the destination should be marked as unreachable for the duration of a hold-down timer before being deleted. The destination should then be polled at a lower frequency using triggered request packets.

- Flow control—To overcome the bandwidth limitations associated with dial-up and low-bandwidth environments, the routing application can perform a form of self-imposed flow control, spreading out routing updates over a period of time.

RIPv1 and RIPv2 compatibility

For compatibility RFC 2453 specifies that packets received by an RIPv1 node that have a version number greater than one should not have their reserved (i.e., must be zero) fields validated. This means that, in theory, an RIPv2 packet should be backward compatible. Unfortunately, this depends on which RIP implementation you are talking to, since vendors may have chosen to ignore this recommendation, and several implementations precede the standard. In order to maintain backward compatibility, the use of the multicast destination address should also be configurable. If multicasting is used, it should be used on all interfaces that support it.

Distance-vector routing enhancements

Distance-vector routing protocols such as RIP and IGRP include a number of additional features (or bug fixes, depending upon your point of view) designed to make routing operations more stable, speed up convergence, and preclude failures such as counting to infinity (which results from the creation of routing loops). These enhancements include the following:

- Triggered updates—Used to speed up the distribution of routing changes rather than waiting for the next announcement interval.

- Split horizon—Routes are not propagated down the interface from which they were learned. Prevents routing loops between adjacent routers.

- Poison reverse—Routes are propagated down the interface from which they were learned with a cost of infinity. Prevents routing loops and speeds up convergence.

- Hold downs—Prevent larger routing updates by imposing a period of calm until the topology is deemed to be sufficiently stable. Prevents counting to infinity.

All of these features are especially important during periods of topological instability. They effectively prevent a bad situation from getting much worse.

3.4.2   Open Shortest Path First (OSPF)

Background

OSPF is currently perhaps the most important open standard IGP for medium to large IP network designs. Many major commercial networks run OSPF backbones, including many sizable Cisco backbones. OSPF has two key characteristics: it is open, in that its specification is in the public domain, and it is based on the shortest path first, or link-state, technology (specifically the Dijkstra algorithm), where the routing database is fully distributed and each router is responsible for calculating the entire routing table independently. OSPF is a hierarchical routing protocol. It distributes routing information between routers belonging to a single Autonomous System (AS).

OSPF was developed by the IGP working group of the IETF, which was formed in the spring of 1988 to design an IGP based on the Shortest Path First (SPF) algorithm for use on the Internet. OSPF was developed to provide efficient and scalable routing for large IP internetworks, primarily due to the failings of existing distance-vector protocols such as RIP and IGRP. The first version of the OSPF protocol was specified in RFC 1131; OSPF version 2 is specified in RFC 1583. OSPF modifications for supporting IPv6 are specified in RFC 2740.

OSPF promotes a hierarchical design, scales well, and converges quickly. It provides features such as a distributed routing database, triggered updates, designated routers, reliable flooding, and explicit support for VLSM and the tagging of externally derived routing information. Optional OSPF features include the authentication of routing updates, equal cost, multipath routing, and routing based on Type of Service (ToS) requests. ToS-based routing is not widely implemented at present, since it is very resource intensive (you need a separate SPF running for each ToS). OSPF is relatively easy to deploy and offers major benefits while demanding more discipline at the design stage.

Packet formats

Figure 3.12 illustrates an OSPF header format.

Figure 3.12
OSPF header format.

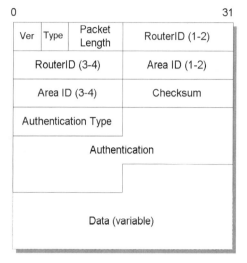

OSPF field definitions

- Ver—Identifies the version number of the OSPF implementation being used.

- Type—Specifies one of the following OSPF packet types:

  - Hello—Sent at regular intervals to establish and maintain neighbor relationships.

  - Database description—Describes the contents of the topological database and are exchanged when an adjacency is being initialized.

  - Link-state request—Requests pieces of a neighbor's topological database. They are exchanged after a router has discovered (through examination of database description packets) that parts of its topological database are out of date.

  - Link-state update—Responses to link-state request packets. They are also used for the regular dispersal of LSAs. Several LSAs may be included within a single packet.

  - Link-state acknowledgment—Acknowledges link-state update packets. Link-state update packets must be explicitly acknowledged to ensure that link-state flooding throughout an area is a reliable process.

  - Each LSA in a link-state update packet contains a type field. There are four LSA types: Router Links Advertisements (RLAs), Network Links Advertisements (NLAs), Summary Links Advertisements (SLAs), and AS external links advertisements.

- Packet length—Specifies in bytes the packet's length, including the OSPF header.

- Router ID—Identifies the packet's source.

- Area ID—Identifies the area to which the packet belongs. All OSPF packets are associated with a single area.

- Checksum—Checks the entire packet contents for potential damage suffered in transit.

- Authentication type—Contains an authentication type. "Simple password" is an example of an authentication type. All OSPF protocol exchanges are authenticated. The authentication type is configurable on a per area basis.

- Authentication—Contains authentication information and is 64 bits in length.

OSPF communication uses a number of variable-length packets for ensuring both neighbor reachability and database distribution. A typical hello packet is shown in Figure 3.13. Notice that the Designated Router (DR) field is blank, because the router that generated this packet was rebooted and had not yet synchronized with any other router; it was not aware of an established DR on the network. Notice also that OSPF does its

```
File:OSPF07.SCP   Type:XYP1820_SCP Mode:••••••• Records:114
===============================================================================
Frame : 61        Len   : 78        Error  : None
T Elapsed: 01:02:26:385   T Delta : 00:00:00:270
-----------------------------[mac]---------------------------------------------
Dest Mac : 01005e000005   Sourc Mac: Xyplex1208e5   Type   : IP
-----------------------------[ip]----------------------------------------------
IP Ver  : 4        IP HLen : 20 Bytes
TOS     : 0x00        Pkt Len : 64        Seg ID  : 0x003a
Flags   : FRAG:X.LAST   Frag Ptr : 0   (8 Octet) TTL    : 1 (Low)
PID     : OSPF ( 89)   Checksum : 0xf4f1 (Good)
Dest IP : 224.0.0.5    Source IP: 156.48.8.4
-----------------------------[ospf]--------------------------------------------
OSPF Ver : 2       Type   : HELLO      Length  : 44
Router ID: 156.48.121.10  Area  ID: 0.0.0.0     Checksum : 0xe963
AU Type : 00          AU Key  : {    }
-----------------------------[hello]-------------------------------------------
Hello Msk: 255.255.255.0  Hello Int: 10        Hello Pri: 1
Options : 00          Dead Int : 40
DR    : 0.0.0.0      BDR  : 0.0.0.0
==============================[data:  0]=======================================
```

Figure 3.13 *OSPF hello packet.*

own checksumming. The hello priority field is used during the election process for designated and backup designated routers.

Link-State Advertisements (LSAs)

Link-State Advertisements (LSAs) include information about a router's adjacencies and are the fundamental data structure used to distribute routing information. There are four different types of LSAs, as follows:

- Type 1 Router Links Advertisements (RLAs)—Describe the collective states of a router's links to a specific area. A router sends an RLA for every interface. RLAs are flooded throughout the entire area and no farther.

- Type 2 Network Links Advertisements (NLAs)—NLAs are generated by Designated Router (DRs) and describe all routers that are attached to a multiaccess network (Ethernet, Token Ring, FDDI, or NBMA). NLAs are flooded throughout the area containing the multiaccess network.

- Type 3 and Type 4 Summary Links Advertisements (SLAs)—Summarize routes to destinations outside an area but within the AS (this is how network reachability information is disseminated between areas). SLAs are generated by Area Border Routers (ABRs) and injected into the backbone (area 0), where they will be flooded and disseminated to other areas. Only intra-area routes are advertised into the backbone. Both intra-area and interarea routes are advertised into the other areas. ABRs also have the job of propagating the reachability of the ASBR (this is how routers learn how to get to external routes outside the AS). Type 3 LSAs are used when the destination is an IP network. Type 4 LSAs are used when the destination is an AS boundary router.

- Type 5 AS external links advertisements—Describe a route to a destination that is outside the AS. These networks are injected into OSPF via redistribution, and it is the Autonomous System Border Router's (ASBR's) responsibility to inject these routes into the AS. These are the only type of LSA that is forwarded everywhere in the AS; all others are forwarded only within specific areas.

A new variation of the AS external LSA, called a Type 7 LSA, is defined for use with not so stubby areas, and is described later in the chapter.

Metrics

The default metric used in OSPF is an arbitrary two-byte integer, and ToS is not supported as standard. ToS is optionally supported through the use of a separate metric for each of the eight combinations created by the three IP ToS bits (delay, throughput, and reliability). For example, if the IP ToS bits specify low delay, low throughput, and high reliability, OSPF calculates routes to all destinations based on this ToS designation. Note that there will be a separate routing table for each ToS combination, so we can see that the overheads of supporting ToS in this manner are quite extravagant.

Timers

OSPF uses a number of timers and variables—some configurable, some constant. The main timers in OSPF network design are as follows:

- HelloInterval—A variable, defaults normally to ten seconds. The hello interval represents the length of time, in seconds, between the hello packets sent by a router on an interface. It must be the same for all routers attached to a common network. The smaller the hello interval, the faster topological changes will be detected but at the expense of increased traffic. For an X.25 PDN network we might choose 30 seconds; for a local area network we might choose ten seconds or less.

- RouterDeadInterval—A variable, defaults normally to 40 seconds. The dead interval represents the number of seconds a router will wait before assuming that a neighbor is down (i.e., since the last hello packet received). This value again must be the same for all routers attached to a common network.

- RxmtInterval—A variable, defaults normally to five seconds. The retransmit interval represents the number of seconds between link-state advertisement retransmissions for adjacencies belonging to an interface. It is also used when retransmitting database description and link-state request packets. The retransmit interval should easily exceed the expected round-trip time between neighbors. A typical LAN value is five seconds; it should, therefore, be set larger on low-speed serial lines and virtual links.

- InfTransDelay—A variable, defaults normally to one second, must be > 0. The interface transit delay represents the estimated time (in seconds) taken to transmit an LSU over an interface. LSAs contained in the LSU must have their age incremented by InfTransDelay before transmission. InfTransDelay should take into account the transmission and propagation delays of the interface.

■ LSRefreshTime—A constant, set to 30 minutes. The LSA aging timer is not configurable. This timer controls how long a self-origi-nated (i.e., not learned) LSA is held in the link-state database before it is considered too old. When the LS age field of an LSA reaches the value LSRefreshTime, a new instance of that LSA is originated. In practice this means that there will be a slow release of all LSAs over time, even though the physical link-states have not changed. This ensures integrity of the database. Note that this behavior differs in dial or demand circuit environments.

■ MaxAge—A constant set to one hour. MaxAge is also not config-urable and represents the maximum age that an LSA can attain. If the LS age field of an LSA reaches MaxAge, it is reflooded in an attempt to flush the advertisement from the routing domain. LSAs of MaxAge are not used in the routing table calculation. MaxAge must be greater than LSRefreshTime.

The hello and dead intervals are often tuned together, according to the network topology and network medium speeds. These affect how often keep-alive messages are sent and how long a neighbor should wait before assuming a peer is down. By speeding up these timers you can improve con-vergence in the case where a peer is not responding. In general you should keep the dead interval as follows:

Dead interval >= 4 × hello interval

For detailed information about OSPF timers and variables, the inter-ested reader is referred to RFC 1587.

VLSM support

OSPF routing updates support Variable-Length Subnet Masks (VLSM), since each route distributed by OSPF has a destination and a mask. With variable-length subnet masks, an IP network can be broken into many sub-nets of various sizes. This provides network administrators with extra net-work configuration flexibility.

Message authentication

OSPF contains an optional authentication field. If enabled, all routers within an area must agree on the value of the authentication field. The authentication field prevents bad routing exchanges and malicious attempts to destabilize the network. Currently there are three modes of operation. By default, a router uses a null authentication, which means that routing exchanges over a network are not authenticated. There are two additional authentication methods: simple password authentication and message digest authentication.

Protocol stack

OSPF runs directly over IP, as protocol 89 (0x59), and supports only Internet Protocol (IP) routing environments (i.e., it is not multiprotocol). OSPF has its own mechanisms for providing reliable delivery and authentication, which we discuss later. OSPF uses two reserved IP multicast addresses when sending and receiving the updates (224.0.0.5 and 224.0.0.6). Implementations may additionally support routing based on the IP Type of Service (ToS) bits in the IP packet header, and OSPF has been adapted for QoS-based routing.

Operation

OSPF is a link-state routing protocol, and each router is responsible for monitoring the state of its attached interfaces and the distribution of this status information to neighbors via Link-State Advertisements (LSAs). LSAs are reliably flooded throughout the AS (note that the term flooding here is possibly misleading, since each LSA has a TTL of one). Once OSPF routers have acquired neighbors and synchronized all link-state information, they run the SPF algorithm to calculate a shortest path tree to each node (specifically, the SPF algorithm used is Dijkstra). Each router within an area maintains an identical database describing the autonomous system's topology. Part of this database reflects an individual router's local state (i.e., the router's attached interfaces and neighbors). OSPF contrasts with distance-vector routing protocols RIP and IGRP, where each router distributes its entire routing tables.

In an OSPF network all routers run the exact same SPF algorithm in parallel. From the topological database, each router constructs a tree of shortest paths with itself as root. This shortest path tree gives the destination in the autonomous system. Externally derived routing information appears on the tree as leaves. OSPF optionally calculates separate routes for each Type of Service (ToS). When several equal-cost routes to a destination exist, traffic is load balanced among them. The cost of a route is described by a single, dimensionless 32-bit metric (either set automatically based on interface bandwidth or configured by the network administrator).

Routing hierarchy

OSPF is purely an Interior Gateway Protocol (IGP) but does provide excellent support for hierarchical designs within Autonomous Systems (ASs). OSPF enables an AS to be partitioned into one or more areas, joined together by a backbone. This leads to two different types of OSPF routing, depending on whether the source and destination are in the same or different areas: intra-area routing (source and destination in the same area) and inter-area routing (source and destination in different areas). This leads to the following four classifications of OSPF routers, as illustrated in Figure 3.14.

- Autonomous System Border Routers (ASBR)—where a router has external interfaces to another AS.

- Backbone Routers (BR)—where each router has its interfaces connected only to the backbone.

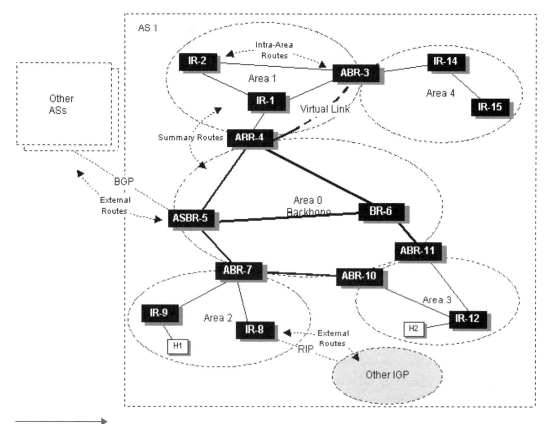

Figure 3.14   *Hierarchical OSPF internetwork showing the four basic router classifications.*

- Area Border Router (ABR)—where a router interfaces to multiple areas (including the backbone).

- Internal Router (IR)—where all interfaces are connected purely within an area.

In Figure 3.14, all areas are directly connected to the backbone apart from Area 4. In cases where a direct physical link to the backbone is not possible, a virtual link must be configured to maintain backbone continuity. The figure shows various types of routing information. Routes originated and targeted within an area are called intra-area routes. Routes that originate from other areas are called interarea or summary routes. Routes that originate from external processes (e.g., RIP, BGP, or different OSPF processes) that are injected into OSPF via redistribution are called external routes. Multiple routes to the same destination are preferred in the following order: intra-area, interarea, external.

Areas

An area is essentially an arbitrary collection of subnetworks. Areas are used to constrain the flooding of link-state updates within manageable bounds. The scope of the Dijkstra algorithm on a router is limited to changes within an area, and all routers within an area hold an identical copy of the link-state database. There are several types of areas, according to the interfaces they have and the kind of routing information they are configured to carry, as follows:

- Stub areas are recommended for simple areas that have only one ABR (i.e., a single exit point). Stub areas carry a default route, intra-area routes, and interarea routes. External routes, such as those redistributed from other protocols into OSPF, are not allowed to be flooded into a stub area. Virtual links cannot be configured through a stub area, and stubs cannot contain an ASBR.

- Totally stubby areas (Cisco proprietary) are sometimes referred to as stub areas without summaries and are recommended for simple configurations where a single router connects an area to the backbone. Totally stubby areas have a single ABR and carry only a default route and intra-area routes. External routes and summaries are blocked.

- Not So Stubby Areas (NSSAs) are stub areas that use default routes, but the restriction on not importing externals is relaxed. NSSAs have the capability of importing AS external routes in a limited fashion. NSSAs may be connected to the backbone at more than one ABR but may not be used as a transit area. NSSAs are designed to be used with moderately complex leaf sites.

- Nonstub areas—that is, plain old areas, contain an ASBR. An area must also be non-stub if a virtual link is configured across it. Nonstub areas are the most resource-intensive type of area. Nonstub areas carry a default route, static routes, intra-area routes, interarea routes, and external routes.

The topology of an area is transparent to other areas and the rest of the AS. By keeping area topologies separate, OSPF passes less routing traffic than it would if the AS were not partitioned. The main advantages of area partitioning are as follows:

- Faster convergence—Each area runs its own instance of Dijkstra, and so the number of nodes in the SPF calculation is limited to the area. This improves convergence and reduces the demand for CPU and memory on routers.

- Better stability—Mission-critical areas of the network can be isolated from areas of potential instability. This partitioning also limits the scope of bad routing data. For example, a flaky wide area network need not bring down the whole server farm every time a link goes down.

- Overall reduction in routing traffic by constraining information on a need-to-know basis.

Routers can be attached to multiple areas concurrently; these routers are called Area Border Routers (ABRs). An ABR maintains a separate topological database for each area and has the responsibility of disseminating routing information or routing changes between areas. The topological database contains the summary of all LSAs received from all routers in the same area.

Backbone

When designing OSPF networks, if multiple areas are configured then one of these areas must be defined as area 0, the so-called backbone. The backbone operates as an area itself, so BRs maintain area routing information just as any area router would. It is generally good practice to start with area 0 before defining other areas. The backbone comprises all ABRs, networks not wholly contained in any area, and their attached routers. Ideally, all areas should be physically connected to the backbone, though in practise this may not be possible and virtual links may be required. The reason for this is that OSPF expects all areas to inject routing information into the backbone. The backbone has the special responsibility of disseminating that information into other areas. Note that the backbone in this context is an abstract routing entity and should not be confused with physical backbone networks such as an ATM or Frame Relay core. An OSPF backbone could, for example, be configured inside a router or over a single LAN segment.

Figure 3.14 shows an example of an internetwork with several areas. In this figure, routers 4, 5, 6, 7, 10, and 11 make up the backbone. If host H1 in area 2 needs to send a packet to host H2 in area 3, the packet is first sent to router 9, which forwards the packet to Area Border Router (ABR) 7. ABR 7 forwards the packet across the backbone to ABR 10, which forwards the packet through ABR 11 onto intra-area router 11 and finally host H2. The backbone topology is transparent to all intra-area routers, and individual area topologies are transparent to the backbone.

Virtual links

Virtual links are essentially unnumbered point-to-point links. Virtual links should be configured between any backbone routers that share a link to a nonbackbone area, as follows:

- Scenario A—To logically connect an area to the backbone that has no direct physical connection.

- Scenario B—To patch the backbone where a discontinuity occurs.

Routing information

There are four potential types of routing information in an area, as follows:

- Default—If an explicit route cannot be found for a given IP network or subnetwork, the router will forward the packet to the destination specified in the default route.

- Intra-area routes—Explicit network or subnet routes must be carried for all networks or subnets inside an area.

- Interarea route—Areas may carry explicit network or subnet routes for networks or subnets that are in this AS but not in this area.

- External routes—When different ASs exchange routing information, the routes they exchange are referred to as external routes. In general, it is desirable to restrict routing information in any area to the minimum required.

ASBRs running OSPF learn about external routes through dynamic exterior gateway protocols, such as BGP-4 or static routes. These externally derived routing data are passed transparently throughout the AS and kept separate from the OSPF link-state data. Each external route can also be tagged by the advertising router, enabling the passing of additional information between routers on the boundaries of the AS.

Neighbor acquisition

When an OSPF router is powered up, it initializes its data structures, checks for functional lower-level interfaces, and then begins to solicit potential neighbors by transmitting regular hello messages (advertising its presence on a subnet using the destination multicast address 224.0.0.5). Any potential neighbors that receive these hello messages will attempt to peer with the transmitter. For two routers to become neighbors they must agree on the following: AreaID, authentication, hello/dead intervals, and stub area flag. If all of these are consistent, then the routers will attempt to establish an adjacency (where link-state databases are synchronized). If there is a Designated Router (DR) on the subnet, then only it will establish adjacencies to minimize overheads.

Adjacencies

In order to establish an adjacency, each router will go through several well-defined states (usually you can view this in the neighbor events on a router). These states include the following:

- Down—No hellos seen yet.

- Attempt—On NBMA networks such as Frame Relay, this indicates that no recent information has been received from the neighbor. Efforts should be made to contact the neighbor by sending hello packets at the reduced rate.

- Init—The interface has detected a hello packet coming from a neighbor; however, bidirectional communication has not yet been established.

- Two-way—There is bidirectional communication with a neighbor. The router has seen its own address in the hello packets originating from its neighbor. The routers decide whether to carry on building an adjacency or not, based on whether one of the routers is a DR or a BDR, or the link is a point-to-point or a virtual link.

- Exchange start—Routers begin to establish the initial sequence number used in the exchange. One router will become the primary and the other will become secondary. The primary router will poll the secondary for information.

■ Exchange—Routers describe their entire link-state database by sending database description packets. At this stage packets could be flooded to other interfaces on the router.

■ Loading—Routers finalize the database exchange. Routers have built a link-state request list and a link-state retransmission list. Any information that looks incomplete or outdated will be put on the request list. Any update that is sent will be put on the retransmission list until it gets acknowledged.

■ Full—The database synchronization process is complete and the neighbors are said to be fully adjacent.

Figure 3.15 shows a typical trace sequence from a real network where two routers become fully adjacent by announcing themselves to each other and exchanging link-state data. The first stage involves both routers describing (using database descriptions) the state of their own topology databases to each other; this establishes which entries in the database the two routers

```
File:OSPF07.SCP   Type:XYP1820_SCP Mode:•••••••  Records:114  A:[••00000]
================================================================================
FRAME HH:MM:SS:ms   LEN S PACKET CONTENT
----- -----------   --- - --------------------------------------------------
 59 00:00:00:069   78   1208e5->000005  IP OSPF Hello
 61 00:00:00:300   78   1208e5->000005  IP OSPF Hello
 62 00:00:00:270   82   1208e6->000005  IP OSPF Hello
 67 00:00:00:458   66   1208e5->1208e6  IP OSPF DataDes
 68 00:00:00:002   66   1208e6->1208e5  IP OSPF DataDes
 69 00:00:00:002  346   1208e6->1208e5  IP OSPF DataDes
 70 00:00:00:002  346   1208e5->1208e6  IP OSPF DataDes
 71 00:00:00:001  134   1208e6->000005  IP OSPF LSUpd
 72 00:00:00:003   66   1208e6->1208e5  IP OSPF DataDes
 73 00:00:00:001   70   1208e6->1208e5  IP OSPF LSReq
 74: 00:00:00:002  134    1208e5->1208e6  IP OSPF LSUpd
 75 00:00:00:085   78   1208e5->000005  IP OSPF LSAck
 77 00:00:00:040   78   1208e6->000005  IP OSPF LSAck
 78 00:00:00:331  134   1208e5->000005  IP OSPF LSUpd
 79 00:00:00:035   82   1208e5->000005  IP OSPF Hello
 80 00:00:00:010  134   1208e6->000005  IP OSPF LSUpd
 81 00:00:00:127  134   1208e6->000005  IP OSPF LSUpd
 82 00:00:00:047   78   1208e5->000005  IP OSPF LSAck
 83 00:00:00:071   82   1208e6->000005  IP OSPF Hello
 85 00:00:00:499  134   1208e6->1208e5  IP OSPF LSUpd
 86 00:00:00:001   78   1208e5->1208e6  IP OSPF LSAck
 87 00:00:00:229   82   1208e5->000005  IP OSPF Hello
 88 00:00:00:270   82   1208e6->000005  IP OSPF Hello
=================================================================================
```

Figure 3.15 *Trace of OSPF neighbors forming an adjacency.*

have in common and which entries they do not have in common. Armed with this knowledge each router will then request all unknown entries from its peer (using link-state requests) until both databases are synchronized. Updates are sent using link-state updates and are explicitly acknowledged using link-state acknowledgments. Once a router becomes adjacent (i.e., synchronized) it will use its own copy of the topological database to calculate a shortest path tree, with itself as root. The shortest path tree is used as the basis for the forwarding table.

Adjacencies are a fundamental part of OSPF, since they determine the distribution of routing protocol packets. These packets are sent and received only between adjacent routers. Once adjacency is established, the routers maintain and monitor the relationship through the use of regular hello messages, which act as keep alives. We can see in packets 87 and 88 that both routers have reached a position where their respective databases are fully up-to-date. Note that even when routers are fully synchronized, each router periodically sends Link-State Advertisements (LSAs) due to an LSA aging process. LSAs are also sent immediately if any interfaces on the router change state. By comparing established adjacencies to link states, failed routers can be quickly detected and the network's topology altered appropriately.

Adjacencies on NonBroadcast MultiAccess (NBMA)

OSPF treats NonBroadcast MultiAccess (NBMA) networks like a regular broadcast media (e.g., Ethernet). However, NBMA networks are typically partial mesh topologies and so cannot provide the multiaccess features that OSPF DR operations require. The DR and BDR, therefore, need to have a static list of all other routers attached to the cloud; this list would normally be configured by the network administrator. There are methods to avoid configuring static neighbors and having specific routers becoming DRs or BDRs on the nonbroadcast cloud. These include the following:

- Point-to-point subinterface—As far as OSPF is concerned, an adjacency is always formed over a point-to-point subinterface with no DR or BDR election. We could, for example, split a serial interface into two point-to-point subinterfaces: S0.1 and S0.2. The only drawback for the point to point is that each segment will belong to a different subnet. Another workaround is to use IP unnumbered interfaces on the cloud. This also might be a problem for some administrators who manage the WAN based on IP addresses of the serial lines.

- Point-to-multipoint interfaces is defined as a numbered point-to-point interface having one or more neighbors. This should work well for people who are migrating into the point-to-point concept with no change in IP addressing on the cloud. Also, they would not have to worry about DRs and neighbor statements. The only drawback for point to multipoint is that it generates multiple host routes (routes with mask 255.255.255.255) for all the neighbors.

■ Broadcast interfaces—This approach is a workaround for statically listing all existing neighbors. The interface will be logically set to broadcast and will behave as if the router were connected to a LAN. DR and BDR election will still be performed, so special care should be taken to assure either a full-mesh topology or a static selection of the DR based on the interface priority.

Designated router

The OSPF concept of a Designated Router (DR) has a very specific meaning and is often misunderstood. There is a common misconception among practicing engineers that DRs are directly associated with areas and that you can have only one DR per area. This is quite incorrect. DRs are used to promote scalability on multiaccess networks (typically LANs, such as Ethernet).

The primary purpose of the DR and BDR is to minimize the number of adjacencies on multiaccess media, so that both bandwidth and router resources are optimized (see Figure 3.16). DRs facilitate a significant reduction in network traffic and in the size of the topological database. Consider the situation where we have five OSPF routers on an Ethernet. Without the concept of the DR (Figure 3.16[a]) each router must establish a full-mesh adjacency with all other routers, which in effect means $4 + 3 + 2 + 1 = 10$ sessions. Clearly, if one of these routers is nominated to be the relay point for all of this link-state information (Figure 3.16[b]), then the number of sessions drops to four, so we can see that this approach will scale much better. The BDR is simply implemented for backup, in case the DR dies—the

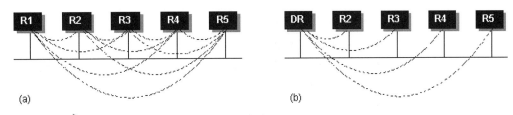

(a) (b)

Figure 3.16 *(a) OSPF full-mesh peering required without designated router (DR) support (adjacencies scale exponentially and so clearly cannot scale). (b) Peering required when router 1 acts as a DR. Note that normally a Backup Designated Router (BDR) would also be used for resilience, so we scale adjacencies linearly as (n × 2) – 2.*

idea being that the BDR also shadows the DR's adjacencies and cuts over quickly when the DR stops working, without all routers having to go through a new election process and resynchronize all their databases.

The election of the DR is established via the hello protocol, where the router with the highest OSPF priority on a segment is elected DR for that segment. The same process is then repeated for the BDR. In the event of a tie, the router with the highest router ID (RID) wins. The default for the interface OSPF priority is one. A priority value of zero is typically used to indicate that an interface should never be elected (typically shown on an OSPF interface as the DROTHER state).

Convergence

One of the most attractive features about OSPF is the ability to quickly adapt to topology changes while using a minimum of routing traffic. There are two components to routing convergence, as follows:

- Detection of topology changes—OSPF uses two mechanisms to detect topology changes. Interface status changes, and failure of OSPF to receive a hello packet from its neighbor within a timing window is called a dead interval.

- Recalculation of routes—Once a failure has been detected, the router that detected the failure sends a link-state packet with the change information to all routers in the area. All the routers recalculate all of their routes using the Dijkstra (or SPF) algorithm. The time required to run the algorithm depends on a combination of the size of the area and the number of routes in the database.

Scalability

The ability to scale an OSPF internetwork will be influenced by several factors, including the following:

- Future-proof network addressing

- Imposing hierarchy and enabling route summarization

- Ensuring that routing resources and bandwidth are adequately provisioned

We now discuss each topic briefly.

Addressing model   OSPF networks should be designed so that areas do not need to be split to accommodate growth. Address space should be reserved to permit the addition of new areas. We covered addressing models and the techniques involved in Chapter 2.

Routing resources and bandwidth provisioning Routing devices should be factored into network growth projections. Scaling is determined by the utilization of memory, CPU, and bandwidth, as follows:

- Memory—An OSPF router stores all link-states for all of the areas that it is configured for. It can also store summaries and externals. Judicious use of route summarization and stub areas can reduce memory overheads substantially.

- CPU—An OSPF router uses CPU cycles whenever a link-state change occurs. Keeping areas small and using route summarization dramatically reduces CPU overheads.

- Bandwidth—OSPF sends partial updates when a link-state change occurs. The updates are flooded to all routers in the area. In a quiet network, OSPF is a quiet protocol. In a network with many probable topology changes you should try to isolate the main culprits from critical resources.

It is possible on some routers to run multiple OSPF processes on the same router (say, to handle different areas discretely); however, it is not recommended since it creates multiple database instances that add extra overhead to the router.

Hierarchy and route summarization As we saw in Chapter 2, hierarchical routing is a key technique used to build very large networks. As networks grow, their use of finite routing resources, such as memory, CPU, and bandwidth, grow; a more efficient design will reduce the overall resource deterioration. In flat network designs the OSPF routing table grows linearly, as the number of IP segments increases (at a rate of one for one). Each OSPF router in a flat network is aware of all network segments. By implementing hierarchical routing we can slow the growth of the routing table sizes to a logarithmic rate, $O(\log[n])$, where n is the number of segments. It is important to note that designing networks using hierarchical routing can prove difficult, and many of the bugs found in OSPF over the years (including some only recently) have been related to this mode of routing support. In general, however, the benefits for large networks far outweigh any disadvantages. As Figure 3.17 illustrates, hierarchical routing is clearly beneficial as networks become very large.

Figure 3.17
Linear versus
logarithmic
growth.

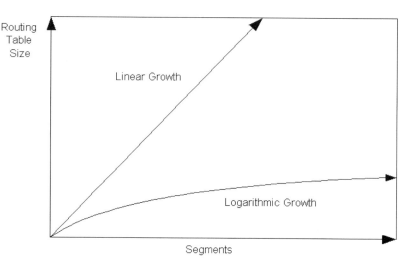

Choosing an exterior gateway protocol

Exterior Gateway Protocols (EGPs) are not really routing protocols; it would be more accurate to call them reachability protocols. The choice of exterior gateway protocols is also somewhat easier than choosing an IGP; essentially it boils down to the following options:

- Static routes have been used for many years in the AS-AS environment, primarily because they are easy to deploy, require no routing protocol, and by their very nature, enforce policy (i.e., no route equals no access). On the downside, static routes do not promote scalability, can be difficult to maintain in a changing environment, and do not respond to topology changes (as mentioned previously, some vendors associate preferences with default routes to enable a limited form of dynamic path selection).

- EGP was the first real protocol to be available in the AS-AS domain and is described in [5, 6]. Unfortunately, it suffers from several design limitations that make it unsuitable for a scalable and robust internetwork design (it requires a single Spanning Tree for a start). EGP has been subsequently declared historical by the IETF and is now obsolete.

- BGP (BGP-4 is the latest incarnation) represents a new generation of AS-AS protocol, and overcomes many of the design limitations of EGP, while also supporting Classless InterDomain Routing (CIDR). BGP-4 is the favored protocol of ISPs and carriers, in combination with static routes.

3.4.3   Border Gateway Routing Protocol (BGP)

Background

Exterior Gateway Protocols (EGPs) are designed to route between groups of routing domains called Autonomous Systems (ASs). The simplest form of exterior gateway protocol is the static route. Static routes are explicit in enforcing policy and are simple to configure and understand. The first dynamic exterior gateway protocol to achieve widespread acceptance was the Exterior Gateway Protocol (EGP). EGP, unfortunately, had several major weaknesses, including its inability to detect routing loops and support multiple paths, which meant it was somewhat limiting for robust internetworking applications such as the Internet. EGP has subsequently been displaced by the Border Gateway Protocol (BGP), another inter-AS routing protocol. Today, BGP is widely deployed over Internet Service Provider (ISP) networks. It addresses the most serious EGP problems, runs over the reliable TCP transport protocol, and includes many other useful enhancements. The latest version of BGP is version 4 (BGP-4) and is defined in RFC 1771. In effect, EGP and all previous versions of BGP are now obsolete. This section, therefore, discusses only the capabilities of BGP-4.

Protocol stack

BGP runs directly over TCP on port 179 (0xb3). The TCP connection is essential in order for the two peer routers to start exchanging routing updates reliably. This contrasts with EGP, which runs directly over IP (port 8) and is essentially a best-effort service. Note that BGP supports only IP routing environments; it is not multiprotocol.

Packet formats

BGP fields

- Marker (16 bytes)—Contains a value that the receiver of the message can predict. This field is used for authentication.

- Length (2 bytes)—Contains the total length of the message in bytes.

- Type (1 byte)—Specifies the message type.

- Data (variable)—Additional fields and/or data associated with the message type.

The BGP packet format is shown in Figure 3.18. All BGP packets use the common 19-byte header. The smallest BGP message is 19 bytes; the largest BGP message supported is 4,096 bytes. RFC 1163 specifies four

Figure 3.18
BGP packet format.

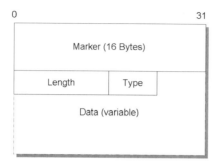

message types: open, update, notification, and keep alive. Keep-alive messages require only the 19-byte header; open, update, and notification messages require additional fields. These message types are defined as follows:

Message types

- Open—The first message sent by each side after a transport connection is established is an open message. If accepted by the recipient, a keep-alive message is returned as confirmation; thereafter, updates, keep alives, and notifications may be exchanged. In addition to the BGP header, open messages define several fields.

    - Version provides a BGP version number and allows the recipient to check that it is running the same version as the sender.
    - My autonomous system provides the AS number of the sender.
    - Hold time indicates the maximum number of seconds that may elapse without receipt of a message before the transmitter is assumed to be dead.
    - BGP identifier—The sender's ID (typically the router ID, though this is implementation dependent).
    - Optional parameter length—The length of a list of any optional parameters included in the message.
    - Optional data—A list of optional parameters and data in <type, length, value> format. This includes the ability to perform authentication.

- Update—BGP update messages provide routing updates to other BGP systems. Network Layer Reachability Information (NLKRI) included in these messages is used to construct a graph describing the relationships of the various ASs. In addition to the common BGP header, update messages include several additional fields, including unfeasible routes length, withdrawn routes, and total path attribute length. These fields provide routing information by listing path attributes corresponding to each network. Path attributes are covered later in this section.

- Notification—Sent when an error condition is detected, and a router needs to inform its peer why it is terminating the connection between them. In addition to the BGP header, notification messages include an error code field, an error subcode field, plus error data. The error code indicates one of six classes of error, some of which have subcodes indicating more specific problems: 1—message header error, 2—open message error, 3—update message error, 4—hold time expired, 5—finite state machine error, and 6—cease. For full details refer to RFC 1771.

- Keep alive—These messages comprise only the BGP header. Keep alives are exchanged between peers periodically to maintain peer integrity (i.e., by keeping the hold timer from expiring).

Operation

Fundamental to the operation of BGP is the concept of routing policy. All routing information passed between BGP routers is normally done under policy control. The network administrator configures routing policy manually, since by default a BGP router is usually configured not to receive or transmit any routing data. BGP routers exchange network reachability information, which basically comprises information on the various Autonomous Systems (AS) that need to be traversed in order to reach other networks. This information is then used to construct a graph of AS connectivity from which routing loops are pruned and with which AS-level policy decisions can be enforced. Each BGP router maintains a routing table that lists all feasible paths to a particular network.

BGP operates as a conventional link-state protocol, in that BGP neighbors initially exchange complete routing information when they peer, after which only incremental updates are used for any detected changes. Although a BGP router maintains a complete routing table, with all feasible paths to a particular network, it advertises only the primary (i.e., optimal) path in its update messages. BGP update messages comprise <network number><AS path> pairs; the AS path contains the string of ASs through which the specified network can be reached. Update messages are sent over TCP to ensure reliable delivery.

BGP peering

A pair of BGP speakers establish a peer or neighbor relationship with other BGP routers by first establishing a reliable transport connection via TCP. Once the connection is up, both routers use open messages to establish a

BGP routing session and exchange values such as the AS number, the BGP version they are running (version 3 or 4), the BGP router ID, and the keep-alive hold time. BGP sessions may begin by using BGP version 4 and negotiating downward to earlier versions if necessary (some routers allow this negotiation to be disabled—for example, in a BGPv4-only network). Once these values are confirmed and accepted the neighbor connection is established. Any state other than established means that the two routers could not become neighbors (and so BGP updates cannot be exchanged). Assuming peering is successful, routing information is then passed between neighbors via update messages, with any errors or special conditions flagged by notification messages. In order to maintain sessions BGP peers regularly exchange keep-alive messages. This exchange is illustrated in Figure 3.19. After the TCP session is established both routers open up the BGP session and update each other with routing information. Thereafter, the session is maintained via keep alive.

During session establishment, BGP peers initially exchange their full BGP routing tables. Thereafter, BGP peers send incremental updates only. In Figure 3.20, where multiple BGP routers are enabled inside an AS, internal BGP (iBGP) is run between these routers (see R10 and R9). Between ASs external BGP (eBGP) is run. Peering is normally done via the loopback interfaces of the routers rather than using real interface addresses (for fault

Figure 3.19

Two BGP routers peering.

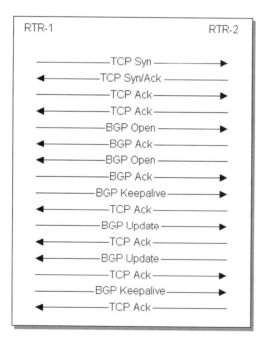

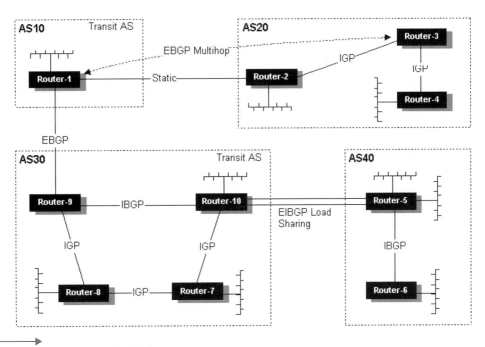

Figure 3.20 *Conceptual BGP design.*

tolerance). Note that between R1 and R3 there is a non-BGP router, so eBGP multihop must be configured from R1 to R3's loopback address and vice versa. A combination of static and IGP routing is required to ensure reachability between R1 and R3. The routing information consists of a series of AS numbers that describe the full path to the destination network. BGP uses this information to construct a loop-free map of ASs.

All BGP speakers within an AS must establish a peer relationship with each other before BGP can exchange routing information with other ASs. In effect this means that iBGP routers inside an AS must be fully meshed logically (to improve scalability BGP-4 provides two techniques to alleviate this requirement—confederations and route reflectors—described later in this chapter). This process ensures that networks within the AS are reachable and is achieved by peering among iBGP routers and by redistributing BGP routing information to IGPs (such as OSPF) that run within that AS. A BGP peer group is a group of BGP neighbors that share the same update policies.

Internal and external BGP

Although BGP was designed primarily as an inter-AS protocol, it can be used within ASs and may also operate over ASs that do not support BGP explicitly, as follows:

- Inter-AS routing is the conventional EGP mode, where two or more BGP routers in different ASs peer with each other directly to maintain a consistent view of the internetwork topology. BGP neighbors communicating between ASs must reside on the same physical network. For example, the Internet uses this type of routing to integrate hundreds of ASs from various universities, corporations, and government bodies. BGP is frequently used for path determination to provide optimal routing within the Internet.

- Intra-AS routing occurs between two or more BGP routers located within the same AS. BGP peer routers within the same autonomous system use BGP to maintain a consistent view of the system topology. BGP also is used to determine which router will serve as the connection point for specific external autonomous systems. Once again, the Internet provides an example of inter-AS routing. An organization, such as a university, could make use of BGP to provide optimal routing within its own administrative domain or AS. The BGP protocol can provide both inter- and intra-AS routing services.

- Pass-through (transit) AS routing occurs between two or more BGP peer routers that exchange traffic across an AS that does not run BGP. In a pass-through AS environment, the BGP traffic does not originate within the AS in question and is not destined for a node in the AS. BGP must interact with whatever intra-autonomous system routing protocol is being used to successfully transport BGP traffic through that AS.

Routers that belong to the same AS and exchange BGP updates are said to be running internal BGP (iBGP), and routers that belong to different ASs and exchange BGP updates are said to be running external BGP (eBGP). Note that eBGP neighbors are typically directly connected (e.g., over a point-to-point WAN link); iBGP neighbors do not have to be directly connected as long as there is an IGP (or static route) that enables the two neighbors to reach each another.

Internal BGP (iBGP)

Internal BGP (iBGP) is the form of BGP that exchanges BGP updates within an AS. This might, for example, be used by a large organization to exchange routing information between different domains under its administrative control. Use of iBGP in this respect is not mandatory; the routes learned via eBGP could be redistributed into an IGP within the AS and then redistributed again into another AS. However, iBGP is more flexible, provides more efficient ways of controlling the exchange of information within the AS, and presents a consistent view of the AS to external neighbors. For example, iBGP provides ways to control the exit point from an AS.

An important point to remember is that when a BGP speaker receives an update from other BGP speakers in its own AS (via iBGP), the receiving BGP speaker will not redistribute that information to other BGP speakers in its own AS. The receiving BGP speaker will redistribute that information to other BGP speakers outside of its AS using eBGP. This is why it is necessary for BGP speakers within an AS to be fully meshed.

External BGP (eBGP)

When two BGP speakers in different ASs run BGP to exchange routing information, they are said to be running external BGP (eBGP). Again, it is not mandatory to run BGP between ASs (one could use static or default routes depending upon the topology), but the advantages in a large dynamic environment far outweigh the additional complexity required. A good example of the application of eBGP is in the design of multihomed ASs connected to the Internet, where multiple service providers are used to provide resilience and possible load sharing.

BGP decision algorithm

When a BGP speaker receives updates from multiple ASs that describe different paths to the same destination, it must choose the single best path for reaching that destination. Once chosen, BGP puts the selected path in its routing table and propagates the path to its neighbors. The decision is based on the value of path attributes (such as next hop, administrative weights, local preference, the origin of the route, and path length) that the update contains and other BGP-configurable parameters. BGP uses the following criteria, in the order presented, to select a path for a destination:

- If the path specifies a next hop that is inaccessible, drop the update.

- Prefer the path with the largest local preference.

- If the local preferences are the same, prefer the path that was originated by BGP running on this router.

- If no route was originated, prefer the route that has the shortest AS path.

- If all paths have the same AS path length, prefer the path with the lowest origin type (where IGP is lower than GP, and EGP is lower than incomplete).

- If the origin codes are the same, prefer the path with the lowest MED attribute.

- If the paths have the same MED, prefer the external path over the internal path.

- If the paths are still the same, prefer the path through the closest IGP neighbor.

- Prefer the path with the lowest IP address, as specified by the BGP router ID.

BGP metrics

BGP uses an abstract routing metric (the inter-AS metric) to determine the best path to a given network. This metric is an arbitrary number that specifies the preference for a particular path and is typically assigned to each path by the network administrator. The value assigned can be based on any number of criteria, including AS count (the number of ASs through which the path passes), stability, speed, delay, cost, and other factors.

BGP attributes

BGP attributes comprise a number of parameters used to maintain path information, such as preferences, next hops, and so on. BGP update messages include variable-length sequences of these attributes, each formatted as a <type, length, value> triple. Attributes are classified as follows:

- Well-known, mandatory—Must be included in an update message and must be recognized by all BGP implementations.

- Well-known, discretionary—May or may not be included in an update message but must be recognized by all BGP implementations.

- Optional, transitive—If the transitive flag is set, then this attribute should be accepted and passed along to other BGP speakers.

- Optional, nontransitive—If the transitive flag is not set, then this attribute should be ignored and not passed along to other BGP speakers.

The attribute type field is a two-byte field that comprises a one-byte flag and one-byte type code. The most significant bit of the flag field indicates whether the parameter is well known (0) or optional (1). The next bit indicates whether the parameter is nontransitive (0) or transitive (1). For full details of these attributes refer to RFC 1771.

Scalability and large-scale designs

For improved scalability you should make use of attributes (especially community). In large BGP networks also make use of peer groups and route reflectors. For stability use loopback addresses for iBGP, generate aggregates, apply passwords, and always filter inbound and outbound.

Because of the increasing size of Internet BGP routing tables there is work underway to research the possibility of imposing additional hierarchy on backbones, enabling the routing database to be partially distributed with a few core super routers holding a complete database.

Route filtering and policy

Route filtering enables a BGP speaker to control what routes to send and receive from any of its peers. Route filtering is, therefore, key to defining routing policy at the AS level. Route filtering is also used to control route importing and exporting from other protocols (such as OSPF or RIP). Note that some implementations of BGP use the term route maps when referring to this capability.

Filtering may be inbound or outbound and available actions include permit or deny. Routes may typically be identified by criteria such as the IP-prefix, source ASN, intermediate ASNs, or specific attributes (the usual method is by AS-path list or Network Layer Reachability Information [NLRI]). Routes permitted through a filter may either be accepted as is or have their attributes modified. Routes that are denied are simply discarded. Attribute manipulation in route filtering is key to establishing successful routing policies and also to enable load balancing and routing symmetry. This requires careful planning and attention to detail.

CIDR and aggregate addresses

BGP-4 supports supernetting (also known as Classless InterDomain Routing [CIDR]), which is a major improvement over BGP-3 and BGP-2. CIDR enables BGP to aggregate routes, combining several distinct routes within a single route advertisement. This minimizes the size of routing tables and reduces the bandwidth overhead, particularly in backbone routers using a single route entry (an aggregate). Note that a BGP router cannot aggregate an address if it does not have a more specific route (i.e., a route with a longer prefix) in the BGP routing table.

Multihoming introduces some interesting problems for applying aggregation rules. In the example in Figure 3.21 we see a customer network, comprising sites in New York and London, multihomed to a single service

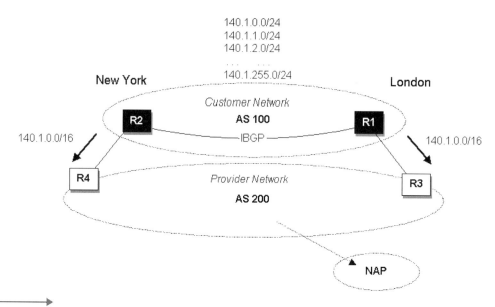

140.1.0.0/24
140.1.1.0/24
140.1.2.0/24
. . .   . . .
140.1.255.0/24

New York   London

Customer Network
AS 100

R2   R1

140.1.0.0/16   IBGP   140.1.0.0/16

R4   R3

Provider Network
AS 200

NAP

Figure 3.21   *BGP aggregation.*

provider at these two locations. The customer has a class B network, which
has been subnetted using a 24-bit prefix. Clearly, it would at first glance
appear pointless to advertise all of these routes to AS 200, since we can simply summarize them using a 140.1.0.0/16 aggregate route. We could also
change attributes for the two aggregates that are advertised, if required. For
example, we could set the MED differently for each of the two links.

Default routes

The default route is by convention expressed as network 0.0.0.0/0 and associated with a next-hop router address, router interface, or network number.
In BGP default routes have the same use as any other routing protocol; they
indicate the last resort route when no other routing information is available
or applicable. There may be a single default route or multiple default routes
pointing to different next hops with different preference levels (i.e., a primary default route with one or more backups in case it fails).

Default routes are clearly useful in single-homed situations, where it
makes little sense to advertise large numbers of external routes when there is
only one way out of the network; however, they may also be used in multihomed scenarios. Figure 3.22 illustrates a customer network (AS 100),
which is multihomed to the same provider (AS 200). Note that if AS 100
used two routers to give two parallel links, then the only additional requirement would be to run iBGP between the two customer routers.

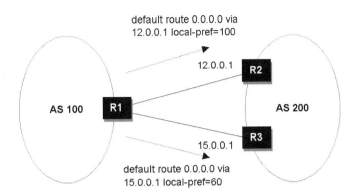

Figure 3.22
BGP default routes.

Static configuration is often preferred because it gives the designer more control and avoids possible routing loops (service providers also tend to filter out dynamically learned default routes to avoid any possible issues).

Backdoor routes

Cisco promotes a concept called backdoor routes. This enables IGP routes to take precedence over eBGP routes where a more direct path is available. This concept relies on eBGP routes being tagged as backdoor routes with an administrative distance of 200 (same as BGP local in Cisco's implementation). In this way learned IGP route will take precedence, since it will have a lower distance. For information on how Cisco applies protocol distances refer to [4].

Multihoming, load balancing, and symmetry

Figure 3.23 illustrates some of the main topology options for BGP when connecting to service providers. Multihoming is an important concern in BGP designs because of the need for resilient Internet access (especially if the business relies on the Internet for e-business functions), the cost of wide area links, and the relative clumsiness of BGP control features used to control routing preferences.

When a customer has multiple paths to the Internet, as shown in Figure 3.23(a) through (e), it is often desirable to apply some form of load balancing on these connections to maximize the available bandwidth. It is also desirable to have control on how traffic flows exit and enter the network. For performance reasons it is generally desirable to have traffic exit and enter the network at the same interface and at an interface closest to the originators. With BGP, administrative control of routing choices is devolved, and there are a number of ways to influence path cost that need to be consistently configured between the provider and a customer network.

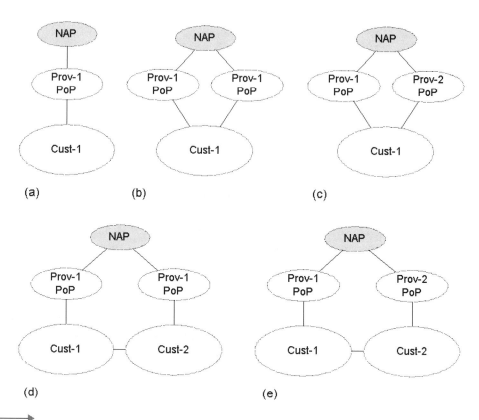

Figure 3.23   *BGP homing topology options. (a) Single homing. (b) Multihoming, single provider. (c) Multihoming, multiple providers. (d) Multiple customers sharing a private iBGP link to a single multihomed provider. (e) Multiple customers sharing a private iBGP link to multiple multihomed providers.*

Without careful design, there is a real possibility of session asymmetry in a multihomed environment. There are several ways to influence path selection with BGP, including the following:

- AS path attribute

- Local preference attribute

- MultiExitDiscriminator (MED) attribute

- Default, partial, and full routing

A key point to be aware of here is the possibility of routing loops, where routing information conflicts, and this is a real possibility where a combination of IGP metrics and default routes are used. Another point to appreciate is that although the path taken by inbound traffic depends on how a customer advertises paths externally, this information may be ignored by the routing policies of other ASs. The only guaranteed way to ensure session symmetry in a multihomed environment is to clearly nominate one link as primary for both incoming and outgoing traffic.

Choosing a router discovery protocol

Most routers today support most, if not all, of the router discovery protocols listed in section 3.3.7. You should, therefore, choose the most appropriate mechanism for your network environment. As a general rule, the preferred solution is the one that imposes the least demand on network and system load, while maintaining some level of automation and dynamic discovery attributes. Using those prerequisites IDRP represents the best choice available today, though it may not be available on all hosts. On legacy host equipment you may be limited to static gateway configuration or passive RIP.

If faced with a large number of end systems with only static gateway configuration available, and it is critical that service is uninterrupted, then all is not lost. An increasingly attractive alternative is to run a protocol such as the Virtual Redundant Router Protocol (VRRP) between multiple routers.

ICMP Router Discovery Protocol (IRDP)

Reference [7] describes a dynamic router discovery mechanism called ICMP Router Discovery Protocol (IRDP), which relies on extensions to ICMP and multicast interfaces. IRDP also scales to more than two routers. IRDP is not a routing protocol; although it facilitates the discovery of nearby routers it does not enable hosts to discover optimal routes to a destination. If a host chooses a poor first-hop router for a particular destination, it should receive an ICMP redirect from that router, indicating a better first hop. IRDP does, however, eliminate the need for manual configuration of router addresses and is independent of any specific routing protocol. IDRP operations require both the end system and router to support the enhanced version of ICMP. Reference [7] specifies two new ICMP router discovery messages: router advertisements and router solicitations.

Operations

Each router periodically multicasts a router advertisement (default address 224.0.0.1, ICMP type 9, code 0) from each of its multicast interfaces, announcing the IP address(es) of that interface. If the router does not support IP multicast, then advertisements are sent using a limited broadcast

(255.255.255.255). Hosts discover the addresses of their neighboring routers simply by listening for advertisements. When a host attached to a multicast link starts up, it may multicast a router solicitation (default address 224.0.0.2, ICMP type 10, code 0) to request immediate advertisements, rather than waiting for the next update. If no advertisements are received, the host may retransmit the solicitation a few times and is then required to back off. Any routers that subsequently start up, or that were not discovered because of packet loss or temporary link partitioning, are eventually discovered through their periodic advertisements. Links that are susceptible to high packet loss or frequent partitioning can be accommodated by increasing the advertisements rate. For each multicast interface on a router the following timers are available:

- MaxAdvertisementInterval—Maximum time allowed between sending router advertisements from the interface, in seconds. Must be not less than four seconds and not greater than 1,800 seconds. Default: 600 seconds.

- MinAdvertisementInterval—The minimum time allowed between sending unsolicited router advertisements from the interface, in seconds. Must be not less than three seconds and not greater than MaxAdvertisementInterval. Default: 0.75 × MaxAdvertisementInterval.

- AdvertisementLifetime—The value to be placed in the lifetime field of router advertisements sent from the interface, in seconds. Must not be less than MaxAdvertisementInterval and not greater than 9,000 seconds. Default: 3 × MaxAdvertisementInterval.

For each of the router's IP addresses on its multicast interfaces the following features are configurable:

- Advertise—A flag indicating whether or not the address is to be advertised. Default: True.

- PreferenceLevel—The preferability of the address as a default router address, relative to other router addresses on the same subnet. A 32-bit, signed, two's-complement integer, with higher values indicating preferability. The minimum value (0x80000000) is used to indicate that the address, even though it may be advertised, is not to be used by neighboring hosts as a default router address. Default: 0.

A router advertisement includes a preference level for each advertised router address. When a host must choose a default router address (i.e., when, for a particular destination, the host has not been redirected or configured to use a specific router address), it is expected to choose from those router addresses that have the highest preference level [8]. A network administrator can configure router address preference levels to encourage or discourage the use of particular routers as default routers. A router advertisement also includes a lifetime field, specifying the maximum length of time that the advertised addresses are to be considered as valid router addresses by hosts, in the absence of further advertisements. This is used to ensure that hosts eventually forget about routers that fail, become unreachable, or stop acting as routers. A network administrator, who wishes to employ advertisements as a supplemental black-hole detection mechanism, is free to configure smaller values. For further information the interested reader is referred to [9].

3.5   Router addressing issues

We discussed several addressing techniques that can be used together with router designs to improve overall performance and preserve bandwidth. These techniques included subnetting, hierarchical addressing (sometimes called route summarization), and supernetting (or CIDR). There are several other related techniques that are commonly implemented on routing platforms, including the following:

- Unnumbered link support

- Multinetting or multihoming

- Broadcast forwarding (including BOOTP forwarding)

3.5.1   Unnumbered links

In large internetworks, there may be many serial point-to-point WAN links between routers, and each serial interface will have an IP address. Each link is effectively a private subnet, and this use of IP addresses has several potential drawbacks, including the following:

- It wastes IP addresses. Since point-to-point links do not usually attach host devices, there is little point in wasting addresses and defining these subnets.

- It becomes difficult to manage, as the network gets larger.

- These point-to-point routes may show up in the routing table, making tables unnecessarily large and slowing down routing calculations and consequently delaying convergence.

A number of proprietary solutions to this problem have been implemented that enable serial interfaces to operate without any IP addresses assigned—a configuration usually referred to as unnumbered links. Modern routing protocols such as OSPF typically support the concept of unnumbered links as an optional feature.

Although generally considered to be extremely useful, there are some potential disadvantages of using unnumbered links in your design; these typically center around troubleshooting, as follows:

- Ping won't be able to test reachability to either the local or remote serial interfaces.

- ICMP Traceroute will lose track of the path over the serial line, since there is no IP address to trace.

- Telnet will not work if you need to connect to the serial interface.

The standards (router requirements) suggest that the RouterID should be used as the remote target whenever a serial IP address is not available in this configuration. In reality, the ability to ping any real IP address or RouterID from a remote network is enough to prove that the serial interface is working, and it is usually possible to telnet either to the RouterID or a LAN interface remotely. The benefits of smaller, cleaner routing tables and simpler configuration management in my view outweigh any of these subsidiary issues.

3.5.2   Multinetting

Multinetting (sometimes called multihoming) was introduced largely to assist network managers in migrating from one IP addressing scheme to another. The concept is quite simple; each physical interface on a router has the ability to support a number of IP addresses of different classes and subnet masks. For example, in the following chart, interface e1 on the router is configured with multiple IP addresses.

Interface	Address	Mask
e1	193.128.66.0	255.255.255.0
e1	120.10.128.0	255.255.240.0
w1	140.40.0.0	255.255.0.0

In operational terms the router sees multiple network interfaces on the LAN port; the fact that they are all sitting on the same physical interface is of no real consequence. This configuration is sometimes referred to as a router on a stick, a lollipop, or a one-armed router. All communication between devices on the dual interface must go via the router. Clearly, this is inefficient if these devices are physically adjacent to each other and connected to the same piece of wire.

Typically, applications of multinetting might be migrating from an illegal network addressing scheme to a legal one. Suppose we had originally built our example network using the unregistered class B network address 120.10.0.0. On a single LAN port/single LAN port router we could still facilitate communications while migrating to a registered class C address. In this case the router would allow LAN-LAN communication transparently but would either filter out or NAT the illegal address when communicating with the wide area (if it were indeed a public network or attached elsewhere to a public network). Once the migration is complete, the LAN interface can be reconfigured by simply deleting the class B address and removing any filters or NAT rules. By this stage all LAN-LAN communication will be direct (avoiding the router).

3.5.3   Broadcast forwarding

Since routers are designed to discard broadcast destination addresses (e.g., 255.255.255.255) and particular source addresses (e.g., 0.0.0.0), applications and services that use such addresses are limited to use on the local network or subnetwork. For example, a client/server application that uses limited broadcasts cannot operate across a router. In most internetworks this is simply not practical, since clients will be widely distributed and the number of servers required in comparison would be quite low. Many such applications still exist; often they were originally intended for LAN use only, and operation over routers was never a design consideration. These applications are most commonly associated with device configuration or directory services (e.g., DNS, NIS, TFTP, and DHCP/BOOTP).

To resolve this problem, a third-party agent is required to transfer broadcast messages between clients and servers. Typically, this agent is implemented as a software feature on router platforms and called broadcast relay (sometimes called broadcast helper or broadcast gateway). This is not a routing function as such but a method of forwarding broadcasts between interfaces in a controlled manner. Because of the different ways in which protocol stacks operate, this feature is also stack specific; there are variants for IP, NetWare IPX, and AppleTalk, for example. In the case of individual services (such as BOOTP), additional packet manipulation is required, so there may be application-specific variations also. For further information on the BOOTP relay agents refer to [10].

3.5.4 Route summarization and CIDR

Two other design techniques, Classless Interdomain Routing Protocol (CIDR) and Route Summarization, are key for developing large-scale network designs.

3.6   Route redistribution

We have seen that there are a number of protocol choices in the intradomain and interdomain space, including a number of legacy protocols, proprietary protocols, and several open standards.

At the AS boundary, interior and exterior routing protocols are typically incompatible. Within an AS there are likely to be multiple IGPs, either for historical reasons or because multiple vendor solutions are being used. The metric schemes associated with all of the routing protocols vary widely and may be incompatible. Even so, we often need to normalize these data to form a holistic view of the network topology. The problem of integrating and mapping routing information from multiple routing domains is dealt with by a process called route redistribution. Redistribution enables routing information derived from one routing protocol to be translated and used by another routing protocol. Redistribution might be used as a quick fix when

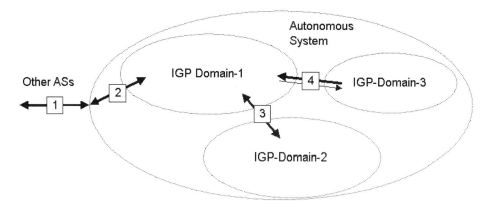

Figure 3.24   *Examples of redistribution interfaces. (1) The AS border interface between exterior routing protocols such as BGP-4 or static routing. (2) The AS border interface between exterior routing protocols and interior routing protocols such as OSPF, EIGRP, and RIP. (3) The interior interface between two different routing domains (e.g., Domain-1 could run OSPF, Domain-3 could run EIGRP). (4) Same as (3), except that redistribution here is not mutual (e.g., Domain-3 runs RIP, and receives only a default route back from OSPF in Domain-1.).*

merging two organizations or for migrating from an old IGP such as RIP to OSPF. Figure 3.24 illustrates some of the key interfaces at which redistribution is likely.

It is important to understand that redistribution has direction, and we can choose to redistribute routing information symmetrically (mutual redistribution) or asymmetrically (hierarchical redistribution). It is also important to appreciate that standards do not really apply here, and the facilities available on a particular router platform are very much vendor dependent. In practice each router will have its own particular idiosyncrasies, and because of the differences inherent to various IGPs and EGPs, redistribution raises several potential problems that require detailed understanding and careful attention to detail. This is especially true at the AS boundary, where the consequences of getting things wrong can be quite extensive.

3.7   Router architecture

This section reviews some of the basic operations and design choices applicable to modern routers. These have a fundamental impact upon price, performance, and the features available from today's commercial router platforms, and, as many engineers recognize, these design choices can significantly influence the network design. Note that here we are primarily interested in packet switching; for an overview of circuit-switching architectures refer to [11].

3.7.1   Router operations

The range of features supported by routers has mushroomed over the last decade, incorporating features such as multiprotocol operations, bridging, and basic firewalling. This is partly because of the drive for tighter integration and also because routers traditionally sit at key boundaries in the network infrastructure. Apart from specialized backbone routers optimized for packet forwarding, routers are becoming almost general-purpose forwarding devices, likely to be involved in the following operations:

- Routing information maintenance—Routers participate in the maintenance and manipulation of routing information and typically maintain locally constructed views of the network topology called routing tables. Routers interact with their neighbors, listening for and generating updates as appropriate in order to maintain a real-time view of the network.

- Layer 3 switching—When routers forward packets (based on routing information), they must create a new outbound Layer 2 encapsulation (since MAC addresses will differ) and generate a new Level 2 checksum (such as the Ethernet FCS). TTL or hop counts should be updated and, if appropriate, Layer 3 checksums should be recalculated.

- Packet classification—Is for manipulation, queuing, and possibly filtering. Some routers provide advanced bandwidth management and QoS features.

- Recording accounting and billing statistics—for example, interface statistics (packets/bytes in/out, error statistics, flow data, and so on).

- Network management—Routers typically support in-band and out-of-band management features such as Telnet, SNMP, ICMP Echo (ping), trace route, and possibly HTTP server. Routers may also support RMON.

- Security/NAT services—If appropriate, perform address translation and packet filtering.

- Tunneling—Routers may originate and terminate secure Virtual Private Networks, (VPNs) and possibly carry nonroutable protocols inside tunnels.

Clearly, some of these operations are extremely complex and resource intensive, and for high-performance routing applications (such as enterprise and backbone nodes) it is important that the architecture of these devices is highly optimized for high-speed forwarding.

3.7.2   Router applications

Routers can be loosely classified into three classes, broadly divided by application: backbone routers, enterprise routers, and access routers. Each class of router is designed to deal with a different set of challenges and is, therefore, broadly differentiated based on factors such as performance, software functionality, port density, media support, and price.

Backbone routers

Backbone routers are used on public networks such as the Internet, telco networks, and large private internetworks. The primary issues here are, therefore, reliability and performance. Backbone routers enable organizations to build large, private international internetworks over high-bandwidth, long-haul trunks. They also enable ISPs and telcos to connect enterprise networks over public networks such as the Internet. The key characteristics of a backbone router are summarized as follows:

- High-speed trunk connectivity

- Performance

- Minimal Layer 3 protocol support

- Hardware fault tolerance

- Software reliability

- Management

- Cost

In the gigabit range there are products such as the M40 (Juniper) and Cisco 7500. Notably, the M40 supports in-service software upgrades (the ability to upgrade the router code online without bringing down the router). At the top end of this class of routers are the so-called carrier class terabit router platforms, for which there are only a small handful of competing vendors (the term carrier class implies extremely high levels of fault tolerance and compliance with the Network Equipment Building Specification [NEBS], a Bellcore originated de facto standard for carrier class equipment). Products in this class include the NX64000 (Lucent), TSR (Avici Systems), Aranea Terabit Router-1 (Charlotte's Web Networks), Pluris 2000 Series TNR (Pluris), Versalar 25000 (Nortel), and the Cisco 12016.

Enterprise routers

Enterprise routers are typically employed within a campus or enterprise network. In this environment there may be thousands of LAN users interfacing with a wide diversity of interfaces. The key characteristics of an enterprise router are summarized as follows:

- Bulk port concentration

- Multiprotocol support

- Service quality

- Additional services

The job of designing an enterprise router is not easy; it must resolve the conflicting design goals of providing a rich feature set at each port, reducing the cost per port, and ensuring ease of configuration, QoS support, and strong management and diagnostic features. Examples of routers in this class include the Cisco AGS+ and 7000 series and the Xyplex 9000 Series.

Access routers

Access routers allow home users and small businesses to access the Internet via an Internet Service Provider (ISP). They are also used in remote offices for central-office connectivity. In the past, access networks began life as modem pools attached to terminal concentrators, serving a large number of low-speed dial-up circuits. In recent years this model has changed dramatically with the emergence of high-speed modems, ISDN, xDSL, and cable modems. ADSL is about to add an extra magnitude of affordable bandwidth into the SOHO environment, and this will increase the load on access routers yet further. The key characteristics of an access router are summarized as follows:

- LAN-WAN interfaces
- Multiprotocol support
- Configuration management
- VPN support
- Voice encapsulation

Examples of routers in this class include the Cisco IGS and 2500 series, the AN range (Bay Networks), and Xyplex 3000 series.

Reducing port costs

Both enterprise and access routers are subject to very tight cost constraints, and stiff competition means there is always pressure to minimize the price per port. This ratio depends on factors such as memory size and type, interface logic, processing architecture, and the complexity of the protocol used between the port and the routing processor. Cost reduction is a serious consideration for all components on these platforms, and a constant concern for designers. Considerations include the following:

- Processor architecture
- Memory
- Buffer memory
- Control protocol

For the interested reader [12] provides an excellent review of this subject.

3.7.3   Router architecture and design

A router is essentially a specialized network computing device optimized for packet switching and as such typically contains CPU, ROM, RAM, some form of bus, possibly flash media, and NVRAM. In order to implement high-speed routing, the architecture of a generic router embodies several key components: a routing processor, switching fabric, and interface cards providing one or more input ports and output ports. While this may seem of academic interest to the casual observer, hard-bitten routing engineers understand all too well the implications of router architecture on performance and scalability in real networks. In the routing world, performance is often critical, especially as we go up the food chain into the backbone domain. The performance characteristics of a router become very exposed when CPU-intensive features such as quality of service are required on top of basic packet forwarding.

Packet switch evolution

We can broadly divide packet switches into three generations, as follows:

- First-generation packet switches—Characterized by a general-purpose processor (e.g., a Pentium) distributing packets to dumb interface cards from main memory. The main bottlenecks are CPU and memory access speeds and possibly the interface adaptor. Such switches are cheap and easy to build and give relatively low performance.

- Second-generation packet switches—Characterized by the more intelligent interface cards, which perform input/output queuing and are capable of offloading the CPU by distribution packets locally (i.e., by performing port mapping) over a shared bus. There is typically a fast-path and slow-path mode of operation, depending upon whether a packet can be switched or routed. The main bottleneck is shared bus contention. Typically these are high-end routers (e.g., the Cisco 7500) and ATM switches (e.g., FORE Systems ASX-200) or hybrid devices such as the Ipsilon (now part of Nokia) IP switching products (a combination of an IP router with an ATM switch, which enables flows to be classified and switched or routed dynamically).

- Third-generation packet switches—Characterized by the ability to perform parallel packet transfers over multiple buses (i.e., a switch fabric). The switch fabric is self-routing; once the port mapper hands over the packet to the fabric it is automatically routed to the appropriate output port where it is queued. The main bottlenecks are the input queue arbiter and the output queue controller (depending upon whether the design has buffers largely at the input or output ports). Typically these are high-end ATM switches or high-end routers with ATM-like switching fabrics.

We will now briefly review the key components of router architecture and their potential impact on features and performance.

Routing processor

The routing processor participates in routing protocols and creates a forwarding table that is used in packet forwarding. The routing processor also runs the software used to configure and manage the router. It handles any packet whose destination address cannot be found in the forwarding table in the line card. Route processing can be implemented in several configurations, including the following:

- Centralized, general-purpose processor
- Centralized, general-purpose processor with hot standby or load-sharing twin processor
- Centralized, general-purpose processor with subsidiary bit-slice processors to prefilter traffic
- Centralized, general-purpose processor with auxiliary processors dedicated to specific tasks
- Fully distributed processing

The architecture employed depends on a number of factors—the class of router, level of fault tolerance required, hardware specification, price, and the following:

- Single processor—Single-processor systems are simpler to implement, but there is a threshold above which throughput will plateau as the offered load increases. Dedicated router platforms can offset this effect (referred to as the von Neuman bottleneck) by limiting the number and speed of interfaces serviced; employing multiple, subsidiary, or auxiliary processors; or enabling load sharing through clustering or stackable routers. Many routers opt for standard CISC processors such as the Intel x86 and Pentium range or the Motorola 680xx series. RISC processors (as implemented in Proteon's CNX 500 router) have largely failed to deliver the level of performance expected.

- Subsidiary processors—Several router vendors have invested effort into offloading the main processor by using subsidiary Bit-Slice Processors (BSPs) on interface cards to prefilter traffic. Another area of development is the implementation of more sophisticated multiple bus architectures. Some of these implementations (such as the Cisco cBus) are essentially facelifts, designed to improve performance in existing product lines without a major redesign and to allow router vendors to move from small numbers of 10 Mbps Ethernet interfaces up to high-performance, higher-density interfaces for technologies such as FDDI, HSSI, and Fast Ethernet.

- Coprocessors—Some router vendors have implemented auxiliary processors to improve performance by offloading nonrouting tasks, such as the Command-Line Interface (CLI), network management, compression, encryption, and encapsulation. This approach was used by Proteon in its CNX600 router design, where the central RISC CPU was supplemented by two AMD 29000 processors.

- Multiprocessors—To date symmetric multiprocessor-like architectures have offered the highest switching rates for routing applications. Some router architectures compromise full symmetric multiprocessing by utilizing one CPU for packet forwarding and the other for general housekeeping. Even if one CPU is idle and the other busy, load cannot be shared because the tasks handled differ. Reference [13] provides some useful insights into why parallel processor designs have to date been applied only for niche, high-end platforms.

Another factor in these design options is whether the routing database itself is centralized, distributed but shared, or fragmented (distributed among routing processors, each with their own routing database). For backbone and large enterprise routers handling many interfaces it is advantageous to have a centralized or closely coupled distributed routing database; however, this requires either substantial horsepower and resources or a highly sophisticated multiprocessor architecture. Some mid-range enterprise and access routers employ a collapsed routing architecture, where each route processor acts like an independent router inside the chassis, connected over a common medium fabric (often internalized Ethernet, FDDI, or ATM cores). Although some highly flexible designs have been deployed, this may mean that internal routes (i.e., routes between cards in the chassis) appear in the routing table just like external routes, potentially slowing down route lookup.

Interface modules

An interface module (sometime called an IO card or line card) is the physical point of attachment for local and wide area circuits to the router. Interface cards typically support one or more physical ports, depending upon the media type, the amount of logic required on the card, and the size of the connectors. Incoming packets are fed into an input port, and outgoing packets are fed to an output port. Many media technologies operate in full-duplex mode, so in some cases the input and output ports may refer to the same physical interface, differentiated only by the direction of traffic flow.

Switching fabric

The switching fabric interconnects input ports with output ports. If the switching fabric has a bandwidth greater than the sum of the bandwidths of the input ports, then packets are queued only at the outputs, and the router is called an output-queued router. Otherwise, queues may build up at the inputs, and the router is called an input-queued router. Fabrics may be physically represented as a traditional backplane (typically one set of large connectors at the back of the chassis) or as a midplane (two opposing sets of connectors in the middle of the chassis). Midplane chassis tend to offer greater flexibility but at the cost of additional complexity. One thing to take special note of is the physical connector presentation. Ideally the backplane/midplane should present female interfaces, since this has the least potential for damage internally. If this is not the case, you run the risk of having to replace the whole chassis if you inadvertently damage the pins of a male connector.

Bus fabric

The traditional and simplest switching fabric to implement is a bus, which interconnects all the input and output ports. It is relatively easy to build a router today using a personal computer equipped with multiple line cards. The problems with this architecture are that the bus is a single point of failure and throughput is constrained by both the capacity of the bus and the overheads imposed by bus arbitration logic.

Shared-memory fabric

In a shared-memory router incoming packets are stored in a shared memory and only pointers to packets are switched. This increases switching capacity. However, there is an intrinsic performance limitation with shared-memory switch fabrics. The speed of the switch is limited to the speed at which we can access memory. Although memory sizes have roughly doubled every 18 months, memory access times have improved by only about 5 percent annually. Unlike crossbar switches, however, shared-memory switches do not suffer from Head-of-Line (HOL) blocking, and multicasting is relatively straightforward to implement.

Crossbar fabric

The crossbar fabric is the simplest form of switching fabric, comprising an $N \times N$ matrix of N input buses, N output buses, and N^2 crosspoints (this can be visualized as 2^N buses). A crossbar radically improves performance by enabling multiple simultaneous data paths to operate through one or more switching fabrics and is at best case N times faster than a second-generation switch.

On the downside, the control status of each crosspoint must be under continuous control for every flow of packets transferred in parallel across the crossbar fabric, and this requires a scheduler. Therefore, with the crossbar architecture, although much improved, the scheduler ultimately constrains performance through the fabric. Furthermore, although a crossbar is internally nonblocking, if multiple packets at the input port want to go to the same destination then output blocking occurs. This can be resolved by either running the crossbar N times faster than the input ports (difficult and expensive) or by placing buffers inside the crossbar. Crossbars do not scale well. Multicasting is complex in a crossbar switch and requires the switch to fabric to be quiet during the period of the multicast.

Hybrid media fabrics

During the mid-1990s some innovative designs emerged that used pseudo-media buses inside the chassis. Some of these devices also implemented a kind of symmetric multiprocessing (promoted by BAY Networks and Xyplex). Some of these implementations were closer to real symmetric multiprocessing than others. For example, Xyplex implemented a highly flexible midplane (as opposed to backplane) architecture in their 9000 series, using three internal Ethernet buses. This design is a form of multiprocessing; however, each route processor operates like a discrete router, even to the point of exchanging routing protocol over the internal media buses. A number of IO ports are dedicated to each processor, and ports can be soft-switched internally or externally, enabling a high degree of flexibility in the design.

This design offers an impressive number of topology options and appears to offer scalability and good fault tolerance. Scalability is limited only by the speed of the internal bus, and individual slots could run different processors to match different types of applications. Each slot is autonomous; in the event of a route processor failing, only the IO ports connected to that slot are affected. Hot swapping is available. Managed load-sharing power supplies are available. The disadvantages are that this is an expensive architecture to implement. Each slot has its own OS and routing processor and requires large amounts of RAM as we move into the backbone domain. Another disadvantage is that routing is taking place internally (e.g., OSPF peering across internal buses) and route entries for internal networks appear in the routing tables.

ATM-like fabrics

In the early 1990s designers began to tackle large ATM switch architectures. Although ATM did not dominate the networking world as predicted, designers of IP routers saw an opportunity to improve throughput and offer (conceptually) mixed-media services by wrapping segmentation and reassembly modules around ATM-like switching fabric cores. With this architecture ATM PVCs are mapped between all ports in the router (i.e., a full-mesh ATM backbone in a box). During the forwarding process, a longest-prefix match determines the destination port for an IP packet. The packet is then fragmented into 53-byte ATM cells and switched over the appropriate PVC to the output port, where it is reassembled back into an IP packet before transmission. From the IP perspective the ATM core could be viewed as a transparent fat pipe; however, this architecture does not allow the possibility of providing different service guarantees, and these designs suffer some of the inherent problems of ATM, including the following.

- ATM switches do not generally provide good support for multicasting. Multicasting requires an ATM VCI to be mapped to multiple VCIs and cells to be replicated either at the input port or within the ATM switch fabric. This degrades the overall efficiency of the switching fabric.

- A subtle problem occurs because traffic control algorithms are usually specified in terms of packets rather than in terms of cells. So, with cell-based fabrics, implementing semantics such as those required by shared filters in RSVP can be a challenge.

Despite these issues, ATM fabrics have appeared in many recent router designs. For further information, the interested reader is referred to [11, 12, 14] for more details of switch design and buffering techniques.

Issues in switch design

Buffering

One of the hardest problems in switch design today is not the fabric design but the buffering component. In short, there are three main buffering techniques, as follows:

- Input queuing is where packets are queued at the input port and pulled off the queue when access to the switching fabric is gained via an arbiter. With FIFO input queuing, however, packets may suffer from head-of-line blocking, which can be avoided by using separate input queues for each output port.

- Output queuing is where packets are queued at the output ports, awaiting scheduling for release onto external interfaces. The problem is where all packets at the input ports are destined for the same output port. Costs can be reduced by assuming a probability for N inputs requiring access to a single output simultaneously, scaling the output port speed accordingly (e.g., the so-called knockout switch—see [14]).

- Shared memory is where the architecture input and output ports share common memory. The output port scheduler removes the packet from memory and passes it to the appropriate output port. Such a device is easy to build, since only headers are switched; however, an $N \times N$ switch must process N packets in a single arrival time, and, since memory bandwidth is usually a major bottleneck, this limits the size of the switch.

For further information on buffering techniques, the interested reader is referred to [14]. For details on performance improvements, and arbitration algorithm design in relation to input queuing, see [15, 16].

Route lookup

Perhaps the single most important performance issue for backbone routers is route lookup time. The operation is based on the most specific (longest) IP prefix. This would be an $O(N)$ operation per packet just to build a set of candidates and is completely unacceptable. This issue is amplified if small packets represent a high proportion of the traffic, since this ultimately means more lookups per second. The two main factors that affect the speed of a route lookup algorithm are memory access time and the data structures used to construct the forwarding table. Performance can be improved in a number of ways, including the following:

- Optimized data structures—Trie-based algorithms [17] optimize storage space at the expense of performing more memory lookups, and, as memory prices drop, this is perhaps the wrong way to go. Recent research indicates that routing tables are essentially quite stable, requiring updates only about once every two minutes [18].

- Hardware-oriented techniques—The most common hardware-oriented solutions to lookup problems are Content Addressable Memories (CAMs) and caches. Both techniques scale poorly with routing table size and, therefore, cannot be used for backbone routers. One approach to solve this problem integrates logic and memory together in a single device, dramatically reducing memory access time.

Another solution is to increase the amount of memory used for the routing table [19], although cost would possibly preclude this for enterprise and access routers. One problem is that as the table grows it becomes very hard to update. Reference [19] describes inexpensive, special-purpose hardware that can be used to perform rapid updates.

- Table compaction techniques—These techniques create complicated but compact data structures for the forwarding table. The table is stored in the primary cache of a processor, enabling route lookup at gigabit speeds. Reference [20] describes such an algorithm.

- Hashing techniques—Hash-based solutions are commonly used for fast lookup problems, but there are problems applying hashing techniques to a forwarding table (given a destination IP address, we do not know in advance what prefix should be used for finding the longest match). Reference [21] offers a scalable, hash-based algorithm to look up the longest prefix match for an N bit address in $O(\log N)$ steps. This algorithm computes a separate hash table for each possible prefix length, and, instead of naively searching for a successful hash, this algorithm does a binary search on the prefix lengths.

Instead of reducing the cost of route lookups, backbone routers can use two techniques to avoid route lookups altogether, as follows:

- Map destination addresses to VCIs at the edge—Backbone networks such as ATM provide a Virtual Circuit Interface (VCI). If edge devices map IP destination addresses to a VCI, then the longest prefix match problem can be avoided in backbone routers. Since VCIs are integers drawn from a small pool, they can be looked up with a single memory access. This approach, however, requires the edge devices to somehow distribute address-to-VCI mappings via protocols such as IP switching and tag switching.

- Table size reduction through routing hierarchy—Another technique is to have backbone routers maintain routes purely for destinations served by that backbone. Since table size is greatly reduced, route lookups are considerably faster. All unknown destinations are routed to gateways at a Network Access Point (NAP), which holds the global routing table. This approach promotes scalability (in particular for BGP).

There are clearly a number of useful solutions to the fast route lookup problem, and several of these techniques will no doubt be incorporated into new generations of router designs. An excellent review of router design trends is given in [12].

3.7.4 Scheduling techniques

The simplest method of scheduling packets from a buffer is to release them in the order of arrival, a strategy commonly referred to as first come, first served (FCFS) or first in, first out (FIFO). Many first-generation routers provided a single FIFO as their own scheduling option (perhaps with one additional queue for control and management traffic). With mixed local and wide area routing there can be a much greater imbalance in line speeds, leading to frequent buffer overflows or timeouts if the amount of remote data is too large to be sustained.

Traffic prioritization and queuing mechanisms have become increasingly sophisticated over recent years and are closely associated with service guarantees. In addition to FCFS/FIFO, queuing strategies currently deployed include priority queuing, custom queuing, Weighted Fair Queuing (WFQ), and Random Early Detection (RED).

3.7.5 Router operating systems

Historically, routers have been viewed as hardware devices optimized for high-speed packet forwarding; consequently, the operating systems implemented in these systems were often not much more than stripped-down schedulers. Many router operating systems are derived from early versions of Free BSD UNIX, and there is increasing interest today in LINUX. Both of these environments have access to a huge suite of essentially free routing software developed over many years and publicly available on the Internet. Over the past decade, however, router hardware has become almost a commodity, and the software component of the router has been increasingly viewed as the true value item. Router vendors such as Cisco have differentiated themselves largely on increasingly rich and sophisticated software functionality, ranging from huge tracts of protocol support to exotic queuing systems and bandwidth management features.

3.8   Summary

This chapter discussed the basics of router networks, including the following:

- The internetworking world is focusing on a unified Layer 3 protocol called IP. IP is particularly well suited for use in an internetworking environment, where several disparate networks need to be connected. Routers (historically called gateways) allow the IP data to be switched between interconnected networks via the Network Layer (Layer 3) part of a packet.

- Scalable routing over large internetworks can be facilitated by imposing hierarchy on the overall design. At the highest level we have the Autonomous System (AS), and this is broken down successively into smaller, manageable domains and areas until we reach the subnet. Hierarchy reduces traffic, reduces load on routers, and assists in minimizing the scope of router misbehavior.

- Routing protocols are broadly divided into two groups: Interior Gateway Protocols (IGPs) and Exterior Gateway Protocols (EGPs). IGPs are broadly divided into two groups, based on the algorithms they use: distance vector and link state. Link-state algorithms scale better than distance-vector algorithms and are generally associated with more sophisticated, modern routing protocols such as OSPF and IS-IS.

- Several mechanisms are available to allow end systems to operate within a routed environment, including Proxy ARP, passive RIP, ICMP Router Discovery (IRDP), and static gateway configuration. Possibly the best dynamic technique available today is ICMP Router Discovery.

- The metrics used by routing protocols vary widely, from simple hops to fine-grained combinatorial metrics (incorporating such features as cost, delay, throughput, etc.). Metrics are fundamental for topology analysis and the creation of effective forwarding databases.

- Router architecture has a fundamental effect on performance and is improving all the time. The first generation of multiprocessor architectures has been deployed, and advances in scheduling, lookup, and queuing algorithms have decreased router switching times considerably over recent years.

- Route lookup time is fundamental to the scalability of routers in the backbone domain. As the number of backbone routes increases, faster algorithms, better data structures, and techniques such as lookup avoidance are increasingly under scrutiny.

References

[1]   T. Kenyon, *High-Performance Network Design: Design Techniques and Tools* (Woburn, MA: Digital Press, 2001).

[2]   Border Gateway Protocol 3 (BGP-3), RFC 1267, October 1991.

[3]   A Framework for QoS-based Routing in the Internet, RFC 2386, August 1998.

[4]   www.cisco.com, Cisco home page.

[5]   Exterior Gateway Protocol (EGP), RFC 827, October 1982.

[6]   Exterior Gateway Protocol Formal Specification, RFC 904, April 1984.

[7]   S. Deering, ICMP Router Discovery Messages, RFC 1256, September 1991.

4

Multicast Network Design

This chapter discusses the special use of multicasts and the protocols required to distribute multicasts throughout an internetwork. Multicasting enables a packet to be distributed from a source to any number of destinations automatically, with the responsibility for packet distribution placed on intelligent network nodes rather than the source itself. For certain types of applications this can be a very efficient way of distributing data to many receivers simultaneously (specifically, highly asymmetrical applications, such as market data feeds, videoconferencing, audioconferencing, database replication, distributed computation, and real-time workgroups). Historically, these applications, either broadcasted data or used multiple TCP unicast sessions from the data feed, to each client. As we have seen already, broadcasts are generally a bad idea on internetworks for several reasons. The unicast solution does not scale and makes poor use of the available bandwidth, since the feed is required to send the same information n times, often along the same physical links. IP multicast, therefore, provides an ideal delivery mechanism for this class of application. With the rise of the Internet, multicasting is likely to play an increasing role in both application and router implementation over the next few years.

The Internet Engineering Task Force (IETF) has introduced a number of standards to provide the infrastructure for multicast support, broadly divided into three areas: multicast addressing, host registration, and multicast routing. Chapter 2 covers the use of IP addresses for multicast use. The Internet Group Management Protocol (IGMP), as described in this chapter, handles registration. Multicast routing, also described in this chapter, is composed of several standards, as follows:

- Distance-Vector Multicast Routing Protocol (DVMRP)

- Multicast Open Shortest Path First (MOSPF), which is an extension to OSPF

- Protocol Independent Multicast (PIM)

- Core-Based Trees (CBT)

A related area of interest is support for real-time applications that use IP multicast, as well as the ability to deliver quality of service guarantees. We will, therefore, briefly cover some of the new protocols introduced in this area also. Readers wishing to keep up to date on this area should refer to [1].

4.1   Multicast application and routing concepts

Before launching into detail about various protocols of importance in multicasting, we need to review some of the key application and technology issues.

4.1.1   Multicast groups

A fundamental part of multicast support is the concept of a multicast group. A multicast group is a logical association of senders and receivers, usually related by application. Groups are usually formed dynamically; receivers request to join or leave a group at will, although statically configured membership is also possible. If there is only one sender, the group is called a point-to-multipoint group. If there are multiple senders, the group is called a multipoint-to-multipoint group. In the IP world a multicast group is associated with a specific class D IPv4 address—for example, 224.0.0.5 is the multicast group used by OSPF routers on which to send hello messages on multiaccess networks. Some of the more important (for this chapter) well-known addresses designated by IANA include the following:

- 224.0.0.1—all systems on the subnet

- 224.0.0.2—all routers on the subnet

- 224.0.0.4—all DVMRP routers

- 224.0.0.5—all OSPF routers

- 224.0.0.6—all OSPF designated routers

- 224.0.0.9—RIP2 routers

- 224.0.0.10—IGRP routers

- 224.0.0.11—mobile agents

- 224.0.0.13—all PIM routers

- 224.0.0.15—all CBT routers

- 224.0.0.18—VRRP

- 224.0.0.22—IGMP

Transient addresses, which may be assigned and reclaimed dynamically, include the following:

- 224.0.1.0 to 238.255.255.255—global scope

- 239.0.0.0 to 239.255.255.255—limited scope

- 239.255.0.0/16—site local scope

- 239.192.0.0/16—organization local scope

For up-to-date assignments, see [2].

4.1.2   Mapping multicasts onto MAC addresses

We learned in Chapter 2 that IPv4 multicasts use the class D address format (with 1110 as the high-order bits and the remaining 28 bits made available for the group address). Reference [3] discusses how IP multicast addresses get mapped onto MAC addresses prior to forwarding on the wire. To recap:

- For Ethernet and FDDI the mapping is straightforward for IPv4; the lower 23 bits of the IP address map onto the lower 23 bits of the MAC address, and the multicast bit is set. For example, 224.0.0.5 translates to 0x01005e000005. With IPv6 a 128-bit multicast address comprises an 8-bit prefix of all ones, a 4-bit flags field, a 4-bit scope field, and a 112-bit identifier. The flags field indicates whether this address is permanently assigned or not. The scope field indicates the application of the address (from a single subnet to global).

- For Token Ring an IP multicast address maps onto a single Token Ring functional address or the all, ones broadcast address. For example, 224.0.0.0 maps to c0-00-00-04-00-c0-00-00-04-00-00 (using the noncanonical format) or ff-ff-ff-ff-ff-ff. This is typically configurable on the interface.

4.1.3   Multicast application models

It is important to understand from the outset that multicasting is inappropriate for most traditional applications. The types of application best suited for multicast distribution are generally characterized by a high degree of asymmetry, the need to send the same information to many receivers simultaneously, and typically (though not always) some real-time constraint. Applications in this class include live market data feeds, videoconferencing, audioconferencing, push applications, streaming media, interactive white-boards, database replication, corporate communications, data warehousing, distributed computation, real-time workgroups, and interactive distance learning. This does not preclude other specialized application types from the benefits of multicasting—for example, applications that synchronize information among multiple nodes or attempt to discover services are likely to benefit from multicasting (in fact the latest generation of routing protocols such as OSPF have made good use of multicasting for some time). For applications suitable for multicasting there are essentially two data distribution models of interest, as follows:

- One-to-many—With this model the application transmits the same information to many receivers simultaneously, so the data flow is one way—for example, applications that transmit real-time stock quotes or news updates.

- Many-to-many—With this model the application shares information between a number of machines simultaneously, so the data flow is bidirectional. Since every receiver is potentially a transmitter, this form of application is in one-to-many mode when sending and many-to-one mode when receiving.

To date, most networked applications have relied almost exclusively on unicast or broadcast delivery mechanisms, with multicasting limited to specialized applications such as routing or control protocols. For certain types of user applications (e.g., market data feeds, multiuser videoconferences, and interactive distance learning) this is a particularly inefficient way to distribute information. These applications have a significant feature in common: large amounts of identical data being sent to many receivers simultaneously. Unicast and broadcast models can be described as follows:

- Reliable unicast model—With a unicast approach this requires discrete sessions to be established from the source to each recipient, and the source must send identical information down each connection. As the number of recipients increases, this approach begins to impose enormous overheads on both the sender and the network, and it cannot scale. The unicast model is reliable because the application makes use of the error detection and correction facilities of reliable transport protocols such as TCP.

- Unreliable broadcast model—The broadcast flooding approach is easier to implement; however, with a broadcast distribution strategy traffic is almost impossible to contain on flat networks. Special relay support is relied on to move traffic across routers. The broadcast model is unreliable because the application makes use of the best-effort facilities of datagram-based transport protocols such as UDP. Broadcasts affect all nodes on a multiaccess network, whether they are interested in the packet or otherwise; it is notable that broadcasts have been outlawed in IPv6.

Both unicast and broadcast mechanisms place increasing load on device CPUs and the network as the number of group members increases. Unicast distribution also requires the server to maintain session states for each individual receiver. Neither of these approaches can scale. In contrast, multicasts are handled differently by the receiver's NIC; a receiving station can be a member of one or more multicast groups, and the NIC can discard any frames not destined for those groups (typically using a high-speed hash function) without interrupting the CPU. Another advantage from the network designer's perspective is that multicasts can be filtered if required, since they can be differentiated from background broadcast traffic. This might be appropriate for additional traffic management purposes or for security (security policies could be applied on devices such as firewalls).

4.1.4   Multicast application design guidelines

Reference [4] describes the host requirements for supporting IP multicast and the default behavioral characteristics of multicast applications, as follows:

- An application must explicitly join a multicast group to receive datagrams destined for that group but need not be a member of a multicast group to send datagrams to it.

- When an application joins a group, it joins on only one local interface.

- When an application sends to a multicast address, outgoing datagrams are sent from only one local interface and have a default TTL of 1.

- All datagrams sent are also, by default, received on the same interface (i.e., datagrams are effectively looped back).

Reference [4] recommends a number of API functions for configuring multicast support. These include the ability to join or leave a multicast group, set the Time to Live (TTL), define local interfaces for multicast transmission or reception, and disable loopback of outgoing multicast datagrams. All of the APIs discussed in the following section support these functions as a minimum.

IP multicast APIs

Most of the major TCP/IP host implementations now offer multicast support, either integrated directly into the OS or via system patches. These implementations also typically support IGMP [4]. The three best-known APIs for UNIX, Windows, and Apple MAC operating systems are as follows (as one would expect, these APIs offer broadly the same functionality).

- Berkeley Sockets Multicast API—The Berkeley Sockets Multicast API is an extension to the Berkeley Socket API for UNIX platforms. While it is the de facto API for IP protocols, Berkeley Sockets is not limited to the IP family. Note that on UNIX systems you must have the relevant kernel patches installed.

- WinSock API—Windows Sockets version 2 (from Microsoft) is designed for 32-bit Windows platforms and is not restricted to IP. WinSock 2 is a subset of Berkeley Sockets (some functions such as ioctls are not supported) but adds Windows-specific functions (such as overlapping IO). WinSock 2 supports the Berkeley Sockets–compatible TCP/IP functions and also defines a set of protocol-independent multipoint APIs that can support IP multicast.

- Open Transport API—The Open Transport (OT) API is defined by Apple Computer, Inc. as its standard interface for creating network applications on Macintosh computers. OT is a superset of the XTI standard networking API defined by the X/Open UNIX vendor consortium (XTI is itself a superset of TLI, another de facto network API). As with Berkeley Sockets and WinSock, OT is protocol independent but also includes some protocol-specific APIs for support of IP multicast.

To meet the requirements set out in [4], basic support for multicasting involves the addition of five new socket options. The Berkeley Socket Multicast API specifies two sets of functions with the prefix IP_ or IPV6_ for IPv4 and IPv6, respectively, as follows:

- ADD_MEMBERSHIP—To join a multicast group

- DROP_MEMBERSHIP—To leave a multicast group

- MULTICAST_IF—To specify the default interface for outgoing multicasts

- MULTICAST_TTL (MULTICAST_HOPS in IPv6)—To specify the scope of outgoing multicasts

- MULTICAST_LOOP—To enable or disable loopback for outgoing multicasts

For further information on these APIs, the interested reader should refer to references [4–11].

Enabling legacy unicast applications for IP multicast

Converting an existing application to use a multicast distribution model can be relatively straightforward. The key issue is whether the application relies on a connection-oriented transport protocol (e.g., TCP) or a datagram-based transport protocol (e.g., UDP). These protocols can be described as follows:

- Unicast datagram-based applications—Datagram-based applications are easier to adapt, since they already assume a message-oriented, unreliable Transport Layer and most likely already have reliability functions built into the application itself. Typically this simply requires remapping a small number of unicast API calls to equivalent multicast-specific API functions. Multicast sources are further required to send traffic to an IP class D destination address and to adjust the IP Time to Live (TTL) according to the desired scope (i.e., according to the number of hops anticipated in the transmission path). They may also be required to disable loopback. In order to receive data from a multicast address the application must bind to a specific port number and join the multicast group.

- Unicast connection-oriented applications—Enabling applications that currently use connection-oriented protocols for multicast support is likely to be difficult, requiring significant redesign. These applications inherently rely on protocols such as TCP to provide reliable, acknowledged data delivery, and IP multicast is inherently unreliable (being based on UDP). Although some commercial products are shipping, standard protocols for reliable multicast are still an area of active research. Reliable IP multicast is discussed in section 4.9.

Design and implementation issues

While multicast applications can be very efficient in bandwidth utilization, they can get out of hand without some constraint in their implementation and delivery mechanisms. In particular, developers of multicast applications should aim for the following goals:

- Constrain the scope of multicast packets—Set the IP datagram TTL value judiciously to ensure that multicast are dropped quickly once they exceed the anticipated radius of the application (generally the TTL equals the number of router hops). Of course, on Internet applications this may not be so easy, and different multicast groups may have different radii at different times, but setting the TTL to 255 is never a good choice. If possible, attempt to dynamically discover the maximum radius of the network as part of the application; if not possible, then make sure this can be tuned through the application to suit different conditions. Multicast routers may implement configurable thresholds beyond which they can drop datagrams before the maximum IP TTL value (255) is reached. Ultimately, these applications will probably use administrative scoping with special multicast addresses rather than a simple TTL.

- Constrain and optimize bandwidth use—As part of the application development process you should characterize how much bandwidth your application requires, under a variety of conditions, and establish how its use of resources scales. If possible dynamically discover what bandwidth is available between senders and receivers and have receivers specify what service characteristic they can support.

- Select address and port numbers carefully—As with any traffic flow over a network, it is important to be able to differentiate that flow, for traffic engineering purposes and security, or to identify the application or group of users in question (from the receiver's standpoint). With multicast application a session can be identified (denoted by a session identifier) using a combination of destination multicast address, source unicast address, transmit and receive port numbers, and protocol. Session identifiers are an important consideration in the design and execution of a multicast application, especially on a public network such as the Internet or MBone. Depending upon the level of granularity applied, multiple application flows could potentially use the same session identifiers and effectively collide. Application developers should take particular care in the choice of multicast address and port number. In some cases the only solution will be to schedule application use, to avoid application collisions.

- Scheduling application use—If you are running several multicast applications, then (if possible) schedule major events (such as a conference or video broadcasts) so that they do not contend for bandwidth. If using the same address and port ranges, this is clearly even more important to avoid service problems.

In a small number of cases, the assignment of one or more permanent IP multicast addresses is warranted for multicast service. For example, standardized (well-known) applications and content providers with constant media streams may justify permanent multicast addresses. Permanent address and port number allocation falls under the control of the IANA [2]. In most cases addresses must be allocated from the available pool of free addresses, and on a large public internetwork there is no foolproof way for an application to select unique addressing parameters, since, by their very nature, multicast service and membership are dynamic. Strategies such as listening on an address for traffic or querying IGMP devices for membership information are, therefore, likely to fail. What is required is a coordinated approach based on a single or shared directory. Note that the MBone makes use of an application called Session Directory (SD), described in section 4.7.2, which resolves the problems of application conflicts.

4.1.5   Deployment issues on local and wide area networks

Local area deployment issues

On a multiaccess LAN, multicasting is relatively easy to implement, since IEEE 802 and other LAN protocols already provide for multicasting at the MAC layer. However, one of the main problems with real network topologies is multicast leakage—specifically, how to stop multicasts from flooding the wire once the multicast frame gets beyond a Layer 3 device. For example, many LANs employ multiport repeaters or multiport switches to collapse parts of the local area backbone for device concentration. If multicast routers are interconnected via such devices, then these concentrators will, by default, inject multicasts into all interfaces (other than the receive interface), whether there are group members attached or otherwise (see Figure 4.1). In this figure, Switch-1 receives incoming multicast packets, which it forwards (as expected) to all interfaces other than the receiving interface. Unfortunately, in this case only two users are interested in receiving these multicasts (situated on Net-1 and Net-3). The server farm and the bridged LAN (Net-4) are also affected unnecessarily. This problem exists regardless of whether or not VLANs are deployed [3]).

Without careful monitoring you might inadvertently be flooding multicasts and wasting valuable bandwidth on parts of the network that should never see this traffic. There are several ways to resolve such problems, including the following:

- Design around the problem—If possible, use private LAN links to interconnect the multicast-enabled interfaces on multicast routers

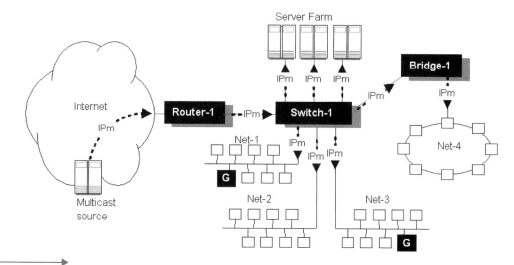

Figure 4.1   *Multicast leaking in a flattened LAN environment.*

(routers are generally configured on a per-interface basis for multicast support).

- Use filtering on intelligent Layer 2 switches—Dumb multiport repeaters will retransmit multicast traffic to all interfaces, and there is very little you can do about it without replacing the device. Buffered Layer 2 switches can usually be configured to block specific multicasts on a per interface basis. While this could become a serious maintenance problem, it will alleviate the problem to some extent. Of course, regardless of whether group members join or leave a group, an interface enabled for multicasting may still be forwarding unwanted multicasts if other active group members exist elsewhere on the switched LAN.

- Deploy multicast-aware switches—Perhaps the most appropriate approach is to use switches that are multicast aware, though this is likely to prove more expensive and require some strategic redesign. In this case there are several options, as follows:

  - GMRP—Use of the relatively recent IEEE 802.1 protocol called the GARP Multicast Registration Protocol (GMRP). This approach requires the host and switch to be GMRP aware and requires a change in the frame MTU size to accommodate additional data.
  - IGMP snooping—Internet Group Membership Protocol (described in section 4.2) can be deployed to operate promiscu-

ously on Layer 2 switches (usually implemented in hardware). The switch can, therefore, examine all packets for join or leave events and reprogram interfaces accordingly.

- Proprietary protocols—Such as the Cisco Group Membership Protocol (CGMP). In contrast to GMRP, CGMP offers a transparent approach to solving the problem through dynamic changes on the switches in response to join or leave events.

It is fair to say that network designers often overlook the deployment of IP multicast applications when the initial design is proposed, which in many cases is understandable. Furthermore, if you have flattened your original network with switches in key areas to take advantage of performance benefits, then this can lead to some nasty surprises when IP multicasting is subsequently enabled. Unfortunately, shared hubs and switches that don't constrain multicast flooding will need to be replaced.

Wide area deployment issues

On wide area networks, and especially on NonBroadcast MultiAccess (NBMA) networks, multicasting can be much more difficult to implement, because the wide area is often characterized by point-to-point links and circuits, as illustrated in Figure 4.2. A new approach to information distribution is required, and this has led to a new generation of multicast protocols specifically geared toward efficient information delivery across wide area internetworks. As we can see in Figure 4.2, the network comprises a number of point-to-point links and a wide area mesh network between routers. Each router attaches one or more LANs. There are several problems to resolve to provide efficient multicast delivery. How does the server know which LANs are used to attach group (G) members? How do group members register for service? What topology should be used to avoid replication? These are just some of the problems that multicast routing protocols have to resolve.

For maximum efficiency we ideally want to send a multicast packet exactly once on each link. The topology formed is a shortest path tree, with the sender at its source. We refer to this as a multicast tree, illustrated in Figure 4.3. As indicated earlier, for a network supporting different multicast groups there are likely to be many logical Spanning Tree distribution topologies at any particular time. In Figure 4.3, note that several networks have been pruned from the tree, since they do not currently have group members. Note also that Net 5 has two possible router interfaces and so R4 has been pruned back automatically, with R5 elected as the designated forwarder (avoiding packet replication on Net 5).

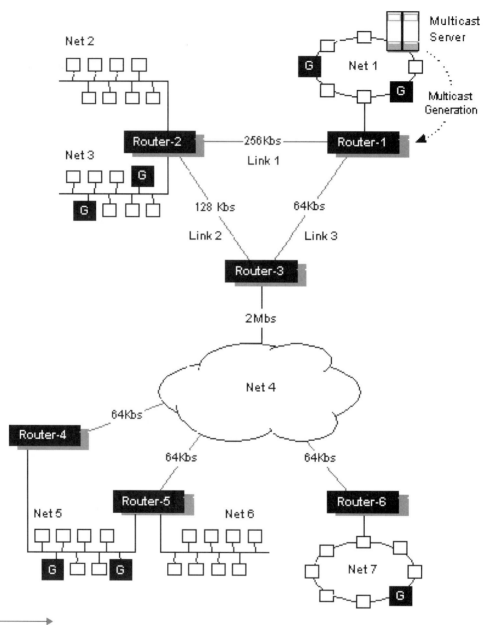

Figure 4.2   *Example internetwork topology required to support multicasting.*

Given that these topologies can vary over time as group membership shifts, one can imagine that there are some interesting problems to resolve. Several of these problems are summarized as follows, and this chapter

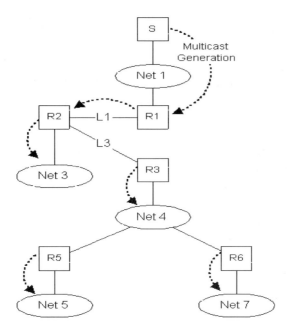

Figure 4.3
Multicast Spanning Tree, rooted at S, for the example network shown in Figure 4.2.

attempts to resolve these and other related questions via a number of protocols and algorithms.

- How does a receiver learn which multicast groups are available?

- How does a receiver register an interest in a group?

- How does a sender discover the set of receivers in a group?

- How does a sender ensure efficient and reliable delivery to all members of the group?

- How does an individual recipient notify the source about problems with delivery?

- How do senders deal with differing network delivery characteristics?

- How does our multicast network scale?

With IP multicasting it is important to recognize that the sender and receiver are decoupled, treated as two separate entities within a multicast group, for a reason. The sender need not know the physical location or address of a receiver; it uses the multicast address as a Rendezvous Point (RP) so that the two parties can communicate. Receivers must join the RP-rooted tree, and senders must register their existence with the RP. In this way the sender is insulated from the recipients, relying upon the network to take care of multicast distribution. Note that the term rendezvous point used in this context is purely an abstraction; some routing protocols implement a physical entity (typically software running on a router) called the rendezvous point to act as an intermediary between senders and recipients.

4.1.6 Common multicast techniques

Multicasting in a wide area network introduces some particular complexities. There are potentially a large number of receivers and many sources. Sources and receivers may join or leave groups even while multicast distribution is in progress. This requires that the multicast trees must be dynamically updated to reflect current status. In multiaccess LANs (such as Ethernet or FDDI) another problem is introduced. If we have multiple access points to these LANs, say via multiple routers (as illustrated in the case of Network-5 in Figure 4.2), then we could end up forwarding duplicate multicasts to each LAN. We need to exploit the broadcast nature of such networks and ensure that only one multicast is forwarded.

If a multicast is to be forwarded to receivers over multiple router hops, then we could simply flood all multicasts throughout the network to ensure that all receivers get the data. For a single application with a well-distributed set of receivers this would work, but for a network supporting several multicast applications and a diverse population of receivers this cannot scale and is potentially highly inefficient (many segments will be receiving unwanted multicasts, which simply wastes bandwidth). Flooding runs the risk of excessive packet replication. We could avoid this by maintaining state information at each router indicating which multicasts have already been forwarded, but this is not very attractive. A better mechanism is, therefore, required for receivers to inform individual routers as to which multicasts they are interested in receiving and how to avoid duplicates.

Reverse Path Forwarding (RPF)

One simple technique for flooding multicasts intelligently is referred to as reverse path forwarding (sometimes called reverse path multicasting). With this technique a router will forward a packet from a source, S, to all its interfaces, if, and only if, the packet arrives on an interface that corresponds to the router's shortest path tree to S. An interface that passes this check is called the RPF interface. An RPF lookup for a source returns the RPF interface and the next-hop information. Packets that are received on interfaces that are not in the Spanning Tree for a particular multicast tree are simply discarded.

Reverse path forwarding allows a data stream to reach all LANs but does not prevent duplicates from occurring entirely, since we use no intelligence on the downstream flooding mechanism. We can extend the technique further by making use of the unicast routing table to control which interfaces to downstream routers are used to flood. If the downstream router, R, is not included in the shortest path tree, then it should not receive multicasts from S. This introduces another potential problem, where multiple equal-cost paths are introduced, but this can be resolved using tie breakers and heuristics, as described later in this chapter. Reverse path forwarding, and its extensions, requires each router to know its shortest path to every source and the shortest path from each neighbor to every source. This information can be recovered from the unicast routing table maintained by IGPs such as RIP, OSPF, and BGP.

Pruning and grafting

Reverse path forwarding ensures that all LANs receive multicasts, but clearly some LANs may not require them. A router attached to a LAN that does not want to receive a particular multicast group can send a prune message to its parent up the shortest path distribution tree, in order to prevent further packets from being transmitted. For example, in Figure 4.3, if group members on Network 7 decide to leave the group or are switched off, then Router-6 can send a prune request up to Router-3. Router-3 will no longer forward multicasts over Network 4 to Router-6 (it must still forward multicasts to Router-5 of course). Prune messages can be associated with a multicast group or with a particular multicast group and a multicast source (in the case where there are multiple senders you could, therefore, decide which sender to register with). In the simple case a router only needs to maintain prune indications on an output interface basis for a whole group. In the latter case a router needs to maintain information on each interface indicating both the group and sender address associations.

The mechanism for adding new branches to the multicast tree is called grafting. If a router receives requests for multicasts (from devices attached to an interface not in the current tree), it can request addition to a multicast tree by sending a graft request to its parent. In our example network (Figure 4.3), if a host on Network 6 decides to rejoin the multicast group, then Router-6 must send a graft request up to Router-3. Note that only one Round-Trip Time (RTT) from the new receiver to the nearest active branch of the tree is required for the new receiver to start receiving traffic.

Expanding ring search

Expanding ring search is a clever technique used to discover resources dynamically. It is used to discover the nearest available resources (e.g.,

IGMP hosts use this technique to discover the nearest multicast server). The technique exploits the Time to Live (TTL) field of IP, exploiting the following information:

- A multicast datagram with a TTL of zero is restricted to a host (i.e., it is internal and should not be transmitted).

- A multicast datagram with a TTL of one is restricted to a subnet (i.e., a router should not forward it).

- A multicast datagram with a TTL greater than one is typically forwarded by routers over several hops, decremented by one at each hop, and eventually discarded when the TTL reaches zero.

By starting with a TTL of one, and then incrementing the TTL by one at each pass, a sender can perform an expanding ring search for a resource until the nearest listening resource responds. On receiving a response the sender locates the closest resource (in hops). For example, a host can use this technique to locate the nearest available server, printer, or gateway.

4.1.7 Multicast routing protocols

It is important to understand that multicast routing is quite different from unicast routing; the differences are subtle but fundamental. Whereas unicast routing is concerned primarily with the destination of a packet, multicast routing is largely concerned with its source. In a sense multicast routing is backward oriented. IP multicast traffic for a particular source-destination group pair (s, g) is transmitted from the source to multiple receivers via a Spanning Tree, which connects all the hosts in that particular group. This implies that in a large internetwork there could be many overlaid Spanning Trees, one for each group, with each topology dependent upon the location and distribution of multicast sources and recipients. Some protocols also support the concept of shared trees (*, g), where several multicast groups share a common tree. Another subtle difference is that multicast routing is generally much more dynamic compared with unicast routing. Multicast routes and multicast traffic flows depend upon the state of a multicast source and whether nodes wish to receive multicasts at any particular time. Multicast routes may, therefore, appear and disappear as part of normal operations.

There are currently a number of multicast routing protocols available for IP, and each uses different techniques to construct its multicast delivery trees. These protocols generally follow one of two basic approaches, depending on the anticipated distribution of multicast group members throughout the network. They can be described as followed:

- Dense distribution model—This model assumes that the multicast group members are densely distributed throughout the network (i.e., many of the subnets contain at least one group member) and that bandwidth is plentiful. Dense-mode multicast routing protocols rely on a technique called flooding to propagate information to all other routers, leaving the responsibility of sensibly pruning back the various multicast trees in the hands of cooperating multicast routers. This operation is sometimes referred to as flood and prune. Dense-mode routing protocols include Distance-Vector Multicast Routing Protocol (DVMRP) and Protocol-Independent Multicast–Dense Mode (PIM–DM).

- Sparse distribution model—This model assumes that the multicast group members are sparsely distributed throughout the network and bandwidth is possibly restricted (e.g., across many regions of the Internet or if users are connected via ISDN lines). Note that sparse-mode routing does not imply that the group has a few members, just that they are widely dispersed. In this case, flooding would unnecessarily waste network bandwidth and could cause serious performance problems. Hence, sparse-mode multicast routing protocols must rely on more efficient techniques to set up and maintain multicast trees, specifically the deployment of intermediate registration agents called Rendezvous Points (RPs) and the use of explicit joins to register interest in a group. The RP initially creates a shared tree (*, g) to enable all multicast groups to deliver traffic via the RP. Sparse-mode routing protocols include Multicast Open Shortest Path First (MOSPF), Core-Based Trees (CBT), and Protocol-Independent Multicast–Sparse Mode (PIM–SM).

Sparse-mode protocols have a number of significant advantages over dense-mode protocols. First, sparse mode offers better scalability, since only routers on the path between a source and a group member must maintain state information. By contrast, dense mode requires state information to be maintained in all routers in the network. Secondly, sparse-mode protocols are much more conservative in their use of network bandwidth, since receivers must explicitly join a group to initiate multicast traffic flow to their particular location. The disadvantages of sparse-mode protocols largely relate to the use of an RP. For example, the RP could prove a single point of failure, either through actual device failure or system overloading (although it is typically possible to deploy RPs in a load-sharing mode). The RP can also become a magnet for multicast traffic leading to nonoptimal paths. Protocols such as PIM–SM solve this problem by switching from a shared tree (*, g) to an optimal shortest path tree for the particular (s, g) multicast pair, once a specified traffic threshold is reached.

All of these multicast routing algorithms and protocols have evolved rapidly over the last few years, and currently there is no absolute winner. This chapter compares and discusses the pertinent features and deployment issues so that useful design choices can be made. We will also investigate strategies for interoperability and discuss some of the new protocols available to support real-time multicast applications.

4.2   Group registration with IGMP

The requirement for a host to be able to join or leave a multicast group is fundamental to multicasting. Membership of a group is interface specific and dynamic (i.e., processes or applications may join and leave one or more groups at will). To support this functionality the Internet Group Management Protocol (IGMP) is used by hosts and routers to communicate multicast group status. (See Figure 4.4.)

IGMP Field Definitions

- Type—Specifies a query or a report. Note that IGMPv2 did away with the IGMPv1 Version field and expects subsequent implementations to recognize messages by their type. Current types include:

  - 0x11—Membership Query. There are two subtypes of membership query messages: general query, used to learn which groups have members on an attached network, and group-specific query, used to learn if a particular group has any members on an attached network. These two messages are differentiated by the group address; a general query uses the all-hosts group address 224.0.0.1, whereas a group-specific query uses the group address being queried. Note that membership query messages are referred to simply as query messages.
  - 0x12—version 1 membership report (for backwards compatibility with IGMPv1)
  - 0x16—version 2 membership report
  - 0x17—leave group: sent to the all-routers group address 224.0.0.2

Figure 4.4   *IGMP message format.*

- Max Response Time (MRT)—Used in membership query messages; in all other messages, it is set to 0 by the sender and ignored by receivers. MRT specifies (in units of 1/10 second) the maximum time allowed before sending a responding report. Modifying this setting allows IGMPv2 routers to tune the leave latency (i.e., the time between the moment when the last host leaves a group and when the routing protocol is notified that there are no more members). It also allows tuning of the burstiness of IGMP traffic on a subnet.

- Checksum—A 16-bit checksum calculated as the ones complement of the ones complement sum of the whole IGMP message (i.e., the entire IP payload). Prior to computing the checksum, the checksum field is set to 0.

- Group Address—In a membership query message, this field is set to 0 when sending a general query and set to the group address being queried when sending a group-specific query. In a membership report or leave group message, this field holds the IP multicast group address of the group being reported or left.

Group membership requests are sent from hosts directly to their nearest multicast router. When a host is multihomed, it can join any group on one or more of its interfaces or subnets. The host keeps track internally of which processes are interested in which group [4]. IGMP uses the expanding ring search technique (described earlier in this chapter) to locate multicast servers. A special range of addresses, 224.0.0.0 through 224.0.0.255, is intended for applications that never need to multicast further than one hop. A multicast router should never forward a datagram with one of these addresses as the destination, regardless of the TTL. For the interested reader IGMPv2 is specified in [12], which updates [4].

4.2.1   Message format

IGMP messages are encapsulated in IP datagrams. IP uses the protocol identifier 2 to indicate IGMP, sets the Type-of-Service (ToS) field to 0, and the Time-to-Live (TTL) field to 1. In IPv4 multicast support is optional, whereas in IPv6 IGMP functionality is integrated into ICMPv6, since all IPv6 hosts are required to support multicasting. Figure 4.4 shows the format of the eight-byte IGMPv2 message.

4.2.2   Operation

The basic operations of IGMP take place between routers and hosts. Multicast routers need to establish whether hosts are interested in specific multicast groups on a specific interface at any particular time (otherwise, if host machines die, how do we know if they are still interested in receiving multicasts?). Routers achieve this by a process of learning. Queries are sent out to the all-hosts multicast address (224.0.0.1) at roughly two-minute intervals to all IGMP-enabled interfaces, and the reports coming back from hosts are used to maintain a database of group memberships associated with each interface, together with a timer for each group membership. Membership requires the presence of at least one active member of a multicast group on a specific interface. When a router receives a multicast datagram, it forwards the datagram (mapped to a corresponding Layer 2 multicast address) on only those interfaces that still have hosts registering an interest in that group. Note that if a router has multiple physical interfaces on a single network, IGMP need run on only one of them. By contrast, hosts must run IGMP on all interfaces that require group membership.

A multicast router running IGMP will assume one of two states with respect to each of its attached network interfaces: Querier or non-Querier. There is normally only one Querier per physical network; so, for example, on a multiaccess LAN, one router is responsible for issuing queries, and the rest stay quiet. The Querier is determined by a simple election process.

IGMP timers

IGMPv2 operations rely on a number of key timers. Most of these timers are configurable; however, if nondefault settings are used, they must be consistent among all routers on a single link. The timers include the following:

- Robustness_Variable (default: 2)—This allows tuning for the expected packet loss on a subnet. If a subnet is expected to be lossy, this variable may be increased. IGMP is robust to (Robustness Variable-1) packet losses. The Robustness_Variable must not be zero and should not be one.

- Query_Interval (default: 125 seconds)—This is the interval between general queries sent by the Querier. By varying this interval an administrator can tune the number of IGMP messages on the subnet; larger values cause IGMP queries to be sent less often.

- Query_Response_Interval (default: 100—i.e., 10 seconds)—This is the max response time inserted into the periodic general queries. By varying this interval, an administrator can tune the burstiness of IGMP messages on the subnet; larger values make the traffic less bursty, since host responses are spread out over a larger interval. Note that (Query_Response_Interval/10) must be less than the Query_Interval.

- Group_Membership_Interval—This is the amount of time that must pass before a multicast router decides there are no more members of a group on a network. This value must be (Robustness_Variable × Query_Interval) − Query_Response_Interval.

- Other_Querier_Present_Interval—This is the length of time that must pass before a multicast router decides that there is no longer another multicast router that should be the Querier. This value must be [(Robustness Variable) × Query_Interval) + (Query_Response_Interval/2)].

- Startup_Query_Interval (default: Query_Interval/4)—This is the interval between general queries sent by a Querier on startup.

- Startup_Query_Count (default: Robustness Variable)—This is the number of queries sent out on startup, separated by the Startup_Query_Interval.

- Last_Member_Query_Interval (default: 10—i.e., 1 second)—This is the max response time inserted into group-specific queries sent in response to leave group messages and is also the amount of time between group-specific query messages. This value may be tuned to modify the leave latency of the network. A reduced value results in reduced time to detect the loss of the last member of a group.

- Last_Member_Query_Count (default: Robustness Variable)—The Last_Member_Query_Count is the number of group-specific queries sent before the router assumes there are no local members.

- Unsolicited_Report_Interval (default:—10 seconds)—This is the time between repetitions of a host's initial report of membership in a group.

- Version_1_Router_Present_Timeout (value: 400 seconds)—This is how long a host must wait after hearing an IGMPv1 query before it may send any IGMPv2 messages.

Querier election process

All multicast routers start up in the Querier state on each attached network. If a multicast router hears a query message from a router with a lower IP address, then it must defer and enter the non-Querier state; so ultimately the router with the lowest IP address wins. If a router has not heard a query message from another router for Other_Querier_Present_Interval, it resumes the role of Querier.

Building group membership tables

As described previously, in order to solicit group membership information a router periodically sends (at Query_Interval) a general query for all attached networks where the router is the Querier. Query messages are sent with a TTL of one to ensure they are not forwarded, and the long interval ensures that IGMP traffic is low. The group address in a query is set to 0, since the router expects a response from a host for every group that contains one or more members. Host membership for the all-hosts multicast group (224.0.0.1) is automatic. Each host that wishes to remain a member of one or more groups replies once for each group. These replies are sent after a random delay to ensure that IGMP does not cause traffic spikes on a subnet. Note that during the startup phase, a router should send Startup_Query_Count general queries more frequently (at Startup_Query_Interval) to the all-systems multicast group (224.0.0.1) in order to precharge its knowledge base.

When a host receives a general query, it sets delay timers for each group of which it is a member on the receiving interface. Each timer is set to a different random value, selected from the range (0 ± max response time], where max response time is specified in the query packet. When a host receives a group-specific query, it sets a delay timer for the specific group being queried, assuming that it is a member on the receiving interface. Subsequent queries may cause this timer to be reset but only if the specified max response time is less than the value of the timer. When a timer expires, the host multicasts a version 2 membership report for that group, with an IP TTL of one. If the host receives another host's report while it has a timer running, it stops its timer for the specified group and does not send a report in order to avoid duplicate reports.

When a router receives a report, it adds the group specified to the receive interface database and sets the timer for the membership at Group_Membership_Interval. Subsequent reports refresh this timer. If no reports are received for a particular group before this timer has expired, the router assumes that the group has no active members on that interface and so the interface is pruned.

Joining a multicast group

To join a group, the host first sends an unsolicited IGMPv2 membership report to the interface on which it requires service. This report is addressed to the multicast group of interest with a TTL of one. To allow for the possibility of the initial membership report being lost, it is recommended that the report is transmitted once or twice after a short delay (Unsolicited_Report_Interval). Multicast routers on the same subnet receive the report and set a flag (if not already set) to indicate that at least one host on the subnet is an active group member. If that branch was previously pruned, the router will graft the subnet onto the distribution tree and start to forward multicasts. Multicast routers must listen to all multicast addresses in order to detect such reports. If other applications or processes on the same subnet subsequently join the same multicast group, there is no need for the host to send another report.

On a large subnet there could be many hosts registering an interest in various multicast groups. To avoid excessive bandwidth spikes, [4] recommends that either a random timer be used by hosts, or, since routers do not care how many hosts are members of a group, only one host need register interest for a group on an interface. Hosts are already listening to registration claims (since they are issued to the multicast group address of interest) and can cancel any pending claims if another host registers interest on the same subnet. This saves wasting resources unnecessarily. If no hosts claim membership of a group within a specified interval, a multicast router will assume that there are no group members on that interface and take appropriate action (such as pruning, if necessary).

Leaving a multicast group

When a host leaves a multicast group, it has one of the two following choices:

- If it was the last host to reply to a query with a membership report for that group, it should send a leave group message to the all-routers multicast group (224.0.0.2). Note that some older implementations use the group multicast destination address, and this should also be supported for backward compatibility.

- If it was not the last host to reply to a query, it may send nothing, since there must be another member on the subnet.

Note that IGMPv1 relied on membership dying out through lack of response; IGMPv2 modifies this behavior to reduce traffic and speed up convergence. A host that cannot maintain status information can always send a leave group message. If a Querier receives a leave group message for a multicast group on an interface that is thought to have active group members, it sends group-specific queries to those groups remaining. If no reports are received after the response time of the last query expires, the routers assume that the group has no local members. Any Querier to non-Querier transition is ignored during this time; the same router keeps sending the group-specific queries. Furthermore, non-Queriers must ignore leave group messages, and Queriers should ignore leave group messages for which there are no group members on the reception interface.

Multicast distribution

IGMP operates effectively as an ES-IS protocol for multicasts; it does not deal with the mechanisms for multicast distribution between multicast routers. There are several multicast routing protocols (such as MOSPF or DVMRP) available for multicast packet routing between multicast routers. Figure 4.5 shows interaction between IGMP and a multicast routing protocol operating in different parts of the topology. Multicasts are transmitted from a sender through a Spanning Tree to the receivers. If none of the hosts on an interface requires multicasts, the branch is pruned. In Figure 4.5, we see that S1 and S2 are multicast servers propagating multicasts on groups A

Figure 4.5
Multicast routing operations with IGMP.

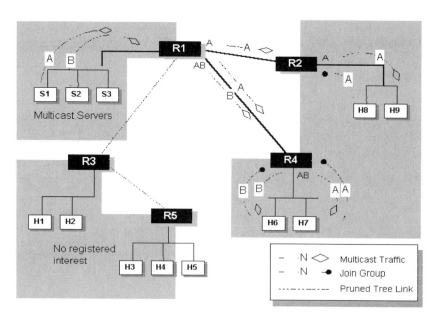

and B, respectively. Shaded areas show current areas where IGMP is running. Hosts 7 and 8 register an interest in group A multicasts, while Host 6 registers an interest in group B multicasts. Routers 3 and 5 prune back the distribution tree to Router 1, since they have no current hosts requiring multicast service. All routers periodically send IGMP requests out on all downstream interfaces to check status. Any host wishing to receive multicasts must issue IGMP report and then respond positively to any future router IGMP requests. The protocol running between routers (i.e., unshaded areas) could be MOSPF or DVMRP.

When a host or a multicast router receives a multicast datagram, its action is dependent upon the TTL value and the destination IP address, as follows:

- A datagram with a TTL of zero is restricted to the source host and should not be transmitted.

- A datagram with a TTL of one will be seen by all hosts on the subnet that are members of the group. Multicast routers decrement the TTL value to zero. Multicast routers view this as a normal occurrence, and they do not send ICMP time-exceeded messages (which would be the norm for unicasts with a low TTL).

- A datagram with a TTL of two (or greater) will be seen by all hosts that are members of the group and all multicast routers (depending upon the actual TTL and the radius of the network). The action of the routers depends on the multicast group address, as follows:

  - [224.0.0.0–224.0.0.255]—Multicast routers will not forward datagrams with destination IP addresses in this range; these addresses are intended for single-hop multicasting applications only. When a host issues a report to these addresses, this informs other hosts on the subnet that the host is a member of the destination multicast group. The exceptions to this rule are 224.0.0.1 and 224.0.0.2.

  - [Other multicast groups]—Datagrams with other destination addresses are forwarded as normal by a multicast router. Each router decrements the TTL value by one at each hop, which allows a host to locate the nearest server using an expanding ring search.

Compatibility with IGMPv1 devices

The changes between IGMPv2 and IGMPv1 were fairly significant and are summarized as follows:

- The IGMPv1 Version and Type fields were combined into a single Type field.

- A new IGMP Type was assigned to version 2 membership report messages, so a router may differentiate between an IGMPv1 and IGMPv2 host report.

- The leave group message type was added.

- The unused field in the membership query message was reallocated to a new max response time field.

- The IGMPv2 specification now specifies a Querier election mechanism.

- The requirements on validity checking for membership queries and membership reports were relaxed.

- The IP router alert option [13] is required to be in all IGMPv2 packets.

For full details, refer to [12], which imposes several requirements to enable backward compatibility. If an IGMPv2 host is deployed on a subnet where there are IGMP hosts that predate IGMPv2, the host must allow its membership report to be suppressed by either a version 1 membership report or a version 2 membership report. If an IGMPv2 router is deployed on a subnet where there are other IGMP hosts that predate IGMPv2, two further requirements apply, as follows:

- If a router receives a version 1 membership report, it must set a timer to note that there are version 1 hosts present that are members of the group for which it heard the report.

- If there are version 1 hosts present for a particular group, a router must ignore any leave group messages that it receives for that group.

Note also that in some older versions of IGMPv2, hosts send leave messages to the remaining multicast group. A router should accept leave messages addressed in this manner for backward compatibility. In all cases, however, hosts must send leave messages to the all-routers address (224.0.0.2). For further details refer to [12].

4.3   Multicast routing with DVMRP

Distance-Vector Multicast Routing Protocol (DVMRP) is a relatively old dense-mode multicast routing protocol, first defined in 1988 [14], although a new version of the protocol (DVMRPv3) is currently the subject of an IETF Internet Draft [15]. DVMRP is used to propagate multicasts through an internetwork by building per source group multicast delivery trees for use within an AS. DVMRP is used for multicast distribution only; routers that are required to distribute both unicasts and multicasts must also run a traditional unicast routing protocol (such as OSPF or RIP).

DVMRP is essentially a flood-and-prune routing protocol (hence, dense-mode). It builds per source multicast trees based upon routing exchanges and then dynamically creates per source group multicast delivery trees by selectively pruning the multicast tree for each source. DVMRP performs reverse path forwarding to determine whether multicast traffic should be forwarded to downstream interfaces. To identify which interface leads back to the source, DVMRP implements its own unicast routing protocol, together with a distributed distance-vector routing algorithm. This unicast routing protocol is similar to RIP and uses a hop-based metric (consequently, the path of multicast traffic may differ from the path of unicast traffic). Using these techniques, source-rooted shortest path trees can be constructed to reach all group members from each source network of multicast traffic. For the interested reader, the application of distance-vector routing to multicast trees is described in [16].

4.3.1 Message format

Figure 4.6 shows the format of the DVMRP message.

DVMRP field definitions

- Type—Always 0x13 for a DVMRP packet.

- Code—Identifies the DVMRP message type, as follows:

    - 1—Probe (for neighbor discovery)
    - 2—Report (for route exchange)
    - 3—Ask neighbors (obsolete)
    - 4—Neighbors (obsolete)
    - 5—Ask neighbors 2 (request neighbor list—diagnostic/troubleshooting)
    - 6—Neighbors 2 (respond with neighbor list—diagnostic/troubleshooting)
    - 7—Prune (for pruning multicast delivery trees)
    - 8—Graft (for grafting multicast delivery trees)
    - 9—Graft ack (for acknowledging graft messages)

- Checksum—A 16-bit checksum calculated as the ones complement of the ones complement sum of the whole IGMP message (i.e., the entire IP payload). Prior to computing the checksum, the checksum field is set to 0.

Figure 4.6
DVMRP message format.

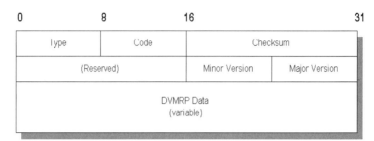

- Minor version—Minor version number of the protocol. Reference [15] specifies 0xFF.

- Major version—Major version number of the protocol. Reference [15] specifies 3.

- DVMRP data—Parameters and data dependent upon the type of DVMRP message. Refer to [15] for details.

DVMRP messages are encapsulated in IP datagrams and are essentially a modified form of IGMP. DVMRP uses the basic IGMP header format, introduces a new type code, and makes use of the Unused field as a subtype that is used to specify the DVMRP message type.

4.3.2 Operation

DVMRP constructs a separate distribution tree for each (s, g) flow initially via reverse path forwarding and flooding techniques. Packets are forwarded out of all interfaces on a distribution tree, initially assuming every branch is part of the multicast group. To optimize delivery trees and deal with dynamic group membership changes, DVMRP relies on pruning and grafting techniques. Pruning eliminates tree branches that have no multicast group members and also eliminates redundant nonshortest paths from any receiver to the source (such as multiple interfaces onto a broadcast LAN).

Terminology

The following terminology is used when describing DVMRP operations:

- Upstream interface—the interface on the shortest path tree back to the source of a multicast group. Sometimes called the reverse path forwarding interface.

- Downstream interfaces—the set of interfaces nominated for multicast forwarding for a particular multicast group. By definition this will not include the upstream interface.

- Received interface—the interface on which a multicast packet is received (which may or may not be the upstream interface).

- Nonleaf network—a network with dependent downstream neighbors for a particular source network.

- Leaf network—a network with no dependent downstream neighbors for a particular source network.

- Neighbor—an adjacent DVMRP router (i.e., a peer router).

- Designated forwarder—a router interface elected to inject packets for a particular multicast group.

- IGMP local group database—a list of active membership information maintained by all IP multicast routers on each physical, multicast-enabled network interface.

- Upstream router—The router responsible for supplying multicasts for a particular (s, g) pair (i.e., the router one hop closer to the source on a particular multicast tree).

Timers

A summary of the key DVMRP timing parameters is given in the following chart (for full details refer to [15]):

Parameter	Value (Seconds)
Probe interval	10
Neighbor timeout interval	35
Minimum flash update interval	5
Route report interval	60
Route expiration time	40
Route hold-down	$2 \times$ route report interval
Prune lifetime	variable (< 2 hours)
Prune retransmission time	3, followed by exponential back-off
Graft retransmission time	5, followed by exponential back-off

Routing process

DVMRP routers use distance-vector routing to establish routing tables of source-based shortest-path multicast trees. The routing process is similar to

RIP. As with RIP, the routing table is propagated to all DVMRP routers, using routing updates in order to provide a consistent view of the network. Initially, each DVMRP router knows only about its local interfaces. In order to learn about the complete network topology it must acquire one or more neighbors. DVMRP routers discover neighbors dynamically by sending neighbor probe messages on multicast-enabled network interfaces and virtual tunnel interfaces. Probes are sent frequently (every ten seconds) to the all-DVMRP-routers multicast address (224.0.0.4). Each probe contains the list of neighbors for which probe messages have been received on that interface. On receiving a probe a router will attempt to establish a full-duplex adjacency with its neighbor.

Each router sends routing updates, comprising the network address and mask of directly connected interfaces, plus all routes received from its neighbors, at regular intervals (default 60 seconds). The metric used in route entries is hop based, and this applies to both standard routing interfaces and tunnel interfaces. Routing metrics comprise the aggregated path cost, as per RIP, but with infinity set to 32. This constrains the network diameter and places an upper bound on convergence time.

As part of the routing exchange process, upstream routers determine whether any downstream routers are dependent on them for forwarding multicasts from particular sources. This is achieved using a technique called poison reverse. When a downstream router selects a particular upstream router as the best next hop to a given source, this is flagged by echoing back the route on the upstream interface with a metric equal to the original metric plus infinity. Hence, legal metric values lie between 1 and 63, as follows:

- 1 to 31 indicates reachable source networks.

- 32 (infinity) indicates unreachable source networks.

- 33 to 63 indicates that the downstream router originating the report depends upon the upstream router to provide multicast datagrams for a particular source network.

When the upstream router sees a metric that lies between 33 and 63, it caches the downstream router address and associated source network in a list associated with that particular interface. This list is used to determine whether to prune back specific IP source multicast trees.

Building multicast trees

When an IP multicast datagram arrives at a DVMRP router, the router checks that the upstream interface matches the received interface. If the interfaces do not match, the packet will be discarded; otherwise, a DVMRP router will forward the datagram to a set of downstream interfaces (including tunnel interfaces), depending upon the state of the interface. If the interface is a leaf network then the IGMP local group database must be consulted. If the destination group address is listed in this database, and the router is the designated forwarder for the source, then the interface is included in the list of downstream interfaces. If there are no group members on the interface, then the interface is removed from the list of downstream interfaces.

Initially, all non-leaf networks (i.e., those with dependent neighbors) should be included in the downstream interface list. This enables all downstream routers to see traffic for a particular (s, g) pair, which they may subsequently prune back (depending upon group membership status for a particular interface) and later reinstate through grafting. Note that this process is applied on a multicast group (s, g) basis, not globally; there may be several overlaid trees with some branches in both a live and pruned state for different multicast groups. Delivery trees are, therefore, calculated and updated dynamically to track the membership of individual groups.

Pruning

If a router determines that all of its downstream interfaces do not meet the criteria for forwarding, it initiates a prune operation by notifying the upstream router that it no longer wants traffic destined for a particular (s, g) pair. This notification is done via a DVMRP prune message upstream to the router to which it expects to forward datagrams from a particular source. When the upstream router receives prune messages, it can remove the interface from its downstream interface list. In the event that the upstream router is able to remove all of its downstream interfaces, it can send a prune message to its upstream router. This process continues until all unnecessary branches are removed from the delivery tree. In Figure 4.7 the multicast delivery tree for this particular service means that links L2 and L6 are logically disconnected, since they are not on the shortest path. In Figure 4.7(a) H7's group membership on Net3 lapses and on R6 DVMRP is informed by IGMP that its local database is empty. R6 sends a prune message to its upstream neighbor, R3, requesting disconnection of the branch from the tree. R3 stops forwarding multicasts for source S. Note that R3 cannot prune itself from the tree, even though it has no hosts requiring multicast service, because it has a downstream dependent neighbor, R5. In Figure 4.7(b) H7 some time later requests multicast service via IGMP. DVMRP is notified on R6, which then sends a graft message to upstream neighbor R3. R3 sends a graft ack, and the branch is reinstated on the multicast delivery tree.

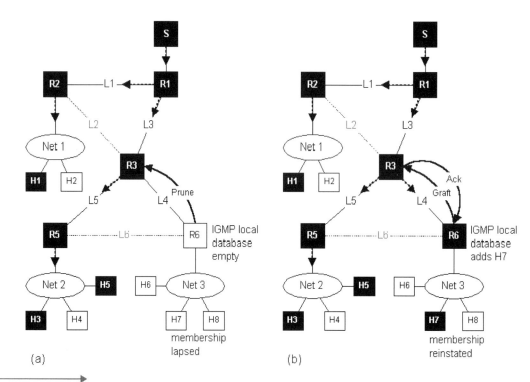

Figure 4.7   *Multicast network running DVMRP between routers and IGMP on the router inter-faces.*

Once branches are pruned back there is no way for routers on these dead branches to know about particular (s, g) flows. To overcome this, DVMPR imposes a lifetime on prune states and periodically resumes the flooding process whenever the prune lifetime expires. If the interface is still a nonleaf, the interface is simply joined back onto the delivery tree. If the multicast datagrams being received are still not required, the prune process is undertaken once more. Note that the lifetime of the prune sent by an upstream router must be equal to the minimum of the lifetime still remaining from the prunes received from downstream routers (each prune message carries its own lifetime parameter).

Grafting

IP multicast promotes the concept of dynamic group membership, so rather than wait for the prune lifetime to expire, hosts on previously pruned branches may proactively initiate multicast delivery at any time. The process starts with a host registering interest in a multicast group via IGMP. Once an interface is known to have interested users, DVMRP routers use graft messages to cancel the prunes that are in place. This is done recursively—all the way back up the multicast delivery tree—with each downstream router sending a graft to its upstream neighbor in turn, until the branch is fully connected. Since there is no way to tell if a graft message sent upstream was lost or the source simply stopped sending traffic, each graft message is positively acknowledged with a DVMRP graft ack message. If an acknowledgment is not received within a graft timeout period, the graft message should be retransmitted, using binary exponential back-off between retransmissions. Duplicate graft ack messages are ignored.

Designated forwarder

If multiple DVMRP routers are attached to the same multiaccess network, then multicast may be duplicated unnecessarily (depending upon the upstream topology). DVMRP automatically prunes back duplicate paths by electing a designated multicast forwarder for each source address (applied on an interface basis). DVMRP routers on a common network will peer and exchange routing updates and will, therefore, have topological knowledge of each other's aggregate metric back to a particular source. The router with the lowest metric to a source is elected to the forwarding state; all other routers must defer. Where routers have the same aggregate path cost, the router with the lowest IP address is elected. In this way DVMRP elects designated forwarders for every source network on every downstream interface.

Tunneling

Since not all IP routers support native multicast routing, DVMRP includes support for tunneling IP multicast datagrams. To achieve this, multicast datagrams are encapsulated in IP unicast packets and then addressed and forwarded to the next multicast router along the destination path. DVMRP treats tunnel interfaces in a manner identical to physical network interfaces, so even if there are several routers that do not support native multicast routing in the intermediate path, these are transparent to the multicast tree. In practice, tunnels generally use either IP-IP [17] or Generic Routing Encapsulation (GRE), although other encapsulation methods can be used. Perhaps the best example of DVMRP tunnel deployment is the MBone (described in section 4.7.2).

Note that in the DVMRP implementations that predate version 3, DVMRP protocol messages were forwarded directly to the unicast tunnel end-point addresses (since they are unicast, they do not actually require encapsulation). Although more direct, it increases the complexity of firewall configuration, since there are multiple flow types to deal with. The latest incarnation of the protocol [15] specifies that all DVMRP protocol messages should be sent encapsulated via the tunnel.

4.3.3   Design issues

The requirement to flood frequently means that DVMRP has limited scalability and is inappropriate for large internetworks with sparsely distributed receivers (i.e., the norm). There is no support for shared trees and the maximum number of hops must be less than 32, constraining the scope of the network. These problems are amplified with early implementations of DVMRP in that they did not support pruning (specifically, DVMRP versions 1 and 2). DVMRP converges slowly, suffering from the same problems as RIP. DVMRP requires a significant amount of state information to be stored in routers (i.e., [s, g] for all pairs). Since route reports may need to refresh several thousand routes each route report interval, routers must attempt to spread the routes reported across the whole route update interval. This reduces the chance of reports becoming synchronized, potentially causing routers to become regularly saturated. It is suggested [15] that route updates be spread across multiple route reports at regular intervals (this also could impact convergence, since this effectively extends the routing update timer).

Having said all this, DVMRP has been used quite successfully for some time on the Internet, where it was selected to provide a multicast overlay network called MBone (described in section 4.7.2). Even so, DVMRP was used largely because of its early availability and its tunneling capabilities. In reality only a minority of routers on the Internet support multicasts, so the logical network created by the overlay is actually much smaller in operational terms.

4.4   Multicast routing with MOSPF

Multicast OSPF (MOSPF) is an extension of the OSPFv2 unicast routing protocol and only works in internetworks that run OSPF (refer to [18] for details). MOSPF is not a separate routing protocol; it operates by including multicast information in a new type of OSPF link-state advertisement, the group membership LSA, which enables each MOSPF router to learn which multicast groups are active on a per interface basis. The multicast extensions in MOSPF have been implemented to reuse the existing OSPF topology database to compute source-rooted shortest-path multicast delivery trees. Although group membership reports are flooded throughout the OSPF routing domain, MOSPF operates as a sparse-mode multicast routing protocol, since it relies on users joining a group before multicast data are for-

Figure 4.8
*OSPF hello
message example.*

```
File:OSPF07.SCP  Type:XYP1820_SCP Mode:oooooooo Records:14
====================================================================
Frame  : 68        Len   : 78         Error  : None
T Elapsed: 01:02:26:385   T Delta : 00:00:00:270
----------------------------[mac]----------------------------
Dest Mac : 01005e000005   Sourc Mac: Xyplex1208e5   Type   : IP
----------------------------[ip]-----------------------------
IP Ver  : 4        IP HLen : 20 Bytes
TOS    : 0x00       Pkt Len : 64       Seg ID  : 0x003a
Flags  : FRAG:X.LAST   Frag Ptr : 0   (8 Octet) TTL   : 1 (Low)
PID   : OSPF ( 89)    Checksum : 0xf4f1 (Good)
Dest IP : 224.0.0.5    Source IP: 156.48.8.4
---------------------------[ospf]----------------------------
OSPF Ver : 2        Type   : HELLO     Length  : 44
Router ID: 156.48.121.10  Area  ID: 0.0.0.0     Checksum : 0xe963
AU Type : 00        AU Key  : {    }
---------------------------[hello]---------------------------
Hello Msk: 255.255.255.0  Hello Int: 10        Hello Pri: 1
Options : MC.E (06)    Dead Int : 40
DR    : 0.0.0.0     BDR   : 0.0.0.0
============================[data:0]==========================
```

warded to an interface. MOSPF builds a multicast distribution tree for each
source-group pair and computes a tree for active sources sending to the
group. The tree state is cached and must be recomputed when a link-state
change occurs or when the cache times out.

4.4.1 Message formats

MOSPF routers advertise their ability to forward multicasts using standard
OSPF hello messages by setting the MC bit in the options field. The example hello packet in Figure 4.8 shows both the E and MC bits set in a standard advertisement, indicating that the router can support both unicast and
multicast forwarding.

4.4.2 Operation

MOSPF forwards a multicast datagram along the shortest path tree, as per
unicast datagrams; however, there are some differences in operation, as
follows:

- MOSPF is responsible for forwarding only multicast datagrams;
  OSPF is still required to forward unicast datagrams using shortest-
  path dynamic routing.

- Unlike unicast datagrams, multicast datagrams are forwarded on the
  basis of both the datagram source unicast address and destination
  multicast address.

- Since there are many potential Spanning Trees, each router will calculate a pruned shortest-path tree on demand for each multicast datagram. Shortest-path trees are built when the first datagram is received and then cached for subsequent use by datagrams with the same source and destination addresses (i.e., they are not recalculated for every datagram in a flow). Pruning occurs because some subnetworks may not require multicast groups to be forwarded to them.

- All routers generate an identical pruned Spanning Tree for a given datagram (unlike unicast operation, where each router generates its own Spanning Tree). There is, therefore, a single path between a datagram's source and its destination group members. Unlike unicast datagrams there is no facility for equal-cost multipath support (optional with OSPF).

- When multicast receivers are located on different interfaces, MOSPF will replicate the source multicast and forward it to all relevant interfaces.

- Network Layer multicasts are mapped onto Data Link Layer multicast, as described previously. MOSPF can be used over NBMA networks, in which case multicasts will be forwarded to neighbors as unicasts, which avoids replication issues and allows selective forwarding.

The OSPF link-state database provides a complete description of the AS's topology. By using the new group membership LSA the location of all multicast group members can be retrieved from the database. The forwarding path for a multicast datagram can be calculated on the fly by building a shortest-path tree rooted at the datagram source address. All branches not containing multicast members are pruned from the tree.

The information cached is actually made up of two sets of data: the group membership information associated with hosts on a particular interface, and a datagram's shortest path tree built on demand for each source/ destination multicast datagram. Note that group membership information is typically retrieved via IGMP (although it can be specified statically on some routers). MOSPF is purely concerned with the distribution trees and router-to-router communications. As with DVMRP, an MOSPF router only needs to know if one host requires multicast service on an interface to include that interface in the distribution tree. Note that IGMP is run only on designated routers in broadcast LANs for maximum efficiency. All other MOSPF routers on that subnet will ignore IGMP information.

MOSPF routers communicate multicast group status information throughout an AS so that other routers can forward relevant multicasts accordingly. This communication is achieved via the group membership LSA. From Chapter 3 you may recall that an OSPF router link advertisement is flooded into each of a router's attached areas, describing the status on cost of each interface into an area. This LSA is modified slightly for MOSPF by the use of a new bit field, the W bit in the Router Type field. This bit indicates that a router is a wildcard multicast receiver, and all multicast datagrams exiting the area should be forwarded to it. This is important, since group membership LSAs are local to an area and never flooded outside that area. Within a group membership LSA, each multicast group that has one or more members is advertised. These LSAs are typically generated by Designated Routers (DRs). Area Border Routers (ABRs) will issue these LSAs into the backbone area.

4.4.3 Design issues

MOSPF is protocol dependent; it works only in OSPF-based networks. Just as in the base OSPF protocol, datagrams (multicast or unicast) are routed as is; they are not further encapsulated or decapsulated as they transit the AS. We discussed in Chapter 3 how OSPF enables an AS to be split into areas and how routers in different areas have only partial knowledge of the AS topology. Clearly, therefore, when forwarding multicasts between areas, the shortest path trees calculated for each datagram may be suboptimal, since the multicast source's neighborhood is approximated by OSPF summary link advertisements or by OSPF AS external link advertisements. More importantly, MOSPF has significant scaling problems in that the Dijkstra algorithm must be run for every multicast (s, g) pair.

Unlike OSPF, MOSPF does not support shared delivery trees. Routers running MOSPF can be intermixed with nonmulticast OSPF routers, and both types of routers can interoperate when forwarding unicast IP data traffic. Unlike DVMRP, however, MOSPF does not support tunneling and, therefore, can be used only in contiguous multicast router networks. MOSPF works well in environments that have relatively few source-group pairs active at any given time. MOSPF is not appropriate for large internetworks with many active senders and receivers. As with OSPF, MOSPF may suffer in environments with a high proportion of unstable links, unless additional damping mechanisms are employed.

4.5 Multicast routing with PIM

Protocol-Independent Multicast (PIM) is a relatively new IP multicast protocol that works with IGMP and with existing unicast routing protocols, such as OSPF, RIP, IS-IS, BGP, and Cisco's IGRP. PIM was developed by the IETF IDMR Working Group and defined in two Internet drafts entitled "Protocol-Independent Multicast (PIM): Motivation and Architecture" and "Protocol-Independent Multicast (PIM): Protocol Specification." As with DVMRP, PIM is independent of any underlying unicast routing protocol (unlike MOSPF, which relies on OSPF). PIMv1 uses the IGMP all-routers multicast group destination address 224.0.0.2, whereas PIMv2 has its own dedicated multicast address, 224.0.0.13. Generally, PIM packet types use a TTL of one to prevent forwarding.

PIM provides design flexibility and resolves potential design scalability problems by offering two operational modes for multicast distribution: dense mode (PIM-DM) and sparse mode (PIM-SM), specified in [19].

The terms dense and sparse refer to the density and proximity of group members. For example, a dense population of group members could be situated on an enterprise LAN. Here many users on different subnets may be interested in using the same multicast application, so there is a high probability that all subnets will require the same multicast feed. In contrast a sparse population may comprise a relatively small number of group members, widely distributed over a disparate network of wide area links. In this case only a small subset of the wide area links available will require multicast service for any particular group. Clearly, these two examples are extremes, and there will be some networks that fall in between the two camps. PIM-DM and PIM-SM are described in the following text.

4.5.1   Dense-mode PIM

Dense-mode PIM (PIM-DM) is currently the subject of an Internet draft [20]. It uses reverse path forwarding (described in section 4.1.6) and in many ways is similar to its predecessor, DVMRP. PIM-DM is, however, simpler than DVMRP in that it does not require routing tables (and is independent of any specific unicast routing protocol). PIM-DM simply forwards multicast packets out to all interfaces (except the receive interface) until explicit pruning occurs. In effect, PIM-DM floods the network and then prunes back specific branches later, based on multicast group member information. DVMRP, by contrast, uses the parent-child relationship and split horizon to recognize downstream routers, as described earlier. Dense mode is most useful when the following conditions occur:

- Senders and receivers are in close proximity to one another.

- There are few senders and many receivers.

- The volume of multicast traffic is high.

- The stream of multicast traffic is constant.

PIM-DM is effective, for example, in a LAN TV multicast environment, because it is likely that there will be a group member on each subnet. Flooding the network is effective, because little pruning is necessary. Note that PIM-DM does not support tunnels.

Operations

When a multicast source starts transmitting, PIM-DM assumes that every downstream system is potentially a group member. Multicast datagrams are, therefore, flooded to all areas of the network. If some areas of the network do not have group members, PIM-DM will prune off the forwarding branch by setting up prune state. The prune state has an associated timer, which, on expiration, will turn into forward state, allowing data to go down the branch previously in prune state. The prune state contains source and group address information. When a new member appears in a pruned area, a router can graft toward the source for the group, turning the pruned branch into forward state. The forwarding branches form a tree rooted at the source leading to all members of the group. This tree is called a source-rooted tree.

In the example network shown in Figure 4.9(a), host S transmits multicast packets destined for multicast group 1 (G1). Router R1 receives this traffic, duplicates each packet, and then forwards them out onto all downstream interfaces to R2 and R3. In the same way, routers R2 and R3 duplicate these packets and forward them to routers R4, R5, and R6. Initially

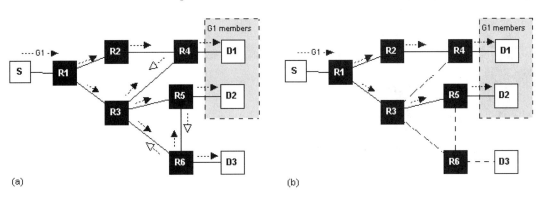

(a)

(b)

Figure 4.9   *PIM dense-mode operation. (a) Shows multicast flooding for multicast group G1 and reverse pruning (either because G1 multicast is not required or duplicate sources are detected). (b) The resulting pruned multicast tree for group G1.*

multicasts are delivered to all hosts via flooding. To optimize delivery the process of pruning is then used. Host D1 is a member of G1, so R5 does not send a prune message. Host D2 is also a member of G1, but notice that R4 receives multicast traffic from both R2 and R3, so R4 prunes back one of these branches. Since host D3 is not a member of G1, R6 also prunes back its feeds. The resulting pruned tree is shown in Figure 4.9(b). Note that this is a logical tree for a specific multicast group. With many multicast sources there are likely to be many overlapping logical trees.

4.5.2   Sparse-mode PIM

Sparse-mode PIM is optimized for environments where there are many multipoint data streams. Each data stream goes to a relatively small number of the LANs in the internetwork. For these types of groups, reverse path forwarding would make inefficient use of the network bandwidth. In relation to PIM-DM, PIM-SM differs in two essential ways: There are no periodic joins transmitted, only explicit triggered grafts/prunes in PIM-DM; and there is no Rendezvous Point (RP) in PIM-DM. PIM-SM assumes that no hosts want the multicast traffic unless they specifically ask for it. It works by defining a Rendezvous Point (RP). The RP is used by senders to a multicast group to announce their existence and by receivers of multicast packets to learn about new senders. When a sender wants to send data, it first sends the data to the RP. When a receiver wants to receive data, it registers with the RP. Once the data stream begins to flow from sender to RP to receiver, the routers in the path automatically optimize the path to remove any unnecessary hops. PIM-SM is most useful when the following conditions occur:

- There are few receivers in a group.

- Senders and receivers are separated by WAN links.

- The stream of multicast traffic is intermittent.

Operations

PIM-SM is designed for sparse multicast regions. For a PIM-SM route to be established there must be a source, a receiver, and a rendezvous point. If any of these are missing, then data in the multicast routing table can be potentially misleading. The basic concept is that multicast data are blocked unless a downstream router explicitly asks for it in order to control the amounts of the traffic that traverse the network. A router receives explicit join/prune messages from those neighboring routers that have downstream group members. The router then forwards data packets addressed to a multicast group, G1, only onto those interfaces on which explicit joins have been received.

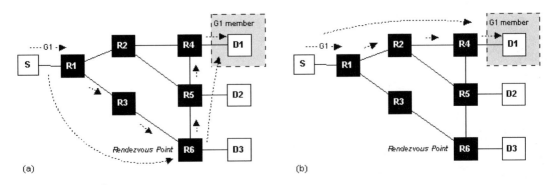

Figure 4.10   *PIM sparse-mode operation. (a) Shows multicast delivery to the rendezvous point (router R6) for multicast group G1. (b) The resulting optimized multicast tree for group G1.*

The basic PIM-SM operation is illustrated in Figure 4.10 and can be described as follows:

- A Designated Router (DR), in this case R1, sends periodic join/prune messages toward a group-specific Rendezvous Point (RP), in this case R6, for each group for which it has active members. The DR is responsible for sending triggered join/prune and register messages toward the RP.

- Each router along the path toward the RP builds and sends join/prune messages on toward the RP. Routers with local members join the group-specific multicast tree rooted at the RP (see Figure 4.10). The RP's route entry may include such fields as the source address, the group address, the incoming interface from which packets are accepted, the list of outgoing interfaces to which packets are sent, timers, flag bits, and so on.

- The sender's DR initially encapsulates multicast packets in the resister message and unicasts them to the RP for the group (see Figure 4.10). The RP decapsulates each register message and forwards the data packet natively to downstream routers on the shared RP tree.

- A router with directly connected members, in this case R4, first joins the shared RP tree. The router can initiate a source's SPT based on a threshold (see Figure 4.10).

- After the router receives multicast packets from both the source's SPT and RP tree, PIM prune messages are sent upstream toward the RP to prune the RP tree. Now multicast data from the source will only flow over the source's SPT toward group members (see Figure 4.10).

The recommended policy is to initiate the switch to the SP tree after receiving a significant number of data packets during a specified time interval from a particular source. To realize this policy the router can monitor data packets from sources for which it has no source-specific multicast route entry and initiate such an entry when the data rate exceeds the configured threshold.

4.5.3 Design issues

The following guidelines are worth observing when using PIM:

- PIM-SM versus PM-DM—PIM sparse mode is generally the preferred way to use PIM. PIM-SM is much more efficient, since it uses an explicit join model, so traffic only flows to where it's required and router state is only created along flow paths. PIM dense mode is simple to configure and useful for small multicast groups (perhaps for small pilot networks). For most applications the flood and prune behavior of PIM-DM is simply too inefficient. Unlike PIM-SM, PIM-DM does not support shared trees.

- Mixed-mode PIM—PIMv2 greatly simplifies the issues for defining a group as sparse or dense. In PIMv1 the router determined the mode; with PIMv2 both sparse and dense groups can coexist on a router interface at the same time (sometimes referred to as PIM sparse-dense mode). With PIMv2 the mode is determined dynamically by testing for the presence of an RP (i.e., if an RP exists for the group; then the mode must be sparse, otherwise, it will operate in dense mode). In rare situations you may want to specifically configure an interface to be sparse or dense—for example, if you are an ISP or if you are connecting to another multicast cloud (i.e., two separate PIM clouds).

- Rendezvous point configuration—If available, use automated techniques to define RP(s), since this avoids configuring an RP on every router and enables simple RP assignment and reassignment. The location of RPs is not especially critical, since SPTs are normally used by default (traffic does not normally flow through the RP, so the RP should not be a bottleneck from the traffic perspective). The exception is where the traffic stays on the shared tree (SPT – Threshold = Infinity).

- Rendezvous point performance considerations—The RP has several resource-intensive tasks to perform and could become a bottleneck in this respect. The RP must process registers and shared-tree joins and prunes; it must also send periodic SPT joins toward the source. PIM routers typically perform the RPF recalculation every five seconds, and you should monitor CPU and memory utilization as the number of multicast routes expands. Overloaded RPs must either have system resources increased (CPU speed, RAM), or you may consider distributing the load across several RPs.

PIM-SM scales much better than PIM-DM, because of its conservative approach to multicast delivery and its low demands on routing resource. PIM-SM is appropriate for wide-scale deployment for both densely and sparsely populated groups in the enterprise. PIM-DM is much more brutal, since it creates an (s, g) state in every router, even when there are no receivers for the traffic, and can cause problems in some network topologies (traffic engineering is virtually impossible). In contrast traffic engineering is possible with PIM-SM, since it uses shared trees rooted at different RPs. PIM-SM is also the basis for Multicast BGP (MBGP) and MSDP interdomain multicast routing [21].

4.6   Multicast routing with CBT

4.6.1   Operation

Core-Based Trees (CBT) is a slimmed-down sparse-mode multicast routing protocol, optimized to support multicast applications such as distributed video gaming and distributed interactive simulation. These applications tend to have many active senders within a single multicast group. Conventional multicast routing protocols (DVMRP or MOSPF) construct a shortest-path tree for each (s, g) pair, meaning that the amount of multicast state information maintained by individual routers is significant. The CBT protocol constructs a single tree that is shared by all members of the group, greatly simplifying the protocols and processes involved.

At the heart of a CBT shared tree is a core router, which is used to build the tree. Routers join the tree by sending a join message to the core. When the core receives a join request, it returns an acknowledgment over the reverse path, forming a new branch of the tree. Join messages need not reach the core before being acknowledged; if the message is intercepted by a router already in the tree (a so-called on-tree router), that router terminates the join and acknowledges it locally. The originating router is then grafted onto the shared tree (see Figure 4.11). In this figure when router R9 wishes to join the tree, it sends a join message back to the core along its reverse path. This message is intercepted by the on-tree router R1, and so the graft can be performed locally, without involving the core.

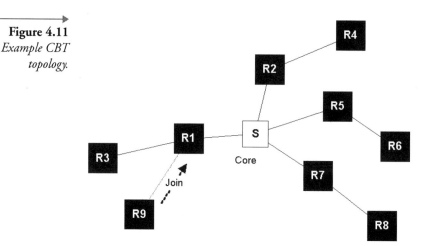

Figure 4.11
*Example CBT
topology.*

4.6.2 Design issues

CBT is relatively straightforward in design. However, because of the simplicity in the tree construction, CBT aggregates traffic onto a smaller subset of links than would be used for traditional source-based trees, resulting
in a large concentration of traffic around the core. This can lead to congestion problems, so some implementations of CBT support the use of load
sharing using multiple cores. To date CBT has not been significantly
deployed. For further information on CBT the interested reader should
refer to [22, 23].

4.7 Interoperability and interdomain routing

We have discussed several different approaches to multicast distribution,
and each has its strengths and weaknesses leading to a somewhat fragmented
installed base. It is clearly desirable for different routing protocols to be able
to interoperate with one another until there is a clear winner. Interoperability approaches can include the following:

- MOSPF is designed to run on top of OSPFv2, so multicast routing
  can be easily introduced into an OSPFv2 routing domain. Interoperability between MOSPF and dense-mode protocols such as DVMRP
  is specified in [18, 24].

- PIM designers are addressing both interoperability between PIM-
  DM and PIM-SM, as well as between PIM and other multicast routing protocols.

- Interoperability between a single CBTv2 stub domain and a DVMRP backbone is outlined in [25].

- An impressive example of the early interoperability in this respect is a network called the Multicast Backbone (MBone), where DVMRP is used to connect multicast-enabled islands via tunneling over the largely unicast-based Internet. An overview of this network is given in section 4.7.2.

Another area we will briefly touch on here is the delivery of IP multicasts between domains (i.e., AS-AS multicast delivery). While an interim solution is available (through a combination of both new and existing technologies), a long-term solution requires a radical examination of possible solutions.

4.7.1 Multicast border routers

There is a fundamental incompatibility between sparse- and dense-mode multicast protocols in the way they approach the construction of distribution trees. Dense-mode protocols are data driven, while sparse-mode protocols rely on explicit join requests. If a dense-mode group is to interoperate with a sparse-mode group (e.g., to form a group that is sparsely distributed over a wide area network but that is densely distributed within a single subnet), there must be a mechanism for allowing the dense group to reach out to the sparse group to request to join. The solution proposed by PIM designers is to have Multicast Border Routers (MBRs) send explicit joins to the sparse group. Note that the same approach would enable PIM-SM to interoperate with other dense-mode protocols, such as DVMRP. For further details on interoperability between different multicast routing protocols via MBRs refer to [24].

4.7.2 Tunneling Multicast Backbone (MBone)

Tunneling is a transition strategy for IP multicast routing. In this context we refer to the encapsulation of multicast packets within IP unicast datagrams, which may then be routed through parts of an internetwork via conventional unicast routing protocols, such as RIP, OSPF, and EIGRP. The encapsulation is added on entry to a tunnel and stripped off on exit from a tunnel. Perhaps the best-known demonstration of multicast tunneling is employed to create an Internet overlay network called the MBone.

The MBone

Multicast packet forwarding is far from uniformly supported on the Internet at present. To gain experience with multicasting, the designers of the Internet decided to create a virtual overlay network on top of the physical infrastructure of the existing Internet. This overlay network is called the Multicast Backbone (MBone). The MBone performed its first worldwide event in March 1992, to support a real-time multicast audioconference over the Internet from an IETF meeting in San Diego. In the original experiment there were 20 sites involved; by 1994 the IETF meeting in Seattle was multicasting to 567 hosts in 15 countries on two parallel channels (audio and video). The multicast routing function was provided by workstations running a daemon process (mrouted), capable of receiving encapsulated multicast packets and processing them as required. Connectivity between these devices was provided using point-to-point IP-encapsulated tunnels, where DVMRP was employed to create logical links between end points over one or more unicast Internet routers. With this early deployment multiple tunnels sometimes ran over the same physical link.

The MBone has grown substantially since 1992, and has subsequently been used for video- and audioconferencing, video broadcasts from international technical conferences, and NASA space shuttle missions. The MBone is probably one of the few places where DVMRP is currently implemented on a live network (although it is understood that the administrators of the

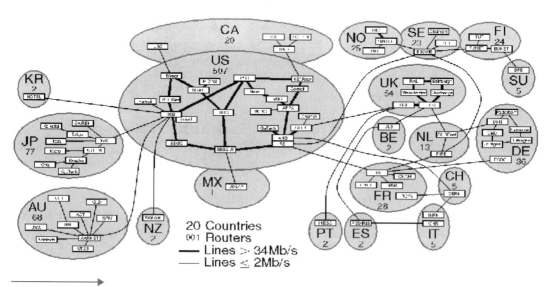

Figure 4.12   *Major MBone routers and links as of May 11, 1994. (Attributed to S. Casner)*

MBone plan to adopt PIM in the future because of its greater efficiency). Figure 4.12 illustrates the MBone status as of May 1994.

MBone access

Multicasting can be supported in commercial multicast routers or in hosts running the multicast routing daemon (mrouted), which uses DVMRP as the routing protocol. Networks that are connected to the MBone must comply with specific requirements for the available bandwidth. For video transmissions, a minimum bandwidth of 128 Kbps is required. For audio transmissions a minimum of 9–16 Kbps is required. The IETF multicast traffic has average transmission rates of 100 to 300 Kbps and spikes of up to 500 Kbps. The interested reader should refer to [26, 27] for further details on the MBone and its architecture.

MBone routing

The basic idea in constructing an overlay network is to create virtual links by tunneling multicast packets inside regular IP unicast packets where the transmission path traverses routers that are not multicast enabled (see Figure 4.13). Since few routers in the Internet today support multicasting, the MBone is overlaid on top of the existing Internet protocols, with multicast routers (mrouters) connected by virtual point-to-point links. Unicast encapsulation hides the multicast data and addressing information inside the payload of a new unicast IP header. The unicast destination address of the new IP header is the tunnel end-point mrouter IP address. When the mrouter at the end of the tunnel receives the encapsulated packet, it strips off the IP header and forwards the original multicast packet. In Figure 4.13, we see that the multicasts being forwarded from Router-1 to Router-4 are sent as multicasts to Router-2 and then encapsulated in IP and tunneled (as unicasts) via Router-3 on to Router-4 (where they are decapsulated). We

Figure 4.13
MBone tunnel. Shaded nodes are multicast-enabled routers forming an overlay network (shown in bold).

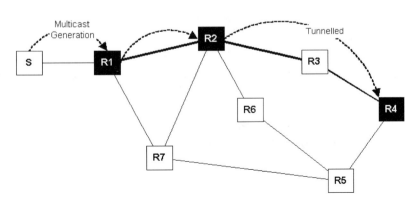

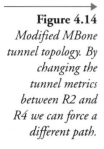

Figure 4.14
Modified MBone tunnel topology. By changing the tunnel metrics between R2 and R4 we can force a different path.

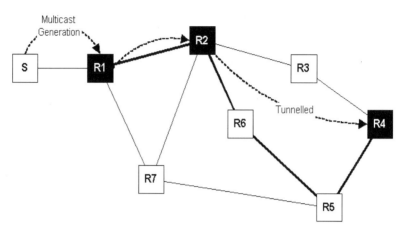

need both unicast and multicast routing tables to support tunneling, since the shortest path for multicasting between R1 and R4 is not necessarily the shortest path for unicasting.

MBone topology is engineered via path metrics, which specify the routing cost for each tunnel (used by DVMRP to select the cheapest path). The lower the metric the lower the cost of forwarding packets through a tunnel. If, in Figure 4.13, we set up two tunnels between Router-2 and Router-4, as R2-R3-R4 and R2-R6-R5-R4, with tunnel metrics 8 and 6, respectively, then the resulting MBone topology will be as illustrated in Figure 4.14.

The MBone also uses a threshold to limit the distribution of multicasts. This parameter specifies the minimum TTL for a multicast packet to be forwarded into an established tunnel. The TTL is decremented by one at every multicast router hop (i.e., it is unaffected by the number of unicast routers traversed). In the future it is envisaged that most Internet routers will be multicast enabled, and this will negate the use of tunneling. The MBone may eventually become obsolete, but this could take some time given the current adoption of multicasting on the Internet.

Example MBone applications

The first multiparty video- and audioconferencing tools to be used over the MBone were developed by the Network Research Group at Lawrence Berkeley National Laboratory (LBNL). Today there are many commercial and noncommercial applications; the following list summarizes some popular MBone applications that are currently available.

- Session Directory (SD)—SD is used to announce MBone sessions.

- Netvideo (NV)—A videoconferencing tool.

- Videoconferencing System (VIC)—A videoconferencing tool.

- INRIA Videoconferencing System (IVS)—See [28].

- Visual Audio Tool (VAT)—An audioconferencing tool.

- Robust Audio Tool (RAT)—An audioconferencing tool.

- Whiteboard (WB)—Provides a shared drawing space for use by videoconference participants.

- MiMaze—A distributed game that runs over the Mbone.

SD is particularly interesting. It can be used by MBone users to reserve and allocate media channels and to view advertised channels. SD advertises session schedules periodically (via a well-known multicast address, 224.2.2.2, and port 4000) and also assigns a unique multicast address and port number to each multicast application session (actually, to each message flow within a session).

The MBone is used widely in the research community to transmit the proceedings of various conferences and to permit desktop conferencing. Most MBone applications run over UDP rather than TCP, since the reliability and flow-control mechanisms of TCP are not practical for real-time broadcasting of multimedia data. The loss of an audio or video packet is acceptable, rather than transmission delays, due to TCP retransmissions. Above UDP most MBone applications use the Real-Time Transport Protocol (RTP), discussed in section 4.8.

4.7.3   Interdomain IP multicasting

There is a perceived need to provide Internet-wide IP multicast, evidenced by the expansion of the MBone and the emergence of new multicast-aware applications. The short-term solution for interdomain multicast routing is functional but relies on an inelegant combination of new and existing technology, as follows:

- An extension to the existing unicast exterior unicast routing protocol BGP4, known as BGP4+, see [29]. BGP4 has been extended to support multicast routes, and this protocol is generally referred to as Multicast Border Gateway Protocol (MBGP).

- Use of an existing interior multicast routing protocol to handle interdomain multicast tree construction. Since broadcast-and-prune methods are not desirable in this regard, the protocol selected is PIM-SM. In this mode PIM-SM treats domains as nodes in a network and determines a multicast tree between domains containing group members.

- A new protocol, called the Multicast Source Discovery Protocol (MSDP), see [21]. The protocol operates by having representatives in each domain announce to other domains the existence of active sources. MSDP is run in the same router as a domain's RP (or one of the RPs). MSDP's operation is similar to MBGP in that MSDP sessions are configured between domains and TCP is used for reliable session message exchange.

While this approach is accepted as a reasonable interim solution, it lacks scalability in the long term, and there is still a perceived need to develop a more integrated long-term strategy. There are several approaches being actively researched at this time, broadly divided into two camps, as follows:

- Border Gateway Multicast Protocol (BGMP)—BGMP was first proposed back in 1998. The basic idea is to construct bidirectional shared trees (*, g) between domains, with only a single RP (BGMP also needs to decide in which domain to root the shared tree). Since address allocation has become an important issue for commercial IP multicast users, BGMP also includes its own address allocation scheme called the Multicast Address-Set Claim (MASC) protocol (although it is not dependent on MASC).

- Root-Addressed Multicast Architecture (RAMA)—The aforementioned approaches to inter-domain multicast do not address related issues such as security, billing, and management. Therefore, several members of the multicast community are attempting to make fundamental changes in the multicast model in an effort to produce a more

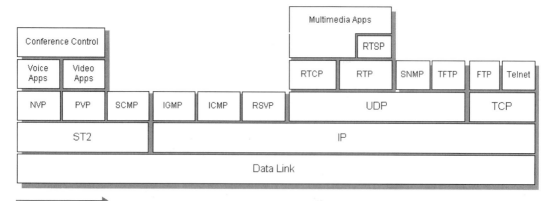

Figure 4.15   *IP multicast and real-time application support protocols in context. For a description of the Streaming Protocol (ST2) and associated higher-level protocols refer to [30].*

comprehensive solution. One proposal is the Root-Addressed Multicast Architecture (RAMA).

Further discussion on this topic is beyond the scope of this book, and the interested reader should keep a watchful eye on forthcoming Internet drafts on this topic.

4.8   Multicast support protocols

Several new protocols have been developed to improve support of real-time multimedia applications, including Real-Time Protocol (RTP), Real-Time Control Protocol (RTCP), and Real-Time Streaming Protocol (RTSP). These protocols are so called because they are designed to support applications with tight delivery constraints (e.g., bounded aggregate transit delay packet interarrival time). Although the protocols are designed from the ground up with large multicast applications in mind, they can happily support unicast traffic. Figure 4.15 illustrates where this new breed of protocols sits within the IP model.

4.8.1   Real-time Transport Protocol (RTP)

RTP is an IETF protocol that provides support for real-time unicast and multicast network applications such as interactive audio and video, although many other applications, such as interactive distributed simulation and control and measurement applications, are also likely candidates. Commercial implementations of RTP and applications that use RTP are currently available for a number of platforms. RTP is also used by the VAT application on the MBone (as described in section 4.7.2). RTP is summarized as follows:

- RTP provides real-time, end-to-end delivery services using existing transport protocols. RTP typically runs on top of UDP (although not mandated), utilizing its multiplexing and checksum services and supplementing these with its own more specialized functions geared toward real-time applications.

- RTP supports simultaneous data transfer to multiple destinations if required (assuming multicasting is supported by the underlying transport). Unlike legacy protocols, RTP embodies the concept of time as part of its delivery mechanism and is now the core protocol for real-time transport on both IP and hybrid MPOA networks. Although time constrained, due to the underlying packet-switched nature of the majority of supported networks, some variation in packet interarrival times is to be expected.

- The RTP header includes fields for sequence numbering and time stamping (32 bit). These functions are performed at source, enabling the receiver to reconstruct the application data flow accordingly. This timing information is necessary to synchronize and display audio and video data and to determine whether packets have been lost or have arrived out of order. For some applications, limited packet loss is not necessarily a problem as long as the real-time characteristics of the source data can be constructed (e.g., a video or audio feed). The source of a stream of RTP packets is called the synchronization source, or SSRC.

- The RTP header specifies the payload type, thus allowing multiple data and compression types. For example, for an audio application the RTP header in each packet indicates what type of audio encoding is employed (e.g., PCM, ADPCM, or LPC). By including encoding details in each packet, senders have the potential to change the encoding during a conference (e.g., to accommodate a new participant that is connected through a low-bandwidth link or to react to indications of network congestion).

- RTP is a best-effort protocol; it does not guarantee timely delivery nor does it provide any quality-of-service guarantees. Packets are not guaranteed to arrive, and when they do they are not guaranteed to be in sequence. QoS facilities are assumed to be provided by protocols such as RSVP.

RTP offers a highly flexible protocol architecture designed to offer scalability, and it is anticipated that RTP services will be integrated within the application framework rather than implemented as a separate layer. Unlike conventional protocols, in which additional functions might be accommodated by making the protocol more general, or by adding an option mechanism that would require parsing, RTP is intended to be tailored through modification and/or additions to the headers as needed. Examples are given in the IETF RTP specification [31], and a companion specification [32] defines a set of payload type codes and their mapping to payload formats (e.g., media encodings).

An RTP session is defined by a particular pair of destination transport addresses (actually a network address plus a port pair for RTP and RTCP). By convention RTP data should be carried on an even UDP port number, and its associated RTCP packets should be carried on the next higher odd port number. Applications may use any such UDP port pair (e.g., the port pair may be allocated randomly by a session management program). A fixed port pair cannot be allocated, because multiple applications are likely to run on the same host, and there are some operating systems that do not allow multiple processes to use the same UDP port with different multicast addresses. However, port numbers 5004 and 5005 have been registered for use as the default pair [32]. The destination transport address pair may be common for all participants (e.g., for IP multicast) or may be different for each (e.g., individual unicast network addresses plus a common port pair). In a multimedia session, each media type (audio, video, etc.) is carried in a separate RTP session with its own RTCP packets. Multiple RTP sessions are distinguished by different port number pairs and/or different multicast addresses.

Since members of the working group join and leave during the conference, it is useful to know who is participating at any moment and how well they are receiving the audio data. For that purpose, each instance of the audio application in the conference periodically multicasts a reception report plus the name of its user on the RTCP (control) port. The reception report indicates how well the current speaker is being received and may be used to control adaptive encodings. In addition to the user name, other identifying information may also be included subject to control bandwidth limits. A site sends the RTCP BYE packet [31] when it leaves the conference.

Mixers and translators

RTP takes into account the likelihood of wide variations in service characteristics across large public networks. Two special intermediate devices (relays) are defined as follows:

- Mixers—Instead of forcing all users to suffer a reduced-quality application feed appropriate for the lowest denominator of the bandwidth available, an RTP-level relay called a mixer may be placed near the low-bandwidth area. This mixer resynchronizes incoming packets into a single packet stream and reconstructs the appropriate packet interarrival spacing for different bandwidth users. These packets might be unicast to a single recipient or multicast on a different address to multiple recipients.

- Translators—Some receivers may have ample bandwidth but may not be directly reachable via IP multicast. For example, they might be behind a firewall that blocks these IP packets. For these sites an RTP-level relay called a translator may be used. Two translators are installed, one on either side of the firewall, with the outside one tunneling all multicast packets through a secure connection to the translator inside the firewall. The translator inside the firewall transmits these packets as multicasts to a multicast group restricted to the site's internal network.

Mixers and translators may be designed for a variety of purposes. An example is a video mixer, which scales the images of individuals in separate video streams and composites them into one video stream to simulate a group scene. Other examples of translation include the connection of a group of hosts speaking only IP-UDP to a group of hosts that understand only ST-II or the packet-by-packet encoding translation of video streams from individual sources without resynchronization or mixing. Details of the operation of mixers and translators are given in [31]. The interested reader should refer to [31–33], for further details on RTP.

4.8.2   **Real-time Control Protocol (RTCP)**

RTCP is the control protocol defined by the IETF to work in cooperation with RTP to provide periodic state information via control packets sent to all participants in a session, using the same packet distribution mechanism as for data. The underlying protocol must, therefore, be capable of multiplexing both data and control packets (typically this is achieved by using separate port numbers in UDP). Feedback of information to the application server can be used both to control performance and for diagnostic purposes. RTCP performs the following functions:

- State information feedback—The main function of RTCP is to provide information to an application regarding the quality of data distribution, in particular the status regarding flow and congestion being experienced by RTP. Each RTCP packet contains transmitter and/or receiver reports that include useful statistics (number of packets transmitted, number of packets lost, interarrival jitter, etc.).

- Identify RTP sources—Each SSRC (i.e., RTP source—see section 4.8.1) is identified by a transport-level identifier within RTCP called the canonical name (CNAME). Since an SSRC may change during an RTP session, perhaps because an application is restarted, the CNAME is used to keep track of all participants in the session. Receivers use the CNAME to identify related data streams within a set of related RTP sessions (e.g., to synchronize audio and video streams).

- Control RTCP transmission rates—In order to constrain control traffic overheads on networks, and to allow RTP to scale, control traffic is limited to at most 5 percent of the overall session traffic. This threshold is regulated by calculating the rate at which RTCP packets are transmitted as a function of the number of participants (and since participants send control packets to everyone else, they can easily work this out).

- Convey session control information—RTCP can optionally be used as a method for conveying a minimal amount of information to all session participants.

Experiments with IP multicasting have demonstrated the value of user feedback from RTCP to diagnose distribution faults. Reception quality feedback is useful for transmitters, receivers, and third-party monitors. For example, a transmitter can regulate its transmission rate based on such feedback; a receiver can determine whether problems are local, regional, or global; and network managers can use RTCP statistics to evaluate the performance of their networks for multicast distribution.

4.8.3   Real-Time Streaming Protocol (RTSP)

Real-Time Streaming Protocol (RTSP) is designed to provide a robust protocol for streaming multimedia in one-to-many applications over unicast and multicast and to support interoperability between clients and servers from different vendors. RTSP can be used with RSVP to set up and manage reserved-bandwidth streaming sessions. RTSP is currently a draft IETF specification, although products using RTSP are available today.

Traditionally, high-volume multimedia data are delivered in maximum-sized packets to optimize bandwidth (reducing the protocol-to-data ratio to maximize efficiency). From the user perspective this often means waiting for large amounts of data to download before a media file can be accessed. The concept behind streaming is to break up data into packets optimized in length for the available bandwidth between the client and server. Once a client has buffered enough incoming packets, it can simultaneously process these packets while receiving and decompressing other incoming packets. This enables the user to start using multimedia applications almost immediately, without having to wait for the whole media file to be downloaded. Typical data sources for streaming applications include both live data feeds and stored clips.

RTSP is designed to work over RTP to both control and deliver real-time content. Although RTSP can be used with unicast in the near future, its use may help smooth the transition for environments transitioning from unicast to IP multicasting with RTP. RTSP is considered more of a framework than a protocol. It is intended to control multiple data delivery sessions and provide a means for choosing delivery channels such as UDP,

TCP, IP Multicast, and delivery mechanisms based on RTP. Control mechanisms such as session establishment and licensing issues are being addressed. The interested reader should refer to [34] for further details.

4.9   Service and management issues

4.9.1   Quality of Service (QoS)

Quality of Service (QoS) is an area of increasing prominence in network design, and there are several reasons why QoS is of particular importance in multicasting. These include the following:

- Guaranteed delivery—Service guarantees are highly desirable for applications that send audio and video or other real-time, high-bandwidth, or mission-critical data; consistent delivery is a concern. QoS considerations for multicast applications include tolerance to jitter, delay, and lost packets. In order to satisfy these requirements, the application must be able to reserve and exercise some control over network resources on an end-to-end basis, adding considerably to the complexity of the routing task.

- Well-defined service characteristics—Multicast routing protocols use a number of techniques to construct multicast trees in order to deliver multicast traffic to group members. The physical paths involved in reaching these users will often vary in bandwidth and quality, as do the traffic conditions across different parts of the network. Multicast delivery trees do not guarantee any specific QoS, leading to potential unfairness in application service (particularly important in applications such as market data feeds). In order to satisfy QoS requirements when setting up a path, routers must include parameters such as delay, bandwidth, loss probability, cost, and jitter in their routing metrics. As we saw earlier, several of these constraints are contradictory, and it might be appropriate to let the user or application define the order in which these parameters are evaluated.

- Traffic engineering—Some multicast routing protocols rely on flooding techniques. With sufficient bandwidth (e.g., a local enterprise), QoS is unlikely to be a problem. However, in relatively low bandwidth environments (such as a wide area network), it is highly desirable that traffic engineering be employed to constrain these application flows within known bounds to preserve bandwidth and keep costs down.

The issue of incorporating QoS routing with the various multicast routing protocols is being actively researched. The Resource Reservation Protocol (RSVP) has been specified by the IETF for use with both IPv4 and
IPv6, and support for IP multicast QoS has been a consideration from the
outset. For various reasons RSVP is unlikely to provide an end-to-end solution across large internetworks, and a longer-term solution to the problems
of reliable IP multicasting is discussed in the next section.

4.9.2   Reliable IP multicast

All of the protocols we have discussed so far assist in the timely and efficient
delivery of multicast traffic to multiple users, but they do not guarantee
delivery. Traditional non–real-time applications (such as file transfer or terminal emulation) already have guaranteed delivery through protocols such
as TCP, which offers full error detection and correction. The new generation of real-time applications requires similar support but without the overhead of a full connection-oriented transport protocol. As specified in [35],
no single reliable multicast protocol is likely to meet the needs of all applications. Therefore, the IETF expects to standardize a number of protocols
that are tailored to meet specific application and network requirements.
This section briefly overviews some of the work in progress and discusses
some of the issues involved.

Requirements

Reference [35] outlines the requirements for reliable multicast protocols
that are to be considered for standardization by the IETF. They include the
following:

- Congestion control—The protocol must be safe to deploy in the
  widespread Internet. Specifically, it must adhere to three mandates: it
  must achieve good throughput (i.e., it must not consistently overload
  links with excess data or repair traffic), it must achieve good link utilization, and it must not starve competing flows.

- Scalability—The protocol should be able to work under a variety of
  conditions, including multiple network topologies, link speeds, and
  the receiver set size. It is more important to have a good understanding of how and when a protocol breaks than how and when it works.

- Security—The protocol must be analyzed to show what is necessary
  to allow it to cope with security and privacy issues. This includes
  understanding the role of the protocol in data confidentiality and

sender authentication, as well as how the protocol will provide defences against Denial of Service (DOS) attacks.

These requirements are designed to ensure that protocols will be safe for widespread Internet deployment.

Design issues

As already intimated, many of the popular real-time applications, such as interactive multimedia, can tolerate some packet loss, and the sequencing and timing services provided by protocols such as RTP ensure that playback is still meaningful. For example, loss of a few frames in a video stream generally makes no difference to the perceived quality of the participants, since the human brain is smart enough to fill in the gaps. However, in a financial application, such as stock trading, loss of even a single packet can be disastrous. Participants in such an application generally demand guaranteed fairness and no loss of data. In the past such applications were implemented by providing each subscriber with a dedicated TCP session, but that approach does not scale, for reasons discussed in section 4.1.3. In a multicast environment it may be important that all updates reach all subscribers so that no group of users has an unfair advantage.

Reliable multicast protocols have the difficult task of providing timely error detection and correction without overburdening the network or compromising scalability. To date this functionality has often been built into the application itself by those wishing to pioneer this technology, with varying degrees of sophistication. For example, the client side of a multicast application could check received sequence numbers (either provided via RTP or through its own application protocol). If sequence numbers are out of order, or missing, then it could simply request resynchronization from the server at the last good event. The problem this raises in a multicast environment, especially in a stock-trading application, is how to update that subscriber in real time, for example:

- Should we send updates via a dynamic reliable unicast session (e.g., a TCP session)?

- Should we use a separate multicast or port address to redistribute lost data?

- Should we send positive acknowledgments for every packet or only negative acknowledgments for missed packets?

- Should we use sender-based Forward Error Correction (FEC) to ensure good throughput (since feedback is not required from receivers)?

- Should we restart the whole multicast advertisement process back at that event to ensure that all parties are in sync and no unfair advantage is given?

- Where should packets be buffered for possible replay? Should this be the responsibility of the server or some intermediate device?

Current status

This is a highly active area of research; several Internet drafts have been submitted related to reliable multicasting, and an Internet Research Task Force (IRTF) has recently been formed to expedite the development of standards-based reliable multicast. There are also a few vendors that offer proprietary reliable IP Multicast solutions designed for different applications and network environments, including support for applications such as multicast file transfer. Surveys of reliable IP Multicast protocols have been conducted as part of the DARPA Multicast Implementation Study (MIST). The interested reader should refer to [36, 37].

Reference [38] describes a reliable multicast transport protocol framework (RMF), which is designed to support reliable end-to-end delivery of multicast data. RMF does not define a specific protocol but provides a supporting framework. RMF guarantees delivery of data to all participants and provides some ordering mechanisms but does not reserve bandwidth (again, the domain of RSVP). RMF is designed to be independent of the underlying Transport and Network Layers.

An implementation called Reliable Multicast Protocol (RMP) is available to academic and research institutions under a no-cost license agreement, and is licensed commercially by GlobalCast Communications; see [39, 40] for further information. Another implementation called the Reliable Adaptive Multicast Protocol (RAMP), developed by TASC, Inc., and the University of Massachusetts at Amherst, is available (with C++ and Java source) from [37].

The Active Error Recovery/Nominee-based Congestion Algorithm (AER/NCA) protocol, developed by the DARPA-sponsored PANAMA project, utilizes active networks to enhance reliable multicast performance in a heterogeneous network. The services offered include repair services, as well as aggregation services for Round-Trip Time (RTT) estimates and congestion control. Version 1.1 of the software and use cases has been released and is available from [41].

Work on congestion control is maturing rapidly via the Reliable Multicast Congestion Control (RMCC) [42] in the IRTF Reliable Multicast

Research Group (RMRG) and has enabled the IETF to charter the RMT working group. Work on reliable bulk transfer is outlined in [43]. For general material and research data on reliable IP multicast, the reader should refer to [1, 44].

4.9.3 Multicast service management

We have discussed the protocols for obtaining multicast group membership (IGMP) and multicast routing (DVMRP, PIM, OSPF, CBT, etc.), as well as protocols for supporting real-time applications (RTP, RTCP, RTSP). However, these protocols merely provide a delivery path; they have no knowledge of the applications they support and therefore cannot disseminate knowledge about applications. We have also seen that there are different models for multicast applications. For example, a conference setup application uses a many-to-many model, whereas permanent guides (analogous to *TV Guides*) uses a one-to-many model, where a listener joins the guide group to find out which IP Multicast sessions are of interest. Given the dynamic nature of multicast services, users and administrators require standard mechanisms for handling multicast application management issues such as the following:

- Service announcements and conference invitations (including the name and subject of the session, time of event, duration)

- Reachability information (i.e., which multicast address and port to use)

- Media types and encodings (audio, video, etc.)

- Security parameters

Currently the configuration of network nodes for multicast services is the responsibility of the network administration staff. Users must be made aware of new services or service changes through mechanisms such as e-mail or the Web, and there is no standard capability to automate service. The IETF Multiparty Multimedia Session Control (music) Working Group is actively developing protocols for the management and coordination of multimedia sessions. To date their primary focus has been to enable conferencing over the MBone and protocols to emerge so far include the Session Description Protocol (SIP), Session Directory Announcement Protocol (SDAP), and the Simple Conference Control Protocol (SCCP). For further details, refer to [45–47].

4.10 Summary

In this chapter we have discussed the following:

- IP Multicast enables many new types of applications and has the potential to significantly reduce network congestion and server load for certain classes of legacy applications. For applications that distribute identical information to multiple users, multicasts represent the best solution available to date; neither unicast nor broadcast mechanisms scale. Furthermore, multicasts are handled more efficiently by the receiver's NIC, and multicasts can be filtered or have security policy applied if required.

- The emergence of networked multimedia applications is driving the development of protocols to support and control multicast packet flows from one or more sources to multiple recipients. IP Multicast traffic for a particular source-destination group pair (s, g) is delivered via a Spanning Tree, which connects all the hosts in the group. Different IP Multicast routing protocols use different techniques to construct these delivery trees.

- IGMP operates effectively as an ES-IS type protocol for multicasts; it allows multicast group members to join or leave a group dynamically and maintains state information on router interfaces that can subsequently be used by multicast routing protocols to determine the delivery tree.

- There are several multicast routing protocols available today, including PIM-SM, PIM-DM, MOSPF, DVMRP, and CBT. There are two basic distribution models: dense mode and sparse mode. Dense mode is generally only applicable to high-density enterprises; for internetworking applications sparse mode is preferred. CBT is optimized for gaming environments by producing a single delivery tree. DVMRP is a dense-mode, distance-vector protocol, now showing its age. MOSPF works well in environments that have relatively few source-group pairs active at any given time. PIM-DM is applicable for small, densely populated, pilot networks. PIM-SM is, for practical purposes, the only scalable solution for multicast routing in interior networks.

- The MBone is an experimental overlay network that supports IP multicasting on the Internet. The MBone uses DVMRP tunneling techniques to interconnect islands of multicast use over unicast backbone. In the future it is envisaged that many more Internet routers will become multicast enabled, and this will eventually negate the use of tunneling (in which case the MBone is likely to become obsolete). This could take some time.

- A new breed of protocols has emerged in recent years to support real-time, reliable multicast distribution. These protocols include RTP, RTCP, RTSP, and RMP. The subject of reliable multicasting is an active area of research and experimentation, and the user is encouraged to keep up-to-date through the list of references and Web sites provided at the end of this chapter.

References

[1]   www.ipmulticast.com, Home site for the IP Multicast Initiative (IPMI). Provides in-depth information including white papers and relevant RFCs on IP multicast. The site also offers a product and services directory and lists members of the IP Multicast Initiative who can be contacted for information and assistance.

[2]   www.isi.edu/in-notes/iana/assignments/multicast-addresses, Current IANA multicast assignments.

[3]   T. Kenyon, *High-Performance Network Design: Design Techniques and Tools* (Woburn, MA: Digital Press, 2001).

[4]   Host Extensions for IP Multicasting, RFC 1112, August 1989.

[5]   R. W. Stevens, *UNIX Network Programming*, vol. I (Englewood Cliffs, NJ: Prentice Hall, 1990).

[6]   S. Deering, "IP Multicast Extensions for 4.3BSD and Related Systems," Stanford University, 1989. See http://portal.research.bell-labs.com/ipmulticast.README.new.

[7]   R. Davis, *Win32 Network Programming* (Reading, M: Addison-Wesley, 1996).

[8]   www.sockets.com, Winsock development home page.

[9]   www.intel.com, Search on Windows Sockets 2 Application Programming Interface, revision 2.2.0.

[10]   www.intel.com, Search on Windows Sockets 2 Protocol-Specific Annex, revision 2.0.3, contains Sockets-compatible multicast APIs in the TCP/IP section and RSVP APIs.

[11]   http://developer.apple.com/macos/opentransport, Apple MAC Open Transport Developer home page.

[12]   Internet Group Management Protocol, Version 2, RFC 2236, November 1997.

[13]   IP Router Alert Option, RFC 2113, February 1997.

[14]   Distance Vector Multicast Routing Protocol, RFC 1075, November 1988.

[15]   T. Pusateri, Distance Vector Multicast Routing Protocol. Internet Draft, draft-ietf-idmr-dvmrp-v3-09.txt, March 2000.

[16]   S. Deering, "Multicast Routing in a Datagram Internetwork," Ph.D. dissertation, Stanford University, Electrical Engineering Dept., 1991.

[17]   IP Encapsulation within IP, RFC 2003, October 1996.

[18]   Multicast Extensions to OSPF, RFC 1584, March 1994.

[19]   Protocol-Independent Multicast–Sparse Mode (PIM-SM): Protocol Specification, RFC 2362, June 1998.

[20]   Estrin, Farinacci, Helmy, Jacobson, and Wei, Protocol Independent Multicast (PIM), Dense Mode Protocol Specification. Internet Draft, draft-ietf-idmr-pim-dm-spec-05.ps, May 1997.

[21]   Multicast Source Discovery Protocol (MSDP). Internet Draft, draft-ietf-msdp-spec-05.txt, February 2000.

[22]   Core-Based Trees (CBT version 2) Multicast Routing: Protocol Specification, RFC 2189, September 1997.

[23]   Core-Based Trees (CBT) Multicast Routing Architecture, RFC 2201, September 1997.

[24]   D. Thaler, D. Estrin, and D. Meyer, Border Gateway Multicast Protocol (BGMP): Protocol Specification. Internet Draft draft-ietf-idmr-gum-01.txt, October 1997.

[25]   A. J. Ballardie, Core-Based Tree (CBT) Multicast Border Router Specification. Internet Draft, draft-ietf-idmr-cbt-br-spec-01.txt, November 1997.

[26]   V. Kumar, *MBone: Interactive Media on the Internet* (New Riders, 1996).

[27]   Several MBONE topology maps are available at ftp://ftp.isi.edu/mbone/:

[28] www-sop.inria.fr/eng/welcome.html, Home page with links for INRIA videoconferencing system.

[29] Multiprotocol Extensions for BGP-4, RFC 2283, February 1998.

[30] D. Minoli and E. Minoli., *Delivering Voice over IP Networks* (New York: John Wiley & Sons, 1998).

[31] RTP: A Transport Protocol for Real-Time Applications, RFC 1889.

[32] RTP Profile for Audio- and VideoConferences with Minimal Control, RFC 1890.

[33] www.cs.columbia.edu/~hgs/rtp, a good source of information about RTP.

[34] www.realaudio.com/prognet/rt/, Research and General Information on RTSP.

[35] Criteria for Evaluating Reliable Multicast Transport and Application Protocols, RFC 2357, June 1998.

[36] gaia.cs.umass.edu/sigcomm_mcast/talk1.html, an overview of Reliable Multicast Protocols from the 8/96 ACM SIGCOMM Multicast Workshop.

[37] www.tascnets.com/mist/doc/mcpCompare.html, MIST Reliable Multicast Protocols Survey.

[38] RMF: A Transport Protocol Framework for Reliable Multicast Applications. Internet Draft <draft-decleene-rmf-01.txt>, February 1998.

[39] www.gcast.com, GlobalCast Communications home site. Commercial implementation of Reliable Multicast Protocol (RMP).

[40] research.ivv.nasa.gov/RMP/Docs/index.html, research information and specifications for Reliable Multicast Protocol (RMP).

[41] www.tascnets.com/panama/AER/index.html, The Active Error Recovery/Nominee-based Congestion Algorithm (AER/NCA) protocol. Version 1.1of the software is available from this site.

[42] M. Handley, S. Floyd, and B. Whetten. Strawman Specification for TCP Friendly (Reliable) Multicast Congestion Control (TFMCC), IRTF Reliable Multicast Research Group (RMRG), work in progress.

[43] Internet Draft <draft-ietf-rmt-buildingblocks-02.txt>, Reliable Multicast Transport Building Blocks for One-to-Many Bulk-Data Transfer. March 2000.

[44] www.stardust.com, publishes several excellent white papers on IP multicasting.

[45] SDP: Session Description Protocol, RFC 2327, April 1998.

[46] SIP: Session Initiation Protocol, RFC 2543.

[47] SAP: Session Announcement Protocol, Version 2. Internet draft draft-ietf-mmusic-sap-v2-01.txt, June 1999.

5

Designing Secure Networks

Network security is a huge subject, which incorporates all seven layers of the OSI model; many of the issues network security raises are sufficiently subtle to require skilled engineers and consultants to understand and tackle them. This chapter focuses on security issues and design solutions with IP-based networks. After discussing the security considerations and planning aspects, we then describe the VPN solutions available in the market today, which is one of the hottest topics in the service provider market. Network security is such a broad topic that this material is necessarily restricted to typical security design issues you are likely to encounter, for which appropriate suitable references are provided. The chapter builds on this framework and deals with the use of security in designing virtual private networks. The following topics are discussed:

- What the key issues are

- What the security threats and vulnerabilities are

- What technologies are available to combat these issues

- How to define a security policy and implement it

- How to design a secure network infrastructure with components available today

- How to avoid single points of failure and bottlenecks with security devices

- Design of secure IP VPNs

Providing security on any network can often have a profound influence on the network topology, design, traffic dynamics, and even the network addressing policy. Security is essentially a game of risk management; you must decide how much time, effort, and money are required to provide an acceptable degree of confidence in the resources you wish to protect. This chapter attempts to cover the salient points of network security, but clearly we have limited space to address this huge topic. For further information, the interested reader is urged to read [1, 23].

5.1   The driving forces and issues behind security

Security products are still relatively immature and weakly integrated. It is, therefore, all the more important that the technologies you select provide a broad, cooperative, and tested security solution that complements the overall security policy you have established. The solution should, at a minimum, satisfy the five primary security functions, as follows:

- Authentication—refers to the process of verifying the validity of a claimed individual or entity and identifying that individual or entity. This process offers confidence that we are who we say we are. A fingerprint is one way of identifying individuals with some degree of confidence.

- Access control—assurance that each user or entity that requests the use of a service is permitted to do so (normally controlled by individual or group access rights). For example, does Fred have the right to download files from BIGSVR over a dial-up line on the weekend?

- Confidentiality—sensitive information must not be revealed to third parties; it should be made available only to the intended recipients. Confidentiality is often referred to as privacy. One way of protecting data is to encrypt it using keys known only to the sender and receiver.

- Integrity—assurance that the data transferred between trusted parties have not been altered or destroyed while in transit. In layman's terms this means that what was sent was actually received.

- Nonrepudiation—assurance that the sender of a message cannot deny being the originator of that message and that the recipient of a message cannot deny the receipt of that message. With applications where payment and goods are exchanged (such as electronic commerce) proof of purchase is vital to gain customer confidence in the process.

Typically this will involve a combination of firewalls, encryption systems, and authentication systems. A layered approach stands a much better chance of alerting you to potential problems. The challenge to provide security for internal networks becomes increasingly difficult as more users access the Internet, internal networks grow in size and complexity, and the range of potential problems expands with new distributed applications and the move toward mobile internetworking. The task of identifying critical or sensitive resources and the threats placed upon them is essentially a process of identifying and quantifying risk. There may be less obvious risks associated with a resource—for example, if confidential user information (age, address, telephone numbers) is held on a networked database, there may be a legal imperative for a company to protect such resources to comply with data protection legislation.

We will first review some of the most common security attacks and illustrate some of the basic vulnerabilities inherent in common data networking protocols and services.

5.1.1   Classifying attacks

Networks need protection against malicious attacks and information leaks from both inside and outside the network, and the former is considerably harder than the latter. Attacks can be classified according to a number of broad characteristics, as follows:

- Denial of Service (DOS)—To disable, severely impair, or corrupt network resources or servers. A DOS attack may be mounted from a single source or multiple sources concurrently. The latter scenario is classed as a Distributed Denial of Service (DDOS) attack. An example of a DOS attack is the SYN flood, described later.

- Impersonation—To gain access to protected services or to falsely create transactions or e-mails. The most basic attack is called IP spoofing, where a hacker uses the IP address of a trusted host to gain access to protected resources.

- Man-In-the-Middle attacks (MITM)—(sometimes referred to as message relay). To gain access to or change information in transit by either relaying session parameters or using keys to fool peers into believing they are communicating directly.

- Sniffing the network—To discover cleartext passwords and sensitive data, using conventional network tools such as Tcpdump or a network analyzer.

- Password and key guessing—To gain access to protected services and data (e.g., by using a brute-force attack, an automated dictionary attack, or planting a virus to discover and e-mail back passwords).

- Viruses—To destroy, disable, or corrupt data or to recover sensitive information such as passwords and keys without the user's knowledge. There are several classes of virus, which we discuss later.

5.1.2 Application and protocol vulnerability

Many of the common network protocols and services in use today were designed originally without any security in mind, and their many vulnerabilities to security threats are widely documented. The IP protocol suite is a good example, designed for straightforward data communications. Although the latest version of IP (IPv6) has mandatory security elements in place, there were no security features built into IPv4 (the protocol was extended subsequently via security options, but these are not widely used). Likewise, TCP, UDP, and many of the services running above them are inherently insecure. This section reviews some of the basic vulnerabilities associated with these services and protocols. It is not meant to be exhaustive; for more information, refer to [3].

ICMP

ICMP is essentially the diagnostic service that runs over IP. There are several exploits based on ICMP, including ping of death, ping sweep, and other hacks based on ICMP redirects and source quench.

Internet Protocol (IP)

IP is a connectionless network service. The next generation of IP (IPv6) includes two key enhancements to improve security: authentication and privacy. IPv6 requires the sender to log in to the receiver. If a sender does not have the prerequisite access rights, he or she cannot access the resource. Privacy is optionally provided by using encryption techniques to protect data. Privacy and authentication are provided by security associations. Either encryption or authentication can be applied first.

User Datagram Protocol (UDP)

Since UDP is connectionless, UDP services are somewhat vulnerable to attack, although many of the original deficiencies have since been resolved. Table 5.1 lists port numbers associated with commonly used UDP protocols.

TCP

TCP is connection oriented. Although more difficult to hack than UDP, there are, nevertheless, well-known hacks that have been used, particularly to deny service. Table 5.1 lists port numbers associated with commonly used TCP protocols. One of the best-known security exploits using TCP is

Table 5.1   *Well-known Port Numbers for UDP and TCP Services*

Application	Protocol	Port No	Application	Protocol	Port No
Reserved	TCP&UDP	0	ISO-TSAP	TCP	102
Remote Job Entry	TCP	5	X.400	TCP	103
Echo	TCP	7	X.400 Sending Service	TCP	104
Discard	TCP	9	SUN Remote Procedure Call (RPC)	UDP	111
Systat	TCP	11	Network News Transfer Protocol (NNTP)	TCP	119
Daytime	TCP	13	Network Time Protocol (NTP)	TCP&UDP	123
NetStat	TCP	15	NetBIOS session source	TCP	139
Quote of the Day (Qotd)	TCP	17	NeWS	TCP	144
File Transfer Protocol (FTP) Data	TCP	20	Simple Network Management Protocol (SNMP)	UDP	161
File Transfer Protocol (FTP) Control	TCP	21	SNMP (traps)	UDP	162
Telnet	TCP	23	Border Gateway Protocol (BGP)	TCP	179
Simple Mail Transfer Protocol (SMTP)	TCP	25	exec	TCP	512
time	TCP	37	rlogin	TCP	513
TACACS	UDP	49	rexec	TCP	514
Domain Name Server (DNS)	TCP&UDP	53	Line Printer Daemon (lpd)	TCP	515
Trivial File Transfer Protocol (TFTP)	UDP	69	talk	TCP&UDP	517
Gopher	TCP	70	ntalk	TCP&UDP	518
Finger	TCP	79	Open Windows (Sun)	TCP&UDP	2000
World Wide Web (HTTP)	TCP	80	Network File System (NFS)	UDP	2049
Kerberos	TCP	88	X11	TCP&UDP	6000+

called the SYN Attack. This uses knowledge of the TCP three-way hand-shake.

Telnet

Telnet is a virtual terminal protocol that runs over TCP (port 23). It is the basic remote access terminal emulator that runs on a range of hosts and operating systems, including native router and firewall OSs. There are several issues with Telnet that are dealt with by a range of authentication mechanisms. From the client perspective one of the potential problems is users leaving authenticated Telnet sessions open.

File Transfer Protocol (FTP)

FTP is used for file transfer and runs over TCP (ports 20/21). It has several security holes. The user name and password used with FTP sessions are transmitted in cleartext and can be accessed by any serious hacker. Anonymous FTP service allows anyone to access a host, without requiring a user account. FTP uses two types of sessions: a control session (TCP port 21) for managing the connection and dynamic data sessions (TCP port 20) for carrying information requested by the user.

Hypertext Transfer Protocol (HTTP)

HTTP is a stateless, object-oriented protocol that runs over TCP port 80. HTTPv1.0 is supported by all Web servers in the market today. A variation, called HTTP-NG (next generation), is being developed to use bandwidth more efficiently. HTTP is highly flexible and makes it difficult to secure resources effectively. You need to be cautious in particular about proxy and gateway applications. HTTP can forward requests to other applications called viewers if it cannot understand the data it receives. HTTP also allows users to execute commands remotely. HTTP allows sensitive log information to be retrieved without authentication. HTTP proxies are men in the middle, the perfect place for a man-in-the-middle attack. A discussion of this is found in section 15 of [4].

Trivial File Transfer Protocol (TFTP)

TFTP runs over UDP. TFTP is mainly used for transferring boot images or configuration data for networked devices that have no local permanent storage and is designed to function without operator intervention. Consequently, it allows unauthorized remote access to file systems, since it does not require a user or password to initiate automated data transfer. For example, on the AIXv3.x operating system remote users could upload /etc/ passwd! One of the problems of TFTP from the firewall perspective is that it dynamically changes ports once a connection is established (i.e., a session starts by using destination port 69 and is then handed off to a new port number from the pool—this clearly cannot be handled by static filters and requires real stateful session and protocol tracking).

Simple Mail Transfer Protocol (SMTP)

SMTP is vulnerable to several attacks. E-mail bombing is an attack that can form a denial-of-service attack by overloading the mail server. In e-mail spamming a malicious user (spammer) sends thousands of copies of an e-mail to several mailing lists. Another twist to this problem is e-mail hijacking, in which the spammer uses your mail relay to forward this spam mail. Potential vulnerability is present, since e-mail servers do not receive the same degree of attention as Web servers, These exploit otherwise legal applications, and security tends to be more lapse. A recent study [5] found that 38 percent of mail servers in .gov domains had security weaknesses.

Domain Name Service (DNS)

DNS is used to convert IP addresses to domain names and vice versa. The protocol has no authentication, and recipients of DNS data automatically assume responses to be valid. There are several techniques that can be employed to modify how the DNS system works, as follows:

- Break into the target network DNS server—Buffer overflow vulnerabilities can be exploited by hackers to deny service. It is possible to break into the machine via a service such as rlogin. By spoofing DNS and redirecting mail users, login details could be collected, and UNIX-based platforms via the rlogin and NFS services could be exploited. Once owned by the attacker, it is easy to modify the information being sent out in response to DNS queries.

- Spoof DNS responses—If a hacker can observe DNS queries, he or she can easily spoof bogus responses. These responses will be believed by other DNS servers or clients implicitly. Places to observe DNS queries are either on the target network, outside the perimeter firewall, or on the same network as the DNS server.

- DNS cache poisoning—Most DNS servers cache the information they process for a finite amount of time, in order to speed up DNS resolution. Unfortunately, there are several techniques used by hackers to poison a DNS cache.

A hacker can corrupt zone information or spoof DNS and offer incorrect name-address associations, causing a denial-of-service attack by rerouting connections or worse, still, allowing the hacker to redirect sensitive information to his or her own machine.

WWW Server Side Includes (SSI)

Many Web servers use some sort of Server Side Include (SSI) to maintain state. This allows a Web server to recognize a previous visitor and maintain the illusion of a session. This may allow the Web user to custom generate HTML code for the particular user. Unfortunately, sometimes the SSI feature is used for security purposes. By spoofing the SSI, a Web user can access other sessions that contain sensitive information.

Other services

There are also a number of nonstandard services that provide value-added services for Internet and WWW access; they are quite sophisticated and difficult to handle from the security perspective. Examples of these services are World Wide Web (WWW), Wide Area Information Service (WAIS), Gopher, and Mosaic. Historically, the PoP and REXEC services have been targets of brute-force attempts simply because they did not have their login failures logged.

Figure 5.1
Growth in complexity of the Microsoft Windows operating systems between 1992 and 2000, showing the estimated number of lines of code used in each OS [2].

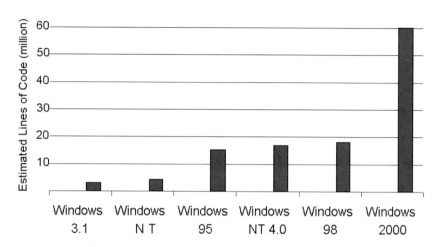

5.1.3   Operating system vulnerability

The ease of use of open network access is in many ways in direct conflict with the provisioning of tight security. Serious vulnerabilities include buffer overruns, inadequate authentication/password protection mechanisms, and the ability to download executable code onto hosts. These types of known vulnerabilities still enable unscrupulous users to crash systems remotely, steal or destroy valuable data, or gather information that enables them to mount a more sophisticated attack later on. Well-known UNIX vulnerabilities exist with services such as echo, chargen, portmap, the r-utilities, rstatd, and tooltalk, and these should be secured, particularly on public-facing servers. Another worrying trend for security designers is the increasing complexity of operating systems (see Figure 5.1). In Figure 5.1 the number of system calls available in Windows also dwarfs other operating systems. For example, Windows NT 4.0 has nearly 3,500 system calls compared with various flavors of UNIX and LINUX with less than 300.

The best approach to protect your OS is to ensure that it is patched at the very latest level and that your firewall and intrusion detection systems are armed with the latest attack signatures. Another factor to consider is the level of certification offered. For further information, refer to [6].

5.1.4   Third-party trust vulnerabilities

Security is largely dependent upon trust, and data networks today often need to allow third parties to access their resources for business or operational reasons based solely on who they are (e.g., extranet applications, VPNs, or home working). Some examples are as follows:

- Accepting named IP addresses through the perimeter firewall—Many network organizations allow remote access to their networks by setting an access filter or firewall rule. In this case authentication is often based solely on source IP address. Some allow complete ranges of IP network or subnetwork addresses from certain ISPs because of the lack of fixed IP addresses. If a hacker can spoof these addresses or owns a machine on the trusted external network, then he or she can easily break into the target network.

- Trusting ISP-originated protocols or services—Aside from DNS there are other types of information, such as routing information (e.g., OSPF or BGP for peering) and network management traffic (for maintenance or SLA monitoring). An Application Service Provider (ASP) may also be hosting a customer server that needs to communicate with internal systems. All of these interactions require communications through the firewall and are potential security holes for a hacker.

- Virtual Private Networks (VPNs)—VPNs rely on secure tunneling protocols to encrypt traffic between two end-points. VPNs may be terminated inside the network at a workstation or server. The firewall then has no way of examining the incoming traffic, so a VPN hijacker could use this tunnel to bypass key security features (such as virus checking) at the perimeter. A hacker may also attempt to defeat the encryption used to protect the tunnel in order to monitor traffic on the wire (either to recover password and key information or to recover sensitive data). Some VPN protocols are more secure than others.

- Modem access—Modems are regularly overlooked as a backdoor route into the network. They may be required for network maintenance or out-of-band management purposes. Often the security on modems is weak, and once compromised a hacker may be able to bypass perimeter defenses.

5.1.5   Well-known attacks

There are many well-known attacks that exploit security weaknesses in operating systems, applications, and protocols. Figure 5.2 illustrates some of the key areas of the IP stack where vulnerabilities are mounted.

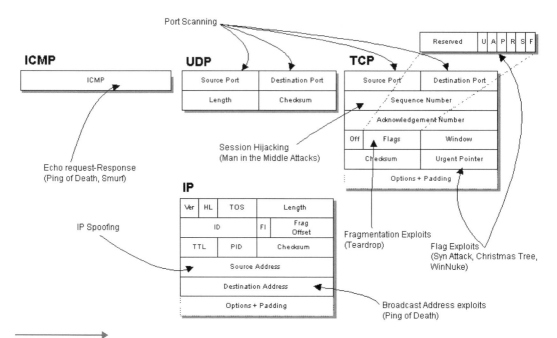

Figure 5.2   *Common protocol features used for IP-based hacking.*

Some of the better-known attacks, together with a brief description, are as follows:

- IP spoofing—The main vulnerability associated with IP spoofing basically involves a hacker masquerading as a trusted client on your network using a trusted IP address. IP's source routing option can be used to discover useful information about your topology. Clearly, on a bridged or switched network you are much more vulnerable to spoofing.

- SYN attack—One of the best known denial-of-service security hacks involves knowledge of the three-way handshake used by all TCP services to open a session. In essence the problem is outlined as follows:

  - Step 1: A TCP host on the internal network receives a perfectly reasonable connection request with the SYN bit set (in the TCP header) to initiate a TCP connection.
  - Step 2: Upon receipt of a SYN packet the host will acknowledge by sending a TCP packet with both the SYN and ACK bits set.
  - Step 3: The host then sets a timer and waits for a reply from the client, which should have the ACK bit set to complete the three-way handshake.

■ Step 4: The host on the internal network receives several more connection requests from different source IP addresses. It goes through steps 2 and 3 for each outstanding connection attempt.

Stateless (filter-based) firewalls may counteract this problem with customized code. Stateful firewalls use a number of methods to resolve the problem; the most common approaches are SYN proxy and SYN relay.

■ Ping of death—The basic idea is that the malicious user sends an illegal echo packet with more than 65,507 bytes of data (IP_header + ICMP_header + MaxIPsize = 20 + 8 + 65,535 = 65,507 bytes). These data will be fragmented and, typically, the receiving station will not process the packet until all fragments have been received, leading to buffer overflows and potential crashes, kernel dumps, and so on. More information on this problem can be found in [7].

■ Ping sweep—A well-known denial-of-service exploit using ICMP is the ping sweep; an ICMP echo request is sent to a broadcast or subnet broadcast IP address, forcing a major traffic spike when all IP members of the network or subnet reply.

■ Smurf—This is a denial-of-service attack that consumes bandwidth. It is mounted by injecting many ICMP echo requests (i.e., ping) into a network with the source address spoofed to match a victim inside that network. The destination address for the faked ping is a network broadcast (e.g., 196.128.32.255 or 140.178.255.255, another variation being 255.255.255.255). This results in the victim being inundated with ICMP echo replies from all IP hosts listening on that network.

■ Land attack—A well-known denial-of-service attack that works by spoofing the source IP address to match that of a victim inside a network and making the destination IP address the same. When sent to certain ports (such as HTTP), this can cause some systems to crash.

■ Teardrop—This is based on UDP, which uses IP fragmentation to attack vulnerable operating systems. The source IP address is invariably spoofed. The basic idea is that after the first fragment is sent, one or more subsequent fragments will overlap the previous fragment (so-called pathological fragmentation). This causes some operating systems to treat the pointer as a negative number (and hence an unsigned integer) memory copy. Unless the host has huge amounts of memory, this will result in a memory write way above the actual memory range, causing a system crash (a known vulnerability on some implementations of LINUX).

- WinNuke—Another denial-of-service attack similar to the land attack (sometimes called OOBNuke) crashes older unpatched Windows systems by typically sending a TCP packet to port 139 (NetBIOS) and setting the so-called Out-of-Band (OOB) flags (in fact, this is the urgent flag in the TCP header, which enables the urgent pointer—see Figure 5.2). The attack will work on other ports Windows is listening to.

- Christmas tree—Another denial-of-service attack based on setting all flags in the TCP header (thereby making many actions placed on the receiver contradictory and forcing a system crash on unpatched systems).

For more detailed information on security exploits, many of the attack signatures required to identify and deal with these hacks are discussed in [6].

5.2   Developing the security policy

One of the first documents many organizations create when tackling security is a security policy. This is basically a list of all activities you will permit on your network and the types of user or network processes allowed to perform them, together with a definition of security levels for various services and data. It is worth reflecting on the definition of security policy offered in [8]: A security policy is a formal statement of the rules by which people who are given access to an organization's technology and information assets must abide.

Given that there are known internal and external threats to your network, you must establish a clear policy for preventing and dealing with security breaches.

5.2.1   Policy components

A security policy should be designed in accordance with a risk assessment of vulnerable resources and what levels of availability or loss the organization can tolerate, with characteristics such as the following:

- It must be understandable and unambiguous. If the policy document is written in such a way as to cause misunderstanding or misinterpretation, then security may be compromised.

- It must be implementable through system administration procedures, publishing of acceptable use guidelines, or other appropriate methods.

- It must be enforceable with security tools, or sanctions where tools are not available or appropriate.

- It must clearly define the areas of responsibility for the users, administrators, and management.

- The more rigorous the security policy, the more expensive the solution, and the more impenetrable the network should be. In an ideal world you should aim to develop a policy document that includes information such as a vulnerability and risk analysis, a privacy policy, an accountability policy, and an authentication policy.

For further information on policy, the interested reader is directed to [8].

5.2.2   Risk analysis

Risk analysis produces a monetary vulnerability assessment, and these data can then be used in financial planning projects when attempting to justify expenditure on security; and it certainly helps to focus attention on critical vulnerabilities. If the annual projected losses exceed the cost of the security measures, then it should be easier to convince senior managers to allocate budgets accordingly.

5.2.3   Attack trees

One useful technique in exploring system vulnerabilities is to create an attack tree of the potential paths and choices a malicious user might take to exploit your system. Figure 5.3 illustrates a partial attack tree with some of the steps that might be considered by a malicious user in attempting to gain a copy of a sensitive client database from a corporate server.

5.2.4   Policy implementation

When implementing policy, there are two basic approaches you can take when configuring software and devices; these form the overall guiding policy from which everything else is derived, as follows:

- Model A: Everything not specifically permitted is denied.

- Model B: Everything not specifically denied is permitted.

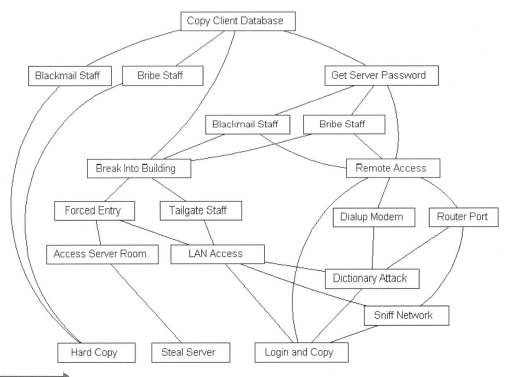

Figure 5.3   *Simplified and incomplete attack tree for getting a copy of a sensitive client database from a corporate server (progress is from top to bottom).*

Anybody serious about security will choose Model A. Policies must be consistent throughout the network. All internetworking devices that relay user and service traffic must be examined to see if they can be included in

Table 5.2   *Various Security Solutions and Their Features*

Technology	Access Control	Encryption	Authent-ication	Address Hiding	Integrity Checking	Session Montoring
AAA Servers	user	no	user	no	no	no
IP Filtering	yes	no	no	no	no	no
NAT	yes	no	no	yes	no	conn
SOCKS	yes	no	client+user	yes	no	conn
SSL	yes	data	system+user	no	yes	yes
Application Proxy	yes	possibly	user	yes	yes	conn+data
IPSec	yes	packet	packet	yes	packet	no
PKI	yes	yes	yes	no	yes	no
Firewall	yes	yes	yes	yes	yes	yes

the policy implementation. This may include routers, bridges, gateways, servers, firewalls, remote access devices, terminal servers, and hosts. Table 5.2 summarizes several major security implementations and demonstrates the various features that are present and absent in each. This table is a useful tool for putting things in perspective when implementing security policy.

5.2.5 Legal issues

Once your security policy has been established, the policy should be reviewed by legal counsel to ensure that it meets all legal requirements.

5.3 Security technology and solutions

Given the potential threats already described, there are a number of technologies available to combat network and system vulnerabilities. Underpinning these technologies are a number of techniques that are typically utilized in various combinations to build products, including the following:

- Encryption: to protect data and passwords

- Authentication and authorization: to prevent improper access

- Integrity checking and message authentication codes: to protect against improper alteration of messages

- Nonrepudiation: to make sure that an action cannot be denied by the person who performed it

- Digital signatures and certificates: to ascertain a party's identity

- One-time passwords and two-way random number handshakes: to mutually authenticate parties of a conversation

- Frequent key refresh, strong keys, and prevention of deriving future keys: to protect against breaking of keys (cryptanalysis)

- Address concealment: to protect against denial-of-service attacks

The security threat is constantly evolving, and a combination of techniques, each dynamically changing to match new threats, must be implemented in order to offer any hope of integrity. Increasingly, many organizations (particularly in the finance sector) are considering migration to a full Public Key Infrastructure (PKI), and next-generation Intrusion Detection Systems (IDS) to complement and further strengthen their security infrastructures. There is increasing research that focuses on systems that adapt and learn proactively, with the ability to feed back

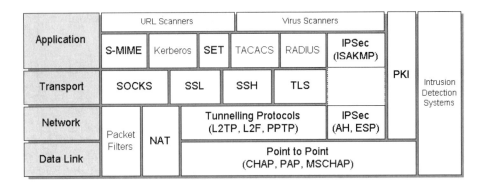

Figure 5.4   *Security solutions in context.*

changes dynamically to perimeter protection systems such as firewalls. (See Figure 5.4.)

This section discusses some of the technologies available today for designing secure networks. The key technologies include the following:

- Network Address Translation (NAT)

- Firewalls, packet filter routers, proxy servers (e.g., SOCKS)

- Remote access security: AAA services, Kerberos, RADIUS, TACACS, PAP, and CHAP

- End-to-end security solutions: Secure Sockets Layer (SSL), SSH, IP Security Architecture (IPSec), S-MIME

- Secure Electronic Transactions (SET)

- Public Key Infrastructure (PKI)

- Virus scanners

- URL scanners

- Intrusion Detection Systems (IDSs)

- Virtual Private Networks (VPNs)

5.3.1   Cryptography

Traditional cryptography is based on the premise that both the sender and receiver are using an identical secret key. This model is generally referred to as secret-key or symmetric cryptography. There are two basic problems with its use: key distribution and scalability.

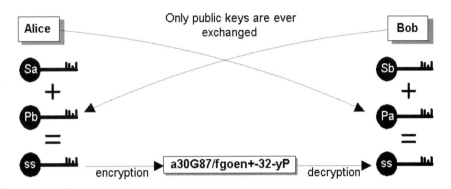

Figure 5.5   *The process of agreeing on a shared secret key, using the Diffie-Helman technique, by exchanging only the public key of the peer.*

The process of key generation, transmission, and storage is referred to as key management.

In the Diffie-Helman (D-H) model, each user holds a pair of keys: a public key and a private key. Public keys are published openly, but each user's private key remains secret and is never transmitted. Each public-private key pair is tightly related mathematically (e.g., via modulo arithmetic); information encrypted with the public key can be decrypted only with the corresponding private key and vice versa. In Figure 5.5, for example, Alice takes her secret key (Sa) and performs a calculation using Bob's public key (Pb) to give the shared secret key (ss). Bob performs a corresponding calculation using his secret key (Sb) and Alice's public key (Pa). The shared secret key is identical in both cases and can be used to encrypt and decrypt.

The real advantage of asymmetric cryptography is that the sender and receiver do not generally need to disclose private keys; another is that the communications channel can be an open or public network (such as the Internet). The problem is that public keys need to be held in a trusted authenticated repository that is accessible to users (Certificate Authority [CA]), and this is an area where the model is less elegant and somewhat controversial.

Encryption algorithms

In symmetric and asymmetric cryptography, messages and data are encrypted, decrypted, or manipulated using a number of specialized algorithms. The simplest algorithm used in cryptographic products (although not strictly a cryptographic technique at all and hardly secure) is an exclusive OR (XOR) operation, whereby bits in the message string are simply flipped. There are several well-known encryption techniques used with symmetric schemes, including the following:

- DES—Data Encryption Standard, as defined in FIPS PUB 46-1. Commonly used for data encryption.

- IDEA—International Data Encryption Algorithm. Commonly used for data encryption.

- CAST—Commonly used for data encryption.

- SkipJack RC2/RC4—RC4 is commonly used for data encryption applications such as IPSec.

There are also a number of additional encryption techniques used with asymmetric schemes, including the following:

- Triple DES—Commonly used for key encryption.

- RSA.

- DSS—Digital Signature Standard.

- MD2, MD4, MD5—RSA Data Security, Inc.'s, Message Digest Algorithms (MD2 is defined in [9]; MD4 is defined in [10]; and MD5 is defined in [11]). MD5 is commonly used for authentication.

- SHS/SHA—Secure Hash Standard/Secure Hash Algorithm. SHA-1 is commonly used for authentication.

Cryptography is the subject of a book in itself, and while I have barely skimmed over it here, I refer interested readers to [1], which covers this subject in the full depth it deserves.

5.3.2 Public Key Infrastructure (PKI)

The Public Key Infrastructure (PKI) builds upon the foundations of asymmetric cryptography to establish a security infrastructure suitable for secure transactions such as electronic commerce. The PKI is a set of hardware, software, policies, and procedures needed to create, manage, store, distribute, and revoke digital certificates based on public key cryptography. (See Figure 5.6.)

The PKI provides services such as key management, certificate distribution, certificate handling, a trusted time service, and support for nonrepudiation. PKI services also require facilities to store an entity's sensitive information. For further information about the PKI, the interested reader is referred to [12].

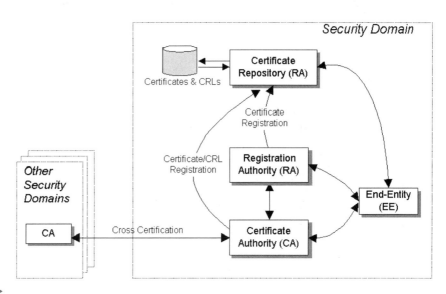

Figure 5.6   *PKI architectural model. Each CA is responsible for a security domain. CAs may perform cross-certification with other CAs.*

X.509 digital certificates

Certificates are cryptographically sealed data objects that validate the binding of a public key to an identity (such as a person or device) via a digital signature. Certificates are issued and held by a trusted third party, in this case Certificate Authority (CA). Certificates are used to verify a claim that a public key does in fact belong to a given entity and prevent a malicious user from using a bogus key to impersonate someone else. The certificate is digitally signed by computing its hash value and encrypting this with an issuer's private key. If any bit is changed or corrupted in the certificate, the recalculated hash value will be different and the signature will be invalid. If the client already possesses the issuer's public key and trusts the issuer to verify the identity of the server, then the client can be sure that the public key in the certificate is the public key of the server. A malicious user would have to know either the private key of the server or the private key of the issuer to successfully impersonate the server. An X.509 digital certificate contains a number of objects, including the following:

- The version number (currently X.509 is at version 3)
- The serial number of the certificate
- The sign algorithm ID (the algorithm type used by the issuer to sign this certificate)

- The issuer's name (the name of the certificate authority that issued the certificate)

- The validity period (the lifetime of the certificate, a valid start and expiration date)

- The subject's name (the user ID)

- The subject's public key

- The issuer's unique ID

- The subject's unique ID

- Optional extensions

- The digital signature of the issuing certificate authority

Certificate data are written in Abstract Syntax Notation 1 (ASN.1) and subsequently converted into binary data along with ASN.1 Distinguished Encoding Rules (DER) to enable certificate data to be independent of specific platform encoding rules. The most widely accepted format for certificates is defined by the ITU-T X.509 international standard; thus, certificates can be read or written by any application complying with X.509.

Digital signatures

A digital signature is the electronic metaphor for a written signature; it provides proof that information sent by a user did indeed come from that user and can be used to prove message integrity. When a message is sent by a user, it can be signed with a digital signature, using the sender's private key. Since all users have access to the sender's public key, the public key can be used to verify the signed message. If the signature can be decrypted using the sender's public key, then only that sender could have created the message using his or her private key. For example, a CA normally signs a certificate with a digital signature computed using its own private key. Anyone can verify the signature by using the CA's public key. If either a message or a certificate is digitally signed, then any tampering with the content is immediately detectable. In this way public key cryptosystems provide both confidentiality (no one can read a message except the receiver) and authenticity (no one can write a message except the sender).

Certificate Authorities (CAs)

Certificates are issued by a Certificate Authority (CA), which can be any trusted central administration willing to vouch for the identities of those to whom it issues certificates and their association with a given key. One way to authenticate entities involves enclosing one or more certificates with every signed message. The receiver of the message would verify the certificate using the CA's public key and, now confident of the public key of the sender, verify the message's signature. There may be several certificates enclosed with the message forming a hierarchical chain, wherein one certificate testifies to the authenticity of the previous certificate. At the end of a certificate hierarchy is a top-level CA, which is trusted without a certificate from any other certifying authority or whose certificate can be self-signed (i.e., the top-level certifying authority uses its own private key to sign its own certificate). Of course, CA's themselves require certificates, and this is part of the reason for this hierarchy. The public key of the top-level CA must be independently known—for example, by being widely published or securely distributed. If the top-level certifying authority has a self-signed certificate, the resulting signature has to be independently known.

Registration Authorities (RAs)

The Registration Authority (RA) is an optional component in a PKI. Often this functionality is bundled with the CA. If a distinct RA is implemented, then the RA is a trusted end entity, certified by the CA and acts as a subordinate server of the CA. The CA can delegate some of its management functions to the RA (e.g., the RA may perform personal authentication tasks, report revoked certificates, generate keys, or archive key pairs). The RA, however, does not issue certificates or CRLs. The RA was introduced to solve an issue where CAs are not sufficiently "Godlike" to authenticate certificates. In essence, the CA-RA model splits responsibilities so that the CA issues keys and the RA authenticates them. RAs are established between users and CAs and may perform user-oriented functions, such as personal authentication, name assignment, key generation, archiving of key pairs, and so on. The standards also define the messages and protocols between CAs, RAs, and users.

Certificate Repositories (CRs)

Because the X.509 certificate format is a natural fit to an X.500 directory, a CR is best implemented as a directory, and it is then able to be accessed by the dominant Directory Access Protocol, the Lightweight Directory Access Protocol (LDAP). Although not recommended, there are other ways to obtain certificates or CRL information if a CR is not implemented in a directory, generally speaking a directory is much the preferred route.

Certificate Revocation Lists (CRLs)

A CRL is a list of certificates that have been prematurely revoked (i.e., invalidated before their scheduled expiration date) and serves to blacklist bad certificates that can be consulted by all interested parties. CRLs are maintained by CAs, and although CRLs are stored in a distributed manner, there may be central repositories for CRLs (e.g., network sites containing the latest CRLs from many organizations).

Current use of public key infrastructures

At the time of writing very few organizations have implemented a PKI. It is considered somewhat immature and expensive, and therefore only large organizations, such as financial institutions, are developing migration plans for deploying a PKI. Many of the larger financial institutions are currently using token cards or starting to implement VPNs. Having said that, PKI components (primarily the cryptographic algorithms) have already been deployed in widely used network protocols and applications, as follows:

- Secure Multipurpose Internet Mail Extensions (S/MIME) is a secure mail application developed by RSA Data Security, Inc. S/MIME is an emerging standard for interoperable secure e-mail and adds digital signatures and encryption to Internet MIME messages. For further information, the interested reader is directed to [13].

- The Secure Electronic Transaction (SET) specification is an open technical standard for supporting e-commerce transactions. The core protocol of SET is based on digital certificates. For further information, the interested reader is directed to [14].

- The Secure Sockets Layer (SSL) protocol uses RSA public key cryptography and is capable of client authentication, server authentication, and encrypted SSL connection. For further information, the interested reader is directed to [15].

- IPSec is a set of specifications for securing IP datagrams using authentication, integrity, and confidentiality services based on cryptography. For further information, the interested reader is directed to [16].

- Point-to-Point Protocol (PPP) uses the Challenge Handshake Authentication Protocol (CHAP), which uses encryption. For further information, the interested reader is directed to [17].

At present the only experience the vast majority of users will have with PKI is using SSL on the Internet to buy products. Nevertheless, warts and all, the PKI is likely to be the cornerstone of future e-commerce. Vendors of PKI solutions and components include Baltimore Technologies [18], Entrust Technologies [19], RSA Security Inc. [20], and VeriSign Inc. [21]. For further information on PKI, the interested reader is referred to [2].

5.3.3 Network Address Translation (NAT)

The basic concepts behind Network Address Translation (NAT) were introduced in Chapter 2, where it was used to combat IP address depletion and resolve illegal IP addressing schemes. NAT also has close associations with network security, because of its ability to hide the details of the network behind a firewall or other NAT-enabled device. When NAT translates IP addresses, it enables devices that communicate with untrusted public networks (such as the Internet) to hide their real addresses. Clearly, from a hacker's perspective, it is much harder to attack a resource where the real address is unknown. Note also that the virtual NAT addresses may not be consistent, since they are assigned on the fly.

NAT must be preconfigured with statically mapped virtual addresses associated with specific services. Figure 5.7 shows the general functionality of NAT. For example, in Figure 5.7 an external name server could have an entry for an internal mail gateway inside the trusted network (Mail Server I). When an external mail server (Mail Server-X) does a lookup via the name server, the name server resolves the public host name of the internal mail gateway to the virtual IP address. The remote mail server can then send a connection request to this virtual IP address. When that request hits the NAT box on the untrusted external interface, NAT resolves the static

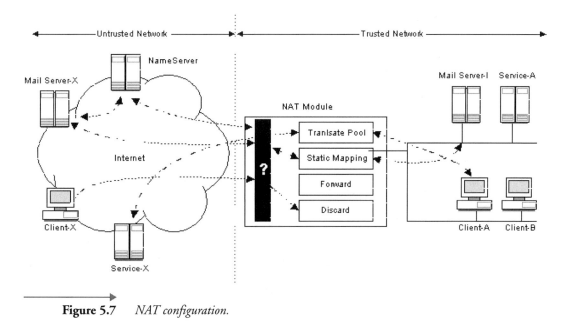

Figure 5.7   *NAT configuration.*

mapping between the public IP address and a secure IP address and forwards the connection request to the internal mail gateway.

NAT also poses particular problems in secure networking environments, as follows:

- Some protocols and services have the unfortunate habit of passing addressing information inside application data (i.e., above the Transport Layer). You can either choose to discard these protocols in your rule base or install a more sophisticated version of NAT that is protocol aware.

- NAT is often run directly on firewalls as an additional security measure. This places an additional processing burden on what may already be a stressed system. It is not unusual to see a 20 percent degradation in overall throughput on firewalls with NAT activated.

- Since NAT changes address information in an IP packet, end-to-end IPSec authentication (if used) will always fail its integrity check under the AH protocol. This is because any change to any bit in the datagram will invalidate the integrity check, generated at source. However, IPSec has many features that negate the need for NAT.

5.3.4   AAA security services

Remote dial-in access has long been recognized as inherently insecure, and the Remote Access Server (RAS) or Network Access Server (NAS) is a vital function of any internetwork. With the rise of mobile computing there is an increasing demand for transparent but secure connectivity to corporate network resources from a variety of mobile computing devices, such as notebook computers, palmtop devices, and WAP-enabled phones for basic e-mail access.

AAA security services model

The triple A (AAA) security model was developed primarily to address the issue of securing remote access, by implementing three functions—authentication, authorization, and accounting—as follows:

- Authentication determines who a user (or entity) is. Authentication can take many forms. Traditional authentication utilizes a name and a fixed password. Most computers work this way; however, fixed passwords have limitations, mainly in the area of security. Many modern authentication mechanisms utilize one-time passwords or a challenge-response query. Authentication generally takes place when the user first logs in to a machine or requests a service of it.

- Authorization determines what a user is allowed to do. In general, authentication precedes authorization, but this is optional. An authorization request may indicate that the user is not authenticated, and in this case it is up to the authorization agent to determine if an unauthenticated user is allowed to use the services requested. In current remote authentication protocols, authorization does not simply provide yes or no answers, but it may customize the service for a particular user. Two of the most popular authentication services are Remote Authentication Dial-In User Service (RADIUS) and Terminal Access Controller Access Control System (TACACS), with Kerberos becoming increasingly popular since its integration with Windows 2000. These services are all described later in this section.

- Accounting is typically the third action after authentication and authorization. But again, neither authentication nor authorization are required. Accounting is the action of recording what a user is doing, or has done. In the distributed client/server security database model, a number of communications servers, or clients, authenticate a dial-in user's identity through a single, central database, or authentication server. The authentication server stores all information about users, their passwords, and access privileges. A central location for authentication data is more secure than scattering the user information on different devices throughout a network. A single authentication server can support hundreds of communications servers, serving up to tens of thousands of users. Communications servers can access an authentication server locally, via a LAN, or over remote wide area circuits. Several remote access vendors and the IETF have been in the forefront of this remote access security effort and the means whereby such security measures are standardized. RADIUS and TACACS are two such cooperative ventures that have evolved out of the Internet standardizing body and remote access vendors.

Fundamental to security is the ability to validate that a user is who he or she says he or she is, and we call this process authentication. There are many techniques available for deploying authentication in a networked environment; several are as follows, in increasing strength:

- Static user name/password
- Aging user name/password

- One-Time Passwords (OTPs) (e.g., S/Key for terminal users, PAP for point-to-point links)

- Token cards/soft tokens (employs OTPs)

- Biometrics (fingerprint, face, and iris scanning)

There are also some services that employ the full AAA model, including Kerberos, TACACS, and RADIUS. We will now briefly review some of the key protocols and services available for authentication.

Static and aging passwords

Static passwords represent the lowest level of authentication available. Experience shows that people are not good at remembering passwords, and therefore passwords tend to be written down and are often easy for a hacker to guess (e.g., the name of your sister or your favorite car). Aging passwords are slightly better in that user are forced at regular intervals to change their passwords. Passwords are easily and rapidly defeated by dictionary attacks, so it is recommended that you choose a password that is an unusual combination of letters and digits.

PAP

The Password Authentication Protocol (PAP) is a way to keep unauthorized remote users from accessing a network. It is typically used to control point-to-point, router-to-router communications and dial-in access. When PAP is enabled, a remote device (e.g., a PC, workstation, router, or communication server) is required to provide a static password known only to the peer device or NAS. If the correct password is not provided, access is denied. PAP is typically supported on router serial lines using Point-to-Point Protocol (PPP) encapsulation. Although effective, it is quite weak in that the password is static, and the password is transferred as plaintext. For further information about PAP, the interested reader is referred to [22, 23].

CHAP

The Challenge Handshake Authentication Protocol (CHAP) is essentially a smarter form of PAP. It is commonly used to control router-to-router communications and dial-in access. When CHAP is enabled, a remote device (e.g., a PC, workstation, router, or communication server) attempting to connect to a local router is challenged to provide a secret. If the correct response is not provided, network access is denied. CHAP is bidirectional; each peer can challenge the other. CHAP also allows for the periodic reissuing of challenges (using different and difficult to predict challenge numbers).

CHAP is becoming popular because it does not require a secret password to be sent over the network. CHAP is typically supported on router serial lines using Point-to-Point Protocol (PPP) encapsulation. Because of its dynamic nature, CHAP is considered more secure than PAP. For further information about CHAP, the interested reader is referred to [23].

Simple Key Management for IP (SKIP)

Simple Key Management Protocol for IP (SKIP) is an authentication scheme developed by Sun. It is commonly integrated into firewalls as a user authentication mechanism because of its simplicity. SKIP has been presented to the IETF Security Working Group. It uses Diffie-Helman 1,024-bit public key–based authentication algorithms for long-term key set up, as well as session and traffic key generation, along with DES, RC2, and RC4–based traffic encryption. SKIP uses one-time passwords (OTPs), which are keys sent unencrypted over the network. Note that keys are not exchanged; SKIP relies on a list of keys. SKIP also includes pipelining of traffic key generation and on-the-fly traffic key changing. A host-based implementation has been implemented, offering a solution to remote network access through authenticated IP tunnels. For further information about SKIP, the interested reader is referred to [24].

Token cards

In recent years a small number of companies have produced tamper-proof smart cards, which typically produce time-based keys for use with authentication schemes. For example, Security Dynamics produces a SecureID card. This scheme works as follows: When users log in, they are prompted for both their user name and a key. The key is generated by the user typing a secret four-digit PIN number into the smart card and then pressing a button to invoke the key-generation algorithm. The key will vary depending upon the time of day. This key is passed to the NAS (or separate token server), which runs the same key-generation algorithm and has a clock synchronized with the card. The card itself is claimed to be tamper proof, and this is a very secure mechanism for dynamic user authentication and is employed by several large organizations, such as financial institutions. It is also supported by several firewalls as an optional authentication scheme. Other vendors in this field include Enigma Logic and DES Card.

Biometrics

Biometrics is an emerging technology to assist in authentication. Currently the main techniques include thumbprint scans, face recognition, iris scans, retinal scans, signature geometry, hand geometry, and voice scans. These techniques work with varying degrees of success, though this is currently limited by the technology available (e.g., thumbprint scans are more reliable than face scans). The technology typically enables the administrator to tune the degree of rigor in the biometric to err on the side of a false-positive or false-negative result (i.e., increase the possibility of impostors fooling the test, or make the system so rigorous that even genuine users have difficulty proving they are who they claim to be). This is again a compromise between security system and ease of use. The general consensus is that biometrics will improve to the point where it will become normal practice as a challenge mechanism to authenticate users' many everyday situations.

Remote Authentication Dial-In User Service (RADIUS)

The Remote Authentication Dial-In User Service (RADIUS) protocol is currently the most popular method for managing remote user authentication and authorization, and was originally designed primarily to manage secure access for dispersed serial line and modem pools, since historically these have proved difficult to administer. RADIUS is a very lightweight, UDP-based protocol. An IETF Working Group for RADIUS was formed in January 1996 to address the standardization of the RADIUS protocol [25]. RADIUS is designed to be extensible; all transactions are comprised of three tuples of variable length <Attribute><Length><Value>. New attribute values can be added without disturbing existing implementations of the protocol.

Because RADIUS is designed to carry authorization data and is widely deployed, it is used as one method for transferring the data required to set up dynamic tunnels for VPNs. For further information about RADIUS, the interested reader is referred to [25].

TACACS

The Defense Data Network (DDN) originally developed Terminal Access Controller Access Control System (TACACS) to control access to its TAC terminal servers. TACACS is now an industry standard protocol, specified in [26]. It is useful, however, to recognize the various flavors of TACACS currently installed in networks. They are as follows:

- TACACS is a simple UDP-based access control protocol originally developed by BBN for the MILNET. TACACS operates in a manner similar to RADIUS and is typically used to protect modem access into a network. TACACS also provides access control for routers, network access servers, and other networked devices via one or more centralized security servers. TACACS receives authentication requests from an NAS client and forwards the user name and password information to a centralized security server. The centralized server can either be a TACACS database or an external security database.

- XTACACS (extended TACACS) is a version of TACACS with extensions that Cisco added to the basic TACACS protocol to support advanced features.

- TACACS+ is another Cisco extension of TACACS. TACACS+ improves on TACACS and XTACACS by separating the AAA functions and by encrypting all traffic between the NAS and the daemon. It allows any authentication mechanism to be utilized with TACACS+ clients and uses TCP to ensure reliable delivery. The protocol allows the client to request fine-grained access control from the daemon. A key benefit to separating authentication from authorization is that authorization (and per user profiles) can be a dynamic process. TACACS+ can be integrated with other negotiations (such as a PPP negotiation) for far greater flexibility.

In all three cases the TACACS daemon should listen at port 49 (the login port assigned for the TACACS protocol). This port is reserved for both UDP and TCP. For further information, the interested reader is referred to [26–28].

Kerberos

Kerberos is an encryption-based security system that provides mutual authentication between the users and the servers in a network environment. Kerberos uses a private key encryption service based on DES. Although Kerberos provides a full AAA service, it is primarily used for authentication. The Kerberos Network Authentication Service version 5 is described in [29]. In a Kerberos environment at least one secure host will be running as the Kerberos server (referred to as the trusted server, or the Key Distributed Center—KDC); all other clients and servers on the network are assumed to be untrustworthy. The trusted server provides authentication services for all other clients and services. Each client and server (referred to as the principals) hold a private DES key. The trusted server holds a database of the names and private keys associated with all clients and servers allowed to use its services. It is assumed that the principals keep their passwords secure. For further information about Kerberos. the interested reader is referred to [30, 31].

5.3.5   Protocol-based security services

Secure Sockets Layer (SSL)

Secure Sockets Layer (SSL) is a de facto security protocol initially developed by Netscape Communications Corporation [32] in cooperation with RSA Security, Inc. [20]. SSL works by using a private key to encrypt data that are transferred over the SSL connection. The main aim of the SSL protocol is to provide a secure, reliable pipe between two communicating applications by providing both encryption and authentication features. It was designed to improve security for services such as HTTP, Telnet, NNTP, and FTP. SSL provides an alternative to the standard TCP/IP socket API, so in theory it is possible to run any TCP/IP socket application over a secure SSL interface without changing the application. SSL version 3 is an open protocol and one of the most popular security mechanisms deployed on the Internet. It is documented in an IETF draft, although the IETF has renamed SSL Transport Layer Security (TLS) [33]. SSLv3 and SSLv2 are backward compatible; the main enhancements in SSLv3 are support for client authentication and more ciphering types in the cipher specification. The SSL protocol provides the following security services:

- Server authentication
- Client authentication (an optional service)
- Integrity of communication over an SSL connection
- Confidentiality of communication over an SSL connection

SSL sits between the Transport Layer and the Application Layer (see Figure 5.4) and is designed to protect the pipe (i.e., IP datagrams) and not individual objects being communicated over the pipe. This means that SSL cannot provide nonrepudiation services or protect individual objects (such as a Web page). SSL is composed of two layers: the SSL Handshake Protocol is the upper layer, comprising a protocol for initial authentication and transfer of encryption keys between the client and server. The SSL Record Protocol is the lower layer and comprises a reliable protocol for encapsulating and transferring data (using a variety of predefined cipher and authentication combinations).

Operation

By convention, Web pages that require an SSL connection are prefixed using the special URL method https: rather than http:. An SSL-protected HTTP transfer also uses port 443, rather than HTTP's default port 80. To access a secure Web server an SSL-enabled browser is required (sites often allow normal HTTP access if the browser does not support SSL, but any transactions are at the user's risk). The two most popular Web browsers, Netscape Navigator and Microsoft's Internet Explorer both support SSL. Today, SSL is primarily used for transmitting private documents or securing transactions over the Internet. SSL has been primarily used for HTTP access, although Netscape has stated an intention to employ it for other application types, such as NNTP and Telnet, and there are several free implementations available on the Internet. Many e-commerce Web sites use SSL to provide secure connections for transferring credit card numbers and other sensitive user data. IBM uses SSL to secure TN3270 sessions. As an example, an SSL session using HTTP is initiated as follows:

- The user requests a document using the special URL prefix https:, either by typing it into the URL, or by clicking on a link (e.g., https://www.testmysecurity.com) via the Web browser.

- The client (an SSL-enabled browser) recognizes the SSL request and establishes a connection through TCP port 443 to the SSL-enabled Web server.

- The client then initiates the SSL handshaking phase, using the SSL Record Protocol as a carrier. At this point there is no encryption or integrity checking built into the connection.

An SSL session operates in two basic states: session and connection. The SSL handshake protocol coordinates the states of the client and the server. In addition, there are read and write states defined to coordinate the encryption in accordance with the change cipher specification messages. SSL has two phases, as follows:

- Phase 1—negotiation and authentication: During this phase the server and client authenticate each other, and the SSL Handshake Protocol negotiates the cipher suites to be used (i.e., the cryptographic algorithms and the Key Exchange Algorithms [KEA] to be used—RSA, D-H). A large number of encryption, hash, and digital signature algorithms are supported by SSL within the specifications (although most real implementations support only a few).

- Phase 2—data: During this phase the raw data are encapsulated in a simple SSL encapsulation protocol (the SSL Record Protocol) and transmitted. The sender takes messages from upper-layer services, fragments them to manageable blocks, and optionally compresses the data. It then applies a Message Authentication Code (MAC), encrypts the data, and transmits the result to the Transport Layer. The receiver takes incoming data from the Transport Layer, decrypts these data, and verifies the data using the negotiated MAC key. It then decompresses the data (if compression was enabled), reassembles the message, and transmits the message to the appropriate upper-layer service.

In practice SSL works well; however, the main problem with SSL is its use of certificates. The SSL authentication and key exchange algorithms are largely based on X.509 certificate techniques, and SSL, therefore, relies on interfacing with a PKI. Most current SSL implementations are, however, not integrated into PKI and have no means to generate or retrieve certificates. It is the user's responsibility to manually check the certificate sent by a server to ensure that the session is, indeed, connected to the intended server. If the certificate does not originate from the organization you are attempting to connect to, then you should be suspicious, since this could potentially be the signature of a man-in-the-middle attack (some companies, unfortunately, source their signature from external organizations and this can be very misleading). There are various competing or overlapping technologies with SSL, such as IPSEC, S-MIME, and SSH.

Secure HTTP (S-HTTP)

S-HTTP was developed by Enterprise Integration Technologies (EIT) (acquired by Verifone, Inc., in 1995). S-HTTP was designed to secure HTTP access and is a superset of the HTTP protocol, which provides a number of security features, including client/server authentication, spontaneous encryption, and request-response nonrepudiation. As with SSL, S-HTTP is also used to secure Web-oriented transactions over the Internet, although SSL is much more commonly deployed. Whereas SSL creates a secure client/server connection, over which any amount of data can be sent securely, S-HTTP is designed to transmit individual messages securely. SSL and S-HTTP can, therefore, be viewed as complementary rather than competing technologies. Both protocols have been approved by the IETF.

S-HTTP uses shared, private, or public keys to authenticate access and ensure confidentiality via encryption and digital signatures. The encryption and signature are controlled through a CGI script. Unfortunately, S-HTTP currently works only on SunOS 4.1.3, Solaris 2.4, Irix 5.2, HP-UX 9.03, DEC OSF/1, and AIX 3.2.4. Note that S-HTTP should not be confused with HTTPS.

SSH

SSH was developed by the Finnish company F-Secure (formerly DataFellows) and essentially provides secure Telnet (and rsh) access, as well as secure file transfer (via SFTP or SCP), replacing the insecure FTP protocol.

SSH can also be used to create a local proxy server for Internet services, providing a secure transmission tunnel for data and e-mail (e.g., PoP, IMAP, SMTP). SSH protects TCP/IP-based terminal connections in UNIX, Windows, and Macintosh environments. Its primary use to date has been for secure remote device configuration. For example, many routers and firewalls have Web servers installed and are now remotely configurable via popular Web browsers. SSH provides a way of securing the Web communication. SSH requires client software to be installed, as well as the SSH server application. For further information, the interested reader is referred to [34].

Secure Multipurpose Internet Mail Extension (S-MIME)

MIME is the official proposed standard format for extended Internet e-mail. Internet e-mail messages comprise two parts: a header and a body. Secure Multipurpose Internet Mail Extension (S-MIME) provides a consistent way to send and receive secure MIME data via the use of digital signatures and encryption. S-MIME is similar in concept to SSL but application specific. It can be used for securing other applications (such as protecting Web pages or EDI messages). S-MIME provides the following cryptographic security services for electronic messaging applications:

- Authentication

- Message integrity and nonrepudiation of origin (via digital signatures)

- Privacy and data security (via encryption).

S-MIME relies on public key technology and uses X.509 certificates to establish the identities of the communicating parties (as defined in RFC 1521). It is typically implemented in end systems and hosts, not in routers or firewalls.

Pretty Good Privacy (PGP)

PGP is a technique for encrypting messages developed by Philip Zimmerman. PGP is one of the most common ways to protect messages on the Internet, because it is effective, easy to use, and free. PGP is based on the public key, which uses two keys. One is a public key that you disseminate to anyone from whom you want to receive a message; the other is a private key that you use to decrypt messages that you receive. To encrypt a message using PGP, you need the PGP encryption package, which is available for free from a number of sources. The official repository is at the Massachusetts Institute of Technology.

Secure Electronic Transaction (SET)

The SET specifications emerged through an agreement by MasterCard International and Visa International to cooperate on the creation of a single electronic credit card system, enabling secure credit card transactions over the Internet. Prior to SET, each organization had proposed its own protocol and each had received support from a number of networking and computing companies. There are several major supporters of the SET specification (e.g., IBM, Microsoft, Netscape, and GTE). SET is a complex standard—for further information, see [14]; this site also maintains a list of cooperating organizations and companies and their status with regard to deploying SET.

IPSec

IP Security (IPSec) is a set of IETF standards for use with IPv4 and IPv6. IPSec provides a standards-based mechanism for protecting IP datagrams, using authentication, integrity, and privacy at the packet level. IPSec can be used to protect IP packets by tunneling them over untrusted networks such as the Internet. The integrity and authentication services are not provided using digital signatures, but use a special form of key seeded hashes called HMAC (Keyed Hashing for Message Authentication—essentially a form of digital signature using symmetric key techniques without the benefit of private-public key technology [35]). This authentication header can be appended to the datagram. Confidentiality is also provided by the IP Encapsulating Security Payload (ESP), which encrypts the complete datagram payload and header and prepends another cleartext header to the datagram. This makes IPSec extremely useful for creating virtual private networks, and there is now growing support from router, firewall, and some host vendors (such as NorTel, Cisco, RAD, Nokia, and Checkpoint).

5.3.6   Firewalls

Firewalls are probably the most widely publicized security technique at present, and many networks have successfully installed first- or second-generation firewall technology. The classic definition of a firewall is a system that enforces security policy between a trusted internal network and an untrusted external network (such as the Internet), as illustrated in Figure 5.8. In this model we trust everybody on the internal network and nobody outside. Access to external resources may be permitted; access to internal resources is not.

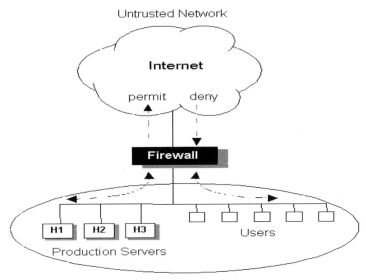

Figure 5.8
*Traditional
firewall concepts.*

Types of Firewalls

Firewalls have evolved from two different directions, and the technology is now finally starting to merge into a hybrid product. First, there are firewalls that have clearly been derived from router implementations. Second, there are firewalls that have evolved from host-gateway implementations, where standard server applications (such as the Telnet daemon on UNIX) have been modified to monitor and relay sessions for secure end-to-end communications. A new generation of products uses a technique called stateful inspection. This uses object-oriented techniques and builds dynamic data structures for flows through the firewall to model and control application behavior. For many network managers it is not a great leap to go from static filters (sometimes called Access Control Lists—ACLs) on routers to a more stateful rule base on a firewall.

Firewalls can be implemented either as an embedded application running on proprietary platforms (such as Cisco's PIX) or as a set of software modules running on general-purpose operating systems such as Windows, UNIX, or LINUX (e.g., Checkpoint's FireWall-1). Firewall architectures can be broadly classified into three groups, as follows:

- Packet-filtering routers/circuit-level gateways

- Proxy servers/application gateways

- Stateful firewalls

Each of these architectures has its own advantages and disadvantages, as discussed in the following text.

Packet-filtering routers

Routers have historically been convenient places to deploy security policy and offer several basic features of interest, including the following:

- Route filtering—Controlling routing information is an important part of the security strategy, and some of the more advanced routing protocols provide features that can be used as part of a security strategy. You may be able to insert a filter on the advertised routes, so that specific routes are not advertised to parts of the network. Routing protocols such as OSPF and ISIS can authenticate other routers before they become neighbors. These authentication mechanisms are typically protocol specific and often quite weak, but they do help to improve network stability by preventing unauthorized routers or hosts from participating in the routing protocol.

- Packet filtering—Many firewalls today are basically routers with advanced filtering techniques. Cisco's terminology for packet filters is Access Control Lists (ACLs), and this term is now commonly understood to be a generic term for packet filters across the industry. Packet filtering is commonly implemented in routers, mainly because the router is often located at positions in the network where traffic and administrative domains are joined. As part of the routing process, packets arriving at an interface are examined and the router compares data in the packet headers with a list of defined filtering rules and makes logical decisions regarding whether or not to forward the packet, discard it, and/or generate events.

When performing packet filtering, the following information is typically examined in IP packets:

- Source IP address

- Destination IP address

- Source TCP/UDP port

- Destination TCP/UDP port

- Encapsulated protocol ID (TCP, UDP, IP tunnel, or ICMP)

- ICMP message type

Many common IP services use well-known TCP and UDP port numbers, and it is often simple to allow or deny these services by configuring address and port information in the filter. For example, a Telnet server listens for connections on TCP port 23 (0x17). By setting a filter on port 23 for a specific interface, Telnet connections can be permitted or denied in either direction. This would, for example, allow us to implement a rule that says that Telnet connections to the Internet are allowed but Telnet from the Internet must be disallowed. For example, under Cisco IOS:

```
define filter 1 if 3 ip addr any tcp port 23 incoming action deny
define filter 2 if 3 ip addr any tcp port 23 outgoing action permit
```

Packet-filtering rules are relatively straightforward and can be used to implement part of a security policy. One of the problems with this approach, however, is the static nature of filters and the level of granularity offered. Application behavior can be very hard to capture in a static filter; some applications are dynamic in their use of ports (NFS, HTML, and TFTP) and may use embedded addresses (such as NetBIOS). For example, NFS uses Remote Procedure Calls (RPCs), where each call can utilize different ports for each connection dynamically. With packet filters we are restricted to protocols up to the socket layer (transport interface). Setting custom filters, which dig deeper into user data, is not a good idea and is potentially very CPU intensive. This leads in to another potential problem performance. As the number of ACLs increases, this is likely to degrade performance significantly on low-end systems due to the time required to parse each of these rules in sequence. Once this starts to become a real problem, it is time to invest in a more stateful firewall (or a router that maintains a connection table that can be hooked into the firewall function). Some routers implement custom code to deal with well-known attacks without sacrificing performance. For example, advanced filtering rules can check IP options, fragment offset, and so on. There may be specific features to handle SYN attacks (these are attacks that exploit the fact that TCP connection requests consume resources on hosts that wait for the three-way TCP handshake to be completed).

Routers operate at the network level and cannot provide a complete solution. They are unable to provide security even for some of the most basic services and protocols. Routers have the following problems when deploying security:

- Packet filters can be difficult to deploy, synchronize, and maintain in a large internetwork.

- Routers only access a limited part of the packet's header information and therefore do not understand content. Higher-level applications are invisible to routers above the socket layer.

- Router ACLs are static; they do not have the flexibility or knowledge to deal with dynamic changes in protocol or application states. To handle more complex, higher-level protocols and applications we need a more stateful monitoring of the traffic flows.

- Routers do not provide the sophisticated event logging and alert mechanisms required for security audits.

Another potential pitfall of general-purpose packet filter–based firewalls is that they can inherit underlying bugs in the operating system (i.e., bugs that may not affect routing operations but can represent serious security flaws when used in a firewall context).

Proxy servers/application gateways

Proxies are usually host implementations of firewalls, comprising two or more network interfaces and supporting relay services for common applications in software. Their primary advantage is their statefulness. Proxies provide partial awareness of protocol states and full awareness of application states. Proxies are also capable of processing and manipulating information. Figure 5.9 illustrates the general model for a proxy. There are several disadvantages in using application-level proxies as firewalls, including the following:

- Each new service requires its own proxy. This limits the ability to respond to new types of services and also severely limits scalability.

- Proxies are not available for UDP, RPC, and other services from common protocol groups.

- Implementation of a specific proxy server is resource intensive and limits performance.

- Proxies may not be aware of issues in lower-level protocols and services.

- Proxies are rarely transparent to users.

- Proxies can be vulnerable to OS and application-level bugs (e.g., if a general-purpose operating system is used and has not been sufficiently tested/hardened for secure environments).

Proxies are effectively the first generation of true firewalls and for many years have been deployed successfully to protect users and services, especially when interfacing with the Internet. As application and traffic demands grow, their relative inflexibility, lack of transparency, and lack of scalability have forced users to look for more powerful hybrid solutions, such as those products supporting stateful technology.

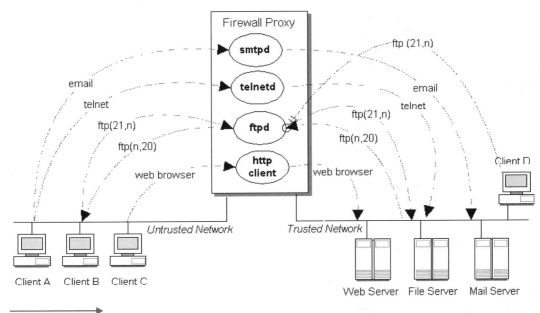

Figure 5.9   *General model for a proxy server handling e-mail, Web, terminal, and file transfer traffic.*

SOCKS

SOCKS is often referred to as a circuit-level gateway, a more transparent version of a proxy where the user does not have to connect to the firewall first before requesting the second connection to the destination server. SOCKS is basically a set of library calls for use on a proxy server. This library must be compiled onto the SOCKS server to replace standard system calls. Special code is required for clients and a separate set of configuration profiles on the firewall. Content servers do not require any modification, since they are unaware that the connection requests are coming from the SOCKS server and not the client. The majority of Web browsers support SOCKS, and you can get SOCKS-enabled TCP/IP stacks for most platforms.

SOCKS operates transparently from the user's perspective. The client initiates a connection to the server using the server's IP address. In practice the session is directed through the SOCKs server, which validates the source address and userID and, if authorized, establishes a connection to the desired server transparently (the session is relayed via the SOCKS server using two sessions). The functionality offered by SOCKS depends on the version of software you are using. SOCKSv4 supports only outbound TCP sessions (it has weak authentication and is, therefore, inappropriate for sessions coming into a trusted network from an untrusted network). SOCKSv5 supports both TCP and UDP sessions and supports several authentication methods, including the following:

- User name/password authentication

- One-time password generators

- Kerberos

- Remote Authentication Dial-In User Services (RADIUS)

- Password Authentication Protocol (PAP)

- IPSec authentication method

SOCKSv5 also supports several encryption standards, including DES, Triple DES, and IPSEC, and the tunneling protocols PPTP, L2F, and L2TP. SOCKSv5 also supports both SKIP and ISAKMP/Oakley key management systems. The SOCKSv5 server listens for connections on port 1080 and supports both TCP and UDP connections. SOCKSv5 is appropriate for use with both outbound and inbound sessions. For additional information, refer to [36–39].

Stateful firewalls

Checkpoint Software Technologies [4] was the first vendor to produce a product employing so-called stateful inspection technology.

The stateful inspection module (implemented in the kernel to minimize context switches) accesses and analyzes data derived from all communication layers. This state and context information is cached and updated dynamically, providing valuable data for tracking both connection-oriented flows (e.g., TCP) and connectionless flows (from protocols such as RPC and those based on UDP). The conceptual architecture of such a system is illustrated in Figure 5.10. The ability to handle stateless services is a significant advantage over proxy servers. When used with a user-configured security rule set, this state information provides the necessary real-time information to make decisions about forwarding traffic, encrypting packets, and generating alarms and events. Any traffic not explicitly allowed by the security rules is discarded by default, and real-time security alerts are generated. This architecture is much more flexible and manageable than the proxy approach, since it takes a generic approach to content. There are advocates of the proxy approach who maintain that it is inherently more secure; however, the market is clearly indicating its preference, with Checkpoint Firewall-1 being the dominant firewall platform today by far.

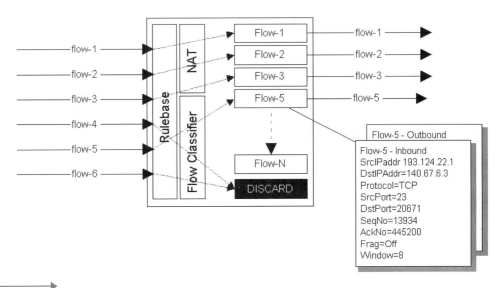

Figure 5.10   *Conceptual architecture of a stateful firewall.*

In Figure 5.10, incoming traffic is compared with the rule-base and, if acceptable, classified as a connection-oriented or connectionless flow/session, based on features such as addressing and port numbers. Once classified the flow is assigned resources (normally a data structure is created to maintain status information and counters on this flow). All activity on a flow is monitored and updated to ensure that the state of the session is known at any particular time. The figure illustrates the type of information monitored for a Telnet session in Flow-5, including caching of sequence numbers to avoid session hijacking. If multiple firewalls are deployed in a clustered configuration, then these session states need to be regularly synchronized.

Personal firewalls

The latest development in firewall technology is the migration of firewall software onto end systems such as laptops, workstations, and servers. Basic features include IP packet filtering rules for inbound and outbound traffic (e.g., the administrator could define a policy that blocks all incoming connections to workstations), a database of predefined network services (such as SMTP e-mail, Windows file sharing, HTTP, and FTP), and IP packet logging for auditing the possible uses as evidence of attempted attacks. At present this technology is fairly immature, but this represents an interesting area for the future. Examples include McAfee's Personal Firewall [41], and F-Secure's Distributed Firewall [34]. Products are also available from Checkpoint [4].

Limitations of firewalls

While traditional firewalls are extremely useful security devices, they are point solutions and do not scale well or provide complete integrity. There is currently a move to implement more pervasive and robust techniques under the umbrella of the PKI. It is important to recognize that the nature of security threats is dynamic. So a firewall is always potentially vulnerable to a new form of attack. The network administrator must be vigilant in examining all relevant event logs and alarms.

5.3.7   Virus protection systems

Viruses probably represent the most immediate security threat to internetworks. A virus is an executable program or code that typically attaches itself to benign objects and replicates itself. A useful database of virus types is maintained by F-Secure [42]. Virus types are generally categorized as follows:

- Viruses are pieces of executable code that are self-replicating. They replicate by attaching to other executable code and so may be distributed throughout an internetwork environment rapidly by piggybacking on data transfers and downloads. Viruses are broadly divided into three classes: file infectors, boot sector viruses, and macros.

- Worms are programs that are specifically designed to search out vulnerable systems and then run on those systems, creating copies and spreading further to other systems. Worms do not require a host program to replicate, and most worms are network aware and do not require user invocation. The ILOVEYOU VB-Script worm is an example of a less sophisticated form that required the user to activate an executable in the form of an e-mail attachment.

- Trojan Horses are executable programs that typically perform some useful or amusing function, while also activating a more malicious function during execution. For example, this could be a game or animated cartoon that secretly destroys files or copies passwords, or a background program that scans the keyboard buffer looking for sensitive information such as credit card data. Perhaps the most infamous example of a Trojan Horse is Back Orifice [LOPHT].

- Logic bombs are executable code that are dormant until activated by some event (such as a change in date). Once the event trigger has occurred, a virus or worm is typically activated. For example, destructive code could be buried unnoticed inside an OS, to be activated on a specific day of a specific year. There have been several well-publicized cases of disgruntled employees engineering such occurrences.

Part of the problem with viruses is that they are now far easier to write and distribute. Viruses are frequently transported in e-mail, most commonly as embedded Visual BASIC for Applications (VBA) macros or attachments to office documents in the form of ActiveX components, Visual BASIC Script (VBS), Java applets, and other forms of applets.

Special antivirus software is now very widely deployed. Most of these tools work by scanning files and e-mail attachments against a database of virus signatures (chunks of code associated with particular viruses). If a match is found, then the file is typically disinfected automatically (by removing the offending code). An important aspect of virus protection is that viruses mutate regularly, and therefore vendors of such products provide regular upgrades for the virus signature library, which must be downloaded frequently to maintain system integrity. There are two general approaches being offered in security solutions today, as follows:

- Centrally managed at the point of ingress—Virus protection may be deployed at the public-private interface, either in dedicated standalone hardware or integrated with the firewall. All untrusted content passing through the firewall is vectored off to the screening device, where content is either disinfected or stripped away before forwarding on to the user.

- End-user managed—Virus protection systems may also be deployed directly on end-system hardware, typically as a background application running on the user's desktop device.

The latter approach may be considerably more expensive, particularly for a large enterprise, since it relies on users to regularly upgrade their virus library. There are many vendors of antivirus software; examples include McAffee's VirusScan [41], F-Secure [34], and Norton's Antivirus [44].

5.3.8   **URL protection systems**

A database of Web or FTP sites is maintained, classified according to a set of criteria (e.g., commercial enterprise, travel, and so on). Permission is set out for users based on what sites may be accessed (typically the policy is to allow access to all sites except for certain site types). The problem with this technology is that new sites are appearing daily, and a high level of manual investigation is required to classify sites. As a consequence, maintenance of the URL classification database is very labor intensive and not guaranteed to be foolproof. Users must also resynchronize databases on a daily basis. URL scanners are typically deployed, either on or closely coupled with firewalls. New URL requests are intercepted and compared with the database and either passed through transparently or rejected. Examples include Web-Sense [45], Symantec I-Gear [44], and Content Technologies MIME-sweeper [46].

5.3.9   E-mail protection systems

E-mail protection is closely linked with virus protection, although e-mail protection tools typically include additional protection against spam attacks and the loss of proprietary information. By guaranteeing that only approved attachments and desired content enter or leave the network, these products ensure that viruses do not enter or leave the network. Examples include Content Technologies MAILsweeper [46], and Symantec Mail-Gear [44].

5.3.10   Intrusion Detection Systems (IDS)

Intrusion Detection Systems (IDSs) are a complementary technology closely associated with firewalls; however, an IDS should only be deployed once strong firewall policy and authentication processes have been deployed. Intrusion detection offers an added layer of security. If the firewall were represented by the checkout staff in a supermarket, then the IDS system would be the plainclothes security staff pounding the aisles searching for shoplifters. While firewalls are good at enforcing policy and handling specific security attacks on a protocol or session basis, they are not currently capable of identifying more sophisticated distributed or composite attacks. IDSs are designed to scan for both misuse attacks and anomalies, either at the packet level or within event logs generated by firewalls, using a combination of rule-based technology and artificial intelligence. For example, an IDS might be configured with a rule to scan for several different types of events over a specific time period. A more dynamic learning IDS might scan events and classify events as interesting, anomalous, or threatening and modify its own rule base on the fly. An important issue IDS must deal with is the reporting of so-called false positives (or metaphorically crying wolf), since this could result in a form of denial of service or at minimum result in a lack of credibility in the IDS system. Note that hackers are already mounting sophisticated attacks to create such problems.

Because of the processing power required, IDSs are typically deployed behind the firewall, running as a second-tier security barrier. Some IDS systems are closely coupled with particular firewall technology, so that anomalous activity picked up by the IDS could, in theory, be fed back into the firewall rule base. A good IDS system should warn you that an attack is taking place at the time of attack, although many IDS systems are much less proactive. This technology is relatively immature, and there is a clear requirement for IDS data collection points to be coordinated, since a standalone IDS is not much use in a large internetwork with multiple ingress and egress points. There is also potential harm in integrating complementary data-gathering technologies, such as RMON, since one of the problems with IDS is the ability to capture and coordinate data in real time from many data sources.

Honeypots and burglar alarms are really subsets of IDS functionality and are therefore described here briefly. A honeypot is typically a server, dressed up to look interesting enough for a hacker to try to attempt access. For example, you could call your server finance.mycompany.com and then populate it with all sorts of interesting data. The idea is to entice the hacker in, and then record all activity to try trace the source and assist possible subsequent prosecution. A burglar alarm is a way of signaling that somebody is using a feature of a system that is not supposed to be used, thereby alarming the network staff to the possibility of an intruder. For example, a dummy user account may sound an alarm if used.

Examples of commercial IDS include Internet Security Systems (ISS) RealSecure [47], Intrusion Detection's Kane Security Monitor [48], Cisco's NetRanger [28], Network Associates CyberCop [49], Axent Technologies OmniGuard-Intruder Alert [50], Trusted Information Systems Stalkers [51], and Advisor Technologies's event log analysis system [52]. There are also many noncommercial tools available, including SHADOW [6]. For further information on IDS systems, the interested reader is referred to [6, 53].

5.3.11 Virtual Private Network

A Virtual Private Network (VPN) is generally characterized as an extension of an enterprise's private intranet across a public network, such as the Internet, creating a secure private pipe or private tunnel.

The term virtual means that the network is simulated to appear to be a single continuous private entity, when in reality it may be a collection of many disparate interconnected networks and technologies. The term private means that information flow over this virtual pipe is encapsulated, encrypted, and authenticated in such a way that it is impenetrable to hackers (i.e., data cannot be eavesdropped and decoded while in transit—at least

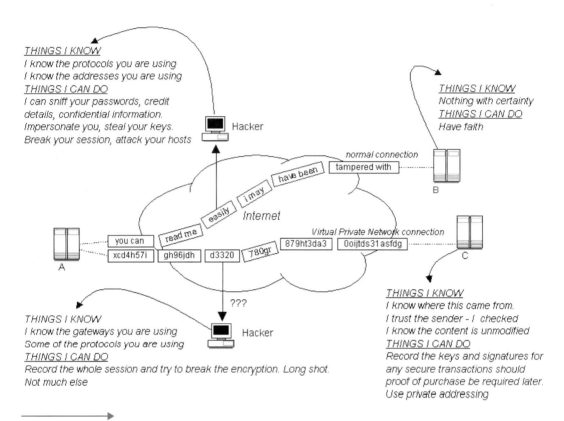

Figure 5.11   *VPN and normal session characteristics.*

that's the theory). In practice VPNs may be established between any intelligent network devices, even between two laptop computers (equipped with appropriate protocol support). Confidentiality may also extend beyond the user data; VPN tunneling enables internal addressing details and application protocols to be obfuscated. Figure 5.11 illustrates the key differences between a normal user connection and a VPN connection, and the information and actions available to a malicious user in each case. In Figure 5.11, Host A has a normal connection to Host B (e.g., a standard TCP session) and a VPN connection to Host C. The VPN connection is encrypted and authenticated and may or may not use tunneling techniques to hide the original site details and protocols. Anybody with access to an Internet backbone or ISP link can retrieve confidential data, keys, and passwords from a standard session, replay the session, mount a man-in-the-middle attack, and retrieve sensitive site topology information. All of these details can be hidden inside a VPN.

Types of VPNs

VPNs can be broadly divided into two basic modes, dial or dedicated, as follows.

- Dial VPNs offer remote access to intranets for mobile users and telecommuters. This is the most common form of VPN deployed today. Figure 5.12 illustrates the concept of a dial VPN for remote users. VPN access is outsourced, with the service provider managing modem banks to ensure reliable connectivity, while the organization manages intranet user authentication. In Figure 5.12, note that access is via the local ISP PoPs (points of presence) and is, therefore, charged at local call rates regardless of end-to-end distance. Many VPNs can be set up in this way, all overlaying each other and completely independent. For example, an enterprise could have a site-to-site VPN to other customer offices and suppliers. Quality (throughput, delay, etc.) is not guaranteed at present. The VPN may not, in fact, allow access to all of the HQ network. For specific customers there can be a DMZ (demilitarized zone) implemented at HQ for semitrusted access over the VPN. Roaming users and home users hook into HQ just as if they were directly connected.

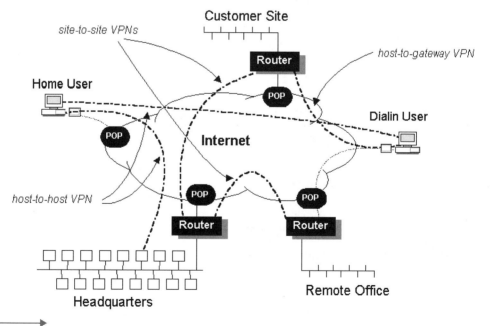

Figure 5.12   *Simple VPN deployment over the Internet.*

- Dedicated VPNs are typically implemented as high-speed connections between private sites connecting multiple users and services. CPE devices such as routers and firewalls typically create the tunnels and enforce policy. Dedicated IVPNs are typically employed to connect the intranet backbone to remote offices or extranet partners over the wide area network.

To counteract this threat VPN traffic is typically authenticated, encrypted, and optionally encapsulated (tunneled) inside a Layer 3 protocol so that its contents are not readily available to other users accessing the same wide area media. Traffic from one virtual network connection passes alongside encrypted and unencrypted traffic from many other public or private networks over a common infrastructure (rather like ships in the night). Sophisticated VPN technologies (such as IPSec) exchange and frequently update encryption keys in a way that makes line tapping, man-in-the-middle attacks, and spoofing virtually impossible.

Issues with VPNs

VPNs are designed to resolve some of the key issues that occur when attempting to transfer data reliably over public networks such as the Internet and between end sites that may or may not run IP protocols or may have private (i.e., unregistered) IP addressing schemes. Some of these problems currently have solutions; others are still being worked on, as follows:

- Protocol encapsulation—Although the Internet and many service provider backbones are based exclusively on IP, many enterprise networks still rely on protocols such as IPX, AppleTalk, and NetBEUI. To carry these protocols over an IP backbone they must be encapsulated and decapsulated at the backbone ingress and egress points, until either protocol conversion or a native IP stack is installed at the enterprise. Encapsulation increases packet sizes.

- Address transparency—For non-IP enterprise networks, tunneling is possibly the best way to carry non-IP traffic over a pure IP core, since end-to-end addressing information is preserved but remains transparent to the core. Furthermore, many IP enterprises have private or unregistered IP addressing schemes that cannot directly interface with the core, and Network Address Translation (NAT) is only a partial solution.

- Security—Any information passed over a public network such as the Internet is open to attack from malicious users or competitors. VPNs use encryption algorithms and public-private key techniques to assure data integrity and strong authentication to assure trust.

- Reliability—The Internet currently has no end-to-end quality of service, and for now we have to expect best-effort delivery in most situations. For many businesses this is simply not acceptable, and this is one of the key factors constraining VPN deployment. Holistic architectures, such as differentiated services, are required to assure end-to-end performance and reliability. Without QoS many enterprises cannot migrate to full-scale VPN deployment, especially those with mission- or time-critical applications. This is an area of intense research.

- Management and maintenance—Diagnosing problems on a private network is hard enough—imagine what the task would be like over a VPN. VPNs running over the Internet could be extremely difficult to debug. There may be several technologies and service providers involved in an end-to-end VPN path, and cooperation between providers will be critical to avoid excessive downtime. Furthermore, with end-to-end VPNs (where the VPN is effectively invisible to the provider) providers may have real problems engineering appropriate QoS and providing any useful reports.

5.4 VPN architectures

Commercial VPN architectures come in several forms, depending upon the service provider and the services offered. Large service providers have the problem of integrating new services with their legacy infrastructure, and a VPN service offered will reflect this. At the other end of the spectrum, start-up providers have very little existing infrastructure and are free to design an IVPN from scratch. Organizations building their own VPN infrastructure can choose to outsource the whole venture or manage it themselves.

5.4.1 Dial VPNs

Virtual dial-up enables many separate and autonomous protocol domains to share a common access infrastructure, including modems, access servers, and ISDN routers. Protocols such as Generic Router Encapsulation (GRE), Point-to-Point Tunneling Protocol (PPTP), Layer 2 Tunneling Protocol (L2TP), and Cisco's Layer 2 Forwarding (L2F) enable tunneling of IP and non-IP link layer protocols (such as HDLC, asynchronous HDLC, or SLIP frames). Using these tunnels, it is possible to insulate protocol and addressing details at the location of the dial-up server and target network from the transport network. This new breed of tunneling protocols allows multiple protocols (such as IP, IPX, and AppleTalk) and unregistered IP addresses (or non-IP addresses) to be tunneled over the Internet. The mechanisms used for virtual dial-up service are intended to coexist with legacy dial-up mechanisms (i.e., an ISP's PoP should be able to simultaneously service ISP clients as well as virtual dial-up clients).

With dial VPNs the service providers provide the remote dial capabilities as part of a VPN service. Subscribers access dial ports by calling a local number to a service provider PoP. Shared dial ports are available to all subscribers to leverage a provider's capital investment. Tunnels provide connections across the public IP network. Subscribers may keep policy control for optimal user authorization and control, along with the security policy server and databases. This function may also be outsourced to the service provider. Dial IP VPNs can be client initiated or NAS initiated.

Client-initiated dial VPNs (voluntary mode)

In a client-initiated dial VPN, a remote client (typically a PC) dials into a local PoP using one of a number of techniques (e.g., dial-up POTS, ISDN, ADSL, etc.), as illustrated in Figure 5.13. The client then requests an encrypted tunnel through to the target intranet to establish a private connection. The secure connection is generally established via IPSec client software running on the PC, in cooperation with a security appliance such as the firewall or router on the corporate intranet access point. Authentication is handled on two levels: the service provider performs basic authentication when a user dials the PoP (e.g., via a RADIUS server on the PoP LAN). This simply establishes the identity of the user. Once the user is authenticated, the dial IP VPN service opens a tunnel to the corporate home gateway, which performs user-level authentication using standard PPP authentication. Since the encrypted tunnel is transparent to the provider, the provider can offer very limited value-added services. Managing client software on a large-scale deployment of mobile user may also impact scalability. For these reasons, many service providers are choosing to implement services where the tunnel is created as part of the service provider network.

In Figure 5.13, the NAS is located in the ISP PoP, typically with an integrated rotary modem capability. For dial-up VPN operation users dial into the NAS, using PPP dial-up software, where they are authenticated (initially at the link level via PPP using PAP or CHAP and then possibly on user-level authentication via a RADIUS server on the PoP LAN). A second

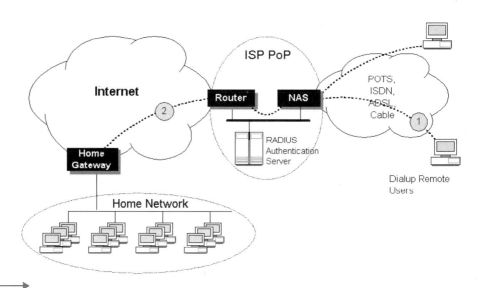

Figure 5.13   *Dial-up VPN operation.*

connection is established through the home gateway via the PoP router or firewall to complete the end-to-end VPN (e.g., by running IPSec at the client).

NAS-initiated dial VPNs (compulsory mode)

In NAS-initiated dial VPNs a service provider NAS initiates the tunnel to the corporate router or home gateway. The IETF standard solution to establish secure tunnels between a user and the home gateway is to use the Layer Two Tunneling Protocol (L2TP). Vendors may also offer proprietary solutions (such as Cisco's Layer 2 Forwarding protocol, L2F). The L2TP standard combines L2F with Microsoft's Point-to-Point Tunneling Protocol (PPTP). To the gateway, L2TP tunnels appear as if the dial users are connecting from a local modem. With L2F or L2TP, users may be authenticated using TACACS or RADIUS servers at the corporate gateway. For additional security, data may be encrypted on a connection or application basis. There are many advantages with managed NAS-initiated dial intranet services. No client software is required on user PCs, greatly simplifying user administration. Since the service provider initiates the tunnel, the provider can also potentially offer premium value-added services, such as reserved modem ports, modem availability guarantees, and priority transport. The NAS can also simultaneously provide both Internet and VPN access. This solution is also more scalable and manageable, since all traffic to a specific destination travels over a single tunnel from an NAS.

5.4.2 Dedicated IVPNs

Dedicated IP tunnels may be created over the Internet using a security appliance such as the firewall or a router supporting IPSec. IPSec is used to create and secure the tunnels, although routers can also create tunnels using a combination of IPsec and Generic Routing Encapsulation (GRE). The tunnel can be used to encapsulate only original packet data (using the original IP address fields for routing) or the whole packet (in which case the original addressing is preserved, and there is the potential for relaying the data). When mapping tunnels onto a physical infrastructure, service providers can provision point-to-point virtual circuits to create IVPNs (e.g., Frame Relay or ATM PVCs). Large service providers (such as telcos or PTTs) use this method to offer IVPNs by leveraging their existing frame or cell-switching infrastructures.

5.5   IP Security architecture (IPSec)

The technologies discussed so far offer the capability to tunnel protocols and user data but do not inherently provide privacy. To satisfy the requirements for scalable, flexible, interoperable VPNs, a major initiative by the IETF Security Working Group has produced a standard called the IP Security Architecture (IPSec). IPSec provides a generic mechanism for the secure transfer of IP-based application data in both public and private networks. IPSec is designed to enable client and gateway products from many vendors to interoperate freely and therefore creates true end-to-end security across multivendor networks such as the Internet. Specifically, as follows:

- IPSec works just above the IP layer, protecting IP datagrams; therefore, any IP-based protocol or application can be automatically secured (unlike protocol-specific mechanisms such as SSL and S-HTTP).

- IPSec is supported as an IPv4 option and as an IPv6 extension header. All IPv6 implementations are required to support IPSec; IPv4 implementations are strongly recommended to do so. Since IPSec works at Layer 3, this enables IPSec to operate transparently over any existing IP infrastructures; existing higher-level protocols and applications do not require any modification.

- IPSec supports standards-based encryption, integrity, and authentication schemes. IPSec is not tied to any particular ciphers and has the flexibility to support emerging, more powerful algorithms as required. Keyed hash algorithms, such as HMAC, combined with traditional hash algorithms, such as MD5 or SHA, are supported for packet authentication. Digital certificates are also fully supported.

- IPSec specifies IKE, a public-key (Diffie-Helman) approach to automatic key management (although other automated key distribution techniques may be used). This is a powerful feature that greatly eases deployment and promotes scalability. Manual key distribution of keys is also supported; for example, KDC-based systems such as Kerberos and other public-key systems such as SKIP could be employed.

- IPSec enables the network administrator to control the granularity at which a security service is offered. For example, a single encrypted tunnel could be created to transport all the traffic between sites, or a separate encrypted tunnel could be established per TCP connection between sites.

It is important to understand that IPSec is limited to tunneling IP applications only; for tunneling non-IP applications it should be used in conjunction with a multiprotocol encapsulation technique such as GRE or L2TP. Having said that, protocols such as NetWare IPX, AppleTalk OSI, and Banyan VINES will happily run over IP instead of their native Layer 3 stacks (e.g., OSI transport class 4 uses IP protocol number 29; VINES uses IP protocol number 83), and where sites are running pure IP at Layer 3, these protocols can be readily tunneled over IPSec.

One of the major strengths of IPSec is that it was developed through open consensus over several years via the IETF (in contrast to technologies such as PPTP, which required several subsequent fixes after security flaws were discovered). IPSec offers flexible building blocks from which robust, secure VPNs can be constructed. Most leading VPN vendors already support IPSec. IPSec is typically implemented on hosts (PCs, servers, etc.) or security gateways (routers, firewalls, or VPN devices), in one of three formats, as follows:

- Native IP implementation is integrated directly into the native IP stack source code and is applicable to both hosts and security gateways.

- Bump-in-the-Stack (BITS) implementation is implemented transparently, between the native IP stack and the local network drivers. Access to the IP stack source code is not required, so this approach may be appropriate for use with legacy systems (usually employed in hosts).

- Hardware assist is another transparent implementation sometimes referred to as a Bump-in-the-Wire (BITW) implementation, applicable to both gateways and hosts. Here, an outboard crypto-processor card is deployed. This is a common design feature of military and high-end commercial network security systems. Usually the BITW device is IP addressable. When supporting a single host, it may be quite analogous to a BITS implementation, but in supporting a router or firewall, it must operate as a security gateway.

This section provides a concise technical review of IPSec and its operations. For further information on IPSec and its components, the interested reader is referred to [54–60].

5.5.1   IPSec concepts and terminology

The IPSec framework comprises three main components, responsible for authentication, privacy, and key management, as follows:

- IP Authentication Header (AH) provides data integrity and data origin authentication and replay protection for IP datagrams. Authentication is applied to the whole IP datagram, including the initial IP header.

- IP Encapsulating Security Payload (ESP) provides data confidentiality (encryption), data origin authentication, data integrity, and replay protection for IP payloads. Here, authentication is applied to the IP datagram beyond the initial IP header.

- Internet Key Exchange (IKE) provides automated setting up of security associations and automated generation and refresh of cryptographic keys.

Fundamental to IPSec is the concept of a Security Association (SA). Both AH and ESP make use of SAs, and a major function of IKE is the establishment and maintenance of SAs. We will discuss each of the above components in turn, after a brief discussion of SAs.

Security Associations (SA)

A Security Association (SA) is an abstraction denoting a secure logical connection between two or more IPSec entities. An SA describes the agreed-upon security services that peer entities will use in order to communicate securely (i.e., an SA is the embodiment of the negotiated security policy between two devices, incorporating the cryptographic algorithms used, keying information, and identifying the participating parties).

There are two basic types of SA: the IKE SA (used for key and SA management) and general-purpose IPSec SAs (used for data transmission). The IKE SA is bidirectional and must be established before any data transfer is

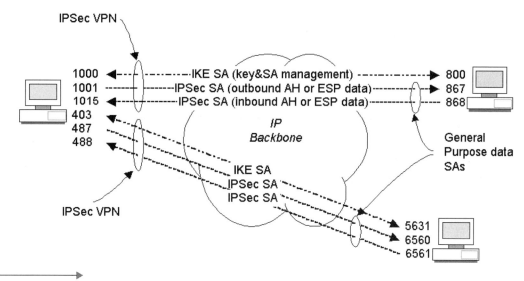

Figure 5.14   *IKE and IPSec Security Associations (SAs) for two VPNs.*

possible. IPSec SAs are unidirectional (simplex). A full IPSec VPN, therefore, comprises at least three SAs: an IKE SA plus two general-purpose SAs
for bidirectional data communication (i.e., an inbound and outbound SA
from the SA initiator's perspective). An SA can be used either for AH or
ESP and may be in either transport or tunnel mode. Figure 5.14 illustrates
the basic SA concepts. In Figure 5.14, we see that each VPN comprises an
IKE SA plus inbound and outbound (relative to the initiator) general-purpose SAs for data transmission. The allocation of SPIs is arbitrary; however,
it is recommended that new SPIs should differ from those recently used.

Each SA is identified by a 32-bit number sitting directly above the IP
layer called the Security Parameter Index (SPI). The SPI is normally allocated dynamically but is fixed for the duration of an SA. The SPI cannot be
encrypted, since it is required to identify the associated SA. A fully qualified
(i.e., unique) SA is identified by the combination of three elements:

<Security Parameter Index, IP Destination Address, Security Protocol>

Security Association Components

- Security Parameter Index (SPI)—This is a 32-bit value used to iden-
  tify different SAs with the same destination address and security pro-
  tocol. The SPI is carried in the header of the security protocol (AH or
  ESP). It has only local significance, as defined by the creator of the
  SA. The SPI values in the range 1 through 255 are reserved by the
  IANA. The SPI value of 0 must be used for local implementation-

specific purposes only. Generally, the SPI is selected by the destination system during the SA establishment.

- IP Destination Address—This address can be a unicast, broadcast, or multicast address. However, currently, SA management mechanisms are defined only for unicast addresses.

- Security Protocol—This can be either AH or ESP but not both.

An SA protects traffic within it via either AH or ESP, but not both. For a connection that requires protection from both AH and ESP a pair of SAs must be configured in each direction as defined in section 5.4.4.

IPSec databases

In order to keep track of SA connection states and the policies in place, an IPSec implementation maintains two databases, as follows:

- Security Policy Database (SPD)—This defines the security services offered to IP traffic, based on factors such as source/destination address, inbound/outbound, and so on. The SPD contains an ordered list of policy entries for inbound and/or outbound traffic. Entries in this database are similar to firewall rules or access control lists. For example, individual entries might specify that traffic to 10.0.0.0 should not go through IPSec processing, traffic to 140.168.0.0 may be discarded, and all other traffic must be processed by IPSec.

- Security Association Database (SAD)—This contains parameter information about each SA, such as AH/ESP algorithms and keys, sequence numbers, protocol mode, and SA lifetime. For outbound processing an SPD entry points to an entry in the SAD (i.e., the SPD determines which SA is applied for a given packet). For inbound processing, the SAD determines how the packet must be processed.

Tunnel and transport mode

IPSec defines two modes of operation for security associations, transport and tunnel mode, as follows:

- Transport mode—This is typically a security association between two hosts. In IPv4 the IPSec header appears immediately after the IP header and any options. In IPv6 the IPSec header appears after the base IP header and extensions but may appear before or after destination options. In both cases the IPSec header appears before any higher-layer protocols (such as TCP or UDP). In transport mode the original IP datagram is secured via IPSec, and therefore registered IP addresses are required if the datagram is to traverse public networks such as the Internet.

- Tunnel mode—In this mode a new IP datagram is constructed and the original IP datagram is fully encapsulated as payload. IPSec tunneling is modeled after [61]. It was originally designed for Mobile IP, an architecture that allows a mobile host to keep its home IP address even if attached to remote or foreign subnets. Tunnel mode is required whenever either end of an SA is operating as a security gateway, where the IPSec traffic is in transit. The IP destination address in the encapsulating header is set to the tunnel endpoint, which is not necessarily the same as the original packet destination. For example, a typical application would be to have two security gateways with an AH tunnel configured to authenticate all traffic between two sites over the Internet.

Figure 5.15 illustrates SAs in both transport and tunnel mode.

The advantages of transport mode are that it adds only a few bytes of overhead per datagram and has a lower processing overhead. Furthermore, since the IP header is passed in the clear, this enables service providers to offer special processing (such as quality of service) at quite a granular level (based on information in the header such as source and destination address, ToS bits, etc.). By contrast, tunneling obfuscates such details, exposing only gateway-to-gateway information. Even so, anything above Layer 3 is likely to be encrypted, so application-specific flow differentiation is not possible. One significant drawback of transport mode is that the IP header is open to abuse by malicious users (i.e., traffic or topology analysis can be performed

Figure 5.15
SAs are defined in either transport mode or tunnel mode.

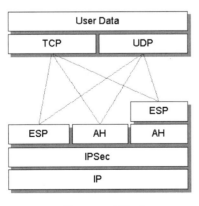

Transport Mode

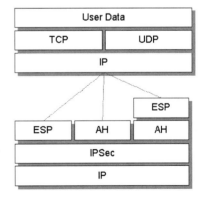

Tunnel Mode

in preparation for a subsequent denial-of-service or spoof attack). Another disadvantage is that the so-called mutable fields within the IP header are not authenticated. Tunnel mode offers complete protection of the encapsulated IP datagram; a malicious user only can determine the tunnel end points and the encapsulation protocol.

Tunnel mode also offers the possibility of using private (i.e., unregistered) addressing schemes and can be used instead of NAT in certain scenarios. A major advantage of tunnel mode is that it enables intermediate network devices (such as a router or firewall) to act as a kind of IPSec proxy for hosts that are not yet IPSec enabled. For example, two sites could be connected using an IPSec VPN via IPSec-enabled routers. Clients and servers on those sites have no IPSec capability; however, IPSec processing can be applied transparently on specified traffic between sites based on access control lists (i.e., the end systems are completely unaware of the gateways—no explicit connection must be made). This enables existing IP networks to reap the benefits of secure VPNs with minimal disruption.

Reference [54] states that a host must support both transport and tunnel mode, whereas a security gateway is required to support only tunnel mode. For all transit traffic security gateways must use tunnel mode; however, gateways frequently use transport mode also (e.g., transport mode may also be used for gateway-to-gateway management traffic such as SNMP or ICMP, where the gateway is effectively operating as a host). It is also common practice for host-to-host connections to be in tunnel mode.

5.5.2 Authentication Header (AH)

The IP Authentication Header (AH) provides integrity and data origin authentication for IP datagrams and also offers optional protection against session replay. Note that replay protection must be implemented by any IPSec-compliant system (regardless of whether it is used or not). Data integrity is assured by a checksum (ICV) generated by a message authentication code (e.g., MD5 or SHA-1); data origin authentication is assured by including a secret shared key in the data to be authenticated; and replay protection is provided by use of a sequence number field within the AH header. In the IPSec vocabulary, these three distinct functions are collectively referred to as authentication.

AH services are connectionless, operating on a per-packet basis. AH authenticates all of the IP datagram, with the exception of a small number of mutable fields in the IP header. These fields are typically modified in transit and cannot be predicted by the receiver. The mutable fields include those shown in the following chart:

IP version 4	*IP version 6*
Type of Service (TOS)	Class
Flags and fragment offset	Flow label
Time to Live (TTL)	Hop limit
Header checksum	

If these fields absolutely must be protected, then IPSec tunnel mode must be used. In tunnel mode the original IP header and associated data are encapsulated inside another IP header, so only the outer IP wrapper changes in transit. The payload of the IP packet (including the original IP header) is considered immutable and can, therefore, be fully protected by AH (or indeed ESP authentication).

AH processing is only performed on unfragmented IP packets. An IP packet that already has AH applied may be fragmented by intermediate routers but must be reassembled at the destination before passing up to the AH process, or else it will be discarded by the AH process. This prevents overlapping fragment attacks (such as teardrop). Packets that fail authenti-

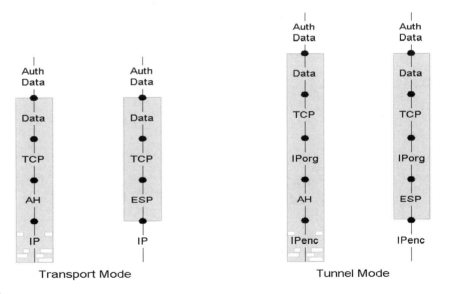

Transport Mode   Tunnel Mode

Figure 5.16   *The shaded area represents the scope of authentication for IPSec transport and tunnel mode using either the AH or the ESP protocol.*

cation are discarded and are not delivered to upper layers to reduce the chance of denial-of-service attacks. (See Figure 5.16.) Note that the patchy authentication of the IP header with AH indicates that certain fields are not authenticated (i.e., so-called mutable fields that are likely to change in transit).

AH header format

AH is identified by protocol number 51, assigned by the IANA. AH can be used either in transport mode or in tunnel mode. In transport mode AH is inserted immediately following the original IP header. If the datagram already has IPSec header(s), then the AH header is inserted before these. In tunnel mode AH is applied to the encapsulating IP header and payload, so the original IP header is fully protected. Note that early IPSec implementations may not support AH in tunnel mode. AH is an integral part of IPv6. In an IPv6 environment, AH is considered a mandatory end-to-end payload and it appears after hop-by-hop, routing, and fragmentation extension headers. The destination options, extension headers may appear either before or after the AH header. The current AH header format and operation are described in [55]. The header format is illustrated in Figure 5.17.

AH Header Fields

- Next Header—The next header is an 8-bit mandatory field that shows the data type carried in the payload—for example, an upper-level protocol identifier such as TCP. The values are chosen from the set of IP protocol numbers defined by the IANA.

Figure 5.17
AH header format.

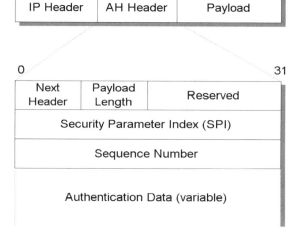

- Payload length—This field is 8 bits long and contains the length of the AH header expressed in 32-bit words, minus 2. It does not relate to the actual payload length of the IP packet as a whole. If default options are used, the value is 4 (three 32-bit fixed words plus three 32-bit words of authentication data minus 2).

- Reserved—This field is reserved for future use. Its length is 16 bits and must be set to 0.

- Security Parameter Index (SPI)—This field is 32 bits in length. It is used to distinguish among different SAs terminating at the same destination and using the same IPsec protocol. An SPI has only local significance. SPI zero is reserved for local implementation-specific applications and should not appear on the wire.

- Sequence number—This 32-bit field is a monotonically increasing counter that is used for replay protection. Replay protection is optional; however, this field is mandatory. The sender always includes this field, and it is at the discretion of the receiver to process it or not. At the establishment of an SA the sequence number is initialized to zero. The first packet transmitted using the SA has a sequence number of one. Sequence numbers are not allowed to repeat. Thus, the maximum number of IP packets that can be transmitted on any given SA is $2^{32} - 1$. After the highest sequence number is used, a new SA and consequently a new key is established. Antireplay is enabled at the sender by default. If, upon SA establishment, the receiver chooses not to use it, the sender does not process this field further. Note that the antireplay mechanism is normally not used with manual key management. Note also that the original AH specification did not discuss the concept of sequence numbers; older IPSec implementations may, therefore, not provide replay protection.

- Authentication data—This is a variable-length field containing a checksum called the Integrity Check Value (ICV). The ICV is calculated on a per-packet basis using an algorithm selected at the SA initialization. The authentication data length is an integral multiple of 32 bits. The ICV is used by the receiver to verify the integrity of the incoming packet. In theory any MAC algorithm can be used to calculate the ICV. The specification requires that HMAC-MD5-96 and HMAC-SHA-1-96 must be supported. It requires keyed MD5. In practice keyed SHA-1 is also used. Implementations usually support two to four algorithms. When performing the ICV calculation, the mutable fields are treated as zero.

5.5.3   **Encapsulating Security Payload (ESP)**

The IP Encapsulating Security Payload (ESP) provides data confidentiality using encryption. ESP can also optionally provide data origin authentication, connectionless (per packet) integrity, and replay protection. When ESP is used to provide authentication functions, it uses the same algorithms used by the AH protocol; however, the scope differs (as illustrated in Figure 5.18). The required services are configurable at SA establishment, with the following restrictions:

- Integrity checking and authentication are always enabled together (i.e., they are mutually inclusive).

- Replay protection is selectable only if authentication is enabled.

- Replay protection is selected only by the receiver.

Encryption is selectable regardless of the other service options. It is strongly recommended that if encryption is enabled, authentication should also be enabled. If encryption alone is enabled, then a malicious user could forge packets and mount cryptanalytic attacks. This is practically impossible when integrity check and authentication are enabled. Although authentication and encryption are optional, at least one of them must be enabled; otherwise, it makes no sense to use ESP at all. As with AH, ESP processing is applied only to unfragmented IP packets. If both encryption and authenti-

Figure 5.18
ESP header and trailer.

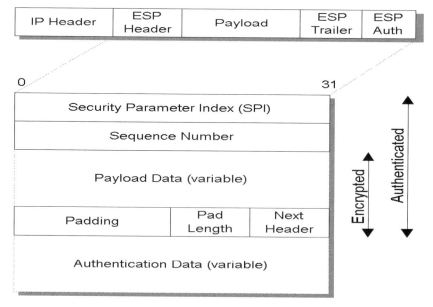

cation are selected, the receiver first authenticates the packet. If authentication fails, the packet is discarded to avoid unnecessary processing and reduce the risk of a denial-of-service attack.

The cryptographic algorithms implemented in IPSec are called transforms. For example, the DES algorithm used in ESP is called the ESP DES-CBC transform [62]. IPSec defines the interfaces into the Public Key Infrastructure (PKI) but does not explicitly specify which PKI; it defines two competing standards: Simple Key Management for Internet Protocol (SKIP) and Internet Security Association Key Management Protocol (ISAKMP). Both are so-called authenticated Diffie-Helman Key Exchange Algorithms (D-H KEAs). Typically, the authentication of the D-H public key material is provided by X.509 certificates, and, therefore, SKIP and ISAKMP do not define the full scope of a PKI and require an interface into an external certificate request-generation technology (such as provided by [18–21]).

ESP packet format

ESP is identified by protocol number 50, assigned by the IANA. The current ESP packet format is described in [56]. The format of the ESP packet is more complicated than that of the AH packet. Actually there is not only an ESP header but also an ESP trailer and ESP authentication data. The payload is encapsulated between the header and the trailer, hence the name of the protocol.

ESP Header Fields

- Security Parameter Index (SPI)—as defined for AH.

- Sequence Number—as defined for AH.

- Payload Data—The Payload Data field is mandatory. It consists of a variable number of bytes of data described by the Next Header field. This field is encrypted with the cryptographic algorithm selected during SA establishment. If the algorithm requires initialization vectors, these are also included here. The ESP specification requires support for the DES algorithm in CBC mode (DES-CBC transform). Often other encryption algorithms are supported, such as triple-DES.

- Padding—Most encryption algorithms require that the input data must be an integral number of blocks. Also, the resulting ciphertext (including the Padding, Pad Length, and Next Header fields) must terminate on a 4-byte boundary, so that the Next Header field is right-aligned. That's why this variable-length field is included. It can be used to hide the length of the original messages, too. However, this could adversely impact the effective bandwidth. Padding is an optional field. Note that encryption covers the Payload Data, Padding, Pad Length, and Next Header fields.

- Pad Length—This 8-bit field contains the number of the preceding padding bytes. It is always present, and the value of 0 indicates no padding.

- Next Header—as defined for AH.

- Authentication Data—This field is variable in length and contains the ICV calculated for the ESP packet from the SPI to the Next Header field inclusive. The Authentication Data field is optional. It is included only when integrity check and authentication have been selected at SA initialization time. The ESP specifications require two authentication algorithms to be supported: HMAC with MD5 and HMAC with SHA-1. Often the simpler keyed versions are supported by the IPSec implementations. Note that the IP header is not covered by the ICV. Note also that the original ESP specification [63] discusses the concept of authentication within ESP in conjunction with the encryption transform. That is, there is no Authentication Data field and it is left to the encryption transform to eventually provide authentication.

Since both ESP and AH provide authentication, one might question why ESP authentication does not cover the IP header, doing away with the need for AH altogether. There are several reasons for this, including the following:

- ESP requires strong cryptographic algorithms to be implemented, and these may be subject to restrictive regulations in some countries, leading to deployment problems with ESP-based solutions. However, authentication is not regulated and AH can be deployed internationally without restriction.

- For many applications only authentication is required. AH is lighter and potentially more scalable than ESP because of the simpler format and lower processing overhead, and in these cases it makes sense to use AH.

- The two protocols combined enable finer control and more flexibility for an IPSec network. By nesting AH and ESP, for example, one can implement IPSec tunnels that leverage the strengths of both.

As with AH, ESP can be used in two ways: transport mode and tunnel mode. In transport mode the original IP datagram is taken and the ESP header is inserted immediately after the IP header. If the datagram already has IPSec header(s), then the ESP header is inserted before any of those. The ESP trailer and the optional authentication data are appended to the payload. ESP in transport mode provides neither authentication nor encryption for the IP header. This is a disadvantage, since false packets might be delivered for ESP processing. In tunnel mode ESP offers complete protection if both encryption and authentication are selected, since the original IP datagram becomes the payload data for the new ESP packet (only the encapsulating IP header is not protected). As with AH, ESP is an integral part of IPv6. In an IPv6 environment, ESP is considered an end-to-end payload and it appears after hop-by-hop, routing, and fragmentation extension headers. The destination option extension headers could appear either before or after the AH header.

5.5.4   Combining IPSec protocols

IP packets transmitted over an individual SA are protected either by AH or ESP but not both. Where the security policy requires a combination of services for a particular traffic flow, it is necessary to employ multiple SAs. The term SA bundle refers to a sequence of SAs through which traffic must be processed in order to satisfy the security policy. The order of the sequence is defined by the policy. Note that the SAs that comprise a bundle may terminate at different end points (e.g., one SA may extend between a mobile host and a security gateway and a second, nested SA may extend to a host behind the gateway). The use of SA bundles means that AH and ESP may be applied alone, in combination with the other, or even nested within another instance. With these combinations, authentication and/or encryption can be provided between a pair of communicating hosts, between a pair of communicating firewalls, or between a host and a firewall. Given the two modes of each protocol, there are a number of possible combinations. Fortunately, only a few combinations make sense. Reference [55] describes the mandatory combinations that must be supported by each IPSec implementation. Other combinations may also be supported, but this could affect interoperability.

SA bundles

As indicated previously, if AH and ESP are required in combination, then multiple SAs must be established in each direction. This group of SAs is referred to as an SA bundle. There are two models for SA bundle creation, as follows:

- Transport adjacency—AH and ESP are applied in transport mode to the same IP datagram, resulting in two distinct SA pairs: one for AH and one for ESP. This method is practical for only one level of combination; there is no advantage in further nesting.

- Iterated (nested) tunneling—AH and ESP are applied in tunnel mode in sequence (i.e., nested). After each application a new IP datagram is created and the next protocol is applied to it. This method has no limit in the nesting levels, though one would normally not nest more than three levels (protocol and processing overheads increase with nesting, and there is the likelihood of fragmentation). Each SA in the bundle can originate or terminate at different nodes along the path. Reference [54] defines three possibilities: all endpoints are identical, one endpoint is the same, or no endpoints are the same. Support for only the latter two is required.

If this were not complicated enough, both transport and nested bundles can be combined. For example, an IP packet with transport adjacency IPSec headers can be sent through nested tunnels. When designing an IPSec VPN, however, it is recommended that you limit the number of times IPSec processing is applied to avoid overburdening the gateways and limiting scalability (this will depend somewhat on the vendor equipment architecture selected). Two stages are sufficient for most applications; it is unlikely that further processing beyond three stages has any real benefit. Note that in order to create an SA bundle in which SAs have different endpoints, at least one level of tunneling must be applied (transport adjacency does not allow for multiple source-destination addresses, because only one IP header is present).

The general principle of the combined use is that IPSec processing upon packet reception should start with authentication followed by decryption. Using this principle, the sender first applies ESP and then AH to outbound traffic (in fact, this sequence is mandated for transport mode IPSec processing). A more subtle issue with combined SAs is whether ESP authentication should be enabled when AH authentication is in use. In practice enabling ESP authentication makes sense only when the ESP SA extends beyond the AH SA (e.g., an encrypted transport connection between two hosts that traverses an AH tunnel between two gateways). In such cases it is strongly recommended that ESP authentication be enabled to avoid potential spoofing attacks. Finally, if packets are received where the origin is unknown, they should be discarded without performing decryption to avoid wasteful processing and reduce the likelihood of a denial-of-service attack.

5.5.5 The Internet Key Exchange Protocol (IKE)

Although the use of security associations is fundamental to IPSec, IPSec does not have an inherent mechanism for creating SAs. The IETF chose to divide functionality into two parts: IPSec provides packet-level processing, while the Internet Key Management Protocol (IKMP) negotiates SAs. After investigating several alternatives (including SKIP and Photuris), the IETF selected as the Internet Key Exchange (IKE) as its standard for configuring IPSec SAs [59]. IKE (previously referred to as ISAKMP/Oakley) supports automated negotiation of SAs and automated generation and refresh of cryptographic keys. Actually, the terms IKE and ISAKMP are not precisely interchangeable; IKE is a hybrid protocol incorporating features from the following:

- ISAKMP provides a framework for authentication and key exchange but does not define them. ISAKMP is designed to be key exchange independent; that is, it supports many different key exchanges. Refer to [57, 58] for further details.

- Oakley describes a series of key exchanges (called modes) and the services provided by each (e.g., Perfect Forward Secrecy [PFS] for keys, identity protection, and authentication). Refer to [60] for further details.

- SKEME describes a versatile key exchange technique that provides anonymity, repudiability, and quick key refreshment. Refer to [64] for further details.

In practice IKE creates an authenticated, secure tunnel between two entities and then negotiates the SA for IPSec. This process requires that the two entities authenticate themselves to each other and establish shared keys. Note that it is not necessary to use IKE, but manually configuring SAs is a laborious and maintenance-intensive process for anything other than a small lab network. In practice IKE will be used for most real-world applications to enable scalable, rapid deployment.

IKE defines a standardized framework to support negotiation of security associations, initial generation of all cryptographic keys, and subsequent refresh of these keys. Oakley is the mandatory key management protocol that is required to be used within the IKE framework. IKE supports automated negotiation of security associations and automated generation and refresh of cryptographic keys. The ability to perform these functions with little or no manual configuration of machines will be a critical element as a VPN grows in size. In addition, the IKE methods have been designed with the explicit goals of providing protection against several well-known exposures, as follows:

- Denial of Service (DoS)—The messages are constructed with unique cookies, which can be used to quickly identify and reject invalid messages without the need to execute processor-intensive cryptographic operations.

- Man in the Middle (MITM)—Protection is provided against the common attacks, such as deletion of messages, modification of messages, reflecting messages back to the sender, replaying old messages, and redirection of messages to unintended recipients.

- Perfect Forward Secrecy (PFS)—Compromise of past keys provides no useful clues for breaking any other key, whether it occurred before or after the compromised key. That is, each refreshed key will be derived without any dependence on predecessor keys.

Operation

IKE requires that all information exchanges must be both encrypted and authenticated so that no one can eavesdrop on the keying material, and the keying material will be exchanged only among authenticated parties. This is required because the IKE procedures deal with initializing the keys, so they must be capable of running over links where no security can be assumed to exist. Hence, the IKE protocols use the most complex and processor-intensive operations in the IPSec protocol suite.

Peer entities must be authenticated to each other before the IKE SA can be established. IKE is very flexible in this regard, supporting multiple authentication methods. The two entities must agree on a common authentication protocol through a negotiation process. At the time of writing the following mechanisms are generally implemented:

- Preshared keys—The same key is preinstalled on each IPSec host. IKE peers authenticate each other by computing and sending a keyed hash of data that includes the preshared key. If the receiving peer is able to independently create the same hash using its preshared key, it knows that both parties must share the same secret, thus authenticating the other party.

- Digital signatures—Each IPSec device digitally signs a set of data and sends it to the other party. This method is similar to the previous one, except that it provides nonrepudiation. Currently both the RSA public key algorithm and the Digital Signature Standard (DSS) are supported.

Both digital signature and public key cryptography require the use of digital certificates to validate the public-private key mapping. IKE allows the certificate to be accessed independently (e.g., through DNSSEC) or by having the two devices explicitly exchange certificates as part of IKE.

The integrity of any cryptography-based solution depends more on keeping keys secret than it does on the strength of the cryptographic algorithms used. With IPSec both parties use a shared session key in order to encrypt the IKE tunnel, negotiated via Diffie-Helman. IPSec employs a set of very robust Oakley exchange protocols, using a two-phase approach, as illustrated in Figure 5.19. As we can see in Figure 5.19, in main mode, messages 1 and 2 negotiate the characteristics of the SAs. Messages 3 and 4 exchange nonces and also execute a D-H exchange to establish a master key (SKEYID). Messages 1 through 4 flow in the clear for the initial Phase 1 exchange, and they are unauthenticated. Messages 5 and 6 exchange the required information for mutually authenticating peer identities. The payloads of these messages are now protected by the encryption and keying material established with messages 1 through 4. Note that if aggressive mode is used instead of main mode, then only four messages are required, but the SA is not authenticated. Quick mode takes three or four messages only (depending upon whether the commit bit is set).

Phase 1—Initializing SAs with IKE

In Phase 1 IKE initially establish SAs and exchange keys between two systems that wish to communicate securely. Throughout this section we refer to the parties involved as Host 1 (H1, the initiator) and Host 2 (H2, the responder). This set of negotiations establishes a master secret from which all cryptographic keys will subsequently be derived for protecting data traffic. In the most general case, public key cryptography is used to establish an IKE SA between systems and to establish the keys that will be used to protect the IKE messages that will flow in the subsequent Phase 2 negotiations. Phase 1 is concerned only with establishing the protection suite for the IKE messages themselves, but it does not establish any SAs or keys for protecting user data.

The SAs that protect the IKE messages are set up during the Phase 1 exchanges. Since we are starting cold (no previous keys or SAs have been negotiated between H1 and H2), the Phase 1 exchanges will use the IKE identity protect exchange (also known as Oakley main mode).

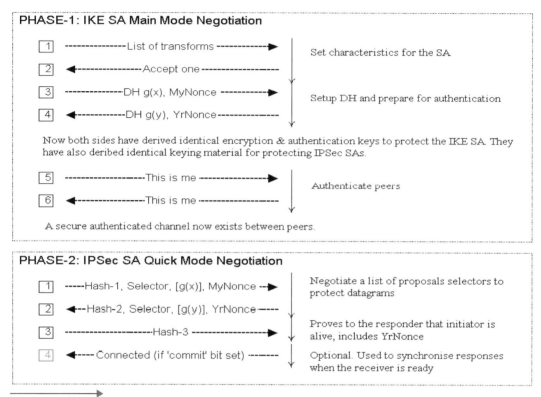

Figure 5.19 *Phase 1 and Phase 2 IKE and IPSec SA negotiations.*

Six messages are needed to complete the exchange, as illustrated in Figure 5.19. As an alternative to main mode IKE supports an option called aggressive mode, used for expedited SA connections (only three messages are exchanged, so this SA is unauthenticated). IKE also offers a solution when the remote host's IP address is not known in advance. IKE allows a remote host to identify itself by a permanent identifier, such as a name or an e-mail address. The IKE Phase 1 exchanges will then authenticate the remote host's permanent identity using public key cryptography, as follows:

- Certificates create a binding between the permanent identifier and a public key. Therefore, IKE certificate-based Phase 1 message exchanges can authenticate the remote host's permanent identify.

- Since the IKE messages are carried within IP datagrams, the IKE peer (e.g., a firewall or destination host) can associate the remote host's dynamic IP address with its authenticated permanent identity.

Phase 2—Initializing protocol SAs for data transfer

Upon successful completion of Phase 1, H1 will initiate the Oakley Phase 2 message exchanges (known as Oakley quick mode) to define the IPSec SAs and keys used to protect IP datagrams exchanged between users. Phase 2 exchanges are relatively simple, since a secure channel has already been established; all that is required is to negotiate the SAs and keys that will protect user data exchanges. In practice Phase 2 negotiations occur much more frequently than Phase 1 negotiations; for example, a typical application of a Phase 2 negotiation is to refresh the cryptographic keys once every two to three minutes. All IKE Phase 2 payloads, except the IKE header itself, must be encrypted using the algorithm agreed upon during Phase 1 negotiations. Phase 2 authentication is achieved through the use of several cryptographically based hash functions. The input to the hash functions is derived partly from Phase 1 information (SKEYID) and partly from information exchanged in Phase 2. Authentication is based on certificates, but the Phase 2 process itself does not use certificates directly (it uses the SKEYI—a material from Phase 1, which was authenticated by certificates). Oakley quick mode comes in two forms, as follows:

- Without a key exchange attribute, quick mode can be used to refresh the cryptographic keys but does not provide the property of Perfect Forward Secrecy (PFS).

- With a key exchange attribute, quick mode can be used to refresh the cryptographic keys in a way that provides PFS. This is accomplished by including an exchange of public D-H values within messages 1 and 2.

Note that although PFS is highly desirable in cryptography, the specifications treat PFS as optional. They mandate that a system must be capable of handling the key exchange field when it is present in a quick mode message but do not require a system to include the field within the message.

Performance issues

IKE Phase 1 uses public key cryptographic operations, which are very processor intensive. Phase 2 uses the less processor-intensive symmetric key cryptography. However, a single IKE Phase 1 negotiation can protect several subsequent Phase 2 negotiations, so in practice Phase 1 negotiations are relatively infrequent. As a general rule one might expect Phase 1 negotiations to be executed once a day or maybe once a week for relatively stable fixed VPNs, with Phase 2 negotiations executed once every few minutes. Clearly, dial-up VPNs are required to execute Phase 1 for the duration of each call.

Using IKE with remote access

The key difference for remote access applications is the use of Oakley to identify the remote host by name, rather than by its dynamically assigned IP address. Once the host identity has been authenticated and the IP address binding is known, the rest of the procedures are identical to those described previously. As indicated, Phase I is only executed once, when the dial-up connection is first initiated. Assuming remote host H1 is dialing into a home network, the key points to note are the following:

- H1's dynamically assigned IP address is placed in the IP header of all IKE messages.

- H1's permanent identifier (e.g., its e-mail address) is placed in the ID field of the IKE Phase 1 messages.

- H1's certificate used in the IKE exchange must be associated with H1's permanent identifier.

- H1's dynamically assigned IP address is used in traffic-bearing datagrams (the destination IP address that is used together with the SPI and protocol type to identify the relevant IPSec SA for inbound processing).

IKE, ISAKMP, Oakley, and SKEME embody many important concepts, and we have skimmed somewhat over the details here. For further information about IKE, the interested reader is referred to [57–60, 64].

5.5.6   Design considerations

IPSec is powerful and very flexible; it offers a wide variety of connectivity scenarios, including gateway to gateway, host to host, and host to gateway (where gateways could be firewalls, routers, dedicated VPN appliances, switches, and RAS/NAS boxes; and hosts could comprise servers, PCs, workstations, laptops, and possibly even PDAs and mobile phones in the future). IPSec's initial applications are to secure communications across public and private networks; however, it may also be used to secure communications across the LAN. Note that all IPv6 devices will incorporate IPSec as standard. Some of the key applications currently being deployed include the following:

- Branch office connectivity over the Internet—Promises dramatic savings on long-haul wide area costs for large internetworks and enables small and medium-sized companies to rapidly deploy low-cost private networks over the Internet. This assumes that the QoS offered by service providers meets business needs.

- Remote access over the Internet—Promises major savings on dial charges for mobile workers and SOHO users. Users dial in to their local ISP and are typically tunneling securely through to the corporate network.

- Extranet and intranet connectivity with partners—IPSec's strong authentication and encryption support means that VPNs can be established to suppliers or partners, each with unique security policies assigned.

- E-commerce security—Since IPSec encrypts and authenticates at the Network Layer, it can be used with other e-commerce protocols such as SSL and SET to enhance security.

IPSec presents excellent opportunities for service providers to provision secure managed services. For dedicated IVPNs the service provider would typically supply, configure, and manage the CPE devices used to construct a VPN. There are already a number of VPN appliances on the market targeted specifically for this application. Providers can bring this service to market very rapidly, since IPSec's transparency means that IVPNs can be deployed without any modification to the service provider infrastructure. Providers can offer basic QoS if they build their IVPN service over a premium IP service (possibly mapped over ATM or Frame Relay). It is also relatively straightforward to provide dial support using IPsec client software on the remote user PCs. Again, this requires no change to the provider infrastructure. We will now examine the most common deployment scenarios for IPSec.

Example design 1: simple end-to-end host security

As shown in Figure 5.20, two hosts are connected through the Internet (or an intranet) without any IPSec gateway between them (standard routing is employed). In this case the hosts may use ESP, AH, or a combination in either transport or tunnel mode. Figure 5.20 illustrates the concept with possible encapsulation formats.

Example design 2: basic VPN support

Figure 5.21 illustrates a very simple VPN created between two IPSec gateways, G1 and G2. In this case the hosts are not required to support IPSec. The gateways are required to support only tunnel mode, either with AH or ESP. This configuration would allow private network addresses to be handled over a public IP network such as the Internet. However, bear in mind that the addressing schemes need to be consistent (e.g., they should not overlap).

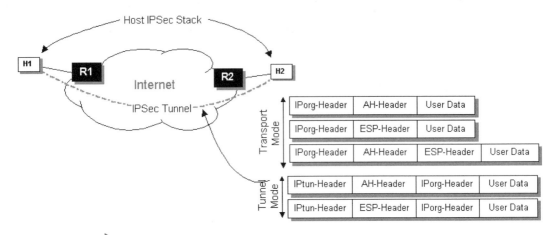

Figure 5.20   *Simple end-to-end security using a host IPSec stack only. Note that IPorg is the original IP header; IPtun is the new IP header created in IPSec tunnel mode.*

It may be desirable to configure tunnels between gateways that combine both AH and ESP support. Some products support this capability, with the encapsulation order configurable via the tunnel policy. Note that this is often termed combined tunneling and should not be confused with iterated tunneling (since the SA bundle comprising the tunnel has identical end points, it would be inefficient to perform iterated tunneling in this case). Instead, one IPSec protocol is applied in tunnel mode and the other in transport mode, which can be conceptually thought of as a combined AH-

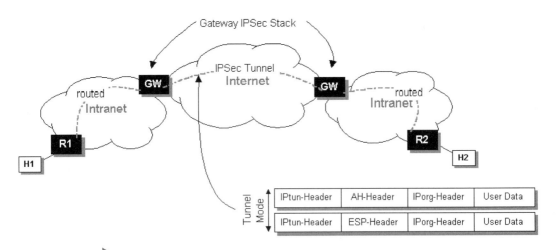

Figure 5.21   *Basic VPN security using gateway IPSec stacks between two intranets. Note that IPorg is the original IP header; IPtun is the new IP header created in IPSec tunnel mode.*

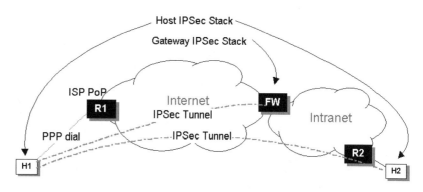

Figure 5.22   *Remote access.*

ESP tunnel. An equivalent approach is to IP tunnel the original datagram and then apply transport adjacency IPSec processing to it. The result is that we have an outer IP header followed by the IPSec headers in the order set by the tunnel policy, and then the original IP packet.

Example design 3: end-to-end security with VPN support

Figure 5.22 illustrates a scenario that is a combination of Designs 1 and 2. Both hosts and gateways are required to support IPSec. The security gateways must be configurable to enable IPsec traffic (including ISAKMP traffic) to be passed for hosts behind them. In this situation one would normally configure the gateways to use AH in tunnel mode, protecting the host traffic, which is set to ESP transport mode.

Note that for enhanced security we could use a combined AH-ESP tunnel between the gateways (if supported), so that the ultimate destination addresses would be encrypted, the entire packet traversing the Internet would be authenticated, and the encapsulated data double encrypted. This is the only case where three stages of IPSec processing might be useful; however, the performance impact is likely to be considerable.

Example design 4: remote access

Figure 5.23 illustrates a secure design—remote access over the Internet to reach a server (H2) in an organization protected by a firewall (FW). The remote host would typically use a PPP dial-in connection to an ISP RAS. The ISP would then onward route using conventional routing. Between the remote host H1 and the firewall, only tunnel mode is required. Between the hosts either tunnel mode or transport mode can be used, with the same choices as in Design 1. A typical configuration would be to use AH in tunnel mode between H1 and FW and ESP in transport mode between H1

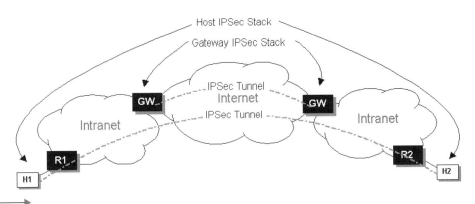

Figure 5.23   *End-to-end security. Both gateways and hosts support IPSec.*

and H2 (note that early IPSec implementations that do not support AH in tunnel mode cannot implement this design). Note that in this case, the sender must apply the transport header before the tunnel header. Therefore, the management interface to the IPsec implementation must support configuration of the SPD and SAD to ensure this ordering of IPsec header application. It may also be possible to create a combined AH-ESP tunnel between the remote host, H1, and the gateway, FW. In this case H1 can access the whole intranet using just one SA bundle.

While the combination of the IPSec protocols in theory leads to a large number of possibilities, in practice only a few (such as those presented previously) are commonly used. Use of other, optional combinations may adversely affect interoperability [54].

5.6   Designing VPNs

5.6.1   Design models

There are two basic design models for building IVPNs: the overlay model and the peer model. These design approaches are differentiated by how tightly coupled the VPN and service provider infrastructure are, which directly influences the level of service and management that can be offered to the user by the service provider.

Overlay model

The overlay model comprises an end-to-end VPN, which normally originates and terminates inside intranet sites and is created by CPE equipment (such as two firewalls). From the provider's perspective the VPN is client initiated, or voluntary. The service provider's backbone is effectively transparent to the VPN, and the VPN routing infrastructure is independent of the provider's routing infrastructure. The advantages of this approach are that the network operates as a single virtual network and has a single management domain. Routing policy can be enforced globally, and Layer 3 troubleshooting can be done without involving the service provider. From the service provider's perspective the VPN is simply IP traffic that it does not need to manage proactively.

The disadvantages of this approach are that all remote sites must be fully meshed to achieve any-to-any connectivity. If two sites are not directly connected, then packets must traverse the provider's backbone twice (i.e., from the source site over the backbone to some intermediate site and then back over the backbone to the target site). This increases latency, degrades efficiency, and may incur additional cost. Since the service provider must provision each virtual connection, a full-mesh topology may simply not scale for many large organizations. Another problem with this approach is that the provider has little visibility of the VPN and may not be able to offer value-added service or the level of QoS granularity required by users.

Peer model

In a peer model the VPN and the service provider network are tightly coupled. The provider's backbone infrastructure peers with the VPN network and routing is well integrated. The service provider has more work to do, proportional to the number of sites. This model enables optimal site-to-site routing to be achieved, because the provider's routing equipment has full visibility over the VPN forwarding requirements. Based on this additional information the provider network could allocate resources much more intelligently than with an overlay model. QoS can be allocated with much better granularity, since the provider network clearly understands what resources each VPN tunnel requires.

The disadvantage of the peer model is that administrative control of the network is fragmented. Layer 3 troubleshooting can be much more complicated, since both the user and provider staff need to cooperate. Since routing information is integrated, misconfigurations on CPE equipment can adversely affect backbone devices and vice versa. Illegal or private addressing schemes inside the subscriber networks must be handled consistently (possibly requiring support for overlapping IP address ranges in different VPNs). Security is also somewhat compromised, since internal addresses and routing topology information are exposed to the ISP (in the overlay model this would all be hidden).

5.6.2   Routing

Tunneling can disguise the operating characteristics of an end-to-end path, masking its true performance and possibly misleading dynamic routing protocols into making poor (and possibly unexpected) forwarding decisions. For example, distance-vector routing protocols (such as RIP) generally select paths based on hop count alone and may prefer a tunnel interface to a real interface (resulting in not-needed traffic being forwarded down the tunnel). A tunnel could traverse a number of different physical links of varying speeds, and a faster path could be available through a non-VPN interface. When configuring tunneling, take note of the media and available bandwidth of the links the tunnel traverses, as well as the metrics used by each routing protocol. Take particular care to avoid inadvertently configuring recursive routing loops (where the best path to the tunnel destination is via the tunnel interface). If a router detects a recursive routing loop, it should ideally shut down the tunnel interface for a predefined hold-down period and issue appropriate alerts or warnings to the network administrator. An indication that a loop has been detected might be that the tunnel interface is up, but the line protocol is down.

Routing loops can be avoided by using different routing protocols for VPN and normal IP network traffic (not always possible), or by setting a high metric for the tunnel interface (so that non-VPN traffic does not get routed incorrectly). You could also keep the IP address ranges for the VPN and non-VPN networks distinct (i.e., use a major address for the tunnel network that differs from the IP network). This will also assist debugging.

5.6.3   Interaction with firewalls

There are commercial firewall products that also originate and terminate VPNs. While this simplifies the configuration and deployment issues, it is unlikely in the short term that such devices will offer sufficient throughput to handle large central site applications without hardware assist. In many cases it is likely that a specialized VPN device will be used together with a packet filtering firewall or stateful firewall, possibly from different vendors. This presents us with several design, management, routing, and security issues, as illustrated in Figure 5.24. Some of these issues can be described as follows:

- VPN fronting the firewall—In Figure 5.24(a), VPN connections will be unencrypted before presenting to the firewall. This compromises end-to-end VPN security (the VPN may also be terminated at a point considered insecure by the intended recipient). There is also no way to

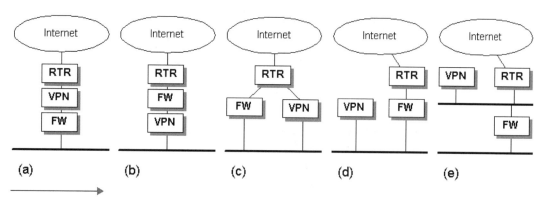

Figure 5.24 *Alternative locations for VPN termination in cooperation with a firewall and router.*

tell which traffic was originally encrypted or if it has been tampered with. The VPN device also requires protection from direct attacks via access lists or policy settings. However, the firewall does not need to be capable of passing IPSec traffic (e.g., proxy firewalls may not), and standard firewall policy can be applied to all VPN traffic.

- VPN behind the firewall—If the VPN device is placed behind the firewall (Figure 5.24[b]), then the firewall cannot access the content and cannot verify whether viruses or illegal activities are being tunneled within the VPN connection. In effect, you need to punch a hole through the firewall to allow VPN traffic through. However, this lends the internal network vulnerable to a possible denial-of-service attack. The firewall needs to be capable of passing IPSec traffic unmodified; conversely, the VPN box has to pass unencrypted (non-VPN) traffic with sufficient throughput. Some VPN boxes do not support filters or access lists. On the plus side this means that the VPN device is also protected by the firewall, and the firewall is not burdened by processing VPN traffic.

- VPN parallel with the firewall—This generally works well for all incoming VPN and non-VPN traffic since each device handles only what is relevant (Figure 5.24[c]). However, the problem lies with routing outbound traffic. Clients typically have only one default gateway set, and this may result in VPN traffic being forwarded to a router or firewall rather than the VPN device, leaving the network unencrypted. If the destination addresses are known in advance (say with a stable site-to-site VPN, or known client VPNs), then it should be possible to configure the router to reflect such traffic back toward the local VPN device using access control lists or policy settings. Again, the VPN device requires protection from direct attacks via access lists or policy settings. Traffic leakage should also be avoided with the VPN box set to drop all non-VPN traffic.

- VPN on a stick behind the firewall—This is generally applicable only to trusted environments, since again a hole must be punched through the firewall to allow VPN traffic in (Figure 5.24[d]). The VPN device is placed in line with the firewall and clients so that encrypted and unencrypted VPN traffic traverses the same physical network. This solution does not scale well, and there may be routing issues with default gateway–directed traffic.

- VPN on a stick fronting the firewall—This is only really applicable where the firewall cannot cope with unfiltered traffic, as well as for small networks (Figure 5.24[e]). Again, the VPN device requires protection from direct attacks via access lists or policy settings.

In practice the VPN system is often placed behind the firewall, as illustrated in Figure 5.25. This offers most of the benefits with minimal complexity. Policy or filtering on both the firewall and router need to accept authorized tunnels to pass through.

5.6.4   Performance

Tunneling is CPU intensive, and encryption is even more so. Expect significant degradation in throughput over normal IP packet forwarding if tunneling is enabled with encryption. Software-based encryption schemes are suitable only for small numbers of site-to-site tunnels. If you intend to ter-

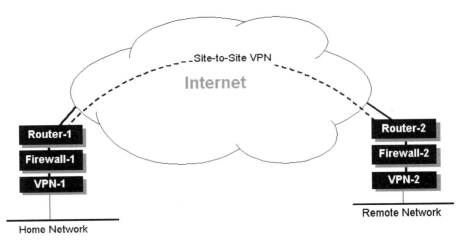

Figure 5.25   *VPN termination between two trusted sites. The firewall and router must be configured to accept any VPN tunneling or key-management protocols.*

minate large numbers of encrypted tunnels (e.g., thousands or tens of thousands at a central site), you really need to select specialized hardware that can perform encryption with hardware assist. It is also highly desirable to select products that offer some form of clustering or HA capability to promote scalability.

Fragmentation

Any protocol that adds overhead is more likely to introduce IP fragmentation issues, since large IP packets may exceed their MTU. Fragmentation is generally to be avoided, since it degrades VPN performance (more packets must be processed, and fragments must be buffered and reassembled in order to perform tasks such as authentication). If the application servers are within your domain, you may be able to reduce their MTU to allow for additional VPN headers.

Another issue with IP fragmentation is the DF (Don't Fragment) bit. Note that IPSec always copies the DF bit setting from the inner to the outer IP header in tunnel mode. This may be overridden, since it may cause problems for some TCP stacks and firewalls (changing this setting should be avoided if at all possible as it may result in suboptimal fragmentation).

5.6.5   Scalability and management

One of the clear indications at present is that new solutions providing real VPN scalability are going to be required. The next-generation IP VPN will require the ability to provision thousands of sites per VPN and thousands of VPNs. This requires simplified management to allow VPN membership and large-scale deployment. Users are demanding any-to-any connectivity for extended intranets and extranets, which requires VPNs to encompass multiple businesses. Support for sophisticated IP intranet applications, such as dynamic bandwidth allocation, application-specific transport characteristics (e.g., voice), and new services and service classes are required. Multicast technologies for multimedia applications and multiple service classes to support mission-critical and time-sensitive traffic such as video and voice will be key to growth.

Meeting these requirements requires a new paradigm for building these highly scalable and capable IP VPNs. This service differs from previous models, because the network is directly aware of the VPNs. As stated earlier, today's VPNs are generally transparent to the network infrastructure, limiting scalability and flexibility.

MPLS-based VPN backbones

MultiProtocol Label Switching (MPLS) is viewed by many as the most appropriate delivery mechanism for providing scalable VPNs over backbone networks (by backbone we mean core-wide area networks, not local backbones). MPLS in essence provides switched and virtual circuit capabilities, called Label-Switched Paths (LSPs) over an IP core. MPLS enables individual or groups of VPNs with similar routing and QoS requirements to be mapped onto LSPs. Clearly, many VPN applications are end to end, and MPLS is not an end-to-end technology since its resource demands are significant. This will require MPLS LSPs to be mapped onto LAN-based VPNs at the edge.

5.7   Summary

In this chapter, we discussed the following:

- Business customers want new approaches to wide area networking that preserve the benefits of low-cost, easy-to-deploy IP-based intranet applications and deliver them to mobile users and branch offices. IVPN solutions are emerging as a viable solution that provides the connectivity, transparency, security, and flexibility required by intranet and extranet applications over public wide area backbones such as the Internet.

- The availability of advanced outsourced IP networking services will give small and medium-sized businesses the ability to deploy global networks at a manageable price, in order to stay competitive against large corporations.

- The groundswell of demand for IVPN services is forcing service providers to plan and implement the deployment of highly scalable IVPNs, preserving the current economic benefits for subscribers while also adding new capabilities and services.

- Layer 2 tunneling protocols such as L2TP and PPTP are a good way of providing cost-effective remote access in mixed-protocol environments; however, they offer no privacy (well, PPTP has extensions for encryption and authentication). Without the complementary use of strong, scalable, security techniques (as provided by IPSec), a Layer 2 tunnel alone does not provide adequate security for today's e-commerce applications.

- An advantage of tunneling protocols such as L2TP and GRE is that providers can offer finer-grained QoS than with IPsec solutions alone (since routers have visibility into IP header information necessary for application-level QoS). In an IPSec packet, the payload protocol and user data are encrypted, obfuscating all of the useful data required to prioritize applications. The disadvantage of a pure encapsulation solution is that by definition it is not secure.

- L2TP enables remote users to connect to a local ISP and tunnel through the Internet to a home network, avoiding long-distance charges. L2TP has emerged as the open standard protocol for multi-protocol Layer 2 tunneling. L2TP should be used over IPSec for true VPN provisioning.

- IPSec is becoming the standard for IP-based VPN applications. IPSec is now a powerful and mature standard with excellent support for authentication, confidentiality, and key management (via IKE). Since IPSec works at the Network Layer, it is totally transparent to applications. While the combination of the IPSec protocols in theory leads to a large number of possibilities, in practice only a few are commonly used.

References

[1]   B. Schneier, *Applied Cryptography* (New York: John Wiley & Sons, 1994).

[2]   B. Schneier, *Secrets and Lies: Digital Security in a Networked World* (New York: John Wiley & Sons, 2000).

[3]   M. Goncalves, *Firewalls Complete* (New York: McGraw-Hill, 1998).

[4]   Hypertext Transfer Protocol—HTTP/1.1, RFC 2616, June 1999.

[5]   www.nta-monitor.com, NTA Monitor home page—leading European security testing organization.

[6]   A. Northcutt, *Network Intrusion Detection: An Analyst's Handbook* (City, State: New Riders Professional Library, 1999).

[7]   www.sophist.demon.co.uk/ping/, Information about ping-of-death fragmentation issues.

[8]   Site Security Handbook, RFC 2196, September 1997.

[9]   The MD2 Message-Digest Algorithm, RFC 1319, April 1992.

[10] The MD4 Message-Digest Algorithm, RFC 1320, April 1992.

[11] The MD5 Message-Digest Algorithm, RFC 1321, April 1992.

[12] A. Arsenault, and S. Turner, Internet X.509 Public Key Infrastructure, PKIX Roadmap. Internet Draft draft-ietf-pkix-roadmap-05.txt, March 10, 2000.

[13] www.rsa.com/smime, RSA page about S-MIME.

[14] www.setco.org/, Information about the SET specifications.

[15] developer.netscape.com/docs/manuals/security.html, NetScape pages about security, including SSL.

[16] www.ietf.org/html.charters/ipsec-charter.html, IETF IPSec Working Group charter.

[17] www.ietf.org/html.charters/pppext-charter.html, IETF PPP Working Group charter.

[18] www.baltimore.com, Baltimore Technologies home page.

[19] www.entrust.com, Entrust Technologies home page for PKI products and solutions.

[20] www.rsa.com, RSA Security Inc. home page.

[21] www.verisign.com, Versisign Inc. home page.

[22] PPP Authentication Protocols, RFC 1334, October 1992.

[23] PPP Challenge Handshake Authentication Protocol (CHAP), RFC 1994, August 1996.

[24] Sun's SKIP Firewall Traversal for Mobile IP, RFC 235, June 1998.

[25] Remote Authentication Dial-In User Service (RADIUS), RFC 2138, April 1997.

[26] An Access Control Protocol, sometimes called TACACS, RFC 1492, July 1993.

[27] D. Carrel, and L. Grant, The TACACS+ Protocol, Version 1.78. Internet Draft draft-grant-tacacs-02.txt, January 1997.

[28] www.cisco.com, Cisco home page.

[29] The Kerberos Network Authentication Service (V5), RFC 1510, September 1993.

[30] web.mit.edu/kerberos/www/, Kerberos information and source code from the Massachusetts Institute of Technology (MIT).

[31] www.isi.edu/gost/info/kerberos/, USC/ISI Kerberos home page.

[32] www.netscape.com, Netscape home page.

[33] The TLS Protocol Version 1.0, RFC 2246, January 1999.

[34] www.fsecure.com, F-Secure home page.

[35] HMAC: Keyed Hashing for Message Authentication, RFC 2104, February 1997.

[36] SOCKS Protocol Version 5, RFC 1928, April 1996.

[37] User name/Password Authentication for SOCKS v5, RFC 1929, April 1996.

[38] GSS-API Authentication Method for SOCKS Version 5, RFC 1961, June 1996.

[39] www.socks.nec.com, SOCKS home page.

[40] www.checkpoint.com, Checkpoint Technologies home page.

[41] www.macafee.com, McAfee home page.

[42] http://www.fsecure.com/virus-info/, F-Secure online database of viruses.

[43] www.lopht.com, Lopht Heavy Industries home page, advisories, tools, and information about security vulnerabilities.

[44] www.symantec.com, Symantec home page for antivirus, firewall, and URL screening software.

[45] www.Websense.com, Websense Inc. (formerly Netpartners Internet Solutions) home page.

[46] www.mimesweeper.com, Content Technologies home page for the MIMEsweeper product range.

[47] www.iss.net, Internet Security System home page (RealSecure).

[48] www.intrucion.com, Intrusion Detection home page (Kane Security Monitor).

[49] www.nai.com, Network Associate home page.

[50] www.axent.com, Axent Technologies home page (OmniGuard/ Intruder Alert).

[51] www.tis.com, Trusted Information Systems home page (Stalkers IDS).

[52] www.advisortechnologies.com, Advisor Technologies home site for intrusion detection event monitoring.

[53] E. Amoroso, *Intrusion Detection: An Introduction to Internet Surveillance, Correlation, Trace Back, Traps, and Response* (City, State: AT&T Laboratories. 1999).

[54] Security Architecture for the Internet Protocol, RFC 2401, November 1998.

[55] IP Authentication Header, RFC 2402, November 1998.

[56] IP Encapsulating Security Payload, RFC 2406, November 1998.

[57] The Internet IP Security Domain of Interpretation for ISAKMP, RFC 2407, November 1998.

[58] Internet Security Association and Key Management Protocol, RFC 2408, November 1998.

[59] The Internet Key Exchange (IKE), RFC 2409, November 1998.

[60] The Oakley Key Determination Protocol, RFC 2412, November 1998.

[61] IP Encapsulation within IP, RFC 2003, October 1996.

[62] The ESP DES-CBC Cipher Algorithm with Explicit IV, RFC 2405, November 1998.

[63] IP Encapsulating Security Payload (ESP), RFC 1827, August 1995, (obsoleted by RFC 2406).

[64] H. Krawczyk, "SKEME: A Versatile Secure Key Exchange Mechanism for the Internet," in *IEEE Proceedings of the 1996 Symposium on Network and Distributed Systems Security,* 1996.

Designing Reliable Networks

Organizations are increasingly reliant on computer networks for business- or mission-critical applications. The scope and size of these networks have expanded so rapidly over the past two decades that considerable effort and expense are now targeted at keeping network resources available, sometimes 24 hours a day, all year. Traditionally this area of network design has been the preserve of large mainframe sites and those sites requiring high levels of protection (such as nuclear power plants). However, the explosion of Web-based business methods means than many more organizations are now eager to maintain high availability in order to minimize service losses (Table 6.1 illustrates the kinds of losses we could expect by industry type and operation). If the network is poorly designed, and insufficient attention is paid to providing availability in core systems, users can experience anything from slow response times to complete loss of service (referred to as downtime) for extended periods. The technical issues in maintaining high availability are both complex and subtle, and it is the network designer's job to balance loss probability against cost, providing guidance to senior management on the likelihood of failures and their impact on the business.

Networks are rarely static environments, and budgets are finite. In practice network designers are required to make a range of pragmatic and technical decisions that address, accept, mitigate, or transfer the risks of failure—all within the constraints of a budget. The designer must also ensure that the solutions provided are scalable, so that additional nodes, services, and capacity can be added without major upheaval and without adversely affecting existing users. Downtime for truly business- and mission-critical systems can equate to losses of millions of dollars per minute; these organizations, therefore, demand high-availability (HA) networks and are often prepared to go to extraordinary lengths to achieve them. HA networks must provide alternate systems and network resources to compensate

Table 6.1   *Average Downtime Costs by Industry Type and Operation (Source: Dataquest—Perspective, September 30, 1996).*

Industry	Operation	Avg Cost per hour Downtime ($K)
Financial	Brokerage	$6,450.0
Financial	Credit Card/Sales Authorisation	$2,600.0
Media	Pay-Per-View	$150.0
Financial	ATM Fees	$145.0
Retail	Home Shopping (TV)	$113.0
Retail	Home Catalog Sales	$90.0
Transportation	Airline Reservations	$89.5
Media	Tee-Ticket Sales	$69.0
Transportation	Package Shipping	$28.0

for critical system or component failures, ideally automatically and with no loss of data.

Failure knows no boundaries in a network design, and the smallest component failure can effectively bring down a whole business without warning (e.g., a failed hard disk controller on your core e-business server could stop all transactions). For practical reasons organizations are invariably broken down into teams responsible for different aspects of IT (desktop support, communications, applications, database, cabling, etc.). When a problem occurs, it is all too common for application staff to blame the network and vice versa. To maintain HA networks, different disciplines must work together, both at the design phase and subsequently. Good diagnostic, monitoring, and management tools can also help.

In practice there are a range of design techniques and vendor solutions available, some standard and some proprietary. Often these techniques are designed to address specific aspects of the design, such as application failure, network failure, system failure, media failure, and component failure. In this chapter we will cover the theoretical assessment of risk and availability, media and topological resilience, load sharing, high-availability protocols, and device and component resilience. Some of the techniques described here are closely related to performance optimization, since by providing resilience through parallel systems or parallel paths we are often able to make use of this extra capacity to provide performance scalability. Performance and resilience are, therefore, frequently tightly bound in network design.

6.1   Planning for failure

When designing a reliable data network, network designers are well advised to keep two quotations in mind at all times:

Whatever can go wrong will go wrong at the worst possible time and in the worst possible way . . .

—Murphy

Expect the unexpected.

—Douglas Adams, *The Hitchhiker's Guide to the Galaxy*

Murphy's Law is widely known and often quoted. While the other directive may appear as humorous nonsense, in practice you should use this to start thinking laterally about failure scenarios you would not normally expect. This exercise can be illuminating.

6.1.1   Terminology

In researching network reliability you will frequently come across terms such as fault tolerance, fault resilience, single/multiple points of failure, and disaster recovery. Differentiating fault tolerance from fault resilience in the literature can be especially difficult, since many vendors use the term "fault tolerance" indiscriminately. In essence, these terms can be defined as follows:

- Failure refers to a situation where the observed behavior of a system differs from its specified behavior. A failure occurs because of an error, caused by a fault. The time lapse between the error occurring and the resulting failure is called the error latency [1]. Faults can be hard (permanent) or soft (transient). For example, a cable break is a hard failure, whereas intermittent noise on the line is a soft failure.

- Single Point of Failure (SPOF) indicates that a system or network can be rendered inoperable, or significantly impaired in operation, by the failure of one single component. For example, a single hard disk failure could bring down a server; a single router failure could break all connectivity for a network.

- Multiple points of failure indicate that a system or network can be rendered inoperable through a chain or combination of failures (as few as two). For example, failure of a single router, plus failure of a backup modem link, could mean that all connectivity is lost for a network. In general it is much more expensive to cope with multiple points of failure and often financially impractical.

- Fault tolerance indicates that every component in the chain supporting the system has redundant features or is duplicated. A fault-tolerant system will not fail because any one component fails (i.e., it has no single point of failure). The system should also provide recovery from multiple failures. Components are often overengineered or purposely underutilized to ensure that while performance may be affected during an outage, the system will perform within predictable, acceptable bounds.

- Fault resilience implies that at least one of the modules or components within a system is backed up with a spare (e.g., a power supply). This may be in hot standby, cold standby, or load-sharing mode. In contrast with fault-tolerant systems, not all modules or components are necessarily redundant (i.e., there may be several single points of failure). For example, a fault-resilient router may have multiple power supplies but only one routing processor. By definition, one fault-resilient component does not make the entire system fault tolerant.

- Disaster recovery is the process of identifying all potential failures, their impact on the system/network as a whole, and planning the means to recover from such failures.

All of these concepts are intimately bound together, and in designing any high-availability solution a rigorous and detailed approach to problem identification and resolution is essential. The designer's goal is to keep the network running no matter what and to maximize the number of failures the network can accommodate without failure while minimizing potential weaknesses. It is also worth restating that high availability does not come cheap. Availability and cost are conflicting constraints on the network design.

6.1.2 Calculating the true cost of downtime

Network designers are largely unfamiliar with financial models [2]. It is, however, imperative in designing reliable networks that the designer gathers some basic financial data in order to cost justify and direct suitable technical solutions. The data may come from line managers or financial support staff and may not be readily collated. Without these data the scale of the problem is undefined, and it will be hard to convince senior financial and operational management that additional features are necessary.

To illustrate the point let us consider a hypothetical consumer-oriented business (such as an airline, car rental, vacation, or hotel reservation call center). The call center is required to be online 24 hours a day, 7 days a week, 365 days a year. The business has 800 staff involved in call handling (transactions), each with an average burdened cost of $25 an hour (i.e., the cost of providing a desk, heating, lighting, phone, data point, etc.). There is a small profit made on each transaction, plus a large profit on any actual sale that can be closed. We assume here that there are on average three sales closed per hour.

Clearly, any downtime represents lost calls, which equates to lost revenue. Worse still, in this kind of operation lost business is typically lost for good, since customers will typically ring a competitor rather than call back later. Our job is to quantify the true cost of downtime and establish what changes to the availability model could improve the situation to the point where the cost of improvements is balanced by acceptable levels of outage. Our starting point would typically be the current network availability. In Figure 6.1 there are four simple cost models, starting with the current availability estimated at 99 percent (i.e., unmanaged). Each of the three subsequent models uses higher availability targets (99.5 percent, 99.9 percent, and 99.99, percent respectively); all other parameters are identical. In Figure 6.1 note that the Cost of Idle Staff is calculated as (Headcount × Burdened Cost × Downtime). Production Losses are calculated as (Headcount × Transactions per Hour × Profit per Transaction × Downtime). Lost Sales are calculated as (Headcount × Sales per Hour × Profit per Sale × Downtime).

Financial models can be instructive. The current network availability, Figure 6.1(a) predicts nearly four whole days of lost business in any year, equating to $8.5 million projected annual lost business unless additional countermeasures are employed. These hard data can be used as a starting point for justifying a range of network and system enhancements; in many cases even relatively modest enhancements could significantly improve availability. In Figure 6.1(b) we can see that an increase of only 0.5 percent availability reduces predicted losses by 50 percent. Note that the cost of meeting very high availability targets tends to rise dramatically; each business needs to draw the line where it sees fit.

6.1.3   Developing a disaster recovery plan

All networks are vulnerable to disruption. Sometimes these disruptions may come from the most unlikely sources. Natural events such as flooding, fire, lightning strikes, earthquakes, tidal waves, and hurricanes are all possible, as

Headcount	800		Headcount	800
Burdened Cost/hour	$25		Burdened Cost/hour	$25
Transactions/Hour per Head	40		Transactions/Hour per Head	40
Profit per Transaction	$0.5		Profit per Transaction	$0.5
Sales per Hour per Head	3		Sales per Hour per Head	3
Profit Per Sale	$35		Profit Per Sale	$35
Availability (%)	99.00%		Availability (%)	99.50%
Downtime per Year (hours)	87.60		Downtime per Year (hours)	43.80
Lost Transactions	2,803,200		Lost Transactions	1,401,600
Cost of Idle Staff ($)	$1,752,000		Cost of Idle Staff ($)	$876,000
Production Losses ($)	$1,401,600		Production Losses ($)	$700,800
Lost Sales ($)	$7,358,400		Lost Sales ($)	$3,679,200
TOTAL LOSSES PER YEAR	$10,512,000		TOTAL LOSSES PER YEAR	$5,256,000

(a)   **(b)**

Headcount	800		Headcount	800
Burdened Cost/hour	$25		Burdened Cost/hour	$25
Transactions/Hour per Head	40		Transactions/Hour per Head	40
Profit per Transaction	$0.5		Profit per Transaction	$0.5
Sales per Hour per Head	3		Sales per Hour per Head	3
Profit Per Sale	$35		Profit Per Sale	$35
Availability (%)	99.90%		Availability (%)	99.99%
Downtime per Year (hours)	8.76		Downtime per Year (hours)	0.88
Lost Transactions	280,320		Lost Transactions	28,032
Cost of Idle Staff ($)	$175,200		Cost of Idle Staff ($)	$17,520
Production Losses ($)	$140,160		Production Losses ($)	$14,016
Lost Sales ($)	$735,840		Lost Sales ($)	$73,584
TOTAL LOSSES PER YEAR	$1,051,200		TOTAL LOSSES PER YEAR	$105,120

(c)   **(d)**

Figure 6.1   *Cost of unavailability in a fictitious call center.*

well as fuel shortages, electricity strikes, viruses, hackers, system failures, and software bugs. History shows us that these events do happen regularly. As recently as 1999 and 2000 we saw the seemingly impossible: power shortages in California threatened to cripple Silicon Valley, and a combination of fuel shortages, train safety issues, and massive flooding in the United Kingdom meant that many staff simply could not get to work. In fact, various studies indicate that the majority of system failures can be attributed to a relatively small set of events. These include, in decreasing order of frequency, natural disaster, power failure, systems failure, sabotage/viruses, fire, and human error. There is also a general consensus that companies that take longer than a full business week to get back online run a high risk of being forced out of business entirely (some analysts state as high as 50 percent). For further information on recent disaster studies, see [3, 43].

The first step in mitigating the effects of disaster is to plan for it, especially if you have mission- or business-critical applications running on your network. In order to capture this process you need to create a Disaster Recovery (DR) plan; a general approach to the creation of a DR plan is, as follows:

- Benchmark the current design—Perform a full risk assessment for all key systems and the network as a whole. Identify key threats to system and network integrity. Analyze core business requirements and identify core processes and their dependence upon the network. Assign monetary values of loss of service or systems.

- Define the requirements—Based on business needs, determine an acceptable recovery window for each system and the network as a whole. If practical specify a worst-case recovery window and a target recovery window. Specify priorities for mission- or business-critical systems.

- Define the technical solution—Determine the technical response to these challenges by evaluating alternative recovery models, and select solutions that best meet the business requirements. Ensure that a full cost analysis of each solution is provided, together with the recovery times anticipated under catastrophic failure conditions and lesser degrees of failure.

- Develop the recovery strategy—Formulate a crisis management plan identifying the processes to be followed and key personnel response to failure scenarios. Describe where automation and manual intervention are required. Set priorities to clearly identify the order in which systems should be brought back online.

- Develop an implementation strategy—Determine how new/additional technology is to be deployed and over what time period. Document changes to the existing design. Identify how new/additional processes and responsibilities are to be communicated.

- Develop a test program—Determine how business- and mission-critical systems may be exercised and what the expected results should be. Define procedures for rectifying test failures. Run tests to see if the strategy works; if not, make refinements until satisfied.

- Implement continuous monitoring and improvements—Once the disaster recovery plan is established, hold regular reviews to ensure that the plan stays synchronized as the network grows or design features are modified.

Disaster recovery models

There are a number of practical approaches to DR, particularly with respect to protecting valuable user and configuration data. These include tape or CD backup, electronic vaulting, server mirroring, site mirroring, and outsourcing, as follows:

- Tape or CD site backup—Tape or CD-ROM backup and restore are the widely used DR methods for sites. Traditionally, key data repositories and configuration files are backed up nightly or every other night. Backup media are transported and securely stored at a different location. This enables complete data recovery should the main site systems be compromised. If the primary site becomes inoperable, the plan is to ship the media back, reboot, and resume normal operations.

  Pros and Cons: This is a low-cost solution, but the recovery window could range from a few hours to several days; this may prove unacceptable for many businesses. Media reliability may not be 100 percent and, depending upon the backup frequency, valuable data may be lost.

- Electronic vaulting—With remote electronic vaulting, data are archived automatically to tape or CD over the network to a secure remote site. Electronic vaulting ideally requires a dedicated network connection to support large or frequent background data transfers; otherwise, archiving must be performed during off-peak periods or low-utilization periods (e.g., via a nightly backup). Backup procedures can, however, be optimized by archiving only incremental changes since the last archive, reducing both traffic levels and network unavailability.

  Pros and Cons: The operating costs for electronic vaulting can be up to four times more expensive than simple tape or CD backup; however, this approach can be entirely automated. Unlike simple media backup there is no requirement to transport backup data physically. Recovery still depends on the most recent backup copy, but this is likely to be more recent due to automation. Electronic vaulting is more reliable and significantly decreases the recovery window (typically, just a few hours).

- Data replication/disk mirroring—Remote disk mirroring provides faster recovery and less data loss than remote electronic vaulting. Since data are transferred to disk rather than tape, performance impacts are minimized. With disk mirroring you can maintain a complete replica file system image at the backup site; all changes made to production data are tracked and automatically backed up. Data are typically synchronized in the background, and when the recovery site is initialized or when a failed site comes back online, all data are resynchronized from the replica to production storage. Note that data may be available only in read-only mode at the recovery site if the original site fails (to ensure at least one copy is protected), so services will recover but applications that are required to update data may be somewhat compromised unless some form of local data cache is available until the primary storage comes online. A disk mirroring solution should ideally be able to use a variety of disks using industry-standard interfaces (e.g., SCSI, Fibre Channel, etc.). An example of a disk-mirroring application is IBM's GeoRM [5]. Note that some applications provide data replication services as add-on features of their products (e.g., Oracle, Sybase, DB2, and Domino).

   Pros and Cons: Data replication is more expensive than the previous two models, and for large sites considerable traffic volumes can be generated. Ideally, a private storage network should be deployed to separate storage traffic from user traffic. Although more optimal, this requires more maintenance than earlier models.

- Server mirroring and clustering—These techniques can be used to significantly reduce the recovery time to acceptable levels. Ideally, servers should be running live and in parallel, distributing load between them but located at different physical locations. If incremental changes are frequently synchronized between servers, then backup could be a matter of seconds, and only a few transactions may be lost (assuming there isn't large-scale telecommunications or power disruption and staff are well briefed on what to do and what not to do in such circumstances). The increasing focus on electronic commerce and large-scale applications such as ERP means that this configuration is becoming increasingly common.

   Pros and Cons: This approach is widely used at data centers for major financial and retail institutions but is often too expensive to justify for small businesses. Server mirroring requires more infrastructure to achieve (high-speed wide area links, more routers, more firewalls, and tight management and control systems).

- Storage Area Networks (SANs) and Optical Storage Network (OSNs)—There is increasing interest in moving mission- and business-critical data off the main network and offloading it onto a privately managed infrastructure called a Storage Area Network (SAN). Storage can be optically attached via standard high-speed interfaces such as Fibre Channel and SCSI (with optical extenders), providing a physical separation of storage from 600 meters to 10 kilometers. Servers are directly attached to this network (typically via Fibre Channel or ESCON/FICON interfaces [5] and are also attached to the main user network. SANs may be further extended (to thousands of kilometers) via technologies such as Dense Wave Division Multiplexing (DWDM), forming optical storage networks. This allows multiple sites to share storage over reliable high-speed private links.

  Pros and Cons: This approach is an excellent model for disaster recovery and storage optimization. It significantly increases complexity and cost (though storage consolidation may recover some of these costs), and it is, therefore, appropriate only for major enterprises at present. One big attraction for many large enterprises is that the whole storage infrastructure can be outsourced to a Storage Service Provider (SSP). This facilitates a very reliable DR model (some providers are currently quoting four-nines (99.99 percent) availability.

As mentioned previously, there are specialized organizations that offer disaster recovery as an outsourced service, including Storage Service Providers (SSPs). Service may include automated response so that key systems on the network are remotely reconfigured or rebooted in the event of failure, through complete service mirroring on their network, so that business can continue even in the event of a total failure of your location. The arguments for and against outsourcing are very much a matter of personal preference and are dependent on the size and type of organization. In-house DR offers more control, potentially lower costs, and tighter security (some organizations may not want data to be seen by a third party). There may be incompatibilities and miscommunication between the staff, systems, and processes used by the outsourcing company and your own; these need to be addressed early on to avoid surprises. Another argument against outsourcing is that under a real disaster situation, the company you have outsourced to will be so busy helping other clients that you may not get the response time you expect (which leads to the ludicrous situation where you might consider having a DR plan to cope with failure of your DR outsourcing company, although cost is likely to prohibit this).

Outsourced DR may be the only sensible option for organizations that either cannot attract skilled IT staff or simply do not want the headache. It is perhaps most appropriate for mainframe scenarios, which are often mission critical, and where skilled operations staff are very hard to come by. To avoid contention, it is perhaps wise to choose one of the major outsourcing companies with an established reputation and the resources to deal with many clients concurrently.

6.1.4   Risk analysis and risk management

Once a basic network design is conceived, one of the major concerns of a network designer is to offer appropriate levels of fault tolerance for key services, systems, and communication links (where "appropriate" is either defined explicitly by the customer or determined against business needs). If you are supplying a network to a customer, from the customer perspective there may be one or more very specific requirements to be met, for example:

1.   There shall be no single point of failure in Equipment Room A.

2.   Service HTTP-2 shall recover from any system failure within 30 seconds.

3.   The routing network shall reconverge around any single point of failure within ten seconds.

A key consideration when planning for high availability, and particularly fault tolerance, is the cost of implementation versus the estimated cost of failure (based on the probability of failure occurring and the duration of downtime prior to recovery). For most organizations, the cost of making a network totally fault tolerant is simply too prohibitive; our real task is to quantify risk and then work out ways of managing it. In terms of network design this is a two-stage process, as follows:

- Risk analysis is the process of collecting all relevant facts and assumptions concerning network outages, and then using this information to estimate the probability and financial impact of such outages. This phase should also identify any potential mitigation techniques and quantify their benefits if deployed.

- Risk management is the process of taking input from the risk analysis phase and using that information to make decisions about which risks to take (i.e., which mitigation techniques to adopt and which vulnerabilities are deemed to be acceptable risks).

While on paper this seems fairly straightforward, in practice there are a number of issues that make this process more of an art than a science, including the following:

- Scope of failure events—Large internetworks are a highly complex mixture of systems and subsystems, and these entities interact with external systems. It is virtually impossible to identify all possible failure scenarios within the bounds of the network, never mind failures caused by external threats such as malicious users. In practice we list only problems that we know about.

- Event probability distribution—The distribution pattern of many naturally occurring events can be modeled using statistical techniques such as Gaussian and Poisson models [2]. These rules do not hold true for malicious users, so classical statistical methods are probably inappropriate.

- Event independence—As discussed in [2], an important concept used frequently in network modeling is the independence of events. With natural events such as floods or earthquakes we can use classical methods of estimating the probability that two events will occur simultaneously by multiplying their probabilities together. However, malicious user attacks against systems typically involve multiple simultaneous events, often related, and possibly not anticipated. To calculate the joint probabilities of events related in an unknown manner is practically impossible.

- Quantifying loss—In practice it is often very difficult to get agreement on the real loss associated with an event after the event has taken place. While there is a substantial body of knowledge on loss valuation available from auditors, different businesses and organizations may place valuations with ranges several orders of magnitude apart.

- Scope of mitigation techniques—We cannot exhaustively list all mitigation techniques. There are simply too many permutations, and no single organization has the time or resource to identify all of them.

- Quantifying reduction in expected loss—In order to quantify the cost effectiveness of various mitigation techniques, we need to calculate the reduction in expected loss. Unfortunately, there is no universally accepted way to do this with any degree of credibility.

- Sensitivity—In practice risk analysis can be very sensitive to detail. For example, a small change in probability or expected loss can influence the choice of one technique over another, and this could have cascading effects on subsequent decisions. Building sensitivity into risk analysis is likely to create a far more complex model.

Much of risk analysis and risk management treat systems as individual entities; however, when things go wrong in networks the failure scenarios are often complex and involve several different systems. We cannot, therefore, assume that system failures are independent, but if we try to calculate all combinations of events and their impacts on all combinations of systems, we are presented with an extremely daunting combinatorial problem. Networking introduces new classes of events and different types of losses and may dramatically change the expected loss reduction associated with different mitigation techniques—and that's just the beginning. This sounds like a classic case for smart software automation; however, there are very few complete packages for analyzing risk in data networks. There are a number of commercial and public domain vulnerability testing tools but very few integrated tools for discovering and quantifying risk. A product called Expert from L-3 Security (now part of Symantec [6]) takes an innovative approach in automatically locating risk and calculating the financial impact; it holds a database of hundreds of known vulnerabilities and thousands of policy safeguards. The downside is that an extensive audit of the network and its systems must be carried out before use; however, this is work that needs to be done never the less.

Regardless of all these seemingly intractable problems and the lack of good tools, it is essential that you perform at least a basic risk assessment. Without this analysis you could overlook critical issues that could be easily remedied. Depending upon the nature of the business, the causes of network or service outages may be easy or hard to quantify. Since we have to start somewhere, the first step is to attempt to identify all critical Single Points of Failure (SPOF).

Identify single points of failure

By analyzing the single points of failure in the network we can make a first stab at quantifying the scope and monetary impact of the most serious failures. This often proves to be a useful and illuminating exercise (the realization that a company's global e-business strategy relies on a flaky four-year-old Ethernet switch be a moment of purgatory for top executives). Figure 6.2 illustrates a simple network with two sites, the corporate headquarters LAN (Site-A), housing valuable customer database, e-business, and mail services; and a remote depot (Site-B), handling warehousing and dispatch. This network has grown and functions reasonably well but offers little in the way of fault tolerance. Let us assume that the corporate LANs are

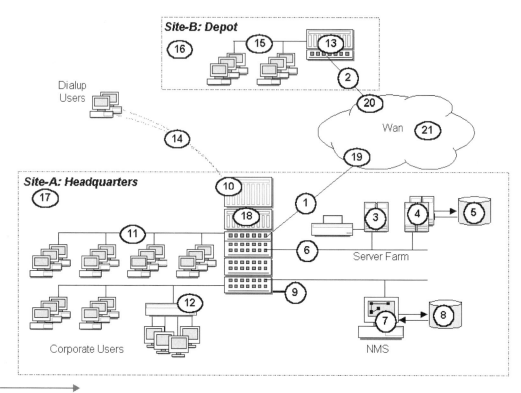

Figure 6.2   *Failure analysis of a simple nonresilient design.*

all switched Ethernet segments, to which a total of 350 users are connected to a single switching concentrator in a central equipment room. At the remote depot, a single Ethernet segment is connected to the corporate headquarters through a single router interface, across a 64-Kbps leased line. Dial-up users can access the router and corporate services via dial-up modem links to an RAS/rotary modem pool at HQ.

Let us determine what the key points of failure are in this design and the effects those failures will have on business operations, as illustrated in Table 6.2. This list is far from exhaustive, but you can begin to see that even with a relatively small network there are many points of failure, some with quite dramatic consequences. Note also that we have only scratched the surface here by identifying the main single points of failure. A more rigorous analysis might identify multiple points of failure in key systems (e.g., failure of two router processes or both power supplies in the HQ router). We may also want to drill down to identify more detailed failure scenarios in the cabling system, failures in connectors or sockets, software failure, disk failures, NVRAM failures, routing failures, and so on.

Table 6.2   *Quick Analysis of Major Points of Failure and Their Immediate Effects on the Example Network in Figure 6.2*

ID	Failure	Effect
1	HQ Wan link	Loss of all communications to HQ. All e-business activities halted.
2	Remote office Wan link	Loss of all communications to remote Depot
3	Web/Mail server	Loss of printing, Intranet and mail services. All e-business activities halted.
4	Database Server	Partial loss of Intranet services. Impact to Sales, Marketing and Finance
5	Database	Major Impact to Sales. Loss on invoices and status information
6	Server LAN	Loss of all HQ printing, Intranet and mail services. All e-business activities halted.
7	NMS	Loss of all control systems and logging information
8	NMS database	Loss of all configuration, logging and audit information
9	Power to Equipment Room	Total loss of all HQ Services. All e-business activities halted.
10	RAS/Modem Rotary	Loss of all remote dialup access to HQ
11	Corporate LAN	Loss of all user access
12	Terminal Server	Loss of all TN3270 access to parts database at Depot
13	Remote Router	Loss of all communications to remote Depot
14	POTS Failure	Loss of all remote dialup access to HQ
15	Depot LAN	Loss of all depot communications and dispatch operations
16	Depot Site	Loss of all depot operations
17	HQ Site	Loss of all HQ operations and services. All e-business activities halted
18	HQ Firewall-Router	Loss of all external access to HQ. All e-business activities halted.
19	WAN to HQ PoP	Loss of all communications to HQ. All e-business activities halted
20	WAN to Depot PoP	Loss of all communications to Depot. Dispatch activities halted.
21	WAN	Loss of all communications. All e-business activities halted.

The next logical step is to categorize and then estimate the costs of each particular failure. If, for example, we turn over an average $50,000 of new business every hour via the HQ Web server, then failures such as 1 and 18 in Table 6.2 are clearly business critical, and the design will almost certainly require modification to provide server mirroring or hot standby facilities. On the other hand, complete failure of the HQ site (e.g., due to an earthquake or bomb) is more difficult to resolve, since it will require substantial site duplication at a different location, possibly via an outsourced disaster recovery program. Each situation needs to be individually assessed on its relative merits to see if a technological solution is feasible and financially justifiable.

Quantifying risk

Fault-tolerant design is essentially a process of identifying and quantifying risk and then balancing those costs against the cost of protection. Once we understand what the risk is, we can deal with it in one of three ways: accept it, mitigate or reduce it, or transfer it (i.e., accept it but insure against it). Ideally, you need to work through each of the services, resources, and data stores available on the network and logically break down their vulnerability, value, and likelihood of being compromised. You can then start to map out who will be allowed to access these resources and what countermeasures you will put in place to minimize the risk of compromise. You can start by asking the following questions:

- How important is the operation of each system/database/link to the business?

- What is the monetary value per hour/minute/second in lost revenue if these services/systems are unavailable?

- How valuable are the data held on any such devices (i.e., the true cost of replacement)?

- What kind of a threat is each resource vulnerable to (disk failure, power failure, denial of service, virus, etc.)?

- What is the likelihood of these threats occurring (0–100 percent)?

- How many times per year would you anticipate such a failure?

- What is the likely recovery time for recovering from such failures?

ALE method

It can be instructive to perform a weighted risk analysis by estimating the risk of losing a resource and the value of that resource and then multiplying them together to get a weighted value. This is more formally known as the Annual Loss Expectancy (ALE) method. ALE is a method of quantifying risk by estimating a loss value per incident and then estimating the number of incidents per year to arrive at an Annual Loss Expectancy (ALE). Here, each item at risk produces a Single Loss Expectancy (SLE), calculated as:

$$SLE = V_x \times E_x$$

where

V_x = the asset value for a specific item, x, expressed as a monetary value (e.g., \$35,000, £100,000, DM 200,000)

E_x = exposure factor for a specific item, x, expressed as a percentage (0–100%) of the asset value.

If we are at risk of losing a database through a virus on an unprotected public file server (Table 6.3, item 5), for which we have no backups (worst-case scenario), then the cost to replace it might be calculated as the time to recreate it—say, two man-years at \$45,000. Given the scenario painted, we could probably assume that the database risk is 75 percent, giving us an SLE of $(2 \times 45 \times 75\%)$—that is, \$67.5K. Note that the manpower cost would almost certainly be higher, since we have not accounted for the true burdened costs (heating, space, expenses, etc.) plus possible lost productivity for other projects for the duration of this fix.

To get an annualized SLE (i.e., an ALE) we simply factor in the predicted number of times that such an event will occur over a year, using the formula:

$$ALE = SLE \times N_x$$

where

N_x = the annual rate of occurrence for a specific event, x.

Using the previous SLE illustration, if we expect to have a virus attack on our database twice in a year then the ALE for database loss is \$135,000. Table 6.3 illustrates how all of the failures listed in Table 6.2 might be quan-

Table 6.3   *ALE Analysis of Major Points of Failure*

ID	Failure	Asset Value	Exposure Factor	SLE	Annual Occurance	ALE
1	HQ Wan link	\$250,000	80%	\$200,000	2.5	\$500,000
2	Remote office Wan link	\$15,000	75%	\$11,250	3.0	\$33,750
3	Web/Mail server	\$250,000	75%	\$187,500	4.0	\$750,000
4	Database Server	\$100,000	20%	\$20,000	3.0	\$60,000
5	Database	\$90,000	75%	\$67,500	2.0	\$135,000
6	Server LAN	\$20,000	25%	\$5,000	4.0	\$20,000
7	NMS	\$10,000	10%	\$1,000	3.0	\$3,000
8	NMS database	\$5,000	10%	\$500	2.0	\$1,000
9	Power to Equipment Room	\$9,000	15%	\$1,350	2.0	\$2,700
10	RAS/Modem Rotary	\$10,000	90%	\$9,000	3.0	\$27,000
11	Corporate LAN	\$25,000	50%	\$12,500	4.0	\$50,000
12	Terminal Server	\$5,000	20%	\$1,000	0.5	\$500
13	Remote Router	\$200,000	75%	\$150,000	1.5	\$225,000
14	POTS Failure	\$20,000	50%	\$10,000	3.0	\$30,000
15	Depot LAN	\$200,000	75%	\$150,000	2.0	\$300,000
16	Depot Site	\$100,000	90%	\$90,000	1.0	\$90,000
17	HQ Site	\$250,000	90%	\$225,000	1.0	\$225,000
18	HQ Firewall-Router	\$40,000	50%	\$20,000	0.3	\$5,000
19	WAN to HQ PoP	\$100,000	10%	\$10,000	1.0	\$10,000
20	WAN to Depot PoP	\$25,000	10%	\$2,500	1.0	\$2,500
21	WAN	\$50,000	75%	\$37,500	0.5	\$18,750

tified using the ALE method. The ALE column can be used as a guide to rank the areas of the design requiring most attention.

Determine recovery times

Once we have identified all single points of failure and quantified risk, we need to determine the likely failure times and the baseline time to fix or recovery time. Whether the fix is automatic or requires manual intervention, you should have answers to the following questions for each failure identified:

- How are maintenance staff notified about a problem? Do monitoring tools alert you to the problem proactively, or are panic calls from users the first sign of trouble?

- How long will it take to track down the cause of the problem for each failed system or component?

- Does the design of the network naturally assist you in focusing on the problem quickly?

- What happens if a failure occurs outside of business hours? How does that affect recovery times?

- How are problems typically resolved for each system (remote reboot, reconfiguration, engineer on site)?

- Are spares held, if so where, and who controls them?

- Are backup configurations maintained? If so, how are they deployed in an emergency?

Without good management diagnostic tools and well-defined procedures, tracking down and resolving problems could conceivably take many hours, and most organizations simply cannot tolerate this level of downtime. Many companies are now relying on their networks as mission-critical business tools, and network downtime could seriously impact both profitability and credibility in the marketplace. As networks become even more tightly integrated and networking software enables files to be more readily distributed, the proliferation of computer viruses is becoming a major issue for maintaining network availability. Viruses such as the ILOVEYOU worm caused widespread chaos at many sites during 2000.

Managing risk

Risk management is the process of making decisions about which risks to take, which risks to avoid, and which risks to mitigate. Risk management is, therefore, a compromise; ultimately money must be spent to mitigate risk, and money may be lost if risks are accepted. Since the output of the risk analysis process can never be flawless, risk management relies on a mixture of common sense and business and basic accounting skills. One of the problems during the risk management phase is that the people making these decisions often may understand very little of the technology. It is, therefore, important that the risk analysis process should reduce the expression of each risk element to its most fundamental and understandable form, so that it can be translated directly into business terms. For example:

> If the HTTP Server (WSELL_2A) loses software integrity, then all pending transactions may be lost and new sessions cannot be serviced because the Telnet daemon may have locked.

should be translated as:

> If the main Web server dies, then no new customers will be able to buy products until it is rebooted, and we are likely to lose data from some of the sales calls in process at the point of failure.

A pragmatic and widely used technique in risk management is the covering technique. This involves listing all anticipated attacks and all possible defenses and then attempting to match appropriate defenses with each attack. Each defensive technique is assessed using a qualitative statement about its effectiveness. The risk manager then decides which attacks to protect against and which not to, based on a subjective view on the impact of each attack on the organization. Clearly, given the absence of numerical data, the risk manager has a great deal of latitude and must consider facts from many different sources in order to reach good decisions (it also implies that you need to choose a good risk manager!).

The following are some approaches we might consider to mitigate the types of failures we have identified in our example network:

- Install a second firewall router at the HQ site, mesh link both routers into the two switches, and then mesh link to both firewalls. Run a fast routing protocol such as OSPF or EIGRP on the internal interfaces of the corporate routers to ensure rapid convergence around failures. Make use of any load-balancing features available, if appropriate.

- Install a backup ISDN link from the remote site to the second HQ router. Configure the ISDN device to auto-dial whenever loss of WAN service is detected at either site.

- Add a second server farm with duplicate servers on a different segment, meshed into the two switches and then into the two firewalls. Front end these servers with a load-balancing device, or use a load-sharing dynamic protocol between the servers, such as HSRP or VRRP.

- Install disk mirroring in key servers and the firewall to protect against hard disk failure.

- Install a UPS at HQ to cover at least four hours of downtime. Consider DC backup via a diesel generator if justified.

The cost of each solution should reflect both the product cost and the cost of deployment. Most of these solutions are straightforward to analyze; however, they become increasingly difficult to cost justify as we work down the list. You need to balance the risk of component or system failure (using data such as MTBF/MTTR) against the scope and monetary impact of downtime due to that particular failure. A failure that affects a single user is unlikely to rate highly, even if the effect is complete downtime for that user.

Whichever model you use, these types of data can be used in financial planning projects when attempting to justify expenditure on fault-tolerant features, and it certainly helps to focus attention on critical vulnerabilities. If the annual projected losses due to system or network component failures exceed the cost of the preventative measures, then it should be easier to convince senior managers to allocate budgets accordingly. Just be aware that much of this process boils down to good judgment, regardless of the number of decimal points your analysis produces.

6.1.5 Availability analysis

In any network it is useful to have some way of quantifying availability and reliability, since this will determine how much money should be spent on avoiding loss of service and where that money should be targeted.

Quantifying availability

A simple way of expressing availability is to use the percentage uptime that a system or service offers, calculated as:

$A\%$ = Operational Time/Total Time

where time is normally expressed in hours. For example, consider a router that fails only once during the year and requires three hours to fix. Availability is calculated as:

$$A\% = [(365 \times 24) - 3]/(365 \times 24)$$

$$A\% = 99.966\%$$

Typical availability values range between 95 percent and 99.99999 percent, depending upon whether a best-effort or carrier-class service is required (as a result, carrier class is often referred to as seven-nines availability). While 95 percent uptime may sound pretty good, it is generally unacceptable for most working networks, since it translates to an average 1.2 hours of network outages per day (as illustrated in Table 6.4). To calculate the availability in hours, use the formula [8,760 × (1 − Availability%)], where 8,760 is the number of hours in a 365-day year. System classification taken from [7].

Wide area digital circuits are typically quoted at least 99.5 percent availability, while analog circuits are quoted at 99.4 percent availability. Highly reliable systems should be available at least 99.9 percent of the time, and most reliable networks operate at approximately 99.95 percent availability, with just over five minutes of downtime per week on average. Public operator networks (so-called carrier class networks) may offer availability from 99.99 percent through to 99.999 percent, although in practice this level of availability may be very expensive to deploy and will usually rely on highly redundant design with a mixture of hot-standby components and clustered solutions. Cost and complexity are the main barriers in moving beyond this level of availability, and increased complexity is itself a contributing factor in reducing reliability.

Table 6.4 *Availability Expressed as a Percentage Off Uptime (Hours = H, Minutes = M, Seconds = S, Milliseconds = MS)*

Network Class	System Class	Availability	Yearly Downtime	Monthly Downtime	Weekly Downtime	Daily Downtime
Best-Effort	1 Unmanaged	90.000000000%	876.00 h	73.00 h	16.85 h	2.40 h
		95.000000000%	438.00 h	36.50 h	8.42 h	1.20 h
	2 Managed	99.000000000%	87.60 h	7.30 h	101.08 m	14.40 m
Reliable		99.500000000%	43.80 h	3.65 h	50.54 m	7.20 m
Highly-Reliable	3 Well-Managed	99.900000000%	8.76 h	43.80 m	10.11 m	1.44 m
		99.950000000%	4.38 h	21.90 m	5.05 m	0.72 m
Mission-critical		99.980000000%	1.75 h	8.76 m	2.02 m	17.28 s
High-Availability	4 Fault Tolerant	99.990000000%	52.56 m	4.38 m	1.01 m	8.64 s
Carrier-Class	5 High-Availability	99.999000000%	5.26 m	26.28 s	6.06 s	863.99 ms
	6 Very High-Availability	99.999900000%	31.54 s	2.63 s	606.46 ms	86.40 ms
	7 Ultra-Availability	99.999990000%	3.15 s	262.80 ms	60.65 ms	8.64 ms
		99.999999000%	315.36 ms	26.28 ms	6.06 ms	0.86 ms
		99.999999900%	31.54 ms	2.63 ms	0.61 ms	0.09 ms
		99.999999990%	3.15 ms	0.26 ms	0.06 ms	0.01 ms
		99.999999999%	0.32 ms	0.03 ms	0.01 ms	0.001 ms

Availability can be expressed mathematically, using a number of components as input, as follows:

- Mean Time Between Service Outages (MTBSO) or Mean Time Between Failure (MTBF) is the average time (expressed in hours) that a system has been working between service outages and is typically greater than 2,000 hours. Since modern network devices may have a short working life (typically five years), MTBF is often a predicted value, based on stress-testing systems and then forecasting availability in the future. Devices with moving mechanical parts such as disk drives often exhibit lower MTBFs than systems that use fixed components (e.g., flash memory). Example MTBFs for a range of network devices are shown in Table 6.5.

- Mean Time To Repair (MTTR) is the average time to repair systems that have failed and is usually several orders of magnitude less that MTBF. MTTR values may vary markedly, depending upon the type of system under repair and the nature of the failure. Typical values range from 30 minutes through to 3 or 4 hours. A typical MTTR for a complex system with little inherent redundancy might be several hours.

In effect, MTBF and MTBSO both represent uptime, whereas MTTR represents downtime. As a general rule, an MTTR of less than one hour and an MTBF of more than 4,000 hours is considered good reliability, since it translates to two failures a year, with a total average yearly downtime of two

Table 6.5   *Example MTBFs for Real Network Devices*

Component	MTBF hours	MTBF years
Managed Repeater Chassis/Backplane	895,175	102.2
Fibre Optic IO Module (chassis based)	236,055	26.9
UTP IO Module (chassis based)	104,846	12.0
Management Module (chassis based)	75,348	8.6
Power Supply	44,000	5.0
Ethernet Transceiver	250,000	28.5
Terminal Server (standalone)	92,250	10.5
Remote Bridge (standalone)	41,000	4.7
Firewall (1 hard drive, 4 * IO card, no CDROM, no Floppy)	36,902	4.2
ATM Switch (3 * IO cards)	54,686	6.2
ATM Switch (16 * IO cards)	34,197	3.9
X.25 Triple-X PAD (standalone)	41,000	4.7
X.25 packet Switch (standalone)	6,000	0.7
Statistical Multiplexer (standalone)	5,300	0.6

hours (i.e., better than 99.98 percent availability). Note, however, that all of these factors represent average values (you could be unlucky and have two or more failures in the first month!). Note also that vendors may quote MTTR values assuming an engineer is already on site; you must also take into account any significant delays in the engineer getting to site from the time the fault call is logged. This may significantly increase the final MTTR and could result in different MTTRs for the same piece of equipment at different sites, depending upon their location and reachability. To simplify matters you may want to take the average MTTR for all of your sites.

Quantifying availability for discrete systems

Simply put, availability is the length of time a system is working compared with the expected lifetime of that system. Availability, A, and its complement, unavailability, U, are calculated as follows (where n is the system number):

$$A_n = \text{MTBF}_n/(\text{MTBF}_n + \text{MTTR}_n) \times 100$$

$$U_n = 1 - [\text{MTBF}_n/(\text{MTBF}_n + \text{MTTR}_n)] \times 100$$

The first equation is effectively the same as dividing operational time by total time, as presented previously. Another way of looking at unavailability is that it represents the probability of failure. The average number of failures, F, in a given time, T hours, is calculated as:

$$F_n = T/(\text{MTBF}_n + \text{MTTR}_n)$$

These methods of quantifying availability are more granular than a simple percentage in that they estimate both the frequency and the duration of system or network outages. For example, a low MTBF of 2,500 hours and an MTTR of 30 minutes indicate that there will be on average 3.5 failures in a year ($T = 8,760$ hours), or one failure every 3.4 months. In each case the downtime is expected to last about 30 minutes (i.e., the MTTR). A better MTBF, say 46,000 hours, indicates only 0.1904 failures per year, or one failure every 5.25 years.

Reliability

Reliability can be defined as the distribution of time between failures, and is often specified by the MTBF for Markovian failures [2]. Reliability, R, is specified as the probability that a system will not fail before T hours have elapsed:

$$R = e^{-t/\text{MTBF}}$$

For example, assume a system with an MTBF of 32,000 hours and a time, T, of one year (8,760 hours); this gives a reliability of 76.05 percent. If we increase the MTBF (say by selecting an alternate system) to 52,000 hours, this increases the reliability to 84.50 percent. For a network of systems in series we can calculate the total reliability, R_t, as follows:

$$R_t = e^{-t\,[(1/\mathrm{MTBF1}+(1/\mathrm{MTBF2})+(1/\mathrm{MTBF3})]}$$

For example, if we had three systems in series with MTBFs of 26,000, 42,000, and 56,000 hours, respectively, the overall reliability for a year would be 49.56 percent.

Quantifying availability in networked systems

Networked systems in series

For a network of devices in series, the total availability, A_t, is calculated as the product of all availabilities:

$$A_t = \prod_{i=1}^{n} A_t$$

Consider the example network in Figure 6.3. We have two switches and two routers in series; both sites are in very remote locations.

Let us assume that the router MTBF is 8,725 hours. The MTTR is calculated as 35 hours (1 hour call logging, 30 hours to ship parts and fly in an engineer, 4 hours to fix); hence, the router availability is 8,725/(8725 + 35) × 100, giving 99.6 percent. The service provider quotes the circuit availability at 99.5 percent. For the purpose of this example we are only interested in the router point-to-point link, so we can calculate the total availability as:

$$A_t = (0.996 \times 0.996 \times 0.995) \times 100$$

$$A_t = 98.71\%$$

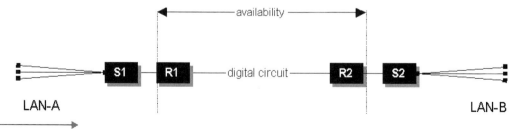

Figure 6.3 *Point-to-point network in series.*

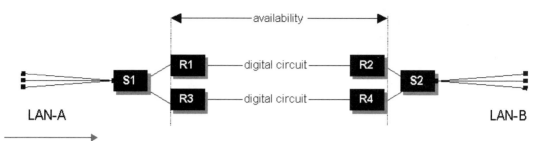

Figure 6.4   *Point-to-point network in parallel.*

Notice that the final result is lower than any of the individual components, as one would expect.

Networked systems in parallel

If we now modify the design to add a second parallel link in parallel, as illustrated in Figure 6.4, we can calculate the total availability as:

$$A_t = \left[1 - \prod_{j=1}^{n} \left(\sum_{i=1}^{n} 1 - A_i \right) \right] \times 100$$

where

j = the number of paths

i = the number of devices in series along those paths.

We can simplify this calculation by first working out the total availability for each path using the equation for solving availability in series. In this case we know from the previous work that this is 98.71 percent for each path. Substituting this result for this example we arrive at the following:

$$A_t = \left[1 - \prod_{j=1}^{2} (1 - 0.9871) \right] \times 100$$

$$A_t = (1 - 0.0129^2) \times 100$$

$$A_t = 99.98\%$$

Notice that the final result is higher than any of the individual components, as one would expect. Availability improves with parallel networks as we add more parallel systems; the converse is true of systems in series.

Combining systems in parallel and in series

To calculate availability for hybrid system, simply work out all the parallel systems first and then treat the whole system as if it were a network in series. For example, in the network illustrated in Figure 6.4, we might want to calculate the end-to-end availability, including the switch and intermediate LAN links. Let us assume that the switches offer 99.7 percent availability, and the LAN cross-connects to the routers offer 99.6 percent availability. We have already calculated the availability of the two parallel paths, so the final calculation is simply a network in series:

$$A_t = (0.996 \times 0.997 \times 0.9998 \times 0.997 \times 0.996) \times 100$$

$$A_t = 98.59\%$$

In summary, with any network design and particularly those with mission- or business-critical data and services, the design must be examined from the top down, starting with the wide area circuit design right down to the component level, identifying all probable single points of failures. There should be a well-defined and documented action plan for analyzing and resolving potential failures, either automatically or manually. Ultimately, networks should be able to heal themselves without requiring human intervention, but today this is not really achievable cost effectively.

The following sections illustrate the technologies and techniques available today to design fault-tolerant networks. These techniques are contrasted and their relative strengths and weaknesses assessed. For further information on risk analysis, the interested reader is directed to [8, 9].

6.2   Network resilience

6.2.1   Topological resilience

From the work presented in [2], you may recall that the basic physical topology chosen for the network has a profound effect on cost, performance, and fault tolerance. Figure 6.5 illustrates how network resilience can be improved by increasing the number of edges per node in the graph (i.e., links per node) and eliminating single points of failure. Clearly, if a node originates in more than one link it has a higher probability of being able to communicate should the topology fail. If we take this to the extreme, each node requires a direct connection to every other node in the graph for complete fault tolerance; we call this a full mesh. The average number of edges, E, is calculated by simply doubling the number of links in the graph and then dividing by the number of nodes. For example, in the partial-mesh

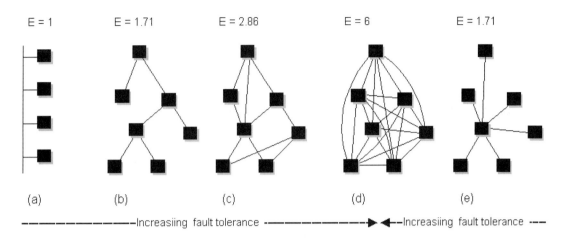

Figure 6.5 *Topological fault tolerance. (a) Bus or multidrop, (b) Tree, (c) Partial mesh, (d) Full mesh, (e) Star.*

network, Figure 6.5(c), this is calculated as $(2 \times 10/7) = 2.86$. As one would expect, for the full-mesh topology, $E = 6$ (i.e., $E = N - 1$, where N is the total number of nodes).

If we look at the example networks in Figure 6.5, we can see subtle differences in the way that failed nodes affect overall connectivity. Both the tree and star topologies have the same average number of edges, but there is a fundamental difference in the impact of node failure. In the tree topology, Figure 6.5(b), a failure at a leaf node (i.e., nodes at the edge of the tree with no downstream edges) affects no other node and does not disconnect the graph (though clearly it would be a bad idea to centralize services at a leaf node). However, failure of a root or branch node within the tree causes a topological disconnect, and two new discrete trees are formed. Depending upon the placement of services within the network, such a break would still allow internodes, communication within the two new trees. On the other hand, in the star topology, Figure 6.5(e), all nodes are effectively leaf nodes except for the central hub node. The hub represents a central point of failure; if this node dies, then the whole network is broken.

Remember that we are only considering network resilience here; there are other factors that must be taken into account. Real network designs are always a compromise and may be subject to many constraints imposed by the technologies employed, site locations, cost, network management, and the existing installed base. For example, in Figure 6.5 the star network generally offers better performance than the tree network (since the star topology has only one hop between any two nodes, but the example tree topology has a worst-case number of hops of three). On the other hand, a star topology is likely to be more expensive, since it requires longer direct circuits. The full pros and cons of all of these topologies are discussed in [2]. For the interested reader [10] includes mathematical techniques used to model reliability in various topologies and methods for predicting connectivity.

In practice it is not unusual to use a combination of techniques—for example, a national wide area backbone may comprise a tree of star networks, with each star collapsing short local access circuits into a central hub site, and each hub site connected over the backbone forming a tree topology. The tree may be supplemented by backup circuits or additional meshing between key sites (to form a partial mesh) for additional resilience, as discussed in the next section.

6.2.2 Resilient wide area networks

Wide area links are used to create internetwork backbones and are often the most expensive and critical component in internetwork design. However, wide area links, especially long-haul links, are relatively less reliable components of an internetwork (partly because of the large distances and number of intermediate systems and carriers involved, and also because of problems associated with the local loop). Furthermore, because of the relatively low bandwidths and high tariffs associated with these links, they are prone to congestion, since they are often operated at high utilization to maximize cost efficiencies, and current traffic engineering practices are not especially intelligent. These factors are all compelling reasons for considering fault tolerance and load-splitting techniques to supplement the design.

Note that adding capacity or additional circuits is not normally a problem, but if you intend to change capacities on a working network or modify routing behavior in any way, then it is advisable to perform some basic modeling beforehand, as the consequences of redirecting flows could lead to unexpected results.

Traditional point-to-point star network

Consider the five-node star network illustrated in Figure 6.6(a). This topology is a traditional regional leased-line network with a central hub site. If any of the satellite nodes or links fail, then no other node is affected (assuming that important services are not placed at a satellite site). However, if the central site equipment fails, then the whole network is broken and no com-

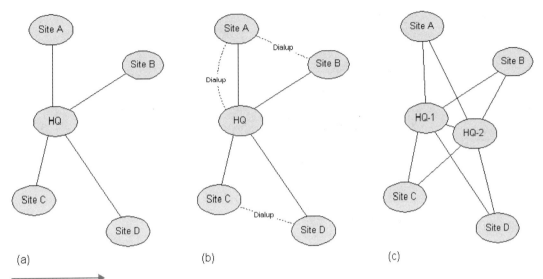

Figure 6.6   *(a) Traditional leased-line star topology. (b) Leased-line star topology, supplemented by dial-up links. (c) Twin star topology with leased lines.*

munication is possible between any of the four satellite sites. To improve fault tolerance there are several options, including the following:

- Add more hub links—Each of the satellite links could be doubled up. This can improve performance through load sharing but will only provide resilience against link failures (if the central site fails, we lose all connectivity) and might be cost prohibitive. This design option clearly does not scale.

- Add dial-up links—Dial backup links (such as provided by ISDN or analog modems) could be utilized as illustrated in Figure 6.6(b). Instead of deploying dial-up in a spoke configuration, dialing between sites is enabled to offer routing around central site failures. For example, on site C this would require the dial-up software to monitor either physical link status on the primary leased line or the reachability to site HQ (this could be achieved through the routing table). If either fails, then the dial-up link would automatically be invoked either to dial-up site D specifically or to a pool of addresses for even greater resilience.

- Add more direct links—Employ partial or full-circuit meshing so that site-to-site communications can continue if the central hub fails.

- Add a second hub—A twin-star network requires a second hub and is inherently more reliable (see Figure 6.6[c]). This requires twice as many hub links but also means that the second hub could be placed at a different location, so that complete failure of the primary hub site can be dealt with. To save costs, the secondary hub links could be dial-up links (e.g., ISDN).

Simple star network topologies offer good performance (fewer hops) but with poor fault tolerance and a higher overall cost. A partial-mesh topology has shorter direct circuits and more inherent resilience.

Dial backup and top-up links

An attractive low-cost option for resilience is the use of dial-up links as backups for the primary backbone interfaces, illustrated in Figure 6.6(b). This feature is sometimes referred to as Dial on Demand Routing (DDR). Since dial-up links are charged primarily on a call-use basis, these facilities can be very cost effective, since they are likely to be idle for much of the time and only called into action when a failure occurs. The tariff is, therefore, likely only to comprise a one-off connection charge and a relatively low monthly rental.

A traditional low bandwidth solution for this would be via features such as DTR dial or V.25bis through external modems. Many routers, for example, include support for at least one of these types of modem support. A more attractive solution is ISDN, since it allows multiple 64-Kbps channels to be bonded dynamically and provides almost instant backup for failed backbone links. Many router vendors offer sophisticated monitoring facilities so that several primary links can be backed up, and different destinations can be dialed depending upon which link failed. When the primary link recovers (possibly after some hold-down timer to avoid link oscillations), the ISDN line is automatically disconnected to avoid further line charges. ISDN vendors may also offer the capability to add bandwidth on demand, a useful way of dynamically topping up the primary link bandwidth if the utilization reaches a configured threshold.

Typical ISDN call-setup times are in the order of a few seconds, depending upon the amount of negotiation required at the link layer. It is worth noting that on some international ISDN connections the call setup time may be in excess of ten seconds (due to additional latency introduced by the convoluted way that end-to-end circuit switch paths are routed).

Improved point-to-point meshing

If a point-to-point network is required, then some simple steps could be taken to improve resilience, ranging from a partial mesh, in topology Figure 6.7(a), to a full mesh (although the costs of a full mesh could be prohibi-

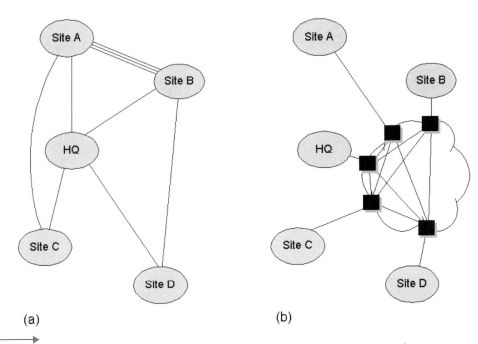

Figure 6.7   *(a) Partial mesh leased line network. (b) Fully meshed leased line network.*

tive). If the backbone is routed, then all of these additional links would be active, and any site-to-site traffic could be offloaded from the HQ site, which previously acted as the transit point for all traffic. Clearly, the additional links will add cost, so, depending upon traffic loads, there could be some waste, since any additional links need enough capacity to carry rerouted traffic in the event of a failure. If there is any form of meshing in the routed backbone, routers can automatically reconfigure around failed WAN links using routing algorithms to calculate alternate routes. This allows services to continue operating, although there may be user disconnection at the point of router reconvergence, depending upon application timeouts.

Load sharing over multiple paths

One of the benefits of multiple parallel links would be the option to split the load over the link pairs, hence reducing response times and increasing throughput. Standard data link protocols such as MLPPP are available to provide this functionality for bridges and routers transparently; if parallel connections are made (sometimes called bonding) between the same router pair, then packets will be delivered in sequence at the far end. If MLPPP is not running, then routing protocols such as OSPF and EIGRP can provide

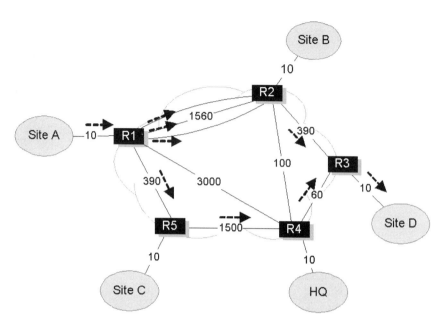

Figure 6.8
*Logical routing
topology where
both multilink and
multipath load
sharing are
employed.*

load sharing. A redundant star is a reasonable topology to choose if there is relatively little traffic between remote sites or mission-critical traffic moving between corporate and remote sites is highly sensitive to delay. Figure 6.8 illustrates a topology where both multilink and multipath routing are available. Here we see that between routers R1 and R2 multilink PPP is used over three parallel links to distribute traffic evenly. This is transparent to any routing protocol. Between Site A and Site D equal cost multipath routing is available via protocols such as OSPF, since the aggregate metrics for the two data paths, A-R1-R2-R3-D and A-R1-R5-R4-R3-D, are equal to 1,960 (note that we assume a directed graph, so the cost from Site A to R1 is zero).

Routers typically support load balancing on either a per packet or a per destination basis. Per packet load balancing, sometimes called round robin, is recommended where the WAN links are relatively slow (e.g., less than 64 Kbps). However, with round robin packets can arrive out of sequence packets at the remote end, so the application must be capable of dealing with this (TCP can handle this but many other applications cannot). For faster link speeds load balancing on a per destination basis is recommended. If firewalls are used in resilient pairs, you may need to use session-based load balancing to ensure sessions are routed explicitly through a particular firewall, since many firewalls cannot tolerate asymmetrical connections or out-of-sequence packets.

Switched service resilience through internal meshing

Figure 6.9 illustrates a more flexible and more resilient topology, using a meshed-switched WAN network such as ATM, X.25, SMDS, or Frame Relay (this may also be more cost effective for higher-bandwidth applications). The service provider is responsible for providing a highly meshed topology inside the cloud, and this offers a higher degree of resilience overall. The nice thing about this option is that the backbone is effectively outsourced, and it is up to the service provider to manage the internals of the network and to ensure that it offers a high level of availability.

One thing to watch here, however, is the number and location of the PoPs provided by the service and how many switches are actually available at the PoP. For example, you may choose to build a highly resilient corporate LAN at HQ, with multiple routers providing separate interfaces from the HQ site into the cloud, thinking that this will provide even better resilience for all corporate services (see Figure 6.9). However, if the PoP distribution is quite sparse, you may find in reality that you are hooking these routers back into a single switch inside the cloud, defeating much of what you thought you were achieving. This situation is not unusual; it is common in developing countries and where providers roll out a new service (typically the provider will deploy PoPs in major population centers first, and then spread out and improve density as the subscriber levels increase). Even in large cities it is by no means guaranteed that you will be diversely routed. This basic topology issue has compromised several very high profile

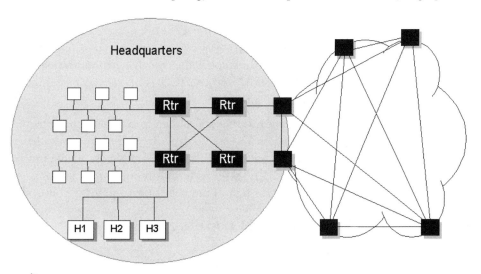

Figure 6.9   *Resilient connections into a switched cloud via dual connections to different PoPs.*

organizations. To be absolutely sure, always check with your service provider.

Link failure detection

So far we have assumed that we know when a WAN link has failed. In reality this is not quite as straightforward as it might seem. Leased lines, for example, do not always fail cleanly; Bit Error Rates (BER) may increase over time until the line becomes effectively unusable, or they may fail cleanly and then bounce back into life several times (sometimes referred to as link flapping). An intermittent problem is much more problematic than a clean failure. Clearly, if this is a routed network, we do not want link-state protocols such as OSPF to be forced to reconverge every time a WAN link oscillates; otherwise, the whole network could be rendered unusable, and for this reason even highly sensitive protocols employ damping features. The mechanisms normally used to detect and handle link failure include the following

- Physical signal monitoring—Low-level software or firmware monitors the state of key signals on the WAN interface and flags any changes to higher-layer protocol layers. Typically some hysteresis is implemented to avoid excessive and continuous transitions. Recognized state changes are reported up to higher-level protocols.

- Link status messages—link status messages are sent across the link to monitor link integrity on a periodic basis. Proprietary serial protocols implement Breath of Life (BOFL) features; while standards-based protocols such as PPP use a feature called Link Quality Monitoring (LQM), where statistical reports on link status are periodically sent over the wire. If the link is unavoidably error prone, then connection-oriented data link protocols such as LAPB may be required to provide buffering and guaranteed delivery.

Signal monitoring capabilities are dependent upon the media type and the hardware components used by the manufacturer in the system design. Link status mechanisms such as PPP's LQM are media independent. Note that some media types provide link monitoring features as standard (e.g., link-pulse monitoring in Ethernet point-to-point copper and fiber).

6.2.3 Resilient LAN topologies

Local area networks are generally more resilient than wide area networks due to their local scope, bandwidth availability, and overall topological robustness. We can summarize a number of common causes of failure in LAN media as follows:

- Cabling failure—Media cable failure (bad termination, cable break, etc.), AUI cable failure.

- Connector failure—Patching failure, loose connectors.

- Concentrator failure—Hub or switch failures.

- Network interface failure—Faulty network interface controller (PC NICs, transceiver failures).

There are also several techniques and tools available to build fault-tolerant LANs—some proprietary, some standards based, including Spanning Tree bridges and switches, source route bridging, redundant link repeater protocols. We discuss these techniques in the following sections.

Backbone design

Local area backbones are a critical part of many enterprise designs. Regardless of advances in distributed applications, the traffic pattern of many networks today is still highly asymmetrical, with users accessing services concentrated at one or more central sites (often for pragmatic reasons such as cost efficiencies and simplified management). It follows that much of the network traffic may be aggregated at these central locations, and high-speed resilient backbones are required to attach high-speed servers and to carry many concurrent user sessions.

A number of popular LAN technologies incorporate fault-tolerance features as standard. FDDI and Token Ring, for example, incorporate dual self-healing rings. Token Ring Multistation Access Units (MAUs) can detect some media connection failures and bypass the failures internally. FDDI dual rings can wrap around failed sections of the ring by moving traffic automatically onto a backup ring. FDDI also incorporates Spanning Tree protocol for resilient meshed concentrator topologies. From a local router, bridge, or switch perspective, media failures can normally be bypassed automatically as long as there are alternate paths available in the network. All of these features enable the network designer to build fairly robust LAN backbones, and it is often easy and relatively inexpensive to deploy or make use of additional cables for topological resilience (much easier than the WAN environment, where additional links can be very costly to deploy).

Figure 6.10 illustrates the two commonly used LAN backbone configurations. Figure 6.10(a) shows a backbone ring topology. Here, total resilience relies on ring nodes to be dual attached; otherwise they run the risk

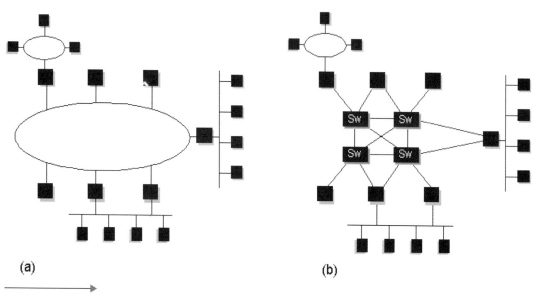

(a)   **(b)**

Figure 6.10   *Topological resilience in LAN backbones. (a) Self-healing fiber ring backbone (e.g.,*
FDDI, Token Ring), (b) Meshed-switched backbone (e.g., FDDI, Fast Ethernet,
Gigabit Ethernet, ATM).

of being isolated in the event of a single point of failure. The ring is easy to
install and manage but may not be flexible enough for some sites and does
not scale well (as the ring grows, the distance between nodes increases, and
often the medium is a shared-access technology such as FDDI). Figure
6.10(b) shows a backbone mesh topology comprising a fabric of interconnected switches. This topology is highly flexible, and switches may be
deployed in a hierarchical or flat configuration to suit the application. The
design is also scalable, new switches can be easily added to increase overall
capacity, and nodes requiring high reliability can deploy many diverse
links. Traffic segmentation and the ability to support full-duplex, point-
to-point links at the switch level means that bandwidth is also managed
more efficiently. For further information on particular media types refer to
[2].

Topological control with routers

Routers and Layer 3 switches maintain loop-free networks using standard
routing protocols (such as RIP, EIGRP, and OSPF) in combination with
path metrics. These protocols typically create multiple Spanning Trees (one
for each source-destination address pair), so traffic routing is much more
efficient than a simple bridged or switched network (which relies on the
Spanning Tree protocol). Routing protocols detect topology problems and

automatically reroute around failed devices or segments. They may also offer load balancing.

Topological control with switches and bridges

Bridges and switches maintain loop-free networks using the Spanning Tree Protocol (STP). STP detects topology loops and automatically reroutes around failed devices or segments. STP creates a single shortest-path tree for the whole network (i.e., a Minimum Spanning Tree, or MST). Ports are placed in a blocking state if loops are detected; this is undesirable for expensive wide area links and several vendors have added proprietary extensions to handle WAN link load sharing in tandem with STP (e.g., Xyplex and Vitalink). For further information, refer to [2].

Topological control with repeaters

At the physical level there are various link and interface monitoring techniques, such as carrier sensing and the use of link-pulse signaling in 10BaseT and FOIRL. These techniques are useful for detecting point-to-point problems and are used to alert higher-level bridging and routing protocols of a possible change in topology. Managed repeaters may also implement a form of proprietary loop control, in particular those with Ethernet connectivity. It is important to understand that there is no standard for resilient link management at the repeater level, although several manufacturers (including Cabletron, Case Communications, Xyplex, and Ungerman-Bass) employ similar techniques in their managed hubs. In this section we refer to this feature generically as Redundant Link Management (RLM). RLM provides controlled topology changes in the event of link or repeater failures. During the late 1980s and early 1990s routers were expensive, often single protocol, and many networks were no more than extended bridged LANs. For mission-critical networks, topological convergence on the order of a few seconds is not uncommon, and the standard Spanning Tree protocol was considered far too slow for such applications. Using RLM and repeaters also removed the requirement for expensive bridges where traffic filtering was not the primary concern.

RLM is typically implemented using a simple master-slave relationship; hubs that operate as a master perform polling of one or more slave hubs. The designer typically configures polling parameters (such as the interfaces used, target addresses to poll for, try intervals, retry counts, etc.). Some implementations allow the designer to set up a number of redundant link groups, where each group is an abstraction for a particular failure scenario. For example, the configuration defines a primary link and two backups for group 1 (shown in the following code segment). The backup links are disabled in software. The primary interface (e0) issues polls for 193.24.2.1 and 193.24.2.21, and the topology remains stable unless either target fails to respond within 3 × 1 seconds (in practice the target addresses could represent the LAN and WAN interface cards on a remote slave hub). In a failure scenario the first backup port in the list is activated and the primary interface is disabled. Note that the backup link may have a completely different target list depending upon the physical topology of the network.

```
Group If  Status   Interval Retry  Targetlist
1     e0  primary  1        3      193.24.2.1 AND 193.24.2.21
1     e1  backup   1        3      190.4.4.1 AND 190.4.4.6
1     e4  backup   1        3      150.20.6.99
```

The protocol used to poll and pass status information is often proprietary (some implementations incorporate standard ping and SNMP operations also). Low-level hardware features (such as link pulse) are often employed to speed up detection of physical link failures. RLM implementations vary significantly; more sophisticated techniques may distribute topology information between hubs, enabling discovery and increased automation. Implementations relying on the simple polling mechanism rely heavily on the designer to ensure that loops are not formed in certain failure scenarios; this is particularly important for designs where multiple hubs are operating as master, and some hubs are both master and slave.

For example, consider the simple designs in Figure 6.11. The first design illustrates a simple topology, with three Ethernet repeaters protected by two pairs of dual fiber links. In this case H2 and H3 will both be polling H1. If either hub fails to receive a response from H1 in the allotted window, it will disable its primary interfaces and swap over to the backup links. Note that this design protects only against cable failure; if H1 dies, then H2 and H3 will most likely oscillate their interface status until H1 comes back online. H1 is a Single Point of Failure (SPOF) for the whole network. In Figure 6.11(b) we see an improved design. No hub is a single point of failure, and we use one less cable. H1 is polling H3 via H2, and in the event of failure, H1 will automatically open up link 1-3 but is configured not to disable its primary interface. This takes care of the event that either link 1-2 or 2-3 dies. If H3 itself dies, then we still have a link between H1 and H2.

RLM is nonstandard, and, therefore, implementations rarely interoperate in multivendor environments (it may be possible to poll devices if a standard polling scheme such as ping is used). RLM traffic is in-band, making it prone to false-positive behavior in very busy networks (in extreme cases links can oscillate during busy periods unless long timeouts are config-

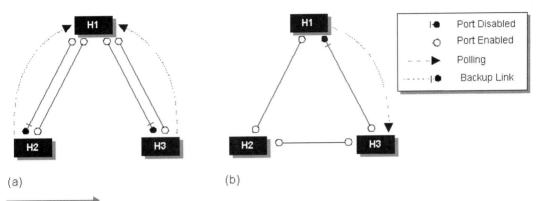

Figure 6.11   *Basic redundant link configurations. (a) A simple star configuration requiring four physical cables to provide link resilience but having a single point of failure at hub H1. (b) An improved configuration with only three cables and no single point of failure.*

ured and damping mechanisms are introduced). Beyond very simple designs there are some challenging subtleties and inconsistencies to resolve, and I would not recommend that you try these. In general it is best to keep the design simple, reduce the number of masters to a minimum, ensure all timers are consistent with the expected failover behavior, and test all scenarios religiously to ensure that there are no surprises. Then document the design thoroughly. While RLM is a very cost-effective way of improving topological resilience, the potential pitfalls and likely maintenance issues make it less and less attractive as fast switches and routers become available as low-cost commodity products.

Segmentation

Segmentation is a widely used design technique in LANs. It reduces the scope of media failure by dividing the network into smaller segments and spreading users and key servers over multiple devices. For example, if you have 200 workstations attached to a single switch, this represents a single point of failure. Adding another switch immediately reduces the impact of a single hub failure to 50 percent of the user base. Both switches could be connected via two backbone links for resilience. Clearly, you can take this model as far as is practical and cost effective. The design becomes more complex as you split device responsibilities, and this complexity manifests itself in the interconnection topology. As a general rule complexity is the enemy of reliability and must also be kept in check.

As discussed in [2], introducing Layer 2 switches (or bridges) partitions the network to create multiple traffic domains. This further improves availability by reducing overall traffic levels. Switches forward traffic intelligently so that traffic is forwarded only to the appropriate LAN segments (instead of being repeated over the whole LAN). Switches also ensure that frame errors such as CRCs are not forwarded. Introducing Layer 3 routers and switches creates partitioning at the Network Layer, improving availability even further. Routers suppress broadcast storms and perform more optimal packet forwarding to reduce overall traffic. Routers also support more intelligent protocols that can resolve topological loops very rapidly (e.g., OSPF).

6.2.4   Resilient end-system topologies

For mission- or business-critical servers it is often appropriate to implement high availability and even fault tolerance. These devices represent a very small percentage of the overall end-system population, and it is particularly important that they remain online. Providing fault tolerance at the user desktop level is, however, likely to be prohibitively expensive for all but a very small number of mission-critical applications (e.g., online traders, critical health care, process control, etc.). There are more cost-effective solutions that can be used to improve availability; even here the cost burden rises significantly with the number of users. These techniques also have a layer of complexity that can make the infrastructure more difficult to manage and maintain.

Multiple network points

Servers are generally installed in or near equipment rooms, so access to multiple network points is generally not an issue. Deploying multiple network outlets at the user desk position can be a relatively inexpensive exercise, if done at the time the cabling system is installed. This technique provides a backup network point. If the primary network connection fails, then the user can manually connect to the second outlet. Unless the second port is permanently online (this would require double the port density in concentrator equipment, with additional costs), the other end of the cable will need to be manually patched by network support staff. Clearly, if the second outlet is wired back to the same card in the same hub, then only cable resilience is provided. For improved availability the second cable should be diversely routed to alternate concentrator equipment. For example, with a dealer desk scenario we could diversely route alternate desk positions to different equipment rooms, so that any single point of failure in the network would take down only a fixed percentage of dealer terminals.

Dual port transceivers

These devices provide two interfaces from the user floor/desk point, which can be diversely routed (see Figure 6.12). The transceiver has limited built-

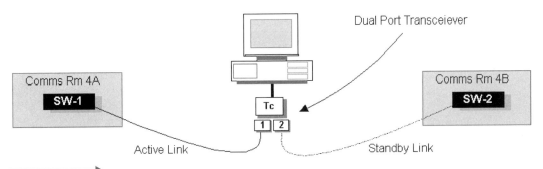

Figure 6.12   *User workstation wired back to two communications rooms using a dual port transceiver connected to different floor outlets.*

in intelligence to sense the status of the primary link and automatically switches to the backup if a failure is detected. The advantage of this approach is that it is transparent to the end user's application stack and requires no intervention by the user.

Dual NICs

Two network interface cards can be installed in the desktop PC/workstation. This provides resilience right inside the user's node and protects against cable and network attachment failure. This approach can, however, prove to be problematical; you should check that the applications and protocol stack are able to cope with multiple interfaces, network, and MAC addresses. You should also ensure that gateway configuration or gateway discovery is handled correctly under all circumstances. It is common practice to install dual NIC cards in mission-critical fault-tolerant servers. Often the protocol stacks in these systems have been modified to accommodate multiple NICs. NIC interfaces should be diversely wired back to different LAN segments or to discrete concentrator equipment.

Backup power and media

A UPS and backup or mirrored hard disk medium can be installed if required. This is rarely applicable for desktop users for cost reasons.

Improving desktop management

As indicated, it is unlikely that you will be able to cost justify high availability at the desktop level, especially in a large network. Even so, there are steps you can take to improve availability of desktop machines through management processes; you should at least take steps to deploy instrumentation that will monitor performance regularly. Desktop devices frequently have outages, and desktop operating systems have a tendency to degrade over time; as new software is installed, deinstallers fail to clean up properly, and disk drives start to underperform. Often these problems go unnoticed on a large network, since users simply reboot, and problems often go unreported. There is a culture of expectation that desktop machines will frequently fail as part of their normal operation (the machine I am writing this chapter on failed to boot properly when started; I simply rebooted and forgot about it).

To improve overall reliability it is recommended that you implement the following measures:

- Instrumentation—Take regular measurements of response times, and maintain statistics on reboots and any protocol errors.

- Control—The responsibility for desktops should be centralized, so that OS versions and vendor platforms can be standardized. This will greatly improve the deployment, maintenance, and fault-analysis processes.

- Classification—Classify the supported platforms according to capacity, performance, and any fault-tolerance requirements—for example, engineer, power user, executive, administration.

- Certification—Initiate a certification process for determining which software will and will not be allowed on the network and which software will be supported on each platform.

- Burn-in—Initiate physical testing procedures for each piece of software before it is allowed on the network. This will ensure that you get first-hand experience of any possible problems in a controlled environment without ending up fire fighting the whole network.

- Build images—For each platform create a standard build image on CD. This will enable you to rapidly deploy or reconfigure failed machines without having to go through a complete install.

- Spares—Maintain a good stock of key spares so that you can quickly replace dead monitors, systems, mice, keyboards, and media.

All of these measures will help to maintain overall reliability in the desktop environment.

6.3   Fault-tolerant, high-availability, and clustering systems

The approach taken for service protection depends largely upon the budget, the relative importance of service outages to the business or organization, and the type of data being protected. The network designer may choose from a basic high-availability solution through to a full fault-tolerant system. These systems can be described as follows:

- Fault-tolerant systems—At the highest level of availability there are fault-tolerant systems (sometimes called Continuous Availability [CA] systems). These systems employ highly sophisticated designs to eliminate practically all single points of failure; consequently, only a small number of vendors can truly claim to have fault-tolerant platforms.

- Fault-resilient systems—At the next level of availability there are fault-resilient systems. These systems employ sophisticated designs to eliminate some single points of failure, so there are basic levels of fault tolerance (e.g., ECC memory, RAID arrays, and multiple network interfaces).

- High-availability systems (clustering and server mirroring)—These techniques rely on external cooperation between multiple systems so that the systems effectively operate as a single logical group resource.

Figure 6.13 illustrates two of these systems.

Fault-tolerant solutions are explicitly designed to eliminate all unplanned and planned computer downtime by incorporating reliability, maintainability, and serviceability features. Fault-tolerant systems claim as much as 99.999 percent uptime (colloquially known as five-nines). High-

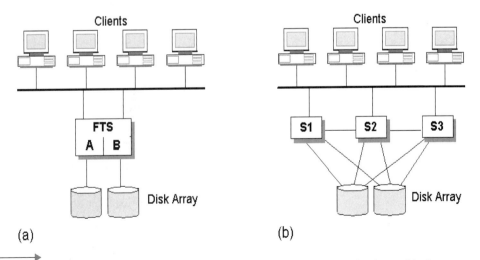

(a)   **(b)**

Figure 6.13   *General architecture for servers in (a) fault-tolerant mode and (b) clustered high-availability (HA) mode.*

availability systems can deliver average levels of uptime in the 99 to 99.9 percent range.

6.3.1   Maintaining service levels

When we talk about system availability, we need to differentiate between data loss, transaction loss, and loss of service. These issues are tackled via different techniques. Data can be protected by recording them simultaneously to multiple storage devices; the most widely used techniques are disk mirroring and RAID. Fault-tolerant systems offer complete protection at the transaction level but are typically very expensive and do not scale. In contrast, HA solutions offer cost-effective and scalable protection; however, transactions may be lost. Regardless of the solution provided, overall service availability depends heavily on the architecture of the applications. Application-based redundancy refers to application-level routines designed to protect data integrity, such as two-phase commit or various data replication processes. Simple applications generally have no protection against transactions lost in midsession; once data are committed they are gone for good. Sophisticated database management systems that support a two-phase commit model are typically much more robust against data loss.

6.3.2   Application models and availability

In general the purpose of improving availability is to protect mission- or business-critical services; it is, therefore, important to understand the dynamics of these services in detail to ensure that the solutions provided are appropriate for, and consistent with, application behavior. Networked applications today often use a multitier architecture based on a client/server or distributed model. For availability purposes, it is useful to consider applications as three layers: communications services, application services, and database services, since the availability issues for each of these layers can be quite different, as follows:

- Communications services include management of the LAN and WAN connections together with higher-level communications and messaging functions (such as routing, store-and-forward messaging, and protocol or data conversion). Systems at this layer typically rely on a large amount of memory-resident data (e.g., connection/session status, queued messages, intermediate results for transactions, and the context of user dialogs). The ability to preserve these critical data against serious failures may be highly desirable for transaction-based services, or services where sessions need to be maintained continuously.

- Application services functions will vary depending upon the application but typically include user interface handling, transaction capture and sequencing, local searching and sorting, computational processing and statistics reporting, event and message logging, and so on. The availability solution most appropriate for this layer will depend largely on the application requirements. Fault-tolerant servers are appropriate when it is important to protect critical, memory-based state information or an in-memory database. If this is not a requirement, then an HA cluster may be more appropriate. In some cases front-end services may mandate stand-in processing, where applications provide continuous client service during periods when back-end databases are unavailable.

- Database services are transaction-based services and typically require a large back-end central database. This is generally implemented as a high-end, scalable server platform architected to handle volume transaction traffic and interface with mass storage systems (either via SCSI/RAID, Fibre Channel, or some other peripheral interface). The recovery issues are fairly straightforward for this layer, since the persistence, data integrity, and recoverability of application data are standard features of all serious database and transaction software.

At a large central site, the three layers are often distributed across several server platforms, in which case it is generally possible to provide a tailored availability solution for each layer. For example, fault-tolerant communications servers can provide continuous availability for higher-level communications services, enabling front-end applications to route messages among multiple back-end systems and to store and later submit transactions if back-end systems are offline. For smaller sites it is normal practice to select a single solution that is most suited for the needs of all three layers.

With fault-tolerant systems much of the hard work is transparent to the network designer, so these systems can be relatively straightforward to implement. However, fault-tolerant systems have finite resources and do not scale (so even FT systems may have to use clustering techniques). HA solutions provide scalability and can provide equivalent availability; an HA solution can be harder to implement, since much of the workings of the HA solution are exposed and may require special tuning or have topological restrictions. Currently there are no generic communications solutions that provide the equivalent level of reliability provided by two-phase commit database management software (although sessions may be maintained by HA solutions, they typically cannot guarantee against transaction loss). Further complications arise from the heterogeneous nature of many communications environments, as well as the need to incorporate existing legacy protocols, multiple operating systems, and a variety of networking devices in the end-to-end delivery path. All of these factors impact reliability.

6.3.3   Fault-tolerant systems

At the high end of the server market there are a number of vendors that offer truly fault-tolerant machines (such as Tandem [11] and Stratus [12]). These machines are designed to eliminate most single points of failure within the internal processor, memory, IO, and power subsystems. They also typically offer multiple network adaptors. Key features to look for in a fault-tolerant system are as follows:

- Replicated hardware subsystems—Some vendors offer the choice of Dual-Modular Redundancy (DMR) or even Triple-Modular Redundancy (TMR) at the hardware level. Systems are monitored constantly and failover is immediate (or at least in the order of milliseconds).

- Online software serviceability—Support for configuration changes, operating-system upgrades, patches, and device driver updates without requiring a system reboot.

- Online hardware serviceability—Hot-swappable drives are an essential component (RAID and otherwise).

- Fast boot methods—Fast dump and reboot to minimize reboot time after a catastrophic OS failure.

- Sophisticated fault-detection logic—Isolates and classifies faults quickly and initiates recovery procedures. The recovery method will depend on whether the failure is hard (repeatable) or transient (not repeatable).

- Hardware failure recovery—Automatic and transparent recovery from hardware failures, including CPU, memory, disk, LAN, I/O, adapter, fans, and power supplies.

- Backup power—A UPS interface is essential for continued short-term operation or graceful shutdown in the event of a major power outage.

- Persistent memory—Some systems offer so-called persistent memory, which enables applications to read and write to selected memory contents even after rebooting the system (this memory is not reinitialized after a reboot). For example, the RAMDISK feature of Windows 2000 could be used to this end.

- Total remote management—Including the ability to reboot remote servers regardless of their state.

- Concurrent backup and restore—The system must be usable during backups and restores (some implementations impose performance or file locking issues, which reduce usability for the duration).

The most resilient of fault-tolerant architectures include full hardware-based fault tolerance. Within these systems, hardware is engineered to include continuous self-checking logic, and all of the main subsystems are physically duplicated (CPUs, main memory, I/O controllers, system bus, power subsystems, disks, etc.). Self-checking logic is typically resident on every major circuit board to detect and immediately isolate failures. Since every separate element of the computer is duplicated, normal application processing continues even if one of these components should fail. In such systems, hardware-based fault tolerance is transparent to application software, and there is no performance degradation if a component failure occurs. Also, logic self-checking allows data errors to be isolated at each clock tick, assuring that erroneous data never enter the bus and, as a result, cannot corrupt other parts of the system. Finally, onboard diagnostics built into continuous availability system architectures often automatically detect problems before they lead to failures and initiate service instantaneously should a component fail.

Conventional computers (even in HA mode) are not fault tolerant; they have many single points of failure that can crash the system running the end user's mission-critical application. Their goal is to recover as soon as possible from a crash, rather than to assure that a crash does not occur in the first place. Recovery times can vary from seconds to many minutes depending on the complexity of the application and the communications involved. Recovery can take much longer if the application must be returned to the point where it was before the failure occurred. In many cases it may actually be impossible to recover the application context, and users may simply have to log in and start again. Disks may have to be resynchronized, databases synchronized, and screens refreshed. If a crash occurs in the middle of a transaction, corrupt data may enter the system, entailing additional time and cost to rectify. Obviously, transaction data also may be permanently lost during a system crash. Conventional computers reconfigured for high availability rely on layered systems software or custom application code residing above the operating system in order to help an application recover from a system crash. These configurations, however, have limited capabilities to identify hardware failures. They cannot detect transient hardware failures, for example. As a result, although the hardware platform may continue to run, the mission-critical software application can be rendered useless by bad data.

While fault-tolerant systems clearly have their advantages, there are several issues with fault-tolerant systems from the designer's perspective: they tend to be very expensive; since the system sits in a single location this is a single point of failure, finite resources mean that for very high traffic volumes there can be scalability issues.

Operating systems

The server operating system can be proprietary or an industry standard OS (such as UNIX or Windows NT/2000). Clearly, the more standard the OS the more likely that more applications will be available to run on the platform. For example, the initial Stratus fault-tolerant platforms ran the proprietary Virtual Operating System (VOS). Stratus subsequently released support for two flavors of UNIX (FTX and HP/UX). Stratus Continuum systems are based on the HP PA-RISC microprocessor family and run a standard version of HP-UX. These systems are reportedly fully ABI and API compatible with HP-9000 servers and can run both HP and third-party software without modification. Stratus recently offered support for Windows 2000 via its Melody fault-tolerant server platform.

Scalability

While fault tolerance can be essential for mission- or business-critical servers, these systems have finite resources. As traffic and transaction levels increase, fault-tolerant systems eventually run out of steam, and an intelligent way of clustering systems (either with or without fault tolerance) is required. Clustering builds availability into a solution through external system redundancy and control procedures, much the same way that fault-tolerant systems internalize those processes. Clustering enables systems to provide scalability through modular addition of further systems into a cooperating group.

Example fault-tolerant application

Fault-tolerant systems are commonly routinely employed to support Automated Teller Machine (ATM) and Point of Sale (POS) card authorization systems, since these systems typically support transactions on a global, 24/7. These systems are characterized by continuously available front-end communications, authorization, and logging service, with back-end mainframe systems handling the customer account databases and settlements. With a fault-tolerant communications front end, service can continue during periods where the back-end systems are unavailable. Another common application is a 24/7 call center, integrated either with a customer service or an order-entry application. By deploying fault-tolerant systems in the call center front-end, the call center can provide temporary processing or transaction capture if the back-end database systems are unavailable. The front end can also route transactions to multiple back-end systems if required.

Fault-tolerant systems may be used to support applications such as mission-critical Intelligent Network (IN) elements and Service Control Points (SCPs). These systems provide application and database services to the voice switches using the SS7 protocol running over WAN links. SCP applications require very high reliability and rely on large in-memory databases to fulfill the subsecond response times required. Network management systems, especially those used in large enterprises or for telecommunications network monitoring, may be deployed using fault-tolerant systems. These applications often keep large amounts of network status information in memory, and some fault-tolerant systems can provide persistent memory for in-context recovery after system failure.

6.3.4   Clustering and high-availability systems

Application and file servers are typically key resources on a network. For many reasons IT managers often prefer to centralize these resources, whether for cost, management, or performance reasons. Since many organizations are heavily dependent on these services, it is imperative that you protect them by deploying some fault-tolerance measures. In the past many enterprise networks were often designed with multiple routers between LAN segments in order to provide redundancy. The effectiveness of this design was limited by the speed at which the hosts on those LANs detected a topology failure and switched to an alternate router. As we have already discussed, many IP hosts tend to be configured with a default gateway or are configured to use Proxy ARP in order to find the nearest router on their LAN. Forcing an IP host to change its default router often requires manual intervention to clear the ARP cache or to change the default gateway. This section describes how this and other problems can be resolved. The main approaches we will consider are as follows:

- Server cluster techniques—Sophisticated software for managing server cluster status.

- Router clustering techniques—Virtual Router Redundancy Protocol (VRRP) and Hot Standby Router Protocol (HSRP).

- Proxy server techniques—Round-robin DNS, network address translation, Proxy ARP, DNS load sharing.

There are many vendors currently offering standard and proprietary-load balancing hardware or software products. The techniques vary widely and have advantages and disadvantages that we will now examine.

Design features of HA systems

Specialized networking devices, such as routers, switches, and firewalls, generally use purpose-built hardware designs, particularly at the high end, that enable fault tolerance or simply improve reliability. These include the following:

- Fault-tolerant power supply—Load sharing managed power supplies with a common power rail.

- DC power supply—To enable backup power generators to provide power should the main AC supply fail.

- Fault-tolerant backplane design—Avoiding single points of failure and improving overall reliability.

- Fault-tolerant processors—Dual processor cards (either hot swap or hot standby) may spread the load and duplicate key live data (such as routing tables or firewall state tables).

- Hot swap line cards—Hot swap interface and processor cards; commissioning can be achieved without taking down the whole system and rebooting.

- Clustering—Logical clustering or stacking to avoid system-level failures.

- Fault-tolerant loading of OS and configuration data—The ability to load the OS and/or configuration data from fast permanent storage with backup sources.

Server mirroring

Server mirroring enables servers to be distributed, eliminating the problems associated with a single location while also enabling more cost-effective platforms to be purchased. With this technique, a backup server simultaneously duplicates all the processes and transactions of the primary server. If the primary server fails, the backup server can immediately take its place without any downtime. Server mirroring is an expensive but effective strategy for achieving fault tolerance. It's expensive because each server must be mirrored by an identical server whose only purpose is to be there in the event of a failure.

This technique generally works by providing hot standby servers. A primary and backup server exchange keep-alive messages; when one stops transmitting, the standby system automatically takes over. These solutions work by capturing disk writes and replicating them to two live servers. Each piece of data written to the volume is captured on the backup server. The backup server is always online, ready to step in (this can take anything from milliseconds to minutes depending upon the architecture of the system). Products in this category are available from several vendors, including Novell (SFT Level III), Vinca Corp (StandbyServer), IBM (HACMP/HAGEO) software, and HP's SwitchOver/UX. A less expensive technique that is becoming more and more popular is clustering.

Clustering techniques

Clustering is a technique generally associated with the grouping of two or more systems together in such a way that they behave like a single logical system. Clustering is used to provide a scalable, resilient solution for mission-critical networking components such as servers, routers, firewalls, and VPN appliances. Clustering is used for parallel processing, for load balancing, and for fault tolerance. Clustering is a popular strategy for implementing parallel processing applications, because it enables companies to leverage the investment already made in PCs and workstations. In addition, it's relatively easy to add new CPUs simply by adding a new PC to the network.

Clustering may be achieved using proprietary protocols and signaling systems or via standard protocols. Protocols such as VRRP or HSRP offer a crude form of clustering for routers.

Clustering software

High-availability server clustering software is available from a number of vendors, including Hewlett-Packard's MC/ServiceGuard [13], IBM's HACMP [5], and Microsoft's Cluster Server software (Wolfpack) [14]. These enable multiple servers, in conjunction with shared disk storage units, to rapidly recover from failures. Whenever a hardware or software failure is detected that affects a critical component (or an entire system), the software automatically triggers a failover from one cluster node to another. Data integrity and data access are preserved using a shared-access RAID system. Application processing and access to disk-based data are typically restored within minutes (recovery times will vary depending upon specific characteristics of the application and system configuration). To ensure proper failover behavior, the user must customize the configuration to match the environment by creating a number of failover scripts. Management of a cluster is generally more complex than for a single system, since multiple systems must be managed and configuration information must be consistent across systems. Software upgrades and other hardware or software maintenance operations can be done with minimal disruption by migrating applications from one node in a cluster to another.

Availability of this software is dependent upon the operating system used. Router and firewall platforms typically rely on proprietary, or at least heavily modified operating systems, which means that this software is unlikely to be available. These devices either implement proprietary clustering protocols or standards-based protocols such as VRRP.

6.3.5   Virtual Router Redundancy Protocol (VRRP)

Virtual Router Redundancy Protocol (VRRP) is a standards-based protocol [15]. VRRP enables devices (normally routers) to act as a logical cluster, offering themselves on a single virtual IP address. The clustering model is simple but effective, based on master-slave relationships. VRRP slave devices continually monitor a master's status and offer hot standby redundancy. A crude form of load sharing is possible through the use of multiple virtual groups. VRRP is similar in operation to Cisco's proprietary Hot Standby Redundancy Protocol (HSRP) [16]. Although primarily used for fault-tolerant router deployment, VRRP has also been employed with other platforms (such as Nokia's range of firewall appliances [17]). The current version of VRRP is version 2.

The real problem VRRP attempts to address is the network vulnerability caused by the lack of end-system routing capabilities on most workstations and desktop devices. The vast majority of end systems interact with routers via default routes; the problem with default gateway functionality is that it creates a single point of failure—if the default router goes down, then all host communications may be lost outside the local subnet, either permanently or until some timer has expired. A mechanism was required to solve this problem quickly and transparently, so that no additional host configuration or software is required. VRRP solves this by clustering routing nodes that reside on a common shared media interface, offering them to end systems under a single virtual IP address. End systems continue to use the default gateway approach; nodes within the VRRP cluster resolve who should forward this traffic. Before proceeding any further let us reflect on the following definitions:

- VRRP router—A router running the VRRP. A VRRP router may participate in one or more virtual routers (i.e., it may belong to more than one virtual group). A VRRP router can be in different states for different virtual groups (it may be master of one group and slave of another).

- Virtual router—This is an abstract object managed by VRRP that acts as a default router for hosts on a shared LAN. Essentially it is a virtual group address and comprises a Virtual Router Identifier (VRID) and a set of associated IP addresses.

- IP address owner—The VRRP router that has the virtual router's IP address(es) as real interface address(es). This is the router that will normally respond to packets addressed to one of these IP addresses (such as ICMP pings, TCP connections, etc.).

- Primary IP address—An IP address selected from the set of real interface addresses (this could be the first address, depending upon the selection algorithm adopted). VRRP advertisements are always sent using the primary IP address as the source address.

- Virtual router master—The VRRP router currently has the responsibility for forwarding packets sent to the IP address(es) associated with the virtual router and answering ARP requests for these IP addresses. If the IP address owner is alive, then it will always assume the role of master.

- Virtual router backup—The set of VRRP routers in standby mode, ready to assume forwarding responsibility should the current master fail.

- Virtual MAC address (VMAC)—The MAC address used by the master when advertising or responding to queries (such as an ATP request).

- Physical MAC address—The real MAC address for a particular VRRP node (i.e., the unique address typically burned into its network hardware).

It is worth pointing out that VRRP is essentially a LAN-based protocol. To my knowledge there are no VRRP implementations available for wide area interfaces (although multiaccess technologies such as Frame Relay or SMDS could conceivably support it). Since the default gateway problem does not manifest itself in the wide area, it makes little sense to use VRRP on WAN interfaces, and dynamic routing protocols generally do a much better job.

Figure 6.14
VRRP packet
format.

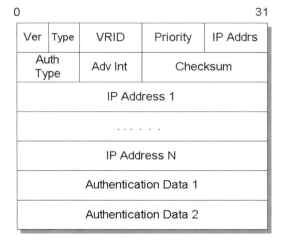

VRRP packet format

VRRP messages are encapsulated in IP packets (protocol 112) and addressed to the IPv4 multicast address 224.0.0.18. This is a link local scope multicast address. Routers must not forward a datagram with this destination address regardless of its TTL, so the TTL must be set to 255. Just to ensure that the packet is not forwarded, a VRRP router receiving a VRRP packet with the TTL not equal to 255 must still discard the packet. The function of VRRP messages is to communicate priority and status information. In a stable state these messages originate from the master only. (See Figure 6.14.)

Field Definitions

- Ver—Specifies the VRRP protocol version of this packet; the current version is 2.

- Type—Specifies the type of this VRRP packet. The only type defined at present is 1; all other types should be discarded.

- VRID—An abstract group identifier that identifies a logical community of cooperating VRRP routers. The VRID must be unique for a particular multiaccess network but may be reused on different multiaccess network interfaces on the same system. The master virtual router advertises status information using the VRID.

- Priority—Specifies the sending VRRP router's priority for the virtual router. Higher values equal higher priority. The priority value for the VRRP router that owns the IP addresses associated with the virtual router (i.e., has a real IP address assigned to one of its interfaces that matches the virtual IP address) should be set to 255 (implementations should ideally assign this automatically). VRRP routers backing up a virtual router must use priority values between 1 and 254, with the default set to 100. The priority value zero (0) has special meaning, indicating that the current master has stopped participating in VRRP. This is used to trigger backup routers to quickly transition to master without having to wait for the current master to time out. A VRRP master router with priority 255 will respond to pings.

- IP Addrs—The number of IP addresses contained in this VRRP advertisement.

- Auth Type—Identifies the authentication method being utilized. Authentication type is unique on a per interface basis. The authentication type field is an 8-bit unsigned integer. A packet with unknown authentication type or that does not match the locally configured authentication method must be discarded. The authentication methods currently defined are as follows:

  - 0—No Authentication
  - 1—Simple text password
  - 2—IP Authentication Header (using HMAC-MD5-96)

- Adver Int—The default advertisement interval is one second, representing the interval between advertisements from the master.

- Checksum—A 16-bit one's complement of the one's complement sum of the entire VRRP message, starting with the version field (where the checksum field is set to 0 for the purpose of this calculation). It is used to detect data corruption in the VRRP message.

- IP Address(es)—One or more IP addresses that are associated with the virtual router.

- Authentication Data—Any associated authentication data.

VRRP operation

VRRP operations are fairly straightforward and are summarized as follows:

- Master election process—VRRP uses a simple election process to dynamically promote master responsibility. The election process is deliberately simple to minimize bandwidth and resource overheads; it implements a very limited state machine and uses a single message type. When VRRP routers first come online, the master is elected via a straightforward highest-priority mechanism. The network administrator typically assigns priorities manually. In a tie, where two routers have equal priority, the router with the higher IP address wins. Once election is complete, the master forwards all traffic as the default gateway for a specific virtual IP address. The exception to this rule is that the real virtual IP address owner should always seize master status if it is functioning properly.

- Backup routers—If the master becomes unavailable (i.e., stops sending VRRP announcements), the highest-priority backup will transition to master after a short delay (the default is three poll intervals, each of one-second duration, plus a random skew time of up to one second). This provides a controlled transition of the virtual router responsibility with minimal service interruption. Note that VRRP routers in a backup state do not send advertisements; they simply monitor the status of the master. A backup router will preempt the master only if it has higher priority. This eliminates service outages unless a more preferred path becomes available. It should also be possible to prohibit all preemption attempts through the configuration interface. The only exception is that a VRRP router will always become master of any virtual router associated with addresses it owns.

- VRRP advertisements—The master sends regular advertisements (by default once a second) to inform slave routers that it is alive. These messages are sent as IP multicast datagrams, so VRRP may operate over any multiaccess LAN media supporting IP multicast. If the master fails to send announcements for a specified time period, a backup router with the next highest priority will take over forwarding responsibility to maintain integrity.

- Virtual groups—Each virtual IP address creates to a logical group, abstracted by a Virtual Router Identifier (VRID). The mapping between VRID and addresses is usually configured manually on a set of VRRP routers by the network administrator. The VRID must be unique to a LAN; however, the same VRID can be reused on other LAN interfaces as long as those LANs are not joined together. In general it is recommended that you use different VRIDs to simplify diagnostics.

- IP and MAC addresses used—To avoid issues with address resolution, a special virtual MAC address is generated and used as the source MAC address for all VRRP announcements sent by the master. This enables devices such as bridges and switches to cache a single MAC address in extended LANs. The virtual router MAC (VMAC) address associated with a virtual router is an IEEE 802 MAC address in the following format (expressed in hex in Internet standard bit order): 00-00-5E-00-01-{VRID}. The first three octets are derived from the IANA's OUI. The next two octets (00-01) indicate the address block assigned to the VRRP protocol. {VRID} is the VRRP virtual router identifier. This mapping provides for up to 255 VRRP routers on a network. For VRRP advertisements the master will use the unicast VMAC as its source address; however, the destination address will use the VMAC with the multicast bit set. For example, for an advertisement for VRID 2 we would see the MAC destination address set to 01-00-5E-00-01-02 and the MAC source address set to 00-00-5E-00-01-02.

- Address seeding—In order to precharge host, bridge, and switch ARP caches VRRP routers use gratuitous ARP messages to advertise their presence. This, together with the use of the VMAC source addresses in all VRRP interactions (including failover to the backup router), is particularly important for efficient multiport bridge and switch operation (VRRPv1 was inconsistent in the use of source addresses, and this caused switches to flood frames onto all ports on occasion).

- ICMP echo (ping) interaction—When a node pings a VRRP master router, or pings through a VRRP router to a remote host, the ICMP response packet from the VRRP router should include the physical (i.e., real) MAC address of the router as its source address, rather than the VMAC address. This is important for diagnosing faults or for remote NMS polling operations (in a VRRP failure scenario, if the VMAC were used as the source address then it would be impossible to distinguish which physical router has failed, and these routers may not necessarily be at the same site). This behavior is not specified implicitly in [15].

- ICMP redirects—ICMP redirects may be used normally when VRRP is running between a group of routers. This allows VRRP to be used in environments where the topology is not symmetric. The IP source address of an ICMP redirect should be the address the end host used when making its next-hop routing decision. If a backup router is currently acting as master, then it must determine which virtual router the packet was sent to when selecting the redirect source address. One method is to examine the destination MAC address in the packet that triggered the redirect. It may be useful to disable redirects for specific cases where VRRP is being used to load share traffic between several routers in a symmetric topology.

- ARP interaction—In contrast to ping operations, when a host sends an ARP request for one of the virtual router IP addresses, the master virtual router must respond using its VMAC address rather than its physical MAC address. This allows the client to consistently use the same MAC address regardless of the current master router. When a VRRP router restarts or boots, it should not send any ARP messages with its physical MAC address for the IP address it owns; it should send only ARP messages that include VMAC addresses. This may entail the following actions:

  - When configuring an interface, VRRP routers should broadcast a gratuitous ARP request containing the VMAC address for each IP address on that interface.
  - At system boot, when initializing interfaces for VRRP operation, delay gratuitous ARP requests and ARP responses until both the IP address and the VMAC address are configured.

If Proxy ARP is to be used on a VRRP router, then the VRRP router must advertise the VMAC address in the Proxy ARP message; otherwise, hosts might learn the real MAC address of the VRRP router.

Example design—simple hot standby

Figure 6.15 illustrates a topology where VRRP is used between two routers to provide resilience for client/server access for two LANs. In this configuration, both routers run VRRP on all interfaces, and on both LAN interfaces both routers simultaneously participate in a single VRRP group. Note that the VRIDs used could be the same in this case, since the two broadcast LANs are physically separate.

End systems on the client LAN (VRID-1) install a default route to the virtual IP address (194.34.4.1), and Router-1 (with a priority of 254 on this interface) is configured as the master VRRP router for that group. Router-2 acts as backup for VRID-1 and only starts forwarding if the master router dies.

End systems on the server LAN (VRID-2) install a default route to the virtual IP address (193.168.32.12), and Router-2 (with a priority of 254 on this interface) is configured as the master VRRP router for that group. Router-1 acts as backup for VRID-2 and starts forwarding only if the master router dies.

This configuration enables full transparent resilience for both clients and servers. The hosts require no special software or configuration and are oblivious to the VRRP operations.

The more observant of you may have noticed that in the topology shown in Figure 6.15, we have effectively created asymmetrical paths across the VRRP cluster; traffic from the client network (VRID-1) is forwarded via Router-1 and is returned from the server network (VRID-2) via Router-2. It would have been just as easy to force the path to be symmetrical by making Router-1 master on both interfaces. In this scenario asymmetry is not a problem, assuming both routers are evenly resourced; in fact, this configuration distributes some of the workload between routers. In cases where the routers have very different performance characteristics (i.e., processor speeds and buffer sizes), this would not be advisable. In such cases the router with the most resources should be configured as master for both interfaces, or at least master for the server side configuration (assuming the bulk of the traffic is server-to-client oriented). Path asymmetry can also be an issue for VRRP routers that also offer firewall applications (session states may be maintained between firewalls), and, depending on the state update frequency, Router-1 and Router-2 may be out of synchronization.

Note also that in this configuration Router-2 is not backed up by Router-1 on the 194.34.4.0 network, and Router-1 is not backed up by Router-2 on the 193.168.32.0 network. This can be achieved by configur-

Figure 6.15
VRRP configuration with resilience for high-speed server farm.

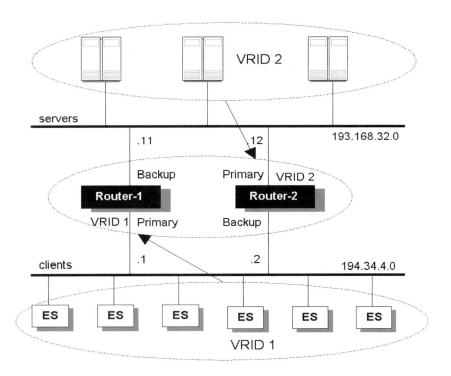

ing another virtual router on each LAN, this time with alternate primary and backup routers. This configuration could be enhanced quite easily to support full load sharing in addition to backup.

VRRP issues

The VRRP default router technique is relatively simple and effective but not without its drawbacks, and there are some subtle VRRP configuration issues that can be difficult to analyze for inexperienced engineers. These include the following:

- Lack of topological knowledge—VRRP is fairly dumb, and the scope of its topological knowledge is generally very narrow. It is typically implemented in isolation, so that there is no interaction with other routing protocols (static or otherwise). In certain scenarios this can lead to serious routing issues. This situation could be improved through tighter vendor integration with dynamic routing protocols, but it would be useful for the standards to address such interplay, even if just for guidance.

- Routing problems and inefficiencies—As indicated previously, VRRP's isolation can lead to serious routing problems, particularly in LAN-WAN scenarios. For example, in Figure 6.16 let us assume that static routes are used on the wide area links. VRRP would typically have no knowledge of the status of these WAN interfaces. Failure of the remote interface 140.0.0.1 would mean that even though router R1 has no remote connectivity, it still remains master for a particular VRID. In this case packets from the LAN destined for the 140.0.0.0 are simply black-holed unless there is manual intervention to force a transition.

Assuming that we run a dynamic routing protocol, or R1's VRRP process somehow gains knowledge of the broken link, it will at best start sending ICMP redirects to clients on the 194.34.4.1 interface, redirecting them to the real IP address of R2. This can lead to further problems, since R2 sees that VRRP operations on the client side are working well (R1 never actually relinquishes master status for VRID-1). This results in routing inefficiencies, since every new user session must be explicitly redirected (some client stacks also handle ICMP redirects badly). To solve this problem some vendors allow the monitoring of specified interfaces, so that transitions on those interfaces automatically trigger a change to the VRRP master status. In this case we could monitor 140.0.0.1, and any failure would be treated as a soft system failure, so the master stops advertising or lowers its priority to force reelection (note that this feature is not specified in the standards).

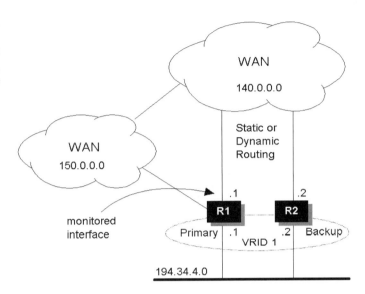

Figure 6.16
VRRP configuration with LAN and WAN interfaces.

This works, but there is yet another subtle problem that this enhancement does not address. Since dynamic routing knowledge is not available to VRRP, in some scenarios it is quite possible that a dynamic routing protocol (e.g., RIP or OSPF) will be announcing a more optimal next-hop address, based on superior topological knowledge. In Figure 6.16 consider a failure of interface 140.0.0.1; assuming circuit monitoring is available, this will result in VRRP transitioning, so that R2 starts forwarding traffic as expected. However, OSPF (running concurrently on R1) may announce a better route to 140.0.0.0 via R1 and network 150.0.0.0 (e.g., there could be problems upstream of R2 at the interface to 140.0.0.0 that VRRP is unaware of). These problems could include the following:

- Scalability—Perhaps a more important issue with the VRRP/default route technique is that it is not a truly scalable solution for LANs with a large workstation population, particularly in load-sharing mode. In a large enterprise it will be cumbersome to configure default gateways for hundreds of PCs by hand. A dynamic service such as DHCP can help; however, the flexibility offered by DHCP depends on the implementation. On a Windows NT machine you can allocate default gateway addresses on a per-subnet basis. This would enable clients to load share very crudely by subnet. There could be huge differences in the actual load distribution, especially if subnets use different services.

- Backward compatibility—There were significant changes between VRRPv2 and VRRPv1 that affect compatibility; VRRPv1 used IP protocol number 99, VRRPv2 uses IP protocol number 112. VRRPv1 also used destination IP multicast 224.0.0.12, VRRPv2 uses 224.0.0.18. VRRPv1 also used an additional IP address to denote the virtual address, whereas VRRPv2 uses real addresses.

- Convergence speed—For standards-compliant implementations the fastest convergence time would be approximately four to five seconds (three polls spaced at one-second intervals plus skew time).

- Duplicate packets—The typical operational scenarios are defined to be two redundant routers and/or distinct path preferences among each router. A side effect when these assumptions are violated (e.g., more than two redundant paths all with equal preference) is that duplicate packets can be forwarded for a brief period during master election. However, the typical scenario assumptions are likely to cover the vast majority of deployments, loss of the master router is infrequent, and the expected duration in master election convergence is quite small (less than one second). Thus, the VRRP optimizations represent significant simplifications in the protocol design while incurring an insignificant probability of brief network degradation.

VRRP is clearly useful but can be problematic for anything other than simple clustering applications. Subtle interactions with ARP, ping, and interior routing protocols often result in confusion for engineers, making diagnostic work protracted. VRRP does not provide efficient load sharing; in practice it distributes traffic on a node-node basis (i.e., not the session or packet level). This means that a heavy traffic producer always goes to the same gateway regardless. For large client populations there is no easy way for a network administrator to automate allocation of default gateways fairly (ironically this is the scenario VRRP would most usefully benefit if used as a quick fix). In summary VRRP is a useful but very basic tool. For real high-bandwidth load sharing and fault-tolerant applications a more granular, more intelligent, transparent clustering technique is required.

6.3.6 Hot Standby Routing Protocol (HSRP)

The Hot Standby Router Protocol (HSRP) predates VRRP and is described in [16]. HSRP is a Cisco proprietary protocol (see Cisco's patent [18]) with functionality similar to VRRP. HSRP handles network topology changes transparent to the host using a virtual group IP address. HSRP has its own terminology, as follows:

- Active router is the router that is currently forwarding packets for the virtual router.

- Standby router is the primary backup router.

- Standby group is the set of routers participating in HSRP that jointly emulate a virtual router.

- Hello time is the interval between successive HSRP hello messages from a given router.

- Hold time is the interval between receipt of a hello and the presumption that the sending router has failed.

HSRP is supported over Ethernet, Token Ring, FDDI, Fast Ethernet, and ATM. HSRP runs over the UDP protocol and uses port number 1985. Routers use their actual IP address as the source address for protocol packets, not the virtual IP address. This is necessary so that the HSRP routers can identify each other. Packets are sent to multicast address 224.0.0.2 with a TTL of 1. As with VRRP, an HSRP group can be defined on each LAN. One member of the group is elected master (the active router), and this router forwards all packets sent to the HSRP virtual group address. The other routers are in standby mode and constantly monitor the status of the active router. All members of the group know the standby IP address and the standby MAC address. If the active router becomes unavailable, the highest-priority standby router is elected and inherits the HSRP MAC address and IP address. HSRP typically allows hosts to reroute in approximately ten seconds. High-end routers (Cisco 4500, 7000, and 7500 families) are able to support multiple MAC addresses on the same Ethernet or FDDI interface, allowing the routers to simultaneously handle both traffic that is sent to the standby MAC address and to the private MAC address. As with VRRP, if multiple groups are configured on a single LAN, load sharing is possible using different standby groups and appropriate default routes in end systems.

Differences between HSRP and VRRP

The main differences between VRRP and HSRP are as follows:

- Both active and standby HSRP routers send hello messages. In VRRP only the master sends hellos.

- HSRP implementation is a little more sophisticated than VRRP in that HSRP uses a more complex state machine and includes more events. The operational results from the user perspective are very similar, except that HSRP produces more traffic.

- Unlike VRRP, [16] mandates that routers participating in HSRP on an interface must not send ICMP redirects on that interface.

- Unlike VRRP, the virtual IP address is not assigned to any real interface (i.e., very much like VRRP version 1). This means that an additional IP address is required for an HSRP deployment.

The same reservations I made for VRRP in sophisticated designs apply to HSRP also. For further information on HSRP, the interested reader is directed to [16, 19].

6.3.7   Proxy server and interception techniques

There are a number of techniques used by gateways and proxies to enable load balancing as a kind of value-added service. These techniques usually work on the premise that since these proxies are often placed in strategic network locations (say in front of a server farm or on the perimeter WAN interface), and they need to modify or respond to requests as part of their basic function, they might add value without the user knowing. Note that the term balancing here is generally misleading, and the term sharing is perhaps more appropriate. Most of these techniques rely on quite crude methods to distribute load, and generally there are no guarantees about the actual load levels. Techniques in this class include the following:

- DNS load-sharing proxies—Domain Name System (DNS) requests can be intercepted and distributed to a cluster of real DNS servers to provide both performance and reliability improvements.

- HTTP load-sharing proxies—A method of distributing requests for Web service among a cluster of Web servers to improve performance and resilience. This technique is often referred to as HTTP redirection.

- FTP load-sharing proxies—A method of distributing requests for FTP service among a cluster of FTP servers to improve performance and resilience. In practice this is generally achieved using network address translation.

- ARP load-sharing proxies—Proxy ARP can be used to provide resilient paths to services and improve performance.

- NAT load-sharing proxies—Network address translation is a common technique for providing resilient paths to services and improving performance.

When deploying proxy load balancers, careful attention should be paid to the design so that the balancer may become a single point of failure. If the load balancer dies, then remote clients may not be able to reach any of the servers in the cluster behind it. Since this functionality is increasingly being integrated into general-purpose load-sharing systems, switches, and firewalls, these devices can often be clustered to provide appropriate levels of fault tolerance. Many of the techniques listed above are closely associated with load sharing and performance optimization.

6.3.8 Other related techniques

There are a number of other protocol techniques used to provide clustered fault tolerance, some standard, some proprietary, including router discovery protocol and IGP default routes.

6.3.9 Combining HA clusters with fault-tolerant servers

An architecture that combines HA clustering and fault-tolerant servers in a front-end/back-end configuration provides customers with the best combination of performance, flexibility, scalability, and availability. High-end servers, combined with MC/ServiceGuard software, provide a robust, scalable, back-end database service. Fault-tolerant servers provide a continuously available front-end communication service. Application services can run on the back end, front end, or both, depending on the specific application requirements. In some cases, the Application Services layer may warrant a separate set of server systems, again depending on the particular application environment and availability needs. This front-end/back-end architecture is actually very similar to the traditional mainframe architecture that has supported enterprise applications for over 30 years. Mainframes have used an intelligent communications controller to offload communications processing from the host (much of this communication is IBM SNA) and to allow routing of transactions among multiple hosts, providing both higher availability and load sharing. The combination of approaches brings the benefits of this traditional architecture to the world of open systems.

Deciding between an HA cluster and a fault-tolerant system will depend on the particular characteristics of the application and operational features of the network. HA clusters are a good choice if the following guidelines are present:

- Database services are the predominant part of the application.

- The recovery model is transaction based.

- Scalability beyond a midrange system is needed.

- Application can accommodate seconds to minutes of recovery time.

- Operations staff is available for cluster management.

A fault-tolerant system is a good choice if the following guidelines are present:

- Communications services or in-memory data are the predominant part of the application.

- The recovery model relies on in-memory data or application state.

- Remote site requires lights-out operation.

- Application requires subsecond recovery time.

6.4   Component-level availability

At the lowest level of an internetwork, we have the individual network devices and discrete systems (i.e., servers, routers, modems, workstations, network printers, etc.). The decision of whether or not to provide backup systems and procedures should these devices fail is largely a matter of assessing risk and relative value. The systems most often targeted for attention are business- or mission-critical servers, key data repositories, wide area routers, and perimeter firewalls—that is, systems where even a small break in service could equate to significant financial or productivity losses. On carrier networks it is expected that systems will operate nonstop at key switching centers and PoPs. On corporate networks there may be similar requirements for systems providing e-commerce applications or intranet service. Some of the key techniques used to improve availability are summarized as follows:

- Passive backplanes and hot swap line cards

- Server mirroring, clustering, distributed processing

- Fault-tolerant power, backup DC power, uninterruptable power

- Backup media, disk mirroring, RAID

- Complete or partial hot or cold standby systems and subcomponents

- Automated and alternate data and boot image sources (Disk, BOOTP, DHCP, etc.)

Standard off-the-shelf commercial products may include limited resilience features; however, at the top end of the market there is a subset of systems available commercially that are referred to as carrier class (a term often misused in product literature and typically requiring at least 99.99999 percent availability). In essence the design of a carrier class system should eliminate all single points of failure, including loss of power, loss of a single interface card, loss of a processor card, loss of configuration data, and loss of recorded data. It is usually mandatory that such a system should be capable of running 24/7. This dictates that it should be possible to make software changes without taking the system down. It is also important that a high level of system integration is provided, together with sophisticated system and environmental management (for proactive signaling of predicted failures in power supplies, fan systems, etc.). True carrier class systems tend to be very expensive, and they may make stringent demands on the environmental conditions provided in the equipment rooms (air quality, temperature control, humidity, etc.).

6.4.1   Backplane design

The internal backplane design of higher-end systems may offer several features that assist fault tolerance, including the following:

- Passive backplane design—So-called passive rather than active backplanes are preferred. Passive backplanes do not require power to operate and so are less prone to failure.

- Multipath backplane design—A single large bus represents a single point of failure. Multiple buses or, better still, multiple switching fabrics, offer multiple paths so that at least partial work can continue in the event of bus failure.

- Backplane connectors—Using female backplane connectors is preferred (i.e., no pins on the backplane). If the backplane has male connectors, then a connector failure (e.g., a bent or broken pin) affects the whole backplane, which may need to be replaced. If male connectors are used on line cards then a connector failure affects only that line card.

- Midplane design—Some backplanes are positioned in the middle of the chassis with connectors at either side, enabling interface cards to be swapped or upgraded without affecting the processing function. With some architectures this may also improve cost efficiency, since cheaper interface cards may operate with a corresponding processor card.

If the product is based on standard system and bus components (e.g., a generic PC chassis running BSD UNIX or LINUX), there may be serious limitations in performance and fault-tolerance features. For example, the

PCI architecture does not enable hot swap, so several vendors have moved to the Compact PCI (cPCI) architecture.

6.4.2   Hot swap

Hot swap is a feature often provided by high-end routing and firewall platforms; it is mandatory in carrier class systems such as high-end backbone routers. In essence this means that we have the ability to replace or install new cards or hardware without taking the system down and rebooting. Clearly, any users serviced by the card being replaced will be affected, but the point is that other users will not. On a large routing concentrator or firewall this is important. Another common product feature included in hot swap is the ability to perform some configuration or updating online (e.g., a firewall or IDS system may update virus signatures online and have them activated without requiring a reboot). A more ambitious target is the capability to patch the operating system or install a completely new operating system online (very hard to achieve in practice). Enterprise and backbone routers generally offer hot swap features, though the implementation and scope is entirely vendor dependent and may be constrained by the internal bus architecture. In practice hot swap architectures are more expensive to implement and require more sophisticated components (e.g., early-earth detection and more sophisticated arbitration logic to ensure that new cards do not interfere with existing systems running on shared buses during bootstrapping or during bus data transfers).

6.4.3   Disk mirroring

Data can be protected by recording them to multiple storage devices simultaneously; the most widely used techniques are disk mirroring and RAID. Disk mirroring is a common technique used for mission-critical devices such as application servers or firewalls. It is often used in online database systems and for the storage of a mission-critical event, policy, or configuration (such as a firewall accounting data), where it is critical that these data be accessible and recoverable at all times. The concepts are quite simple: a backup disk drive is dynamically synchronized with the primary drive so that all write operations are performed on both drives simultaneously. Typically there is a simple synchronization protocol and/or some watchdog hardware to ensure that the backup drive contains identical, or near identical, data. The second drive may be located in the same physical device or (for additional resilience) on a mirrored device elsewhere in the network. For true resilience ensure that the drive farm is accessible by mul-

tiple disk controllers. For further information on such products, refer to
[20, 21].

6.4.4 **Redundant Array of Inexpensive Disks (RAID)**

Redundant Array of Inexpensive Disks (RAID) is a technology that enables
multiple inexpensive PC-style hard disks to be logically clustered so that
they appear as a large single hard disk (normally achieved using SCSI).
This flexibility enables higher performance and resilient configurations.
RAID is available at several levels, designed to suit various applications, as
follows:

- Level 0—High-speed mode, using a technique called striping, where
  blocks of data are written to multiple disks concurrently and can be
  read back into memory concurrently. This significantly increases
  overall disk access times. No fault tolerance is provided, since all disks
  are used to provide aggregate capacity.

- Level 1—Offers disk mirroring in addition to striping. Two copies of
  data are simultaneously written on different drives.

- Level 2—Similar to Level 1 but with additional bit-level error detec-
  tion/correction distributed over all drives. Performance can be seriously degraded for small files (it is not suitable for server
  applications). Only 70 percent of the total disk space is available for
  data.

- Level 3—Similar to Level 2 but with bit-level error detection/correc-
  tion applied to a single drive called the parity disk. Disk write operations are sequential, seriously degrading performance (again, it is not
  suitable for server applications). Approximately 85 percent of disk
  space is available for data.

- Level 4—Similar to Level 3 with optimized error detection/correction
  at the sector level (rather than bit-level), offering higher performance.

- Level 5—Similar to Level 4 but with additional bit-level error detec-
  tion/correction distributed over all drives. This enables concurrent
  read and write operations, significantly improving performance.
  Approximately 85 percent of disk space is available for data. This
  mode requires more expensive intelligent disk controllers.

For true resilience ensure that the drive farm is accessible by multiple
SCSI controllers. It is not unusual to see a server communicating with a
fault-tolerant RAID using a single SCSI controller card (representing an
SPOF).

Peripheral switching

Peripheral switching places an intelligent switch on the SCSI chain between the server and the disk farm (typically a RAID device). This is a logical extension of the matrix switches used for many years on large mainframe sites to move huge numbers of peripherals from one mainframe channel to another. A typical example of peripheral switching could be as follows. Two RAID devices are connected to the switch along with two servers. One server is primary, the other an active backup. Each server owns one of the RAID devices. In the standby server, a background application runs, which periodically polls the primary and performs small disk reads to ensure operation. If the test fails, it waits a configurable period to retry. After a second failure it signals the switch to move the failed server's RAID device to the secondary. The secondary then mounts the volumes and starts the appropriate applications.

6.4.5   **Reliable power**

Power faults are common in large networks; in fact, some studies report that nearly 50 percent of claims for computer damage relates to power surges. Power faults are difficult to predict; they can be caused by pulled power cords, tripped circuit breakers, and regional or national power failures due to adverse weather conditions (such as lightning strikes or high winds) or brown-outs due to network overload. For each network design you need to include the probability and scope of power failure in your risk analysis. Before going much further, some definitions are in order, as follows:

- Power surges occur when the voltage exceeds the recommended level for a brief time; this can happen if a heavy load is removed from a circuit quickly. Typically a surge lasts for half the AC period or possibly longer. In the United States (60 Hz) this would be approximately 1/120th of a second; in Europe (50 Hz) this would be 1/100th of a second. Surges are potentially very damaging for electrical components.

- Power sags are temporary drops in voltage below the recommended level. A typical example is switching on a power shower at home where you might see the light dim slightly for a few seconds. Typically, power sags will be restricted locally to the same electrical circuit and should not affect modern computer equipment.

- Brownouts are power sags that are much longer in duration. They are typically caused when the network is overloaded and the resulting supply becomes diluted. This could be caused by millions of television viewers all switching on coffee-makers during the intermission of a major television event. European equipment is more tolerant of brownouts than U.S. equipment, since it is typically designed to cope with the much lower U.S. voltages (110 V).

- Power spikes are very short overvoltages. They can be caused by electrical storms or devices such as fluorescent lights, photocopiers, heaters, and air conditioners. Most power supplies include some measure of protection from everyday spikes, but spikes caused by lightning are potentially very harmful to electrical equipment and may cause severe damage. Spikes of ±100 volts are not uncommon even in major city power grids. It is, therefore, recommended that clean power sources always be used for sensitive computer equipment.

- Noise has a variety of sources; examples include RFI, computer equipment, and distance lightning. Typically there will be noise even on a clean electrical supply, but as noise becomes more serious it will have effects similar to those of power surges and spikes.

- Blackouts are periods of total power loss. The duration is unpredictable since there are a number of reasons, some due to natural phenomenon. A typical example would be loss of overhead supply cables to a region due to high winds or heavy snow. The effects of a blackout are unpredictable, since it is effectively the same as switching the power off on your equipment while in the middle of some operation. Having said that, blackouts are typically preceded and followed by sags, surges, and spikes and these may cause real damage.

Preventative measures

There are several basic approaches to providing a fault-tolerant power supply, including the following:

- Source your main power supply from different providers. This option is currently more widely available in the United States than in Europe. It may be possible to get power from different power grids using the same supplier, but this can be very expensive.

- Ask your provider if it can provide surge-protected supplies. This is likely to cost more money.

- Install surge suppressers. These devices protect against overvoltage problems such as surges and spikes. This can be an expensive option, and one should also consider that the additional voltage is typically redirected to the ground. Since your LAN infrastructure is likely to be grounded to the same ground, this is hardly desirable, and there are specialized devices you can buy to address this problem.

- Install voltage regulators. These are passive devices designed to damp out temporary voltage anomalies. Since they cannot create power, these devices cannot cope with power sags unless supplemented by batteries. Batteries are trickle charged in normal operation and brought into play during power sags to provide extra voltage. Power sags are quite common and so such a device may be a cost-effective solution.

- Install AC filters. These are passive devices and essentially less powerful voltage regulators without battery backup. AC filters essentially smooth out noise. Top-end voltage regulators typically include AC filters as standard.

- Install an Uninterruptable Power Supply (UPS). A UPS is essentially a battery system designed to cope with short-term power loss. Some UPS systems may cooperate with servers (such as Novell) so that they signal imminent failure prior to battery loss, allowing the server to gracefully shut down. You should ensure that the UPS produces a waveform your systems can tolerate during the switchover between main AC and battery AC, since many UPS systems produce a square AC wave, which some power supplies will not tolerate.

- Ensure that all equipment and cabling are correctly grounded. This is especially true for tall buildings (where a potential difference can be created between upper and lower stories) and industrial complexes (where grounding may be problematic).

It is common to protect key resources such as servers, firewalls, and backbone routers with one or more UPS systems. You should also note that many mid- to high-end devices (such as routers) support DC operation rather than AC. This is because many service providers require their telecommunications exchanges to run on a –48 DC supply, since this is much easier to back up with batteries than AC. Devices such as the Cisco 4000 and 7000 and the Bay BLN and BCN nodes support DC mode operation.

Multiple power supplies

Localized power failures can be avoided by the use of redundant power supplies in key servers, firewalls, and routers. Often these power supplies can be implemented in a load-sharing configuration, thereby extending the life of the power supplies. High-end managed devices may also interface power supplies to a common management bus, so that the status of each power supply can be monitored and alarms sent in the event of any significant status change. This level of integration may even allow power supplies to be switched on and off remotely via a network management station or Telnet session.

6.4.6 Boot and configuration data

The operating system and configuration data of devices such as servers, routers, gateways, and firewalls are vulnerable to corruption. These systems often rely on hard or floppy disk media for holding OS or configuration data. A moving media subsystem is generally more prone to failure than static media such as NonVolatile RAM (NVRAM). For mission-critical applications (such as firewalling, server clustering, or backbone routing) designers typically demand at least some degree of fault tolerance in the media subsystem. Operating system and key configuration data can be loaded from a number of sources, including the following:

- Hard disk, tape

- Flash EPROM, ROM/PROM

- NVRAM (holding system configuration data)

- SCSI RAID for OS, configuration and logging data

- Reboot from local CD or floppy disk

- The capability to reboot automatically over the network, using protocols such as BOOTP, RARP, DHCP, MOP, and TFTP

Fault tolerance loading should be implemented so that failure of one source forces the node to try alternate sources. Note that general-purpose OSs can be quite large, and this may restrict loading to some forms of mass storage (hard disk or tape) for practical purposes. In this case mirrored hard disks or RAID configurations should be considered. In many cases a mass storage device is required for high-volume storage, such as event logging. In the event of catastrophic disk failure, some devices can automatically switch over to pump logging data to a remote system over the network.

6.4.7 Standby modules and spares

The internal architecture of a mission-critical device may lead to critical single points of failure. For example, if a router uses a single module to perform the routing processor function, then if this card fails all routing dies with it. Carrier class devices often allow the use of multiple modules for critical system functions such as routing. These modules may either be in a cold-standby state (i.e., the device simply monitors the live module using some form of watchdog and performs no activity until the primary module fails) or hot standby (where load could be distributed between modules, and either module is capable of taking over if the other dies). The approach you should take is as follows:

- Identify all single points of failure in the system. Get the MTBF of each component from the vendor.

- Scope the impact of any failures. Does it just affect the users connected to that card or the whole system functionality? How would you rectify the problem?

- Identify whether the application justifies additional fault-tolerant measures. A single firewall to the Internet may be a critical resource. If you cannot justify multiple firewalls, then it would be wise to consider at least system fault tolerance.

- Identify what possible warnings can be generated to indicate failure (SNMP traps on low disk space, environmental problems, etc.).

- Identify what fault-tolerant features are available. What are the switchover times for each option? What is the impact on users (session loss, no affect)?

At the very least, most networks now carry some spares at key locations and document procedures for dealing with component failure. On a large international network spares holding could represent a substantial part of the overall network cost, and there is a potential issue of maintaining current revision levels of hardware and software. In such cases it is worth investigating spares provision as part of an outsourced maintenance contract.

6.5   Example resilient network design

Some organizations will go to great lengths to provide complete resilience. It is not unusual for a financial trading network to completely duplicate its floor infrastructure and locate it in separate sites, connected by one or more fast backbones. This is clearly an expensive option, but some organizations simply cannot afford to be offline under any circumstances. Such organizations may be targeted by terrorists and extortionists, since disruption of their networks can be so important as to threaten not only their livelihood but also the regional economy. For these networks it is useful to base the design on military metaphors. All core systems must be duplicated. Command and control systems must be proactive, automated, and fully distributed. The worst-case scenario of a catastrophic site failure must be accounted for in the design.

6.5.1   Backbone design

In our example we illustrate some of the techniques used to design such a fault-tolerant network (note that this design is fictitious and simplified for brevity). In this network we have two major exchanges: New York and London. New York generates 80 percent of the business and is, therefore, considered to be sufficiently important to warrant a mirrored site configuration (XChange-A and XChange-B). Information exchange between London and New York is critical; therefore, both a private backbone and backups via dial-up primary rate ISDN are deployed. Secure VPNs are also configured over the Internet. The VPN is provisioned by a service provider offering a Service-Level Agreement (SLA) with tight bandwidth and availability guarantees. The main backbone design is outlined in Figure 6.17. Note in this figure that both New York exchanges are dual linked by local high-speed Gigabit Ethernet links. Boston and New York are connected via a private T1 bundle, with the option for ISDN top-up and backup via multiple PRI links. New York is dual linked to the Internet, using different service providers for additional resilience.

Note that this network is expensive and could be optimized further. At current tariff rates the three 2-Mbps international leased circuits alone are likely to incur annual charges in excess of $2 million (excluding any local taxes, such as VAT). Once the basic design is complete, it would be worth checking on further service options, particularly for the most expensive links. Higher-bandwidth leased lines (say a single 6-Mbps service) could be cheaper, and Frame Relay should provide a more flexible and cost-effective solution in this scenario.

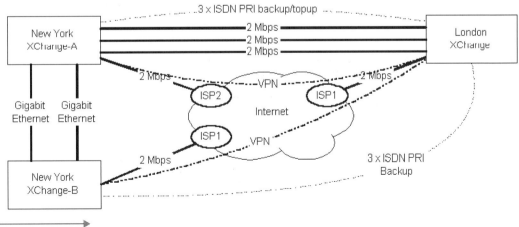

Figure 6.17   *Fault-tolerant backbone design.*

6.5.2　Building design

If we now examine New York XChange-A in more detail, we can see in Figure 6.18 that there are high levels of resilience built into a single multi-story building. Floor resilience is provided by dual-switching hubs, and wiring at the floor level is interleaved to ensure 50 percent of desk positions are covered in the event of a complete riser failure. Hub resilience is achieved via Spanning Tree protocols. Dual routers are provided for subnet routing and wide area access. The links between routers are in fact live for routing traffic and backup for data (forced using standard routing metrics). In the computer rooms all services are mirrored. Both intranet and Internet access are dual connected. Both UPS and backup DC power are available.

Specifically, the following guidelines are in place:

- All key network elements (routers, switches, firewalls, servers) are duplicated.

- Server mirroring is operating between XChange-A and XChange-B.

- All key external communication paths are duplicated.

- Both local and intersite bandwidth are overprovisioned to cope with both fast market conditions and a catastrophic site failure.

- Trader dealing desks are fed from alternate risers and different physical equipment to cope with complete riser or device failure.

- Multiple power sources are deployed. Different power supply companies service the central computer rooms. Backup power is available as short-term UPS battery backup and a longer-term DC diesel generator.

- All routers are running OSPF for intranet applications. This offers fast recovery around failures (typically in the order of seconds).

- As well as being resilient this design is scalable, since performance is balanced between different locations; services appear to be identical externally.

Note that this is only a top-level physical view. We would also need to cover the operation of the command and control protocols running over this infrastructure in much greater depth. A complete design would go into much finer detail and would include a complete survivability analysis together with crisis management plans.

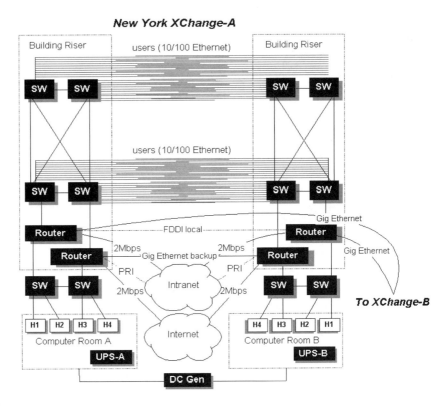

New York XChange-A

Figure 6.18   *Total resilience in a building environment.*

6.5.3   **Floor design**

The cost of providing complete end-user resilience for a large user population is generally too prohibitive and often leads to an inflexible design that is hard to maintain. As Figure 6.18 illustrates, the user networks at New York XChange-A are diversely routed to different risers with some overlap; the purpose of this overlap will now become clear. For applications such as online trading, it is important that simple network failures do not wipe out whole groups of dealers. Since these users may be physically located in very close proximity, this is a definite possibility, absent careful design.

In this particular design we have chosen to interleave the wiring for desk positions so that no single point of failure will take out a complete trading group (as illustrated in Figure 6.19). The cabling for each adjacent desk position is diversely routed back to different equipment rooms so that any single point of failure in the network would take down only a fixed percent-

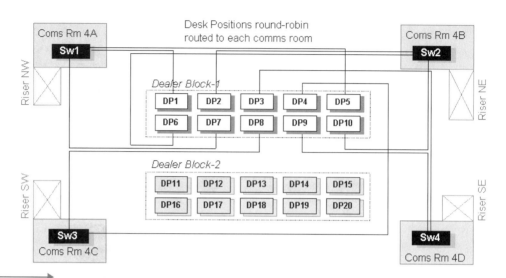

Figure 6.19   *First floor conceptual wiring plan at New York XChange-A, Floor 1.*

age of dealer terminals. In this example there are in fact four risers and four communications rooms per floor. This means that a single point of failure would take out only an average 25 percent of terminals in any dealing area. Note that this is partly influenced by the number of desks organized into a block. In this example desks are arranged in groups of ten. This means that should switches SW1 or SW2 fail, then three out of ten desks will be lost. Should switches SW3 or SW4 fail, then two out of ten desks will be lost.

One of the problems particular to financial trading networks is fairness. For example, it would not be fair if one trader were to consistently receive share prices several seconds earlier than a colleague. This is a particular problem for the network designer, since the very act of diversely routing transmission paths for high availability may incur additional hops and cable lengths. The fact that different paths are taken also means that the traffic dynamics along those paths are likely to vary. All of these factors affect latency, and it is the designer's job, in cooperation with the users, to provide performance that is within acceptable windows.

6.5.4   Testing the design

A critical part of a high-availability design is the testing phase. While in theory everything may look fine, it is imperative that you test all of the identified failure scenarios in order to establish confidence in the design and to assess the true recovery times. You will need to run live traffic through the network and break components of the design systematically, recording all key data and ensuring that the results are clearly documented.

In practice our example design needs to be explored in considerably more depth. We would need to cover routing infrastructure, dealer applications, external feeds, and traffic engineering problems in considerable detail. However, this should hopefully give a sample of the kinds of issues that need to be addressed when designing any fault-tolerant network.

6.6   Summary

In this chapter we discussed the following:

- Most organizations today require at least some measure of fault tolerance in their networks. The degree of resilience offered on any network is a compromise between risk and cost. For mission- or business-critical applications, such as a public network service provider's switching center, very high levels of availability will be required (say 99.99 percent or greater), as well as carrier class equipment.

- Resilience is the best approach from the top down. Potential failures should be identified from the wide area circuit design down to component level. Once these failures are identified, a plan for resolving each failure, together with associated cost, should be devised.

- Techniques such as multilink and multipath load sharing are important in the wide area, where backbone links are typically expensive, congested, and critical to the successful operation of the network.

- Protocols such as VRRP and HSRP enable key devices such as routers and firewalls to be deployed in a fault-tolerant configuration, transparently to end users.

- HA clusters and fault-tolerant systems both provide effective availability solutions. Each has specific advantages depending upon the environment and problems to be solved. In some cases, a combination of HA clusters and fault tolerance is appropriate.

- Fault tolerance often goes hand in hand with performance scalability, since the use of parallel paths or multiple system, often has a performance benefit.

References

[1]   K. Norvag, "An Introduction to Fault-Tolerant Systems," IDI Technical Report 6/99, Norwegian University of Science and Technology, July 2000.

[2]   T. Kenyon, *High-Performance Network Design: Design Techniques and Tools* (Woburn MA: Digital Press, 2001)

[3]   www.drj.com/special/stats/tari.htm, information about recent disasters.

[4]   www.fema.gov/library/lib01.htm. information about recent disasters.

[5]   www.ibm.com, IBM home page.

[6]   www.symantec.com, Symantec home page.

[7]   J. Gray and A. Reuter, *Transaction Processing: Concepts and Techniques* (San Mateo, CA: Morgan Kaufmann Publishers, 1993).

[8]   www.sra.org, The Society for Risk Analysis, home page.

[9]   www.riskworld.com, Risk World home page.

[10] A. Kershenbaum, *Telecommunications Design Algorithms* (New York: McGraw-Hill)

[11] himalaya.compaq.com, Tandem home page (part of Compaq).

[12] www.stratus.com, Stratus home page.

[13] www.hp.com, Hewlett-Packard home page.

[14] www.microsoft.com, Microsoft home page.

[15] Virtual Router Redundancy Protocol, RFC 2338, April 1998.

[16] Cisco Hot Standby Router Protocol (HSRP), RFC 2281, March 1998.

[17] www.nokia.com, see security products.

[18] United States Patent Office, Patent Number: 5,473,599, Standby Router Protocol, December 5, 1995.

[19] www.cisco.com, Cisco home page. See links for HSRP.

[20] www.arcoide.com, Arco Computer Products, Inc., home Web page. Supplier of disk mirroring products.

[21] http://teak.wiscnet.net/linux-mirror-cookbook, Linux disk mirroring cookbook.

7

Network Optimization

Designing an internetwork is just the starting point. To get the best out of it you must systematically fine-tune key areas of the design to improve performance, preserve critical bandwidth, and minimize operating costs. Network optimization is typically performed soon after the network design is complete, and it must be performed periodically throughout the lifetime of the network to ensure that changes in traffic dynamics are monitored and responded to. It is possible to improve even a good network design considerably through judicious configuration, tuning, and the use of specialized software and hardware tools. However, before attempting optimization you should know the baseline characteristics of the network, its systems, and its protocols. Typically, the acceptance stage is the best time to collate baseline data; failing that, you should at least characterize the key systems before attempting to optimize. Without this database you have nothing with which to make comparisons later, and this could lead to wasted time and effort. During the capacity-planning phase you may have also identified potential bottlenecks; again this, may help to focus your attention if performance problems occur [1].

The complex interactions between users, applications, protocols, and systems create dynamic loads on a network that are often hard to predict at the design phase. As networks expand, it becomes all the more important to understand, control, and optimize traffic over the network to preserve valuable bandwidth (and possibly meet service guarantees). This active form of control is often referred to as policy. Traffic engineering policy comprises a set of rules that govern the distribution of traffic throughout the network. Examples include the following:

- To regulate backbone traffic to a maximum of 25 percent average bandwidth during the workday, with one-minute peak traffic not exceeding 70 percent utilization.

- To ensure that all nonessential traffic is filtered off the backbone.

Table 7.1 *Optimization Techniques and Their Benefits*

Optimisation Techniques	Reduces Latency	Conserves Bandwidth	Routing Performance	Protocol Performance	Application Performance
Traffic Prioritisation & Queuing	✓	✓		✓	✓
Packet Filtering		✓		✓	✓
Load Sharing	✓		✓	✓	✓
Caching Techniques	✓	✓	✓	✓	✓
Hierachical Routing		✓	✓		
Data Compression	✓	✓			
Protocol Tuning		✓		✓	✓
Proxy Services	✓	✓		✓	✓
Keepalive/Local ACK Spoofing	✓	✓			
Storage Optimisation	✓	✓		✓	✓

■ To ensure that communication between remote departments occurs transparently, irrespective of the differences in technology employed.

To implement policy there are many standards-based and proprietary tools and technologies available to the network designer—some with only system-level context and others with network-wide scope. Lack of integration in multivendor environments is currently a major issue, and careless use of these tools may result in contradictory or inconsistent behavior. Unfortunately, there is no magic wand. Table 7.1 lists a number of techniques available today and the main benefits achieved by using those techniques.

This chapter deals with the technologies that you are likely to encounter and use in the optimization process. We take a broadly hierarchical approach, starting at the backbone level and working down to specific protocol tuning options. In Chapter 8 we take a much broader view of traffic policy by introducing architectures used to provide network Quality of Service (QoS). This is an area of much recent interest and research, especially in the Internet and backbone environments. There is now a concerted effort to improve QoS provisioning in the IP environment, and this bodes well for the future. In Chapter 9 we present an overall policy management framework. For further details and a more formal discussion of performance analysis, the interested reader is referred to [2].

7.1 Optimizing network bandwidth

Traffic control is a major technical problem on public networks such as the Internet. There is a severe lack of skilled resources, and service providers are often struggling to maintain equipment that is either underpowered or sub-optimal in its configuration. There have been many examples of misconfig-ured routers diverting traffic accidentally onto congested paths, and often these problems take hours to resolve due to poor diagnostics or lack of cen-tralized management. It is also not unheard of for service providers to deploy routers that do not have enough processing power or memory to effectively manage their own routing tables (especially if these devices have been in situ for some years and have not been upgraded). Regardless of whether the network is public or private, many of the challenges we must face in traffic engineering are the same.

In this section we will look at ways in which we can improve bandwidth utilization and overall performance on an internetwork. These techniques focus primarily on ways to keep unwanted traffic off the backbone and any other critical network segments. Even though intelligent devices such as bridges, switches, and routers already perform traffic segmentation, there are many cases where you can improve matters through the use of packet fil-tering, route filtering, spoofing, or other protocol management tools. Rout-ers are becoming ever more sophisticated at dealing with traffic intelligently and may offer advanced features such as priority queuing, combinatorial metrics, and proxy services. All of these features are described in this chapter.

7.1.1   Optimizing routing

Routing protocols and related addressing issues were described extensively in Chapters 2 through 4; this section summarizes techniques already dis-cussed in those chapters and provides references where appropriate. There are a number of key points to consider in optimizing routing and switched networks, including the following:

- Routing protocol selection—Select the best routing protocol for the environment. On anything other than very small internetworks (more than ten routers) choose a protocol that scales well and con-verges quickly. Protocols such as OSPF, Integrated IS-IS, and EIGRP are all strong candidates. If interoperability is important to you, choose only industry-standard protocols such as OSPF and IS-IS.

- Tuning—Tune timers and configuration parameters to improve con-vergence times, according to the available bandwidth and resources (e.g., OSPF has a hello interval and dead interval, which can be changed to speed up convergence at the cost of additional bandwidth and processing).

- Impose hierarchy—Use a hierarchical addressing model so that route summarization can be enabled, particularly in large networks. With route summarization, routers can reduce many routes to a single advertisement. This can significantly reduce load on the network, reduce router processing overheads, and reduce the perceived complexity of the network.

- Load sharing—Configure load sharing down multiple physical and logical paths where possible to make the best use of the available bandwidth (an analogy would be to use parallel rather than serial communications to achieve greater throughput). Techniques include:
    - Point-to-point link sharing (e.g., Multilink PPP)
    - Multipath bridging (typically proprietary techniques such as Xyplex's Fully Distributed Redundant Bridging (FDRB) technique)
    - Multipath routing (OSPF Multipath, IGRP, and EIGRP load sharing)

- Reduce the number of active protocols—Where possible, minimize the number of routing protocols running on your backbone and on the network as a whole. This frees up router CPU and memory resources as well as conserving valuable WAN and LAN bandwidth.

- Configure route filters—If possible add routing filters to avoid router processing of unnecessary routes.

- Tune path costs—Most designers will exert some control over routing metrics to improve control over the paths that traffic takes through the internetwork. For various reasons path costs selected automatically by routers may not be optimum.

In recent years new techniques have emerged to make more efficient use of wide area links, including QoS-Based Routing, Constraint-Based Routing (CBR), and MultiProtocol Label Switching (MPLS).

7.1.2 Eliminating unwanted traffic

Networks can generate a surprising level of unwanted traffic—that is, traffic present on networks or subnetworks that has no place being there. Often this is symptomatic of legacy applications and routing protocols that rely heavily on broadcasts, or it may be due to suboptimal configuration of networking devices and protocol stacks. With bandwidth becoming an increasingly critical resource, it is important that the network designer eliminate unwanted traffic both during the design phase and after implementation.

The process of elimination is essentially a three-phase strategy, in the following order:

- Phase 1—Disabling unwanted or unnecessary protocols
- Phase 2—Tuning protocols or optimizing traffic flows by design
- Phase 3—Filtering out unwanted traffic

In an ideal world we would approach this problem in the order presented, starting by eliminating problems at the source (by designing unwanted protocols out of the configuration altogether). In practice the biggest initial gains tend to be from Phase 2 and Phase 3, since the bulk of unwanted traffic is not due to Phase 1 issues (however, it makes little sense to install packet filters throughout the network to stop a protocol that can be discarded at the source).

Disabling unnecessary protocols

Networked systems usually have default settings that are designed to assist the network administrator in deploying systems quickly (i.e., a network metaphor for plug and play). For example, when enabling a routing protocol via the command line, this may enable that protocol on all IP interfaces. While this is very useful at the commissioning phase, it can lead to significant levels of unwanted traffic later, especially if one imagines this problem multiplied by hundreds of nodes. Key things to look out for are as follows:

- Routing or bridging protocols running on interfaces where they are not required. For example, a router interface may have RIP and OSPF enabled when only OSPF is required on that interface. RIP should be explicitly disabled at that interface to stop periodic broadcasts.

- Boot protocols, commonly left enabled by default on devices such as terminal servers. These are typically broadcast solicitations (e.g., BOOTP, DHCP, DEC MOP, RARP). If the device is only booted locally or via one of these mechanisms, then all others should be disabled.

The standard configuration for network devices should be designed to disable all unnecessary protocols and protocol activities per interface. Unfortunately, for legacy installations there is no easy way to determine which settings are redundant after the event. In this case you may have no choice but to take detailed packet traces and search for anomalous events (such as protocols and messages appearing on networks where they are clearly not required). Broadcasts and multicasts are always worthy of close examination, since these are particularly significant in degrading network system performance. You will also need to review the configuration of each class of device.

Reducing broadcast traffic

Legacy routing protocols and LAN applications often communicate using broadcasts. There are also emerging applications and protocols that support multicast operation. As we saw earlier, broadcasts and multicasts may be forwarded to network segments where they are not required (often referred to as broadcast radiation and multicast leakage). Broadcast and multicast handling is also fundamentally different from unicast handling from the host perspective (with broadcast packets the network device driver must interrupt the processor for each broadcast packet received, even though the majority of packets received will be discarded). The level of background broadcast traffic, therefore, directly affects the performance of all network-attached hosts. Relatively modest broadcast rates (up to 100's per second) can cause serious system degradation, even though link utilization is not significant. This area of the design, therefore, requires careful examination.

At extreme levels of broadcasts (1,000's per second) networks can suffer what is colloquially referred to as a broadcast storm, and flat bridged/switched networks are particularly vulnerable. Although rare, these events can completely disable a network, forcing a major reboot. The causes of broadcast storms are typically the result of misconfiguration (e.g., inconsistencies or errors in filter settings), major hardware or software malfunction (e.g., a PC card throwing out spurious frames), or a serious design flaw (e.g., a loop). It is important, therefore, that the network designer implements ways of containing the scope of these packet types. Broadcasts are especially difficult to block on flat networks, since filters may need to extend well into the user data part of the frame to differentiate applications. In switched networks multicasts may be dealt with using multicast-aware switches (using protocols such as GARP and GMRP), and broadcasts can be contained to some extent using VLANs [1]. We will now examine some of the common sources of broadcast and multicast traffic.

Sources of multicasts and broadcasts

There are many sources of broadcasts and multicasts; the main culprits are LAN-based servers, workstations, routers, and LAN-originated applications, as follows:

- IP routing announcements—RIP-enabled routers transmit entire routing table updates as broadcasts (or multicasts with RIPv2) every

30 seconds. RIP allows only 25 routes to be transmitted per packet (using 554-byte packets). On a 300-router network with a routing table of 1,000 entries this would equate to 40 packets per router update. This produces a broadcast rate of 400 per second ($300 \times 40/30$). This consumes an average of 1.8 Mbps, assuming that the updates are spread evenly. If updates become synchronized (as they tend to do without some built-in randomization or scheduling), the traffic level will be 30 times worse. For a router pair on a relatively slow point-to-point serial link, this represents a traffic spike of 177 Kbps in each direction every 30 seconds. For this reason most designers would limit the number of RIP routers to about a dozen.

- IP workstations—IP workstations cache on average between 5 and 50 addresses per hour and regularly transmit broadcast ARPs at an average rate of 25 per hour (or 0.0069 ARPs per second). Therefore, a network with 2,000 IP endstations would produce approximately 14 ARP broadcasts per second.

- Multicast applications—Multicasting is an effective way to distribute some types of application data (e.g., video and audio conferencing), and these applications can be particularly bandwidth intensive (a typical packet video application can generate a 7-MB stream of multicasts). We saw earlier how multicasts in a bridged or switched enterprise LAN could be leaked to all segments, affecting all users (whether they wish to participate in the application or not) and degrading overall performance.

- NetWare service announcements—Novell's NetWare Operating System is still quite widely used on LANs and for LAN servers. NetWare servers use Service Advertisement Protocol (SAP) broadcasts to regularly announce their presence.

- NetWare routing announcements—NetWare routers use Router Information Protocol (RIP) broadcasts (these are IPX packets, not IP) to regularly announce their presence.

- NetWare client solicitations—NetWare clients use broadcasts (e.g., Get-Nearest-Server) to locate NetWare servers.

- NetWare version 4 management—SNMP-based network management applications (such as NetExplorer) regularly broadcast packets to discover changes in the network.

- AppleTalk multicasts—AppleTalk uses multicasting extensively to advertise and solicit services and to resolve addresses. When AppleTalk stations boot up, they issue a series of mainly multicast packets (perhaps 20 or more) to resolve network address and local zone information.

- AppleTalk Chooser—The AppleTalk Chooser is particularly broadcast intensive. The Chooser enables the user to select shared network services. It uses AppleTalk multicasts to find file servers, printers, and other services. When the user opens the Chooser and selects a type of service (e.g., a printer), the Chooser transmits 45 multicasts at a rate of one packet per second. If left open, the Chooser sends a five-packet burst with a progressively longer delay. If left open for several minutes, the Chooser reaches its maximum delay and transmits a five-packet burst every 270 seconds.

- AppleTalk broadcasts—Several other AppleTalk protocols are broadcast intensive—for example, the Name Binding Protocol (used to bind a client to a server), the Router Discovery Protocol (an implementation of RIP), and AutoRemounter (the system initialization service, part of the Mac OS).

In order to constrain broadcast radiation, it is important that flat networks be broken up using routers (or VLAN-enabled switches). Where possible, limit the size of RIP networks to no more than a dozen routers, especially where low-speed WAN links are present. On bridges and switches, if possible use level-2 packet filters to discard multicast traffic from segments where this traffic is not required. Multicast-aware switches (e.g., those supporting GARP, GMRP, and GVRP) can also help control this traffic more efficiently. For further information about the IPX protocol suite, refer to [3]; for further information about the AppleTalk suite, refer to [4].

Filtering techniques

Packet filtering is a traffic management technique widely used in routers, bridges, and switches for reducing intersite or interdomain traffic. Filtering is often employed to keep unwanted traffic off the backbone and to preserve bandwidth on heavily utilized segments. Filters can also be used to implement basic security measures. Note that the term Access Control List (ACL) is effectively synonymous with packet filtering (although ACL is Cisco terminology). Even so, the implementation of packet filters differs widely across vendor platforms; you cannot assume that the same syntax or functionality is available throughout a multivendor network. This can lead to policy implementation issues and inconsistencies. Several smaller vendors have implemented a Cisco-like Command-Line Interface (CLI) to help simplify maintenance (based on the assumption that most internetwork engineers will already be familiar with this CLI).

Packet filters

A packet filter is a set of one or more logical rules that are examined whenever a new packet arrives at an interface. If an incoming packet meets one or more of these rules, then a set of actions are invoked, such as accepting the packet, discarding the packet, logging its occurrence, alerting an NMS, and so on. Depending upon the platform (bridge, switch, router, firewall, etc.), filters may be available at Layer 2, Layer 3, Layer 4, or even application layers. Typical capabilities include the following:

- Interface control—The ability to configure individual filters on either all or named LAN and WAN interfaces, by direction (incoming, outgoing), possibly down to subinterface specifications for protocols such as ATM and Frame Relay (e.g., forward if-3:dlci 7).

- Level 2 filtering criteria—Source Mac address, destination Mac address, EtherType.

- Level 3 filtering criteria—IP protocol type (e.g., OSPF = 89), source or destination IP address/subnet mask/prefix.

- Level 4 filtering criteria—Filter on the source or destination UDP or TCP port (e.g., Telnet = TCP port 23).

- Special flags—The ability to filter on key protocol flags (e.g., the TCP SYN bit).

- Prioritization—The ability to specify an order of precedence for a sequence of filters (in some products this may simply be the order in which filters are created or listed in the filter table).

- Actions—Accept, forward [to all interfaces: to named interfaces], deny/discard, log, and so on.

- Logical pattern matching—The ability to match specified fields by using content and offset, associated with logical AND, OR, and XOR operators.

Consult the vendor documentation to assess the facilities of the products on your network.

Examples

A modern multiprotocol router is likely to support filtering at several layers of the protocol stack, as follows:

- Layer 2 type filter—The type filter is extremely useful for a broadbrush approach to filtering. Entire protocol stacks can be discarded with a simple type filter. For example, a filter could be configured to

discard DEC LAVc (EtherType 0x6007) traffic on WAN router interfaces. This could be used to prevent VAX cluster broadcasts from
being transmitted over wide area circuits. On a Xyplex bridge CLI we
could type the following command to invoke this filter:

```
define filter type 6007 discard all
```

The following chart lists some other common protocol types (in
hexadecimal) that you may wish to include in Layer 2 access lists.

Protocol	Type
IP	0800
DEC MOP	6001, 6002
DEC LAT	6004
ARP	0806
Novell	8037, 8038
AppleTalk	809b

The ability to discard frames by protocol type is a powerful tool
but may lack sufficient granularity for some scenarios (e.g., it does
not allow you to differentiate TCP services from UDP services).

- Service type filter—Traffic filters based on service type are often used
  as part of a policy-based access control for backbone services. Service
  filters use access lists applied to particular protocols (e.g., IPX, UDP)
  or applications (e.g., SMTP, DHCP). For example, assume we have a

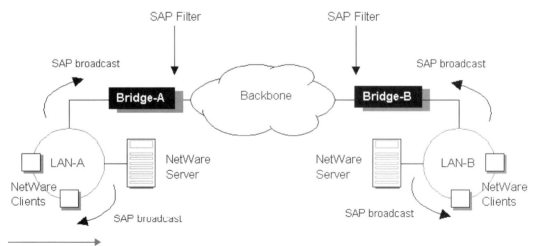

Figure 7.1   *Policy implementation using SAP packet filtering.*

wide area network with two Novell NetWare LANs, as illustrated in
Figure 7.1. Policy mandates that you discard all unnecessary backbone traffic and that LANs of a certain size must offer file and print
services locally. To meet these requirements we could filter Service
Advertisement Protocol (SAP) messages at the router egress, since
there is no reason for services to be advertised remotely (unless
remote backup services are also mandated).

- Area and network filter—Area, or network-based, filters are used to
  police the selective transmission of traffic based on network addressing fields. They can be applied on either incoming or outgoing ports,
  or both.

- Security filter—An example of a simple ACL on a Cisco router is
  shown in the following code segment. This rule is a basic security filter that denies any TCP connections from network 140.12.00.0 into
  network 193.128.78.0. Just to be awkward, Cisco uses an inverted
  mask format (i.e., mask bytes in reverse order) in its syntax:

```
access-list 90 deny tcp 140.12.0.0 0.0.255.255
193.128.78.0 0.0.0.255 established
```

The field called established refers to the SYN bit in the TCP header,
which is set whenever a TCP station wishes to initiate a new connection as
part of a three-way handshake.

Issues with packet filters

There are several limitations of packet filtering, especially when used in
large internetworks, including the following:

- Statelessness—Packet filtering is a simple-to-use, crude but effective
  mechanism for controlling traffic; hence, it is widely used. Packet filters depend on static information. This lack of statefulness means that
  they cannot readily cope with more dynamic protocols such as HTTP.

- Processing overhead—ACLs tend to be CPU intensive (if not implemented in programmable hardware), since the router must parse this
  whole list of ACLs every time a new packet arrives. You should, therefore, aim to keep the number of ACLs to a minimum and prioritize
  ordering according to event frequency.

- Lack of management—ACLs need to be implemented across the network in a controlled manner. Without central policy management they
  can quickly get out of control, become inconsistent, and become a real
  maintenance problem, especially in large multivendor enterprises.

- Planning and transparency—A potentially serious problem with filters is that they need to be carefully planned and require that you have full knowledge of network operations to avoid errors. For example, you may install a filter that discards unnecessary BOOTP broadcasts without first checking where all devices on a segment are booted from. Even though the network could work fine for many months, a subsequent power outage may result in devices failing to reboot, by which time you will have forgotten about the modification. This could be both difficult and time consuming to debug, especially on remote sites.

Policy management systems enable multivendor ACLs to be centrally managed and distributed. In this way packet filters can be used as part of an overall security policy.

7.1.3 Compression techniques

Data compression techniques, when applied to networking, are most effective when there are patterns of repetition in data flows. Fortunately, data networking offers two major areas for data compression techniques to attack, as follows:

- Protocol repetition—Much of today's internetworking traffic is connectionless, and this leads to great inefficiency in protocols. Within application flows, all the way down the stack there are repetitions on a packet-by-packet basis to ensure successful delivery. For example, TCP headers (port IDs), IP headers (IP addresses), and MAC headers (MAC addresses and types). On a point-to-point link or virtual circuit much of this repetition is redundant since there is only one path for data to follow.

- Data repetition—Much of the user data encapsulated in protocol traffic contains repeated patterns that can be compressed. Since text data are derived from a relatively small alphabet, the frequency in which characters occur in a data stream can be used to compress data using techniques such as Huffman encoding [5]. Note that image data is often precompressed before transmission and is therefore hard to compress further (in fact it may result in some data expansion, as described later).

Telnet is quite inefficient; user keystrokes are typically transmitted as padded 64-byte packets. HTTP uses a large number of small packets, resulting in high overhead per unit of data transferred. All of this overhead greatly reduces the real data throughput of expensive wide area links and should be optimized if possible, especially on low-speed links.

Compression ratio and data expansion

The term compression ratio is a relative measure of the amount of data input versus the amount of data output, expressed as follows:

Compression Ratio = Size of Output Stream/Size of Input Stream

The term "compression factor" is the inverse of the compression ratio. Currently the efficiency of the modern compression techniques results in compression ratios of anywhere between 0.5 and 0.02.

A compression ratio greater than one indicates negative compression (i.e., expansion of the original data). This can occur where the original data are either random or have already been compressed (in which case these data will appear almost random, since, by definition, many of the patterns of repetition will have been removed). If you compress data at several levels in the protocol stack then this may actually result in more data being generated than intended (termed data expansion). For example, a JPEG image sent over a WAN link may expand if V.42bis compression is used, due to additional symbol data being produced. Fortunately, LZ-based algorithms are precise enough to allow determination of the worst-case maximum expansion size. For example, Stac LZS, described shortly, specifies a maximum expansion size of 12.5 percent over the original data size.

Compression techniques used in networking

There are a number of standards-based and proprietary techniques that have historically been used to optimize wide area bandwidth; these include the following:

- Lempel-Ziv (LZ) dictionary method derivatives (e.g., V.42bis and Stac)—These techniques compress entire packets by ratios of up to 4:1. Reference [6] provides details about the Lempel-Ziv compression algorithm. The use of Stac compression over PPP links is defined in [7].

- Run-Length Encoding (RLE) is a widely used technique, sometimes called Data Frame Multiplexing (DFM) or Repetitive Pattern Suppression (RPS). RLE operates on the simple premise that if n occurrences of a data element, d, occur in a data stream, they can be replaced by the pair nd. The number of occurrences, n, is referred to as the run length. In practice an escape character is normally used to indicate that the next sequence is a run length pair (encoded as

<escape><count><data>), and to avoid data expansion for short repetitions the minimum run length is 3. The compression factor for RLE can be expressed as:

$$S/[S - R(N - 3)]$$

where S is the length of the string to be compressed, and the string contains R repetitions of average length, N. For example, for a piece of text 2,000 characters long, with 20 repetitions of average length 12, the compression factor is 1.099. RLE is also useful for image compression, since adjacent pixels often have the same characteristics (e.g., color). In general, the less complex the image the better the results achieved.

- Microcom Network Protocol (MNP) is a commonly used set of data compression algorithms developed by Microcom, Inc. MNP defines a number of classes. MNP Class 5 is widely used in modems and uses a two-stage process comprising run length encoding followed by adaptive frequency encoding. MNP Class 5 (MNP5) uses a repetition count when three or more identical bytes appear in an input stream. This means that a run length of only three results in four characters being output (i.e., data expansion). The compression factor for MNP5 is similar to that of RLE:

$$S/[S - R(N - 4)]$$

MNP Class 7 (MNP7) is a more sophisticated variation of MNP5, which combines run length encoding with a two-dimensional variant of adaptive Huffman encoding. MNP7 can be very efficient, especially where the input data comprise natural language text.

- ITU-T fax compression recommendations—Early data compression standards include T1 (Group 1) and T2 (Group 2). These have since been made obsolete by T4 (Group 3) and T6 (Group 4). T4 is designed to work on all fax machines that attach to the PSTN (currently operating at speeds up to 9.6 Kbps). T6 is designed to operate with fax machines connected to the ISDN (with speeds of 64 Kbps). Both methods can provide a compression ratio of 10:1 or higher [8].

- TCP header compression—TCP header compression, described in [9], is based on a simple premise: Much of the data in the TCP header are repeated during a sustained transfer and thus are unnecessary. By squeezing all but the most essential data, compression can reduce the TCP header from 20 bytes down to 5 bytes (and even 3 bytes in some cases).

- Proprietary header compression techniques—A variety of proprietary techniques have been used over the years, including zero fill padding suppression, a proprietary technique to reduce the minimum packet size by removing pad characters and indicating how much packing is required. MAC header compression is a proprietary technique where Ethernet frame headers are reduced from 14 bytes to approximately 2 bytes by setting up partial state information at each end of a WAN link. LAT header compression is a proprietary technique where DEC LAT headers can be reduced from 7 bytes to 2 bytes by setting up partial state information at each end of a WAN link. Many other techniques exist and these are typically vendor dependent.

Proprietary techniques require both routers to be from the same vendor and are largely dying out with the advancement of more effective standards-based technologies. The majority of WAN devices for use on low-speed links (i.e., modems, routers, FRADs, etc.) now support the PPP protocol. Virtually all PPP implementations support TCP header compression, and many support variations of LZ (such as Stac or V.42bis) as a negotiable option (via PPP's Compression Control Protocol (CCP) [10]). Reference [11] provides an excellent discussion of generic compression technology.

Stac LZS compression over PPP

All dictionary-based compression methods are based on the work of J. Ziv and A. Lempel back in the late 1970s (referred to as LZ77 and LZ78). Stac Electronics developed an enhanced compression algorithm called Stac LZS, based on work published in [6]. Stac LZS is commonly used on low-speed (under 2 Mbps) wide area links as a standard negotiable option with the PPP protocol. The LZS algorithm is designed to compress most file types as efficiently as possible (even string matches as short as two bytes are effectively compressed). It uses the previously examined input data stream as a dictionary, and the encoder uses a sliding window [11], which comprises a look-ahead buffer and the current dictionary. LZS supports single or multiple compression histories, and with circuit-based technologies such as Frame Relay the latter can significantly improve the compression ratio of a communications link by associating separate compression histories with separate virtual circuits. As indicated previously, the maximum expansion of Stac LZS is specified as 12.5 percent in [7]. This has implications on a point-to-point link for the Maximum Receive Unit (MRU) size, as follows:

- An MRU that is 12.5 percent larger than the size of a normal packet, should be negotiated ideally. In this way, packets can always be sent compressed regardless of expansion, since they will never exceed the MRU.

■ In the case where the MRU has not risen and the expansion plus compression header exceeds the size of the peer's MRU for the link, the PPP packet must be sent uncompressed, and the transmitter must reset the affected compression history.

For further information, the interested reader is referred to [7].

Software or hardware compression

Compression may be software or hardware based and typically operates on a point-to-point basis, with both devices at either end of a link compressing and uncompressing data. The major router vendors all offer compression as part of their software. Software compression is very CPU intensive, and if you enable compression on several WAN links, you should monitor CPU utilization to ensure that sufficient resources are available (for this reason vendors often limit the number of interfaces and speeds they will support, particularly on lower-specification access routers). Several vendors now offer plug-in modules that perform hardware compression and offload this activity from the main processor. Standalone hardware devices are also available that sit between the router and the WAN link (behind the NTU or CSU/DSU in the United States [1]). These devices generally offer good compression ratios (typically in the range of 2:1 to 4:1). Many of the emerging VPN devices also offer data compression, although these devices may be less efficient if data are already encrypted (since this tends to scramble any repetition).

Design guidelines

There are a few caveats with all compression techniques when used in real network designs, as follows:

■ Ensure that the Maximum Receive Unit (MRU) on point-to-point links takes account of the maximum data expansion expected of the compression algorithm used.

■ Compression generally works best on relatively low-speed WAN links (typically less than 2 Mbps and possibly only up to 64 Kbps with some software implementations). In practice this means that as the link speed increases, the processing power required to keep up ultimately becomes a bottleneck. On very high speed links, compression may actually reduce throughput below the rate at which uncompressed traffic would be forwarded.

- Compression is often employed on a point-to-point basis over wide area links (e.g., using PPP). Over a large internetwork several stages of compression and decompression may take place. This is inherently inefficient; for bulk data compression end-to-end solutions are preferable.

Note that some ISPs may be unwilling to enable compression on their CPE equipment, since it offers them no capability to compress that traffic further over more expensive backbone links (and you are effectively not given the opportunity to use more bandwidth than provided). Check with your provider.

7.2   System-level traffic engineering

Traffic engineering concerns the manipulation of network traffic in order to better optimize network resources (and possibly meet quality of service requirements). In Chapter 8 we deal with the network view of traffic engineering; here we are concerned primarily with traffic manipulation techniques within systems such as routers and switches. In practice the main techniques of interest include scheduling disciplines and bandwidth managers. Most routers provide facilities that enable network designers to exercise some control over packet. These techniques have particular value at the LAN-WAN interface, where speed mismatches and high-circuit tariffs mean that traffic flowing over the wide area interface needs to be actively managed, partly to make the best use of the bandwidth and partly to ensure that business- and mission-critical traffic gets priority access. As the processing capacity and resources available on modern routing and switching platforms have improved over the years, an increasingly sophisticated range of techniques has become available to control bandwidth allocation. Using these techniques the network designer can now exercise, with a high degree of granularity, the way in which applications are classified and prioritized.

7.2.1   Conservation law

It is important to consider at the outset that the fixed nature of circuit bandwidth means that prioritization has consequences. By improving the performance of one particular traffic flow over another, we are, by definition, penalizing other traffic on that circuit. This is referred to as the conservation law. More formally we can express this as follows [12]:

$$\sum_{i=1}^{n} p_i q_i = \text{constant}$$

where pi is the product of the mean arrival rate and the mean service time for connection i, and qi is the waiting time at the scheduler for connection i. Note that this law applies to work-conserving scheduling systems (where the scheduler is idle only when the queue is empty) and is independent of the particular scheduling discipline. In practice this means that improving the mean delay for one particular flow results in increased average delays for other flows sharing that circuit.

7.2.2 Traffic-shaping techniques

Traffic shaping (sometimes called intelligent bandwidth management) is an admission control technique, whereby bandwidth is allocated to specified applications at the egress port of a switch or routing device (normally a wide area interface). The idea is to apply some control on the amount of bandwidth allocated to each application, thereby enabling mission- or business-critical applications to have guaranteed bandwidth and background applications (such as Web browsing) to be constrained within set performance bounds. Bandwidth managers are designed to understand the operating requirements of different applications and manage priority queues dynamically according to policy requirements (e.g., policy may dictate that SAP should always have priority over Web browsing and push applications). Implementations vary widely. Features may include the following:

- The ability to identify application flows by address, port number (i.e., application), ToS bits, packet length, and so on.

- The ability to create sophisticated traffic profiles (based as token bucket or other credit-based schemes), guaranteeing fixed bandwidth on a per-flow or a per-application basis, and allowing applications to burst in a controlled manner during off-peak periods.

- The ability to dynamically allocate queue depth; for example, if videoconferencing session latency rises above some predefined threshold, the bandwidth manager can allocate more bandwidth. Advanced bandwidth managers may work on both outbound and inbound traffic and use more efficient algorithms to control congestion. Products may throttle outbound and inbound TCP traffic (e.g., by changing TCP window sizes and transmitting TCP acknowledgments at a controlled rate).

- The ability to quench sources selectively in periods of congestion.

- The use of automated discovery techniques to assess bandwidth management needs. The products can analyze which applications generate the most traffic and suggest an appropriate bandwidth management policy. The policy can then be fine-tuned to meet an organization's requirements.

Traffic shaping can be useful for applications where bandwidth costs are high and wide area circuit speeds are moderate (wide area interface between 56 Kbps and 384 Kbps). The level of bandwidth granularity offered may mean in practice that there is no added value for lower-speed circuits (e.g., if the implementation offers a minimum bandwidth allocation of 64 Kbps per application, then anything less than a 128-Kbps circuit cannot be subrated). Note that traffic shaping is a purely local bandwidth reservation technique; it has no end-to-end significance and so must be used in cooperation with broader strategies (such as RSVP) to provide service guarantees over an internetwork. If used in isolation, traffic shaping is only really applicable for point-to-point circuits or for private backbones (where you have complete control of all node configurations). It has questionable value when interfacing with a public backbone, unless specific SLAs are mapped directly onto the application flows at the point of egress. Where SLAs are mapped, traffic shaping could be used, for example, to enable an ISP to offer different service classes (e.g., gold, silver, and bronze). Without strict SLA mapping or tight integration with a higher-level QoS strategy, traffic enters a free-for-all fight for bandwidth as soon as it enters the backbone. It is also worth noting that not all traffic types can be managed (e.g., inbound ICMP and connectionless UDP packets may be unmanaged).

Traffic shaping functionality may be integrated directly into edge router and switching products or may be provided as a standalone platform placed between the routing node and the circuit. The class of products was pioneered by companies such as Packeteer (rather than managing queues to prioritize or reserve bandwidth, the approach they adopted was to manage TCP/IP flows proactively, by measuring the RTT of packets to assess the level of congestion and quenching senders of low-priority traffic in busy periods). There are now several other products available in this class, utilizing a variety of reservation, prioritization, scheduling and congestion control techniques, including Check Point (Floodgate), Nokia (integrated rate shaping software), and products from Allot Communications.

Token bucket

Token bucket is a widely used strategy for shaping traffic and forms part of the Integrated Services (IS) model. Token bucket defines a data-flow control mechanism where a sender adds characters (tokens) at periodic intervals into a buffer (bucket). New packet arrivals are queued and will be processed only if there are at least as many tokens in the bucket as the length of the packet. This strategy allows a precise control of the time interval between two data packets on the network. In practice it enables many traffic sources to be easily defined and provides a concise description of the load imposed by a flow.

The token bucket system is specified by two parameters: the token rate, r, which represents the rate at which tokens are placed into the bucket, and the bucket capacity, b, (see Figure 7.2). Both r and b must be positive. The parameter r specifies the long-term data rate and is measured in bytes of IP datagrams per second. The value of this parameter can range from 1 byte per second to 40 terabytes per second. The parameter b specifies the burst data rate allowed by the system and is measured in bytes. The value of this parameter can range from 1 byte to 250 gigabytes. The range of values allowed for these parameters is intentionally large for possible future network technologies (network elements are not expected to support the full range currently). In Figure 7.2, the bucket represents a counter that controls the number of IP octets that can be transmitted at any time. The bucket fills with octet tokens at a rate, r, up to the bucket capacity. Arrivals are queued and packets can be processed only if there are sufficient octet tokens to match the IP data size. When a packet is processed, the bucket is drained of the corresponding number of tokens. If a packet arrives and there are

Figure 7.2
*Token bucket
scheme.*

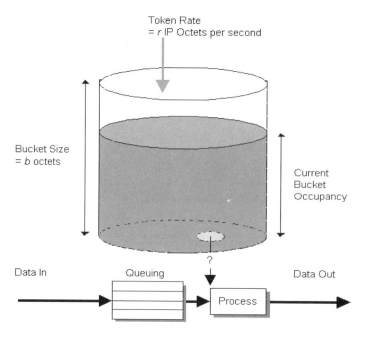

insufficient tokens, then the packet exceeds the Tspec for this flow and may be relegated to best-effort service. Over time the average IP data rate is r, and b is a measure of the degree of burstiness allowed.

Traffic that passes the token bucket filter must obey the rule that over all time periods, T, the amount of data sent does not exceed $rT + b$, where r and b are the token bucket parameters. There are two additional token bucket parameters that form part of the Tspec: the minimum policed unit, m, and the maximum packet size, M. The parameter m specifies the minimum IP datagram size in bytes. Smaller packets are counted against the token bucket filter as being of size m. The parameter M specifies the maximum packet size in bytes that conforms to the Tspec. Network elements must reject a service request if the requested maximum packet size is larger than the MTU size of the link. Summarizing, the token bucket filter is a policing function that isolates the packets that conform to the traffic specifications from the ones that do not conform.

7.2.3 Scheduling techniques

A router is a closed system, and from the network perspective should be treated as a micronetwork in itself. When a packet enters the system, it is important to understand what happens to that packet as it is processed, classified, placed on output queues, and subsequently dispatched. When designing a network, it is imperative that you understand how each system deals with high-priority or time-sensitive traffic. For example, if the router becomes saturated with low-priority traffic, does it start discarding all traffic (including high-priority traffic) arriving at input ports, or does it make space for these packets by clearing out low-priority traffic from queues? How many queues does the router have? How is mission-critical traffic handled? How is delay- or jitter-sensitive traffic handled? This is an area where vendors offer differentiation, and many of the schemes offered are implementation specific. Aside from the obvious requirements for prioritizing mission- or business-critical traffic, increasingly network users are demanding granular quality of service guarantees for a whole range of applications and services. It is, therefore, essential to have control over flow classification and scheduling processes, and most high-end routers today implement a sophisticated range of queuing algorithms that can be configured to meet a particular policy requirement.

One of the dilemmas for router designers is that the more sophisticated the queuing strategy, the more likely that additional processing resources are consumed, and this also affects overall system throughput and response times. For many network applications (particularly multimedia) what we are striving for are minimum service guarantees; for example, it may be more important to have bounded latency and jitter than high throughput. No queuing discipline is right for all scenarios, so there is often a balance to be made between complexity and performance. Different queuing strategies are applicable, depending upon the service requirements of your network and the levels of congestion expected.

Another subtle issue for designers is that routing strategies tend to focus mainly on output queuing. If packets are allowed to enter a system freely (i.e., without any congestion control at the input side), prioritization can become ineffective. For example, a system that employs sophisticated techniques to ensure that control traffic (e.g., OSPF, VRRP, Spanning Tree, etc.) is always prioritized over user data at its output queues, may still fail to maintain network integrity if the system is besieged by user data packets at the input port. This can be a particular problem where large bursts of small packets originating on high-speed LANs are destined for lower-speed WANs. The designer must ensure that control packets are not dropped at the input port due to lack of buffer space or processing resource or aged out of internal queues due to other processing demands. If control traffic is not serviced in a timely manner, this may lead to network instability, which can further aggravate congestion.

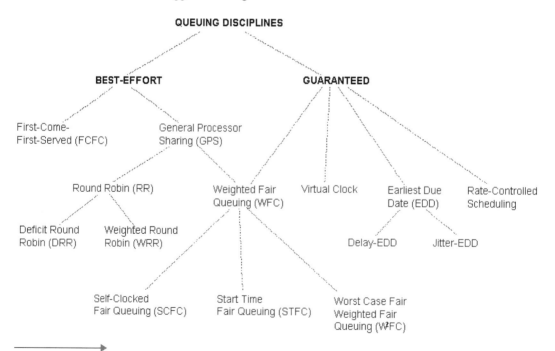

Figure 7.3   *A classification of queuing disciplines.*

Figure 7.3 illustrates a broad classification of the better-known strategies today. For the interested reader, [13] provides an excellent description of scheduling disciplines. We will concentrate in this section on a subset that is typically deployed on internetworking equipment today. We cover the following:

- First-in/First-Out (FIFO) or First-Come/First-Served (FCFS) queuing
- Priority queuing
- Custom queuing
- Weighted Round Robin (WRR)
- Weighted Fair Queuing (WFQ)
- Class-based Queuing (CBQ)

Some of these queuing models are standard, and some are proprietary; however, network designers should be familiar with all of them. You should check with your router vendor about the queuing strategies supported by your specific platform.

FIFO queuing (or FCFS)

FIFO queuing is an open technology that offers simple store-and-forward functionality; it is often implemented as the most basic queuing strategy in a wide range of networked devices (it also has many other applications in IT). Packets are stored in a queue and serviced strictly in the order they arrive, so the next packet processed is always the oldest, and packets arriving at a full queue are discarded. FIFO queuing is the least demanding of system resources. The data structures used to implement FIFOs can, therefore, be extremely simple, and enqueue/dequeue operations are very fast (since we never have to search/insert/move entries, performance is constant, O[1]). FIFO queues require very little user configuration (at most you will be able to configure the queue size and maximum age timer for entries in the queue). The disadvantage is that FIFO queuing cannot accommodate prioritized traffic (packets wishing to minimize delays cannot jump the queue).

In practice even low-end routers that support FIFO queuing implement some form of prioritization, although this may not be visible to the user. Mission-critical routing and control traffic is typically placed in a separate FIFO queue and dispatched in preference to user data, as illustrated in Figure 7.4. This simple queuing model ensures that network integrity is maintained even under periods of heavy congestion (e.g., OSPF hello messages would always be dispatched on time). Note, however, that even with this enhancement there is no prioritization of application traffic and therefore

Figure 7.4
Enhanced FIFO queuing.

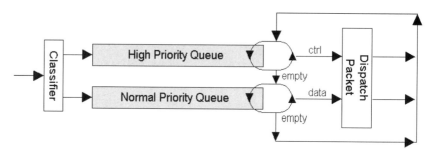

no ability to offer QoS guarantees. As we will see in the remainder of this section, sophisticated queuing disciplines often achieve granular prioritization by implementing multiple FIFO queues.

Priority queuing

Priority queuing is a widely used scheduling technique that enables the network designer to classify traffic by priority, directing traffic into different FIFO queues. Traffic may be classified according to a number of criteria (protocol and subprotocol type, receive interface, packet size, or source and destination IP address) and then queued on one of four (or possibly more) output queues (e.g., high, medium, normal, or low priority). High-priority traffic is always serviced first. If a priority queue overflows, excess packets are discarded and source quench messages may be sent to slow down the packet flow (if supported by that protocol).

You may be able to adjust the output queue length on priority queues. Figure 7.5 illustrates the principles of priority queuing. With some implementations additional fine-tuning may be possible on designated protocols (e.g., IP ToS bits or IBM Logical Unit [LU] addressing). This enables more

Figure 7.5
Priority queuing.

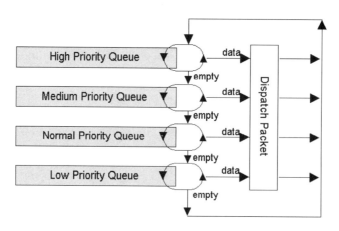

granular control for mission-critical or time-sensitive applications, such as IBM SNA, multimedia, or SAP environments.

Priority queuing is useful on low-speed serial links where the WAN link may be frequently congested. If the WAN link never becomes congested, then this strategy could be overkill. Priority queuing introduces a problem in that packets classified onto lower-priority queues may get treated unfairly, either by not servicing them in a timely manner or by ignoring them so long that they are aged out of the queue and never get serviced (generally forcing a retransmission by the source).

Custom queuing

Custom queuing is a technique promoted by Cisco that is designed to address the unfairness problem with priority queuing; it is designed to cope with a wider range of applications with different bandwidth or latency requirements. Different protocols can be assigned different amounts of queue space, and a set of queues (up to 17 in Cisco's IOS) is handled in a round-robin manner (as shown in Figure 7.6). The first queue (Queue 0) is serviced first and is reserved for control messages (such as routing or signaling protocols); the remaining queues are user configurable. Priority is promoted by allocating more queue space to a particular protocol. Each queue has a transmission window to stop any particular protocol from hogging the system indefinitely. The effect of custom queuing is to reserve bandwidth for defined protocols. This enables mission-critical traffic to receive a guaranteed minimum amount of bandwidth at any time while remaining fair to other traffic types. For example, you could reserve 45 percent of bandwidth for SNA, 25 percent for TCP/IP, 15 percent for NetWare, and the remain-

Figure 7.6
Custom queuing.

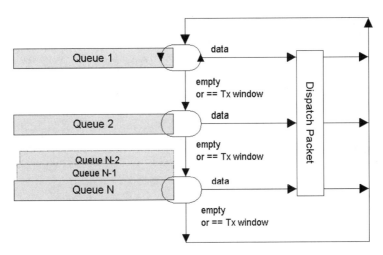

ing 15 percent to be shared among other protocols. Although bandwidth is reserved, it can be made available to lower-priority traffic if it is currently unused.

Custom queuing is designed for environments that wish to ensure a minimum service level for a number of applications and is commonly used in internetworking environments where multiple protocols are present. Custom queuing guarantees a minimum bandwidth for each application at the point where links become congested. Many organizations also use this strategy for delay-sensitive SNA traffic, because of these bandwidth reservation capabilities. Custom queuing is ultimately fairer then priority queuing but not so strong when prioritizing a single dominant application.

Weighted Round Robin (WRR)

Weighted Round Robin (WRR) is an open technology and one of the simplest scheduling algorithms. It works by dispatching packets from priority queues in a round-robin manner, taking a fixed number from each according to the priority weighting configured. For example, if three priority queues are established (high, medium, and low), and a weighting of 5:2:1 is defined, then each dispatch cycle takes five packets from the high priority queue, two from the medium-priority queue, and one from the low-priority queue. While fast and effective, at times of congestion incoming packets may be discarded because no buffer space is available in the appropriate queue (sometimes referred to as tail dropping). Lost packets typically lead to retransmissions, further aggravating the congestion problem. WRR is implemented in products from Cabletron, Extreme Networks, Lucent, and 3Com.

Weighted Fair Queuing (WFQ)

WFQ uses a flow-based queuing algorithm based on Time-Division Multiplexing (TDM) techniques to divide the available bandwidth among flows that share the same interface. WFQ is an open technology and is implemented in several commercial switching and routing products (note that an algorithm called Packet by Packet Generalized Processor Sharing [PGPS] is identical but was developed independently, so we will simply use the term WFQ). One of the chief aims of WFQ is to avoid bandwidth starvation for low-priority traffic (a problem with most other priority-based scheduling strategies in times of congestion).

WFQ works by computing the time a packet would require to complete if a GPS server had been used, and then tags packets with these data (the finish number). This tag determines the priority order for scheduling.

WFQ is designed to ensure that response times are consistent for both high- and low-volume traffic by allocating a time slice for each flow and processing them in a round-robin fashion. For example, if there are 30 active FTP sessions (high volume) and 50 active Telnet sessions (low volume), each flow identified will receive the same time slice of processor activity in turn, regardless of the arrival rate. Additional bandwidth for specific flow types is assigned by adjusting weights based on criteria such as the IP precedence/ Type-of-Service (ToS) bits. Flows with higher weights are processed more frequently. The use of weights allows time-sensitive traffic to obtain additional bandwidth, so a consistent response time is guaranteed under heavy traffic.

WFQ provides an algorithm to classify data streams dynamically and then sort them into separate logical queues. The algorithm uses discriminators based on the network layer information available (e.g., IP source and destination address, protocol type, port numbers, and ToS bits). Using this information WFQ could differentiate two Telnet sessions, for example, and then assign them to different queues. Note that some non-IP protocols are much harder to classify; for example, SNA sessions cannot be differentiated, since in DLSw+ SNA traffic is multiplexed onto a single TCP session (similar to IBM's Advanced Peer to Peer Networking [APPN], SNA sessions are multiplexed onto a single LLC2 session). The WFQ algorithm treats such sessions as a single conversation. For this reason, this algorithm is not generally recommended for SNA environments either with DLSw+ TCP/IP encapsulation or APPN.

With WFQ, round-trip delays for the interactive traffic are predictable. WFQ also has many advantages over priority queuing and custom queuing. Priority queuing and custom queuing require the use of access lists; the bandwidth must be preallocated, and priorities have to be predefined. WFQ classifies individual traffic streams automatically without these administrative overheads. For the interested reader, WFQ and two other variations of WFQ: Self-Clocked Fair Queuing (SCFQ) and Start-Time Fair Queuing (SFQ) are more formally described in [13]. WFQ is implemented in commercial products from Cabletron, Extreme Networks, and 3Com.

Class-Based Queuing (CBQ)

Class-Based Queuing (CBQ) is an open technology defined by leading members of the Internet community. CBQ works by classifying received traffic and then shaping that traffic prior to dispatch according to user criteria. Once traffic has been classified, it is shaped according to user-defined criteria. Traffic shaping is where specific resources such as bandwidth and burst times are allocated to traffic based on classification, as follows:

■ For Web-surfing applications a traffic class could be defined with a maximum bandwidth and the ability to burst above this bandwidth only if spare capacity is available, as illustrated in Figure 7.7. Without some form of traffic shaping at the application level, the only way to deal with this issue is to overprovision the network by adding more bandwidth.

■ A router could allocate specific wide area circuit bandwidth to different classes of traffic. Classes could be constructed for TCP and UDP traffic, multicast traffic, and for traffic originating from particular sites. The multicast traffic class could be configured to use more than its allocated bandwidth in periods where there is spare circuit capacity available.

In the absence of reservation protocols such as RSVP, network designers can use fields in the packet headers to manually classify traffic. For example, we could use the IP source and destination address, protocol field, and ToS bits. We might also use criteria such as groups of addresses, subnets, domain names, interface data, or even individual applications (e.g., by TCP/UDP port). If reservation protocols are used with CBQ, then flows could dynamically request reservations for higher-priority service (in fact, CBQ has been shown to work well with RSVP [14]).

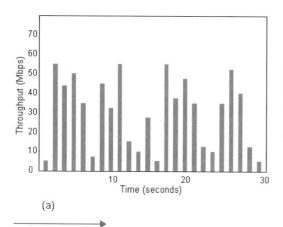 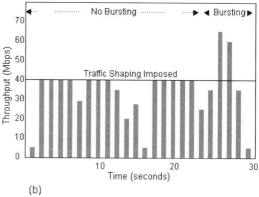

Figure 7.7   *The effects of an applied CBQ class to a Web-browsing application. In (a) the traffic is unconstrained and has regular bursts above 50 Mbps, affecting other services. In (b) the traffic class applied limits the maximum available bandwidth to 40 Mbps.*

One of the major strengths of CBQ is its ability to dedicate bandwidth to classes while independently assigning priorities to those classes. For example, a router could have a high-priority real-time class and a lower-priority non–real-time class, each with a different bandwidth allocation. Packets in the real-time class will receive priority scheduling as long as sufficient bandwidth is available and as long as the arrival rate for that class does not exceed its allocated bandwidth. CBQ is a powerful and extremely flexible traffic management tool. For example, one possibility would be to have a single high-priority class for controlled load traffic; for flows to use RSVP as the reservation protocol; and for the router to use admission control algorithms, statistical multiplexing of controlled load traffic in a single class, and FIFO queuing within the controlled load class. This scenario is discussed in [15]. Another possibility would be to use CBQ with RSVP for guaranteed service, with a new CBQ class created at the router for each flow that is granted guaranteed service. This scenario is discussed in [16]. The interested reader is referred to [14] for further information. CBQ is implemented in commercial products from Cabletron and 3Com.

7.2.4 Congestion avoidance

So far we have discussed techniques for classifying and scheduling packets that are received by a network system. These techniques work well only if congestion-control mechanisms are in place to avoid overloading the system. Of particular interest are a number of congestion-avoidance techniques [17], as follows:

- DECbit is a binary feedback scheme for congestion avoidance [18]. DECbit is an early example of congestion detection at the gateway (i.e., router); DECbit gateways give explicit feedback when the average queue size exceeds a certain threshold.

- Random Early Detection (RED) is a selective discard technique similar to DECbit. Some aspects of RED gateways are specifically targeted at TCP/IP networks, where a single marked or dropped packet is sufficient to indicate congestion to the Transport Layer. This differs from the DECbit, where the Transport Layer protocol computes the fraction of arriving packets that have the congestion indication bit set [19].

- Source-based congestion avoidance is a technique applicable to end systems (including ICMP source Quench and TCP Vegas).

In the following text, we discuss the application of RED, which is used commercially in routers and switches for TCP/IP internetworks.

Taildrop

Although scheduling techniques work well in managing packet flows through a network system, they suffer a common problem during periods of congestion. Since buffer space is a finite resource, under very heavy loads all space will be allocated and new arrivals must be discarded indiscriminately (i.e., without regard for different classes of service). This phenomenon is referred to as taildrop. The problems associated with taildrop are potentially serious, especially for TCP/IP networks; they are as follows:

- All mission- or business-critical traffic is dropped at the input port regardless of whether or not lower-priority traffic is currently enqueued.

- When packets are discarded, TCP goes into a slow-start phase. Since packets are dropped indiscriminately, many sessions are affected. While this relieves the congestion, it is effectively like pulling on the emergency break every time you approach a red light.

- Since many TCP sessions may be affected, and all go into slow-start, this results in a situation called global synchronization, where dramatic oscillations of both congestion and low utilization occur, rather than a graceful easing off.

- Congestion is likely to be caused by one or more bursty traffic sources. Since packets are discarded during congestion periods, these sources are unfairly penalized. Taildrop is effectively biased against bursty senders.

For TCP this kind of bursty packet loss is particularly damaging, leading to overall inefficiency in TCP throughput for all network users. Furthermore, this problem cannot be addressed by simply increasing the memory available for queues, especially if the traffic profile is self-similar. The chaotic nature of self-similar traffic means that traffic is likely to burst beyond resource limits regardless [1]. We therefore need a way to intelligently preempt congestion that backs off senders gracefully.

RED gateways

Random Early Detection (RED) is a technique designed to address the problems associated with taildrop in TCP/IP networks and provide a mechanism for controlling average delay. It is modeled on the simple FIFO queue and can be implemented with most routing or switching nodes. The term RED gateway is generally applied to a router running the RED algorithm ([19, 20], although in practice other devices could just as easily implement the technique.

RED works by monitoring the queue length, and when it senses that congestion is imminent, senders are notified to modify their congestion window. Since there is no way to explicitly inform all senders that congestion is pending (since senders may be using a variety of protocol stacks) and some senders cannot be trusted to back off, RED notifies senders implicitly by discarding packets at random sooner than they would normally need to be. Note that this is not the same as dropping all packets during congestion; the result is that some senders are forced to retransmit lost packets and back off. For example, this forces TCP to decrease its congestion window sooner than it would normally have to. Note that other protocols may respond less well to packet loss (e.g., Novell NetWare and AppleTalk are not sufficiently robust in this regard); therefore, you should not use RED if a high proportion of the traffic is composed of these protocols.

Operation

RED drops packets from the queue based on the queue length and a discard probability. Whenever the queue length exceeds a drop level and the next packet arriving has a drop probability greater than some predefined threshold, the packet is dropped (this is called a random early drop). RED computes the average queue length, Q_{avg}, using a weighted running average, as follows:

$$Q_{avg} = (1 - W) \times Q_{avg} + \text{Weight} \times Q_{last}$$

where

$$0 < W < 1$$

Q_{last} is the length of the queue when last measured.

In practice W (i.e., weight) is set to 0.002, and the queue length is measured at every new packet arrival. RED uses two queue length thresholds (TH_{min} and TH_{max}) to determine whether or not to queue a packet, according to the following logic:

```
if (Qavg <= THmin)
queuePkt ();

else if ((Qavg > THmin) && (Qavg < THmax))
{
P = dropProbability();
if ( dropArrival(P) )
```

```
discardPkt ();
else
queuePkt();


}
else if (Q_avg >= TH_max)
discardPkt ();
```

So, if the average queue length is lower than the minimum threshold, all new arrivals are queued as normal, and if the average queue length exceeds the maximum threshold then all new arrivals are dropped. Packets arriving when the queue length is between the two thresholds are dropped with probability P, where P is calculated as follows:

$$P_{tmp} = P_{max} \times (Q_{avg} - TH_{min})/(TH_{max} - TH_{min})$$
$$P = P_{tmp}/(1 - N_{arr} \times TempP)$$

N_{arr} represents the number of new arrivals that have been successfully queued while Q_{avg} was between the two thresholds. P_{max} is typically set to 0.02 [19], so when the average queue length is midway between the two thresholds the router starts to drop 1 in every 50 packets. The difference between the two thresholds should ideally be greater than the increase in the average queue length in one RTT, and TH_{min} should be set sufficiently high to enable high link utilization to be sustained in bursty traffic conditions. In practice the probability of dropping a packet for a particular flow is roughly proportional to the amount of bandwidth that flow is consuming at the router.

The RED algorithm is implemented in a number of commercial products, including those from Cabletron and Cisco. Cisco implements variations of RED, such as Weighted Random Early Discard (WRED) in its edge routing products (where WRED generally drops packets selectively based on IP precedence) and VIP-Distributed WRED for high-speed backbone platforms. Note that there may be performance issues when mixing different queuing and congestion avoidance schemes. For further details about RED, the interested reader is referred to [19, 21].

7.3 Load-splitting and load-sharing techniques

One of the ways you can scale up device performance is by spreading the traffic load between multiple devices. There are several ways to achieve this; the following list is not meant to be exhaustive:

- DNS, ARP, NAT, HTTP, and FTP load balancers

- IP load balancers (integrated OS features or specialized systems)

- Generic load-sharing protocols such as the VRRP and HSRP

- Policy-based routes

- Port hashing techniques

The key to this problem is to split traffic and allow each device to deal with a fair proportion of the overall traffic. The first issue to address is whether to do this on a per-packet basis or on a flow basis. The per-packet mechanism (e.g., round robin) is likely to result in fairer resource allocation but is also more likely to result in problems with retransmissions (if end systems cannot resequence packets); it may also be harder to debug and generate accounting data. If the load is to be spread among firewalls, state synchronization may rely on flows being handled deterministically (the flow, or session, goes in via one interface and returns back through that interface rather than sessions being asymmetrical).

7.3.1   An introduction to server load-sharing algorithms

Load-sharing server clusters, fronted by a proxy server, are a common technique used on internetworks, since they offer both resilience and scalable performance. Server clusters can be application specific (a DNS load sharer) or generic IP application servers. There are a number of algorithms available to iterate new sessions fairly between servers in a group. Load can be distributed nonintelligently or intelligently, based on cost, delay, server status, and other factors. It is useful to consider two environments for server load sharing: the case where the proxy server is local to the servers and the case where the proxy server is remotely located, as follows:

- Local proxy server algorithms assume that all server pool members are at equal or nearly equal proximity to the proxy server; hence the load distribution can be based solely on either resource availability or system load on remote servers. Network costs are irrelevant in this scenario.

- Remote proxy server algorithms assume that all server pool members have equal resource availability, and the criterion for selection would be proximity, or network cost, required to reach these servers.

The two topologies are illustrated in Figure 7.8. There are basically two approaches we can use to monitor session load on server pool members: nonintrusive and intrusive. Nonintrusive algorithms use simple heuristic techniques to distribute requests. Intrusive algorithms require protocol

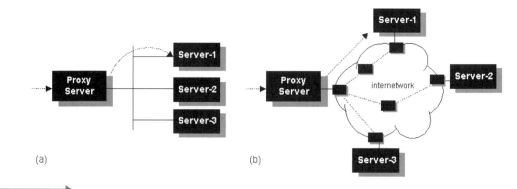

Figure 7.8   *(a) Local proxy configuration. (b) Remote proxy configuration.*

interaction between each member of the server group and the proxy server, so that real-time status information can be passed between them.

Local load-sharing algorithms

With local proxy servers the selected algorithm should ideally use precise knowledge of real-time resource availability and system load for each host in the server pool, so that selection of the host with maximum unutilized capacity would be the obvious choice. However, this is not so easy to achieve. Some common nonintrusive algorithms are as follows:

- Round robin—A scheme where a server is selected from a list on a round-robin basis, without regard to load on the host. If a particular server is busy or down, this algorithm may take no notice unless additional interactive techniques are used.

- Random—A scheme where a server is selected from a list at random, without regard to load on the host. If a particular server is busy or down, this algorithm may take no notice unless additional interactive techniques are used.

- Domain—A scheme where a server is selected from a list regarding proximity to the client based on domain names, without regard to load on the host. If a particular server is busy or down, this algorithm may take no notice unless additional interactive techniques are used.

- Least load first—This is an improvement over the round-robin approach in that the host with the least number of sessions bound to it is selected to service a new session. This approach is not without its drawbacks. Each session is assumed to be as resource consuming as any other session, independent of the type of service the session represents, and all hosts in the server pool are assumed to be equally resourceful.

- Least traffic first—A further improvement over the previous algorithm is to measure system load by tracking packet counts or byte counts directed from or to each of the member hosts over a period of time. Although packet counts are not the same as system load, it is a reasonable approximation.

- Least weighted load first—This would be an enhancement to the first two. This allows administrators to assign weights to sessions (based on likely resource consumption estimates of session types) and weights to hosts (based on resource availability). The sum of all session loads by weight assigned to a server, divided by weight of the server, would be evaluated to select the server with the least weighted load to assign for each new session. Say, FTP sessions are assigned 5 times the weight (5x) of a Telnet session (x), and server S3 is assumed to be 3 times as resourceful as server S1. Let us also say that S1 is assigned one FTP session and one Telnet session, whereas S3 is assigned two FTP sessions and five Telnet sessions. When a new Telnet session needs assignment, the weighted load on S3 is evaluated to be $(2 \times 5x + 5 \times x)/3 = 5x$, and the load on S1 is evaluated to be $(1 \times 5x + 1 \times x) = 6x$. Server S3 is selected to bind the new Telnet session, since the weighted load on S3 is smaller than that of S1.

Distributed load-sharing algorithms

When the proxy and server cluster, are geographically separated over large distances, the cost to reach them could vary markedly. In this case the load algorithm could use cost information to select servers based on proximity to the client. The algorithm would need to access routing tables for metric and reachability data from protocols such as OSPF to build a true cost of accessing a server in the group. The following algorithms are nonintrusive:

- Weighted least load first algorithm—The selection criteria would be based on cost of access to server and the number of sessions assigned to server. The product of cost and session load for each server would be evaluated to select the server with the least weighted load for each new session. Assume the cost of accessing server S1 is twice as much as that of server S2. In that case, S1 will be assigned twice as much load as that of S2 during the distribution process. When a server is not accessible due to network failure, the cost of access is set to infinity and no further load can be assigned to that server.

- Weighted least traffic first algorithm—An improvement over the previous algorithm would be to measure network load by tracking packet count or byte count directed from or to each of the member hosts over a period of time. Although packet count is not the same as system load, it is a reasonable approximation. So, the product of cost and traffic load (over a fixed duration) for each server would be evaluated to select the server with the least weighted traffic load for each new session.

Intrusive load-sharing algorithms

All of the previous algorithms determine the capacity of servers using heuristic techniques. In practice it is necessary to use closely coupled techniques for accurate remote prediction and status monitoring of system capacity. This class of algorithm is called intrusive, since work is required on the part of the host system. Intrusive algorithms fall into the following broad categories:

- Round-trip time—A scheme where a server is selected from a list based on knowledge acquired using ping to periodically determine round-trip times between the proxy and each of the destination servers. The server with the shortest round-trip time should be selected. This algorithm has no regard for true load on the host, but clearly the lack of response indicates that the server in unavailable or very slow (ping is not a reliable method of testing server load, since higher-layer software and protocols are not exercised by ICMP). This method can be used in conjunction with heuristic techniques reasonably effectively.

- Exercising content—Advanced load balancers can run scripts to trigger real application interaction to test the true response time of servers for specific applications. For example, a simple HTTP session could be periodically activated to test Web server response time. Clearly, this places some additional background load on the server but still remains transparent. This is a very granular way of measuring performance on servers running multiple services concurrently, since services such as FTP and HTTP can all be explicitly measured with reasonable accuracy.

- Agent-based monitoring—Remote agent software can be deployed on each server node. This interacts with monitoring software on the proxy server, providing detailed status reports concerning resource availability. The remote agent software needs to be run in the background so it does not consume excessive resources on the server.

Communications between the agent and monitor may be via either standard or proprietary protocols (e.g., SNMP or RMON). Typically this software is configurable, to allow the network administrator to tune features such as the update/measurement interval according to local conditions.

Although active algorithms are a little more complex to implement and deploy, they offer a more optimal solution for accurate load distribution, at the price of sacrificing additional resource on the server pool.

Dead host detection

One of the problems with server clusters is detecting host availability and dynamically adjusting for this as part of the normal load-sharing operations. In a naive implementation, where this functionality is not included, client sessions could be directed to unreachable host addresses (e.g., where the server is down). Many heuristic approaches are available, including the following:

- Sending pings periodically to each server in the cluster would be one way to determine availability.

- Another approach would be to track traffic originating from a host in the group when it is assigned new sessions. If no activity is detected in a few seconds, that server should be declared dead and taken out of service temporarily until further activity is detected (or the proxy explicitly tests the server status).

Note that although ping is commonly used, it is potentially misleading if used to assess response times, since a host may turn around pings very quickly even if other resources on the system (such as disk IO) are overloaded.

TCP and UDP session use

By convention TCP/IP servers use TCP and UDP ports 0 to 1,023 to listen for incoming connections. Clients typically select source ports in the range of 1,024 to 65,535. However, this convention is not always adhered to; some clients use source port numbers in the 0 to 1,023 range, and some applications listen on ports in the 1,024 to 65,535 range.

7.3.2   DNS load sharing

A DNS load balancer can be used to improve both performance and network reliability by offering a cluster of DNS servers to the network under a single host name. This system acts as a proxy server by intercepting name resolution requests for a particular service and then cycling through a table of alternate IP addresses distributing DNS requests to servers, based on their availability. This functionality only benefits users of DNS; it is not a general-purpose load-sharing system. DNS load balancers can be broadly divided into two groups, as follows:

- Nonintelligent DNS load balancers distribute DNS requests in a round-robin manner without any knowledge of server status. This is not strictly a load-balancing method, since there is no real way of knowing what load the hosts are currently experiencing, and we are distributing traffic by session, not by packet (with a large number of sessions the traffic will be expected to average out but there is no guarantee). This mode is often called round-robin DNS. An example of this technology is Bind—the DNS implementation included with many UNIX implementations and available under Windows NT. Bind does not assess the current status of each DNS server, and so it may forward DNS requests to a server that is overloaded or out of service. For further information on Bind, see [22, 23].

- Intelligent DNS load balancers improve functionality by being aware of the load and availability of each DNS server in a cluster. A small process runs on each server and reports back to the load balancer. This functionality is being increasingly embedded into high-speed switching and routing devices, and also being integrated into general-purpose load-sharing systems, switches, and firewalls. Examples include the ArrowPoint (now part of Cisco) range of content-aware switches, Metainfo's IP/Load Balancer, and Cisco's Local-Director.

The advantages of DNS proxies are that they are protocol transparent, simple to deploy, and offer improved performance and reliability. However, these advantages may be negated where name servers and Web browsers cache the IP address returned by the DNS server (commonly done for local performance advantages). These systems may also ignore the DNS Time-To-Live (TTL) value, defeating the possibility of dynamically adjusting load per session. When deploying DNS load balancers, careful attention should be paid to the design. A DNS load balancer may become a single point of failure. A load balancer advertises its name and address to other DNS servers on the Internet, which cache the information. If the load balancer dies, remote clients may not be able to reach any of the DNS server clusters behind it until the cache in their local DNS server expires. The default timeout for DNS entries in many UNIX implementations is five minutes (some servers may be configured to retain DNS information for more than 40 days). Since this functionality is increasingly being integrated into general-purpose load-sharing systems, switches, and firewalls, these devices can often be clustered to provide appropriate levels of fault tolerance. The interested reader is directed to [24–26] for further details about the operation of DNS. Reference [27] documents DNS support issues for load balancing.

7.3.3 HTTP load sharing

HTTP load sharing proxies (sometimes referred to as logical HTTP servers or HTTP redirectors) can be used as a method for distributing requests for Web services. This functionality is limited to Web traffic only. As with DNS, load balancing is implemented as a proxy service, and this has the advantage of being simple to implement and transparent. From the user's perspective there is only one Web server, whereas in reality there may be several servers, often located physically at different sites for additional resilience. Note that Web servers do not necessarily have to be on a particular interface on the proxy (e.g., if this functionality is implemented in a firewall, some Web servers may be behind the firewall, others may be accessible via the Internet).

In effect redirection means that the client browser effectively has two HTTP sessions (although the client is generally unaware of this). The client initially makes an HTTP request to the proxy. The proxy recognizes the destination URL as a logical server and selects the most appropriate server (based on its load-balancing algorithm). The proxy then notifies the client that the URL is being directed via the URL redirection feature of HTTP, redirecting the client to a specific IP address. In practice, this functionality can be negated if the user caches URLs locally as bookmarks, since the HTTP proxy will be bypassed. HTTP load sharing may be implemented in standalone devices or integrated into general-purpose load balancers, such as ArrowPoint's content-aware switches, Cisco's LocalDirector, and Checkpoint's Firewall-1.

7.3.4 FTP load sharing

FTP load-sharing proxies (sometimes referred to as logical FTP servers) can be used as a method for distributing requests for FTP services. This functionality is limited to FTP traffic only. As with HTTP, load sharing is implemented as a proxy service, and this has the advantage of being simple to implement and transparent. From the user's perspective there is only one FTP server, whereas in reality there may be several servers, often located physically at different sites for additional resilience. As with HTTP load sharing, FTP servers do not necessarily have to be on a particular interface on the proxy. However, in this case, unlike HTTP load sharing, there is no explicit redirection; all server sessions are handled through the proxy.

The client initially makes an FTP request to the proxy. The proxy recognizes the destination IP address or name as a logical server and selects the most appropriate server (based on its load-balancing algorithm). The proxy then performs network address translation on the session so that the client is unaware of the true destination server. Address translation is performed in both directions (so that even FTP back connections are handled properly). FTP load sharing may be implemented in standalone devices or integrated into general-purpose load balancers, such as ArrowPoint's content-aware switches, Cisco's LocalDirector, and Checkpoint's Firewall-1.

7.3.5   ARP load sharing

Proxy ARP can be used to provide resilient paths to services and spread load. For example, assume we have a client connected to a LAN-A. The client has an IP address 140.4.3.1 and a mask 255.255.0.0. There are two routers connected to LAN-A, and both remotely connect to LAN-B, which attaches to a server. The server uses IP address 140.4.2.1 and a mask 255.255.255.0. Both routers run proxy ARP. When the client wishes to connect to the server, it believes that the server is locally attached (since it uses a natural class B mask). It, therefore, ARPs locally. Both routers receive the ARP and will respond with their own MAC addresses. The client will cache the MAC address from the most recent ARP response and send the packet addressed to the server's IP address and one of the router's MAC addresses. The relevant router will forward the packet onto LAN-B. This approach is simple and transparent but does have some drawbacks. If one of the routers dies, then all client sessions using that router will eventually time out. Clients will then have to generate a new ARP request, which should be responded to by the working router. All further sessions will be directed to this single router. If the failed router recovers, it will not be used until sessions are broken or new clients come online. ARP timers are quite long, and it may take considerable time for the load to be evenly distributed between routers. For further information on basic ARP and Proxy ARP operations, the interested reader is referred to [28].

7.3.6 **NAT load sharing**

Network Address Translation (NAT) dynamically changes source and destination IP addresses (and possibly ports) as IP packets traverse the NAT system. NAT is typically employed for security applications or to convert
private IP addresses to registered IP addresses (NAT operations are
described in [29]). Since this is a critical function, NAT systems are often
incorporated in firewalls or perimeter routers placed at strategic locations
on the network. In a client/server environment, this gives a NAT system the
opportunity to distribute sessions among different servers by dynamically
changing the destination IP address to match one of several servers in a
hunt group. For complete transparency, packets returned from the servers
must traverse the NAT device so that addresses are flipped back to their
original forms and forwarded to the client. Since NAT operates at the IP
layer, it is not tied to a specific service.

An enhanced version of NAT called Load Share Network Address Translator (LSNAT) is described in [RFC2391]. LSNAT extends NAT to offer
load sharing across a pool of servers, instead of directing requests to a single
server. LSNAT uses real-time load-sharing algorithms to transparently distribute the load across a server group. This enables servers to scale in large
internetwork environments. Unlike traditional NAT, LSNAT devices initiate translations on inbound sessions by binding each session represented
by a tuple (client address, client TCP/UDP port, virtual server address,
server TCP/UDP port) to one of the servers in the cluster, selection based
on a real-time load-sharing algorithm. A virtual server address is a globally
unique IP address that identifies a physical server or a group of servers that
provide similar functionality. In essence, when a client sends a request to a
server (using virtual address), the LSNAT system transparently redirects the
request to one of the hosts in the server pool, chosen using a real-time load-
sharing algorithm. Multiple sessions may be initiated from the same client,
and each session could be directed to a different host based on load balancing across server pool hosts at the time. If load sharing is desired for just a
few specific services, the configuration on LSNAT could be defined to
restrict load sharing for just the services desired.

To check if a server is up, NAT-based load-balancing solutions need to
sacrifice an actual client request, and so a server outage is typically perceived
only as a result of a timeout of one of these real client requests. NAT devices
often only map affinity or stickiness based on the client's IP address, not at
the port level. This means that once a client has contacted a server, then all
traffic from that client that is intended for other applications is forwarded

to the same server. This drastically restricts configuration flexibility, in many cases rendering the sticky capability unusable in the real world. There are some other limitations worth noting, as follows:

- All requests and responses within a session flow (e.g., Telnet) between a client and server must be routed via the same LSNAT system. Once a node is assigned to service a session, that session is bound to that node until termination. Reference [30] recommends operating LSNATs on a single border router to a stub domain in which the server pool would be confined. This would ensure that all traffic directed to servers from clients outside the domain and vice versa would necessarily traverse the LSNAT border router.

- LSNAT is not able to switch loads between hosts in the middle of sessions. This is because LSNATs measure load in granularity of sessions. Once a session is assigned to a host, the session cannot be moved to a different host until the end of that session.

- The servers in the cluster must be functionally equivalent—that is, each of the nodes in the cluster should be capable of supporting client sessions with no discernible difference in functionality.

- Addresses owned by LSNAT cannot be used on the host platform. For example, in the case where the virtual server address is the same as an interface address on an LSNAT router, server applications (such as Telnet) on LSNAT-enabled routers should be disabled for external access on that specific address.

NAT operations introduce additional overhead and latency, as well as queuing delay in the load balancer. Traffic is also typically asymmetrical, with much higher volumes passing downstream to the client. These factors limit the potential scalability of NAT solutions, unless the NAT systems can be clustered (e.g., by grouping firewalls or routers running NAT using protocols such as VRRP or HSRP). Note that some NAT systems mandate that the NAT device be installed as a kind of bridge and will not permit bridges of any other kind to be installed in parallel. All traffic must pass through the NAT devices, whether it is required to be NATed or not. This forces the server group to be located on a private segment behind the NAT system and restricts the flexibility of NAT to include remote WAN servers in the hunt group. It may compromise resilience unless the NAT systems can be clustered. For further information, the interested reader is referred to [30].

7.3.7 IP load balancers

IP load balancers are generic devices that sit in front of a group of IP servers (e.g., a Web farm), sharing the load between these servers. Broadly speaking, load balancers can be divided into two groups, as follows:

- Nonintelligent—These systems operate without knowledge of the server status. The most widely used load balancer in this class is Destination Address Rotary Translation (a software feature included in Cisco's IOS). IOS simply farms out requests for a given destination IP address to the next server in the group using a round-robin algorithm. Each server has a unique IP address; however, clients use only the address advertised by IOS. This system has no knowledge of the changing loads or availability of servers in the group.

- Intelligent—More sophisticated IP load balancers are required to optimize large commercial Web and e-commerce sites. These systems track server status and are generally specialized hardware devices placed between the Internet router and the server farm. Requests can be allotted using a number of algorithms, such as round robin, random, dedicated servers based on domain name or IP address, or based on server status (CPU utilization, response time, etc.). Typically the designer can configure how these systems operate.

Assessing server status is actually quite hard to achieve with any degree of accuracy. For example, CPU utilization statistics on UNIX servers can be misleading; under some conditions these values can be artificially high. As we saw earlier, measuring response time by simply pinging servers may produce inaccurate results, since a server's CPU and network adapter may return fast responses even though the disk subsystem is overloaded. Some of the more sophisticated products in this class create a load index to analyze several key criteria (response time, throughput, number of concurrent connections, etc.). Instead of simply using ping, some of these products may actually request content to assess real-life application performance and may include the ability to run customized scripts as part of the status-testing algorithm. On high-end load balancers, servers can be brought in and out of service dynamically, and content can be moved around (using FTP) as demand increases. Because of their strong fault tolerance, IP or DNS load balancers complement proxy caches. Among the vendors with products are Alteon Networks., ArrowPoint, Foundry, Checkpoint, Cisco, Bright Tiger Technologies, Coyote Point System, F5 Labs, Hydraweb Technologies, and Resonate.

7.3.8   VRRP and HSRP

Virtual Redundant Routing Protocol (VRRP) and Hot Standby Routing Protocol (HSRP) are both relatively dumb protocols that rely on the default gateway feature configured on end systems. The basic idea is that devices (typically routers) within a cluster offer themselves as a virtual IP address. While these protocols are essentially designed to provide a hot standby device, they allow multiple virtual IP groups to be configured, and so traffic can be shared dynamically among several devices, and resilience is offered concurrently. Figure 7.9 illustrates a topology where VRRP is used between two routers to provide both load sharing and resilience for client/server access.

In this configuration, both routers run VRRP on all interfaces, and on both LAN interfaces both routers will simultaneously participate in two VRRP groups. Half of the end systems install a default route to the IP address of Router-1 (194.34.4.1); the remaining end systems install a default route to the IP address of Router-2 (194.34.4.2). Router-1 is elected as the master for VRID 1, with a priority of 254, with Router-2 providing backup. In the same way Router-2 is elected master for VRID 2, with Router-1 providing backup. If either master should fail, the backup will automatically kick in. For example, if Router-1 dies, then Router-2 will

Figure 7.9
VRRP configuration with load sharing and resilience for a server farm.

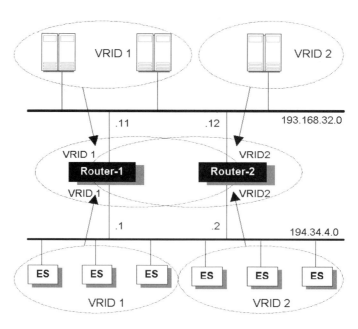

operate as master for virtual IP addresses 194.34.4.2 and 194.34.4.1 until Router-1 resumes activity. On the server-side LAN we are doing effectively the same thing. Note that VRID-1 and VRID-2 are used on both LANs but are effectively operating as different groups.

This configuration enables load sharing through the routers, while also providing full redundancy and transparency. If more horsepower is required, then more than two routers could be configured in parallel.

7.3.9   Port hashing techniques

This technique may be implemented in switches or routers as a hash function to control flow destination based on flow criteria. Normally this is generally a proprietary feature, and the output of the function may be deterministic or non-deterministic (i.e., the designer can predict which physical interface will be used to output a flow based on input, or load balancing is entirely dynamic). Assume, for the sake of simplicity, that our hash function simply takes two addresses and outputs an interface ID using an XOR function, using bit positions to associate an interface. In this case we assume the switch has 16 interfaces, so we use a 4-bit mask to determine which port to use. Let us assume that an IP packet arrives with source address 195.66.3.6 and destination address 140.10.128.3:

```
11000011 01000010 00000011 00000110 = 195.66.3.6    // Class C address
10001100 00001010 10000000 00000011 = 140.10.128.3  // Class B address
XXXXXXXX XXXXXXXX XXXXXXXX XXXX1111 0.0.0.15         // Interface Mask
-------------------------------- logical_XOR
XXXXXXXX XXXXXXXX XXXXXXXX XXXX0101 = 5              // The Interface!
```

Note that I am not recommending this particular algorithm, just illustrating the concept. For a switch with only four active interfaces (as used in our example) the function could be configured (or could reconfigure dynamically) to adjust the length of the bit mask and, if necessary, wrap around if the number of active ports is not a power of 2. For more granular flow classification, the algorithm could hash the IP source and destination address and destination TCP or UDP port to generate an output interface. This would enable differentiation of applications such as FTP, SMTP, and Telnet.

If this algorithm is deterministic (as in our example), we would simply need to cable up the network topology consistently to be sure that flows are sent and received down the same path (this may be important for applications such as stateful firewalls); in effect we are demultiplexing flows

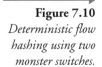

Figure 7.10
*Deterministic flow
hashing using two
monster switches.*

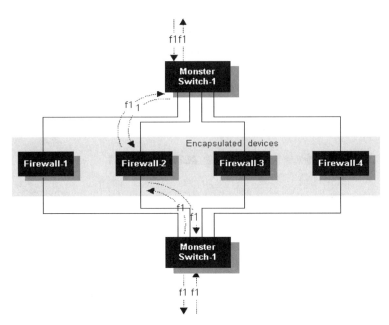

through a physical infrastructure and then aggregating them on the other side. In Figure 7.10, we use this concept to scale firewall performance using high-speed switches (capable of operating at up to wire speed). The physical wiring in this case would typically be 10/100 Ethernet. The basic idea is that the bottleneck device (typically a device doing a lot of work, in this case a firewall) should be encapsulated (in the topological sense) inside a number of higher-speed devices. The encapsulated device sees only a proportion of the overall traffic, since the switch presorts flows and allocates them to specific physical interfaces. This enables devices such as firewalls to be scaled as many times as there are available interfaces at the switch. In Figure 7.10, a session is identified (f1) on Switch-1 and hashed to a specific interface. Physical cabling ensures that this interface is fed into Firewall-2, which simply outputs into Switch-2. The flow return is directed down the same physical path (this means that the hash function used on Switch-2 must be consistent, and cabling must reflect the output of the function to ensure that the return path is consistent.

The main design restrictions are associated with the hash function and the physical topology. The hash function must have sufficient granularity to pick out application flows to enable a reasonable load distribution. On the other hand, the function needs to be fairly simple to avoid too many processing overheads per packet. There is therefore a trade-off between making

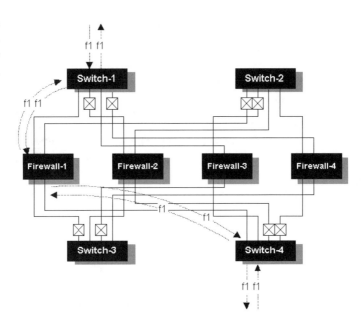

Figure 7.11
Deterministic flow hashing.

this function fast and sufficiently fair. The other main issue is that the physical topology may need to be symmetrical and should exhibit consistently throughout. If a physical interface or cable breaks on either side of the encapsulated device, the flow send and return paths could be inconsistent. This may not be a problem if the encapsulated device does not need to maintain flow state information (a router), but this may be unacceptable to a more sophisticated device such as a firewall (e.g., if stateful inspection is being used). In this case the switch could implement a simple polling feature to test available paths and force interfaces to forward consistently on both sides, or some form of state synchronization could be used between switches to ensure that the hash function output is consistent for all flows.

Since this is a flow-based function, we are not talking about true load balancing. The actual load imposed on each encapsulated device will depend on the applications used and the number of flows. In a large network with reasonably diverse flows the loading should be evenly distributed. If one dominant source is present, loading may be less evenly spread. Note also that some commercial solutions use modulo-based hash functions; this will lead to uneven distribution depending upon the number of switches. If the switch runs into performance issues (assume the external paths in the topology are Gigabit Ethernet) it is possible to scale the switch design, as illustrated in Figure 7.11.

Distributed hashing techniques

Some implementations take a more intelligent approach to traffic flow distribution by clustering devices and using hashing techniques to allocate flows among group members. In general there are two methods employed, as follows:

- Autocratic model—See Figure 7.12(a). Here we elect a master flow distributor for the cluster. The master receives all incoming packets, and, based on the flows identified and the number of members in the cluster, flows are bounced back and directed to individual group members for processing.

- Democratic model—See Figure 7.12(b). Here we use a stateful protocol between group members to distribute flow allocation (a master may still be elected for controlling flow state updates, but this is analogous to the role of the designated router in a link-state protocol). This is really an improvement on the first technique in that traffic is no longer redirected through the single master device. Each group node knows which flows to handle and which ones to discard. The downside is that all traffic needs to be seen by all members of the cluster.

At first it may seem that the autocratic method adds little value, since we need to process and classify all incoming traffic at the master in order to decide how to distribute it. However, consider a device such as a firewall or VPN termination node. These devices perform significant packet processing functions (particularly if high-speed encryption is required for thousands of concurrent sessions). For this class of device, simply classifying and bouncing incoming traffic between cluster nodes is a negligible overhead in terms of this overall processing requirement.

In either model it is important that the algorithm handle cluster node introduction and removal dynamically. This is a fundamental requirement, since we need to deal gracefully with a cluster member malfunction (including failure of a master), so as not to cause major disruption to the whole group. For applications such as VPN, stateful firewalls, or transaction processing, it is also highly desirable that flows be switched transparently in the event of a failure, so that sessions remain alive regardless. For these applications it may also be desirable that flows be handled symmetrically, so that send and return flows for each individual application session are routed through the same cluster node. We have also assumed so far that nodes in the cluster have equivalent resources (processor speed, memory size, etc.). With either model, more sophisticated algorithms may allow nodes to be mixed, with the flow allocation reflecting any differences in processing

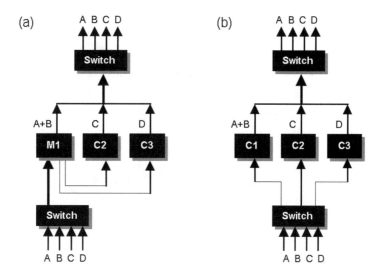

Figure 7.12 *Distributing flows using hashing techniques. Here, four flows (A, B, C, and D) are fed into the cluster. (a) An autocratic model, where a master (M1) is elected and performs flow distribution at the ingress port. (b) A democratic model, where each node is aware of the flow states being handled by other members of the cluster.*

capability. Note that in both designs a single switch is used on either side of the cluster; in practice, this could be deployed as multiple switches for scalability and high availability.

7.4 Optimizing applications

7.4.1 Use of multicasts

Many legacy network applications still rely on unicast or broadcast distribution techniques to push data out to users. For example, a market data feed may be distributed to each subscriber via individual TCP sessions. Applications that distribute essentially the same information to many users would be much better served by multicasting. If the application is developed in-house, it may be well worth reexamining the application architecture to see if this is possible. Several leading application providers in the financial arena have already implemented, or are considering the use of, multicasts. Clearly, if the application is multicast based and is to be used over an internetwork, a suitable distribution mechanism needs to be in place. This requires a routing infrastructure based on protocols such as IGMP, MOSPF, PIM, and DVMRP.

7.4.2   Wide area tuning issues

In wide area networks there are a number of points to consider when optimizing applications, including the following:

- Sun's Network File System (NFS) runs over UDP and has a default retransmission timeout of 700 ms. A full datagram is 8,192 bytes (six frames). Therefore, if NFS sends a complete datagram over a 64-Kbps leased line, this will take over a second. The timer must be increased to approximately two seconds, or the datagram size in the NFS end systems must be decreased to 3,000 bytes or less. The latest versions of NFS adjust timeout and message size dynamically to suit the WAN delay characteristics.

- Satellite links typically have a Round-Trip Time (RTT) of 500 ms or more. Too large a message size gives best efficiency but increases the probability of error. Lowering the message size decreases errors but loses efficiency due to encapsulation overheads.

- Bridges cannot modify the message size, since this would result in fragmentation. However, routers can, so they can optimize the MTU to improve throughput according to the WAN delay characteristics. In a situation where Token Ring is being bridged to Ethernet over the wide area, you can either set the MTU for all Token Ring interfaces to 1,500 bytes or use routers. Source Route (SR) bridges report the MTU size available for the path and how much would be possibly used.

7.4.3   Proxy services

A router or switch can act as a proxy for services that are not available locally. In a sense they are acting as surrogates, pretending to originate a service that is actually hosted elsewhere, and for this reason this functionality is often referred to as spoofing. Proxy services also improve application performance by minimizing latency and preserving valuable wide area bandwidth. Typical examples of proxy services include the following:

- Service announcements—A router or switch may have to pretend that it is a server if resource-discovery frames are issued on a remote LAN and there is no server locally. Examples include the following:

  - NetWare NCP servers broadcast Service Advertisement Protocol (SAP) messages regularly. In a remote dial-up environment, where there is no local server, a router may spoof SAP broadcast announcements and respond to Get-Nearest-Server requests from clients (i.e., act as a SAP proxy).

■ Banyan VINES networks may require a router to respond to local VINES clients requesting network addresses.

■ Address resolution services—For example, there are circumstances where a router must support Proxy ARP to offer MAC to IP address resolution where subnetting is not supported on end systems.

■ NetBIOS name caching enables a router to maintain a cache of mappings between NetBIOS server and client names and their MAC addresses. This avoids the overhead of transmitting broadcasts between NetBIOS clients and servers in a Source Route Bridging (SRB) environment. As a result, broadcast requests sent by clients to find servers (and by servers in reply to their clients) can be sent directly to their destinations, rather than being broadcast across the entire bridged network. The router also notices ·when any host sends a series of duplicate query frames and limits retransmission to one frame per period (the time period is typically configurable).

■ Routing announcements—Proxy services are commonly employed where routing protocols are used over dial-up or low-bandwidth WAN links. For example:

  ■ NetWare routers broadcast Routing Information Protocol (RIP) messages regularly.

  ■ IP Routing Information Protocol (RIP) announcements need to be constrained and spoofed by local spoofing or low-demand services.

  ■ OSPF LSAs need to be constrained by running in low-demand mode.

For remote dial applications where there is a single satellite site (i.e., a stub network), it is often easier to implement static routes than use a low-demand dynamic routing protocol.

■ Keep-alive spoofing—Spoofing is commonly employed where LAN operating systems are used over dial-up or low-bandwidth WAN links. For example:

  ■ Novell NetWare has a number of features that require spoofing. For example, NetWare Core Protocol (NCP) servers may send keep-alive messages to all connected clients every five minutes to establish their status. NetWare IPX and SPX Watchdog packets must also be spoofed. Finally, NetWare issues regular serialization queries to check that installations are properly licensed; these also must be spoofed.

- Data link acknowledgments (e.g., LLC2)—The majority of enterprises use the connectionless form of link layer (LLC Type 1), which is more an encapsulation format than an actual protocol. Some enterprises, however, (especially those dominated by IBM) use connection-oriented SDLC and LLC Type 2. These protocols create and maintain session states and are not supported natively over the Internet. If SDLC or LLC2 is tunneled end to end over IP, this will most likely result in timeouts, since the full round-trip time could be orders of magnitude higher than normally expected. To avoid this problem some routers enable data link sessions to be spoofed locally; both the local and remote nodes have data link sessions with their local routers and not with each other (no Layer 2 traffic is sent over the Internet). This preserves backbone bandwidth and ensures sessions stay active. This feature is often called local ACK.

- Applications that send regular TCP ACKs as keep-alives must be spoofed at routers or switches over dial-up links. In practice this is hard to achieve, and since both ends of the link must keep state and be prepared to synchronize once the link is active again.

As indicated, proxy services are commonly used on dial-up links, since it would be ill advised to let regular announcements and keep-alives cause the link to stay up permanently (or cause regular dial-ups) and since we are likely to be charged for both call setup and uptime (e.g., ISDN). Proxy services are also a good general technique for conserving backbone bandwidth.

7.4.4   Caching techniques

On any large internetwork where data sources are distributed, one of the prime areas for optimization is concerned with the way in which content is moved around. If we analyze the movement of content on a public backbone such as the Internet, we begin to see consistent patterns emerging. A significant proportion of that content may be moved again and again, often over large distances from the origin server to the recipient. This leads to two problems, as follows:

- Latency—There is a noticeable delay between the recipient requesting content and that content being delivered.

- Congestion—Moving the same content over the backbone many times wastes valuable bandwidth.

Both these issues are intimately linked. If congestion increases, this contributes to additional latency. If latency is excessive, sessions may time out, leading to retransmissions and further contributing to congestion. In order to counter these delays and preserve valuable backbone capacity, significant research activity has taken place in recent years leading to the implementation of caching systems.

Caching basics

Caching systems monitor content utilization statistically and store copies of frequently used data closer to the users, so that future requests can be serviced locally. Caching is a generic technique for improving performance and has been applied almost universally at the network system and microcomponent level. As with compression techniques, caching relies on repeatability for its efficiency. If on a particular network content is moved only once, then caching adds no value.

In practice, placing caching systems at strategic points on an internetwork brings several major benefits: Average latency is reduced, backbone capacity is increased, and resource utilization of origin servers is diminished. Overall caching systems can significantly improve scalability and prove very cost effective (wide area circuit costs make up a substantial part of the IT budget, so reducing backbone utilization means that either downsizing or increased productivity is possible). Whenever a user requests information, the request is redirected to a nearby cache server. The server checks whether duplicate content is held in cache. If found, the server returns the content to the requester. If not found, the server retrieves the original data from the origin server, delivers the content to the requester, and possibly caches this new content.

Caching system design issues

Designing a highly efficient caching system is not easy. Some of the key problems that cache systems have to address are as follows:

- Optimizing content—Since caching systems have finite resources, they operate by analyzing user requests statistically. In principle, the more the same content is requested, the higher the probability that the content will be cached. When users request content, if that content resides in cache, we term this a cache hit; otherwise, it is termed a cache miss. The more requests can be serviced from cache, the higher the hit rate. The decision to cache a requested object needs to be made quickly. To optimize resources the server needs to employ sophisticated statistical techniques to analyze the most frequently accessed content, together with actual content size. This must be implemented dynamically, so that changes in use patterns at different times of the day or different days of the week are reflected in the cache population.

- Synchronization—Cached content may become out of date and must be periodically refreshed. Most cache managers include synchronization mechanisms to regularly query the origin server to ensure that data held locally are current. Ideally this should be asynchronous (i.e., done in background mode). If a large proportion of the content is changing rapidly, caching systems either present inaccurate data (if synchronization intervals are too long) or become less efficient (since the caching system is spending much of its time pulling down updates). Note also that Web browsers often implement local caching at the desktop device; again, if this content is changing, the user must remember to manually refresh these data.

- Capacity and responsiveness—System performance is determined largely by the architecture and the implementation of the cache server, such as the operating system, whether the server uses multiple threads, queuing strategies, load balancing, and so on. If only a modest amount of cache resources (CPU, RAM, disk) are available and content is changing frequently, the hit rate will be relatively low. In busy systems it is important to ensure that cache retrieval latency and cache size restrictions do not become a bottleneck. The ability to respond to user requests in a timely manner is determined by a number of techniques used to maximize cache hit rate, including the structure of cache hierarchies and content optimization.

- Reliability and availability—Since caching is essentially a transparent enhancement to a normal network operation, it is usually possible to continue operations if a cache server fails (albeit with degraded performance). Having said that, loss of caching systems may violate user QoS guarantees. It is, therefore, highly beneficial to design in some level of fault tolerance or high availability (perhaps through clustering techniques) to minimize service disruption.

- Management and control—As with any sophisticated network-wide resource, it is important to be able to easily install, configure, and maintain cache servers. Even though cache clusters may be distributed over large distances, they need to be centrally managed, with the ability to download consistent policy. Management should include event logging and statistical reporting capabilities, together with tight security mechanisms.

- Scalability—Since cache server resources are finite, they must be monitored regularly. If too many users are directed to a particular cache server, performance can degrade, causing more able users to circumvent the cache. If caching systems become overloaded, more cache servers need to be installed to share the load. It is desirable for large caching systems to scale performance close to linearly, O(n). In the general case, where a significant number of the remote objects are being requested by many users, the real problem is how to design a cache server architecture that scales to keep pace with demand. The size of disk arrays and disk seek times may not create a bottleneck, but caching software must manage large amounts of data concurrently (both for writing new content to be cached, and reading cached content). The physical organization and access of data on disk is a potential issue, since general-purpose file layouts and operating system file IO functions may not be sufficiently optimized for specialized applications. Very large caches are effective but also the most difficult to implement, since they typically require some form of clustering or load sharing to scale beyond the limitations of a single system.

To provide scalability, some caching systems are hierarchical. There are two types of hierarchical caches: sibling and parent-child. In the sibling model, a cache server that does not have the request content sends a request to all other servers in the group for that content. The parent-child model is a vertical hierarchy; the child cache server only asks its parent for a resource. Both designs are supported by the Internet Cache Protocol (ICP) version 2, a lightweight query-response protocol used for communicating between Web caches (specified in [31, 32]. For most organizations using multiple cache servers the sibling model is probably adequate. But if an organization's ISP also uses a cache server, a parent-child design can significantly reduce traffic on ISP backbones.

Applications that benefit from caching

In an internetwork environment network caching benefits a number of content delivery services. In general the most suitable services are those where fairly static content is requested and delivered frequently and repeatedly (e.g., documents, Web pages, video clips, certificates, etc.). Promising applications include the following:

- HyperText Transfer Protocol (HTTP)—HTTP content is perhaps the most obvious example of content that is frequently and repeatedly accessed. The increased use of embedded objects in Web content means that file sizes are also increasing.

- File Transfer Protocol (FTP)—FTP servers are commonly used to store boot images, documents, configuration data, driver updates, and so on. Since the average file size transferred by FTP tends to be larger than a typical HTML file, FTP users can benefit even more from local caching.

- Network News Transport Protocol (NNTP)—Frequent news updates are delivered to large numbers of subscribers [33]. Usenet news is one of the biggest sources of inbound Internet traffic for ISPs. Many organizations and smaller ISPs no longer maintain full Usenet feeds for their networks. Instead, they use a larger ISP's upstream news server but only pull down selected articles of interest to end users.

- Real-Time Streaming Protocol (RTSP)—Internet video and audio applications transfer literally hundreds of megabytes to registered users.

- Public Key Infrastructure (PKI) services—Certificate Revocation Lists (CRLs) may be cached locally to reduce latency. This is especially beneficial for transaction-oriented applications where latency is critical.

It is possible to use a cache with dynamic Web content, since even these pages tend to contain a large proportion of static content. With Web caching, 40 percent or more of browser requests can typically be offloaded from the network and serviced locally. To illustrate the point let us consider what happens when a user requests Web and FTP content without caching, as illustrated in Figure 7.13. If we assume several thousand LAN users, every new user requiring the same content causes both HTTP requests and the content to repeatedly traverse the network. All of these users are subject to the end-to-end latency of hauling megabytes of data over the network, and the network is effectively wasting bandwidth sending the same content repeatedly (and often concurrently) to the same destination. In Figure 7.13, the content requested could, for example, be a static HTML page (with links to other files and embedded graphics) or a dynamically created page (created by a search engine, database query, or Web application). Dynamically created pages typically have some static components. FTP requests are dealt with in a similar manner.

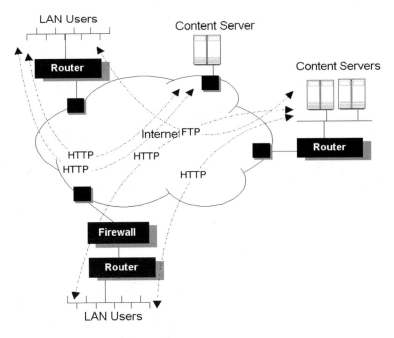

Figure 7.13   *Web browsing and FTP file requests without caching. (1) The Web browser issues an
HTTP request for a Uniform Resource Locator (URL), which refers to a specific Web
page on a particular server (also known as an HTTP server or origin server) attached to
the Internet. (2) The request is forwarded to the server through standard IP routing. (3)
The HTTP Content Server returns content to the Web browser one file at a time (which
typically comprises a sequence of large packets).*

There is clearly room for improvement. We can reduce latency and also
preserve valuable backbone bandwidth by distributing frequently used content closer to the users. As illustrated in Figure 7.14, content may be cached
inside the perimeter firewall at the user site, at the local ISP, or at some
other Network Access Point (NAP) or Point of Presence (PoP) closer to the
user site. For an ISP, traffic reduction could provide substantial savings in
circuit utilization and represent additional capacity (up to one-third of an
ISP's operating costs may be attributed to recurring circuit costs). For a user
organization, placing cache inside the perimeter firewall may provide substantial performance benefits if all content must be scrutinized by the firewall. For example, if all incoming content must be checked for viruses
(notoriously slow), cached content will already have been decontaminated
and is, therefore, instantly available. As can be seen in Figure 7.14, cache
servers could be placed behind the user's firewall, on the local LAN, or even
at the ISP PoP. In this case only requests for new content (infrequently

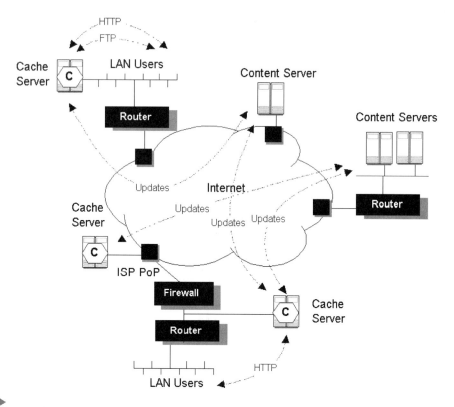

Figure 7.14 *Web and FTP transactions with caching.*

accessed content or content that has aged out) or content synchronization updates are sent over the wide area. Local cache servers service all requests for frequently accessed content, reducing both WAN bandwidth and transaction latency.

Deploying cache in an internetwork

How to deploy cache servers

There are several approaches to implementing cache server architectures. The model used depends on several factors, including where the cache is implemented, the primary purpose of the cache, and the nature of the traffic. Caches can be deployed with varying degrees of transparency, as follows:

- Nontransparent—In order to make use of cache servers, network administrators must reconfigure Web browsers and FTP client software on all end stations to point at the cache instead of the Internet at large. In this case the cache acts as a proxy agent. Nontransparent caches are often components of larger proxy servers acting as part of an overall gateway or firewall solution.

- Semitransparent—A semitransparent cache can be implemented by mass dynamic configuration of browsers. Both Microsoft and Netscape provide tools that enable this to be achieved, and browser plug-ins are available to provide automatic configuration. This approach is better than hard configuration but does require some maintenance effort on an ongoing basis.

- Transparent—A transparent cache is invisible to browsers and other systems. It operates by listening to network traffic and intercepting and responding as appropriate. Some router and application-aware switching products enable you to redirect all outbound content queries (e.g., HTTP requests) to one or more local cache servers. This approach is completely transparent and requires no end-system modifications; changes to the cache server configuration need only be reflected at the router or switch, and attempts to circumvent the local cache are blocked. It may also be possible to use intelligent load sharing using algorithms on the router or switch to distribute load between cache clusters and improve availability.

For service providers or large internetworks a transparent or semitransparent configuration is preferable, since it minimizes maintenance and support overheads and avoids service disruption if caching components fail. Users automatically receive the benefits of caching without any knowledge of its activities, and caching server designs can be modified without having to reconfigure client machines manually.

Where to deploy cache servers

The most promising locations for caching systems are points where the network aggregates large volumes of traffic (choke points such as PoPs, edge routers, etc.), points where many sessions need to be examined (e.g., perimeter firewalls), and points where there is a significant financial or performance cost associated with moving content upstream (e.g., the LAN-WAN interface, satellite links, etc.). These locations generally present the cache server with a high visibility of network traffic, enabling the cache to deal with more requests and store more content locally while improving performance and conserving upstream bandwidth.

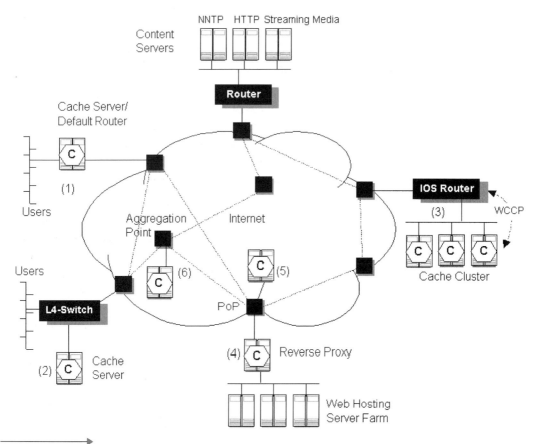

Figure 7.15   *Cache deployment options. Note that cache locations are highlighted with a C.*
(1) Cache server acting as a default gateway. (2) Layer 4 switches can route requests for
cacheable data (HTTP, NNTP, etc.) to the cache server while forwarding all other
requests to the Internet. (3) Web Cache Control Protocol (WCCP) implemented in a
Cisco IOS-based router. Port 80 (HTTP) requests are routed to the cache servers, while
other requests are routed to the Internet. (4) In front of a Web farm to reduce load on
content servers. (5) At an ISP Point of Presence (PoP) to serve requests locally. (6) At an
aggregation point at the edge of the Internet to reduce bandwidth requirements.

A number of common cache locations are illustrated in Figure 7.15 and
are discussed in the following list:

- Deploying cache in the default router—See Figure 7.15(1). The
cache server can be configured as a default router for all Internet traffic. This approach is highly transparent and requires no browser configuration but does require the cache server to operate as a full router,
making it a mission-critical component of the network. Some high-

end routers support policy-based routing, which enables them to get around this issue by operating as a default router and forwarding only HTTP (TCP Port 80) traffic to the cache server. In the event of cache server failure, policy routing can be configured to bypass the server, forwarding all HTTP traffic as normal.

- Deploying cache in Layer 4 switches—See Figure 7.15(2), Layer 4 switches are increasingly being used to interface with cache servers. These are typically high-performance switching devices that can differentiate traffic flows in hardware and make rapid forwarding decisions based on protocols above the IP level (such as UDP or TCP port information). Some of these devices parse into the application space to identify individual HTTP sessions or URL requests. Based on these data, these switches can direct HTTP, FTP, and other application traffic to the caches and forward other traffic as standard.

- Clustering with Web Cache Control Protocol (WCCP)—See Figure 7.15(3). WCCP is a protocol developed by Cisco Systems [34]. It enables Web caches to be transparently deployed using Cisco IOS-based routers. WCCPv1 runs between a router functioning as a Web redirector and a cluster of out-of-path proxies. The protocol enables one or more proxies to register with a single router to receive redirected Web traffic. It also allows one of the proxies, the designated proxy, to dictate to the router how redirected Web traffic should be distributed across the cluster. WCCP does not require any changes to the network architecture; HTTP traffic is redirected transparently to the Web cache instead of the origin server.

- Web Hosting/Reverse Proxy Configuration—See Figure 7.15(4). By using a cache server configured in a reverse proxy configuration, frequently accessed content on the hosted Web sites can be cached, providing improved performance while reducing the ISP's equipment costs. Here the caching server sits in front of one or more Web servers, intercepting traffic to those servers and acting as a proxy for those servers. This also enables traffic spikes to be handled without affecting overall performance. Distributed cache servers in this mode also reduce bandwidth requirements by providing a lower-cost method of content replication compared with replicated Web servers. The proxy servers will request dynamic and other short-lived content from the origin servers as and when required. This enables content from the site to be served from a local cache instead of from the origin server. Benefits include the ability to enable load balancing, provide peak-demand insurance to assure availability, and provide dynamic mirroring of content for high availability.

- NAPs, exchanges, and PoPs—See Figure 7.15(6). The major distribution points on the Internet are NAPs, exchanges, and PoPs (and so-called SuperPoPs). These are ideal places for implementing caching solutions, because they are aggregation points for large volumes of traffic. By caching frequently accessed content, service providers can free up additional bandwidth by eliminating redundant data transfers. Locating a cache at these aggregation points optimizes upstream link utilization and provides improved service to subscribers. As requests for content are made, the PoP resident cache stores the content locally, making it readily available to subsequent users. The economics of locating caches at NAPs are likely to continue to improve as ISPs employ more sophisticated traffic-engineering measures and optimize their pricing structures.

- Satellite interfaces—Satellite links are expensive and notoriously slow (with latencies often exceeding 500 ms). Locating caching systems at the user side of a satellite link makes good sense, since it preserves bandwidth over the link and significantly improves latency.

- International gateways—Wide area circuit tariffs vary widely around the world [1]. This makes it important for ISPs to optimize the use of expensive Internet uplink connections at gateway points between the provider's own network infrastructure and access points for international traffic (often high-volume Web content from the United States to other parts of the world). By caching upstream content, providers can significantly reduce costs and bandwidth utilization.

- Access network concentrators—High-speed access links to customer premises and businesses are increasingly being provided through broadband cable and xDSL services [1]. Providers offering these services need to compensate for the relatively slow performance of the Internet in order to improve access to content for their customers, and caching locally in the access network is a good solution.

- Perimeter gateways—Caching at or behind a perimeter gateway reduces upstream bandwidth requirements and provides improved service to users. If the gateway is a firewall, the performance gain could be significant, since these devices often have to perform extensive content analysis before forwarding to users (e.g., virus checking). Since the content is cached behind the firewall, this process is no longer required whenever the user requests content that is cached.

One of the problems in deploying a large distributed cache system is how to locate caches transparently. Reference [35] describes HyperText Caching Protocol (HTCP), an experimental protocol for discovering HTTP caches and cached data, managing sets of HTTP caches, and monitoring cache activity. The IETF is also working on a protocol called Web Proxy Autodiscovery Protocol (WPAD). WPAD is also designed to automatically locate caches and services on the network without requiring user configuration.

Capacity planning

Determining how large a cache to maintain is a trade-off between the cache hit rate and the cost of configuring disk storage. Cache capacity can range from single cache servers to clusters of servers to distributed cache hierarchies. The more content that is cached, the higher the hit rates will be for retrieving content but the higher the cost of maintaining the cache will be. Although more caches are better, each installation has to be evaluated on its own merits. Undersizing the cache will fail to provide the desired benefits, but oversizing the cache can waste resources. In general, if a scalable caching solution is used, it is best to start with a conservative amount of capacity and have a plan to expand capacity incrementally to meet demand.

Benchmarks have shown that even modest cache hit rates (of approximately 30 to 40 percent in a moderately loaded Network Access Point [NAP]) can reduce the amount of outbound bandwidth that has to be configured by the equivalent of several T3 lines. This means that a provider can deliver more content to customers with less outlay for bandwidth, effectively providing more bandwidth per dollar. This allows service providers to better manage their network build-out, which is critical since it may not always be available to add.

To get a sense of the magnitude of the possible economic benefits to network access providers, assume that one T3 line carries 45 Mbps of data and 40 percent of that is HTTP traffic. A conservative cache hit rate of 40 percent would take 40 percent of Web traffic off the backbone. Caching additional protocols, such as NNTP and FTP, would result in even greater savings. Just using HTTP traffic for this example, the access provider would have a 16 percent reduction in backbone traffic ($0.40 \times 0.40 = 0.16$). If bandwidth costs are estimated at \$1,000 per Mbps per month, then a network cache in front of a metered T3 with Internet access can save an ISP \$7,200 per month or \$86,000 per year. For a large ISP with multiple T3 lines, these savings can add up quickly.

Cache performance metrics

Definitions of cache performance metrics are as follows:

- Response time is the primary metric of cache performance. This is the mean time taken for a requested content to be delivered to the user. In terms of Web page content this includes all objects encapsulated by that page. A typical HTML page is made up of many embedded objects, such as GIF and JPEG images and sounds, Java applets, and so on. The browser must individually retrieve each object before it can completely render the page. A user's perception of Web performance is based on the time it takes to access completely each page. Individual page latency varies significantly, depending upon the number of objects encapsulated and the different types of objects (simple pages can have less than ten objects and rich pages can contain 50 or more objects, some of them more complex).

- Hit ratio is the percentage of requests served by the cache, as a proportion of all requests, and central to any measurement of cache performance. Response time metrics are heavily influenced by those requests that lie within the hit ratio (faster) and those outside (slower). A low hit ratio of 20 percent means that 80 percent of requests are required to traverse the entire network in order to communicate with the origin server, while only 20 percent of requests are serviced locally.

- Response time under load indicates how network scalability is affected by the ability of caching systems to deliver consistent response times as cache load increases. For example, at any given time, there will be many concurrent HTTP object requests to the cache, and the load on the cache is the rate at which it is delivering requested objects to clients. HTTP object access times will also vary with the load. As the load increases, the time to retrieve a given object from cache is likely to increase, and hence the response time for a complete page is likely to increase. If the load on a cache exceeds a threshold where the cache stops responding consistently to requests, then the caching system effectively acts as a performance bottleneck.

In effect every cache miss degrades response times and places more unnecessary traffic on the backbone. The challenge in designing efficient caching systems is that in order to achieve a high hit ratio more resources need to be made available to that system to maintain connection states, and the management of these additional resources may limit scalability. As the system is loaded, we should ideally be looking for a fairly constant average response time until the load threshold of the system is reached; the response time should not oscillate as load is increased. At very high loads there will be internal system limitations that come into play (such as disk and memory access times). Some cache systems may also store content using off-the-shelf general-purpose file systems; this is likely to be a significant performance constraint. A dedicated high-performance caching system will almost certainly require a highly optimized storage system to minimize the number of disk seek and I/O operations per object. High-performance caches also query origin servers using asynchronous checks for content freshness, since synchronous checks would penalize response times. For further details of performance analysis and methodologies applicable for modeling Web performance, the interested reader is referred to [36].

Measurement techniques

Most network cache performance measurement techniques are derived from benchmarks designed for measuring Web server performance. They use synthetic workloads, assume that all objects are cacheable, and try to simulate, if not eliminate, the behavior of the Internet by using local servers and isolated networks. They focus on throughput only. A more realistic test tool is available from [37]. This test is end-user oriented and focuses on the Web page response time that users of a cache would experience. It measures this under different loads on the cache. It uses real workloads derived from traces collected at network access points and accesses objects live on the Internet (including approximately 2,500 URLs of popular business-oriented Web pages). The workloads are generated using URLs from existing Web proxy access logs. For these tests, we used workloads derived from the sanitized weekly access logs maintained by the National Laboratory for Applied Network Research (NLANR) [38].

Cache products

One of the best-known caches deployed on the Internet is Squid, a public domain UNIX tool maintained by the National Laboratory for Applied Network Research (NLANR). Squid caches Web and FTP content, as well as DNS lookups. It also supports hierarchical caching, allowing a group of caches to improve performance through cooperation. Several vendors sell commercial caching software, including CacheFlow [37] and Proxy Server from Netscape Communications Corp. (a Squid derivative). Proxy Server from Microsoft Corp. and Bordermanager from Novell, Inc. also support hierarchical caching. NNTP Cache, a freeware UNIX product, caches Usenet news.

7.5   Optimizing protocols

7.5.1   Frame and packet size

In packet-switched networks, packet size has a significant influence on throughput and efficiency. Smaller packets clearly incur more overhead than larger packets, since the ratio of protocol and encapsulation headers to actual user data is proportionally much higher. Therefore, the user data throughput of a link decreases as packet size decreases (even though the number of bytes passed over the link may be the same). The advantage of smaller packets in packet-switched networks is that they have a much better chance of getting through without error, and hence fewer retransmissions are likely. Line quality clearly plays an important part in deciding optimum packet size. On high-quality lines larger packets are less likely to become corrupted.

This phenomenon produces a bell-shaped curve [1]), where throughput increases as packet size increases but then begins to degrade. The optimum packet size is found to be the highest point in the curve. For example, an IP network suffers from low throughput with very small packet sizes but will also degrade when packet sizes are too large (due to fragmentation). The goal is to increase packet size to just below the point where fragmentation is needed and increase buffers accordingly to compensate for transmission delays. This will generally vary by packet service; in networks where each node must read an entire frame before transmission (Frame Relay, etc.), very large packets should be avoided. In many cases you will have to use trial and error. For example, you could start with a packet size of 1,500 bytes and measure performance as this value is increased or decreased.

When vendors document the throughput supported by their equipment, they often do so using the minimum packet size. While this may not be the most efficient data rate, it leads to the highest raw throughput numbers possible (usually expressed in Packet Per Second [PPS]). These numbers may bare no relation to the traffic characteristics of your network, so beware. Reference [39] suggests the following frame sizes to be used in throughput tests:

- Ethernet: 64, 128, 256, 512, 1,024, 1,280, 157 bytes
- Token Ring: 54, 64, 128, 256, 1,024, 157, 2,048, 4,472 bytes
- FDDI: 54, 64, 128, 256, 1,024, 157, 2,048, 4,472 bytes

7.5.2   Fragmentation

Fragmentation (sometimes called segmentation) occurs frequently in packet-switched internetworks and can be a significant factor in degrading performance. Fragmentation occurs when one media technology cannot support the Maximum Transmission Unit (MTU) of another, in which case it must break up packets and insert the appropriate encapsulation for each fragment before forwarding. The remote end system typically has the responsibility of reassembling these smaller fragments, although intermediate devices such as routers or firewalls may also need to reassemble fragments for security reasons (some security attacks attempt to conceal malicious activity within fragments). Clearly, this additional encapsulation overhead and the increase in the number of packets transmitted decrease overall throughput and add both latency and additional bandwidth overheads to the network. As a consequence, applications that routinely generate very large packets (such as NFS) may exhibit poor performance and occasionally time out, due to excessive delays and subsequent retransmissions (wasting yet more bandwidth). Where possible, set higher-level protocols and applications to limit their MTU to the maximum packet size supported on the network. This may compromise the efficiency of these applications on local networks, but this may be an acceptable trade-off. For the interested reader, [40] provides a formal analysis of optimal fragmentation algorithms in computer networks.

7.5.3   Window sizes

Connection-oriented protocols often use the concept of a window to enable the transmission of multiple packets in sequence before requiring an acknowledgment. This is inherently more efficient than requiring a separate acknowledgment for each packet transmitted, as long as all packets within the window reach their destination intact. The larger the window size, the more system resources are consumed at the receiver, since the recipient must buffer and check all packets in the sequence until the receive window is filled, at which point an acknowledgment can be sent. Theoretically, the optimal window size can be expressed as:

WindowSize = CircuitBandwidth × CircuitDelay

To maximize throughput the transmit window should be large enough to fill the pipe with data completely before stopping and waiting for an acknowledgment. In packet-switched internetworks, protocol window sizes are often tuned at packet-switched nodes (such as routers) to meet the characteristics of the circuit media. Broadly speaking window size can be increased on reliable networks (such as high-speed fiber-optic links with low Bit Error Rates [BER]) and decreased on less reliable networks (such as analog leased lines or X.25 PSNs). Large windows are usually a bad idea on low-speed links or links with potentially high bit error rates, since packet loss or timeouts may result in frequent retransmissions and could dramatically degrade performance.

Some protocols monitor session throughput and will automatically adjust window sizes, timers, and retransmission attempts to suit. For example, TCP will dynamically adjust both its transmit and receive window sizes based on throughput using a number of well-documented mechanisms. As a general rule window size should not be modified without a thorough understanding of the circuit quality and buffering capabilities on the intermediate network. Setting the wrong window size could be disastrous. In cases where performance problems are observed, you could potentially identify performance problems elsewhere in the network by examining changes in TCP window size within a detailed packet trace.

7.5.4 Tuning TCP/IP

TCP/IP is a general-purpose protocol suite and, therefore, it may be possible to tune up and improve performance on mission- or business-critical resources such as network servers. There are several factors that affect TCP/IP application performance, as follows:

- Every TCP connection starts with a three-way handshake (SYN, SYN-ACK, ACK) and this can take 500 ms or more to complete (depending on the length and characteristics of the end-to-end path). All TCP applications require that a session be established before user data can be transferred.

- TCP also uses a sliding window algorithm for efficient bulk data transfer. The loss of even one TCP packet in the window sequence requires the whole block of data to be retransmitted.

- TCP's built-in slow-start algorithm, intended to cut down on congestion and traffic spikes, has the effect of degrading throughput by effectively dampening TCP's ability to transfer data rapidly at session start up.

- TCP's Nagle algorithm [41] is designed to reduce small packet traffic by batching small packets for a round-trip time; under some circumstances, there can be a waiting period of 200 ms before data are transmitted.

Since applications such as Web browsing or FTP can involve dozens of connections, connection latency is incurred by each new session. The Nagle algorithm can also impact applications that require near real-time feedback such as some X-Windows applications (and may be disabled by setting the TCP_NODELAY flag via the Socket API).

Of particular importance is TCP's behavior in response to packet loss. When a TCP sender detects a dropped segment, it retransmits that segment and then adjusts its transmission rate to half of what it was previously by going into slow start. Although this back-off behavior is responsive to congestion, problems occur when many TCP sessions are affected simultaneously, as is the case with tail drop in overloaded routers. This situation can be improved using techniques such as RED gateways, as discussed in section 7.2.3.

Tunable parameters

With most TCP/IP implementations (including Windows 95, 98, and NT and Solaris v2) there are a few parameters you should be able to override default settings for, including the following:

- IP Maximum Transmission Unit (MTU)—determines the maximum packet size.

- TCP Maximum Segment Size (MSS)—determines the maximum segment size.

- IP Path MTU Discovery (PMTUD)—a probe algorithm that may be disabled or enabled.

- TCP window size—not normally configurable by the user, but some applications may change default settings.

In some cases it may actually be necessary to change these values if problems are encountered with data transfers involving maximum sized packets (where data transfers with short packet lengths work fine). If sessions hang or time out, then it is likely that there is a problem due to fragmentation or inconsistent MTU sizes within the network. Often this is observed as a unidirectional problem, with large data transfers succeeding in one direction but failing in the other. This can be a particular problem where mixed-media bridging is deployed, where different MTU sizes are configured and there is no capability to fragment (FDDI to Ethernet or Ethernet to Token Ring). Another potential problem could occur when a router interface

MTU is set correctly, but the router cannot forward datagrams of that size over the interface (perhaps due to buffering limitations, a malfunctioning CSU/DSU/modem, bad cable, or software/firmware failures). In this case the router may generate any useful ICMP messages, because the states that trigger such events are not entered. Finally, tunneling protocols such as GRE and L2TP introduce additional packet overheads on links that may not be taken into account when configuring MTU sizes.

TCP MSS and IP MTU

The TCP Maximum Segment Size (MSS) parameter specifies the maximum amount of TCP data in a single IP datagram that the local system can accept (i.e., specifically the maximum amount of data it is willing to reassemble). Theoretically, the MSS could be as large as 65,495, but in practice it is usually much lower to avoid fragmentation (hosts typically subtract 40 bytes from the MTU of the output interface to calculate the MSS, where 40 is the combined size of an IPv4 and TCP header). For example, the MSS value for an Ethernet interface would typically be set to 1,460 bytes (i.e., 1,500 − 40). To set the maximum MSS to 1,460 on Solaris 2, for example, we would use the command $ ndd -set /dev/tcp tcp_mss_max 1,460.

Note that if the MSS is set larger than the MTU, then IP datagrams must be fragmented into several packets when transmitted. Receiving stations must be prepared to accept the same MSS size. Note also that if you change the interface MTU on a router or end station, then all systems connected to the same broadcast domain must be configured with consistent MTUs. If systems on the same broadcast domain use different MTUs, they may exhibit problems communicating (large packets are discarded if sent from stations with a larger MTU to stations with a smaller MTU).

PMTUD

Prior to Path MTU Discovery (PMTUD), the default MTU used by most IP systems was set to 576 bytes. This is the minimum size that must be supported by any IP node when communicating over different subnets and leads in many cases to throughput inefficiency, since often we could use much larger packets to transfer bulk data. PMTUD is an algorithm that attempts to maximize data transfer throughput by first discovering the largest IP datagram that may be sent without incurring fragmentation by probing the network. PMTUD is implemented in relatively new TCP/IP stacks and described in [42]. PMTUD works by setting the Don't Fragment (DF) flag in the IP header of a probe packet. Initially very large probes are sent, with the size being progressively reduced until a successful end-to-end transmission is achieved. Unsuccessful transmissions are indicated by the ICMP message Type 3, Code 4 (fragmentation needed and DF set), which is returned by intermediate routers along the path if the MTU of the next-hop interface will not support this packet size [43].

There are a number of scenarios where PMTUD will not work, and the IP sender will continue to use a large MTU with consequent retransmissions. Essentially these problems revolve around the need for PMTUD to see an explicit ICMP failure message to know the path MTU status. Some routers may not generate ICMP's errors, or intermediate routers may discard ICMPs from farther upstream. There are also potential host stack problems where received ICMP messages may be misinterpreted or filtered before PMTUD can process them. In these cases you will need to disable PMTUD on the sending stations. To disable PMTUD on Solaris 2, for example, we would use the command `$ ndd -set /dev/ip ip_path_mtu_discovery 0`. This causes the IP sender to send IP datagrams with the DF flag clear. This may result in fragmentation if the MSS value exceeds intermediate media MTU values, so it may also be beneficial to lower the MSS if fragmentation issues are evident.

TCP window size

Generally it is not possible to configure TCP window sizes from the user's interface; it may be an option available to programmers wishing to optimize performance if they have direct access to the stack. Reference [44], for example, illustrates the potential for larger window sizes than the standard TCP window of 65,535 bytes, when TCP is used over very high–speed pipes with long delays (e.g., high-bandwidth satellite channels and long-distance transcontinental fiber-optic links).

In recent years there have been some innovative approaches to these problems, including plug-in Web server and browser software, which reduces handshaking latency by transmitting data in the first TCP packet of a connection and selectively retransmits only dropped packets in a sequence rather than the whole window. These modifications are reported to boost Web browsing performance by a factor of three or more. They might also assist transaction-based services, such as credit card authorization (where short data messages could be sent as part of the connection request and the session could be quickly terminated—rather like X.25's expedited data facility). The disadvantage is that they require special software to be installed on all server and client platforms.

7.6   Optimizing storage

For the last two decades storage space has been both limited and relatively expensive; hard disks, for example, have been largely restricted to the MB range on all but very large mainframes. However, memory and media costs have continued to fall, to the point where today's laptop computers are available with over 80 GB of disk storage and over 64 MB of main memory. With front- and back-office applications generating huge amounts of critical data, storage management has become a high priority for enterprise administrators and network designers.

Traditionally, data have been stored locally on application, file, and database servers. On these systems, there is a loose hierarchy of storage components, in terms of expense, speed, and the average volume of data stored. We can rank each component in descending order of speed and decreasing cost per MB as follows:

- CPU registers
- Cache memory
- Main memory
- Extended memory
- Fast hard disk
- Slow (or compressed) hard disk
- Tape or optical library
- Vaulted tape (offline)

Clearly, the storage components with the fastest access time are typically the most expensive. In order to optimize data access time, the general theory is to place the most volatile (frequently accessed) data into higher-speed storage components. However, cost constraints mean that it is highly unlikely that all useful data could be placed in memory, so the current focus is on high-speed bulk disk storage solutions for the majority of applications. In fact, a combination of fast disks, compressed disks, and an automated tape library are commonly employed to provide a complete storage solution.

7.6.1   Disk compression techniques

Disk compression techniques are effective, useful, and widely available. Compression increases the apparent capacity of disks by encoding the data to take up less physical space. Disk compression may be performed in hardware (by a disk controller) or via software. In the latter case compression will require resources from the system CPU and is normally done in the background. Current techniques achieve an average of 2:1 compression ratio and up to 4:1 depending on the type of data. Although compression and decompression are transparent to applications, there is typically a small performance hit. Performance for compressed disks is generally slower than for noncompressed disks, especially for sequential write applications. In effect, disk compression allows the network designer to trade performance for storage at a lower cost per megabyte. When deploying disk compression, it is important to scope out the performance bounds through thorough testing.

7.6.2   Hierarchical Storage Management (HSM)

In practice the great majority of online data is used infrequently. Given that storage space is at a premium and archiving is a lengthy process that often renders the network unusable for several hours, it makes sense to organize data in such a way that space is optimized and to automate backup procedures so that they are both transparent and unobtrusive to network users. Any new methodology must also address the basic user requirements for data; critical data need to be available quickly, data that are required to be available for extended periods must be archived, and mechanisms must be in place to prevented data loss. Hierarchical Storage Management (HSM) is a powerful method of classifying and managing data according to use patterns in order to better optimize storage. In broad terms three classes of data can be defined, as follows:

- Level 1: Online material—where data must be immediately accessible on a 24/7 basis.

- Level 2: Near-line material—which must be accessed periodically, but not necessarily immediately or 24/7.

- Level 3: Offline material—historical archives that are accessed infrequently but may be required to comply with legal, business, or security policy rules.

Level 1 material is normally held directly on the server. Level 2 material is migrated to a storage device such as a Magnet-Optical (MO) disk jukebox or tape library. Level 3 material is typically held in a tape storage library and stored offline in a vault (ideally fireproof). In practice both tape and optical libraries offer data recovery in the order of a few minutes, although data transfer rates for tape tend to be higher than for optical at present. An HSM server uses policy rules set by the network administrator to decide how data should be made available, and data are migrated transparently to the appropriate storage mechanism. The network administrator should ideally be able to set high watermarks so that critical online storage is managed dynamically, with less frequently accessed data migrated off the server in peak periods. Data may be statistically monitored to allow frequently used data to automatically move to faster storage and seldom used data to move to slower storage. As a general rule, data are not migrated until they are backed up.

Some HSM systems offer file tracking, which is integrated with directory services and operating system services (such as Novell's NDS). This can enable file pointers to be updated so that they remain consistent regardless of the data location. Other systems provide file stubs, which are managed in a separate database. IBM OS/400, for example, supports Media and Storage Extensions (MSE) and supports dynamic data retrieval [IBM]. From the user's perspective all files appear to be available; some just take longer to access than others since they are migrated from different storage devices to the server on demand. In effect, HSM operates like an intelligent caching system. Using HSM it is not unusual to reduce server storage demands to less than 5 percent of previous storage requirements. Aside from optimizing and consolidating precious server storage space, this data management technique can dramatically reduce backup times, which in turn increases network availability.

7.6.3 NAS and SANs storage strategies

Currently there are three main ways in which bulk storage is implemented, as follows:

- Server attached storage—Disk drives and other persistent storage media are installed directly in application, file, and database servers, typically via interfaces such as IDE and SCSI. The traditional way of increasing storage is to add another disk or a larger server. This legacy solution has served the industry well for many years but does not scale and increases the Total Cost of Ownership (TCO). Since storage is not managed holistically at the enterprise level, there is likely to be substantial spare capacity that is effectively wasted.

- Network Attached Storage (NAS)—NAS systems connect to the network using traditional LAN protocols such as Ethernet and TCP/IP. The system typically has an IP and/or other network address. NAS systems include intelligent disk arrays, online tape backup devices, or

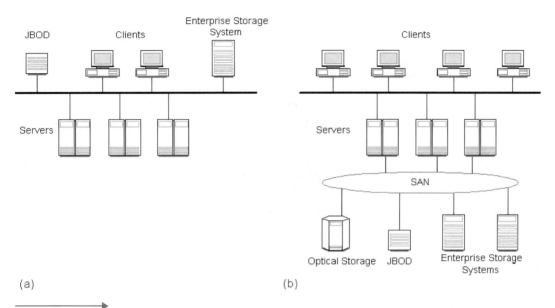

(a)   (b)

Figure 7.16   *(a) Network Attached Storage (NAS), and (b) Storage Attached Network (SAN) topologies.*

Just a Bunch of Disks (JBOD) connected to a network controller. See Figure 7.16(a).

- Storage Attached Networks (SANs)—SANs separate storage devices from processing devices (servers or mainframes) via dedicated, high-speed Enterprise Systems Connection (ESCON) and Fibre Connection (FICON) [45]; Fiber Channel; and SCSI links. See Figure 7.16(b).

Note in Figure 7.16 that although the NAS network is traditionally easier to manage and deploy, all storage-related traffic is inline with user traffic, wasting valuable bandwidth and degrading overall network performance. In the SAN topology all storage-related traffic is offloaded to a private network, improving both data and network access speeds.

With the increased use of multimedia and the reliance on mission- and business-critical applications, such as e-business, Customer Relationship Management (CRM), Sales Force Automation (SFA), and Enterprise Resource Planning (ERP), large enterprises are now deploying bulk storage in the terabyte range. Storage requirements for these large organizations are predicted to increase to tens and even hundreds of terabytes over the next few years. In order to facilitate high availability at this level, application and database servers are typically located at different sites, with all critical data mirrored between them. To provide scalability, load balancing is configured across the cluster, with high-speed optical fiber between sites.

7.6.4 Optical Storage Networks (OSN)

Current wide area network solutions provided by legacy operators are perceived to be bandwidth poor, very expensive, and slow to deploy, particularly as viewed by large enterprises. Companies are either suffering these inadequacies or installing their own private fiber links between sites. Neither situation is sustainable, because the demands for bandwidth are escalating, and the need to manage, optimize, and consolidate storage over this infrastructure represents a significant cost and maintenance burden for many organizations.

The potential of optical networks has been predicted for years, and with the emergence of new DWDM equipment that is both protocol and bit rate independent and the substantial increase in fiber-optic cable deployments, there is now a real foundation for a high-performance network infrastructure. Optical Storage Networks (OSN) employ DWDM technology as a wide area transport backbone to connect high-speed servers and storage components. This enables organizations to consolidate ESCON, Fiber Channel, and 100/1,000 Ethernet circuits onto the same optical fiber (by multiplexing feeds at different wavelengths). OSNs also offer the potential to aggregate voice, data, and storage networking traffic on a single, high-bandwidth, fiber-optic infrastructure that spans campus, metropolitan, and intercity networks. It is likely that this will be offered as a managed service through a combination of Storage Service Providers (SSPs) and Optical Service Providers (OSPs).

The evolution of OSNs and increased deployment of Fibre Channel are likely to have a significant impact on enterprise storage strategies over the next decade. As such, network planners should pay particular attention to the design of Fibre Channel SANs to ensure that they have a clear migration path to OSN in the future. Once OSNs are deployed, organizations may begin to consider the possibilities of extending the advantages of optical networking to traditional data network applications. Since an OSN is effectively a high-speed private WAN backbone, it could, for example, be used to support applications such as distributed server clustering (server-to-server protocols could be directed across the OSN rather than in-band). OSNs might also be useful for out-of-band management applications; this would, for example, enable the network to be monitored and configured even if the main backbone is offline.

7.7 Summary

We have seen that there is a confusing arsenal of tools available to assist in improving internetwork performance—some standard and some proprietary. Many of these solutions can be used together to good effect, although you should exercise caution and ensure that the solutions used are complementary. It is especially important as part of any optimization process to first baseline the network, identify potential bottlenecks, and only then begin to change operating parameters.

In this chapter, we also discussed the following:

- Routing and addressing hierarchy is key for large-scale internetwork design. It is critical that router performance is optimized and that valuable WAN bandwidth is preserved by using features such as route summarization where possible.

- Load splitting and clustering techniques are often the only effective way to provide scalability for CPU-intensive devices such as firewalls and Web servers.

- Caching is a generic technique that is used in many areas of IT. The principal theme of caching is to localize copies of information that are used frequently, in order to minimize the number of remote transactions and reduce latency. Caching has become especially important as a way of improving performance for Web-based applications.

- Bandwidth managers and load balancers play complementary roles. Proxy servers such as Squid work with any of these technologies.

- There could be potential conflicts between standalone bandwidth managers and routers that implement their own prioritization and queuing techniques. Some bandwidth managers, for example, claim that by shaping traffic they prevent router prioritization routines from ever being invoked in the first place, thus avoiding any conflicts.

- Data compression is a good generic technique for use on low-bandwidth wide area links (typically below 2 Mbps). It may be implemented in hardware or software. It is also applicable for optimizing storage media such as hard disks.

- Storage is becoming a critical resource for large-scale enterprise networks. Techniques such as Hierarchical Storage Management (HSM), Network Attached Storage (NAS), Storage Attached Networks (SANs), and Optical Storage Networks (OSNs) are increasingly being deployed to solve the space and performance problems associated with managing and moving terabytes of data over today's networks.

References

[1]   T. Kenyon, *High-Performance Network Design: Design Techniques and Tools* (Woburn, MA: Digital Press, 2001).

[2]   R. Jain, *The Art of Computer Systems Performance Analysis* (New York: John Wiley & Sons, 1991).

[3]   L. Chappell, *Novell's Guide to NetWare LAN Analysis* (Alameda, CA: Sybex, Inc., 1993).

[4]   G. S. Sidhu, R. F. Andrews, and A. B. Oppenheimer, *Inside Apple-Talk* (Reading, MA: Addison-Wesley, 1993).

[5]   M. A. Weiss, *Data Structures and Algorithm Analysis in C,* 2nd ed. (Reading, MA: Addison-Wesley, 1997).

[6]   A. Lempel and J. Ziv, "A Universal Algorithm for Sequential Data Compression," *IEEE Transactions on Information Theory,* vol. IT-23, No. 3, May 1977.

[7]   PPP Stac LZS Compression Protocol, RFC 1974, August 1996.

[8]   www.itu.ch, The International Telecommunications Union (ITU) home page.

[9]   Compressing TCP/IP Headers for Low-Speed Serial Links, RFC 1144.

[10]   The PPP Compression Control Protocol (CCP), RFC 1962, July 1996.

[11]   D. Saloman, *Data Compression The Complete Reference* (New York: Springer-Verlag, 1998).

[12]   L. Kleinrock, *Queuing Systems*, vol. 2: *Computer Applications* (New York: Wiley Interscience, 1975).

[13]   S. Keshav, *An Engineering Approach to Computer Networking* (Reading, MA: Addison-Wesley, 1997).

[14]   ftp.ee.lbl.gov/floyd/cbq.html, The CBQ Web page—useful links to papers and source code for CBQ.

[15]   ftp://ftp.ee.lbl.gov/papers/admit.ps.Z, Comments on measurement-based admissions control for controlled-load services.

[16]   ftp.ee.lbl.gov/floyd/cbq.html, Notes on CBQ and guaranteed service.

[17] R. Jain and K. K. Ramakrishnan, "Congestion Avoidance in Computer Networks with a Connectionless Network Layer: Concepts, Goals, and Methodology," in Proceedings of the IEEE Computer Networking Symposium, Washington, DC, April 1988.

[18] K. K. Ramakrishnan and R. Jain, "A Binary Feedback Scheme for Congestion Avoidance in Computer Networks," *ACM Transactions on Computer Systems*, vol. 8, no. 2, 1990.

[19] S. Floyd and V. Jacobson, "Random Early Detection Gateways for Congestion Avoidance," *IEEE/ACM Transactions on Networking*, August 1993.

[20] S. Floyd and K. Fall, "Router Mechanisms to Support End-to-End Congestion Control," in *Proceedings of SIGCOMM '97*, 1997.

[21] www-nrg.ee.lbl.gov/floyd/, Sally Floyd home page; excellent links for research papers on congestion avoidance and queuing strategies.

[22] P. Albitz, and C. Liu, *DNS and BIND* (Cambridge MA: O'Reilly & Associates, 1997).

[23] www.isc.org, The Internet Software Consortium Web site—contains source for the BIND application.

[24] Domain Names—Concepts and Facilities, RFC 1034, November 1987.

[25] Domain Names—Implementation and Specification, RFC 1035, November 1987.

[26] DNS Extensions to Support IP Version 6, RFC 786, December 1995.

[27] DNS Support for Load Balancing, RFC 1794, April 1995.

[28] Ethernet Address Resolution Protocol: Converting Network Protocol Addresses to 48.bit Ethernet Addresses for Transmission on Ethernet Hardware, RFC 826, November 1982.

[29] The IP Network Address Translator (NAT), RFC 1631, May 1994.

[30] Load Sharing Using IP Network Address Translation (LSNAT), RFC2391, August 1998.

[31] Internet Cache Protocol (ICP), Version 2, RFC 276, September 1997.

[32] Application of Internet Cache Protocol (ICP), Version 2, RFC 277, September 1997.

[33] Network News Transfer Protocol, RFC 977, February 1986.

[34] Cisco Web Cache Control Protocol V1.0. Internet Draft draft-ietf-wrec-web-pro-00.txt, June 1999.

[35] Hyper Text Caching Protocol (HTCP/0.0), RFC 2756, January 2000. (Experimental).

[36] D. A. Menasce and A. F. Almeida, *Capacity Planning for Web Performance* (Englewood Cliffs, NJ: Prentice Hall, 1998).

[37] www.cacheflow.com, Caheflow home Web site—useful white papers on caching technology.

[38] ftp://ircache.nlanr.net/Traces/, Weekly access log files maintained by the National Laboratory for Applied Network Research (NLANR).

[39] Benchmarking Methodology for Network Interconnect Devices, RFC 2544, March 1999.

[40] A. Orda and R. Rom, "Optimal Packet Fragmentation in Computer Networks," Department of Electrical Engineering, Technion—Israel Institute of Technology, Haifa, Israel, March 1994.

[41] Congestion Control in IP/TCP Internetworks, RFC 896, January 1984.

[42] Path MTU Discovery, RFC 1191, November 1990.

[43] Internet Control Message Protocol, RFC 792, September 1981.

[44] TCP Extensions for High Performance, RFC 1323, May 1992.

[45] www.ibm.com, IBM home Web site.

8

Quality of Service

This chapter discusses Quality of Service (QoS) and the related subject of traffic engineering. QoS is becoming increasingly important for both private intranets and the Internet and is beginning to have a fundamental affect on the way we design networks, particularly large public networks like the Internet. It is notable that the long-term requirement for QoS mechanisms is a hotly debated topic. It is proposed in some quarters that the increased use of fiber optics, together with Wavelength Division Multiplexing (WDM), will make bandwidth so abundant and inexpensive in the future that QoS will be redundant. Unfortunately, experience tells us that these benefits rarely get passed on to users quickly, if at all, since many service providers still operate virtual monopolies in many regions of the world. We are likely to require more QoS features for the foreseeable future. Although this chapter is concerned with service quality, in reality most IP internetworks today provide only one class of service, called best effort (which essentially means no guarantees for delivery, bandwidth, or response times). In effect, all traffic has the same priority. Over the last decade use of the Internet has increased dramatically for both private and business users. The commercial use of the Internet in particular is a key driver for the implementation of end-to-end service guarantees for e-commerce and business-critical applications; this requires classification and special handling of packet streams at the session or flow level. Businesses are beginning to require tighter Service-Level Agreements (SLAs) from service providers to ensure smooth operations, availability, and guaranteed response times. The SLA comprises a set of parameters that specify such characteristics as bandwidth, buffer use, priority, and CPU use for different types of data.

Another important development is that as bandwidth has increased, so has the ability for application developers to make use of it with new innovative applications. The latest generation of real-time multimedia applications (e.g., interactive videoconferencing and audioconferencing) requires much tighter service guarantees than legacy applications such as FTP, Telnet, and e-mail. Legacy applications are relatively low-bandwidth consumers, fairly insensitive to variable delay (jitter), and do not tolerate packet loss. Real-time applications, on the other hand, are typically high-bandwidth consumers, will often compensate for a degree of packet loss, and are usually sensitive to jitter. Video is especially bandwidth intensive (high-quality video can demand tens of megabytes per seconds), while audio can be transferred over 64-Kbps channels with reasonable quality (CD-quality audio might consume up to 1 Mbps). With both the increase in legacy traffic and the emergence of a new generation of real-time applications, there is now a serious requirement to resolve contention intelligently, by providing defined assurances from the network. Finally, a relatively new application, Virtual Private Networks (VPNs), means that both business and private users will no longer make do with best-effort performance. Providing SLAs at the VPN level can be extremely difficult.

QoS makes no sense from the user perspective unless it is end to end, and in order to provide end-to-end service assurances to meet various application scenarios it is likely that several service classes will be required. One service class will provide predictable Internet services for organizations that do business on the Web. These organizations will be willing to pay more in order to ensure that their services are reliable and timely. This service class may be differentiated as a gold, silver, and bronze service, with decreasing quality and cost. Another service class will be geared toward real-time applications such as Internet telephony and videoconferencing, ensuring tight bounds on delay and jitter. It is likely that organizations will be willing to pay a premium for this service. The best-effort service will remain for those customers who need only connectivity. As we will see in this chapter, one of the most significant problems with providing true end-to-end QoS is that most internetworks are likely to comprise many disparate technologies. Mapping QoS requirements between many different LAN and WAN network technologies can be difficult at best and is likely to require additional protocol standards and a new generation of high-speed switching products. To this end we will discuss two broad architectures developed by the IETF for providing end-to-end QoS: differentiated services and integrated services (including the resource reservation protocol). We also discuss routing and switching enhancements necessary for traffic engineering and scalability, specifically constraint-based routing and multiprotocol label switching.

8.1   Quality-of-service models

QoS is not a new concept; several models have been proposed and implemented over the years to offer quality of service, with varying degrees of success. Often these mechanisms have been tied to specific media or offered as proprietary solutions by vendors. What has been conspicuously lacking until recently is an overall architecture for handling QoS on an end-to-end basis for traffic moving from private to public networks over a variety of media types. One of the other key stumbling blocks in the past was how to provide a generic QoS when there are multiple protocols to consider. Now we are beginning to see that IP has become pervasive enough to simplify this task. We can broadly classify these alternative models into the following categories:

- Service marking

- Label switching

- Integrated services/RSVP

- Static per hop classification

- Relative priority marking/differentiated services

These models are discussed briefly in this section. First we need to define how traffic is to be identified, since this is fundamental to the provision of any service level.

8.1.1   Traffic differentiation and flow handling

Over recent years there has been increasing emphasis on a more intelligent approach to dealing with IP datagram traffic. Datagrams are fine for delivery; however, to offer value-added services such as quality of service we need a higher-level view that can pick out individual packets and associate them with a particular session context. In reference [1] the concept of the packet train was introduced; a more widely used term for this association is flow.

Flows

So far we have mentioned the term "flow" without really defining it. A flow is an abstraction that is fundamental to several major technologies used in traffic engineering, switching, network security, and quality of service. It is useful to reflect on some of the definitions provided in the standards. Reference [2] defines a flow as follows: IP flow (or simply flow) is an IP packet stream from a source to a destination (unicast or multicast) with an associ-

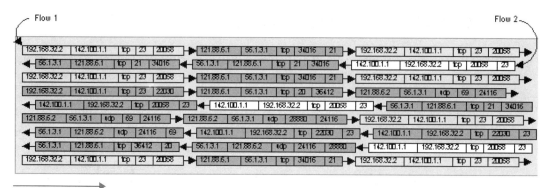

Figure 8.1   *Flow identification. Here we see two flows highlighted amidst background traffic.*

ated Quality of Service (QoS) and higher-level demultiplexing information. The associated QoS could be best effort.

Reference [3] defines a microflow as a single instance of an application-to-application flow of packets that is identified by source address, source port, destination address, destination port, and protocol ID.

We define a flow as a distinguishable stream of related datagrams that results from a single user activity and requires the same quality of service. For example, a flow might comprise a transport connection or a video stream between a specific host pair (see Figure 8.1). We define a flow to be simplex. Thus, an *N*-way teleconference will generally require *N* flows, one originating at each site. In order to provide scalable traffic engineering solutions, flows with similar service requirements may be combined to form an aggregated flow.

In practice there are many flows to consider, depending upon the level of granularity required. We could, for example, single out an individual FTP connection between two nodes by isolating flows at the TCP or UDP port level. For some applications it may be appropriate to use higher-level fields to identify flows. However, as granularity increases it becomes increasingly difficult to achieve flow classification efficiently in real time, especially if the fields of interest are not at fixed offsets (this is one area for vendor differentiation).

Once flows are identified the packets they contain can be handled in a manner consistent with policy rules. Currently the Internet handles IP packet forwarding in a fairly democratic manner; all packets effectively receive the same quality of service, since packets are typically forwarded using a strict FIFO queuing discipline. For new QoS models, such as integrated services, a router must be capable of identifying and implementing an appropriate service quality for each flow. This requires that routers support flow-specific states and represents a fundamental change to the Internet model (the Internet architecture was founded on the concept that all flow-related states should be a function of end systems [4]).

As indicated, recognizing flows in real time is not without its problems; it depends upon the protocols used; the presence of addressing, port, or Service Access Point (SAP) fields; and whether or not the system performing flow identification is smart enough to be stateful. For example, in Figure 8.1 there are UDP flows within the background traffic (specifically a TFTP session on port 69). TFTP illustrates a particular problem for flow identification, since it uses ports dynamically (the well-known port 69 is not used beyond the connection phase, and a new port is allocated from the pool). In order to identify all packets that form part of the same TFTP flow, stateful monitoring of session and recognition of events within the TFTP payload are required. When dynamic ports are used, it is necessary to track the session from the outset; otherwise, it may be impossible to determine the application type and the appropriate QoS. As we shall see later, flow states can be implemented as soft states in devices such as routers to provide transparency.

Flow handling

Within an intermediate system, such as a router, incoming traffic needs to be unambiguously sorted so that it can be handled appropriately. For example, if SAP traffic from a particular network is to be given dedicated bandwidth and assigned a certain priority, then this traffic needs to be separated from the mass of incoming packets and then queued and scheduled for release to meet the policy objectives. To achieve all this we need specialized system components, each with a clearly delineated responsibility, as follows:

- Admission control

- Packet classifier

- Packet scheduler

Figure 8.2 illustrates how the various flow-handling components interwork in a generic system.

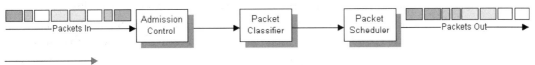

Figure 8.2   *Integrated services model for a host and a route.*

Admission control

When a packet arrives at an interface (e.g., a router wide area port), it may need to convince admission control that it should be given special treatment. Admission control contains the decision algorithm that a device uses to determine if there are sufficient resources to accept the requested QoS for a new flow. If there are not enough free resources, accepting that flow could impact earlier guarantees, so the new flow must either be rejected (in the IS model) or handled on a best-effort basis (with some feedback mechanism to inform the sender). If the new flow is accepted, then the packet classifier and packet scheduler are configured to handle this new flow so that the requested QoS can be realized.

Packet classifier

A classifier is a component of a system that defines how the system should sort incoming traffic (packets, frames, or cells) into appropriate groups in order that they can be scheduled with the appropriate service level. For example, a classifier could be used to differentiate real-time traffic from non–real-time traffic, multicast traffic from unicast traffic, TCP for UDP traffic, or traffic based on specific ToS settings. Classifiers can be broadly divided into two types, as follows:

- Flow classifiers—are applicable to IP unicast and multicast traffic only, typically using criteria such as the IP protocol number, IP source-destination address/mask, and source-destination port number (or range of ports). On a system where multiple classifiers are implemented, there needs to be a method of determining which classifier has preference if the packet classification data are sufficiently ambiguous to be handled by more than one controlled classifier. For example, classifiers can be numbered so that the lower-numbered classifier takes preference if there is a conflict.

- Nonflow classifiers—are applicable to both switched and routed traffic, and operate using criteria such as the protocol type (e.g., IP = 0x0800), a cast type (unicast, multicast, or broadcast), or IEEE 802.1p priority tag values (as described later).

For the purpose of this chapter we are primarily interested in flow classifiers. Since much of the data-networking world is now exclusively IP-oriented, considerable research and development effort is focused on IP packet classification. Flow classifiers are divided into different types, depending upon the service model implemented (e.g., in the IS model, classifiers are divided into multifield and behavior aggregate classifiers; these are described later in this chapter). Nonflow classifiers are appropriate for switched VLANs, multiprotocol LANs, and local area networks where protocol stacks do not support Layer 3 information (e.g., DEC LAT traffic).

The flow classifier identifies packets of an IP flow in hosts and routers that will receive a certain level of service. To realize effective traffic control, each incoming packet is mapped by the classifier into a specific traffic class. All packets that are classified in the same class get the same treatment from the packet scheduler. The choice of a class is based upon the source and destination IP address and port number in the existing packet header or an additional classification number, which must be added to each packet. A class can correspond to a broad category of flows. For example, all video flows from a videoconference with several participants can belong to one service class. But it is also possible that only one flow belongs to a specific service class.

Packet scheduler

The packet scheduler manages the forwarding of different flows in hosts and routers, based on their service class, using queue management and various scheduling algorithms. The packet scheduler must ensure that the packet delivery corresponds to the QoS parameter for each flow. A scheduler can also police or shape the traffic to conform to a certain level of service. The packet scheduler must be implemented at the point where packets are queued. This is typically the output driver level of an operating system and corresponds to the link layer protocol.

An early application of flows—IP switching

Ipsilon Networks, Inc. (now integrated into Nokia Telecommunications) raised a few eyebrows in the mid-1990s with an innovative technique, whereby IP sessions were mapped dynamically onto connection-oriented ATM VCs. This feature, called IP switching, enabled IP for the first time to benefit directly from ATM prioritization and QoS mechanisms. The basic idea was to route datagram IP traffic as normal, while monitoring traffic for any identifiable flows. Note that Ipsilon's definition of a flow is "a sequence of IP packets sent from a particular source to a particular destination sharing the same protocol type, type of service, and other characteristics as determined by information in the packet header."

Flows are classified as long-lived and short-lived. Table 8.1 illustrates some typical examples. Once a flow is identified, an ATM VC can be established dynamically, and this identified flow is then taken out of the routing path and switched directly over the ATM VC.

Table 8.1 *Typical Flow-Oriented Traffic From the Types of Data That Normally Do Not Qualify as a Flow*

Long-Lived Flows	Short-Lived Flows
FTP Data	DNS Query
Telnet Data	SMTP Data
HTTP Data	NTP
Web Image Downloads	POP
Multimedia (audio/video)	SNMP

Ipsilon's implementation requires two hardware devices: an IP switch (incorporating an ATM fabric) and a switch controller (a fairly standard UNIX routing platform incorporating flow classification software). IP switching operates as follows:

- At system startup, each IP node sets up a virtual channel on each of its ATM physical links to be used as the default-forwarding channel.

- An ATM input port on the IP switch receives incoming traffic from the upstream device on the default channel and forwards it to the IP switch controller.

- The IP switch controller forwards packets over the default-forwarding channel. It also performs flow classification to assess suitability for switching out of the slow routed path. Short-lived flows, or unidentified packet streams, are ignored and continue to be forwarded using hop-by-hop store-and-forward routing.

- Once a long-lived flow is identified (e.g., an FTP session), the switch controller asks the upstream node to label that traffic using a new virtual channel.

- If the upstream node concurs, the traffic starts to flow on the new virtual channel. Independently, the downstream node also can ask the IP switch controller to set up an outgoing virtual channel for the flow.

- When the flow is isolated to a particular input and output channel, the IP switch controller instructs the switch to make the appropriate port mapping in hardware, bypassing the routing software and its associated processing overhead. Long duration flows are thus switched out of the slow routing path (using cut-through switching) and mapped directly onto ATM SVCs.

This design enables IP switches to forward packets at rates limited only by the aggregate throughput of the underlying switching engine. First-generation IP switches supported up to 5.3 million pages per second throughput, and since there is no need to reassemble ATM cells into IP packets at intermediate switches, throughput remains optimized throughout the IP network.

The technology introduced by Ipsilon is now obsolete (largely due to a lack of mindshare rather than respect for the technology and the fact that the technique was also ATM specific). Cisco recognized the potential threat this technology posed to its market dominance and countered strongly with its own technology, tag switching. Tag switching [5] classifies traffic by inserting special tag fields into packets as they enter the ingress to the backbone. Tags specify QoS requirements such as minimum bandwidth or maximum latency. Once a packet is tagged it can be switched through the network quickly without being reclassified. At the egress point the tag is removed by another tag-switching router. Cisco's implementation is currently available only in its high-end product lines (such as the 7000 series routers and BPX switches), and to some extent this has slowed deployment, since these are not edge devices. As discussed later in this chapter, the IETF is developing a standards-based tagging scheme called MultiProtocol Label Switching (MPLS), a superset of tag switching and related technologies such as the Ipsilon IP switching. MPLS incorporates scalability features such as flow aggregation onto large trunks. Both tag switching and MPLS require routers and switches to maintain flow state information, and this requires massive amounts of switch memory for backbone links. Nevertheless MPLS is a key technology for the future and is of particular interest for backbone scalability and virtual private networking.

Standard models for ensuring consistent behavior

The purpose of these components is to collectively enable an individual device (such as a router) to comply with policy based on the Service-Level Agreement (SLA) contracted between the user and the service provider. One piece that is missing here is how to coordinate multiple devices in a network so that they all behave consistently when dealing with incoming traffic. There are a number of fundamentally different approaches to this problem, including the following:

- The original IP model uses simple service marking via the Type of Service (ToS) field to indicate how the flow should be handled. IPv6 implements relative priority marking.

- The differentiated services model uses relative priority marking to enable recipients to clearly identify the class of traffic received.

- The integrated service model uses explicit signaling protocol to reserve resources across a network of routers in advance of sending data.

- Label switching, as implemented by ATM and MPLS, is used to set up virtual circuits, where the QoS state is maintained for the duration of the circuit.

We now briefly review these various models.

8.1.2   Service marking

Simple service marking model

An example of a service marking model is IPv4 Type of Service (ToS), as defined in [6], and illustrated in Figure 8.3. With IPv4 ToS, an application could mark each packet with a request for a particular type of service, which could include requests to minimize delay, maximize throughput, maximize reliability, or minimize cost. Intermediate network nodes may select routing paths or forwarding behaviors that are engineered to satisfy this service request.

The precedence field in IPv4 is defined in [6] as follows:

111—Network Control   11—Flash

110—Internetwork Control   010—Immediate

101—CRITIC/ECP   001—Priority

100—Flash Override   000—Routine

The ToS bits in IPv4 are defined in [6] as follows:

Bit 3:   0 = Normal Delay   1 = Low Delay

Bit 4:   0 = Normal Throughput   1 = High Throughput

Bit 5:   0 = Normal Reliability   1 = High Reliability

Bits 6–7:   Reserved for Future Use

Reference [7] redefines the use of the ToS bits to single enumerated values rather than as a set of bits each with specific meaning. It also assigns bit 6 for ToS applications, as follows:

xxx1000:   minimize delay

xxx0100:   maximize throughput

xxx0010:   maximize reliability

xxx0001:   minimize monetary cost

xxx0000:   normal service

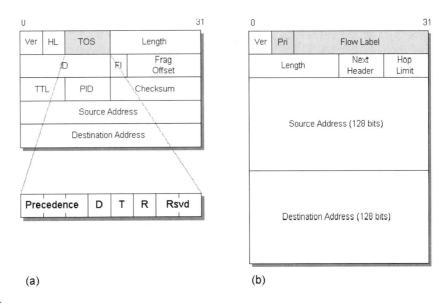

Figure 8.3   *IPv4 and IPv6 QoS-related fields.*

This model is subtly different from the relative priority marking model offered by IPv6. The ToS markings defined in [8] are very generic and do not span the range of possible service semantics. Furthermore, the service request is associated with each individual packet, whereas some service semantics may depend on the aggregate forwarding behavior of a sequence of packets (a flow). The service-marking model does not easily accommodate growth in the number and range of future services (since the codepoint space is small) and involves configuration of the ToS forwarding behavior association in each core network node. Standardizing service markings implies standardizing service offerings, which is outside the scope of the IETF. Note that provisions are made in the allocation of the Differentiated Services (DS) codepoint to allow for locally significant codepoints, which may be used by a provider to support service-marking semantics.

IPv6 class of service model

IPv6 incorporates two major enhancements to support Class of Service (CoS): traffic differentiation field and the flow label, as follows:

- Traffic differentiation: IPv6 is able to differentiate two traffic types: congestion controlled and noncongestion controlled. Congestion-controlled traffic tolerates delays in the face of network congestion (e.g., File Transfer Protocol—FTP). Non-congestion-controlled traffic requires a smooth delivery under any load (e.g., isochronous content such as streaming audio and video where there would be tight constraints on jitter).

8.1.3 Label switching

Examples of the label-switching (or virtual circuit) model include Frame Relay [9], ATM [10], and MPLS. In this model path forwarding state and traffic management or QoS state is established for traffic streams on each hop along a network path. Traffic aggregates of varying granularity are associated with a label-switched path at an ingress node, and packets or cells within each label-switched path are marked with a forwarding label that is used to look up the next-hop node, the per hop forwarding behavior, and the replacement label at each hop. This model permits finer granularity resource allocation to traffic streams, since label values are not globally significant but are only significant on a single link. Resources can, therefore, be reserved for the aggregate of packets or cells received on a link with a particular label, and the label-switching semantics govern the next-hop selection, allowing a traffic stream to follow a specially engineered path through the network. This improved granularity comes at the cost of additional management and configuration requirements to establish and maintain the label-switched paths. In addition, the amount of forwarding state maintained at each node scales in proportion to the number of edge nodes of the network in the best case (assuming multipoint-to-point label-switched paths), and it scales in proportion with the square of the number of edge nodes in the worst case, when edge-edge label-switched paths with provisioned resources are employed.

8.1.4 Integrated services and RSVP

Integrated Services (IS) builds upon the Internet's best-effort model with support for real-time transmission and guaranteed bandwidth for specific traffic flows. A flow is an identifiable stream of datagrams from a unique sender to a unique receiver (e.g., a Telnet session over TCP or a TFTP session over UDP). In most applications two flows are necessary (one in each direction). Applications that initiate flows can specify the required QoS (bandwidth, maximum packet delay, etc.).

The integrated services model relies upon traditional datagram forwarding in the default case but allows senders and receivers to exchange signaling messages, which establish additional packet classification and forwarding state on each node along the path between them [11]. In the absence of state aggregation, the amount of state on each node scales in proportion to the number of concurrent reservations, which can be potentially large on high-speed links. This model also requires application support for the Resource Reservation Protocol (RSVP) signaling protocol. Differentiated services mechanisms can be utilized to aggregate integrated services state in the core of the network [12].

A variation of the integrated services model eliminates the requirement for hop-by-hop signaling by utilizing only static classification and forwarding policies that are implemented in each node along a network path. These policies are updated on administrative time scales and not in response to the instantaneous mix of microflows active in the network. The state requirements for this variation are potentially worse than those encountered when RSVP is used, especially in backbone nodes, since the number of static policies that might be applicable at a node over time may be larger than the number of active sender-receiver sessions that might have installed reservation state on a node. Although the support of large numbers of classifier rules and forwarding policies may be computationally feasible, the management burden associated with installing and maintaining these rules on each node within a backbone network that might be traversed by a traffic stream is substantial.

8.1.5 Relative priority marking and differentiated services

Examples of the relative priority-marking model include IPv4 precedence marking as defined in [6], IEEE802.5 Token Ring priority [13], and the default interpretation of 802.1p traffic classes [14]. In this model the application, host, or proxy node selects a relative priority or precedence for a packet (e.g., delay or discard priority), and the network nodes along the transit path apply the appropriate priority forwarding behavior corresponding to the priority value within the packet header. The Differentiated Services (DiffServ, or DS) architecture can be thought of as a refinement to this model, since it more clearly specifies the role and importance of boundary nodes and traffic conditioners and since its per hop behavior model permits more general forwarding behaviors than relative delay or discard priority.

DiffServ is a much simpler and more scalable solution than the integrated services model, since it does require additional signaling protocol. With DiffServ, traffic entering a network is classified and possibly conditioned at the boundary, and then assigned to different behavior aggregates. DiffServ uses the existing Type of Service (ToS) field in the IPv4 header [8]. Bits in this field have been reallocated by DiffServ to characterize the service characteristics required (in terms of delay, throughput, and packet loss). DiffServ specifies how the network should treat each packet on a hop-by-hop basis, using the ToS field. The ToS field is marked at the edge (access point) of the network by Customer Premises Equipment (CPE), such as routers. Since DiffServ operates at Layer 3, it can work transparently over any Layer 2 transport (ATM, Frame Relay, ISDN, etc.), and since it relies on embedded ToS marking, it places no additional burden on the network. Equipment that supports DiffServ needs to be able to interpret and act upon ToS settings in real time, and this does require additional CPU power. DiffServ is currently viewed as the most flexible method of supporting Virtual Private Networks (VPNs), when used in combination with traffic engineering mechanisms such as MultiProtocol Label Switching (MPLS).

8.1.6   Vendor approaches to QoS

Equipment manufacturers have taken a number of approaches to enable bandwidth policy management and service specifications at both the access point and the core. The QoS features, supported in hardware and/or software, can be broadly categorized as follows:

- Guaranteed bandwidth: A feature that enables a high probability that bandwidth will be available at all times. Excess traffic is discarded, delayed, or counted and billed.

- Committed information rate: A feature that allows a minimum amount of bandwidth to be guaranteed. Transmitters can send at a higher rate up to a specified maximum. Excess traffic is discarded, delayed, or counted and billed.

- Rate shaping: A feature that regulates bandwidth for a flow so that it does not exceed a specified maximum. Excess traffic is delayed.

- Expedited service: A feature that defines service classes. A customer's traffic is compared against the Service-Level Agreement (SLA). Excess traffic is discarded, delayed, or counted and billed.

- Congestion management: A feature that allows traffic policies to be specified, based on maximizing throughput during congestion conditions. Typically there is a precedence upon which packets are dropped.

- Resource reservation: A feature that enables end-to-end reservation of resources to guarantee service quality.

Table 8.2   *QoS Features Supported by Leading Networking Vendors*

Vendor	Guaranteed Bandwidth	Committed Info Rate	Rate Shaping	Expedited Service	Congestion Management	Resource Reservation
Cisco	yes	yes	yes	yes	yes	yes
Ascend	yes	yes	yes	yes	yes	yes
Lucent	yes	yes	yes	yes	yes	yes
Bay Networks	yes	yes	yes	yes	no	no
3Com	yes	yes	no	yes	yes	yes
Nokia	yes	yes	yes	no	no	no
Fore Systems	no	no	no	no	yes	yes
Packeteer	yes	yes	yes	no	no	no
Yago	yes	yes	no	yes	no	no
Xedia	yes	yes	yes	yes	no	no
Structured Internetworks	yes	yes	no	no	no	yes
Resonate	no	no	no	no	yes	no
Foundry Networks	yes	yes	no	yes	yes	no
BlazeNet	yes	yes	no	no	no	no
ArrowPoint	yes	yes	yes	yes	no	no
LanOptics	yes	yes	no	no	no	no
InfoHighway	no	no	yes	yes	yes	yes
Internet Devices	yes	no	no	yes	no	no

Table 8.2 illustrates the broad approaches supported by leading net-working vendors in the area of QoS. Note that devices such as routers implement a range of queuing disciplines to support QoS requests, ranging from simple FIFO strategies through to more sophisticated techniques such as Weighted Fair Queuing (WFQ) and Class-Based Queuing (CBQ).

8.1.7   Service-Level Agreements (SLAs)

In order for an organization to expect better than best-effort service from its service provider, it must have a Service-Level Agreement (SLA) with that provider. The SLA basically specifies the service classes supported and the amount of traffic available to each class. It is the provider's responsibility to provision the network to cope with the service commitments made. At the ingress of the service provider's network (typically an access router), packets are classified, policed, and possibly shaped. The rules used by these processes and the amount of bandwidth and buffering space required are derived from the SLA. SLAs may be static or dynamic. Static SLAs are negotiated on a regular (e.g., monthly and yearly) basis. Dynamic SLAs are negotiated on demand, through the use of a signaling protocol such as RSVP.

The Internet Service Provider (ISP) market is extremely competitive, and there is increasing focus on both the specification and monitoring of

SLAs (we will review some monitoring tools shortly). The most common SLA guarantees are round-trip latency, packet loss, and availability (uptime per month), as follows:

- Round-trip latency—Internet Round-Trip Time (RTT) is fairly predictable (currently between 200 and 400 ms on average), and SLAs offered by service providers generally specify 80–150 ms depending upon the region (e.g., UUNET offers 85 ms U.S. RTT and 120 ms transatlantic RTT at the time of writing). One point to be aware of is the difference between average and peak latency. Peak latency is the delay imposed during a worst-case congestion period (i.e., this is the worst latency value we would ever expect to see). If an SLA specifies average latency, then in reality users could expect to see much worse delays at periods of high congestion.

- Packet loss is also an important factor in maintaining good performance. As packet loss approaches 30 percent over the Internet, there are likely to be so many retransmissions taking place that the service is effectively unusable. A good rule of thumb is that 10 percent packet loss would severely impair performance, and greater than 15 percent makes the service effectively unavailable. Most service providers do not currently offer this feature.

The SLA comprises a series of traffic rules or mandates, expressed in sufficient detail to be measurable, as follows:

Rule 1: 95 percent of in-profile traffic delivered at service level B will experience no more than 50 ms latency.

Rule 2: 99.9 percent of in-profile traffic delivered at service level C will be delivered.

Rule 3: 99 percent of in-profile traffic delivered at service level A will experience no more than 100 ms latency.

The SLA should also specify the level of technical support required. For example, you may require 24-hour, 7-day support, with a maximum 2-hour response time for a particularly mission-critical network. A more general specification would be 12-hour, 5-day support, with a 4- or 8-hour response time. The SLA should also include details of any compensation due should the provider not meet the agreement.

Service providers have to date concentrated on providing SLAs on backbone access. With the emergence of Virtual Private Networks (VPNs), it is likely that SLAs will need to be extended right into the customer premises; however, this raises the possibility that two or more service providers may be required to match guarantees, with the local area parts of the VPN network managed by private companies or outsourced. The technologies involved differ markedly between the local and wide area networks, making service prediction difficult (e.g., several T1 links fed into Gigabit Ethernet and then distributed as switched and shared Ethernet or Token Ring LANs). In the local area there are currently many different techniques for offering service guarantees; some LAN technologies offer no guarantees. Efforts are currently focusing on using a common tagging format to ensure that frames can be classified and handled uniformly regardless of the technology used, and the IETF is focusing on the DiffServ model as an overall architecture to provide end-to-end SLAs. We will discuss these technologies and issues in detail shortly. For the foreseeable future SLA homogenization between LANs and WANs may be simply unworkable without tight design and technology constraints; however, this is likely to be commonplace in the future as reliance on networks for business processes increases and service providers begin to invade the local area with managed service offerings.

Monitoring SLAs

One of the obvious problems with QoS in the real world is that a customer attached to a public network places significant trust in the service provider once the SLA is in place. For some organizations this honor system may be unacceptable, since the operation of a business may depend to a large degree on the availability of network links to customers and partners. These organizations may wish to monitor the SLA and may also expect restitution if significant loss of service or service quality occurs. There are a number of vendors offering SLA monitoring tools that compile and present activity reports for a range of WAN services. This information can (in theory) be used to force providers to offer compensation if the SLA guarantees falls short in practice.

Before purchasing a monitoring tool you should first examine the SLA. No product can help you if your SLA is poorly defined or badly negotiated. The looseness of many agreements makes it easy for providers to ignore significant service shortfalls and the corresponding compensation due to customers. The interested reader is referred to standards bodies such as the Frame Relay Forum [15] and the Telemanagement Forum (formerly known as the Network Management Forum) [16] for tips on designing better SLAs. These bodies are defining key parameters that can be used in setting up SLAs, and this is an active area for collaborative discussion. It is worth noting that some carriers have standard SLAs that are nonnegotiable. In these cases if you are unhappy with the SLA and you cannot exert sufficient commercial pressure, then your only choices are either to talk to other providers or to live with the SLA offered.

Features of commercial monitoring tools

Monitoring tools come in a variety of guises. Some products have been designed from the ground up; others are extensions of existing network management and monitoring systems. In any case, it is important when deploying these systems to understand how a product gathers information, what level of granularity is available, and what kind of polling mechanisms are used. In general they comprise the following elements:

- Data collection models—Products may be purely software (data collection modules installed on key network components, with collection from standard networking devices) or a combination of software and dedicated hardware (in the form of remote monitoring probes or CSU/DSUs). Probes are typically more expensive than CSU/DSUs, but they can track much more information, since they are able to access the upper layers of the protocol stack. CSU/DSU-based solutions are limited to Physical Layer statistics and may be limited in geographic scope (these products may not be certified or compatible for international networks).

- WAN interfaces—Monitoring tools can typically monitor traditional WAN technologies such as Frame Relay, ISDN, and leased lines. Not all tools currently support ATM, and none can currently be used to monitor Internet services.

- External data feeds—Products use a number of external interfaces to capture real-time data (e.g., SNMP, RMONv1 and RMONv2, serial interfaces, CLI capture, proprietary protocols, and management systems such as HP Openview). These data can be consolidated with data captured by their own agents (if deployed).

- Predictive features—Predictive capabilities can be extremely useful when considering the position of the products within the infrastructure:

  - Trend analysis can be used to graphically highlight key performance patterns and areas requiring additional capacity in the future. Many vendors offer this capability as part of their products. Forecasting also fits here; it makes use of statistical analysis to let network managers predict overall future performance based on current metrics.

- What-if analysis allows users to model and test scenarios for their possible impact on performance. For example, a link can be temporarily broken (in software) to determine how an outage would affect other circuits.

- Traffic shaping—Some vendors incorporate traffic shaping and filtering facilities into their products to help in maintaining QoS proactively at the edge. These features can be used to optimize the use of WAN bandwidth. This also adds an extra level of control that could be used to extend service-level guarantees to in-house users. Some products in this class can be set up to identify periods of congestion and can then allocate bandwidth dynamically to keep mission-critical applications alive.

- Data capture and storage—On a large high-speed network, database requirements can be brutal, with respect to both storage space and database access speed (particularly Write actions). Consider the number of objects required to be stored from multiple feeds if all data are to be recording in real time. Many products have filtering capabilities to reduce the amount of data captured. Some customers may, however, insist that all pertinent data be recorded.

- Reporting features—An important feature of these products is report generation. Pay particular attention to Web accessibility, frequency of report generation, composite measurement capabilities, security, and customization. Database products offering SQL-based interfaces enable data to be easily exported to other reporting tools and databases.

- Diagnostic features—Troubleshooting features range from basic threshold alarms that can be set when traffic patterns vary (something nearly every vendor offers) to more complicated event correlation tools and packet-decoding features. If customers discover a problem, they can pay to have it corrected immediately and then (in theory) get the provider to reimburse them later on.

Key metrics to monitor

Given the importance of SLAs one would assume that there are standard metrics to monitor for each technology type. In fact only the Frame Relay Forum has begun to make progress on this issue at the time of writing. The ATM Forum has discussions under way, but no documents have yet been drafted. The Telemanagement Forum (TMF) has established definitions and documents for joint use by carriers and their customers, but much of this work pertains specifically to theoretical models carriers can use in setting up customer service systems. The types of metrics you need to focus on include the following:

- Network availability (uptime)—Armed with standard network equipment (such as a router) you can track availability by recording how long a service is up over a specified period of time, and these products also typically maintain statistics on error rates, throughput, utilization, and so on.

- Circuit error rates (e.g., bit error rate, CRC failure rate)—Again, standard network equipment typically maintains statistics on error rates. Specialized equipment such as BERT testers can also be employed.

- Throughput—Throughput is important as a measure of efficiency; not all products are currently able to provide a consistent way to measure the amount of data successfully delivered.

- Network latency (delay) and possibly jitter (variability of delay)— Several monitoring products can track network latency, delay, and response time. They typically use the ICMP ping facility to reach an agent at the other end of the link, measuring how long it takes to get a response. Some products can track the response time of specific applications running over WAN circuits. These intelligent monitoring agents can run alongside popular business applications, monitoring time stamps to measure how well the application is responding.

- Circuit stability (oscillations in link up/down status)—Link oscillations can cripple a network, even if they represent only minor downtime at the WAN interface. For example, in a routed intranet, if the WAN link is part of an OSPF routing domain, each oscillation could force the network to reconverge frequently; this could lead to packet or even session loss.

It is important to fully understand the implications of the SLA specifications. For example, an SLA specifying 99 percent uptime per month on a particular circuit may seem more than adequate. In practice this could mean that the user experiences over seven hours of downtime on a regular basis with the carrier still meeting its SLA. If your business demands no more than 30 minutes downtime per month, you would be looking to specify at least 99.932 percent availability. Clearly, there are cost implications here. For further information on useful parameters refer to [15, 16].

Challenging an SLA

Recording data is one thing; challenging a service provider on SLAs is not quite so straightforward. Capture agents must collect data at frequent intervals in order to present a realistic view, and reports must be unambiguously timestamped and clearly identify the resources being tracked. Before investing in monitoring tools, you must discuss with your provider what it is prepared to reasonably accept in terms of SLA challenges. From the provider's perspective it is conceivable that you could be running inadequate tools to provide a credible challenge or that you could in some way alter the data. There are currently no hard rules or standards concerning what carriers will accept as proof of poor performance, other than their own measurements. Providers are likely to use their own tools, and these could offer much greater resolution than your own, or they might use commercial products that you could purchase and mirror at your site. Organizations that cannot afford to buy additional tools, or simply do not have the resources to manage the process, can outsource this activity to an independent service monitoring agency. Another subtle problem with SLA metric recording is security. If you cannot prove that the data collection devices are secure, then it is possible for a provider to argue that the data you have collected could have been tampered with. Surprisingly, only a few commercial products currently have security features that extend beyond simple password control. A small number of products now support SSL and integral firewall features

Key vendors

Key vendors of SLA monitoring solutions include ADC Kentrox, Concord Communications, Digital Link, Hewlett-Packard, Infovista, Ion Networks, The Knowledge Group, Netscout Systems, Netreality, Paradyne, Quallaby, Sync Research, and Visual Networks.

8.2   Traffic engineering with policy and QoS constraints

If a network does not provide adequate delivery, customers will be unhappy and will press for price reductions or compensation or possibly switch to a new provider. At the most basic level the provider must provision a number of circuits with adequate capacity and sufficient geographic coverage to meet customer needs. Once the physical topology exists, the job of controlling the traffic over that topology to maximize efficiency must be tackled.

Once we have control, users can be offered service quality and delivery guarantees. Clearly, we cannot build a successful QoS model without first deploying mechanisms to engineer traffic so that we can shape and direct individual traffic flows at will.

8.2.1   Traffic engineering

Traffic engineering is the process of mapping and managing traffic flows over a physical network infrastructure, with the aim of optimizing the use of that infrastructure. To date, this mapping has been handled in a fairly crude manner, with the emphasis placed on connectivity and a best-effort packet delivery service. Traffic flows are still largely controlled by unicast Interior Gateway Protocols (IGPs) and a mixture of standard and proprietary queuing features implemented in access devices. Planners who have implemented an ATM core into their design have access to better traffic engineering capabilities than legacy backbones, but this does not solve the end-to-end QoS problem in large heterogeneous internetworks [1].

Measuring traffic on backbones

If you are designing an entirely new backbone, the traffic data available will be a mixture of theoretical projections and the results of any empirical testing [1]). Traffic engineering can, therefore, start even before the network is installed, through a mixture of good design, simulation modeling, and pilot testing. If the backbone is already installed, it is important to baseline the traffic dynamics before attempting to engineer traffic flows, starting by establishing how much traffic is passing through the backbone ingress and egress points. This is vital for estimating future growth and capacity expansion plans. Traffic statistics provide the raw data for traffic engineering, enabling a designer to plan and optimize circuit provisioning.

Building a traffic matrix from an ATM core is quite straightforward, since ATM switches provide detailed per PVC statistics. When analyzed over time, these statistics provide the designer with good visibility about which circuits are underutilized and which circuits are experiencing growth. Each PVC can be provisioned to support specific traffic engineering requirements. If a path begins to suffer frequent congestion problems, it can be reconfigured accordingly. ATM is not without its drawbacks, however (such as its limitations in multicast support and the continuing debate over fixed cells versus frames for data traffic). Traffic engineering solutions cannot rely on ATM; they must be independent of the underlying infrastructure.

Building a traffic matrix with a routed core is more difficult, due to lack of accuracy and lack of granularity. For example, studies show that as much as 99 percent of the routing information in the current Internet is inaccurate [17]. Furthermore, traffic statistics maintained on backbone trunks do not typically differentiate traffic that is either entering or exiting a PoP from traffic that is transiting that PoP. You could improve matters by sampling traffic over time (say by capturing 1 out of every 100 packets), with the intention of capturing a statistically significant portion, but in practice this may be difficult to accomplish on high-speed trunks (running at OC-48 or even higher rates).

Network planners, therefore, require traffic engineering support capabilities that are similar if not better than those provided by ATM but with the flexibility of a routing overlay network. Ideally any emerging solution should combine the advantages of both while eliminating any disadvantages. This has led to the development of a relatively new technology called MultiProtocol Label Switching (MPLS). MPLS is proposed as the solution to underpin traffic engineering in large service-provider networks and is described later in this section.

Problems with least cost routing

Interior gateway protocols (such as OSPF) are essentially all opportunistic. They rely on shortest path forwarding techniques, creating a single least-cost path per source-destination network pair; paths are typically optimized for a single arbitrary metric, administrative weight, or hop count. While this approach has served the industry well for many years, it does not optimize resources, leading to scalability problems, unevenly distributed traffic, congestion, and gross bandwidth waste. Simple routing metric schemes do not provide sufficient granularity or flexibility for optimizing individual traffic flows over large, meshed heterogeneous internetworks. Routers and circuits that are in the shortest path often become congested, while resources on longer (but equally viable) paths remain underutilized. To combat this problem, some IGP protocols provide a form of load splitting over multiple paths (e.g., OSPF Equal-Cost Multi-Path [18], IS-IS [19], and EIGRP's load sharing over mixed speed circuits). These features are, however, still inadequate for load optimization on backbone networks and add complexity (e.g., load splitting may result in packets delivered out of sequence, and the designer is often required to engineer metrics to force paths to be used). Aside from these very basic traffic engineering problems, conventional routing protocols cannot hope to support the fundamental requirements of a QoS infrastructure—namely, differentiated flow handling.

The way forward

We have arrived at a point where this rigid best-effort approach is no longer suitable for business needs. The boom-and-bust nature of the resulting traffic dynamics has meant that many service providers have mitigated congestion by simply overprovisioning bandwidth. On a large network with expensive high-speed trunk circuits this typically results in huge cost and bandwidth inefficiencies. We need a new way of engineering traffic to maximize the bandwidth available by smoothing out uneven network utilization dynamically. The offered load must be handled in a more deterministic manner, and a number of well-defined service profiles should be available to meet the requirements of different applications (e.g., interactive, batch, video, voice, etc.). Consequently, traffic engineering is currently one of the hottest topics for service providers and standards bodies such as the IETF. Traffic engineering offers the flexibility to shift traffic flows away from the shortest path onto longer but less congested paths. A number of important techniques have emerged in recent years to assist in this process, as follows:

- QoS-Based Routing (QBR) improves on traditional routing by recognizing and responding dynamically to multiple service-related constraints rather than simple metrics. QBR classifies flows and then directs traffic along forwarding paths that can meet QoS requirements.

- Policy-Based Routing (PBR) improves on traditional routing by assigning forwarding paths to flows based on administrative policy rather than simple metrics. This offers administrators direct control over the forwarding paths selected.

- Constraint-Based Routing (CBR) is a combination of QBR and PBR. CBR automates the traffic engineering process, helps to avoid congestion, and provides graceful performance degradation where congestion is unavoidable. The problems introduced by optimizing multiple constraints are, however, daunting.

- MultiProtocol Label Switching (MPLS) is a forwarding scheme that combines high-speed switching techniques with traditional routing intelligence. Labels are inserted into traffic flows to enable intermediate devices to switch traffic quickly without having to consult routing tables. MPLS provides the granularity and performance required to handle flow-based traffic. MPLS adds scalability and is proposed as a technology that underpins QBR, PBR, and CBR in wide area backbones.

We will now discuss each briefly in turn.

8.2.2   QoS-Based Routing (QBR)

QoS-Based Routing (QBR) is a forwarding mechanism used to find paths that have a high probability of meeting the request service quality for flows (or aggregate flows). QBR does not include mechanisms for reserving resources; consequently, it is generally used in conjunction with a resource reservation function (such as RSVP). QoS-based routing is defined in [2] as a routing mechanism under which paths for flows are determined based on some knowledge of resource availability in the network as well as the QoS requirement of the flows.

Simple forms of QoS-based routing, based on IP's Type of Service (ToS) field, have been proposed in the past. For example, with OSPF, a different shortest-path tree can be computed for each of the eight ToS values in the IP header. Such mechanisms can be used to select specially provisioned paths but do not completely assure that resources will not be overbooked along the path. As long as strict resource management and control are not required, mechanisms such as ToS-based routing are useful for separating whole classes of traffic over multiple routes (e.g., this might work well with the emerging differential services initiative). The downside of this approach is that it consumes significant routing resources (e.g., the Dijkstra algorithm must be run for every shortest path tree).

A number of different QoS-based routing models have been proposed in recent years (for both unicast and multicast routing), each designed to address different types of problems. These schemes often make different assumptions about the state of the network and rarely work together. The IETF has developed a common framework [2], which can accommodate different kinds of algorithms. This framework offers a hierarchical model with two levels: intradomain QoS-based routing and interdomain QoS-based routing. This model is compatible with the routing hierarchy discussed previously, which has the concept of Autonomous System (AS) as the highest-order entity. Under QoS-based routing, the path assigned to a flow would be determined based on the QoS requirements for that flow, as well as knowledge of resource availability in the network. The main objectives of QoS-based routing are as follows:

- Dynamic determination of feasible paths—QoS-based routing should identify a path that has a good chance of accommodating the QoS requirements for a given flow. Feasible path selection may be subject to policy constraints (such as path cost, provider selection, etc.).

- Optimization of resource use—A network state-dependent QoS-based routing scheme can assist in the efficient utilization of network resources by improving total network throughput. Such a routing scheme can be the basis for efficient network engineering.

- Graceful performance degradation—State-dependent routing can compensate for transient inadequacies in network engineering (e.g., localized congestion conditions), providing better throughput and a more graceful performance degradation as compared to a state-insensitive routing scheme.

In a large heterogeneous multivendor internetwork such as the Internet, however, QBR raises a number of serious issues because of the lack of integration or any centralized administration and because of the scalability and performance problems that occur [2]. Many of these problems are common to Constraint-Based Routing (CBR) issues. For the interested reader [20] provides comprehensive coverage of the issues involved in QoS routing, including formal analysis of key algorithms and heuristics used for QoS routing solutions.

8.2.3   Policy-Based Routing (PBR)

Policy-Based Routing (PBR) provides a mechanism for expressing rules and controlling packet forwarding based on policies defined by the network administrator. This is necessary to regulate network access; otherwise, all users could simply demand premium service quality. It is also necessary to take account of nontechnical issues, such as political, security, management, or budgetary concerns, or just matters of personal preference. PBT provides a powerful and flexible routing model that complements legacy routing protocols. With PBR the routing decision is not based simply on topology knowledge and metrics but on administrative policies. For example, the following policies could be defined:

Policy Rule 1:   Prohibit all e-mail traffic from using the international link WME-10 for security reasons, even if the link exceeds bandwidth and delay requirements.

Policy Rule 2:   R&D traffic is not permitted to transit the HQ backbone network.

Policy Rule 3:   Interactive traffic originating from PROD_LAN will be routed via next-hop router 181.4.3.1, while all other traffic will be routed via next-hop router 181.4.3.2.

PBR enables network planners to implement policies that selectively force packets to take different paths through the network, and it provides mechanisms to mark packets so that certain types of traffic receive preferential service when used in combination with scheduling techniques. For example, ISPs could use PBR to route traffic originating from different user groups or sites through different Internet connections. Enterprise network administrators could use PBR to distribute interactive and batch traffic over lower-cost wide area circuits, leaving mission- or business-critical traffic free to use high-bandwidth switched pipes.

PBR improves over legacy routing techniques by enabling packet flows to be routed using a criterion other than destination address. This means that traffic can be better distributed over the available links rather than taking the shortest path, leading to better overall utilization and lowering the probability of congesting the most attractive circuits. For example, policies could assign specific flows to forwarding paths based on criteria such as the following:

- End system, network, or subnet source address

- Application type (e.g., FTP, TFTP, Telnet, SMTP, DNS)

- Protocol type (e.g., IP, IPX, AppleTalk, SNA)

- Packet size (e.g., packets greater than 1,000 bytes could be routed differently from small packets)

Forwarding decisions may be specified quite tightly or with a degree of flexibility. For example, a particular flow could be directed to exit a router via a specific physical interface or list of interfaces. Alternatively, the flow could be directed to use a list of default routes, specific next-hop IP addresses, or a list of next-hop addresses. By offering multiple choices the availability of forwarding paths is improved.

Currently policy-based routing implementations are generally statically configured, and the features available are largely vendor-specific (since router/switch vendors implement scheduling and congestion control mechanisms in different ways on their platforms). Flows are typically classified at edge routers using filters or Access Control Lists (ACLs). Once classified, packets can be marked before injecting into the backbone by setting values in the IP precedence/ToS (IPv4) or flow label (IPv6) fields (see Figure 8.3). Different classes of service can be assigned to these tagged packets as they traverse the backbone by configuring resources (such as scheduling or congestion control facilities) to meet specific priority or delay requirements.

Note that PBR is effective but requires that all routers behave in a consistent manner in order to achieve service guarantees. In a multivendor network, routing and switching nodes may have dissimilar capabilities and be tuned differently to achieve similar behavior.

8.2.4   **Constraint-Based Routing (CBR)**

Constraint-Based Routing (CBR) evolved from earlier work on QoS-based routing but has a much broader scope. CBR paths are calculated subject to multiple constraints, including both QoS constraints and policy constraints. CBR aims to automate path selection using feedback from the network to meet flow requirements but within overall policy control. CBR can be considered a superset of both QBR and PBR. CBR uses a sophisticated approach to traffic engineering attempts to identify viable paths to meet the QoS requirements for a particular flow (or flow aggregate), based on multiple constraints [2]. Resolving forwarding paths at the flow level results in better overall circuit utilization and lower mean delay. Examples of constraints include availability, monetary cost, hop-count, reliability, delay, jitter, and Class of Service (CoS). CBR takes this further by considering the kind of policy constraints introduced in section 8.2.3. Path selection is influenced by dynamic information, such as flow characteristics, resource availability, resource utilization, topological status, and any static or dynamic policies defined by the network administrator.

Implementing CBR in a real-time network environment is far from easy, and there are several major issues to resolve, including the following:

- Routing granularity—the level of detail used to calculate routes.

- Maintaining topology state data—how to disseminate this additional dynamic state data quickly, without introducing significant overheads on circuit or processing entities.

- Topological stability—how to maintain stability if CBR is constantly altering the traffic dynamics.

- Optimizing the topology—with contradictory constraints the routing problem becomes difficult.

In order to perform CBR, a router or switch needs regular feedback on the state of a number of metrics concerning network utilization and availability. There must be a mechanism to distribute this additional state information. Once accurate information is collated, the router must compute routes based on additional constraint information.

Routing granularity

The granularity used to calculate routes with CBR has a fundamental influence on the efficiency of the overall network utilization produced with CBR. By granularity, we mean the amount of detail used as input to the routing calculation. Conventional routing is typically based upon destination address only; however, with CBR we may also be interested in routing calculation using source and destination addresses, class information, trunk capacity and utilization, delay, or flow data. As granularity increases so does the flexibility of the route calculation, leading to better efficiency in resource utilization and improving overall network stability (attractive high-capacity links are less likely to become swamped with traffic if the calculation is more sensitive to other factors such as delay and utilization). However, routing with multiple constraints, especially where constraints are contradictory, is difficult.

Maintaining topology state information and topological stability

As indicated, most current shortest-path–based IGPs are not adaptive. If the shortest path is congested, there is generally no feedback to reflect this in the link metric (i.e., a congested link could be considered temporarily unavailable; however, its metric still makes it attractive, and there is only one path to choose from for any (s, d) pair). Circuit utilization will vary with the state of active traffic flows, and to select optimum forwarding paths to meet QoS requirements a CBR-enabled router must be aware of the state of available resources at the time when the forwarding decision is made. This knowledge could be disseminated via a special signal protocol, or via extensions to existing IGP protocols. For example, bandwidth information could be distributed via extended OSPF (QOSPF) or IS-IS link state advertisements [21, 22].

The Spanning Trees produced by CBR are likely to be much more dynamic than dynamic routing protocols (the Spanning Tree topology created by conventional routing rarely changes once the network is stable). One major challenge here is the dynamic nature of bandwidth availability, since this can introduce stability problems for adaptive routing schemes. If the response to such dynamic feedback is overly sensitive, this can lead to routing instability, unless mechanisms are put in place to compress routing oscillations. In particular, in-band adaptive routing is even more vulnerable to instability, since it may actually contribute to existing problems by flooding state information too frequently over the very same links that are over-utilized. If network utilization is changing frequently, the router spends too much time recomputing routing tables and can become unresponsive. A trade-off must, therefore, be made between the need to maintain accurate state information and the need to minimize flooding to dampen topology changes. In practice it may be advantageous to use imprecise state information to make routing decisions rather than attempt to be overly accurate. Typically a hold-down timer is used to restrict the frequency of state advertisements, making the system less reactive. Reducing the computation complexity of the routers also helps to improve stability.

Routing table structure and size

The routing table structure and size depend directly on routing granularity and path metrics. The computation and storage overheads of CBR are, therefore, likely to be considerable when compared with conventional routing. Implementations may need to minimize the memory and CPU overheads of CBR. In practice, it may be advisable to run the IGP as normal for best-effort traffic and run CBR on demand to compute routes for new flows. This essentially trades computation time for a smaller storage requirement. Alternatively, coarse routing granularity could be used or techniques such as hop quantization (i.e., dividing all hop-count values into a few classes to reduce the number of columns in the routing table).

Optimizing routes

The routing algorithms used in CBR and the complexity of such algorithms, depend on the type and number of metrics to be included in route calculation [20]. We know that some of these constraints may be contradictory (e.g., cost versus bandwidth, delay versus throughput). It turns out that bandwidth and hop count are generally more useful constraints than delay and jitter, because very few applications cannot tolerate an occasional violation of such constraints, and since delay and jitter can be determined by the allocated bandwidth and hop-count of the flow path, these constraints can be mapped to bandwidth and hop-count constraints, if required. Another factor is that many real-time applications demand a certain amount of bandwidth. The hop-count metric of a route is also important, because the more hops a flow traverses, the more resources it consumes. For example, a 1-Mbps flow that traverses two hops consumes twice as many resources as one that traverses a single hop. Note that calculating optimal routes subject to constraints of two or more additive and/or multiplicative metrics belongs to a class of problem referred to as NP-Complete and must be resolved using heuristic techniques.

In CBR, routes can be precomputed for each traffic class or computed on demand (triggered by the receipt of the QoS request of a flow). Either way, a router will have to compute its routing table more frequently with CBR than with conventional dynamic routing, since routing table computation can be triggered by significant bandwidth changes in addition to topology changes. This additional complexity means that the computation overhead with CBR can be very high. Practical approaches to reducing this overhead include using a timer to reduce the computation frequency, choosing bandwidth and hop count as constraints, and using administrative policy to prune unsuitable links before calculating the routing table (e.g., if a flow has a maximum delay requirement, satellite links may be pruned before the routing table computation). With practical implementations of CBR there is also a trade-off between resource conservation and load balancing. A CBR scheme could choose one of the following options as a viable path for a flow:

- Shortest-distance path—This approach is basically the same as dynamic routing. It emphasizes preserving network resources by choosing the shortest paths.

- Widest-shortest path—This approach emphasizes load balancing by choosing the widest paths. It finds paths with minimum hop count and, if there are multiple such paths, the one with largest available bandwidth.

- Shortest-widest path—This approach makes a trade-off between the two extremes. It favors shortest paths when network load is heavy and widest paths when network load is moderate. It finds a path with largest available bandwidth and, if there are multiple such paths, the one with the minimum hop count.

The last two cases consume more resources, which is not efficient when the network utilization is high. A trade-off must be made between resource conservation and load balancing. Simulations showed that the first approach consistently outperforms the other two for best-effort traffic, regardless of the network topology and traffic dynamics.

In practice, CBR must be implemented and deployed with care; otherwise, the cost of instability and increased complexity may outweigh the benefits. Since CBR is a superset of conventional dynamic routing, it is possible CBR may replace dynamic routing in the future as processing and memory resources in routers and switches continue to improve. A good example of a new intradomain CBR protocol, based on an existing dynamic routing protocol, is QOSPF. For the interested reader [20] provides comprehensive coverage of the issues involved in constraint-based routing, including formal analysis of key algorithms and heuristics used for routing unicast and multicast traffic under QoS constraints.

8.2.5   MultiProtocol Label Switching (MPLS)

MultiProtocol Label Switching (MPLS) is an emerging technology aimed at delivering improved IP traffic engineering tools to enable service providers to more easily manage, monitor, and meet various SLAs across their backbones. MPLS is basically a forwarding scheme, combining label swapping with Network Layer routing, having evolved from Cisco's tag switching. MPLS uses the intelligence in routers and the speed of switches to provide a mechanism to map IP packets onto reliable circuit-oriented protocols such as ATM and Frame Relay. MPLS is designed to offer scalability and efficiency. Since this scheme is independent of underlying protocols, it is called MultiProtocol Label Switching. MPLS is currently an Internet draft [23], and the initial effort from the MPLS working group is focused on developing a label-swapping standard for Layer 3 switching with IPv4 and IPv6. The core technology will subsequently be expanded to incorporate multiple Network Layer protocols. MPLS is not confined to any specific Data Link Layer technology. It can work with any medium over which Network Layer packets can be passed between Network Layer entities. The group started with Cisco's tag switching and IBM's Aggregate Route-Based IP Switching (ARIS). The issue of ATM interworking was not solved by tag switching, because cell and PDU interleaving occurs when the tag is identified with the VCI.

MPLS uses Layer 3 routing information to build forwarding (routing) tables and allocate resources. It uses Layer 2 (ATM, Frame Relay, etc.) to then forward the information over the appropriate path. A special MPLS label, attached to the IP header, is associated with a specific entry in the forwarding table and specifies the next hop. Flows that have common routing and service requirements typically take the same path through the network. The main benefit is a consistent level of service for flows that are of higher priority. A router that supports MPLS is called a Label Switch Router (LSR). An LSR examines only labels in packets to be forwarded. In order to work MPLS requires the deployment of Label Switching Routers (LSRs) in the network, which obviously affects how quickly this technology will be deployed. Implementations are being deployed now. A Label Distribution Protocol (LDP) is required to distribute labels in order to set up Label-Switched Paths (LSPs). A definition of QoS is incorporated into the MPLS header, which contains a 20-bit label, 8-bit TTL field, 3-bit class of service, 1-bit stack indicator, next header type indicator, and checksum.

MPLS is targeted for deployment on backbones initially. LSRs in the core or provider's PoP will interwork with the CPE. For example, a customer could be running CBQ to classify traffic and DiffServ to mark IP ToS, so that the provider network understands what service is required (as agreed upon in the SLA). The network edge devices will then map the DiffServ/ToS specification into the QoS field of the MPLS header, so that the service specification is preserved on an end-to-end basis as packets traverse the core.

Operation

The key feature provided by MPLS is the ability to provide Label-Switched Paths (LSPs), similar to Permanent Virtual Circuits (PVCs) in ATM and Frame Relay networks. An LSP is created by the concatenation of one or more label-switched hops, enabling a packet to be forwarded from one LSR to another across the backbone network. An LSR that receives an IP packet can choose to forward it along an LSP. It does this by encapsulating the packet inside an MPLS header and then forwarding it to another LSR. The labeled packet will be forwarded along the LSP by each LSR in turn until it reaches the end of the LSP, where the MPLS header will be removed and the packet will be forwarded based on Layer 3 information (such as the IP destination address). The key point here is that the path chosen for the LSP is not necessarily the IGP's shortest path, as illustrated in Figure 8.4.

Figure 8.4
Router backbone, with some routers supporting MPLS.

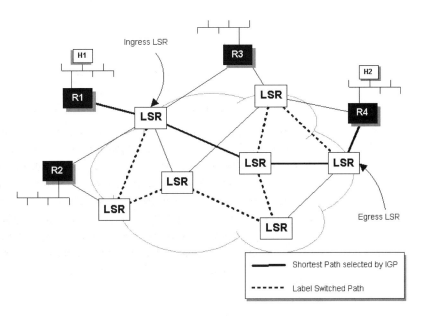

Figure 8.5
Label-switched
forwarding table.

InboundLBL	OutBoundIF	OutBoundLBL
20	5	210
256	4	650
50	1	32
8	6	760
37	3	10

The forwarding process of each LSR is based on the concept of label swapping. The labels are bound to IP prefixes and are link-local. When a packet containing a label arrives at an LSR, the LSR examines the label and uses it as an index into its forwarding table. Each entry in the forwarding table contains an inbound label, which is mapped to a set of forwarding information that is applied to all packets that carry the same inbound label (see Figure 8.5).

If an LSR receives a packet on Interface 2 with a label set to 50, the LSR uses the outbound data to forward the frame to Interface 1, with a new label of 32.

Traffic engineering with MPLS

Traffic enters and exits a backbone network from the network's border routers. In the context of traffic engineering, the border routers are called the ingress and egress points to and from the network. Traffic engineering is accomplished with MPLS by establishing LSPs between ingress points and egress points. We have already defined traffic engineering as the mapping of traffic onto a physical topology. This means that the real traffic engineering task for MPLS is determining the path for LSPs. There are several ways to route an LSP, including the following:

- Calculate the full path for the LSP offline and statically configure all LSRs in the LSP with the necessary forwarding state. This is analogous to how some ISPs are currently using ATM.

- Calculate the full path for the LSP offline and statically configure the head-end LSR with the full path. The head-end LSR then uses the Resource Reservation Setup Protocol (RSVP) as a dynamic signaling protocol to install forwarding state in each LSR. Note that RSVP is being used only to install the forwarding state, and it does not reserve bandwidth or provide any assurance of minimal delay or jitter. The Juniper Networks engineers were involved in specifying the new label object, explicit route object, and record route object for RSVP that allow it to operate as an LSP setup protocol.

- Calculate a partial path for the LSP offline and statically configure the head-end LSR with a subset of the LSRs in the path. The partial path that is specified can include any combination of strict and loose routes. For example, imagine that an ISP has a topology that includes two east-west paths across the country: one in the north through Chicago and one in the south through Dallas. Now imagine that the ISP wants to establish an LSP between a router in New York and a router in San Francisco. The ISP could configure the partial path for the LSP to include a single loose-routed hop of an LSR in Dallas, and the result would be that the LSP will be routed along the southern path. The head-end LSR uses RSVP to install the forwarding state along the LSP.

- Configure the head-end LSR with just the identification of the tail-end LSR. In this case, normal IP routing is used to determine the path of the LSP. This configuration doesn't provide any value in terms of traffic engineering, but the configuration is easy and it might be useful in situations where services such as Virtual Private Networks (VPNs) are needed.

In all these cases, any number of LSPs can be specified as backups for the primary LSP. If a circuit on which the primary LSP is routed fails, the head-end LSR will notice because it will stop hearing RSVP messages from the remote end. If this happens, the head-end LSR can call on RSVP to create forwarding state for one of the backup LSPs.

Note that some vendors are extending their MPLS implementation to support CBR so that the network itself can participate in traffic engineering. This enables the head-end LSR to calculate the entire LSP based on certain constraints and then initiate signaling across the network. A key feature required to extend MPLS for CBR is bandwidth reservation. If we provide LSRs with the ability to request bandwidth, respond to such requests, and advertise the state of their bandwidth allocation, then LSP setup could be performed by negotiating with the network (and could take into account bandwidth on a given trunk already committed to flows between specific nodes). The advertisement of available and committed bandwidths could be provided through IS-IS or OSPF type-length-value attribute extensions.

Performance considerations

One misconception about MPLS is that it significantly enhances forwarding performance in routers. We know that IP forwarding is based on a longest-match lookup, while MPLS is based on an exact-match lookup (the same kind of lookup as the VPI/VCI lookup in ATM). Traditionally, fixed-length lookups in hardware are considerably faster than longest-match lookups in software. However, recent advances in silicon technology allow ASIC-based route lookup engines to run just as quickly, forwarding packets at line rates. The real benefit of MPLS is the increased traffic engineering capabilities that it offers.

MPLS benefits

The following should be considered when a possible MPLS deployment is discussed:

- Growth of the Internet is exceeding the L3 processing capacity of traditional routers.

- Enables routing to leverage the price, performance, and maturity of Layer 2 switching.

- ATM switches can be augmented with IP routing.

- MPLS forwarding is independent of current and future enhancements to Network Layer protocols.

- Works over any Layer 2 datalink technology (e.g., ATM, Frame Relay, Ethernet, SONET, etc.).

- Offers more efficient traffic engineering capabilities.

- Uses label stacks rather than IP-OVER-IP encapsulation for tunnels.

- Offers explicit routes.

- ISP's need to support and deliver special services.

Previously, it was suggested that any emerging solution providing traffic engineering across the optical Internet must combine the advantages of ATM and routed cores while eliminating the disadvantages. Let's conclude this section by examining how well MPLS meets this challenge, as follows:

- An MPLS core fully supports traffic engineering via LSP configuration. This permits the ISP to precisely distribute traffic across all of the links so the trunks are evenly used.

- In an MPLS core, the per LSP statistics reported by the LSRs provide exactly the type of information required for configuring new traffic engineering paths and deploying new physical topologies.

- In an MPLS core, the physical topology and the logical topology are identical. This eliminates the *n*-squared problem associated with ATM networks.

- The lack of a cell tax in an MPLS core means that the provisioned bandwidth is used much more efficiently than in an ATM core.

An MPLS core converges the Layer 2 and Layer 3 networks required in an ATM-based core. The management of a single network reduces costs and permits routing and traffic engineering to occur on the same platform. This simplifies the design, configuration, operation, and debugging of the entire network. MPLS support for a dynamic protocol, such as RSVP, simplifies the deployment of traffic-engineered LSPs across the network. Future MPLS support for CBR achieves the same control as manual traffic engineering but with less human intervention, because the network participates in LSP calculation.

8.3   LAN and WAN media QoS features

Before dealing with large-scale architectures for QoS, it is worth investigating what facilities are available at the media level for different local and wide area technologies. These facilities represent the lowest interface available for mapping priority and service-quality requests, and, as we will see, features vary markedly.

8.3.1   LAN QoS features

General IEEE 802 service model

The IEEE 802 service model uses an abstraction called the User Priority Value (UPV) to group traffic according to the Class of Service (CoS) required. The UPV may or may not be physically carried over the network, depending upon the facilities offered by the media type, as follows:

- Token Ring/IEEE 802.5 carries this value encoded in its FC octet.

- Ethernet/IEEE 802.3 does not carry it. Only the two levels of priority (high/low) can be recovered, based on the value of priority encoded in the start delimiter (SD).

- IEEE 802.12 may or may not carry it, depending on the frame format in use.

The revised IEEE 802.1D standard (incorporating 802.1p and 802.1Q) defines a consistent way to carry the value of the UPV over a bridged network comprising Ethernet, Token Ring, Demand Priority, FDDI, or other MAC layer media, and is described in the following text.

IEEE 802.1p and IEEE 802.1Q

Unlike protocols such as FDDI and Token Ring, Ethernet does not offer any useful priority facilities. To address this problem IEEE 802.1p (part of a revised 802.1D bridging standard) uses a special 3-bit field called the user priority value. The user priority value is encoded within a tag field defined by another standard, IEEE 802.1Q (also part 802.1D), which is designed to support VLAN tagging via a 32-bit tag header inserted after the frame's MAC header (note that support for IEEE 802.1p does not imply that VLANs need to be implemented). The 802.1Q tag header comprises the following:

- Three priority bits are used for signaling 802.1p switches.

- One bit identifies optional token-ring encapsulation.

- Twelve bits are used for the virtual LAN ID applied to virtual LAN membership.

- Sixteen bits are used to modify the EtherType frame.

The IEEE ratified the 802.1p standard in September 1998. 802.1p offers two major functions, as follows:

- Traffic class expediting—The 802.1p header includes a 3-bit field for prioritization called the User Priority Value (UPV), which enables packets to be grouped into one of eight traffic classes. Higher-priority traffic gets through faster; lower-priority traffic may be dropped if resources are oversubscribed.

- GMRP multicast filtering—The 802.1p standard also offers the capability to filter multicast traffic dynamically, in order to stop multicast leaking in switches. This facilitates dynamic registration of multicast groups, ensuring that traffic is delivered only to those who request it.

UPV to traffic type mappings are listed as follows in increasing priority order (for further information see [24, 25]. Note that the value 0, the default, best effort, has a higher priority than value 2, standard.

- 1—binary 001: Background, loss-eligible traffic

- 2—binary 010: Standard (spare)

- 0—binary 000: Best-effort default, invoked automatically when no other value has been set

- 3—Binary 011: Excellent effort (for business-critical traffic such as SAP)

- 4—binary 100: Controlled load (for applications such as streaming multimedia)

- 5—binary 101: Video, interactive, and delay-sensitive (less than 100 ms latency and jitter)

- 6—binary 110: Voice, interactive, and delay-sensitive (less than 10 ms latency and jitter)

- 7—binary 111: Network control (reserved traffic for control protocols such as RIP and OSPF)

This mapping enables support for policy-based QoS by specifying a Class of Service (CoS) on a frame basis. Lower-priority packets are deferred if there are packets waiting in higher-priority queues. This enables the differentiation of real-time data, voice, and video traffic from normal (best effort) data traffic such as e-mail. This solution benefits businesses that want to deploy real-time multimedia traffic and providers offering SLAs that extend into the LAN environment.

The IEEE specifications make no assumptions about how UPV is to be used by end stations or by the network nor do they provide recommendations about how a sender should select the UPV (the interested reader is referred to [26]). In practice the UPV may be set by workstations, servers, routers, or Layer 3 switches. In host devices 802.1p-compliant Network Interface Cards (NICs) are able to set or read the UPV bits. Hubs and switches can use this information to prioritize traffic prior to forwarding to other LAN segments. For example, without any form of prioritization a switch would typically delay or drop packets in response to congestion. On an 802.1p-enabled switch, a packet with a higher priority receives preferential treatment and is serviced before a packet with a lower priority; therefore, lower priority-traffic is more likely to be dropped in preference. The basic operations are as follows:

- Unless a host computer has properly negotiated QoS with the network, the host should only mark packets transmitted with a best-effort priority value. If the host computer has a packet scheduler installed, the host uses the appropriate QoS signaling components to negotiate with the network for higher 802.1p priority values.

- Routers and Layer 3 switches use packet payload information such as TCP and UDP port numbers to differentiate application flows. This information can be used together with network administrator-defined policies to classify any untagged packets.

- Since Layer 2 switches cannot see data above the MAC layer, the 802.1p specification enables them to understand packet priorities but not perform classification.

- In addition to these functions, switches and routers must employ multiple output queues (so-called multiqueue hardware) for each port to be capable of processing priority requests effectively. The 802.1p specification assumes multiqueue hardware implicitly in that it recommends how the various traffic classes should be assigned in systems with multiple queues per port.

- IEEE 802.1D defines static priority queuing as the default mode of operation of switches that implement multiple queues; the UPV is really a priority only in a loose sense, since it depends on the number of traffic classes actually implemented by a switch.

The general switch algorithm is as follows. Packets are queued within a particular traffic class based on the received UPV, the value of which is either obtained directly from the packet, if an IEEE 802.1Q header or IEEE 802.5 network is used, or is assigned according to some local policy. The queue is selected based on a mapping from UPV (0 through 7) onto the number of available traffic classes. A switch may implement one or more traffic classes. The advertised IntServ parameters and the switch's admission control behavior may be used to determine the mapping from UPV to traffic classes within the switch. A switch is not precluded from implementing other scheduling algorithms, such as weighted fair queuing and round robin.

Issues with 802.1p

There are several open issues with 802.1p, including the following:

- IEEE 802.1p specifies no admission control protocols. It would be possible to give network control priority to all packets and the network would be easily congested. Currently this is viewed as the responsibility of NIC drivers (i.e., self-regulating and therefore potentially open to abuse).

- IEEE 802.1p does not limit the amount of resources a particular application consumes. A mechanism to negotiate a guaranteed QoS for each application, end to end, according to the network policy maintained by local network administrators would be a useful improvement.

- Interoperability has been a major problem but is being addressed through initiatives such as the Subnet Bandwidth Manager (SBM) [YAV98]. This specification deals with how to deliver end-to-end QoS to and from the Ethernet to other networks.

- Some older network analyzers may not decode 802.1p protocol information properly.

Several of the leading switches now support the standard. For example, 3Com supports 802.1p in several products via its DynamicAccess software with its industry-leading EtherLink and EtherLink Server NICs, at the core with the CoreBuilder 3500 Layer 3 switch, and now in the wiring closet with the new SuperStack II Switch 1100 and 3300 software. At the desktop, Microsoft supports 802.1p in its Windows 98 and Windows 2000 operating systems, including other QoS mechanisms such as differentiated services and RSVP. Support for 802.1p priority was included in NDIS 5.0.

Ethernet/IEEE 802.3

There is no explicit traffic class or UPV field carried in Ethernet packets. This means that UPV must be regenerated at a downstream receiver or switch according to some defaults or by parsing further into higher-layer protocol fields in the packet. Alternatively, IEEE 802.1p with 802.1Q encapsulation may be used to provide an explicit UPV field on top of the basic MAC frame format. For the different IP packet encapsulations used over Ethernet/IEEE 802.3, it will be necessary to adjust any admission control calculations according to the framing and padding requirements, as listed in the following chart.

Encapsulation	Frame Overhead	IP MTU
EtherType	18 bytes	1,500 bytes
EtherType + IEEE 802.1D/Q	22 bytes	1,500 bytes
EtherType + LLC/SNAP	24 bytes	1,492 bytes

Note that the packet length of an Ethernet frame using the IEEE 802.1Q specification exceeds the current IEEE 802.3 MTU value (1,518 bytes) by 4 bytes. The change of maximum MTU size for IEEE 802.1Q frames is being accommodated by IEEE 802.3ac [28].

Token Ring/IEEE 802.5

The Token Ring standard [29] provides a priority mechanism to control both the queuing of packets for transmission and the access of packets to the shared media. The access priority features are an integral part of the token-passing protocol. The Token Ring priority mechanisms are implemented using bits within the Access Control (AC) and the Frame Control (FC) fields in either a token or a frame. Token Ring has the following characteristics:

- Access priority is indicated by the first three bits (called the token priority bits) of the AC field.

- Token Ring also uses a concept of reserved priority, which relates to the value of priority that a station uses to reserve the token for the next transmission on the ring. Reservation of a priority level is indicated in the last three bits (the reservation bits) of the AC field by a node requiring higher transmission priority. When a free token is circulating, only a station having an access priority greater than or equal to the reserved priority in the token will be allowed to seize the token for transmission. If the passing token or frame already contains a priority reservation higher than the desired one, the ring station must leave the reservation bits unchanged. If, however, the token's reservation bits have not yet been set (i.e., binary 000) or indicate a lower priority than the desired one, the ring station can set the reservation bits to its required priority. A node originating a token of higher priority enters priority-hold state (also called a stacking station in the IEEE 802.5 token-passing ring standards). Readers are referred to [27] for further discussion of this topic.

- The last three bits of the FC field of an LLC frame (the user priority bits) are obtained from the higher layer in the UPV parameter when it requests transmission of a packet. This parameter also establishes the access priority used by the MAC. The UPV is conveyed end-to-end by the user priority bits in the FC field and is typically preserved through Token Ring bridges of all types. In all cases, 0 is the lowest priority.

A Token Ring station is theoretically capable of separately queuing each of the eight levels of requested UPV and then transmitting frames in order of priority. Table 8.3 lists the recommended use of the priority levels (note that different implementations of Token Ring may deviate from these definitions). A station sets reservation bits according to the UPV of frames that are queued for transmission in the highest-priority queue. This allows the access mechanism to ensure that the frame with the highest priority throughout the entire ring will be transmitted before any lower-priority frame.

Table 8.3   *Recommended Use of Token Ring User Priority*

Priority bit Settings		Description
Dec	Binary	
0	000	Normal user priority - None Time-Critical data
1	001	Normal user priority - None Time-Critical data
2	010	Normal user priority - None Time-Critical data
3	011	Normal user priority - None Time-Critical data
4	100	LAN Management
5	101	Time-Sensitive data
6	110	Real-Time-Critical data
7	111	MAC Frames

To prevent a high-priority station from monopolizing the LAN medium and to make sure the priority eventually can come down again, the protocol provides fairness within each priority level. To reduce frame jitter associated with high-priority traffic, Annex I to the IEEE 802.5 Token Ring standard recommends that stations transmit only one frame per token and that the maximum information field size be 4,399 bytes whenever delay-sensitive traffic is traversing the ring. Most existing implementations of Token Ring bridges forward all LLC frames with a default access priority of 4. Annex I recommends that bridges forward LLC frames that have a UPV greater than 4 with a reservation equal to the UPV (although the draft IEEE 802.1D [30] permits network management to override this behavior). The capabilities provided by the Token Ring architecture, such as user priority and reserved priority, can provide effective support for integrated services flows that require QoS guarantees.

For the different IP packet encapsulations used over Token Ring/IEEE 802.5, it will be necessary to adjust any admission control calculations according to the framing requirements listed in the following chart.

Encapsulation	*Frame Overhead*	*IP MTU*
EtherType + IEEE 802.1D/Q	29 bytes	4,370 bytes
EtherType + LLC/SNAP	25 bytes	4,370 bytes

Note that the suggested MTU specified in RFC 1042 [24] is 4,464 bytes, but there are issues related to discovering what the maximum supported MTU between any two points within and between Token Ring subnets is. The MTU reported here is consistent with the IEEE 802.5 Annex I recommendation.

Fiber Distributed Data Interface (FDDI)

The FDDI standard [29] provides a priority mechanism that can be used to control both packet queuing and access to the shared media. The priority mechanisms are implemented using mechanisms similar to Token Ring; however, access priority is based upon timers rather than token manipulation. For the discussion of QoS mechanisms, FDDI is treated as a 100-Mbps Token Ring technology using a service interface compatible with IEEE 802 networks. FDDI supports real-time allocation of network bandwidth, making it suitable for a variety of different applications, including interactive multimedia. FDDI defines two main traffic classes, as follows:

- Synchronous traffic—Used by nodes requiring continuous transmission capability (say for voice or videoconferencing applications); it can be configured to use synchronous bandwidth. The FDDI SMT specification defines a distributed bidding scheme to allocate FDDI bandwidth.

- Asynchronous traffic—Bandwidth is allocated using an eight-level priority scheme. Each station is assigned an asynchronous priority level. FDDI also permits extended dialog, where stations may temporarily use all asynchronous bandwidth.

Synchronous data traffic is supported through strict media access and delay guarantees and is allowed to consume a fixed proportion of the network bandwidth, leaving the remainder for asynchronous traffic. Stations that require standard client/server or file transfer applications typically use FDDI's asynchronous bandwidth. The FDDI priority mechanism can lock out stations that cannot use synchronous bandwidth and have too low an asynchronous priority.

100BaseVG/IEEE 802.12

IEEE 802.12 is a standard for a shared 100-Mbps LAN and is specified in [31]. The MAC protocol for 802.12 is called demand priority. It supports two service priority levels: normal priority and high priority (ensuring guaranteed bandwidth). Data packets from all network nodes (hosts, bridges, and switches) are served using a simple round-robin algorithm. Demand priority enables data transfer with very low latency across a LAN hub by using on-the-fly packet transfer. The demand priority protocol supports guaranteed bandwidth through a priority arrangement, as follows:

- When an end system wishes to transmit, it issues a request.

- This request is sent to a switch and is handled immediately if there is no other active request (i.e., on an FCFS basis).

- When a packet is transmitted to the hub, the hub determines the appropriate output port in real time and switches the packet to that port.

Demand priority is deterministic in that it ensures that all high-priority frames have strict priority over frames with normal priority, and even normal priority packets have a maximum guaranteed access time to the medium (in a situation where a normal priority packet has been waiting at the head of an output queue for more than packet promotion [i.e., 200–300 ms] its priority is automatically promoted to high priority [31]).

Essentially there are three mechanisms for mapping UPV values onto 802.12 frames, as follows:

- With 802.3 frames the UPV is encoded in the Starting Delimiter (SD) of the 802.12 frame.

- With 802.5 frames the UPV is encoded in the user priority bits of the FC field in the 802.5 frame header.

- IEEE 802.1Q encapsulation may also be used, encoding the UPV within the 802.1Q tag.

In all cases, switches are able to recover any UPV supplied by a sender. The same rules apply for 802.12 UPV mapping in a bridge. The only additional information is that normal priority is used by default for UPV values 0 through 4, and high priority is used for UPV levels 5 through 7. This ensures that the default Token Ring UPV level of 4 for 802.5 bridges is mapped to normal priority on 802.12 segments.

Integrated services can be built on top of the 802.12 medium access mechanisms. When combined with admission control and bandwidth enforcement mechanisms, delay guarantees as required for a guaranteed service can be provided without any changes to the existing 802.12 MAC protocol. Note that since the 802.12 standard supports the 802.3 and 802.5 frame formats, the same framing overhead issues must be considered in the admission control computations for 802.12 links.

8.3.2   WAN QoS Features

SMDS

SMDS provides mechanisms to facilitate QoS for data traffic by supporting a number of access classes to accommodate different traffic profiles and equipment capabilities. The provider configures access classes at the time of subscription. Access classes define a maximum sustained information rate, SIR, as well as the maximum burst size, N, allowed. This is implemented as a leaky bucket scheme. Five access classes, corresponding to sustained information rates 4, 10, 16, 25, and 34 Mbps, are supported for the DS-3 access interface, implemented through credit management algorithms. These algorithms track credit balances for each customer interface. Credit is allocated on a periodic basis, up to some maximum, and as packets are sent to the network, the credit balance is decremented. This credit management scheme essentially constrains the customer's equipment to some sustained or average rate of data transfer. This average rate of transfer is less than the full information-carrying bandwidth of the DS-3 access facility. The credit management scheme is not applied to DS-1 access interfaces.

Frame Relay

Frame Relay uses a simplified protocol at each switching node, omitting flow control. Performance of Frame Relay networks is, therefore, greatly influenced by the offered load. When the offered load is high, some Frame Relay nodes may become overloaded, resulting in a degraded throughput; hence, additional mechanisms are required to control congestion, as follows:

- Admission control—This ensures that a request for resources, once accepted, is guaranteed. A decision is made whether to accept a new connection request based on the requested traffic descriptor and the network's residual capacity. The traffic descriptor comprises a set of parameters sent to switching nodes at call setup time (or service subscription time), which characterizes the connection's statistical properties. The traffic descriptor consists of the following elements:

  - Committed Information Rate (CIR)—The average rate (in bits per second) at which the network guarantees to transfer information units over a measurement interval, T, where $T = Bc/CIR$.
  - Committed burst size—The maximum number of information units that can be transmitted during the interval T.
  - Excess burst size—The maximum number of uncommitted information units (in bits) that the network will attempt to carry during the interval T.

The public network is obliged to deliver all data submitted to the network that comes within the user's CIR when the network is operating normally. Therefore, public networks should be sized according to the CIRs from all access devices (the available bandwidth must always be greater than the total CIR). Some service providers will offer an absolute guarantee of data delivery within the CIR period, while others will offer only a probability of guaranteed delivery.

ATM

The architecture for services provided at the ATM layer consists of the following five service categories [10]:

- CBR—Constant Bit Rate
- rt-VBR—Real-Time Variable Bit Rate
- nrt-VBR—Non-Real-Time Variable Bit Rate
- UBR—Unspecified Bit Rate
- ABR—Available Bit Rate

These service categories relate traffic characteristics and QoS requirements to network behavior. Service categories are differentiated as real-time or non-real-time. There are two real-time categories, CBR and rt-VBR, distinguished by whether the traffic descriptor contains only the Peak Cell Rate (PCR) or both PCR and the Sustainable Cell Rate (SCR) parameters. The three non-real-time categories are nrt-VBR, UBR, and ABR. All service categories apply to both VCCs and VPCs.

There are no mechanisms defined within ATM to bound error or loss rates, since ATM relies on the quality of the underlying physical infrastructure. Traditional ATM links (such as SONET/SDH and DS3) exhibit very low bit-error rates; however, the amount of cell loss depends very much on the architecture of ATM switches and terminal equipment (some switches are known to lose cells, even at fairly low traffic levels, but this should improve as the technology matures). The ATM layer offers error detection and single-bit error correction (optional) on cell headers but no payload protection. AAL1 detects errors in sequencing information but does not provide payload protection. AAL3/4 and AAL5 both support error detection, 3/4 on a cell-by-cell basis and 5 on a complete-packet basis. ATM does not offer an assured service; to date, the only truly reliable end-to-end ATM service is that provided via the Service-Specific Connection-Oriented Protocol (SSCOP), a protocol that runs over AAL5. SSCOP is used by the ATM signaling protocol, Q.2931.

There is an implicit contract that includes specific QoS guarantees for bandwidth, delay, delay variation, and so on with every virtual channel. However, there is not yet consensus on the level of commitment implied by these guarantees or the conditions that may void them. Consequently, experienced quality of service may vary widely from vendor to vendor and from one traffic environment to another. There will have to be agreements made on what constitutes acceptable service for the various classes of ATM and how that service will be provided. Developing mechanisms to ensure quality of service in ATM is one of the most important topics that the ATM Forum is currently investigating.

8.4   Integrated Services (IS)

The fundamental service model of the Internet, exemplified in the best-effort delivery service of IP, has remained essentially unchanged for over 20 years. This model has serviced legacy applications such as file transfer and terminal access well, but routing delays and congestion mean that real-time applications do not work so well on a best-effort Internet. The Integrated Services (IS) model is intended to solve these problems by becoming a key component of future Internet architecture. This new Internet architecture includes support for both the current best-effort services and emerging real-time services. IS is designed to optimize network resources for real-time applications such as videoconferencing, video broadcast, and audioconferencing. These applications all require guaranteed QoS in order to offer acceptable quality. IS enables Internet traffic to be separated into legacy best-effort traffic and real-time data flows requiring guaranteed QoS. IS defines two service classes specifically designed for real-time traffic, as follows:

- Guaranteed service—intended for applications requiring a fixed delay [32].

- Predictive service—intended for applications requiring prognosticate delay [32].

IS integrates (hence the name) all of these services over a common link, using a scheme called controlled link sharing. IS is also designed to work equally well with multicast as well as unicast traffic. The IS model is specified by the IETF in [11].

8.4.1   Implementation model

There are four main components required in an implementation of IS; these comprise the packet scheduler, the admission control routine, the classifier, and the reservation setup protocol. These are discussed briefly below.

- Reservation setup protocol. IS use the reservation protocol (RSVP) for the signaling of the reservation messages. The IS instances communicate via RSVP to create and maintain flow-specific states in the end-point hosts and in routers along the path of a flow. An application that wants to send data packets in a reserved flow communicates with the reservation instance RSVP. The RSVP protocol tries to set up a flow reservation with the requested QoS, which will be accepted if the application fulfilled the policy restrictions and the routers can handle the requested QoS. RSVP advises the packet classifier and packet scheduler in each node to process the packets for this flow adequately. If the application now delivers the data packets to the classifier in the first node, which has mapped this flow into a specific service class complying to the requested QoS, the flow is recognized with the sender IP address and is transmitted to the packet scheduler. The packet scheduler forwards the packets, depending on their service class, to the next router or, finally, to the receiving host. Because RSVP is a simplex protocol, QoS reservations are made only in one direction: from the sending node to the receiving node. If the application in our example wants to cancel the reservation for the data flow, it sends a message to the reservation instance, which frees the reserved QoS resources in all routers along the path, so the resources can be used for other flows.

- Admission control. The admission control contains the decision algorithm that a router uses to determine if there are enough routing resources to accept the requested QoS for a new flow. If there are not enough free routing resources, accepting a new flow would impact earlier guarantees and the new flow must be rejected. If the new flow is accepted, the reservation instance in the router assigns the packet classifier and the packet scheduler to reserve the requested QoS for this flow. Admission control is invoked at each router along a reservation path to make a local accept/reject decision at the time a host requests a real-time service. The admission control algorithm must be consistent with the service model. Admission control should not be confused with policy control, which is a packet-by-packet function processed by the packet scheduler. It ensures that a host does not violate its promised traffic characteristics. Nevertheless, to ensure that QoS guarantees are honored, the admission control will be concerned with enforcing administrative policies on resource reservations. Some policies will be used to check the user authentication for a requested reservation. Unauthorized reservation requests can be rejected. Admission control will play an important role in accounting costs for Internet resources in the future.

- Packet classifier. The packet classifier identifies packets of an IP flow in hosts and routers that will receive a certain level of service, so that each incoming packet is mapped by the classifier into a specific class. All packets that are classified in the same class get the same treatment from the packet scheduler.

- Packet scheduler. The packet scheduler manages the forwarding of different packet streams in hosts and routers, based on their service class, using queue management and various scheduling algorithms. The packet scheduler must ensure that the packet delivery corresponds to the QoS parameter for each flow.

In order for an application requiring guaranteed service or controlled-load service to make use of QoS, it must establish the end-to-end path and reserve resources along that path via the resource setup protocol prior to transmitting any data. The decision of whether or not to allocate resources is the responsibility of admission control. If granted, each router along the path must place all incoming packets associated with that flow in specific queues, according to multifield classification performed by the classifier. The scheduler then releases packets in accordance with the QoS specification.

To support the IS model, an Internet router must be able to provide an appropriate QoS for each flow. This function is called traffic control. Figure 8.6 shows the implementation model for a router and host. It is important to note that a router must determine the forwarding path for a packet on a per-packet basis. This procedure must be highly optimized, and in most

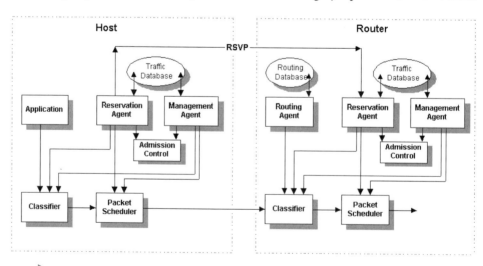

Figure 8.6   *IS model for a host and a router.*

commercial routers this typically requires hardware assist. For efficiency, a common mechanism should be used for both resource classification and route lookup.

Before describing these services in more detail we need to enlarge on our earlier discussion of flows.

8.4.2 Flows

The IS model, and especially RSVP, relies on the classification of related datagrams into flows (we defined flows earlier in section 8.1.1). There are three basic concepts related to flows that are fundamental to the IS model: sessions, flow specifications, and filter specifications.

Sessions

A session is a data flow that can be identified by its destination. The term session is used rather than destination to emphasize the soft-state nature of the flow. Once a reservation is made by a router for a particular destination, the router classifies this as a session and allocates resources for its duration. A session is defined as follows:

- Destination IP address (unicast or multicast)

- IP protocol ID (e.g., TCP, UDP)

- Destination port number (e.g., Telnet)

If the destination IP address is multicast, the destination port may not be required, since different multicast applications typically use different addresses rather than different ports. Packets that cannot be identified as belonging to a session are given a best-effort delivery service.

Flow descriptors

A reservation request issued by a destination end system for a particular flow is called a flow descriptor. A flow descriptor defines the traffic and QoS characteristics for a specific flow of data. The flow descriptor comprises a filter specification (filterspec) and a flow specification (flowspec), as follows:

- Flowspec—Used by an application to specify a desired QoS for a flow. Routers will process packets for this flow using a set of preferences based on active flowspecs. The flowspec contains the following elements: service class, Rspec, and Tspec. The service class identifies the type of service requested and includes information used by routers to merge requests. Flowspecs also contain a set of parameters collectively referred to as the invocation information, divided into two groups: Traffic Specification (Tspec) and service Request Specification (Rspec). The Tspec describes the traffic characteristics of the requested service and is represented with a token bucket filter. Rspec specifies the QoS required by the application for the flow and may comprise parameters such as a specified bandwidth, maximum packet delay, and maximum packet loss rate. The flowspec is transported by the reservation protocol, passed to admission control, and then to the packet scheduler. Note that the information derived from Tspec and Rspec and used by the scheduler is not directly visible to RSVP.

- Filterspec—The filterspec identifies the set of packets for which the flowspec is requested. Therefore, the filterspec, in combination with the session, defines a flow on which the desired QoS is to be offered. The information from the filterspec is used in the packet classifier. Filterspec comprises two elements: source IP address and source port number (e.g., for UDP/TCP). The filterspec is used to identify a specific subset of the packets associated with a session.

Traffic shaping

The IS model uses a token bucket strategy to shape traffic to meet reservation requests. This enables many traffic sources to be easily characterized, provides a concise description of the load imposed by a flow, and simplifies the process of resource reservation. Traffic shaping provides input parameters to the policing function.

8.4.3   Service classes

In addition to the basic best-effort service the IS model defines two additional service classes: a guaranteed service [32] and a controlled load service [33].

Controlled load service

The controlled load service is designed to support applications that are highly sensitive to congestion conditions in the Internet (such as real-time applications). The controlled load service is also designed for applications that can tolerate a reasonable amount of packet loss and delay, such as audio- and videoconferencing software. These applications work well on lightly loaded networks but degrade rapidly as network load increases and congestion occurs. If an application selects the controlled load service for a specific flow, then the performance of that flow will not degrade as the network load increases. The controlled load service offers only one fixed service level, with no optional features in the specification. The service simulates a best-effort service over lightly loaded networks. In effect the service offered is equivalent to that experienced by best-effort (uncontrolled) traffic under lightly loaded conditions. This means that a very high percentage of transmitted packets will be successfully delivered to the destination, and the transit delay for a very high percentage of the delivered packets will not greatly exceed the minimum transit delay.

Any router that accepts requests for controlled load services must ensure that sufficient bandwidth and processing resources are available. This can be achieved with active admission control. Before a router accepts a new QoS reservation, represented by the Tspec, it must consider all key resources (link bandwidth, router or switch port buffer space, and computational capacity for packet forwarding). The controlled load service class does not accept or make use of specific target values for control parameters such as bandwidth, delay, or loss. Applications that use controlled load services must be capable of dealing with small amounts of packet loss and occasional packet delays.

QoS reservations using controlled load services must provide a Tspec that consists of the token bucket parameters, r and b, together with the minimum policed unit, m, and the maximum packet size, M. It is not necessary to supply an Rspec, since controlled load services do not provide functions to reserve a fixed bandwidth or guarantee minimum packet delays. Controlled load service provides QoS control only for traffic that conforms to the Tspec provided at setup time. Clearly, the service guarantees apply only to packets that respect the token bucket rule (i.e., over all time periods, T, the amount of data sent cannot exceed $rT + b$).

Guaranteed service

The guaranteed service is designed to deliver datagrams from the source to the destination within a guaranteed delivery time. This means that every packet within a flow that conforms to the traffic specifications will arrive at worst case at the maximum delay time specified in the flow descriptor. For example, real-time multimedia applications, such as video and audio broadcasting, can use streaming technology. These applications cannot insert datagrams that arrive after their allotted playback time. The guaranteed service is extremely demanding in its specification for end-to-end delay control, and hence it is useful only if it is supported by every router along the reservation path (other service models in the intermediate path may have much weaker delay control mechanisms). It is important to understand that packet delay has two components, as follows:

- A fixed transmission delay. The fixed delay depends on the path taken, which is selected not by guaranteed service but by the setup mechanism. All data packets in an IP network have a minimum delay that is limited by the propagation velocity of the media and the turn-around time of the data packets in all routers on the routing path.

- A variable queuing delay. The queuing delay is determined by guaranteed service, and it is controlled by two parameters: the token bucket (in particular, the bucket size, b) and the requested bandwidth, R. These parameters are used to construct the fluid model characterizing the end-to-end behavior of a flow.

The fluid model specifies a service level for a flow that is equivalent to having a dedicated link of bandwidth R. In effect each flow has its own independent service specification that is not influenced by other flow requirements or activities. The definition of guaranteed service is based on the premise that the fluid delay of a flow obeying a token bucket (r, b), being served by a line with bandwidth R, is bounded by b / R (where $R \geq r$). In practice guaranteed service offers an end-to-end service rate, R, where R represents a proportion of bandwidth reserved along the routing path and not the bandwidth of a dedicated line. In this model, Tspec and Rspec are used to set up a flow reservation. The Tspec is represented by the token bucket parameters. The Rspec contains the parameter, R, that specifies the bandwidth for the flow reservation. Guaranteed service does not minimize jitter, but it does control the maximum queuing delay. Applications that have demanding real-time requirements (such as real-time distribution of share prices) will almost certainly require guaranteed service.

8.4.4 Resource reservation protocol (RSVP)

Resource reservation protocol (RSVP) is a key component of the IS architecture and is defined in [34]. RSVP is a connection-oriented signaling protocol designed to establish QoS-compliant paths through an end-to-end network connection by reserving bandwidth and resources in advance. RSVP is designed to meet the demands of real-time voice and video applications as well as legacy best-effort traffic. For example, a video server may ask RSVP to reserve a path to a specific destination, with bounded delay and jitter, in order to deliver a real-time videoconference feed.

RSVP runs over IP (protocol 46) and is designed to operate in both IPv4 and IPv6 environments. It exploits the Type of Service (ToS) field in the

IPv4 header and the flow label field in the Ipv6 header. RSVP can be viewed as a Session Layer service; it does not transport user data or perform routing functions. RSVP is designed to operate with both unicast and multicast routing protocols, using the local routing database on each routing node to obtain active path information. Once the path is reserved, data are delivered using a combination of conventional transport and routing protocols. Note that all the hosts, routers, and other network infrastructure elements between the receiver and sender must support RSVP along the end-to-end reservation path to maintain the path state and integrity. All devices in the path must agree to observe the RSVP call request parameters before user traffic is allowed to flow. These parameters may include mandatory flow specifications, such as the maximum frame transmission rate, long-term average frame transmission rate, maximum frame jitter, and maximum end-to-end delay. In order to satisfy these requirements, each intermediate RSVP element must reserve sufficient resources, such as bandwidth, CPU, memory, and buffers, for the specified flow.

RSVP requests are simplex (i.e., unidirectional). Therefore, the RSVP model differentiates between senders and receivers. RSVP also uses the concepts of flows and reservations. Reservations are receiver initiated (i.e., along the reverse delivery path to the sender) and made on behalf of individual packet flows. Routers in the reservation path may merge reservation requests from multiple downstream receivers, as they propagate the requests toward the sender. The receiver maintains the resource reservation for that flow for the duration. RSVP identifies flows by a combination of the destination IP address and destination port. All flows have an associated flow descriptor, which specifies the QoS requirements. Note that RSVP does not understand the contents of the flow descriptor; this object is processed by system-level traffic control functions (i.e., the packet classifier and scheduler). Depending upon the state of the network and the system resources available, any intermediate RSVP element along the upstream path can accept or reject reservation requests.

Most network applications require full-duplex services, since each sender may also act as a receiver (e.g., an interactive videoconference). In such cases two RSVP sessions must be created, one for each peer. Each receiver sends a reservation request to its associated sender, where the contents of the request depend upon the capabilities of the receiver (e.g., network interface speed, display capabilities, throughput, etc.). This model also accommodates the different QoS requirements for heterogeneous receivers in large multicast groups. The sender does not need to know the characteristics of all possible receivers to structure the reservations. For example, a high-per-

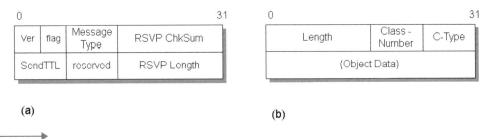

Figure 8.7   *(a) RSVP common header. (b) RSVP object header.*

formance workstation and a standard PC wish to receive a high-quality MPEG stream from a video server. The default frame rate for the video stream is 30 fps, with an unconstrained data rate of 1.5 Mbps. In this case the PC does not have enough processing power to decode the video stream at the full rate; it can only cope with 10 fps. Initially the video server uses RSVP to signal to the two receivers that it can offer the video stream at 1.5 Mbps. In this case the workstation issues a reservation request for the full 1.5 Mbps; the PC issues a reservation request for a flow with 10 frames per second and a data rate of 500 Kbps.

RSVP messages format

RSVP messages comprise a common header, followed by a variable number of objects. The number and type of these objects depends on the type of message. Message objects contain information necessary to make resource reservations—for example, the flow descriptor or the reservation style. In most cases, the order of the objects in an RSVP message is immaterial. Reference [34] recommends a specified order, but implementers should accept the objects in any order. Figure 8.7(a) shows the common header of an RSVP message. The RSVP objects that follow the common header consist of a 32-bit header and one or more 32-bit words. Figure 8.7(b) shows the RSVP object header.

Common header field definitions

- Version—a 4-bit RSVP protocol revision (currently 1).

- Flags—a 4-bit field. No flags are defined yet.

- Message Type—an 8-bit field that indicates the message type:
    - 1. Path
    - 2. Resv
    - 3. PathErr

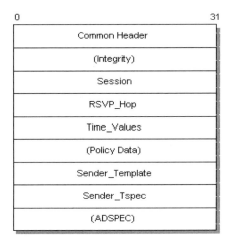

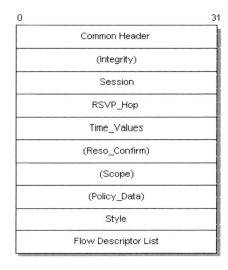

(b)   (b)

Figure 8.8   *Path reservation message format. (b) Resv message format.*

- 4. ResvErr
- 5. PathTear
- 6. ResvTear
- 7. ResvConf

- RSVP Checksum—a 16-bit field. May be used by receivers of an RSVP message to detect transmission errors.

- Send_TTL—an 8-bit field that contains the IP TTL value.

- RSVP Length—a 16-bit field that contains the total length of the RSVP message including the common header and all objects that follow. The length is counted in bytes.

We have already seen the operation of the RSVP Path and Resv messages. Figure 8.8 shows the RSVP Path and RESV Message formats. The integrity object must follow the common header if it is used. The style object and the flow descriptor list must also occur at the end of the message. The order of all other objects should follow the recommendation in [34].

RSVP message field definitions

- Length—a 16-bit field that contains the object length in bytes. This must be a multiple of 4. The minimum length is 4 bytes.

- Class-Number—Identifies the object class. The following classes are defined:

  - Null—set to zero. The length of this object must be at least 4, and any multiple of 4. The object can appear anywhere in the object sequence of an RSVP message. The content is ignored by the receiver.

  - Session—contains the IP destination address, the IP protocol ID, and the destination port to define a specific session for the other objects that follow. The session object is required in every RSVP message.

  - RSVP_HOP—contains the IP address of the node that sent this message and a logical outgoing interface handle. For downstream messages (e.g., path messages) the RSVP_HOP object represents a PHOP (previous hop) object, and for upstream messages (e.g., RESV messages) it represents an NHOP (next hop) object.

  - Time_Values—contains the refresh period for path and reservation messages. If these messages are not refreshed within the specified time period, the path or reservation state is canceled.

  - Style—defines the reservation style and some style-specific information that is not in flowspec or filterspec. The style object is required in every Resv message.

  - Flowspec—specifies the required QoS in reservation messages.

  - Filterspec—defines which data packets receive the QoS specified in the flowspec.

  - Sender_Template—contains the sender IP address and additional demultiplexing information used to identify a sender. Required in every path message.

  - Sender_Tspec—defines traffic characteristics of a data flow from a sender. Required in all path messages.

  - Adspec—advertises information to the traffic control modules in the RSVP nodes along the path.

  - Error_Spec—specifies an error in a PathErr, ResvErr, or a confirmation in a ResvConf message.

  - Policy_Data—contains information that allows a policy module to decide whether an associated reservation is administratively permitted or not. It can be used in path, Resv, PathErr, or ResvErr messages.

  - Integrity—contains cryptographic data to authenticate the originating node and to verify the contents of an RSVP message.

- Scope—contains an explicit list of sender hosts to which the information in the message are sent. The object can appear in a Resv, ResvErr, or ResvTear message.
- Resv_Confirm—contains the IP address of a receiver that requests confirmation for its reservation. It can be used in a Resv or ResvConf message.

- C-Type—specifies the object type within the class number. Different object types are used for IPv4 and IPv6.

- Object contents—varies by object type, maximum length is 65,528 bytes.

For a detailed description of the RSVP message structure and the handling of the different reservation styles in reservation messages, please refer to [34].

RSVP operation

The core operations in RSVP involve the setup and tearing down of paths and the reservation of resources along those paths. The path is the route taken by a packet flow through one or more routers from the sender to the receiver. All packets that belong to a particular flow will follow the same path through the network (i.e., typically the shortest path [s,d] created by an IGP such as OSPF or DVMRP).

Path setup, reservation, and teardown

In order to create a path, an RSVP sender uses the following process:

- The sender first issues a path message that traverses the network to the intended destination of the flow. The path message contains traffic parameters that describe the QoS requirements for a particular flow. In order to forward this message, RSVP consults routing tables in each router (created by conventional routing protocols).

- When the path message reaches the first RSVP router, the router caches the IP address from the RSVP hop field within the message (in this case the address of the sender). Then the router overwrites the last hop field with its own IP address and then forwards the modified path message to the next router in the path.

- This process continues until the message has finally reached its destination (the receiver), by which time each router in the path will know the address of the previous router and the path can be accessed in reverse.

Figure 8.9
*RSVP path
definition process.*

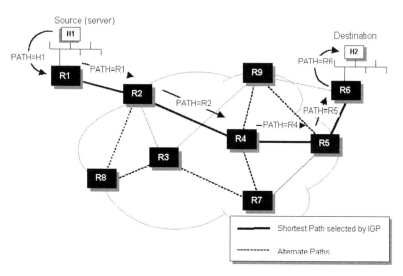

- At this point the receiver(s) knows that a sender can accommodate any QoS requirements of the flow and that all routers along the end-to-end path are aware that there may be pending resource reservations issued for this flow (which they may or may not accept, depending upon their status).

Figure 8.9 shows the process of the path definition.

If a receiver now wishes to make QoS requests for the flow, it goes through the following steps:

- The receiver transmits a reservation (Resv) message to the sender. This message contains the QoS requested from this receiver for a specific flow, as represented by the flow descriptor (comprising a filter-spec and a flowspec). The Resv message is directed to the last router in the path with the address it received and cached from the path message.

- Since each RSVP-enabled router on the end-to-end path has already cached the previous hop IP address (taken from the path message), Resv messages are simply forwarded in the reverse direction to the sender, and each router in the path examines the resource reservation request to see if it can be accommodated.

If required, a receiver may request confirmation that a request was accepted by including a confirmation request in its Resv message. Each router will return a ResvConf message if the reservation was established successfully. Figure 8.10 illustrates this process.

Figure 8.10
RSVP Resv message flow.

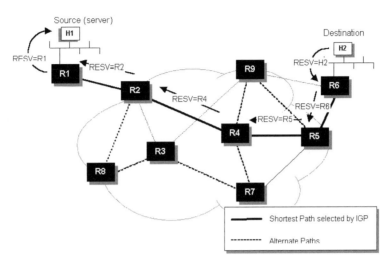

At each intermediate node, the following actions are undertaken in order to service the request:

- Process the reservation request—The RSVP process passes the QoS request to the admission control and policy control instance within the node. Admission control establishes whether the node has sufficient resource to support the new flow. Policy control checks that the requesting application is authorized to make such requests.

  - Reject the request—If either admission control or policy control tests fail, then the reservation request is rejected and a ResvErr error message is sent back to the receiver.
  - Accept the request—If both tests succeed, the node uses the filter-spec information to configure the packet classifier and the flow-spec information to configure the packet scheduler. The packet classifier will now recognize all packets belonging to this new flow, and the packet scheduler will use the QoS defined by the flowspec to determine how best to queue and schedule packet release on the outgoing interface(s).

- Forward the reservation request—If the request is accepted, it is forwarded to the next upstream RSVP node in the direction of the sender.

Note that the admission and policy control utilize information from underlying integrated services mechanisms, which are not part of RSVP and are to some extent implementation dependent (different routers have different queuing strategies).

If the reservation request does eventually reach the sender, then the sender knows that QoS reservation was accepted and configured in each router in the delivery path, and, by implication, all nodes in that path are RSVP enabled (even if a single router in the path does not support RSVP, the service cannot be guaranteed, and only a best-effort service is effected). The application can then begin to send packets downstream to the receivers. The packet classifier and the packet scheduler in each router ensure that these packets are handled and forwarded according to the requested QoS. It is important to understand that resource reservations are maintained in soft state. This requires that once established, each sender must periodically transmit Path and Resv messages to refresh the path and QoS state data for each flow it originates. This allows route changes to occur dynamically without resulting in protocol overhead. A reservation will be canceled if RSVP does not send refresh messages.

Tearing down paths

Path and reservation states can be explicitly deleted using RSVP teardown messages. There are two message types, as follows:

- PathTear messages travel downstream from the point of issue to all receivers, deleting the path state and all dependent reservation states in each RSVP-enabled device along the path.

- ResvTear messages travel upstream from the point of issue to all senders, deleting reservation states in each RSVP-enabled device along the path.

Any RSVP-enabled device that detects a state timeout should issue a teardown request automatically, so it is not strictly necessary to explicitly tear down an old reservation. However, it is recommended that all hosts issue a teardown request when an existing reservation is no longer required, since in a busy network this will release resources immediately.

Multicast operations

Although RSVP supports conventional unicast operations, it was designed primarily with multicast applications in mind, since multicasting offers a challenging scenario for resource reservation on public networks such as the Internet. For multicast operations a host sends IGMP messages to join a host multicast group as standard, and then sends RSVP messages upstream to reserve resources along the delivery path of that group. Note that conventional multicast routing protocols are still responsible for the delivery tree topology. RSVP is designed to scale efficiently for large multicast delivery groups, so reservation requests need only travel to a point where the multicast delivery tree merges another reservation for the same multicast stream. This receiver-oriented design can accommodate large multicast groups and dynamic group membership.

In a multicast environment, a receiver could be receiving data from multiple senders, and the set of senders to which a Resv message is directed is called the scope of that request. Note that with multicast operations, the Resv message that is forwarded upstream after a successful reservation may differ from the request that was received from the downstream node, for the following two reasons:

- In a multicast environment, reservations made for a common multicast source on different downstream branches are merged together as they travel upstream. This is necessary to conserve router resources and promote scalability.

- The traffic control mechanism could modify the flowspec on a hop-by-hop basis.

In fact, a reservation request travels upstream along the multicast delivery tree until it reaches a point where an existing reservation is equal to, or greater than, that being requested. At this point, the request is simply folded in with the reservation already in place; there is no need to forward it any farther. For example, in Figure 8.11, H3 sends a Resv message back toward H1 after receiving a path message. Router R7 accepts the request and forwards it upstream to R4. When R4 examines the request, it sees that H2 already has an identical QoS request in place back through R2; it accepts the request (after checking with its own admission control or policy control for the downstream interface) but does not forward it any farther upstream.

RSVP reservation styles

As described previously, receivers of multicast multimedia applications may receive flows from different senders. In the reservation process, a receiver must initiate a separate reservation request for each flow it wants to receive. However, RSVP provides a more flexible way to reserve QoS for flows from different senders. A reservation request includes a set of options that are called the reservation style. One of these options deals with the treatment of reservations for different senders within the same session. The receiver can establish a distinct reservation for each sender or make a single shared reservation for all packets from the senders in one session. Another option defines how the senders for a reservation request are selected. It is possible to specify an explicit list or a wildcard that selects the senders belonging to one session. In an explicit sender-selection reservation, a filterspec must

Figure 8.11
*RSVP behavior
with multicast
flows.*

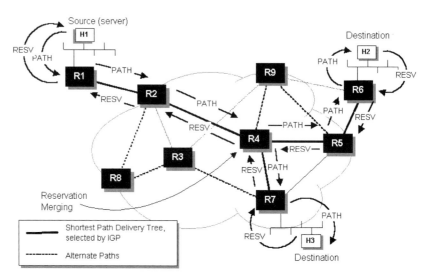

identify exactly one sender. In a wildcard sender-selection, the filterspec is
not needed.

Table 8.4 shows the reservation styles that are defined with this reservation option, as follows:

- Wildcard-Filter (WF) uses the options shared reservation and wildcard sender selection. This reservation style establishes a single reservation for all senders in a session. Reservations from different senders
  are merged together along the path so that only the biggest reservation request reaches the senders. A wildcard reservation is forwarded
  upstream to all sender hosts. If new senders appear in the session—for
  example, new members enter a videoconference—the reservation is
  extended to those new senders.

- Fixed-Filter (FF) uses the option's distinct reservations and explicit
  sender selection. This means that a distinct reservation is created for
  data packets from a particular sender. Packets from different senders
  that are in the same session do not share reservations.

- Shared-Explicit (SE) uses the option's shared reservation and explicit
  sender selection. This means that a single reservation covers flows
  from a specified subset of senders. Therefore, a sender list must be
  included in the reservation request from the receiver.

Shared reservations (WF and SE) are generally used for multicast applications. For these applications it is unlikely that several data sources trans-

Table 8.4   *RSVP Reservation Attributes and Styles*

Sender Selection	Reservation Attribute	
	Distinct	Shared
Explicit	Fixed-Filter Style (FF)	Shared-Explicit Style (SE)
Wildcard	(undefined)	Wildcard-Filter Style (WF)

mit data simultaneously, so it is not necessary to reserve QoS for each sender. For example, an audioconference could be directed to ten identically equipped receivers, each with a 64 Kbps back to the sender. With a fixed-filter reservation, all receivers must establish nine separate 64-Kbps reservations for the flows from every other sender. This is overkill, since we know that audioconferences generally operate on the principle that only one or two people speak at the same time, and most audioconferencing software today uses silence suppression (if a person does not speak, then no packets are sent). Therefore, it would be appropriate in this case to reserve a total bandwidth of maybe 128 Kbps for all senders, if every receiver makes one shared reservation of 128 Kbps for all senders. If the shared-explicit style is used, all receivers must explicitly identify all other senders in the conference. If the wildcard-filter style is used, then the reservation applies to every sender that matches the reservation specifications (e.g., if the audioconferencing program transmits data to a special TCP/IP port, the receivers can make a wildcard-filter reservation using this destination port number).

RSVP APIs

A receiver can make a reservation request for itself or on behalf of another application. To do so requires a set of RSVP-relevant APIs. There are currently a number of standard RSVP API proposals that multicast application programmers should be aware of for possible future enhancement of their applications. These include the following:

- RSVP Application Programming Interface (RAPI)—for Sun OS/ BSD: v4.0, describes a set of APIs that provide low-level access to the protocol services.

- WinSock 2 Application Programming Interface (API) specification— has a set of easy-to-use, protocol-independent QoS-sensitive APIs that will map to RSVP services.

- The WinSock 2 protocol-specific annex—specification has some RSVP protocol-specific APIs available for low-level access to the protocol services.

Vendors have implemented host RSVP stacks both above and below the Winsock layer. Another approach is to use an RSVP proxy, which runs independently of the real application, making RSVP reservations on its behalf.

8.4.5 Design considerations

There are a number of issues with the IS model, including the following:

- Scalability—One key issue with the IS model is scalability. Fundamentally this is limited by the state that would be required in the network for RSVP on links with very high levels of statistical multiplexing. The size of the state tables expands relative to number of flows; with a large, busy network this can consume a significant portion of router processing power and memory. As a direct consequence, at present only high-end router platforms typically support RSVP.

- End-to-end RSVP support—A key drawback with the IS model is that it requires unanimous support for RSVP between the end systems to offer QoS guarantees. Although intermediate routers and routing domains can happily coexist without needing to support RSVP, this reduces the guarantee to no better than best-effort unless static service-level agreements can be mapped at intermediate non-IS domains. More router manufacturers are beginning to support RSVP; however, its support is difficult, and it is typically supported on the high-end, more expensive platforms.

- Pricing model—The issue of pricing structure is fundamental to the widespread deployment of RSVP. It is expected that service providers will charge premiums for RSVP QoS reservations. Consider a flow traversing the global Internet. It is very unlikely that this flow would receive special handling from all of the routers along a path unless those routers have a real incentive to do so, in preference to handling other flows with the same level of care. Furthermore, on a free network most users would eventually request special handling, negating its value, so there needs to be a way of dissuading such practice. The most likely mechanism to promote the required behavior is differential pricing. However, it is difficult to imagine a practical pricing model to handle bandwidth reservation and billing across multiple carrier networks. This issue still requires further research and definition.

- Maintaining acceptable best-effort support—If the IS model is to be adopted for the Internet, it must ensure that the current best-effort traffic characteristics are still maintained. It would be unacceptable for some routers to be so busy handling RSVP reservations that they could not process the default best-effort traffic. This could even be a policy decision for ISPs. For example, an ISP could specify that one-half of the routing capacity is reserved for RSVP flow reservations and the other half for the best-effort traffic.

- Performance—An important consideration when running the IS model over an internetwork is the traffic control overhead in RSVP-enabled routers. This may degrade the routing performance of under-powered devices or devices without hardware assist. As the number of data flows handled by a router increases, more RSVP sessions must be handled by the RSVP agent, and more CPU time and memory capacity will be utilized. The computational resources required for routers to inspect and handle these packets in a priority order are likely to be significant. Approaches such as tag switching are being developed to alleviate this issue. Another area of research is enhancing RSVP to use routing services that provide alternate and fixed paths. In the meantime router manufacturers must ensure that in high-traffic situations a router is not too busy managing RSVP sessions instead of routing packets and maintaining the network integrity.

- Real-time applications—Protocols such as RTP can complement RSVP by allowing applications to respond to the underlying network performance. For multimedia, the audio and video are carried in a separate RTP session with RTCP packets controlling the quality of the session. Routers communicate via RSVP to set up and manage reserved-bandwidth sessions.

These limitations are considerable barriers to IS deployment, and the jury is still out. Even if eventually successful, it will be some time before end-to-end RSVP services are available on the Internet. Currently IS is perhaps best employed in corporate intranets, providing end-to-end QoS for multimedia and other real-time applications.

8.5   Differentiated Services (DS)

The Differentiated Services (DS) concept is currently under development at the IETF DS working group. The DS specifications are defined in a number of IETF Internet drafts, but currently no RFC is available. Since the concepts involved are still in the development phase, some of the information and references are likely to change. The goal of DS development is to provide differentiated classes of service for Internet traffic to support various types of applications and specific business requirements. DS offers predictable performance (delay, throughput, packet loss, etc.) for a given load at a given time. A key advantage of DS over the IS model is that DS provides a scalable service for the Internet without the need for per flow state and signaling at every router hop. It eliminates the need to store information about each flow and can be deployed without requiring expensive and complicated end-to-end signaling (e.g., RSVP).

8.5.1   Service marking

DS-enabled networks classify packets according to one of a small number of aggregated flows, based on bit settings within the one-byte ToS field of the IPv4 header and the traffic class byte in the IPv6 header. The IETF DS working group has proposed to redefine the structure of this field in DS-capable networks, and this revised field is referred to as the DS byte (overriding the IPv4 TOS byte specifications in [8]). Figure 8.12 illustrates the structure of the DS byte.

Field definitions

- DSCP—Six bits of the DS field are used as a Differentiated Services CodePoint (DSCP) to select the traffic class a packet will experience at each node.

  - 000000—The IETF working group recommends this value for the default best-effort Per Hop Behavior (PHB).
  - 101100—The IETF working group recommends this value for the Expedited Forwarding (EF) PHB.

- CU—A two-bit Currently Unused (CU) field is reserved and can be assigned later.

The traffic class specified in the DS byte indicates whether packets should receive special handling or the default best-effort delivery. All network traffic inside a domain receives a service that depends on the traffic class specified in the DS byte. To provide SLA-conforming services, the following mechanisms must be combined in a network:

- Setting bits in the DS byte (ToS octet) at network edges and administrative boundaries.

- Using DS bits to indicate how packets are treated by the routers inside the network.

Figure 8.12
The DS byte format.

- Conditioning marked packets at network boundaries in accordance with the QoS requirements.

The DS architecture currently provides service differentiation in one direction and is, therefore, asymmetric. Development of a complementary symmetric architecture is a subject of further work. Unlike IS, QoS guarantees with DS are static and stay for a long term in routers. This means that applications using DS don't need to set up QoS reservations for specific data packets. All traffic that passes DS-capable networks can receive a specific QoS. The data packets must be marked with the DS byte, which is interpreted by the routers in the network.

8.5.2   Per Hop Behavior (PHB)

Every DS-enabled network device must have access to information on how packets with different DS codepoints (DSCP) should be handled. This is referred to as the Per Hop Behavior (PHB). PHB describes the treatment a packet receives by each network node along the forwarding path. PHBs need to be defined in all routers in a DS-capable network in order to provide predictable end-to-end services. The PHB is basically a set of parameters that can be used by a router to determine how packets are scheduled for dispatch to an output interface.

There are a number of scheduling and congestion avoidance techniques available in commercial products today. DS requires routers with sophisticated scheduling disciplines to prioritize outbound packets and control the queue depth (using algorithms such as WFQ and RED) to minimize congestion on the network. Routers with only FIFO queuing cannot provide service differentiation and may potentially suffer periodic congestion. The exact handling a packet will receive inside a router is very much vendor dependent. For example, an IP packet could be forwarded to a router with eight different queues (0 = high priority, 8 = low priority), and the DS byte can be used to select which queue is most appropriate for forwarding the packet. Alternatively, a router can have a single queue with multiple drop priorities for data packets. The router uses the DS byte to select the drop preference for the packets in the queue. A value of zero would indicate that the router is most likely to drop this packet; whereas a value of seven means that the router is least likely to drop this packet.

To ensure that the PHBs in each router are consistent, a number of standard PHBs will be defined in future DS specifications (see Figure 8.12). All routers in a DS domain must know which service a packet with a specific PHB should receive. PHBs will be defined in groups. A PHB group is a set of one or more PHBs that can only be specified and implemented simultaneously, because of queue servicing or queue management policies that apply to all PHBs in one group. A default PHB must be available in all DS-compliant nodes. It represents the standard best-effort forwarding behavior available in existing routers. When no other agreements are in place, it is assumed that packets belong to this service level. Another PHB that is proposed for standardization is Expedited Forwarding (EF). EF requires high-priority treatment and is typically used for network control traffic (such as OSPF routing updates).

8.5.3   Design considerations

The attraction of the DS model when compared to the IS model is that it builds on existing best-effort service components without a major hardware and software overhaul. This makes it much more viable for service providers and equipment vendors alike. Since the DS model relies on soft-state information, it is considerably more flexible both to deploy and enhance.

Differentiated services domains

The setup of QoS guarantees is not made for specific end-to-end connections but for well-defined DS domains. The IETF working group defines a DS domain as a contiguous portion of the Internet over which a consistent set of differentiated services policies are administered in a coordinated fashion. It can represent different administrative domains or autonomous systems, different trust regions, and different network technologies, such as cell or frame-based techniques, hosts, and routers. A DS domain comprises boundary components that are used to connect different DS domains to each other and interior components that are used only inside the domains. A DS domain normally comprises one or more networks under the same administration. This could be a corporate intranet or an ISP. Administrators of a DS domain are responsible for ensuring that adequate resources are provisioned and reserved to support the SLAs offered by the domain. This should be regularly monitored.

Boundary nodes

All data packets that travel from one DS domain to another must pass a boundary node, which can be a router, host, or firewall. A DS boundary node that handles traffic leaving a DS domain is called an egress node, and a boundary node that handles traffic entering a DS domain is called an ingress node. Normally, DS boundary nodes act both as ingress node and egress node depending on the traffic direction. The ingress node must make sure that the packets entering a domain receive the same QoS as in the previous domain. A DS egress node performs conditioning functions on traffic that is forwarded to a directly connected peering domain. The traffic conditioning is done inside a boundary node by a traffic conditioner. It classifies, marks and possibly conditions packets that enter or leave the DS domain. Figure 8.13 shows the cooperation of the traffic conditioner components. A traffic conditioner consists of the following components:

- Classifier—A classifier selects packets based on their packet header and forwards the packets that match the classifier rules for further processing. The DS model specifies two types of packet classifiers:

  - MultiField (MF) classifiers that can classify on the DS byte as well as on any other IP header field (e.g., the IP address and the port number, similar to an RSVP classifier).
  - Behavior Aggregate (BA) classifiers, which classify only on the bits in the DS byte.

- Meter—Traffic meters measure if the forwarding of the packets that are selected by the classifier corresponds to the traffic profile that describes the QoS for the SLA between customer and service provider. A meter passes state information to other conditioning functions to trigger a particular action for each packet that either does or does not comply with the requested QoS requirements.

- Marker—DS markers set the DS byte of the incoming IP packets to a particular bit pattern. The PHB is set in the first six bits of the DS byte so that the marked packets are forwarded inside the DS domain according to the SLA between service provider and customer.

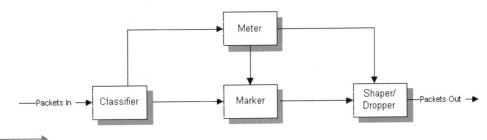

Figure 8.13   *DS traffic conditioner.*

■ Shaper/dropper—Packet shapers and droppers cause conformance to some configured traffic properties, (e.g., a token bucket filter). They use different methods to bring the stream into compliance with a traffic profile. Shapers delay some or all of the packets. A shaper usually has a finite-size buffer, and packets may be discarded if there is not sufficient buffer space to hold the delayed packets. Droppers discard some or all of the packets. This process is known as policing the stream. A dropper can be implemented as a special case of shaper by setting the shaper buffer size to zero packets.

The traffic conditioner is primarily used in DS boundary nodes (although it may also be used in interior nodes). The main purpose of traffic conditioning in a boundary node is to ensure that consistent service mappings are applied as packets transit multiple domains (since different DS domains may support different PHB groups, the same entry in the DS byte can be interpreted differently in different domains). For example, routers inside Domain A may have only four queues available, whereas routers inside Domain B may have eight queues. For packets that require high-priority service originating in Domain A, the traffic conditioner must ensure that packets forwarded to Domain B have their PHBs mapped accordingly. In practice the DS byte may be remarked at every boundary component to ensure that the SLA is not violated. A Traffic Conditioning Agreement (TCA) within the SLA specifies the classifier rules (e.g., metering, marking, discarding, and traffic shaping) required to meet the SLA. The TCA parameters must be distributed to all boundary components of a DS network in order to guarantee that packets traversing different DS domains receive a consistent end-to-end level of service.

Interior nodes

Interior nodes (i.e., routers with traffic management features) within a DS domain control the forwarding behavior for packets based on the contents of the DS byte. Since the DS byte is not normally modified within a DS domain, all interior routers must implement consistent forwarding policies. Packets with different PHB settings will receive different levels of service (depending upon the particular QoS-PHB mapping). Since all interior routers within a domain use the same policy functions for incoming traffic, traffic conditioning within an interior node is simply handled by the packet classifier. The classifier selects packets based on their PHB value (or other IP header fields) and then passes these packets to scheduling functions within the node, where they are prioritized and dispatched from queues in a manner appropriate to the required service quality. When packets reach the edge of a domain, they are processed by a boundary router, where they are potentially remarked (to ensure consistent PHB) before being forwarded to the next domain.

Source domains

A source domain is a domain that contains one or more nodes that originate traffic that receives a particular level of service (e.g., a video server within a customer domain requesting a specific delay and throughput quality). Both traffic sources and intermediate nodes within a source domain can perform traffic classification and conditioning functions, and traffic may be marked by the traffic sources directly or by intermediate nodes before leaving the source domain. The first PHB marking of data packets is not done by the sending application; packets are marked by the source host platform or an intermediate router. Applications are, therefore, unaware of DS functions (which is in direct contrast with the IS model, where most applications must be modified to support RSVP). Packets are identified using their IP address and source port. For example, a customer has an SLA with a provider network that guarantees high-priority handling for packets sent by a videoconferencing application. The DS network must implement an appropriate policy to match this requirement. The videoconferencing application transmits packets using a specific port that can be recognized by MultiField (MF) classifiers; an MF classifier can examine the IP address and port number of an individual packet and so differentiate between different applications. Hence, if the source host contains a traffic conditioner with an MF classifier, it can mark IP packets with the appropriate PHB value (i.e., by setting the DS codepoint), as they are being made ready for dispatch. If the source host does not possess this functionality, then the first router encountered in the source domain that supports traffic conditioning handles the initial PHB marking by classifying packets and then setting the correct DS codepoint. Note that the use of the DS codepoint effectively aggregates flows with similar service requirements. The source DS domain is responsible for ensuring that all aggregated flows forwarded to external domains conform to their SLA requirements. The boundary node of the source domain should also monitor incoming traffic to establish that service levels are conformed to and may police, shape, or remark packets if necessary.

8.6 Integrating QoS

As indicated, quality of service is a highly active area of research and experimentation, with several competing and complementary technologies. Over the next few years it is anticipated that these technologies will begin to integrate, since without true integration between LAN, MAN, and WAN envi-

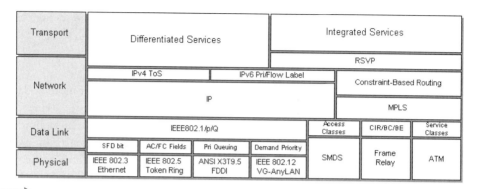

Figure 8.14   *Pieces of the QoS jigsaw puzzle in context.*

ronments there is no hope of providing true end-to-end service quality. If different QoS mechanisms are to be run in each of these environments (and this is to be expected), then clear interfaces and service mappings must be defined and adhered to. To this end several initiatives are underway, particularly within the IETF. Perhaps before discussing some of these initiatives it is worth placing the components of the various QoS and traffic engineering architectures in context, as illustrated in Figure 8.14. Note that this figure does not imply protocol stack choices or combinations; it merely places the various components in their logical position.

8.6.1   Using RSVP with DS

There are several fundamental issues with RSVP and the IS model that hinder widespread adoption, particularly over the Internet. In particular RSVP's reliance on per flow state and per flow processing raises scalability concerns. This complexity means that only a minority of hosts generate RSVP signaling, and many applications may never generate RSVP signaling. For these reasons it may be applicable to deploy IS only in intranets, and use DS over the Internet backbone. This is currently the subject of a draft RFC [35].

Figure 8.15 illustrates an example: Two RSVP-capable customer intranets are connected to the Internet backbone, running DS. Within the DS domain, Boundary Routers (BR) may condition incoming and outgoing traffic at the backbone ingress and egress. Note that the boundary routers are not required to run RSVP; they are expected to implement the policing functions of the DS ingress router. The routers in the DS network must provide a set of per hop behaviors that support an appropriate end-to-end service quality, enabling the mapping of RSVP flow reservations to an

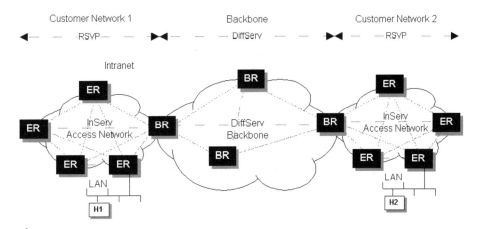

Figure 8.15   *The transit (backbone) network is running DiffServ for scalability and ease of deployment. RSVP is run on the stub (access) networks between the edge routers and the backbone routers.*

appropriate DS service class. The edge boundary routers that join the DS and IS domains support both RSVP and DS functions. The RSVP component must be able to process path and Resv messages, but it is not required to support packet classification or hold RSVP states. The DS component provides an admission control function for the DS network. If a static SLA is used at the IS-DS boundary, then the admission control service could just be a simple table that specifies the QoS for each service level. If the SLA is dynamic, then the admission control service communicates with counterparts within the DS network to make decisions based on the capacity of the network.

RSVP signaling is used to provide admission control to specific service levels in the DS and the IS network. If an RSVP reservation message from the IS domain arrives at an edge boundary router, the RSVP flow descriptor must be mapped to a PHB that represents the corresponding service level in the DS network. The edge router appends the PHB value to the RSVP reservation message, which is carried to the sending host. The sending host then marks all outgoing packets with this PHB value. This approach allows end-to-end QoS guarantees for RSVP applications in different intranets that use the DS Internet as backbone.

8.6.2   Using RSVP with 802.1p

In order to offer true end-to-end QoS from LAN to other network media, we need a way to bind RSVP and IEEE 802.1p together. Reference [27] defines a signaling protocol for RSVP-based admission control over IEEE 802 networks called the Subnet Bandwidth Manager (SBM). SBM conveys 802.1p priorities between Layer 2 switches. It also maps Class of Service (CoS) between RSVP clients and RSVP-enabled networks, describing how LAN hosts, switches, bridges, and routers should operate to enable LAN-based resources to be reserved for RSVP-enabled data flows. For the interested reader, [24] specifies a framework for providing IS over shared and switched LAN technologies.

8.6.3   Using 802.1p with ATM

An increasing number of customers are deploying 802.1p on their switched Ethernet LANs to queue packets using priority. 802.1p prioritizations may be mapped to high-speed ATM switch uplinks provided that the uplinks support both 802.1p and PNNI/LANE. The ATM uplink can request QoS Available Bit Rate (ABR) for those packets destined to travel across the ATM fabric. ABR enables a connection to use whatever bandwidth is currently available, so theoretically the switch could request different ABR QoS profiles for different 802.1p priorities. This does not provide all of ATM's QoS features to Ethernet, but it does enable Ethernet prioritization over ATM.

8.6.4   Using DS with IPSec

IPSec considers the DS field (or ToS field) an immutable field in an IP header; therefore, changes made to the DS field in transit do not compromise end-to-end security. If IPSec is used in tunnel mode, then different DS domains may be supported. Here, the outer IP header and the encapsulated IP header correspond to two different DS domains, and the tunnel end points delimit the two DS domains.

8.6.5   Interoperability with constraint-based routing

Constraint-Based Routing (CBR) is a complementary technology to many of the technologies described in this chapter, as follows:

- CBR with DiffServ—DS and CBR are complementary. CBR may be used to assist in the delivery of DS since the QoS requirement of the flow and the load of the networks are considered in selecting the best path.

- CBR with RSVP—RSVP and CBR are also complementary. The next hop of the RSVP path message determined by CBR might be different from that calculated by dynamic routing, since the QoS requirement of the flow and the load of the networks are considered in selecting the next hop.

- CBR with MPLS—MPLS and CBR together provide a powerful traffic engineering tool. Given a set of routes MPLS uses its label distribution protocol to set up the LSPs. The routing agent is transparent to MPLS and vice versa. If these routes are determined by CBR instead of a dynamic routing protocol, then this makes it possible to do CBR with traffic trunk granularity, without having to perform flow classification within the core routers. MPLS provides per LSP statistics that offer CBR very precise information on traffic levels between every ingress-egress pair, enabling CBR to compute better routes for setting up LSPs.

8.6.6   QoS policy management

In a large QoS-enabled internetwork, especially in a multivendor environment, conventional ways of managing control and configuration data do not scale. It is critical in this environment, where customers are paying for service differentiation, that systems behave consistently. All network entities should ideally be configured under a single policy-based framework, so that service differentiation can be expressed in business terms and then translated into specific device behavior. For example, the network planner may wish to create predefined service classes (e.g., bronze, silver, or gold) and then have routers and switches utilize queuing and congestion control features to support these service classes. If conflicting policy information exists in parts of the network, packets may not receive the requested level of service in certain domains, and the SLA made between customer and provider could be violated. In dynamic network environments it is also necessary to support flexible policy definitions so that behavior can be altered dynamically in the face of certain events (e.g., time of day, network overload, link loss, etc.).

Reference [36] describes a preemption priority policy element for use by signaled policy-based admission protocols (such as RSVP and COPS). For other RSVP policy-related specifications, see [37, 38].

8.7   Summary

In this chapter we discussed the following:

- Customers negotiate Service-Level Agreements (SLAs) with service providers. The SLA specifies what services the customers will receive.

SLAs can be static or dynamic. For static SLAs, customers can transmit data at any time. For dynamic SLAs, customers must use a signaling protocol such as RSVP to request services on demand before transmitting data. SLA monitoring is still an immature technology, and it is not clear what a carrier will or will not accept as proof of a failing SLA. For an ISP or carrier SLA monitoring is not an option, but an end-user network needs to consider the cost-benefit of implementing such tools or outsourcing this activity.

- The ingress routers of ISPs are configured with classification, policing, and remarking rules. The egress routers of ISP networks are configured with reshaping rules. Such rules may be configured manually by network administrators or dynamically by some protocol such as LDAP or RSVP. ISPs must implement admission control in order to support dynamic SLAs. Classification, marking, policing, and shaping/reshaping are only done at the boundary routers. Core routers are shielded from the signaling process. They need only implement two queues with strict priority. They process packets based solely on their DS fields.

- Constraint-Based Routing (CBR) can be used to compute the routes subject to QoS and policy constraints. The goal is to meet the QoS requirements of traffic and to improve utilization of the networks. QoS offers a more sophisticated approach to traffic engineering by taking into account multiple constraints and attempting to distribute traffic more evenly over the available bandwidth while maintaining the QoS requirements for a particular flow. The advantages of CBR over traditional routing are the ability to satisfy QoS requirements of flows and improved network utilization. The disadvantages of CBR are increased communication, computation and storage overheads, longer paths consuming more resources, and potential routing instability. CBR is similar to the dynamic/adaptive routing techniques in telephone networks and ATM networks. CBR must be implemented and deployed with care; otherwise, the cost of instability and increased complexity may outweigh the benefits.

- With MPLS, Label-Switched Paths (LSPs) are established between each ingress-egress pair. At the ISP ingress routers, labels and Class of Service (CoS) fields are determined from the classification and routing results. MPLS headers are then inserted into the packets. Core routers process packets based on their labels and COS fields only. Labels are removed before packets leave an MPLS domain. MPLS and constraint-based routing can be used together to control the path of traffic so as to avoid congestion and improve the utility of the networks.

- The relatively recent ratification of 802.1p is enabling QoS convergence in the LAN environment. Setting priority bits and implementing class-based forwarding are significant steps toward multimedia convergence and policy-enabled networking. While most vendors today agree that 802.1p/Q is the mechanism to tag frames for prioritization, there is no uniform approach to implementing the underlying queuing mechanisms to control priority flows.

- One of the first attempts to provide QoS through the Internet was via a signaling protocol called Resource Reservation Protocol (RSVP). RSVP uses end-to-end signaling to set up and tear down IP connections, each having specific service characteristics. Intermediate nodes (such as routers and switches) are expected to reserve the resources necessary to satisfy a particular application service specification. RSVP is now part of an overall architecture for QoS developed by the IETF, called Integrated Services (IS). RSVP only defines the connection setup mechanisms; other technologies are required to allocate and ensure that the resources are in place.

- There are still major issues to resolve with the DS model if is to be deployed across the global Internet. RSVP must be deployed on all routers in the end-to-end path of a flow. RSVP session processes are complex, and RSVP is difficult to scale, since it places more processing load on heavily utilized backbone nodes. Moreover, the pricing model and intercarrier billing mechanisms for RSVP are far from resolved. These issues are considerable barriers to widespread IS over public backbones, and there is some consensus that IS is perhaps better employed in enterprise environments, mapping onto DS at the backbone edge.

- Differentiated Services (DS) is an alternative end-to-end QoS model proposed by the IETF. A key advantage of DS over the IS model is that DS provides a scalable service for the Internet without the need for per flow state and signaling at every router hop. It eliminates the need to store information about each flow and can be deployed without requiring expensive and complicated end-to-end signaling (e.g., RSVP). DS networks classify packets according to one of a small number of aggregated flows, based on the setting of bits in a ToS field in each packet's IP header.

References

[1]   T. Kenyon, *High-Performance Network Design: Design Techniques and Tools* (Woburn, MA: Digital Press, 2001).

[2]   A Framework for QoS-based Routing in the Internet, RFC 2386, August 1998.

[3]   Blake et. al., Architecture for Differentiated Services. Internet draft, draft-ietf-diffserv-arch-02.txt, October 1998.

[4]   D. Clark, "The Design Philosophy of the DARPA Internet Protocols," in *Proceedings of ACM SIGCOMM '88*, August 1988.

[5]   Cisco Systems, Tag Switching Architecture Overview, RFC 2105, February 1997.

[6]   Internet Protocol, RFC 791, September 1981.

[7]   Type of Service in the Internet Protocol Suite, RFC 1349, July 1992. (obsoleted by RFC 2474).

[8]   Definition of the Differentiated Services Field (DS Field) in the IPv4 and IPv6 Headers, RFC 2474, December 1998.

[9]   ANSI T1S1, DSSI Core Aspects of Frame Rely, March 1990.

[10]   Traffic Management Specification version 4.0. The ATM Forum Technical Committee, af-tm-0056.000, April 1996.

[11]   Integrated Services in the Internet Architecture: An Overview, RFC 1633, June 1994.

[12]   Y. Bernet, R. Yavatkar, P. Ford, et al., A Framework for Use of RSVP with DiffServ Networks. Internet draft <draft-ietf-diffserv-rsvp-00.txt>, June 1998.

[13]   ISO/IEC 8802-5 Information Technology—Telecommunications and Information Exchange between Systems—Local and Metropolitan Area Networks—Common Specifications—Part 5: Token Ring Access Method and Physical Layer Specifications (also ANSI/IEEE Std 802.5-1995), 1995.

[14]   ISO/IEC Final CD 15802-3 Information Technology—Telecommunications and Information Exchange between Systems—Local and Metropolitan Area Networks—Common Specifications—Part 3: Media Access Control (MAC) Bridges, (current draft available as IEEE P802.1D/D15), September 1998.

[15]   www.frforum.com, Frame Relay Forum home page.

[16] www.tmforum.org, Telemanagement Forum home page.

[17] C. Labovitz, G. R. Malan, F. Jahanian, "Internet Routing Instability," *IEEE/ACM Transactions on Networking,* vol. 6, no. 5, October 1998, 515–528.

[18] OSPF version 2, RFC 2178, July 1997.

[19] C. Villamizar, and T. Li, IS-IS Optimized Multipath (IS-IS OMP). Internet draft: draft-villamizar-isis-omp-00.txt, October 1998.

[20] S. Chen, "Routing Support for Providing Guaranteed End-to-End Quality of Service." Ph.D. dissertation, University of Illinois, May 1999.

[21] R. Guerin, S. Kamat, A. Orda, et al., QoS Routing Mechanisms and OSPF Extensions. Internet draft, draft-guerin-QoS-routing-ospf-03.txt, January 1998.

[22] Z. Zhang, C. Sanchez, B. Salkewicz, et al,. QoS Extensions to OSPF. Internet draft: draft-zhang-qos-ospf-01, September 1997.

[23] R. Callon, P. Doolan, N. Feldman, et al., A Framework for Multiprotocol Label Switching. Internet draft, draft-ietf-mpls-framework-02.txt, November 1997.

[24] M. Seaman, A. Smith, and E. Crawley, Integrated Service Mappings on IEEE 802 Networks (work in progress). Internet Draft, draft-ietf-issll-is802-svc-mapping-01.txt, November 1997.

[25] W. Lidinsky, IEEE Standard P802.1D Information Technology—Telecommunications and Information Exchange between Systems—Common Specifications—Part 3: Media Access Control (MAC) Bridges: Revision, 24.11.1997, 1997.

[26] A. Ghanwani, J. W. Pace, V. Srinivasan, et al., A Framework for Integrated Services Over Shared and Switched IEEE 802 LAN Technologies. Internet draft, draft-ietf-issll-is802-framework-07.txt, June 1999.

[27] R. Yavatkar D. Hoffman Y. Bernet Y, et al., SBM (Subnet Bandwidth Manager): A Protocol for RSVP-based Admission Control over IEEE 802-style Networks. Internet draft: draft-ietf-issll-is802-sbm-07.txt, November 1998.

[28] ISO/IEC 15802-3 Information Technology—Telecommunications and Information Exchange between Systems—Local and Metropolitan Area Networks—Specific Requirements—Supplement to Carrier Sense Multiple Access with Collision Detection (CSMA/CD) Access

Method and Physical Layer Specifications—Frame Extensions for Virtual Bridged Local Area Network (VLAN) Tagging on 802.3 Networks, IEEE Std 802.3ac-898 (supplement to IEEE 802.3 1998 edition), 1998.

[29]   ISO/IEC 8802-5 Information Technology—Telecommunications and Information Exchange between Systems—Local and Metropolitan Area Networks—Common Specifications—Part 5: Token Ring Access Method and Physical Layer Specifications (also ANSI/IEEE Std 802.5-1995), 1995.

[30]   ISO/IEC 15802-3 Information Technology—Telecommunications and Information Exchange between Systems—Local and Metropolitan Area Networks—Common Specifications—Part 3: Media Access Control (MAC) Bridges (also ANSI/IEEE Std 802.1D-1998), 1998.

[31]   IEEE Standards for Local and Metropolitan Area Networks: Demand Priority Access Method, Physical Layer, and Repeater Specification for 100-Mbps Operation, IEEE Std 802.12-1995, 1995.

[32]   Specification of Guaranteed Quality of Service, RFC 2212, September 1997.

[33]   Specification of the Controlled Load Network Element Service. RFC 2211. September 897.

[34]   Resource Reservation Protocol (RSVP)—version 1, Functional Specification, RFC 2205, September 1997.

[35]   E. Bernet et al., A Framework for Use of RSVP with DiffServ Networks, draft-ietf-diffserv-rsvp-00.txt, June 1998.

[36]   Signaled Preemption Priority Policy Element, RFC 2751, January 2000 (proposed standard).

[37]   RSVP Extensions for Policy Control, RFC 2750 (proposed standard).

[38]   Identity Representation for RSVP, RFC 2752, January 2000 (proposed standard).

9

Network Management

This chapter is concerned with the management and maintenance of inter-networks. Management should be tackled as a proactive task and should form an integral part of your design strategy. Maintenance is all too often a reactive task, dealing with unforeseen problems and diagnosing network failures. Network management becomes a key concern as networks grow in both size and complexity. As the number of devices, services, users, and sites begins to multiply, so do the network manager's activities and responsibilities. In a large commercial internetwork, it may be critical to identify problems and resolve them in a matter of minutes. You need to identify and resolve problems before they become serious enough to jeopardize the business. Remote devices may need to be monitored, closed down, and restarted. Faults must be clearly reported, understood, and acted upon. Inefficiency, overloading, and degraded performance should be diagnosed and resolved proactively. To achieve all this, management centers and managed devices must be capable of communicating with one another. These functions are commonly referred to as a Management Information Services (MIS). If the network is designed properly from the ground up, the MIS should be used as a proactive tool to monitor the network and work out where performance can be improved and cost savings made. Value-added services (such as advanced network monitoring and modeling tools) can be built into this basic structure. In a badly designed network you will spend the majority of your time fire fighting.

Perhaps the two classic vendor architectures are DEC's DECnet and IBM's SNA. Both architectures have strong emphasis on management and introduce very comprehensive and well-integrated management models. In the IP world SNMP has been around since the late 1980s, but since no single vendor controls this architecture the management model is less comprehensive. Nevertheless, from an internetwork point of view SNMP currently dominates the installed base, and even proprietary systems often have gateways into the SNMP domain.

Network management and control represents a potentially exciting area for further investment in the application of artificial intelligence. Networks are destined to evolve from disjoint, inarticulate, and helpless organisms to intelligent, self-maintaining entities capable of keeping themselves in peak performance with minimal intervention from the network manager. Serious network outages are regularly caused by simple cable breaks, loose connectors, faulty hardware, and misconfigured software. These problems could be better resolved through good design choices and proactive management tools (especially tools that distribute intelligence across the network); this represents a promising area for further research.

9.1   Network management technologies

9.1.1   The Network Management System (NMS)

In a well-run network, network management allows managers to take control of the network rather than the other way around, and the network management system (sometimes called the network operations center) is likely to be the focal point for network status monitoring and reporting. Many large commercial networks have dedicated rooms for network management facilities, often with multiple in-band management stations along with out-of-band control facilities. At the heart of most network management systems is a live network map. This is typically a set of hierarchical object maps presented on a Graphical User Interface (GUI). Various icons are used to represent the class and status of the different devices being managed. Figure 9.1 illustrates a typical map showing a number of color-coded devices indicating normal operation and unreachable or fault condition

Management interfaces can be either passive or active. A passive interface allows the network administrator to access important information such as system status, protocol events, and traffic statistics. An active interface enables the administrator to modify device status and control activities on a device (such as enabling a port, disabling a routing protocol, etc.). Clearly, one of the key issues with active interfaces (and to some extent passive interfaces) is security, in that the remote party must be a trusted user. Security has limited the scope of SNMP deployment for many years.

Toolbar   Network Map

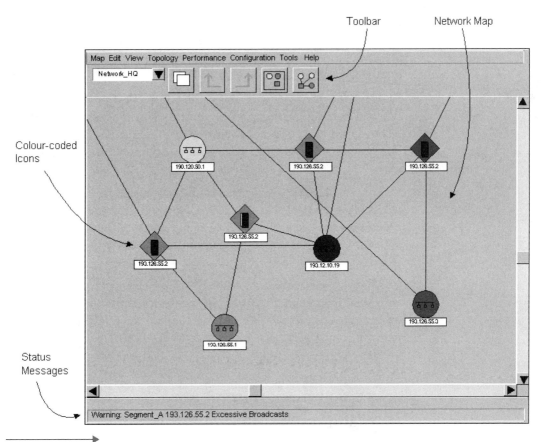

Figure 9.1 *A typical Graphical User Interface (GUI) showing a network map.*

There is more to network management than the network map however. The ISO Management Framework breaks down network management into the following categories:

- Configuration management—During the initial implementation of any large internetwork configuration management is the most important facet of network management. It covers areas such as installation, booting, inventory management, and reconfiguration. In a multivendor environment it may be difficult to maintain consistent procedures here, and this is just one area of network management that needs significant future development.

- Performance management—Performance management is key to capacity planning, trend analysis, and baselining [1]. It is also important for performance tuning and optimization. The results of performance monitoring should ideally be fed back into any tools used to design the network so that the model can be validated. Some of the more sophisticated design tools are now able to do this, albeit in a limited fashion.

- Fault management—Covers areas such as troubleshooting, diagnostics, and locating and fixing failed devices. This is probably one of the better served areas of network management, although there is still a long way to go towards the goal of automating most of these procedures.

- Security management—As networks have increased in size and businesses move more of their operations onto the network, security has become a major concern. Security management includes topics such as alerting unauthorized access via alarms and traps and coordinating security policy over large internetworks.

- Accounting management—Accounting management is concerned with how the running costs of the network are captured and ultimately billed to users. This is possibly the least well-developed area of network management today.

To assist this functionality, a network management station may offer features such as the following:

- Graphical User Interface (GUI)

- Autotopology discovery (difficult in mixed-media multivendor networks)

- Database support (either proprietary or standard, increasingly accessible via the Lightweight Directory Access Protocol—LDAP)

- Both in-band and out-of-band management interfaces

- Embedded ping and Telnet support (either for diagnostics, inventory management, configuration management, reachability testing where no SNMP stack exists, or as part of autodiscovery)

- Reporting capabilities and detailed network statistics (standard objects plus many vendor-specific additions)

- Trouble ticketing

- Conversion of traps/events to alerts for centralized management

There needs to be a data collection and transport architecture underpinning all of these features to glue all of the relevant pieces together. The main choices to date are Simple Network Management Protocol (SNMP), Common Management Information Protocol/Common Management Information Service (CMIP/CMIS), and IBM's NetView. Some of the main vendors offering network management platforms, complete architectures, and management tools are discussed in section 9.1.6. First we discuss some of the underlying technology used to build network management frameworks.

9.1.2   Simple Network Management Protocol (SNMP)

Background

Nowadays it seems almost impossible to mention the words network management without using SNMP in the same sentence. SNMP has become synonymous with network management due to its rapid deployment and the fact that, for the most part, it works well and is compact enough to be implemented on most low-level devices. SNMP was designed to operate over large internetworks and is primarily concerned with monitoring and isolating faults. SNMP is not really designed for end system management or high-level configuration management.

SNMP is based on the Simple Gateway Management Protocol (SGMP) router protocol; the original architects are Jeff Case, James Davin, Mark Fedor, and Martin Schoffstall. Cisco, ACC, and Proteon introduced the first SNMP-products in 1988. At the time there was still much debate about OSI and IEEE management schemes, but these were soon drowned in a tidal wave of SNMP-enabled products. SNMP is now supported by practically every manufacturer of network devices. SNMP is the de facto standard for multivendor network management. It was primarily developed for use with TCP/IP networks and was endorsed by the U.S. Internet Activities Board (IAB) in April 1988. SNMP is now extremely well supported as agent software running in devices such as repeaters, bridges, routers, and switches. From the management station perspective, implementations range from basic management tools built with UNIX command-line utilities or simple Windows dialog boxes (which are often freely available) up to sophisticated network management systems with built-in expert systems costing thousands, or even millions, of dollars.

The key advantages of implementing SNMP are that it is vendor independent, simple to implement, and relatively small (in terms of protocol stack requirements). Early studies suggested that SNMP could be implemented in as little as 64 KB of RAM, whereas OSI's CMIS/CMIP required as much as half a megabyte (plus additional connection-oriented processing overheads). This is important for keeping costs down in devices where there

is precious little memory and possibly no requirement for a transport protocol (such as in a modem or multiplexer). Critics of the protocol, however,
argue that it is insecure (especially version 1) and makes device configuration very cumbersome (since SNMP has no concept of data grouping).
Today, SNMP is supported by numerous commercial platforms and is
widely available as public domain source code. SNMPv1 is documented in
[2]; SNMPv2 is documented in [3–7].

Architecture

SNMP is based on a manager-agent interaction, running a client/server
model over connectionless UDP (although transport over TCP and other
protocols is possible). Typically the agent collects real-time data (called
managed objects) from the device on which it is resident. The manager
polls the agents for information on a regular basis to keep track of the status
of resources (see Figure 9.2). The NMS then processes the data locally.
Agents cannot request information from an NMS (hence they cannot perform tasks such as user validation on SetRequests). An SNMP manager (the
client) has the ability to issue the SNMP commands and be the end point
for traps being sent by the agent (the server).

The manager uses commands to either retrieve data (using a Get command) or change data (using a Set command) from the Management Information Base (MIB) located in the agent. An agent can notify a manager of
an event using the Trap command.

SNMP also supports the concept of a proxy agent. This is a type of gateway and provides the ability to manage remote non-SNMP devices over
proprietary protocols. The management station must interface with the
non-SNMP devices using other protocols (possibly proprietary) and then
publishes any relevant data into the SNMP domain by placing these data in
the local MIB.

Aside from the client/server architecture, the key components of the
SNMP model comprise the Structure of Management Information (SMI),
the Management Information Base (MIB), and the Simple Network Management Protocol (SNMP).

SMI

The Structure of Management Information (SMI) is defined in [5, 8]. The
SMI organizes, names, and describes object information in order to standardize how information can be accessed consistently. Objects are defined
using SMI encoding rules. The SMI states that each managed object must
have a name, syntax, and an encoding, as follows:

- The name (referred to as an Object Identifier, or OID) uniquely identifies the object.

- The syntax defines the data type, such as an integer or a string of octets.

- The encoding describes how the information associated with an object is serialized for transmission between machines.

SMI defines the Basic Encoding Rules (BER) for representing managed objects and uses a subset of Abstract Syntax Notation (ASN.1) encoding for message formats (see section 9.1.4 and [2]). SNMP uses four simple types: INTEGER (32-bit unsigned), OCTET STRING, OBJECT IDENTIFIER, and NULL. Managed objects are referenced using a unique OID, and values associated with these objects are stored as strings or integers. Note that the NULL type is used by programmers to customize data types. SNMP also permits two constructor types (sometimes referred to as aggregate types): SEQUENCE and SEQUENCE OF. These are used to generate lists and tables. Finally, SNMP supports a small numbers of application-wide types, as follows:

- NetworkAddress—This represents an address from one of possibly several protocol families. Currently, only the Internet protocol family is present. The type is defined in ASN.1 as CHOICE.

Figure 9.2
Basic SNMP architecture.

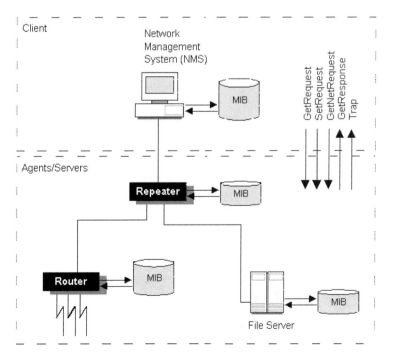

- IpAddress—A 32-bit IP address. It is defined as an OCTET STRING of length 4, in network byte order.

- Counter—A nonnegative integer, which increments until it reaches a maximum value, at which point it wraps around and starts increasing again from zero. The maximum value is 2^{32-1} (4294967295 decimal).

- Gauge—A nonnegative integer, which may increase or decrease but which latches at a maximum value. The maximum value is 2^{32-1} (4294967295 decimal).

- TimeTicks—A nonnegative integer, which counts the time in hundredths of a second since some epoch. The description of the object type identifies the reference epoch.

- Opaque—Offers the capability to pass any form of encoding transparently as an OCTET STRING. A conforming implementation need only be able to accept and recognize opaquely encoded data (it does not need to be able to unwrap these data).

Note that the restricted 32-bit integer size of counters has caused some concern for long-term statistical analysis on large or extremely busy networks. If these counters wrap, there is no obvious way of knowing how many times they have cycled, and so data are effectively lost or are meaningless unless collated regularly.

MIB

An MIB defines groups of managed objects, some of which are mandatory according to the protocol modules implemented in the managed device. The objects are defined independently from SNMP and arranged into a hierarchical tree, divided into four broad object classifications (directory, mgt, experimental, private), as illustrated in Figure 9.3. The major object branches are as follows:

```
1                       iso
1.3                     org
1.3.6                   dod
1.3.6.1                 internet
1.3.6.1.1               directory
1.3.6.1.2               mgmt
1.3.6.1.2.1             mib-2
1.3.6.1.2.1.2.2.1.3     ifType
1.3.6.1.2.1.10          transmission
1.3.6.1.2.1.10.23       transmission.ppp
1.3.6.1.2.1.27          application
1.3.6.1.2.1.28          mta
```

```
1.3.6.1.3              experimental
1.3.6.1.4              private
1.3.6.1.4.1            enterprise
1.3.6.1.5              security
1.3.6.1.6              SNMPv2
1.3.6.1.7                 mail
```

The mgt (management) subtree is mandatory for objects under SNMP and is the subtree used to identify objects that are defined in IAB-approved documents. The experimental subtree is used to identify objects used in Internet experiments, and objects here are potentially migrated into the mgt branch [9]. The directory branch is reserved for future use. For a complete list of assigned numbers relating to the subtrees, consult [10]. The private subtree is used to identify objects defined unilaterally (i.e., for vendor-specific extensions). Note that it is also strongly recommended for vendors to register themselves under the private.enterprise subtree 1.3.6.1.4.1.

Examples of networking-related enterprise OIDs are as follows (there are over 1,000 registered entries referenced in [10]).

Figure 9.3
MIB tree hierarchy.

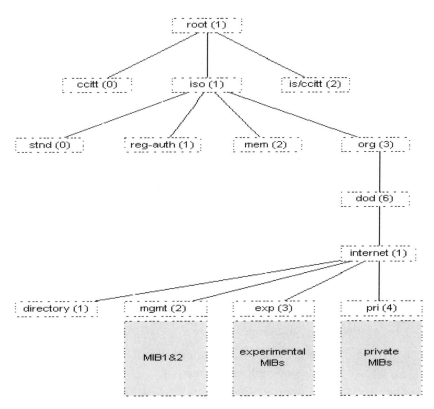

1	Proteon	164	Rad Data Communications Ltd.
2	IBM	166	Shiva Corporation
5	ACC	193	Ericsson Business Communications
9	Cisco	211	Fujitsu Limited
16	Timeplex	232	Compaq
23	Novell	233	NetManage, Inc.
33	Xyplex	238	Netrix Systems Corporation
34	Cray	303	Hughes
35	Bell Northern Research	311	Microsoft
36	DEC	351	Stratacom
42	Sun Microsystems	353	ATM Forum
43	3Com	434	EICON
52	Cabletron Systems	437	Grand Junction Networks
56	Castle Rock Computing	475	Wandel and Goltermann Technologies
72	Retix	484	kn-X Ltd.
75	Ungermann-Bass	559	Sonix Communications, Ltd.
81	Lannet Company	562	Northern Telecom, Ltd.
94	Nokia Data Communications	594	British Telecom
99	SNMP Research	838	Xedia Corporation
111	Oracle	897	Sybase, Inc.
119	NEC Corporation	946	Bay Technologies Pty Ltd.

One of the most important generic MIBs is called MIB-II [11], which supersedes MIB-I [12]. Objects within an MIB are referenced by traversing the tree using a dot-delimited string of short names or integer OIDs. For example, an object in MIB-II could be prefixed by 1.1.3.6.1.2.1 or iso.org.dod.internet.mgmt.mib2 (note that root uses OID = 1 but has no name). Figure 9.4 illustrates an example GetRequest for the object 1.3.6.1.2.1.1.1.1.1.1.1.1.0 in its decoded form.

MIB-I defines 126 generic objects and is fairly limited in scope. The latest MIB standard (MIB-II, see [11]) defines several extensions for routing and media support. These include DS3, PPP, and Frame Relay support; better EGP monitoring; improved access to application information; and IEEE 802.1d STA, Token Ring, and DECnet Phase IV support. MIB-II defines the ten function groups as follows:

- System—textual description of the entity being managed.

- Interface (IF Table)—tabular description of the network interfaces.

- Address Translation (AT Table)—translation tables for physical addresses.

- IP—addresses, indicators, and counters for IP decisions on datagrams and routing information.

- ICMP—the error input and output statistics.

- TCP—information of TCP connections, and transmission.

- UDP—information on datagrams.

- EGP—information on the exterior gateway neighbors.

- Transmission—information on different types of transmission media.

- SNMP—information on SNMP for use by applications using SNMP statistical information.

An SNMP agent does not have to implement all groups; however, if an agent implements a group then it must implement all the managed objects within that group. Note that MIB-1 and MIB-II have the same OID. MIB-II is a superset of MIB-1.

Vendors can create their own private MIBs using the private.enterprise tree; these are normally described in an ASCII text file using ASN.1 BER. In the past, some vendors did not publish their MIB extensions and produced their own proprietary management applications, mainly for competitive reasons. Thankfully, those days are long gone, and nowadays these private MIBs are often freely published on vendor Web sites or may be obtained by contacting the vendor directly. For a management application

```
File:SNMP01.ENC      Type:SNIFFER_ENC  Mode:oooooo  Records:16
==============================================================================
Frame    : 5              Len     : 87              Error   : None
T Elapsed: 12:09:09:636   T Delta : 00:00:00:002
------------------------------[mac]-------------------------------------------
Dest Mac : Xyplex027c33   Sourc Mac: Sun   02be59   Type    : IP
------------------------------[ip]--------------------------------------------
IP Ver   : 4              IP HLen : 20 Bytes
TOS      : 0x00           Pkt Len : 73              Seg ID  : 0x450d
Flags    : FRAG:v.LAST    Frag Ptr : 0    (8 Octet) TTL     : 60
PID      : UDP ( 17)      Checksum : 0x5ae  (Good)
Dest IP  : 193.128.88.59  Source IP: 193.128.88.173
------------------------------[udp]-------------------------------------------
Dest Port: SNMP [  161]              Src Port : 4401
Length   : 53                        Checksum : 0x0000
------------------------------[snmp]------------------------------------------
Version  : 1
Community: "public"
Command  : GetRequest
RequestID: 17
ErrStatus: 00
ErrIndex : 00
Object ID: 1.3.6.1.2.1.1.1.1.1.1.1.1.1.0.
String   : ""
=============================[data:   0]======================================
```

Figure 9.4 *Example GetRequest for 1.3.6.1.2.1.1.1.1.1.1.1.1.0.*

to access these private objects it must be aware of them and understand their context. Once downloaded you can incorporate these private objects onto an NMS platform via an ASN.1 compiler. The compiler is often supplied with the management application, but you could use a public domain MIB compiler (see [13, 14] or one of the many commercial compilers).

Private extensions typically comprise performance, routing, hardware status, and configuration management objects. Over time, some of these extensions make it into the standard MIBs, and as the standard MIBs expand, the management of devices in a multivendor network will become simpler and less proprietary.

SNMP

SNMP [2] is a simple request-response protocol and is predominantly asymmetric in operation; most communications are initiated from an intelligent management application and directed toward one or more relatively dumb agents (SNMPv2 redresses the balance a little by introducing peer communication via the inform command). The SNMP agent resides on the device being managed (such as a router) and acts upon Get or Set requests from the NMS by interacting with local MIB objects. The only autonomous operation an SNMPv1 agent can perform is the transmission of Traps to the NMS. The management application is normally accessible through a local or remote graphical user interface; the agent usually has no user interface.

SNMP is transport independent, the preferred transport platform being UDP (using ports 161 and 162) over IP (see Figure 9.5). UDP port 161 is used to send and receive all data-related SNMP messages. UDP port 162 is used exclusively for Traps. There may also be circumstances in which SNMP is required to run directly over some other protocol stack (generally this is not the case), as follows:

- If the SNMP UDP/IP stack cannot be tunneled.

- The managed node is accessible only via a proprietary protocol.

- The UDP/IP encapsulation is seen as too great an overhead.

- The host network is pure OSI or some other non-IP architecture.

- The application requires low-bandwidth out-of-band management and, therefore, minimal overhead.

- There is no current or future requirement for internetworking on a large flat network.

SNMP has been ported over a number of different protocol stacks, including TCP, OSI Connectionless-mode Transport Service (CLTS), OSI

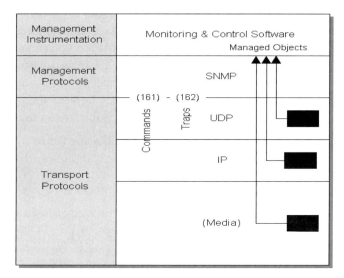

Figure 9.5
*Basic SNMP
protocol stack and
object interaction.*

Connection-Oriented Transport Service (COTS) [15], AppleTalk DDP [16], Novell IPX [17], SLIP/PPP, ATM, X.25 tunneling, LLC/LLC2, and Ethernet MAC layer framing (EtherType 0x814C). As a general rule there is not much benefit in running SNMP over anything other then UDP, since it is so widely implemented, although a number of users do perceive the need for a guaranteed transport service (such as TCP or OSI Transport Class 4). Direct mappings over Data Link or Physical Layer protocols have questionable value, since they cannot be routed, and this severely limits the scope of network management. Another issue to be resolved with non-UDP implementations is interoperability; there would clearly need to be some form of transport gateway if two different implementations were to communicate. The interested reader is directed to [4, 18, 19] for further information on possible transport mappings and their implications.

SNMP message structure

SNMP entities normally communicate via UDP messages within IP datagrams. A message must be entirely contained in a single datagram (no fragmentation is allowed). SNMP packet formats are described using ASN.1. ASN.1 basically fills the role of external data representation (XDR). The message format uses the basic encoding rules of ASN.1, structured as follows:

```
INT     Version ID
BYTE    *Community Name
BYTE    *Data
```

The data field comprises one or more SNMP Protocol Data Units (PDUs). The maximum SNMP message size is limited by maximum UDP message size (65,507 bytes). All SNMP implementations must be capable of receiving packets up to at least 484 bytes in length. Message lengths greater than 484 bytes may be rejected, although support for larger messages is recommended. Some SNMP implementations may not handle packets exceeding 484 octets or may misbehave on receipt of such messages.

Each SNMP PDU contains the following fields:

- PDU type—the command type

- Request ID—request sequence number

- Error status—zero if no error—otherwise one of a small set

- Error index—if nonzero, indicates which of the OIDs in the PDU caused the error

- List of OIDs and values—values are null for get and get next requests (values are supplied by agents in response PDUs)

In SNMPv1, Trap PDUs differ from the standard PDU and contain the following fields:

- Enterprise—identifies the type of object causing the Trap

- Agent address—IP address of agent that sent the Trap

- Generic Trap ID—the common standard Traps

- Specific Trap ID—indicates a proprietary or enterprise Trap

- Timestamp—indicates when the Trap occurred in time ticks

- List of OIDs and values—OIDs that may be relevant to send to the NMS

SNMPv2 Trap PDUs were modified to use the standard PDU format.

Service primitives

SNMP operations are invoked by a small number of primitives, as defined in [2]. SNMP supports the following functions:

- Get Request/Response

- Set Request/Response

- GetNext Request/Response

- GetBulk Request/Response (introduced in SNMPv2)

- Trap

- Inform Request/Response (introduced in SNMPv2)

Get

GetRequests retrieve object information from a client MIB. They can retrieve only one object at a time and are unsuitable for bulk retrieval. A request is not explicitly acknowledged, but if successful the client will respond with the appropriate data and an error indication using a GetResponse.

Set

SetRequests are used to modify an MIB object or variable, and a successful operation will be responded to by a SetResponse. The client will respond with appropriate data and an error indication if not successful.

GetNext

GetNextRequests are used to simplify table transversal and simplify MIB browsing. GetNextRequest references a pointer to the last retrieved object and so does not require an exact name to be specified; when invoked, it simply returns the next object in the MIB (hence, MIBs must be strictly ordered sets, and, depending upon the implementation, GetNextRequests can exhibit some anomalies).

GetBulk

GetBulkRequests are used to alleviate the burden of programming multiple GetNextRequests; in effect that is precisely what they do automatically to retrieve multiple rows of table data. The implementation of GetBulk is, unfortunately, still problematic. Refer to [20] for full details of GetBulk.

Inform

Inform is used for unsolicited messages for manager-to-manager (M2M) communications. This could also be used for distributed management or by a networking device wishing to retrieve information from the management application. Several vendors have retrofitted this command to their SNMPv1 stacks.

Trap

Traps are used for unsolicited messages, triggers, and alarms. A Trap might be generated on a significant alarm condition, such as link failure or authentication failure. In SNMPv1 the Trap primitive used a form of PDU different from the other commands. In SNMPv2 the Trap PDU was made consistent, and traps are named in MIB space (enabling manager-to-manager communications). The original mandatory Trap list specifies the following conditions:

- 0: coldStart

- 1: warmStart

- 2: linkDown

- 3: linkUp

- 4: authenticationFailure

- 5: egpNeighborLoss

Many products do not implement all of these Traps, since they are not all relevant to every device type supporting SNMP (egpNeighborLoss being a good example). Vendors can assign additional Traps (starting at 6) for custom events via a special Trap called the enterprise Trap (see [21, 22]. Trap is the only PDU sent by an agent to one or more nominated Trap servers (usually one or more NMSs) on its own initiative.

One of the problems with Traps is that when a number of failures occur, many Traps could be generated, blocking up event logs and potentially causing congestion. To work around this, a managed node may be configured to send Traps only when specific thresholds have been reached (e.g., a transparent bridge could send a Trap when 90 percent of its filter table is in use). Newer MIBs specify management objects that control how Traps are sent. An even better solution is the concept of Trap-directed polling. With this model the managed node sends a single trap to the NMS when an extraordinary event occurs. It is then up to the NMS to poll in the vicinity of the problem by initiating further communications with the managed node or neighboring managed devices (the NMS is clearly in a better position to determine what the cause of the problem might be, since it has the big picture of the network).

Table traversal with GetNextRequest

In SNMPv1 the most important use of GetNextRequest is the traversal and retrieval of data from tables within the MIB. GetNext supports multiple arguments, enabling efficient data retrieval; it is interesting to note that other management protocols such as OSI employ extremely complex mechanisms for traversing management information. SNMP data retrieval is, however, not especially efficient from a traffic perspective. Use of the GetNextRequest for bulk data retrieval can have a noticeable impact on network performance; hence, it is worth understanding. An example SNMP exchange is outlined in the following chart. Here an SNMP management application is attempting to retrieve the destination address and next-hop gateway address for all entries in a routing table. The table is accessed via an SNMP agent residing on a remote routing node. Assume in this example that the routing table has only three entries, as follows:

```
Destination          NextHop              Metric
195.160.12.23        195.160.12.1         100
20.0.0.50            89.1.1.42            40
10.0.0.99            89.1.1.42            20
```

The management station sends a GetNextRequest PDU to the SNMP agent, containing several operands representing three columns of data in the first row of the routing table, as follows:

```
GetNextRequest ( ipRouteDest, ipRouteNextHop, ipRouteMetric1 )
```

The interaction between the NMS and agent proceeds as follows:

```
MANAGEMENT APPLICATION                                              SNMP AGENT
              <- GetResponse (( ipRouteDest.195.160.12.23 = "195.160.12.23" ),
                       ( ipRouteNextHop.195.160.12.23  = "195.160.12.1" ),
                              ( ipRouteMetric1.195.160.12.23 = 100 ))

GetNextRequest ( ipRouteDest.195.160.12.23, ->
              ipRouteNextHop.195.160.12.23,
              ipRouteMetric1.195.160.12.23 )

                      <- GetResponse (( ipRouteDest.20.0.0.50 = "20.0.0.50" ),
                            ( ipRouteNextHop.20.0.0.50 = "89.1.1.42" ),
                                  ( ipRouteMetric1.20.0.0.51 = 40 ))

GetNextRequest ( ipRouteDest.20.0.0.50, ->
              ipRouteNextHop.20.0.0.50,
              ipRouteMetric1.20.0.0.50 )

                      <- GetResponse (( ipRouteDest.10.0.0.99 = "10.0.0.99" ),
                            ( ipRouteNextHop.10.0.0.99 = "89.1.1.42" ),
                                  ( ipRouteMetric1.10.0.0.99 = 20 ))

GetNextRequest ( ipRouteDest.10.0.0.99, ->
              ipRouteNextHop.10.0.0.99,
              ipRouteMetric1.10.0.0.99 )
```

When there are no further entries in the table, the SNMP agent returns those objects that are lexicographically next in the order within the MIB (i.e., when the returned prefix differs from the requested prefix, this indicates the end of the table). In this example we would expect to see a final response from the agent with the prefix ipRouteIfIndex instead of ipRouteDest (since this is the next object in MIB-II). From a traffic perspective, each row retrieved produces a pair of SNMP poll-response packets. If large data tables are periodically retrieved from multiple agents, this can lead to a significant amount of background management traffic (imagine a backbone node routing table). For this reason SNMPv2 introduced a new primitive called GetBulk, but unfortunately its use is still problematic.

SNMP security

SNMP by default allows anybody to configure or access data on a remote device. Although it is in the interests of simple management, clearly this represents a considerable security compromise. In SNMPv1 there are several basic mechanisms to control access, as follows:

- Community names

- Limit management requests to specific devices

- Disable the Set capability

The community name (or community string) is a case-sensitive ASCII string (an OctetString, of 0–255 octets). Every managed device belongs to a community; the default community string is Public. Community names are a simple way of restricting configuration and monitoring access; the community name, in effect, operates like a simple password for a group of devices. A group of routers, for example, could belong to the community TERABIT; this would mean that only management applications configured with the same community string would be able to manage these routers. Note that the main NMS on a large internetwork would generally be configured to manage multiple communities. Community names are useful but not very secure, since they are statically configured, sent over the network in cleartext, and hence vulnerable to attack. Even if these strings could be encrypted, some countries might not permit this option if local encryption legislation were particularly restrictive (so remote management over international boundaries could be compromised).

SNMP-enabled internetwork devices usually allow you to configure one of more Trap clients by IP address. If this facility is configured on the managed device (i.e., the agent), any attempts to configure or retrieve data from that device by an untrusted management application could raise an alarm via a Trap message.

Because of the relative weakness of community strings and the potential for damaging mission-critical equipment, many vendors disable the Set capability on their agents by default; several do not implement it at all. In secure environments these devices would typically be configured via the local console, via remote password-protected Telnet sessions into the CLI

Table 9.1   *Comparison of Secure SNMP and SNMPv2 Performance, Measured in SNMP Primitives Per Second (Tests Conducted at Carnegie Mellon University, Pittsburgh, PA)*

	Secure SNMP	SNMP2
No Security	210	3300
Authentication Only	195	2910
DES Encryption	110	1600

or, even better, via a secure remote HTTP access in combination with SSH or SSL (i.e., a secured Web-based browser interface). Once configured these devices would then be purely monitored via SNMP; no configuration changes would be allowed. SNMPv2 and SNMPv3 have enhanced SNMP's security architecture as described in the following text.

SNMPv2

SNMPv2 is an interim standard documented in [6] (with the MIB specified in [7]). SNMPv2 does, however, provide several useful enhancements, including the following:

- Performance improvements, as indicated in Table 9.1.

- A new primitive called GetBulk, for optimized bulk data retrieval.

- A richer set of messages for use between the NMS and the agent. This includes an acknowledgment for Set primitives as well as the ability for an agent to indicate it has a problem servicing a request (so the NMS doesn't persistently retry, as in SNMPv1).

- Multiprotocol support. SNMPv2 offers better abstraction at the Transport Layer interface to enable support for non-IP-based transports.

- A new set of manager-to-manager (M2M) communication features that standardize the role of the Mid-Level Manager (MLM) for hierarchical management models.

SNMPv2 also integrates several security enhancements [23]: Secure SNMP, the Simple Management Protocol (SMP), and the Party-based SNMPv2. Each of these efforts incorporates industrial-strength security, and these efforts were integrated into the SNMPv2 Management Framework [5–7]. However, this framework had no standards-based security and administrative framework of its own and relied on multiple frameworks, including the Community-based SNMPv2 (SNMPv2c), SNMPv2u, and SNMPv2*. Unfortunately, SNMPv2c was endorsed by the IETF but had no security and administration framework, and both SNMPv2u and

SNMPv2* had security but lacked IETF endorsement. Aside from this standards muddle, SNMPv2 offered DES for authentication and encryption, which was problematic for international users since U.S. manufacturers were restricted by legislation from exporting strong encryption outside the United States. Consequently, SNMPv2 received a mixed reception and the whole security issue has been revisited and addressed in SNMPv3.

SNMPv3

SNMPv3 is a new version of SNMP under development but builds upon much of the early work done by the authors of SNMPv1 and SNMPv2. One of the key focal points for SNMPv3 is a definition of security and administration that enables secure management transactions, including manager-to-agent, agent-to-manager, and manager-to-manager transactions. This work comprises authentication and privacy, authorization and view-based access control, and standards-based remote configuration (of particular importance for managed VPNs). Refer to [23] for a full discussion of these features.

Implementations of the SNMPv3 are already being developed by several vendors and research organizations, including ACE*COMM, AdventNet, AGENT++, BMC Software, Cisco (IOS version 12.0[3]T), IBM Research, and SNMP Research. For the interested reader, an active Web page for SNMPv3, including many useful links, is maintained by the Simple Times [24]. See also [RFC2570], [23, 25–28].

SNMP V1, V2, and V3 coexistence

There are two generally accepted approaches for migrating between SNMPv1, SNMPv2, and SNMPv3 environments: bilingual managers and proxy agents. For further details on these strategies refer to [29]. IBM Research [30], for example, already has a multilingual SNMPv1, v2c, and v3 stack.

Resilience

SNMP's simplicity and connectionless operation provide a degree of robustness. The connectionless nature of SNMP leaves the recovery and error detection up to the NMS and even up to the agent. Neither the NMS nor the agents rely on one another for continuous operation (a manager can continue to function even if a remote agent fails and vice versa). Even if an agent fails, it can send a Trap to the NMS if it subsequently restarts, notifying the NMS of its change in operational status. The NMS can periodically poll agents to test their availability.

Although SNMP is typically used over UDP, it is transport independent. UDP, being connectionless, is thought by many to be better suited for network management than a connection-oriented transport, particularly when the network is failing and routing can oscillate. UDP minimizes the stress placed on the network (i.e., no resources are tied up as with maintaining connections), leaving the agent and NMS implementations with the responsibility for error recovery. This contrasts directly with OSI's preference for a connection-oriented approach to network management (using OSI transport class 4). Some users may, however, require a connection-oriented transport, if the network is especially unreliable or if specific guarantees are required to ensure reliable message delivery (in the IP world this could be provisioned using TCP). The argument against this is that it is precisely when the network is most unreliable that connection-oriented protocols place the most stress on the network, potentially making the situation worse.

Performance issues

The connectionless mode of SNMP means that the management application is not required to maintain long-term state information for management sessions (just short-term state information for pending requests or replies). This greatly reduces the CPU and memory overheads on the host NMS platform, and, in theory, the management application needs only to run one client process to manage a large internetwork. However, for performance reasons it is usual for the management application to spawn off multiple client processes to increase throughput (avoiding blocking and queuing problems during management traffic burst or multiple pending events).

SNMPv1 is by definition simple, but the request-response polling model (together with the very limited primitive support) means that it is by no means an efficient way to move bulk management data around the network. We saw earlier that to get the contents of a routing table from a large backbone router via SNMP requires that the table is retrieved a row at a time with successive SNMP GetNextRequests. This means that there will be a UDP request and response for every routing entry (literally thousands in a backbone node), and each request includes a variable OID string and community name. This potentially induces significant traffic overheads on the network and significant latency in data retrieval.

All currently active SNMP frameworks (SNMPv1, SNMPv2c, and SNMPv3) are inefficient in terms of the number of bytes needed to transfer MIB data over the network. There are three main reasons for this inefficiency: the Basic Encoding Rules (BER), the OID naming scheme (lots of repetition), and what is referred to as the GetBulk overshoot problem. Nevertheless, SNMPv1 is considerably slower than its successors. Relative testing performed at Carnegie Mellon University demonstrates how Secure SNMP and SNMPv2 compare (in units of management transactions per second).

Reference [20] describes an algorithm that improves the retrieval of an entire table by using multiple threads in parallel, where each thread retrieves only a portion of the table. This requires a manager that supports multiple threads and that has knowledge about the distribution of instance identifiers in the table. This algorithm does not reduce the total number of request-response PDU exchanges but does improve latency, because several threads gather data simultaneously. The downside for achieving reduced latency is bursty SNMP traffic, which can overload the agent or impact user traffic (since SNMP traffic is most likely in-band). Things get worse if the network starts to drop packets, since retransmission timers must expire and subsequent retransmissions must get through for the retrieval process to continue. SNMPv2 offers a new primitive called GetBulk, which is designed to resolve this issue. Unfortunately, the manager may not know the size of the table to be retrieved and therefore must guess a value for the max-repetitions parameter. Using small values for max-repetitions may result in too many PDU exchanges. Using large values can result in the agent returning data that do not belong to the table being probed. These data will be sent back to the manager to be discarded. In the article "Bulk Transfers of MIB Data" [31] a new operator called getsubtree is proposed to counter this problem.

Another issue for performance is the management hierarchy. In a large internetwork you must seriously consider systems that can be implemented from the top down. If every management system receives all of the management data, then they will quickly become overloaded. It is relatively easy to define which objects an NMS will manage, but some systems may not support an NMS hierarchy, whereby a central backbone NMS manages multiple local Mid-Level Managers (MLMs). There is nothing in the SNMP specifications that describes such a model. With this type of model you should also investigate systems with resilient databases and possibly hierarchical access control schemes to support different classes of users.

Summary of SNMP advantages and disadvantages

The key advantages of SNMP are as follows:

- Its design is simple, easy to understand, and easy to implement on a large internetwork.

- It puts relatively low stress on network bandwidth and resources (compared with connection-oriented management models).

- Public domain or freeware code is widely available. The SNMP API is relatively simple to use to design applications. A particularly nice API for C++ programmers called SNMP++ is documented in [32].

- SNMP has a huge installed base. All major vendors of internetwork hardware (bridges, switches, routers, etc.) design their products to support SNMP.

The disadvantages to SNMP are as follows:

- SNMP is inefficient. The traffic overhead created by using SNMP to monitor multiple devices does not scale well (solutions such as RMON, described shortly, are preferable).

- SNMP lacks a standard model for hierarchical management implementations and interaction. This limits scalability and requires proprietary models to be deployed.

- SNMP security is poor. There are large security holes that allow network intruders to access SNMP data carried over the network. The key weaknesses include data privacy, authentication, and access control. SNMPv2 and Secure SNMP have added security mechanisms that combat these failings. SNMPv3 further develops this work into a consolidated set of standards.

- SNMP is considered by many to be too simple. The information it manipulates is neither sufficiently detailed nor sufficiently well organized to cope with large, demanding internetworks. Some of these problems are being addressed via SNMPv2 and SNMPv3. For example, SNMPv2 allows for more detailed specification of variables and optimizes table retrieval. There are also two new PDUs for manipulating objects in tables.

9.1.3   Remote Network Monitoring (RMON)

Remote Network Monitoring (RMON) is an MIB implementation designed to optimize remote performance monitoring and to offload much of the bandwidth and resource overheads incurred by the SNMP polling model. It relies on local devices called smart agents (implemented in devices such as routers and switches) to gather much of the data for subsequent collection. These agents are often referred to as Data Collection Modules (DCMs) or probes. Probes can be remotely configured by a network manager to set custom thresholds on specific events and report SNMP traps.

RMON is defined by a set of MIBs (see [33, 34]). Reference [34] defines nine major groups of information, most of which are generic object groups relevant to all LANs. It also includes MIB objects that were specifically developed for monitoring remote Ethernet segments. It is worth pointing out that an RMON-compliant agent or manager only has to support a subgroup of information within one major group. There have been two major releases of RMON, called RMONv1 and RMONv2.

RMONv1 provides network managers with a host of new functions they could not get from SNMP-based tools and also allows for storing performance histories on designated segments and triggering alarms for specific network conditions.

RMONv2 provides data about traffic at the Network Layer in addition to the Physical Layer. This enables administrators to analyze traffic by protocol type. RMONv2 also allows managers to check performance all the way to the individual port level on RMON-enabled routers or switches. It also allows a single RMON probe to monitor multiple protocol types on a single segment and provides much more flexibility in the way probes are configured for later reporting and for measuring network response times.

RMONv1 was dogged by high implementation costs and a number of incompatibility issues between vendor implementations. Another problem is that system resource requirements can be significant, especially if RMON features are enabled on all interfaces. Features such as per interface packet capture are superb for remote diagnostics, but unfortunately most existing enterprise and access router architectures would simply stop forwarding (or at least struggle) without an additional hardware assist. These issues have not disappeared with RMONv2. Another issue affecting deployment is that RMONv1 vendors have added proprietary extensions to their products in an effort to make their products more attractive to network managers. Again, there is the potential here for incompatibility. Currently RMON is being deployed with some caution, partly due to the issues described here and partly due to cost, and many customers are sticking with RMONv1 until implementations stabilize. Over time improvements in CPU performance, memory, prices, and system architecture will reduce costs and improve performance, enabling users to make the most out of what RMON has to offer.

Operation

An RMON agent works offline; it is a noninteractive monitor sitting on a LAN segment. An RMON agent is remotely configured and activated via a management application, enabling it to collect traffic and performance data on local interfaces. The agent reads and copies each frame on its local segment, updating counters based on the contents of the frame. Typically this information is cached at the agent until a remote management application requests it to be uploaded. The management application is not actively involved in the data collection. RMON uses preemptive monitoring. By continuously capturing and caching performance data in real time, an RMON application can look for anomalies in traffic patterns over time or perform trend analysis. Traffic surges or rising error rates can be detected and alarmed before the problem becomes critical. The agent can be configured to recognize when specific thresholds have been exceeded and to generate SNMP traps when these events occur. As part of the diagnostic process additional information within the RMON MIBs can be extremely useful in further qualifying the nature of the fault.

The RMON MIBs can hold detailed information about LAN operations, such as Nearest Active Upstream Neighbor (NAUN) order of the Token Ring adapters on the segment [1] or the source and destination MAC addresses of the stations with the most network traffic. This level of detail can be used to help isolate performance problems or perform trend analysis for capacity planning. A single RMON agent can support several remote RMON managers. A table is maintained within the agent of what information (and at what intervals) is to be sent to specific manager IP addresses. This is done through the alarm and event groups within RMON MIBs. Other information is routinely collected by the agent, captured in memory, and reported within GetResponse replies to a remote SNMP manager.

RMON MIB groups

Reference [34] defines the function and organization of the RMON MIB groups, as follows:

- 1—Statistics. Records, packets, octets, broadcasts, collisions, discards, fragments, and errors.

- 2—History. Caches multiple samples from the statistics group to be used for operations such as trend analysis.

- 3—Alarm. Enables thresholds and sampling intervals to be set in order to specify alarm conditions.

- 4—Host. Provides a table of active nodes and basic per node statistics.

- 5—HostTopN. Extends the host table by offering user-defined sorting capabilities (processed at the agent).

- 6—Matrix. Summarizes the traffic and error counts between pairs of nodes.

- 7—Filter. Offers user-defined packet filters for use as trigger or termination events for capturing activities.

- 8—Capture. Packets that pass the defined packet filters are copied and stored locally.

- 9—Event. Enables the user to create event logs or send SNMP Traps from the agent.

Several of the RMON groups in the MIB contain control and data tables. Control tables contain control parameters that specify which statistics you want to access and collect. You can view and change many entries in a control table. Data tables contain statistics the agent collects; usually you can only view entries in these tables. The following sections describe the function of each group and the tables that each group defines. Refer to [34] for more detail.

Statistics group

The statistics group records data that the agent measures on network interfaces. On an Ethernet interface the agent creates one entry for each Ethernet interface it monitors and places the entry in the EtherStatsTable. The EtherStatsTable also contains control parameters for this group. As an example of the kind of statistics maintained, reference [34] defines the following objects:

```
EtherStatsEntry ::= SEQUENCE {
    etherStatsIndex                    INTEGER (1..65535),
    etherStatsDataSource               OBJECT IDENTIFIER,
    etherStatsDropEvents               Counter,
    etherStatsOctets                   Counter,
    etherStatsPkts                     Counter,
    etherStatsBroadcastPkts            Counter,
    etherStatsMulticastPkts            Counter,
    etherStatsCRCAlignErrors           Counter,
    etherStatsUndersizePkts            Counter,
    etherStatsOversizePkts             Counter,
    etherStatsFragments                Counter,
    etherStatsJabbers                  Counter,
    etherStatsCollisions               Counter,
    etherStatsPkts64Octets             Counter,
    etherStatsPkts65to127Octets        Counter,
    etherStatsPkts128to255Octets       Counter,
    etherStatsPkts256to511Octets       Counter,
    etherStatsPkts512to1023Octets      Counter,
```

```
        etherStatsPkts1024to1518Octets        Counter,
        etherStatsOwner                       OwnerString,
        etherStatsStatus                      EntryStatus
}
```

History group

The history group contains a control and data collection function. The control function manages the periodic statistical sampling of data from networks and specifies control parameters, such as the frequency of data sampling, in the historyControlTable. The history function records periodic statistical samples from Ethernet networks—for example, interval, start time, and number of packets. This function places the statistical samples in the etherHistoryTable.

Host group

The host group identifies hosts on the network by recording the source and destination MAC addresses in good packets and places the information in the hostTable. This group also records the time it discovered a host on the network in the hostTimeTable. The hostControlTable specifies control parameters, such as which monitoring operations the agent performs, and contains some information about the monitoring process.

HostTopN group

The HostTopN group ranks hosts according to a statistic type. For example, you might want to rank the hosts by the number of errors they generate. Control parameters for this group appear in the hostTopNControlTable, and data this group generates appear in the hostTopNTable.

Matrix group

The matrix group stores statistics for an interchange between hosts at different addresses. This group's control parameters, such as number of hosts, appear in the matrixControlTable. When the matrix group receives information from a good packet, it places data in both the matrixSDTable and the matrixDSTable.

Filter group

The filter group specifies what type of packets the agent should capture. Filter control parameters, such as the minimum length of the packets to capture, appear in the filterTable. Associated with each filter is a channel (a specific path along which data flow). Control parameters in the channelTable define how and where the filtered packets flow.

Capture group

The capture group enables the capture of packets that satisfy the filter group control parameters for a particular interface. Control parameters in the bufferControlTable specify how to transfer data from the channelTable to the captureBufferTable. For example, you can specify the maximum number of octets from each packet that the group should store in the captureBufferTable.

Alarm group

The alarm group allows you to set an alarm threshold and a sampling interval to enable the RMON agent to generate alarms on any network segment it monitors. Alarm thresholds can be based on absolute or delta values so that you can be notified of rapid spikes or drops in a monitored value. Each alarm is linked to an event in the event group. An event defines an action that will be triggered when the alarm threshold is exceeded. The alarm group periodically takes statistical samples from variables in the agent and compares them with previously configured thresholds. The alarm table stores configuration entries that define a variable, a polling period, and threshold parameters. If the RMON agent determines that a sample crosses the threshold values, it generates an event.

The RMON agent monitors any variables that resolve to an ASN.1 primitive type of integer (integer, counter, gauge, or TimeTick) in this way. You can specify rising or falling thresholds, indicating network faults such as slow throughput or other network-related performance problems. You specify rising thresholds when you want to be notified that an alarm has risen above the threshold you specified. You specify falling thresholds when you want to be notified that the network is behaving normally again. For example, you might specify a falling threshold of 30 collisions per second to indicate a return to acceptable behavior.

Event group

The event group allows for the generation of an SNMP trap, the generation of a log entry, or both, for any event you choose. An event can occur when the sample variable exceeds the alarm threshold or a channel match event generated on an agent. The RMON agent can deliver traps to multiple NMSs. You can typically set up events to either record the monitoring information or to notify the NMS.

The event group includes an event table and a log table. The event table defines the notification that takes place when an event is triggered. One form of notification is to write an entry in the log table. Each entry in the event table identifies an event that can be triggered and indicates an action, such as writing a log entry to the log table or sending an SNMP trap to the NMS. The event can trigger any of the following actions:

- The system sends an SNMP Trap to the network management station.

- The management station is notified immediately. The management station determines how to react to the SNMP Trap.

- The system logs the event in the log table in the agent system.

- The management station can retrieve the information stored in the log table for further analysis. For example, the information collected can be used to select proper threshold values.

- The system sends an SNMP trap and logs the event in the log table.

The log table is a read-only data table for the network management station. It records each event that needs to be logged. It provides the event number, an index that distinguishes occurrences of the same event, the time at which the event occurred, and the event description. You are not required to configure the log table.

RMON summary

RMON is widely recognized as a very useful multivendor tool for efficient remote monitoring, diagnostics, and data collection. RMON management applications are passive, relying on other device management applications to provide change and control operations. It is up to the manager to decide what data should be monitored and what thresholds and alarm conditions to set. RMON can be invaluable in monitoring LAN health and performance and as a guide to longer-term capacity planning. In medium to large internetworks RMON is preferable for traffic monitoring to SNMP polling, since RMON records data passively and does not skew the overall traffic data with additional background management traffic.

9.1.4   Common Management Information Service/ Protocol (CMIS/CMIP)

Background

The OSI defined a complete set of specifications for network management, with two major components: Common Management Information Protocol (CMIP) and Common Management Information Service (CMIS). CMIS defines the services used, and CMIP defines the protocol that carries those services. The OSI management model uses an object-oriented approach. Managed objects all exhibit the same exterior appearance and accept the same set of commands. Part of the OSI standards is the Guidelines for the Definition of Managed Objects (GDMO). This standard provides a common way to define the objects being managed by a manager.

CMIP's basic design is similar to SNMP, whereby PDUs are employed as variables to monitor a network. CMIP, however, contains 11 types of PDUs and it employs much richer and more complex data structures with many attributes. Specifically these are as follows:

- Variable attributes represent the variable's characteristics.

- Variable behaviors are actions of that variable that can be triggered.

- Notifications generate an event report whenever a specified event occurs.

CMIS/CMIP was designed to make up for the shortcomings of SNMP and offers a more powerful and scalable network management platform. Research and development were heavily funded by governments and several large corporations. CMIS/CMIP has had several false starts; initially it was considered unattractive by the user community, because it imposed major overheads on memory and processing resources when compared with SNMP (particularly back in 1988). Its reliance on the OSI Connection-Oriented Transport Service (COTS) protocol also caused great resistance. Unfortunately, further problems with its implementation, the usual standards overkill and delays and high deployment costs, have effectively stalled any widespread deployment. Implementations of CMIS/CMIP are currently used to manage carrier networks (i.e., PTTs, RBOCs, Inter-LATA carriers, etc.); however, it is very expensive to deploy and consequently is rarely seen in enterprise networks. The enterprise market is likely to remain dominated by SNMP for the foreseeable future.

Architecture

CMIP is the basic framework for OSI network management and is largely based on Digital's proprietary protocol architecture. CMIP managers manage CMIP agents and can communicate with many different types of objects. The CMIP applications fall into five categories, as follows:

- Fault

- Configuration

- Accounting

- Performance

- Security

The Management Information Service (MIS) within OSI is provided by an Application Layer entity called the Systems Management Application Entity (SMAE). Since part of SAME's function is to monitor the status of the OSI protocol layers, it has a direct interface to all layers (otherwise it would have to rely on lower layers operating correctly to ensure management reachability—see Figure 9.6). SMAE gets its information about each level of protocol from an MIB. The MIB interfaces directly to each OSI protocol layer.

Clearly, it would be overkill for devices such as routers to implement the full seven-layer OSI protocol stack. For such devices a minimum communication capability is provided by the use of an OSI subprofile (a thin slice of the OSI seven-layer stack, with just enough features in layers 3 through 7 to manage the device). Even so, many vendors in the IP world consider this to be an unacceptable overhead, since the protocol stack may be required solely for self-management (running a seven-layer OSI stack on a modem does seem like overkill).

Figure 9.6
OSI management structure.

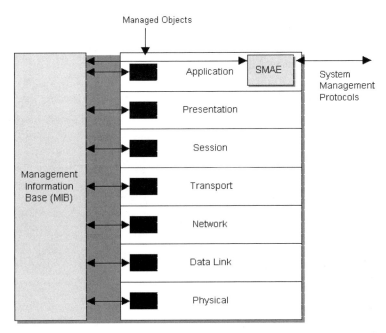

Protocol

CMIP uses the full OSI Application Layer protocol over a Connection-Oriented Transport Service (COTS), although CMIP was initially defined for use over X.25. A management station must establish a virtual circuit between itself and a managed node before any useful management functions can be performed. This has some implications on network performance, as follows:

- When the network is already congested, the connection-oriented CMIP protocol will only add more burden. Unfortunately, this is when management is needed most.

- In COTS mode CMIP requires a minimum of three packets (handshaking) for any meaningful management interaction.

- Active management sessions mean that more resource (CPU, RAM) is required on CMIP-enabled devices to maintain these stateful connections.

Subsequently, there have been efforts to standardize the use of CMIS/CMIP using other transports. Common Management Services and Protocol over TCP/IP (CMOT) and Common Management Services and Protocol over LAN (CMOL) are two examples. CMOT is a protocol configuration proposed by the IETF, where CMIP is available over a connection-oriented TCP stack or a connectionless UDP stack, defined in [35]. To support this functionality in the IP environment a streamlined OSI session, presentation, and application service is offered over TCP/IP, including a Lightweight Presentation Protocol (LPP), as defined in [36]. LPP uses two well-known UDP/TCP port numbers; the CMOT manager uses port 163 and the CMOT agent uses port 164. It is fair to say that none of these transport variants has gained any significant interest from the wider user community; SNMP continues to dominate the installed base.

Primitives

CMIS provides the following primitives:

- Get
- Set
- Event
- Create
- Delete
- Action

SNMP puts restrictions on the use of complex items (such as lists); CMIP does not. Unlike SNMP, CMIP distinguishes between objects and their attributes (e.g., an object may be a port on a hub, and an associated attribute might be its state).

ASN.1

Abstract Syntax Notation One (ASN.1) is a formal language used to define an abstract data format, enabling information to be exchanged between systems at the binary level regardless of machine architecture. In other words, ASN.1 is the Esperanto of data representation. ASN.1 provides two basic representations for information: a human-readable format and an encoded format for use by communications protocols. ASN.1 is an ISO OSI protocol standard [37], broadly equivalent to ITU/T X.409. ASN.1 normally encodes data using the Basic Encoding Rules (BER) [38], although this is not mandatory.

ASN.1 is used by both CMIS/CMIP and SNMP to encode management information; it is used to define both managed objects and PDU formats. Managed objects are described as ASN.1 OBJECT-TYPEs, which comprise five fields (OBJECT DESCRIPTOR, SYNTAX, ACCESS, STATUS, and DESCRIPTION). Typical object definitions are illustrated in the standard MIB-II interfaces group [11].

The five fields are described as follows:

- OBJECT DESCRIPTOR (Name) is a textual name for the object. In our example, ifAdminStatus.

- SYNTAX defines the data type associated with the object. ASN.1 constructs are used to define this structure (note that in SNMP the syntax of ASN.1 is not used). The ASN.1 type ObjectSyntax defines three categories of object syntax: Simple, Application-Wide, and Simply Constructed. Examples include INTEGER, OCTET STRING, NetworkAddress, Counter, Gauge, TimeTicks, SEQUENCE, and SEQUENCE OF.

- ACCESS defines the level of access permitted for the object. It can be either read-only, read-write, write-only, or not accessible.

- STATUS defines the managed objects implementation requirement (Mandatory, Optional, or Obsolete).

- DESCRIPTION is a textual description of the object.

For further information, the interested reader is referred to [37–41].

Performance

CMIP is more powerful than SNMP and generally enables more efficient operations. As we have already discussed, CMIS/CMIP in COTS mode can represent a significant burden on internetworking equipment such as bridges, repeaters, and routers and is unlikely to gain much support from users (since this adds both cost and complexity). Only the carriers can currently afford the luxury of a full OSI management implementation.

CMIP advantages and disadvantages

CMIP has several advantages over when compared with SNMP, as follows:

- CMIP variables not only relay information to and from the terminal (as in SNMP), but they can also be used to perform tasks that would be impossible under SNMP. For instance, if a terminal on a network cannot reach its file server a predetermined amount of times, CMIP can notify the appropriate personnel of the event. With SNMP, however, the management application would have to explicitly keep track of how many unsuccessful attempts to reach a file server a terminal has incurred. CMIP results in a more efficient network management system, since less work is required by a user to keep updated on the status of the network.

- CMIP addresses many of the shortcomings of SNMP. For instance, it has built-in security management devices that support authorization, access control, and security logs. The result of this is a safer system than the installation of SNMP; no security upgrades are necessary.

- CMIP was funded by governments and several large corporations. One can deduce that CMIP not only has a very large development budget, but also that when (and if) it becomes a widely available protocol it will have numerous immediate users—namely, the governments and corporations that funded it.

The disadvantages of CMIP are summarized as follows:

- CMIP has a relatively small installed base and little user acceptance.

- CMIP takes more system resources than SNMP (some say by a factor of ten). In other words, very few systems would be able to handle a full implementation of CMIP without massive network modifications (such as the installation of extra memory and new protocol agents).

- CMIP is difficult to program, which greatly slows down deployment and requires more skilled staff to implement interfaces and applications.

9.1.5   Configuration management

In many texts about network management, configuration management receives little attention. In real networks, however, configuration management is arguably the single most critical system management discipline. Configuration management determines how your network and systems will operate and provides input to many different important processes (including problem, change, and asset management). Configuration management can also impact scalability; in multivendor networks the general lack of integration of configuration management systems can be a major factor in delaying the rollout of new services. We can broadly divide configuration management into two functions, as follows:

- Planning and administration—Managing a large enterprise requires careful planning and control to meet business objectives and avoid network outages. Planning includes functions such as inventory control, configuration design, change control, connectivity information, financial modeling, recovery procedures, and optimization. The main objectives of this phase are to provide cost-effective use of resources and to meet business objectives in a timely manner.

- Operations—In this phase the live configuration of systems is implemented and monitored. This function is responsible for the correct day-to-day operation of the network, in particular the performance and availability of systems on that network.

In an ideal world these functions will be tightly integrated, with well-defined information flows between them. Networks are live entities and so the two processes are often in a state of flux.

In practice, configuration management is one of the most difficult and time-consuming management disciplines and is one of the hardest to quantify in terms of the value to the business. For example, deploying hundreds of routers in remote locations may require skilled engineers at each site if remote configuration management features are poor. For any large service provider this is simply unacceptable, since skill shortages are likely to limit rate of service rollout according to the number of free engineers. A better solution is to configure all nodes centrally, either prior to shipping or over a dial-up line (meaning that a less skilled engineer can be used to connect the

right cables and power up the device). For maintenance purposes all configuration data need to be collated and held centrally, so that any remote failures can be recovered quickly.

The need for automation and integration

In anything other than very small networks, configuration management
demands some level of automation, both to reduce the number of skilled
engineers and to reduce the possibility of errors. Many organizations invest
huge amounts of money developing their own configuration management
functions, either through script files or custom software. SNMP, the de
facto management standard, is particularly weak in the area; SNMP Set and
Get simply do not scale, and due to security weaknesses many devices disable Set altogether.

Traditionally, the configuration of networking equipment has for the
most part been carried out using a combination of Telnet and a vendor-specific Command-Line Interface (CLI). One big advantage of these techniques is that they are fast and relatively low bandwidth, meaning that they
are also suitable for out-of-band management in emergencies (Telnet can be
combined with dial-back modem or ISDN support to facilitate remote
access if the network is down). The network administrator would typically
configure a number of scripts at the central site, and then download them
to each device over a Telnet or console connection. For a large, managed
service these script files may be identical for all, or defined, groups of nodes.
Often the only difference is that a unique IP address is required for each
device (for a remote Telnet connection this requires either that the device
preconfigured with an IP address or that it can be reached via a modem
connection initially). This approach has served the industry reasonably well
for several years but has several drawbacks, including the following:

- The user is required to learn a number of different CLIs.

- Text-based CLIs provide variable degrees of assistance; some are
  extremely terse.

- Security is often poor (usually just a plain ASCII password, transferred unencrypted over the wire). Secure protocols such as SSL and
  SSH may be available, but this really depends on the vendor.

Many experienced engineers still prefer to use CLIs, since, once learned,
they can be very efficient interfaces for rapid configuration and diagnostics.
As indicated, CLIs often support scripting for bulk network configuration
(such as injecting hundreds of large static routes into a routing table). In a

large network this could be the only way of ensuring the timely rollout of equipment.

Web-based configuration management

In recent years HTTP (Web)–based browser management interfaces have become increasingly common as the standard way to manage distributed systems (such as routers and firewalls—see Figure 9.7). This interface is especially easy to implement, requiring a simple HTTP server running on the remote device, with hooks into the system configuration interface and system databases. The major benefit for users is that they simply run a standard Web browser on the client (such as Netscape Navigator or Microsoft Internet Explorer) and connect to the remote device's IP address or domain name. The management interface, therefore, has the appearance of a set of customized Web pages (often with links for additional help to the vendor's home Web site).

This type of interface has been used primarily for configuration management (configuring interfaces, enabling protocols and basic statistics) and so complements the NMS rather than replacing it. The advantages of this approach are obvious: Web browsers are installed on almost all PCs today as

Figure 9.7
*Nokia's Voyager
HTTP interface
for firewall
configuration
management.*

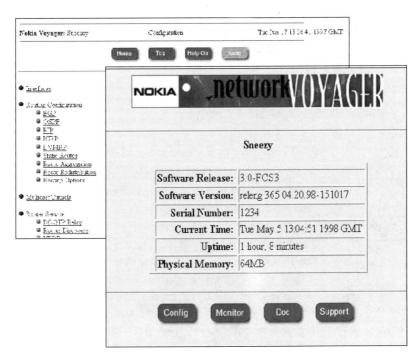

part of the operating system, and most users are now comfortable using this point-and-click interface (thus alleviating the need to learn a new command set for different vendor equipment). Another major advantage is that standard security mechanisms are readily available for this type of interface to ensure that the remote party is trusted—for example, the SSH and SSL protocols. The main disadvantage of this approach is that it tends to be slow; it does not scale when deploying hundreds of devices. Some Web-based systems do, however, include the facility to download configuration scripts from within the interface by simply pressing a button.

Large-scale configuration management

Sophisticated configuration management systems are already emerging to automate and control large-scale parameter and OS image deployment. These systems typically maintain a complete network database of location data, version numbers, addressing information, time last updated, and the methods used (e.g., SSL/TLS, SSH, Telnet, etc.). Implementations can enable the network planner to customize standard templates for different equipment types (routers, switches, by vendor, etc.), together with the ability to organize templates into logical groups (either by device class or some other useful hierarchy, such as network topology or site geography).

9.1.6 Network management platforms and implementations

In this section, we briefly discuss the different types of network management products available commercially or via public domain or shareware repositories. The list of products is representative but not exhaustive.

MIB browsers and development kits

At the noncommercial end of the scale there are numerous MIB browsers, mostly public domain or offered as part of a development kit. These tools offer basic MIB interrogation and data retrieval features (by exercising primitives such as Get, Set, etc.) and the ability to send Traps manually. Their primary use is for testing and demonstrating SNMP implementations, but they can offer limited diagnostic capabilities. Figure 9.8 shows a simple SNMP browser available as part of the HP SNMP++ development kit. SNMP++ offers an excellent object-oriented C++ class library API, which is available on both Windows and a number of UNIX environments. The source code is available free, subject to the inclusion of a copyright notice. The interested reader is referred to [32].

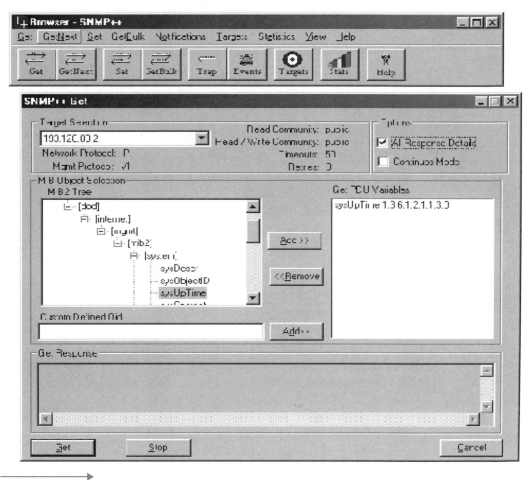

Figure 9.8   *HP++ SNMP browser tool. An example showing the Get primitive being configured for MIB-II.*

We mentioned earlier the standard ISODE SNMP implementation, which is freely available and widely implemented. Public domain source code is also freely available from both the Massachusetts Institute of Technology (MIT) and Carnegie Mellon University (CMU). A respected commercial network management development environment is SNMPc from Castle Rock [42]. SNMPc runs under Windows 98 and NT and provides an integrated MIB compiler plus excellent programming APIs. The APIs include a simple DLL-based API, the WinSNMP de facto standard API, and a Windows DDE-based API (programmable from Visual BASIC and from many Windows applications, such as Microsoft Excel).

Vendor management products

Many of the larger networking vendors have in the past developed their own management systems. Often this was used as a way to lock in customers to a single-vendor solution. With the proliferation of networking systems there are now very few vendors that can offer complete end-to-end solutions with best-of-breed products in all categories; therefore, customers tend to buy routers, firewalls, and servers from different vendors. Having spent years of man-effort developing these management systems and not recovering their costs, hardware vendors have either given up on the mission to create a complete framework or sold off their network management businesses (e.g., Retix split off Network Managers, and Cabletron Systems recently relinquished control of its Spectrum products). Examples of vendor- or domain-specific management products include the following:

- Cisco: CiscoWorks and StrataSphere

- NorTel/Bay Networks: Optivity

- Novell: NetWare Manager

- Apple Macintosh: MacSNMP

While some of these products may claim to be generic management solutions, it is rare to find a management system in this class as the sole NMS in a multivendor network (with the possible exception of Spectrum). Framework vendors tend to be independent specialists.

Network management frameworks

Historically, some of the key vendors offering complete network management architectures included Hewlett-Packard, Digital Equipment, IBM, Tivoli, CA, and Sun Microsystems. Today there are several high-end commercial network management implementations, including Computer Associates, Unicenter TNG [43]; Tivoli, Tivoli Management Environment (TME), NetView [44]; Hewlett-Packard (HP), HP OpenView ITSM, Network Node Manager [45].

Most of these platforms are SNMP based, but several also offer an OSI/CMISE stack. Some of the more sophisticated management platforms (so-called management frameworks) are expensive—prices start around $50,000 and typically reach millions of dollars. Frameworks typically offer a whole range of facilities, including the following:

- Hierarchical Manager-of-Manager (MoM) model, with a centralized event management console and distributed Mid-Level Managers (MLMs)

- Distributed GUIs (e.g., X Windows, Java GUIs, HTTP browser access)

- Security management tools (AAA services)

- SLA management

- Database management tools, resilient or mirrored object databases, often LDAP enabled

- Software distribution tools (version control, remote boot and configuration)

- Topology management (automated discovery via SNMP, Telnet, ping, routing tables, ARP caches, etc.)

- Inventory management (semiautomated database population of software and hardware revisions, device types, location data, addressing information, etc.)

- Element management (via product-specific modules (PSMs)

- Alarm and event consolidation (via overall topology knowledge, Trap-directed polling, or a rulebase)

- Help-desk management

There is an increasing trend for hooking these frameworks into business processes, so that purchasing, deployment, inventory, and maintenance processes can be integrated into a (supposedly) seamless architecture. From a data management perspective this makes good sense, since it can significantly speed up processes and greatly reduce the potential for error, especially if all these systems interface via common APIs. However, this market is still relatively immature; many customers still do not appear to be getting value for money, since often these systems are cumbersome to use and require significant after-sales consultancy and customization [46]. In large multivendor networks the scope of these products means that they cannot always fulfill what is promised (or expected) out of the box. Some frameworks appear to be a thinly disguised mishmash of acquired products, hammered together with varying degrees of success. Nevertheless, these frameworks ultimately represent the best hope for large-scale integrated management. The alternative leaves network managers struggling with piecemeal solutions and hard-to-maintain in-house tools.

We briefly review two of the most important network management frameworks.

Hewlett-Packard (HP) has been very proactive in the area of network management, and HP OpenView is probably the best-known generic NMS platform on the market today. HP OpenView is well known for its SNMP support, but it also offers an OSI/CMISE stack. Its protocol stack is based on the International Standards Organization Decode/Encode (ISODE) releases. This can be run over the Lightweight Presentation Protocol (LPP) directly over UDP (i.e., the Common Management over TCP/IP, or CMOT, implementation). HP offers a base OpenView product as well as a distributed product. It also offers a very useful MIB browser. HP Open-View is based on object-oriented principles, with objects registering via an Object Registration Service (which provides services such as mapping names to network addresses). The OpenView Application Programmers Interface (API) offers a high degree of functionality and has been used successfully by many developers to produce their own enhanced variations of OpenView—either rebagged or relabeled products (e.g., DEC, IBM, and NCR/AT&T). The interested reader is referred to [45].

IBM's network management architecture is called NetView. NetView is designed to manage IBM's mainframe and associated devices and is one of the few proprietary management architectures to survive in the wake of SNMP. NetView runs on an IBM mainframe with terminal access via an application called NetView/PC. After the initial release of NetView, IBM began integrating other network management modules under the control of NetView, and the NetView protocols were opened up so that other network management systems could be hooked in (via the Application Programming Interface/Communication Services, API/CS. This provides an interface to NetView, access to DDM file transfer, and protocols for exchanging alarms and data). IBM has developed problem-solving strategies in this software and combined them with a comprehensive database of network status information; this creates a powerful tool, which may be extended and customized to meet particular customer needs. IBM LAN equipment (hubs, bridges, etc.) is managed via its LAN Manager Agent (not to be confused with Microsoft LAN Manager NOS). IBM's 6611 router is managed via SNMP. IBM's NetView 6000 application runs on an IBM RS/6000 host (running AIX) and was developed from HP's Open-View network management platform. NetView 6000 offers full SNMP management, together with a gateway into proprietary NetView (SNA) devices and the LAN Manager platform. It offers a highly integrated platform for mixed IBM/multivendor environments. For example, SNMP Traps can be converted into SNA alerts and vice versa. The system also has a strong device discovery capability and provides network monitoring for fault and performance measurements.

Element management

As we have already seen, standard MIBs contain only a subset of the management objects needed to run a real-life network, although more objects are being included over time. The major router, switch, and bridge vendors have spent years enhancing and differentiating the functionality of their devices, to the point where there are now many private objects (MIB enterprise extensions) used for advanced status or statistical data, together with objects associated with proprietary protocols. Without access to these objects the scope of a management console would be limited to generic MIB functionality.

Most vendors now publish their private MIBs on the Internet, and you can easily compile these private MIBs onto your management platform; however, depending on the capabilities of the SNMP browser you are using, you may have to do a considerable amount of work to make the best use of these raw objects. Most, if not all, high-end enterprise management frameworks include element management modules (sometimes called Product-Specific Modules, or PSMs). These modules not only include private.enterprise MIB data but may also include associated graphical device representations (detailed chassis views, card views, etc.), interactive status data, and remote configuration capabilities. One of the main headaches for a network management vendor is keeping PSMs current with device hardware and software changes, especially where a large number of PSMs are supported.

9.1.7 Basic implementation models

So far we have talked about the tools and techniques available. There are several ways to implement a management model in an internetwork, and we will discuss the various benefits and trade-offs of the approaches available.

Implementing hierarchical management

On a very small network there may be no need to consider management hierarchy—a single NMS will work fine. As the network grows, the amount of traffic and system overhead (CPU, RAM) imposed by management starts to become significant. As a general rule management traffic should not be running at more than 5 percent of the maximum bandwidth on conventional LANs (Ethernet, Token Ring, and FDDI). The problem is that most network management architectures rely on polling, in-band, to gain real-time data from key devices.

There is a direct trade-off between the amount of traffic created and the usefulness of the data retrieved, against factors such as the following:

- The number of devices polled

- The number of objects required for each poll

- The polling frequency

- The available link bandwidths and bottlenecks

On a large network you will need to consider distributing some of load and constraining polling locally. For example, assume we have a 100-node network spread over three LAN subnets and linked to a central site via 64-Kbps links, as illustrated in Figure 9.9. Assume we are interested in monitoring ten objects from each agent, each of which returns an integer (32-bit) variable, and we want to monitor these every 30 seconds. With a single NMS located in the central site, using SNMP, we would need to issue a single Get request for each object, resulting in ten Gets and ten Responses. Assuming an average packet size of 90 bytes (including the community string and object IS, etc.), we are looking at the following amount of data:

$$\text{Total Traffic} = 90 \text{ (bytes)} \times 8 \text{ (bits)} \times 100 \text{ (nodes)}$$
$$= 72{,}000 \text{ bps}$$

This represents a worst case of 24,000 bps, or 37.5 percent of each 64-Kbps link, in each direction (assuming full-duplex operation), every 30 seconds. This does not take into account any latency in issuing the requests or receiving the responses. It would be tempting to divide this traffic by 30 (i.e., time), but unless you have configured the management application to schedule these requests evenly, the NMS is likely to process these operations as fast as it can, leading to a significant spike of management traffic. These figures also do not take into account queuing delays on intermediate routers [1], so there will be additional latency there. If the load incurred is seriously affecting user traffic, we could try to reduce the number of objects we are monitoring, but this might be a serious compromise in what we are trying to achieve. Even so, be ruthless about the number of objects polled; make sure that they are all really necessary and that no duplication is taking place.

One solution to this would be to place at least one polling agent in each subnet so that all device polling is constrained within the relatively fast LANs; this concept is sometimes referred to as the Mid-Level Manager (MLM) model (see Figure 9.10). The central NMS (a Manager-of-Managers, or MoM) could poll these MLMs periodically, using a more efficient means of uploading these bulk data at relatively quiet periods of the day.

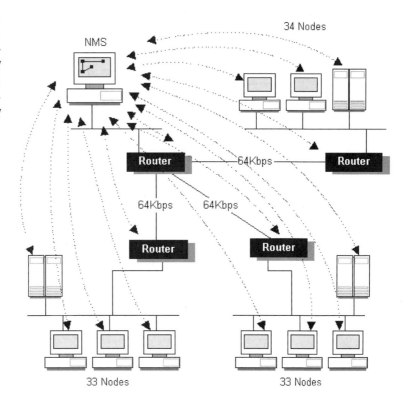

Figure 9.9
Simple one-tier centralized management, with three remote subnets connected via 64-Kbps links.

The MLM could either be another NMS or some management-enabled networking device (such as a concentrator or hub). Another solution would be to use more intelligent agents (such as RMON agents) to do most of the real-time collection locally in each of the end systems and network devices. Note that there are no SNMP standards for MoM or MLM communications, and this has essentially been left for the vendors to define.

In-band or out-of-band management

Most traditional management systems use in-band data collection schemes. As we have discussed, if you can keep the overhead to less than 5 percent, then, under normal conditions, this is a perfectly reasonable approach. The problem is, however, that when the network starts to fail, the NMS is using the network for data transport; this is likely to lead to loss of valuable data and events, and the management system can end up imposing more load on the network (e.g., if it retransmits) just when the network needs all the bandwidth it can get (especially one that is COTS based).

There is no simple solution to this. An out-of-band management system costs more money and adds complexity to the network. We can try to min

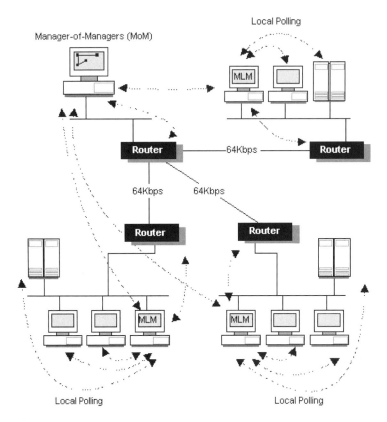

Figure 9.10
Manager-of-Manager (MoM) concepts offering a hierarchical and distributed management design.

imize this by using relatively low-cost media for management traffic (such as dial-up ISDN or modem links, or spare switch ports and LAN segments), but in practice this is rarely done, unless the network is mission critical or especially large. On some networks this may not be optional, and cost may be less of an issue. If a service provider guarantees availability as part of the SLA, the provider may have no choice but to install a highly rugged management architecture, with out-of-band access where appropriate. A network with many remote offices in inaccessible locations may also deem cost to be secondary.

Out-of-band management is, however, an attractive technique for remote configuration management, especially for internetworks where remote devices are very inaccessible or are located in areas of less skilled or no skilled staff. For example, a router housed in a remote military observation post could be equipped with a spare dial-up modem port for remote access should the primary link fail. One of the issues commonly associated with out-of-band management is security.

9.2   Network troubleshooting tools

This section is concerned with how you maintain an operational network. Specifically we will look at the tools and techniques you will need to identify problems on your network and remedy them. Essentially, these fall into the following categories:

- The NMS

- Device statistics and log output

- Software diagnostic tools such as ping, traceroute, tcpdump, netstat, and dig

- Advanced protocol analyzers and network testers

We are almost at the end of this book. Readers who require comic relief during this discussion should refer to [47].

9.2.1   Using the NMS

Your first port of call should be the network management system itself. If properly set up, it should enable you to focus on specific problems to which you can then apply more sophisticated techniques. If you suspect a problem, the first thing you will want to do is get a fix on its location and isolate the nature of the problem using the following tools:

- Network map—Examine the network status map and see if there are any obvious clues regarding the location of the problem. Many NMS GUIs use color-coded icons to indicate the status of a device or link.

- Event logs—Examine network management event logs for any specific Traps, alarms, or events. Examine generic event logs on the management station, such as Syslog, if available.

- Monitoring—You could have proactively configured the NMS to monitor specific MIB objects on key nodes in advance (e.g., interface status, retransmission counters, etc.).

A naive implementation of the management application may indicate many failures, and this could make life difficult if you are trying to isolate the problem (e.g., failure of a single WAN link may cause a number of icons to indicate failure status). A more sophisticated management application may use some form of artificial intelligence or a rule base to lock down more precisely on the problem, or it may implement Trap-directed polling. However, remember that the NMS controls only objects that are managed able and in its object database. If the problem is due to an intermediate device, such as an unmanaged modem, it may not show up on the NMS in any obvious way.

In the standard MIB-II there are many objects that are good candidates for proactive monitoring, including the following:

- ifOperStatus in the interfaces table. Reports up, down, or testing status for a specific interface.

- ipRouteEntry in the IP routing table. You could monitor mission-critical routing entries.

- icmpInRedirects in the ICMP group. You could monitor for excessive redirects, indicating some type of system, routing, or interface failure.

- tcpRetransSegs in the TCP group. You could monitor for excessive retransmissions.

You should explore the MIB contents and see if there are any objects of particular relevance for your environment. Bear in mind the previous discussion on performance with SNMP polling, so keep the number of objects to a minimum and set a reasonable polling interval (one that does not create too much traffic but does give you enough warning about a potential problem). To preserve traffic in large internetworks it may be wise to configure your own enterprise Traps or use RMON probes.

9.2.2   **Router troubleshooting features**

Most internetworking devices provide built-in diagnostic features. For example, you would expect a router to provide basic statistics on packet or protocol behavior, interface status, routing topology status, and some protocol event messages (either logged locally in RAM or sent to Syslog). These tools can be invaluable for debugging network or connectivity problems, and you should familiarize yourself with the facilities available. For example, on a Xyplex router it is possible to view the status of a wide area interface via the CLI, as shown in the following code segment:

```
SHOW LINK W1 STATUS
Link: W1 (A-B)                           Type: WAN

 ~tive State:              Running                       Current   High   Average
    ~e Circuit:            Default       percent Utilization:   0        4         0
       ~ion:               Disabled      Error Rate:        0        0         0
          ~:               N/A
          ~:               N/A                            Current   High   Maximum
       ~ation:             0             Output Queue:        0        1      1082
```

```
            DCE DEVICE                            Current    High    Total
Cable:                          V35    Link Downtime:      0        2        2
Transmit Link Speed (KBPS):  55.900    Link Down Count:                      0
Receive Link Speed (KBPS):   55.900    Last Occurred:
                 Current    Changes
CTS:            Observed          1
RTS:            Asserted          0
DCD:            Observed          1
DSR:            Observed          0
DTR:            Asserted          0
Ring:               N/A           0
```

Here we can see link utilization, link errors, transitions in interface signals, and whether the link has gone down at any point. Farther up the protocol stack we might, for example, monitor the status of OSPF neighbors to find out why routing databases are not synchronizing, as shown in the following code segment:

```
MONITOR OSPF NEIGHBOR SUMMARY
08-00-87-01-FF-82 (ROUTER-C)              BR/460        Uptime: 000 01:13:27

   Area/Interface    Router ID      Nbr IP Addr        State   Mode Priority
   193.128.4.2       0.0.0.0        1 (E1)             Down    None        0
   193.128.4.2       193.128.4.1    193.128.4.1        Full Master         1
```

There may be a large number of displays to get familiar with, some more relevant than others. Often the vendor may be able to advise you what the most useful commands and displays for troubleshooting are.

Some router vendors allow you to configure SNMP Traps for key events, and this enhances the standard Trap functionality described earlier in this chapter. For example, ICMP network unreachable events could trigger specific Traps, indicating the offending source and destination network addresses. These Traps can be sent to one or more nominated Trap hosts configured by the system administrator and could be particularly useful if configured on a default router to indicate the presence of Martian Hosts [1].

9.2.3   Software diagnostic tools

In this section, we will investigate a number of software tools and services used for testing various aspects of internetwork operation. The main tolls of interest include the following:

- Ping—A tool that performs basic reachability tests of network operation.

- TraceRoute—A tool that can help diagnose routing problems.

- Netstat—A tool that is useful for examining network or routing status.

- TCPdump—A tool that can be used as a basic protocol analyzer.

- Nslookup and Dig—Tools that are useful for studying DNS.

The following standard services are not described here, but you may wish to explore these further in [48]:

- Echo—A service that echoes characters back to the sender (port = 7)

- Chargen—A service that sends a complete ASCII character set continuously (port = 19).

- Finger—A service that discovers the real name of a user from his or her UserID (port = 79).

- Discard—A service that acts as a sink point for data (port = 9).

- Daytime—A service that gives the date and time (port = 13).

Although these diagnostic tools are extremely useful, many are not advanced enough to give expert interpretation or even identification of the problems on your network. They give basic packet event and timing data, which you must interpret. You need to invest time in understanding the protocols involved to know what to expect in order to devise a testing strategy that will quickly lock in on possible problems. Experience and a methodical approach help great deal, and anybody working in this area is strongly recommended to keep a notebook and write down anything important as you build up your knowledge.

Ping

Ping (packet internet groper) is probably the most useful debugging tool for internetworks and the first thing most engineers will use as part of the problem-solving strategy. Ping takes its name from a submarine sonar search, in which a short sound burst is transmitted underwater. If there are other objects present, a reflection is echoed back (which makes a sound like a ping). Ping is implemented over IP using the standard ICMP echo function [49]. Ping is primarily used to test reachability, but it can also be used to gather basic statistics about network performance and reliability. Ping performs the following operations:

- Ping sends one or more probe packets (an ICMP echo request) to a specified destination IP address and then waits for a reply. If you understand the topology of your network, you can easily backtrack from the destination, testing reachability along the expected delivery path until you find where the problem is.

- It can generate multiple echo requests (with a specified data size) in batches, allowing you to test for percentage packet loss.

- It inserts a unique sequence number in each probe packet and reports back the sequence numbers received. By running ping for several minutes you can determine if packets have been dropped, duplicated, or reordered.

- It checksums each packet sent and received, enabling you to detect if damage or corruption has occurred.

- It inserts a timestamp in each packet, which is echoed back. This can be used to compute the time taken for each packet exchange (i.e., the Round-Trip Time [RTT]). Run ping for several minutes to determine if the round-trip delays are consistent. Ping normally reports timestamps in milliseconds (ms), although the resolution may be limited to the nearest 10 or 20 ms.

- It reports other useful ICMP error messages (such as target host or subnet unreachable).

The following are some of the typical problems you may experience when debugging with ping:

- Discarded packets

- Fluctuating Round-Trip Times (RTT)

- Unstable connectivity

- Ping works but some applications fail

Ping options

Under MS-DOS version 4.10.2222, ping supports the following options.

MS-DOS Option Definitions

- −t—Ping the specified host until stopped.

- −a—Resolve addresses to hostnames.

- −n count—Number of echo requests to send.

- −l size—Send buffer size.

- −f—Set Don't Fragment flag in packet.

- −i TTL—Time To Live.

- −v TOS—Type of Service.

- –r count—Record route for count hops.

- –s count—Timestamp for count hops.

- –j host-list—Loose source route along host-list.

- –k host-list—Strict source route along host-list.

- –w timeoutt—Timeout in milliseconds to wait for each reply.

BSD UNIX implements a much richer version of ping. The following are some of the most useful ping options under BSD.

BSD UNIX option definitions

- –c Count—Send count packets and then stop. To stop manually type Control-C. This option is useful for scripts that periodically check network behavior.

- –f Flood—Send packets as fast as the receiving host can handle them, at least 100 per second. This is a useful way to stress test a production network. Exercise with caution on a live network, since high-performance workstations can consume large amounts of bandwidth.

- –l Preload—Send preload packets as fast as possible, and then change to normal behavior. Good for finding out how many packets your routers can handle as a burst.

- –n—Numeric output only. Use this when, in addition to everything else, you've got nameserver problems and ping is hanging trying to give you a nice symbolic name for the IP addresses.

- –p Pattern—Pattern is a string of hexadecimal digits with which to pad the end of the packet. This can be useful if you suspect data-dependent problems, since links have been known to fail only when certain bit patterns are presented to them.

- –R Record—Use IP's Record Route option to determine what route the ping packets are using. This can be problematic, since the target host is under no obligation to place a corresponding option on the reply, so consider this a bonus if it works.

- –r—Bypass the routing tables. Use this when, in addition to everything else, you've got routing problems and ping can't find a route to the target host. This works only for hosts that can be directly reached without using any routers.

- –s Size—Set the size of the test packets. You should check large packets, small packets (the default), very large packets that must be fragmented, and packets that are not a power of two. Read the manual to find out exactly what you're specifying here—BSD ping doesn't count either IP or ICMP headers in the packet size.

- –V—Verbose output. Displays other ICMP packets not normally considered interesting.

Ping is available on practically all variations of UNIX, LINUX, and Windows95/NT and is often implemented on many internetworking devices as part of the diagnostic suite. There are several variations, and you may find that not all the options are available or consistent. BSD UNIX offers a fully featured ping, freely available for many host systems. Ping is also a nonprivileged command on most systems. Most Windows implementations have only the basic features implemented. Refer to the documentation on the platform for further details. The options available are very much platform dependent. Syntax varies markedly and on networking hardware (such as a router CLI) ping may be implemented with very limited functionality. The general format for using ping is as follows:

```
ping [options] <destinationIPaddrs>
```

Using ping

Many TCP/IP systems have a special IP address called the localhost or loopback interface (specifically, 127.0.0.1; no packets sent to this address must appear outside a host). Pinging the loopback interface is a good way to exercise the internal network configuration and IP stack, although the extent of testing is implementation dependent (good implementations test all the way down to the hardware interface, but many implementations test only down to the IP layer). Problems found in a loopback test are rare but are cause for further investigation (if you cannot ping your local address, it is unlikely you will be pinging anywhere else either). The following ping test shows a sequence of ten echo responses over the loopback interface on a UNIX host (the reports will vary by OS). Note sequence numbers with each reply. The TTL values are also reported, as are the round-trip times. Both are very consistent. At the end of the session, statistics are reported.

```
bozo$ ping -c10 localhost
PING localhost (127.0.0.1): 56 data bytes
64 bytes from 127.0.0.1: icmp_seq=0 ttl=255 time=2 ms
64 bytes from 127.0.0.1: icmp_seq=1 ttl=255 time=2 ms
64 bytes from 127.0.0.1: icmp_seq=2 ttl=255 time=2 ms
64 bytes from 127.0.0.1: icmp_seq=3 ttl=255 time=2 ms
64 bytes from 127.0.0.1: icmp_seq=4 ttl=255 time=2 ms
64 bytes from 127.0.0.1: icmp_seq=5 ttl=255 time=2 ms
64 bytes from 127.0.0.1: icmp_seq=6 ttl=255 time=2 ms
64 bytes from 127.0.0.1: icmp_seq=7 ttl=255 time=2 ms
```

```
64 bytes from 127.0.0.1: icmp_seq=8 ttl=255 time=2 ms
64 bytes from 127.0.0.1: icmp_seq=9 ttl=255 time=2 ms

--- localhost ping statistics ---
10 packets transmitted, 10 packets received, 0 percent packet loss
round-trip min/avg/max = 2/2/2 ms
bozo $
```

The next ping test illustrates how a WAN link is performing by pinging a remote router on the other side of a 128-Kbps link.

```
laurell 8 >ping hardy
PING hardy (193.128.56.2): 56 data bytes
64 bytes from 193.128.56.2: icmp_seq=0 ttl=254 time=36.134 ms
64 bytes from 193.128.56.2: icmp_seq=1 ttl=254 time=27.473 ms
64 bytes from 193.128.56.2: icmp_seq=2 ttl=254 time=29.243 ms
64 bytes from 193.128.56.2: icmp_seq=3 ttl=254 time=39.151 ms
64 bytes from 193.128.56.2: icmp_seq=4 ttl=254 time=28.922 ms
64 bytes from 193.128.56.2: icmp_seq=5 ttl=254 time=39.181 ms
64 bytes from 193.128.56.2: icmp_seq=6 ttl=254 time=31.221 ms
...
64 bytes from 193.128.56.2: icmp_seq=30 ttl=254 time=816.691 ms
64 bytes from 193.128.56.2: icmp_seq=31 ttl=254 time=36.105 ms
64 bytes from 193.128.56.2: icmp_seq=32 ttl=254 time=853.323 ms
64 bytes from 193.128.56.2: icmp_seq=33 ttl=254 time=678.253 ms
64 bytes from 193.128.56.2: icmp_seq=34 ttl=254 time=331.213 ms
64 bytes from 193.128.56.2: icmp_seq=35 ttl=254 time=27.931 ms
64 bytes from 193.128.56.2: icmp_seq=36 ttl=254 time=273.661 ms
64 bytes from 193.128.56.2: icmp_seq=37 ttl=254 time=131.990 ms
64 bytes from 193.128.56.2: icmp_seq=38 ttl=254 time=29.141 ms
...
laurell 9 >
```

The initial timings show consistent link behavior with an average RTT of approximately 31 seconds. However, about 30 seconds into the trace, we see large RTT fluctuations (nearly a whole minute for some packets). Since we are transferring 56 bytes of data, plus an 8-byte ICMP header, plus a 20-byte IP header, plus link encapsulation (assume 10 bytes), this gives 94 byte packets. At 128 Kpbs, 94 bytes should require approximately 5.875 ms to transfer ($94 \times 8/128,000$). For a two-way exchange (i.e., an ICMP echo request and echo response) we would expect at least twice this delay plus some host processing time (say 10–20 ms in total). We can assume the initial RTT values indicate other traffic on the link and possible queuing latency, but the values from packet 30 onward indicate serious link congestion.

Potential problems

In some situations ping may be unable to help. These situations include the following:

- Some routers silently discard undeliverable packets. Others may believe a packet has been transmitted successfully when it has not been. (This is especially common over Ethernet, which does not provide link-layer acknowledgments.) Therefore, ping may not always provide reasons why packets go unanswered.

- Ping cannot tell you why a packet was damaged, delayed, or duplicated. It cannot tell you where this happened either, although you may be able to deduce it.

- Ping cannot give you a blow-by-blow description of every host that handled the packet and everything that happened at every step of the way. It is an unfortunate fact that no software can reliably provide this information for a TCP/IP network.

- Application-level faults may not be detected by ping, since it tests only the IP layer.

- In secure environments ICMP echo may be disabled on sensitive hosts or devices to avoid potential hacking techniques.

Traceroute

TCP/IP provides very limited capabilities for tracing routes, restricted to the IP record route options. These are poorly specified, not reliably implemented, and often disabled for security reasons—hence, they cannot be relied upon as diagnostic tools. Traceroute is, therefore, a best-effort tool hacked together to work around these limitations; it may not work in all circumstances—nevertheless, it can be surprisingly useful. The traceroute program attempts to trace the path a packet takes through the network by transmitting a series of UDP probe packets to a specified IP address (using UDP port 33434) and then waits for ICMP replies. A group of probe packets (usually three) are initially sent with a minimum valid TTL value (i.e., one). The TTL (within the IP header) is then incremented for each subsequent test, usually up to a value of 30. In an internetwork, every router that forwards these packets will subtract one from the packet's current TTL. If the TTL reaches zero, the packet lifetime has expired and the packet must be discarded. Traceroute relies on the fact that routers normally send an ICMP time exceeded message back to the sender whenever they discard packets due to a zero TTL value. By starting with small TTL values that quickly expire, traceroute forces routers along the active route to generate these ICMP messages, so we can identify which routers are in the path and in which order. For example, a packet sent with TTL = 1 should produce a message from the first router in the path; using the IP address of the inter

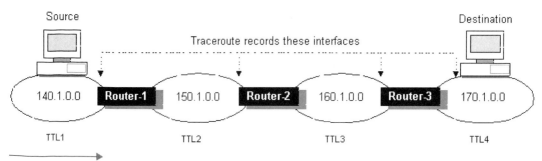

Figure 9.11   *Traceroute recording example.*

face it transmits the ICMP timeout messages on the receiving interface. A packet with TTL = 2 generates a message from the second router and so on, as illustrated in Figure 9.11. If the packet eventually reaches the specified destination, the receiving node will return an ICMP port-unreachable packet (since 33434 is not a well-known port). Refer to [49] for full details of ICMP error codes.

For each batch of probe packets traceroute displays the IP addresses reported back, and DNS is used to convert this into a symbolic domain address. Round-trip times are also reported for each packet in the group. Traceroute reports any additional ICMP messages (such as destination unreachable) using a rather cryptic syntax (!N means network unreachable; !H means host unreachable). Once a group of packets has been processed (this could take several seconds), the next group (TTL + 1) begins transmitting, and the whole process repeats.

Traceroute options

Here's a list of common traceroute options.

Traceroute option definitions

- −m max-ttl—At some TTL value, traceroute expects to get a reply from the target host. Of course, if the host is unreachable for some reason, this may never happen, so max-ttl (default 30) sets a limit on how long traceroute keeps trying. If the target host is farther than 30 hops away, you'll need to increase this value.

- −n—Numerical output only. Use if you're having nameserver problems and traceroute hangs trying to do inverse DNS lookups.

- −p port—Base UDP port. The packets traceroute sends are UDP packets targeted at strange port numbers that nothing will be listening on (we hope). The target host should ignore the packets after generating port-unreachable messages. Port is the UDP port number that traceroute uses on its first packet, and increments by one for each subsequent packet. My traceroute uses 33434 (yours probably does too). Change this if a program on the target host might be using ports in roughly the 33434–33534 range.

- –q queries—How many packets should be sent for each TTL value. The default is 3, which is fine for finding out the route. If you're more interested in seeing RTT values from each hop, I'd suggest increasing this number to 10.

- –w wait—Wait is the number of seconds packets have to generate replies before traceroute assumes they never will and moves on. The default is 3. Increase this if pings to the target host show round-trip times longer than this.

Potential problems

Traceroute has already been described as potentially unreliable, not because of any fault in the application itself but due to external issues that could occur and make its findings questionable. These issues include the following:

- Routing policy—Increasingly features such as policy-based routing are being used on routers to support quality-of-service requirements. Routing policy may cause traceroute to generate routes that have no relevance to the forwarding paths used by applications.

- Lack of or bad responses—Some routers do not send back ICMP time-exceeded packets, or they manipulate the TTL field incorrectly. Some end systems do not return ICMP port-unreachable messages, causing traceroute to take a long time to timeout.

- Routing oscillations—During the running of a traceroute test, probe packets should follow a consistent route, but this is not always the case. If the network is unstable, packets may be routed differently and the resulting reports may be confusing. Run the test several times to be sure.

- No forwarding addresses—Traceroute reports only one IP address from each router (normally the receiving interface address). The forwarding interface is not explicitly exposed, and with unnumbered WAN links this could be impossible to deduce.

- Routing problems—The router does not have a route back to the sender or may have a route via a different interface than the one on which it received the probe packet. In these cases, you may receive no reply at all or a response from an IP address that is inconsistent (i.e., some other interface on the same router or even the loopback address).

The bottom line is that traceroute can be very useful, but treat its output with some degree of scepticism. Use other tools to validate its reports if you are unsure.

Netstat

Netstat is a useful status tool, available on most TCP/IP implementations. Netstat can be used to display a number of protocol or interface statistics. It can also be used to display the contents of the routing table (so you can see if the host node is learning routes as expected). Again the syntax and facilities will vary between platforms. The options available for MS-DOS version 4.10.2222 are shown in the following list.

MS-DOS NetStat option definitions

- –a—Displays all connections and listening ports.

- –e—Displays Ethernet statistics. This may be combined with the –s option.

- –n—Displays addresses and port numbers in numerical form.

- –p proto—Shows connections for the protocol specified by proto; proto may be TCP or UDP. If used with the –s option to display per protocol statistics, proto may be TCP, UDP, or IP.

- –r—Displays the routing table.

- –s—Displays per protocol statistics. By default, statistics are shown for TCP, UDP, and IP; the –p option may be used to specify a subset of the default.

- interval—Redisplays selected statistics, pausing interval seconds between each display. Press CTRL+C to stop redisplaying statistics. If omitted, Netstat will print the current configuration information once.

Using Netstat

We can examine the routing table by using the –r option, as shown in the following code segment.

```
C:\WINDOWS>netstat -r

Route Table
```

```
Active Routes:

    Network Address              Netmask     Gateway Address           Interface    Metric
           127.0.0.0          255.0.0.0           127.0.0.1           127.0.0.1        1
        192.168.32.0      255.255.255.0      192.168.32.200      192.168.32.200        1
      192.168.32.200    255.255.255.255           127.0.0.1           127.0.0        1
      192.168.32.255    255.255.255.255      192.168.32.200      192.168.32.200        1
           224.0.0.0          224.0.0.0      192.168.32.200      192.168.32.200        1
     255.255.255.255    255.255.255.255      192.168.32.200             0.0.0.0        1

Active Connections

   Proto   Local Address        Foreign Address         State
```

In this example there are no active connections.

In our next example we can combine the –s and –p options to display a subset of the available protocol statistics, as shown in the following code segment.

```
C:\WINDOWS>netstat -s -p icmp

ICMP Statistics

                              Received    Sent
        Messages              69          69
        Errors                0           0
        Destination Unreachable  0        0
        Time Exceeded         0           0
        Parameter Problems    0           0
        Source Quenches       0           0
        Redirects             0           0
        Echos                 33          33
        Echo Replies          33          33
        Timestamps            0           0
        Timestamp Replies     0           0
        Address Masks         0           0
        Address Mask Replies  0           0
```

Tcpdump

Tcpdump is a basic packet analyzer, originally released on UNIX and subsequently supported on SunOS, Ultrix, and most BSD revisions. For the following examples I used a version ported onto DOS (there are also reports of a port to LINUX). It was originally written by Van Jacobsen to analyze TCP performance problems but can now be used for analyzing a variety of IP protocols and encapsulations, such as TCP, DNS, NFS, SLIP, or Apple-Talk. It may be difficult to get tcpdump to work on some UNIX systems, since it requires the interface to be in promiscuous mode.

Using tcpdump

The easiest way to use tcpdump is to run it in interactive mode and use the −i switch to specify the network interface to be used. Summary information for every Internet packet received or transmitted on the interface will be displayed on the screen. The following example trace shows VRRP traffic in normal operation. Since we are looking at all traffic, there is also ICMP traffic generated by a ping request.

```
bozo[admin]# tcpdump -i eth-s1p2
tcpdump: listening on eth-s1p2
06:12:00.630249 192.168.32.12 > 224.0.0.18:   VRRPv2-adver 20: vrid 32 pri 255
06:12:01.630144 192.168.32.12 > 224.0.0.18:   VRRPv2-adver 20: vrid 32 pri 255
06:12:02.630132 192.168.32.12 > 224.0.0.18:   VRRPv2-adver 20: vrid 32 pri 255
06:12:03.630107 192.168.32.12 > 224.0.0.18:   VRRPv2-adver 20: vrid 32 pri 255
06:12:03.822585 192.168.32.100 > 192.168.32.12:   icmp: echo request
06:12:03.822659 192.168.32.12 > 192.168.32.100:   icmp: echo reply
06:12:04.630083 192.168.32.12 > 224.0.0.18:   VRRPv2-adver 20: vrid 32 pri 255
06:12:04.831643 192.168.32.100 > 192.168.32.12:   icmp: echo request
06:12:04.831684 192.168.32.12 > 192.168.32.100:   icmp: echo reply
06:12:05.630082 192.168.32.12 > 224.0.0.18:   VRRPv2-adver 20: vrid 32 pri 255
^C
10 packets received by filter
0 packets dropped by kernel
```

The following example trace illustrates tcpdump in verbose mode. Again this trace shows VRRP traffic in normal operation plus ICMP traffic generated by a ping request. Verbose mode is useful for more detailed packet data, but it may swamp the display, making it difficult to analyze and debug problems.

```
bozo [admin]# tcpdump -ev -i eth-s1p2
tcpdump: listening on eth-s1p2
06:14:10.630215 0:0:5e:0:1:20 1:0:5e:0:0:12 0800 54: 192.168.32.12 > 224.0.0.18:
VRRPv2-adver 20: vrid 32 pri 255 int 1 sum ff27 naddrs 1 192.168.32.12 (ttl 255, id
1845)
06:14:10.807724 0:80:c7:bf:52:9c 0:0:5e:0:1:20 0800 74: 192.168.32.100 >
192.168.32.12: icmp: echo request (ttl 32, id 16643)
06:14:10.807800 0:0:5e:0:1:20 0:80:c7:bf:52:9c 0800 74: 192.168.32.12 >
192.168.32.100: icmp: echo reply (ttl 255, id 1846)
06:14:11.630110 0:0:5e:0:1:20 1:0:5e:0:0:12 0800 54: 192.168.32.12 > 224.0.0.18:
VRRPv2-adver 20: vrid 32 pri 255 int 1 sum ff27 naddrs 1 192.168.32.12 (ttl 255, id
1847)
06:14:11.810506 0:80:c7:bf:52:9c 0:0:5e:0:1:20 0800 74: 192.168.32.100 >
192.168.32.12: icmp: echo request (ttl 32, id 16899)
06:14:11.810551 0:0:5e:0:1:20 0:80:c7:bf:52:9c 0800 74: 192.168.32.12 >
192.168.32.100: icmp: echo reply (ttl 255, id 1848)

   ets received by filter
    s dropped by kernel
```

,9

Tcpdump provides several other important options, as well as the ability to specify an expression to restrict the range of packets you wish to see. Refer to the tcpdump "man" page under UNIX or the relevant help or Readme file under DOS or Windows.

Potential problems

Potential problems include the following:

- No output—Check to make sure you're specifying the correct network interface with the –i option, which I suggest you always use explicitly. If you're having DNS problems, tcpdump might hang trying to look up DNS names for IP addresses; try the –f or –n options to disable this feature. If you still see nothing, check the kernel interface; –tcpdump might be misconfigured for your system.

- Dropped packets—At the end of its run, tcpdump will inform you if any packets were dropped in the kernel. If this becomes a problem, it's likely that your host can't keep up with the network traffic and decode it at the same time. Try using the tcpdump –w option to bypass the decoding and write the raw packets to a file; then come back later and decode the file with the –r switch. You can also try using –s to reduce the capture snapshot size.

- Messages that end with [|rip] and [|domain]—Messages ending with [|proto] indicate that the packet couldn't be completely decoded, because the capture snapshot size (the so-called snarf length) was too small. Increase it with the –s switch.

Nslookup and dig

Nslookup is a comprehensive tool for diagnosing DNS problems and is included in the BIND distribution. There are too many applications for nslookup to be covered here, so rather than do it an injustice the interested reader is directed to [50], where a whole chapter is dedicated to its use. Domain information groper (Dig) is another useful diagnostic tool that works in a way similar to nslookup and is also included in the BIND distribution. Some engineers prefer dig's user interface to that of nslookup. In short, both dig and nslookup are command-line tools that enable you to issue queries to DNS servers; the replies are then reported on the display (nslookup can be run interactively or noninteractively, depending on the scope of action required). In effect they allow you to act as a DNS resolver.

For example, you can retrieve a list of root servers by typing the following command line:

```
percent dig @a.root-servers.net . ns > db.cache
```

9.2.4 Advanced diagnostic tools

There are many commercial tools on the market for diagnosing network problems. They broadly fall into the following categories:

- Media and cable testers

- Multiprotocol protocol analyzers

- Traffic generators and application simulators

We will not dwell on the first category of products; there are many vendors of media testers—see [51] for representative examples such as the DSP-2000 handheld cable analyzer.

Protocol analyzers

Network protocol analyzers are one of the key tools used by network engineers to identify subtle network, application, or protocol issues. They range in complexity from handheld or PC-based packet capture tools (see Figure 9.12) to sophisticated custom hardware offering simultaneous multiport packet capture, expert analysis, and simulation/playback. Each packet is typically timestamped with millisecond resolution and checked for CRC errors and media errors, such as being too short or too long. So-called expert analyzers will check for errors or notable events based on analysis of multiple packet streams by identifying which stream each packet belongs to and analyzing each flow individually. This requires data structures to be maintained to keep track of items such as source and destination addresses, port numbers, protocol IDs, timestamps, and flags. Expert analysis requires inherent knowledge of how various protocols and applications work, as well as tracking of the key state machine events.

Historically the prime vendors of this equipment include companies such as Network Associates, Inc. (Santa Clara, CA), Wandel & Goltermann Technologies, Inc. (Triangle Park, NC), and Hewlett-Packard Co. (Palo Alto, CA). Examples of widely used network analyzers today include the following:

- Network Associates, Inc.—Sniffer, NetXRay [52]

- HP range of network analyzers (e.g., 4950) [45]

- Wandel & Goltermann Technologies network analyzers and testing suites [53]

- Radcom Equipment, Inc. (e.g., Enlite, Wirespeed 622 ATM Analyzer, Prismelt Analyzer) [54]

- Fluke range of handheld protocol analyzers (e.g., 680 Series Enterprise LANMeter) [51]

- Tekelec range of network analyzers

- Novell LANAlyzer

- IBM's DatagLANce Network Analyzer

The Sniffer product from Network Associates, Inc. has become something of a benchmark product, used by many companies because of its

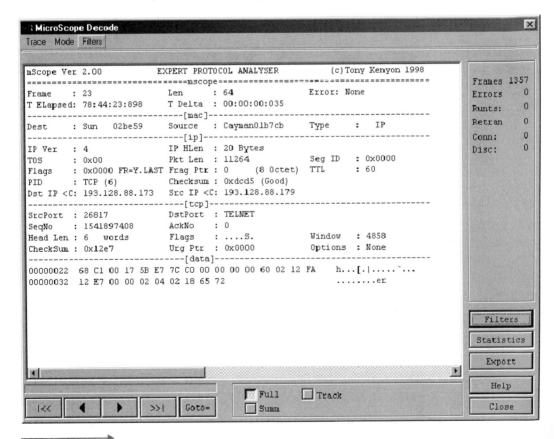

Figure 9.12   *A PC-based network analyzer, showing detailed protocol decoding of a TCP/IP frame over an Ethernet interface.*

robustness, its broad protocol decoding abilities, and the ability to add custom decodes. HP also has a history of producing quality products, and W&G offer high-end, high-performance analyzers. RAD is relatively new to the market but offers a number of products, including wire-speed ATM analyzers. At the basic level these devices will give you useful statistics on the major performance parameters, such as the following:

- Network utilization

- Symbol and receive length errors

- Average and peak frame rates

- Bytes transmitted

- Hardware flow control

- Unicast and multicast distribution

- Protocol distribution

- Bad frames, too-short too-long frames, bad CRC

- Total and current frames/cells sent and received by VPI/VCI or DLCI

  For serious work the key features to look out for are as follows:

- A full suite of protocol decodes

- A wide range of WAN options (Frame Relay, T1/T3, E1/E3, ATM, X.25, PPP, etc.)

- Extensive custom filtering capabilities

- The capability to add custom decodes

- Real-time capture and translation

- Expert protocol or application analysis

- The ability to edit traces and playback for simulation work

- Multiinterface capture (typically LAN and WAN)

- High-speed media support (100-Mbs Ethernet, Gigabit Ethernet, etc.)

- The ability to distribute multiple capture devices and centrally manage them

- Trace file export options (ASCII and other trace formats)

  Some of these features are discussed in the following text.

Expert or no expert

Without an expert mode option the engineer needs to be extremely well acquainted with the protocols and services of interest. A basic analyzer will decode frames and provide timestamps, flag analysis, and rudimentary error checking (long and short frames, CRC errors, etc.). Some protocol suites may not be decoded fully, depending upon the level of sophistication of the analyzer. These basic devices are effectively stateless in that the more subtle protocol state issues are not observed, since the analysis is essentially based on discrete frames. More sophisticated expert analyzers are more protocol aware and more stateful in operation. These devices are aware of the state machines used by common protocol stacks, so they know that FTP uses a fixed control session and dynamic data sessions on different port numbers and can associate several related flows. They may even include very high level application support for protocols such as SQLnet and have a much broader set of decodes. Network Associates, Inc., for example, claims support for more than 400 protocol decodes. This level of support can save valuable hours digging through traces and mapping out protocol interactions by hand.

Some devices may offer automated fault and performance management functions, which can be integrated with your network management. These tools automatically detect and pinpoint problems while monitoring the network and forwarding alarms with events to an NMS as required. Bottlenecks, protocol violations, and even problems such as duplicate addresses and misconfigured routers can be identified automatically and flagged to the NMS.

Edit, playback, and simulation

For any serious work you will also need the ability to modify and play back traces. This gives you the ability to simulate either failure or heavy load conditions in the lab and get a better handle on the problem. You may also want to stress test a live network as part of the commissioning stage. If your analyzer lets you edit frames, this will allow you to adjust a trace from a live network to suit your test environment. For example, you may need to change IP addresses in a whole range of packets. Note that if you did this, you would typically have to modify any TCP or UDP checksums, so any tool that can do this automatically is extremely useful.

Real-time capture, multiple interfaces

Another useful feature of more advanced devices is multiport real-time capturing. This allows you to capture a LAN and WAN port concurrently. You can then map the two traces together (both are timestamped), and this can resolve subtle issues when diagnosing problems over wide area links.

High-speed, real-time capture

As network media increase in bandwidth (e.g., Gigabit Ethernet or ATM OC-3 and OC-12), analyzers have a much tougher job to keep up. Not only do they have to capture all frames comfortably (missing frames equals missed problems), but they have to do at least some measure of translation and analysis in real time. For example, when capturing ATM you may wish to display open and closed Switched Virtual Circuit (SVC) connections in real time while capturing cells. Gigabit Ethernet operates at approximately 1.4 million frames per second, so real-time capture and translation is no small task. Software-based analyzers, which run on standard PCs using off-the-shelf adapter cards, are unlikely to keep up with these kind of speeds for the foreseeable future; you will need dedicated hardware. Vendors of custom-designed analyzers claimed to operate at gigabit rates are Network Associates, Inc. [52], Wandel & Goltermann Technologies, Inc. [53], and Hewlett-Packard Co [45].

Trace format export and import

The lowest common denominator here might be ASCII or Comma Separated Value (CSV) format. This at least allows you to read a trace from different sources via a standard word processor (ASCII) or spreadsheet (CSV). Of course, you will not be able to perform any further protocol analysis in this format; you are at the mercy of the tool that exported the file. Network Associates was probably the first major vendor in this field to publish its internal (proprietary) trace file format. They chose to implement a simple but elegant <Tag><Length><Value> schema for storing records, and this is much easier to translate than a bulk memory dump. Subsequently many other vendors supported the import and export of this file format. The Sniffer file format is the closest thing to a standard among competing manufacturers, and this is important for any support organization, where traces may be coming in from the field in different file formats. It is far easier to convert traces and analyze on a common platform than to have an array of different analyzers back at the main office just to read different file formats.

9.2.5 Selecting the right tools for the job

Before you dust off the analyzer, the most useful approach for locating problems is the NMS and tools such as ping, traceroute, and tcpdump. You can waste considerable time running around your network taking traces at exactly the wrong spots, so the first job you must do in the event of a network failure is attempt to isolate the problem. You may narrow this down to a particular LAN or WAN segment and then you can focus in on the problem. In many cases you will resolve the problem without taking a trace.

For small networks or day-to-day use a cheaper PC-based analyzer can be extremely useful. These tools are essentially software applications running over standard NICs and may be restricted in the interface types supported (often LAN only, sometimes only Ethernet). A good example is illustrated in Figure 9.12. The tcpdump utility is useful but really quite limited; but if you cannot afford even a PC-based analyzer, this may be your only option. For serious debugging you will need a more sophisticated LAN/WAN analyzer, probably more than one. If you have taken a proactive approach with your management strategy by deploying remote monitoring agents or RMON probes, a network analyzer will complement these tools well. Much as your finance department may balk at the price for these devices, the cost of failing to diagnose a problem quickly enough may dwarf the product cost. Choose a tool with high-performance capabilities, with the capability to add more modules as your network grows or new media types are added. You need a wide range of protocol decodes, even on an IP-only internetwork; remember that there will be Windows devices potentially churning out Novell, NetBIOS, and who knows what else. To lock in quickly on problems choose an analyzer with some form of expert capability, and playback mode is a must.

9.3   Policy-based management

In recent years the scale and complexity of internetworks and the huge amount of control information required to configure and maintain them have led to the requirement for an overall policy-based management architecture. This architecture must integrate many different facets of network operations, provide a consistent repository for control data, and provide timely responses to policy queries. Policy should be defined and controlled centrally and then translated automatically into specific system configuration parameters, ready for download to network systems and devices. The intention is to abstract much of the complexity of individual device configuration and operating systems from the network planner, so that more time can be spent optimizing the design, rather than on learning the intricacies of how a dozen or so different products work. Policy-based management is intended to significantly reduce the time, effort, and cost associated with deploying large internetworks and reduce the burden maintenance and troubleshooting by ensuring that all systems in the network behave consistently. It turns out that there are several important areas of network operations that benefit from an overall policy model, including the following:

- Quality of service (e.g., 802.1p, differentiated services, ToS)

- Network security and VPN management (e.g., firewall policy, IPSec VPN policy, ACL management)

- Traffic engineering and bandwidth allocation (e.g., routing policy, ACL management)

- Routing policy [55]

- Address management (e.g., DHCP policy, NAT policy)

- Storage management (e.g., HSM policy)

Policy management characterizes the response of the network as a whole to specific traffic behavior, user behavior, application behavior, and system behavior. Policy should reflect the needs of an organization as whole, individual groups within the organization, and the way that an organization interfaces with the outside world. Policy management utilizes other facets of traditional management systems, such as configuration management, to effect those changes in behavior and be sufficiently granular to effect changes based on time of day and day of week.

9.3.1 Policy defined

Policy is a set of rules associated with services (such as security, bandwidth, etc.), where these rules define the criteria for obtaining those services. A rule comprises one or more conditions and actions, typically represented as a tuple:

IF <conditions> THEN <actions>

A rule, therefore, describes the conditions that must be met before the specified actions can be taken. For example, a high-level policy rule might be:

Rule: On the backbone, SAP traffic flows from HQ should get higher priority than those from remote offices.

We can break this down as:

CONDITION: If the traffic flows are identified as SAP and originate from the HQ network.

ACTION: Assign higher priority to these flows.

In practice policies can be complex and numerous; policies can be defined recursively, which means that a policy could contain other policies. A policy group is an aggregation of policy rules or an aggregation of policy groups.

Policy management services must be able to identify and resolve policy conflicts and must be flexible enough to support both static and dynamic operations (i.e., the ability to enforce policy rules loaded at system startup and the ability to enforce policy rules based on events). The IETF Policy Framework working group is addressing the need for a policy framework definition language, a policy architecture model, and policy terminology. Although much of the initial focus is on QoS policy, this work is generic in scope. The policy metamodel links high-level business requirements (e.g., such as those specified in an SLA), to low-level device implementation mechanisms (such as rules for access control or the configuration of queues to handle a particular service class). In Figure 9.13, master policy may reside on a dedicated policy server or a directory server (in some implementations it may even reside on the management console). Policy-enabled devices such as switches and routers typically cache policy locally to reduce latency in policy queries. Legacy devices must be configured directly from a standalone policy server. For high-availability applications a redundant policy server may be available.

Figure 9.13
Policy management deployment.

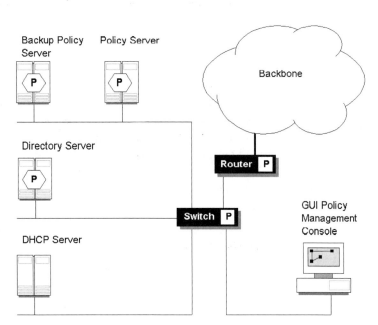

9.3.2 Components of a policy management system

The basic components of a policy management system are as follows:

- Policy console—to enable GUI or command-line access to policy functions (such as setting QoS policies)

- Policy servers—to hold policy data at different sites

- Policy repository—typically a Directory Service (LDAP) or RDBMS (such as Oracle or SQL Server) to provide centralized storage for policy profiles

- Policy distribution protocols—used to download policy (SNMP, TFTP, COPS, CLI, etc.)

There are other so-called policy peripherals, which may be offered with a policy management system, including the following:

- Policy proxy agents—to implement policies in network devices (e.g., a policy-enabled switch)

- Integrated DHCP or WINS/NIS servers—for address allocation and management

- Integrated security servers—for authentication or certificate management

- Baselining tools—for checking that policy is effective by first characterizing the network

- RMON probes—for remote performance monitoring

Policy console

Policy rules are created, edited, and viewed at the central policy console, with changes sent to the policy repository. The policy console is also responsible for other functions, such as checking for possible conflicts between policy rules. The interface is typically an object-oriented GUI (although some vendors have implemented a text-oriented CLI). The user typically creates or modifies a set of policy profiles that characterize the behavior of systems. For example:

- The default security policy could be defined for a class of device called PerimeterFirewalls.

- The default QoS policy could be defined for a class of device called EnterpriseRouters. This would define how these devices should treat different types of traffic in order to meet specified QoS requirements.

- The default routing policy could be defined for a class of device called BackboneRouters.

Policy repository

A policy repository is a dedicated server that is responsible for policy storage and retrieval. Policy must be centralized for consistency, and in large, multi-vendor internetworks it is essential to use a standardized vendor-independent format for storing policy profiles. The IETF Policy Framework working group defines a core information model and schema [56]. The policy core schema is based on LDAP [57] and comprises 13 classes, including policyGroup, policyRule, policyCondition, and policyAction. There must be standardized mechanisms to distribute policy information to clients; currently this can take several forms, as follows:

- A centralized Directory Server, such as an LDAP Server, Microsoft's Active Directory Service (ADS), or Novell's Novell Directory Service (NDS)

- A standard Relational Database Management System (RDBMS), such as SQL Server, Oracle, or Sybase

- A highly optimized proprietary database format

In practice there are examples of all three types of implementation in commercial products, including hybrid combinations; the prime concerns for implementers are performance, scalability, and flexibility. For example, policy rules for different service levels could be stored in directories as LDAP schema and be downloaded to devices that implement policy (such as hosts, routers, firewalls, policy servers, or proxies) via LDAP. The Directory-Enabled Networks (DEN) initiative is also of great interest for policy management systems, so much so that the DEN standards have been incorporated into Distributed Management Task Force (DMTF) and Common Information Model (CIM).

Policy server

The policy server (referred to as the Policy Decision Point [PDP]) makes decisions based on the policy rules it retrieves from the policy repository. The policy server can also retrieve information from other entities (such as authentication server or SNMP agents). The policy server can also translate abstract rules into low-level vendor-specific rules. The policy server is responsible for communicating policy to client systems (such as switches, routers, and firewalls). One policy server can manage multiple policy clients in the same administrative domain.

Policy servers can be implemented as standalone systems (e.g., as software running on a Windows NT, Solaris, or UNIX platform), or they can be embedded within networking systems (such as switches and routers). To improve scalability, some vendors take a two-tiered approach (rather like the Manager-of-Managers concept introduced earlier) that uses a server manager to download policies to a number of standalone servers. For high-availability applications, systems may be deployed with redundant policy servers. To improve performance policy may be cached inside policy-enabled devices such as switches and routers. This operates rather like caching systems, except that the content of interest here is policy. Any requests for policy not in the cache must be forwarded to a policy server, and cached policy must be synchronized regularly to avoid inconsistencies. If the policy server is also embedded in the same system, the policy request will be resolved locally, and the embedded policy server must fetch policy from the central policy repository.

Policy clients

Policy clients (referred to as the Policy Enforcement Points [PEPs]) represent the physical execution point for policies (e.g., a router, switch, or firewall). As indicated previously, the separation of PDP and PEP functions is a logical distinction; both functions are often implemented in the same network device. Once policy has been communicated and accepted, it is up to the client device to enforce policy according to its individual functional capabilities. For example, in response to a QoS policy, a router could use internal scheduling mechanisms and admission control features to meet policy requirements. Note that the main prioritization schemes associated with policy manipulation in commercial products today include 802.1p, Differentiated Services, and ToS.

Policy distribution

Policy needs to be fetched from the central policy repository and held on policy servers. Policy also needs to be communicated between policy servers and policy clients (such as a router or switch). This requires some form of messaging protocol. Unfortunately, there is a huge installed base of equipment that is not policy enabled, so there is no universally accepted way to achieve this.

Most vendors today use SNMP and LDAP to distribute policy to clients. SNMP is not viewed as a long-term solution due to its weak security, connectionless deployment, and its inefficiency for bulk data transfers. LDAP also has similar limitations; however, only embedded-server vendors tend to use it for fetching policy profiles from the central policy repository (i.e., the less time-critical part of policy distribution). Several vendors have reverse engineered Cisco's IOS Command-Line Interface (CLI), enabling configuration commands to be fed directly into Cisco hardware over Telnet. Vendors are also showing increased interest in a relatively new IETF protocol called Common Open Policy Service (COPS), developed initially for QoS policy distribution between policy servers and policy clients and optimized for high performance. We will briefly review COPS here.

Common Open Policy Service (COPS) protocol

Common Open Policy Service (COPS) is a simple client/server query-response protocol. It was initially designed to support policy control over QoS signaling protocols, although the model is extensible so that other policy clients can be supported in the future. COPS requires that at least one policy server exists in each administrative domain; it is used to exchange policy information between the policy server (PDP) and its clients (PEPs). The COPS protocol is reliable, utilizing a single persistent TCP connection between the PEP and a remote PDP (the PDP listens on a well-known TCP port, 3288). All COPS messages include a common eight-byte header, incorporating a one-byte OpCode. Current operations include the following:

- Request (REQ)
- Decision (DEC)
- Report State (RPT)
- Delete Request State (DRQ)
- Synchronize State Req (SSQ)
- Client-Open (OPN)
- Client-Accept (CAT)
- Client-Close (CC)
- Keep-Alive (KA)
- Synchronize Complete (SSC)

COPS makes no assumptions about the methods used by the policy server; all it requires is that the server returns decisions to policy requests. The basic model for interaction between a policy server and its clients is compatible with the framework document for policy-based admission control [58]. For further information on COPS, the interested reader is referred to [59]. Reference [60] discusses COPS applications with RSVP.

9.3.3 Design and implementation issues

While all of this sounds great in theory, unfortunately, given the major discontinuities in multivendor networks, the task of integrating all of this functionality into a seamless architecture is far from easy. It is important to note that the physical implementation of the policy server can significantly affect scalability, cost, and performance, as follows:

- Standalone servers reduce the number of policy profiles, since with the embedded approach each client maintains its own profile. However, standalone servers have finite resources and can distribute policy to only a finite number of network devices before they become a bottleneck. The number of devices capable of being managed by a policy server varies widely, with estimates ranging between 5 and 500. A two-tier architecture is advisable for very large networks. Another problem with standalone managers is that they are often run on general-purpose platforms. These platforms may not be sufficiently rugged for nonstop operations. During outages policy may be unavailable even though the client switch or router continues to operate.

- Embedded servers are claimed to scale better and provide higher availability. With the embedded approach each switch or router is loaded with its own policy server, and client-to-server overheads are greatly reduced and do not impact on the network. Embedded servers do, however, require more resources (processor and memory), which increase the platform price. This could increase the cost of a design significantly if many hundreds of systems are involved.

Standalone managers are useful in the interim, since they enable network planners to apply policy to legacy networking equipment (e.g., routers and LAN switches that either cannot be upgraded or do not have sufficient memory or processing capacity to run policy code). For the foreseeable future, policy managers will require a mixture of standard and proprietary methods to work in large, multivendor networks. There is also a substantial installed base of legacy equipment that does not support new standards, such as Differentiated Services and COPS, and possibly never will.

For the interested reader, [61] provides some excellent background information on policy, the applications of directories, and middleware in policy-based management.

Vendors

Examples of vendors of policy managers and embedded policy servers include Orchestream, Xedia, Check Point, Cabletron, Cisco, IBM, HP/Intel, Lucent, Extreme Networks, Fore Systems, 3Com, Xylan, Aponet, Class Data Systems, Packeteer, IP Highway, and Newbridge Networks.

9.4   Summary

In this chapter we discussed the following:

- SNMP is the dominant management framework for enterprise and IP-based internetworks. However, SNMP lacks features that promote scalability in large internetworks—for example, there is no support for hierarchical management, using techniques such as Mid-Level Management (MLM). In the carrier space CMIS/CMIP has been successfully deployed, but it remains unattractive to the average network manager. IBM has a largely proprietary but sophisticated architecture for its mainframe management model called NetView.

- There have been efforts to broaden the attractiveness of CMIS/CMIP IP and enterprise environments; examples include CMOT and CMOL. It is fair to say that none of these transport variants has gained any significant interest from the user community, and SNMP continues to dominate the installed base.

- HTTP-based managers are becoming the de facto way of performing configuration management on remote devices. Security mechanisms such as SSH and SSL can be built into these interfaces for peace of mind.

- For medium to large internetworks network management can impose unacceptable overheads on bandwidth, CPU, and device memory. A distributed and hierarchical management model needs to be deployed to optimize the available bandwidth.

- RMON is a very useful tool for remote monitoring and data collection in multivendor networks. It is up to you to decide how and what data should be monitored and what thresholds and alarm conditions to set. RMON can be invaluable in monitoring LAN health and performance and as a guide to longer-term capacity planning.

- Ping, traceroute, tcpdump, netstat, and dig are invaluable tools for IP internetwork diagnostics. Beyond these tools you need to use advanced protocol analyzers.

- Policy-based management is a critical emerging technology finally beginning to unite multivendor networks by abstracting network configuration and holding policy data in consistent, centrally managed repositories. Once in place this will significantly relieve the burden of network administration, especially in large, multivendor enterprises. There is some way to go yet in making policy management a practical reality.

References

[1]   T. Kenyon, *High-Performance Network Design: Design Techniques and Tools* (Woburn, MA: Digital Press, 2001).

[2]   Simple Network Management Protocol, STD 15, RFC 1157, May 1990.

[3]   Introduction to SNMPv2, RFC 1441, March 1993.

[4]   Transport Mappings for SNMPv2, RFC 1449, April 1993.

[5]   Structure of Management Information for Version 2 of the Simple Network Management Protocol (SNMPv2), RFC 1902, January 1996.

[6]   Protocol Operations for Version 2 of the Simple Network Management Protocol (SNMPv2), RFC 1905, January 1996.

[7]   Management Information Base for Version 2 of the Simple Network Management Protocol (SNMPv2), RFC 1907, January 1996.

[8]   Structure and Identification of Management Information for TCP/IP-Based Internets, RFC 1155, May 1990.

[9]   Reassignment of Experimental MIBs to Standard MIBs, RFC 1239, June 1991.

[10] Assigned Numbers, RFC 1700, October 1994.

[11] Management Information Base for Network Management of TCP/IP-Based Internets: MIB-II, RFC 1213, March 1991.

[12] Management Information Base for Network Management of TCP/IP-Based Internets, RFC 1156, May 1990.

[13] ftp.uu.net, MOSC (Managed Object Syntax Compiler). Publicly available (copyrighted) Yacc-based SNMP MIB Compiler.

[14] ftp.synoptics.com, SMIC. Publicly available (copyrighted) SNMP MIB Compiler.

[15] SNMP over OSI, RFC 1418, March 1993.

[16] SNMP over AppleTalk, RFC 1419, March 1993.

[17] SNMP over IPX, RFC 1420, March 1993.

[18] SNMP over Ethernet, RFC 1089, February 1989.

[19] R. L. Townsend, *SNMP Applications Developer's Guide* (New York, NY: VNR Communications Library, 1995).

[20] Bulk Table Retrieval with the SNMP, RFC 1157, October 1990.

[21] A Convention for Defining Traps for Use with the SNMP, RFC 1215, March 1991.

[22] M. T. Rose, *The Simple Book: An Introduction to Management of TCP/IP-Based Internets* (Englewood Cliffs, NJ: Prentice Hall, 1991).

[23] Introduction to Version 3 of the Internet Standard Network Management Framework, RFC 2570, April 1999.

[24] www.simple-times.org, *The Simple Times.* Publishes quality materials on SNMP and provides good links for network management information.

[25] SNMP Applications, RFC 2573, April 1999.

[26] User-Based Security Model (USM) for Version 3 of the Simple Network Management Protocol (SNMPv3), RFC 2574, April 1999.

[27] View-Based Access Control Model (VACM) for the Simple Network Management Protocol (SNMP), RFC 2575, April 1999.

[28] Coexistence between Version 1, Version 2, and Version 3 of the Internet Standard Network Management Framework, RFC 2576, March 2000.

[29] Coexistence between Version 1 and Version 2 of the Internet Standard Network Management Framework, RFC 1452, April 1993.

[30] http://www.watson.ibm.com, IBM Research Web site.

[31] "Bulk Transfers of MIB Data," *The Simple Times,* The Quarterly Newsletter of SNMP Technology, vol 7, no. 1, March 1999.

[32]   P. E. Mellquist, *SNMP++, An Object-Oriented Approach to Developing Network Management Applications* (Des Moines, IA: Prentice Hall PTR, Hewlett-Packard Professional Books, 1997).

[33]   Remote Network Monitoring Management Information Base Version 2 Using SMIv2, RFC 2021, January 1997.

[34]   Remote Network Monitoring Management Information Base, RFC 1757, November 1994.

[35]   Common Management Information Services Protocol over TCP/IP (CMOT), RFC 1095, April 1989.

[36]   ISO Presentation Services on Top of TCP/IP-Based Internets, RFC 1085, December 1988.

[37]   Information Processing Systems—Open Systems Interconnection—Specification of Abstract Syntax Notation One (ASN.1), International Organization for Standardization, IS 8824, December 1987.

[38]   Information Processing Systems—Open Systems Interconnection—Specification of Basic Encoding Rules for Abstract Notation One (ASN.1), International Organization for Standardization, IS 8825, December 1987.

[39]   Information Processing Systems—Open Systems Interconnection—Specification of Abstract Syntax Notation One (ASN.1), International Organization for Standardization, IS 8824, December, 1987.

[40]   ITU-T Rec. X.680, Abstract Syntax Notation One (ASN.1)—Specification of Basic Notation, 1994.

[41]   ITU-T Rec. X.690, Specification of ASN.1 Encoding Rules: Basic, Canonical, and Distinguished Encoding Rules, 1994.

[42]   www.catelrock.com, Home page for Castle Rock's SNMPc.

[43]   www.cai.com, Computer Associates International home page for CA Unicenter.

[44]   www.tivoli.com, Tovoli Systems, home page for Tivoli TME.

[45]   www.hp.com, Hewlett-Packard Co. (HP) home Web site.

[46]   Framework Fraud?, *Data Communications International,* September 1999, 33–42.

[47]   RITA—The Reliable Internetwork Troubleshooting Agent, RFC 2321, April 1998.

[48] K. Washburn, J. T. Evans, *TCP/IP: Running a Successful Network* (Reading, MA: Addison-Wesley 1993).

[49] Internet Control Message Protocol, DARPA Internet Program Protocol Specification, September 1981.

[50] P. Albitz, and C. Liu, *DNS and BIND* (Cambridge, MA: O'Reilly & Associates, 1997).

[51] www.fluke.com, Fluke test equipment home page.

[52] www.nai.com, Network Associates, Inc. home Web site.

[53] www.wg.com, Wandel & Goltermann Technologies, Inc. (W&G), home Web site.

[54] www.radcom-inc.com, Radcom Equipment, Inc., home page for protocol analysis equipment.

[55] Routing Policy System Replication, RFC 2769, February 2000 (proposed standard).

[56] B. Moore, E. Ellesson, J. Strassner, Policy Framework Core Information Model. Internet draft: draft-ietf-policy-core-info-model-02.txt, October 1999.

[57] J. Strassner, et. al., Policy Framework LDAP Core Schema. Internet draft: draft-ietf-policy-core-schema-06.txt, November 1999.

[58] A Framework for Policy-Based Admission Control, RFC 2753, January 2000.

[59] The COPS (Common Open Policy Service) Protocol, RFC 2748, January 2000 (proposed standard).

[60] COPS Usage for RSVP, RFC 2748, January 2000 (proposed standard).

[61] Network Policy and Services: A Report of a Workshop on Middleware, RFC 2768, February 2000.

Mathematical Review

Much of the research literature available to the network designer may often appear impenetrable, since the language used to express ideas involves advanced mathematical notation. Although this book is not heavily numerical, it is assumed that the reader has a basic grasp of mathematics, as the use of mathematical conventions in some areas of network design is unavoidable. In this appendix we briefly review a selection of the more common techniques applicable to data communications design theory.

A.1 Operators

$+$	Add	$\times$	Multiply
$-$	Subtract	$\div$	Divide
$=$	Equals	$\neq$	Not equal to
$\cong$ or $\approx$	Approximately equal to	$<$	Less than
$>$	Greater than	$\leq$	Less than or equal to
$\geq$	Greater or equal to	$\wedge$	Raised to the power of
$\sqrt{}$	The square root of	$\rightarrow$	Tends to or approaches

A.2 Numbers

Real numbers are numbers that can take a positive, negative, or zero value. For example:

$-400, -20, -11.75, -3, 0, +1, +3.76, +1000$

Integers are whole numbers, positive or negative, that have no fractional parts. For example:

−400, −20, −11, −3, 0, +1, +3, +1000

Rational numbers are fractional numbers and may be positive or negative. Rational numbers include fractions that are less than one, those that are greater than one (so-called *improper* fractions). Formally stated, rational numbers have the form *a*/*b*, where *a* and *b* are integers, *b* cannot be zero, and there are no common factors (i.e., 4/6 should be reduced to 2/3). Note that *b* can equal 1, so all integers, including zero, can be seen as rational numbers with a value of *b* equal to 1. For example:

−7/2, −1/4, 0/1, +1/8, +1/4, +3/2, +16/1

Irrational numbers are a form of rational numbers where *a* and *b* are non-integer. Irrational numbers can be produced in a number of ways; for example, π is irrational, and the square root of any *prime* number is irrational (e.g., √2 or √13). For example:

2.2360679, 3.1415926

A Prime number is a whole number that is greater than 1 and has no common factors other than 1 and itself (i.e., it cannot be divided by two integers that are greater than 1). Every natural number greater than 1 is either prime or can be expressed as a product of primes (e.g., 28 = 2 × 2 × 7). Prime numbers have many useful applications in cryptography, as discussed in Chapter 15. Examples include:

2, 3, …, 17, 19, 23, …, 47, …, 101, …, 1093,

Infinity is itself not a number. In effect, it is an unbounded value; we may therefore use the phrase *infinitely large* or *infinitely small* to represent inconceivably large or small values respectively. The term *infinitesimal* means a value whose limit is zero. Infinity is normally represented by the symbol ∞.

A.3   Summation

Summation of a series of numbers is frequently used in statistical and communication theory. A shorthand notation is used to represent a series of additions:

Σ (Sigma), used to denote "the sum of."

where the general form is:

$$\sum_{Initialization\_Condition}^{Termination\_Condition} \left(variable\ expression \right)$$

For example:

$$\sum_{i=1}^{n} x_i$$

represents the sum of the series $X_1 + X_2 + X_3 + \ldots X_n$. To illustrate, if $n = 4$ and the series of numbers is $\{1, 2, 3, 4\}$, then this operation would produce the result 10. Note that the variable expression must be summed before any external operator can be applied; so for example:

$$\sum_{i=0}^{n} x_i^2 \neq \left(\sum_{i=0}^{n} x_i \right)^2$$

This is clearly demonstrated using the previous example series $\{1, 2, 3, 4\}$ and $n = 4$.

$$1^2 + 2^2 + 3^2 + 4^2 \neq (1 + 2 + 3 + 4)^2$$

$$30 \neq 100$$

Summation is frequently used with more complex variable expressions, such as summation of a series of products:

$$\sum_{i=1}^{n} x_i y_i$$

It is important to recognize here that the *first* instance of x is multiplied by the first instance of y and so on through the series. There are a number of other basic rules applicable to summation operations, these include:

Rule 1: The summation of the sum of two variables is equal to the sum of the two summations of those variables:

$$\sum_{i=1}^{n} \left(x_i + y_i \right) = \sum_{i=1}^{n} x_i + \sum_{i=1}^{n} y_i$$

Rule 2: The summation of the subtraction of two variables is equal to the difference between the two summations of those variables:

$$\sum_{i=1}^{n} \left(x_i - y_i \right) = \sum_{i=1}^{n} x_i - \sum_{i=1}^{n} y_i$$

Rule 3: The summation of a constant n times is equal to the product of n and that constant:

$$\sum_{i=1}^{n} c = cn$$

Rule 4: The summation of the product of a constant and a variable is equal to the product of the constant and the summation of that variable:

$$\sum_{i=1}^{n} cx_i = c\sum_{i=1}^{n} x_i$$

A.4   Sets

A collection, class, or listing of mathematical objects is called a set. The objects in the set are referred to as *elements* or *members*. The *universal set* is the complete set of objects applicable to the object context (for example, if we were interested in performing operations on sets of *prime* numbers between 0 and 20, then the universal set would be {2, 3, 5, 7, 11, 13, 17, 19}). For statistical applications we are largely interested in sets of *numbers*; however, in areas of design such as topology analysis we may wish to manipulate a set of *objects* such as *edges* or *adjacencies* (described in Chapters 4 and 6). A set can be described using precise mathematical notation. Once described, there are algebraic operations that can be performed on sets using additional notation.

$\{a,b,c,d,e, \ldots z\}$	the set of elements from a to z
ϕ	the empty set
A'	the complement of set A (i.e., A becomes the *universal set* minus the intersection of set A and the universal set)
$n(A)$	the number of elements in set A
$\cup$	union of two sets (i.e., those elements common or unique to both sets)
$\cap$	intersection of two sets (i.e., those elements common to both sets)
$\in$	is a member/element of (e.g., $3 \in \{1, 2, 3\}$).

∉   is not a member/element of (e.g., $3 \notin \{1, 2, 4, 8\}$).

⊆   is a subset of (e.g., if every element of set T is a member of set S, then $T \subseteq S$).

⊂   is a proper subset of (e.g., $T \subset S$ in the above example, if an element $s \in S$, and $s \notin T$).

For example: the set containing 0 and 1 is denoted as $\{0, 1\}$. The set of even numbers between 2 and 500 is denoted as $\{2, 4, 6, \ldots, 500\}$. Regarding subsets, set S =$\{2, 4, 6\}$ has 8 distinct subsets: $\{2, 4, 6\}$, $\{2\}$, $\{4\}$, $\{6\}$, $\{2, 4\}$, $\{2, 6\}$, $\{4, 6\}$, plus the empty set $\{\}$, denoted as ϕ.

DNS Top Level Domain Codes

The following list of DNS Top Level Domain (TLD) codes comprises information from various sources, including RFC 1700 and some personal observations. Any errors or omissions are, therefore, my own. The list includes both country codes (CCs) and generic TLDs (highlighted in bold).

Domain	Country or Organisation	Domain	Country or Organisation
AG	Antigua And Barbuda	JP	Japan
AL	Albania	KM	Comoros
AQ	Antartica	KN	Saint Kitts and Nevis
AR	Argentina	KR	Republic of Korea
ARPA	ARPA Internet	LC	Saint Lucia
AS	Austria	LK	Sri Lanka
AU	Australia	LU	Luxembourg
BB	Barbados	**MIL**	Military
BE	Belgium	MY	Malaysia
BG	Bulgaria	MX	Mexico
BO	Bolivia	NA	Namibia
BR	Brazil	**NATO**	North Atlantic Treaty Organisation
BS	Bahamas	**NET**	Network Entities
CA	Canada	NI	Nicaragua
CH	Switzerland	NL	Netherlands
CL	Chile	NO	Norway
CN	China	NZ	New Zealand
CO	Colombia	**ORG**	Organisations
CR	Costa Rica	PE	Peru
CS	Czech Republic	PG	Papua New Guinea
DE	Germany	PH	Philippines
DK	Denmark	PL	Poland
DM	Dominica	PR	Puerto Rico
DO	Dominican Republic	PT	Portugal
EC	Ecuador	PY	Paraguay
EDU	Education	SE	Sweden
EG	Egypt	SG	Singapore
ES	Spain	SR	Suriname
FI	Finland	SU	USSR
FR	France	TH	Thailand
GB	Great Britain	TN	Tunisia

Domain	Country or Organisation	Domain	Country or Organisation
GOV	Government	TR	Turkey
GR	Greece	TT	Trinidad and Tobago
HK	Hong Kong	TW	Taiwan
HU	Hungary	UK	United Kingdom
IE	Ireland	US	United States of America
IL	Israel	UY	Uruguay
IN	India	VC	St Vincent and the Grenadines
INT	International Entities	VE	Venezuela
IS	Iceland	YU	Yugoslavia
IT	Italy	ZA	South Africa
JM	Jamaica	ZW	Zimbabwe

C

IP Protocol Numbers

Within the IP header there is an 8-bit field that identifies the next higher-level protocol (in IPv4 this field is called Protocol, in IPv6 it is called Next Header). The following list of IP protocol identifiers comprises information from various sources, including RFC 1700 and some personal observations. Any errors or omissions are therefore my own. The list provided here is not exhaustive. For a complete up-to-date list of port assignments see the IANA URL below:

URL = ftp://ftp.isi.edu/in-notes/iana/assignments/protocol-numbers

C.1   IP Protocol Assignments

Decimal	Keyword	Protocol
0	—	Reserved
1	ICMP	Internet Control Message
2	IGMP	Internet Group Management
3	GGP	Gateway-to-Gateway
4	IP	IP in IP (encapsulation)
5	ST	Stream
6	TCP	Transmission Control
7	UCL	UCL
8	EGP	Exterior Gateway Protocol
9	IGP	any private interior gateway
10	BBN-RCC-MON	BBN RCC Monitoring
11	NVP-II	Network Voice Protocol
12	PUP	PUP
13	ARGUS	ARGUS

Decimal	Keyword	Protocol
14	EMCON	EMCON
15	XNET	Cross Net Debugger
16	CHAOS	Chaos
17	UDP	User Datagram
18	MUX	Multiplexing
19	DCN-MEAS	DCN Measurement Subsystems
20	HMP	Host Monitoring
21	PRM	Packet Radio Measurement
22	XNS-IDP	XEROX NS IDP
23	TRUNK-1	Trunk-1
24	TRUNK-2	Trunk-2
25	LEAF-1	Leaf-1
26	LEAF-2	Leaf-2
27	RDP	Reliable Data Protocol
28	IRTP	Internet Reliable Transaction
29	ISO-TP4	ISO Transport Protocol Class 4
30	NETBLT	Bulk Data Transfer Protocol
31	MFE-NSP	MFE Network Services Protocol
32	MERIT-INP	MERIT Internodal Protocol
33	SEP	Sequential Exchange Protocol
34	3PC	Third Party Connect Protocol
35	IDPR	Inter-Domain Policy Routing Protocol
36	XTP	XTP
37	DDP	Datagram Delivery Protocol
38	IDPR-CMTP	IDPR Control Message Transport Proto
39	TP++	TP++ Transport Protocol
40	IL	IL Transport Protocol
41	SIP	Simple Internet Protocol
42	SDRP	Source Demand Routing Protocol
43	SIP-SR	SIP Source Route
44	SIP-FRAG	SIP Fragment
45	IDRP	Inter-Domain Routing Protocol

Decimal	Keyword	Protocol
46	RSVP	Reservation Protocol
47	GRE	General Routing Encapsulation
48	MHRP	Mobile Host Routing Protocol
49	BNA	BNA
50	SIPP-ESP	SIPP Encapsulation Security Payload
51	SIPP-AH	SIPP Authentication Header
52	I-NLSP	Integrated Net Layer SecurityTUBA
53	SWIPE	IP with Encryption
54	NHRP	NBMA Next Hop Resolution Protocol
55	MOBILE	IP Mobility
56	TLSP	Transport Layer Security Protocol via Kryptonet key mgt
57	SKIP	SKIP
58	IPv6-ICMP	ICMP for IPv6
59	IPv6-NoNxt	No Next Header for IPv6
60	IPv6-Opts	Destination Options for IPv6
61	—	any host internal protocols
62	CFTP	CFTP
63	—	any local network
64	SAT-EXPAK	SATNET and Backroom EXPAK
65	KRYPTOLAN	Kryptolan
66	RVD	MIT Remote Virtual Disk Protocol
67	IPPC	Internet Pluribus Packet Core
68	—	any distributed file system
69	SAT-MON	SATNET Monitoring
70	VISA	VISA Protocol
71	IPCV	Internet Packet Core Utility
72	CPNX	Computer Protocol Network Executive
73	CPHB	Computer Protocol Heart Beat
74	WSN	Wang Span Network
75	PVP	Packet Video Protocol
76	BR-SAT-MON	Backroom SATNET Monitoring
77	SUN-ND	SUN ND PROTOCOL—Tempora'

Decimal	Keyword	Protocol
78	WB-MON	WIDEBAND Monitoring
79	WB-EXPAK	WIDEBAND EXPAK
80	ISO-IP	ISO Internet Protocol
81	VMTP	VMTP
82	SECURE-VMTP	SECURE-VMTP
83	VINES	VINES
84	TTP	TTP
85	NSFNET-IGP	NSFNET-IGP
86	DGP	Dissimilar Gateway Protocol
87	TCF	TCF
88	IGRP	IGRP
89	OSPFIGP	OSPFIGP
90	Sprite-RPC	Sprite RPC Protocol
91	LARP	Locus Address Resolution Protocol
92	MTP	Multicast Transport Protocol
93	AX.25	AX.25 Frames
94	PIP	IP-within-IP Encapsulation Protocol
95	MICP	Mobile Internetworking Control Pro.
96	SCC-SP	Semaphore Communications Sec. Pro.
97	ETHERIP	Ethernet-within-IP Encapsulation
98	ENCAP	Encapsulation Header
99	—	any private encryption scheme
100	GMTP	GMTP
101	IFMP	Ipsilon Flow Management Protocol
102	PNNI	PNNI over IP
103–111	—	Unassigned
112	VRRP	Virtual Router Redundancy Protocol (VRRP)
113	PGM	PGM Reliable Transport Protocol
114	—	any 0-hop protocol
115	L2TP	Layer Two Tunneling Protocol
116	DDX	D-II Data Exchange (DDX)
117	IATP	Interactive Agent Transfer Protocol

Decimal	Keyword	Protocol
118	STP	Schedule Transfer Protocol
119	SRP	SpectraLink Radio Protocol
120	UTI	UTI
121	SMP	Simple Message Protocol
122	SM	SM
123	PTP	Performance Transparency Protocol
124	ISIS over IPv4	
125	FIRE	
126	CRTP	Combat Radio Transport Protocol
127	CRUDP	Combat Radio User Datagram
128	SSCOPMCE	
129	IPLT	
130	SPS	Secure Packet Shield
131	PIPE	Private IP Encapsulation within IP
132	SCTP	Stream Control Transmission Protocol
133	FC	Fibre Channel
134–254	Unassigned	
255	Reserved	

D

UDP and TCP Port Numbers

The following list of port numbers comprises information derived mainly from RFC 1700. Any errors or omissions are, therefore, my own. The port numbers are divided into three ranges, as follows:

- Well-known ports are those from 0 through 1,023.
- Registered ports are those from 1,024 through 49,151.
- Dynamic and/or private ports are those from 49,152 through 65,535.

The list provided here is not exhaustive. For a complete up-to-date list of port assignments see the IANA URL: URL = ftp://ftp.isi.edu/in-notes/iana/assignments/port-numbers.

D.1   Well-known port numbers

Ports are used in protocols such as TCP and UDP to identify the end points of logical connections that carry long-term conversations. For many applications it is useful to have the service port predefined, so that clients connecting to a server know what port to connect to for widely used applications such as FTP, Telnet, DNS, and so on. These ports are sometimes called well-known ports or assigned ports. These ports are controlled and assigned by the IANA, and on most systems can be used only by system (or root) processes or by programs executed by privileged users. The assigned ports take only a small part of the available port space, for many years restricted to the range 0–255. Recently, the range has been expanded by the IANA to 0–1,023.

Keyword	Decimal	Protocol	Description
—	0	TCP, UDP	Reserved
tcpmux	1	TCP, UDP	TCP Port Service Multiplexer
compressnet	2	TCP, UDP	Management Utility
compressnet	3	TCP, UDP	Compression Process
#	4	TCP, UDP	Unassigned
rje	5	TCP, UDP	Remote Job Entry
#	6	TCP, UDP	Unassigned
echo	7	TCP, UDP	Echo
#	8	TCP, UDP	Unassigned
discard	9	TCP, UDP	Discard
#	10	TCP, UDP	Unassigned
systat	11	TCP, UDP	Active Users
#	12	TCP, UDP	Unassigned
daytime	13	TCP, UDP	Daytime
#	14	TCP, UDP	Unassigned
#	15	TCP	Unassigned [was netstat]
#	15	UDP	Unassigned
#	16	TCP, UDP	Unassigned
qotd	17	TCP, UDP	Quote of the Day
msp	18	TCP, UDP	Message Send Protocol
chargen	19	TCP, UDP	Character Generator
ftp-data	20	TCP, UDP	File Transfer [Default Data]
ftp	21	TCP, UDP	File Transfer [Control]
#	22	TCP, UDP	Unassigned
telnet	23	TCP, UDP	Telnet
	24	TCP, UDP	any private mail system
smtp	25	TCP, UDP	Simple Mail Transfer
#	26	TCP, UDP	Unassigned
nsw-fe	27	TCP, UDP	NSW User System FE
#	28	TCP, UDP	Unassigned
msg-icp	29	TCP, UDP	MSG ICP
#	30	TCP, UDP	Unassigned
msg-auth	31	TCP, UDP	MSG Authentication

Keyword	Decimal	Protocol	Description
#	32	TCP, UDP	Unassigned
dsp	33	TCP, UDP	Display Support Protocol
#	34	TCP, UDP	Unassigned
	35	TCP, UDP	any private printer server
#	36	TCP, UDP	Unassigned
time	37	TCP, UDP	Time
rap	38	TCP, UDP	Route Access Protocol
rlp	39	TCP, UDP	Resource Location Protocol
#	40	TCP, UDP	Unassigned
graphics	41	TCP, UDP	Graphics
nameserver	42	TCP, UDP	Host Name Server
nicname	43	TCP, UDP	Who Is
mpm-flags	44	TCP, UDP	MPM FLAGS Protocol
mpm	45	TCP, UDP	Message Processing Module [recv]
mpm-snd	46	TCP, UDP	MPM [default send]
ni-ftp	47	TCP, UDP	NI FTP
auditd	48	TCP, UDP	Digital Audit Daemon
login	49	TCP, UDP	Login Host Protocol
re-mail-ck	50	TCP, UDP	Remote Mail Checking Protocol
la-maint	51	TCP, UDP	IMP Logical Address Maintenance
xns-time	52	TCP, UDP	XNS Time Protocol
domain	53	TCP, UDP	Domain Name Server
xns-ch	54	TCP, UDP	XNS Clearinghouse
isi-gl	55	TCP, UDP	ISI Graphics Language
xns-auth	56	TCP, UDP	XNS Authentication
	57	TCP, UDP	any private terminal access
xns-mail	58	TCP, UDP	XNS Mail
	59	TCP, UDP	any private file service
	60	TCP, UDP	Unassigned
ni-mail	61	TCP, UDP	NI MAIL
acas	62	TCP, UDP	ACA Services
#	63	TCP, UDP	Unassigned
covia	64	TCP, UDP	Communications Integrator (CI)

Keyword	Decimal	Protocol	Description
tacacs-ds	65	TCP, UDP	TACACS-Database Service
sql*net	66	TCP, UDP	Oracle SQL*NET
bootps	67	TCP, UDP	Bootstrap Protocol Server
bootpc	68	TCP, UDP	Bootstrap Protocol Client
tftp	69	TCP, UDP	Trivial File Transfer
gopher	70	TCP, UDP	Gopher
netrjs-1	71	TCP, UDP	Remote Job Service
netrjs-2	72	TCP, UDP	Remote Job Service
netrjs-3	73	TCP, UDP	Remote Job Service
netrjs-4	74	TCP, UDP	Remote Job Service
	75	TCP, UDP	any private dial-out service
deos	76	TCP, UDP	Distributed External Object Store
	77	TCP, UDP	any private RJE service
vettcp	78	TCP, UDP	vettcp
finger	79	TCP, UDP	Finger
www-http	80	TCP, UDP	World Wide Web HTTP
hosts2-ns	81	TCP, UDP	HOSTS2 Name Server
xfer	82	TCP, UDP	XFER Utility
mit-ml-dev	83	TCP, UDP	MIT ML Device
ctf	84	TCP, UDP	Common Trace Facility
mit-ml-dev	85	TCP, UDP	MIT ML Device
mfcobol	86	TCP, UDP	Micro Focus Cobol
	87	TCP, UDP	any private terminal link
kerberos	88	TCP, UDP	Kerberos
su-mit-tg	89	TCP, UDP	SU/MIT Telnet Gateway
dnsix	90	TCP, UDP	DNSIX Security Attribute Token Map
mit-dov	91	TCP, UDP	MIT Dover Spooler
npp	92	TCP, UDP	Network Printing Protocol
dcp	93	TCP, UDP	Device Control Protocol
objcall	94	TCP, UDP	Tivoli Object Dispatcher
supdup	95	TCP, UDP	SUPDUP
dixie	96	TCP, UDP	DIXIE Protocol Specification
swift-rvf	97	TCP, UDP	Swift Remote Vitural File Protocol

Keyword	Decimal	Protocol	Description
tacnews	98	TCP, UDP	TAC News
metagram	99	TCP, UDP	Metagram Relay
newacct	100	TCP, UDP	[unauthorized use]
hostname	101	TCP, UDP	NIC Host Name Server
iso-tsap	102	TCP, UDP	ISO-TSAP
gppitnp	103	TCP, UDP	Genesis Point-to-Point Trans Net
acr-nema	104	TCP, UDP	ACR-NEMA Digital Imag. & Comm. 300
csnet-ns	105	TCP, UDP	Mailbox Name Nameserver
3com-tsmux	106	TCP, UDP	3COM-TSMUX
rtelnet	107	TCP, UDP	Remote Telnet Service
snagas	108	TCP, UDP	SNA Gateway Access Server
pop2	109	TCP, UDP	Post Office Protocol - Version 2
pop3	110	TCP, UDP	Post Office Protocol - Version 3
sunrpc	111	TCP, UDP	SUN Remote Procedure Call
mcidas	112	TCP, UDP	McIDAS Data Transmission Protocol
auth	113	TCP, UDP	Authentication Service
audionews	114	TCP, UDP	Audio News Multicast
sftp	115	TCP, UDP	Simple File Transfer Protocol
ansanotify	116	TCP, UDP	ANSA REX Notify
uucp-path	117	TCP, UDP	UUCP Path Service
sqlserv	118	TCP, UDP	SQL Services
nntp	119	TCP, UDP	Network News Transfer Protocol
cfdptkt	120	TCP, UDP	CFDPTKT
erpc	121	TCP, UDP	Encore Expedited Remote Pro.Call
smakynet	122	TCP, UDP	SMAKYNET
ntp	123	TCP, UDP	Network Time Protocol
ansatrader	124	TCP, UDP	ANSA REX Trader
locus-map	125	TCP, UDP	Locus PC-Interface Net Map Ser
unitary	126	TCP, UDP	Unisys Unitary Login
locus-con	127	TCP, UDP	Locus PC-Interface Conn Server
gss-xlicen	128	TCP, UDP	GSS X License Verification
pwdgen	129	TCP, UDP	Password Generator Protocol
cisco-fna	130	TCP, UDP	Cisco FNATIVE

Keyword	*Decimal*	*Protocol*	*Description*
cisco-tna	131	TCP, UDP	Cisco TNATIVE
cisco-sys	132	TCP, UDP	Cisco SYSMAINT
statsrv	133	TCP, UDP	Statistics Service
ingres-net	134	TCP, UDP	INGRES-NET Service
loc-srv	135	TCP, UDP	Location Service
profile	136	TCP, UDP	PROFILE Naming System
netbios-ns	137	TCP, UDP	NETBIOS Name Service
netbios-dgm	138	TCP, UDP	NETBIOS Datagram Service
netbios-ssn	139	TCP, UDP	NETBIOS Session Service
emfis-data	140	TCP, UDP	EMFIS Data Service
emfis-cntl	141	TCP, UDP	EMFIS Control Service
bl-idm	142	TCP, UDP	Britton-Lee IDM
imap2	143	TCP, UDP	Interim Mail Access Protocol v2
news	144	TCP, UDP	NewS
uaac	145	TCP, UDP	UAAC Protocol
iso-tp0	146	TCP, UDP	ISO-IP0
iso-ip	147	TCP, UDP	ISO-IP
cronus	148	TCP, UDP	CRONUS-SUPPORT
aed-512	149	TCP, UDP	AED 512 Emulation Service
sql-net	150	TCP, UDP	SQL-NET
hems	151	TCP, UDP	HEMS
bftp	152	TCP, UDP	Background File Transfer Program
sgmp	153	TCP, UDP	SGMP
netsc-prod	154	TCP, UDP	NETSC
netsc-dev	155	TCP, UDP	NETSC
sqlsrv	156	TCP, UDP	SQL Service
knet-cmp	157	TCP, UDP	KNET/VM Command/Message Protocol
pcmail-srv	158	TCP, UDP	PCMail Server
nss-routing	159	TCP, UDP	NSS-Routing
sgmp-traps	160	TCP, UDP	SGMP-TRAPS
snmp	161	TCP, UDP	SNMP
snmptrap	162	TCP, UDP	SNMPTRAP
cmip-man	163	TCP, UDP	CMIP TCP Manager

Keyword	*Decimal*	*Protocol*	*Description*
cmip-agent	164	TCP, UDP	CMIP TCP Agent
xns-courier	165	TCP, UDP	Xerox
s-net	166	TCP, UDP	Sirius Systems
namp	167	TCP, UDP	NAMP
rsvd	168	TCP, UDP	RSVD
send	169	TCP, UDP	SEND
print-srv	170	TCP, UDP	Network PostScript
multiplex	171	TCP, UDP	Network Innovations Multiplex
cl/1	172	TCP, UDP	Network Innovations CL/1
xyplex-mux	173	TCP, UDP	Xyplex
mailq	174	TCP, UDP	MAILQ
vmnet	175	TCP, UDP	VMNET
genrad-mux	176	TCP, UDP	GENRAD-MUX
xdmcp	177	TCP, UDP	X Display Manager Control Protocol
nextstep	178	TCP, UDP	NextStep Window Server
bgp	179	TCP, UDP	Border Gateway Protocol
ris	180	TCP, UDP	Intergraph
unify	181	TCP, UDP	Unify
audit	182	TCP, UDP	Unisys Audit SITP
ocbinder	183	TCP, UDP	OCBinder
ocserver	184	TCP, UDP	OCServer
remote-kis	185	TCP, UDP	Remote-KIS
kis	186	TCP, UDP	KIS Protocol
aci	187	TCP, UDP	Application Communication Interface
mumps	188	TCP, UDP	Plus Five's MUMPS
qft	189	TCP, UDP	Queued File Transport
gacp	190	TCP, UDP	Gateway Access Control Protocol
prospero	191	TCP, UDP	Prospero Directory Service
osu-nms	192	TCP, UDP	OSU Network Monitoring System
srmp	193	TCP, UDP	Spider Remote Monitoring Protocol
irc	194	TCP, UDP	Internet Relay Chat Protocol
dn6-nlm-aud	195	TCP, UDP	DNSIX Network Level Module Audit
dn6-smm-red	196	TCP, UDP	DNSIX Session Mgt Module Audit Redir

Keyword	Decimal	Protocol	Description
dls	197	TCP, UDP	Directory Location Service
dls-mon	198	TCP, UDP	Directory Location Service Monitor
smux	199	TCP, UDP	SMUX
src	200	TCP, UDP	IBM System Resource Controller
at-rtmp	201	TCP, UDP	AppleTalk Routing Maintenance
at-nbp	202	TCP, UDP	AppleTalk Name Binding
at-3	203	TCP, UDP	AppleTalk Unused
at-echo	204	TCP, UDP	AppleTalk Echo
at-5	205	TCP, UDP	AppleTalk Unused
at-zis	206	TCP, UDP	AppleTalk Zone Information
at-7	207	TCP, UDP	AppleTalk Unused
at-8	208	TCP, UDP	AppleTalk Unused
tam	209	TCP, UDP	Trivial Authenticated Mail Protocol
z39.50	210	TCP, UDP	ANSI Z39.50
914c/g	211	TCP, UDP	Texas Instruments 914C/G Terminal
anet	212	TCP, UDP	ATEXSSTR
ipx	213	TCP, UDP	IPX
vmpwscs	214	TCP, UDP	VM PWSCS
softpc	215	TCP, UDP	Insignia Solutions
atls	216	TCP, UDP	Access Technology License Server
dbase	217	TCP, UDP	dBASE Unix
mpp	218	TCP, UDP	Netix Message Posting Protocol
uarps	219	TCP, UDP	Unisys ARPs
imap3	220	TCP, UDP	Interactive Mail Access Protocol v3
fln-spx	221	TCP, UDP	Berkeley rlogind with SPX auth
rsh-spx	222	TCP, UDP	Berkeley rshd with SPX auth
cdc	223	TCP, UDP	Certificate Distribution Center
#	224–241	TCP, UDP	Reserved
#	242	TCP, UDP	Unassigned
sur-meas	243	TCP, UDP	Survey Measurement
#	244	TCP, UDP	Unassigned
link	245	TCP, UDP	LINK
dsp3270	246	TCP, UDP	Display Systems Protocol

Keyword	Decimal	Protocol	Description
#	247–255	TCP, UDP	Reserved
#	256–343	TCP, UDP	Unassigned
pdap	344	TCP, UDP	Prospero Data Access Protocol
pawserv	345	TCP, UDP	Perf Analysis Workbench
zserv	346	TCP, UDP	Zebra server
fatserv	347	TCP, UDP	Fatmen Server
csi-sgwp	348	TCP, UDP	Cabletron Management Protocol
#	349–370	TCP, UDP	Unassigned
clearcase	371	TCP, UDP	Clearcase
ulistserv	372	TCP, UDP	UNIX Listserv
legent-1	373	TCP, UDP	Legent Corporation
legent-2	374	TCP, UDP	Legent Corporation
hassle	375	TCP, UDP	Hassle
nip	376	TCP, UDP	Amiga Envoy Network Inquiry Protocol
tnETOS	377	TCP, UDP	NEC Corporation
dsETOS	378	TCP, UDP	NEC Corporation
is99c	379	TCP, UDP	TIA/EIA/IS-99 modem client
is99s	380	TCP, UDP	TIA/EIA/IS-99 modem server
hp-collector	381	TCP, UDP	hp performance data collector
hp-managed-node	382	TCP, UDP	hp performance data managed node
hp-alarm-mgr	383	TCP, UDP	hp performance data alarm manager
arns	384	TCP, UDP	A Remote Network Server System
ibm-app	385	TCP, UDP	IBM Application
asa	386	TCP, UDP	ASA Message Router Object Def.
aurp	387	TCP, UDP	Appletalk Update-Based Routing Protocol
unidata-ldm	388	TCP, UDP	Unidata LDM Version 4
ldap	389	TCP, UDP	Lightweight Directory Access Protocol
uis	390	TCP, UDP	UIS
synotics-relay	391	TCP, UDP	SynOptics SNMP Relay Port
synotics-broker	392	TCP, UDP	SynOptics Port Broker Port
dis	393	TCP, UDP	Data Interpretation System
embl-ndt	394	TCP, UDP	EMBL Nucleic Data Transfer
netcp	395	TCP, UDP	NETscout Control Protocol

Keyword	*Decimal*	*Protocol*	*Description*
netware-ip	396	TCP, UDP	Novell Netware over IP
mptn	397	TCP, UDP	Multi Protocol Trans. Net.
kryptolan	398	TCP, UDP	Kryptolan
#	399	TCP, UDP	Unassigned
work-sol	400	TCP, UDP	Workstation Solutions
ups	401	TCP, UDP	Uninterruptible Power Supply
genie	402	TCP, UDP	Genie Protocol
decap	403	TCP, UDP	decap
nced	404	TCP, UDP	nced
ncld	405	TCP, UDP	ncld
imsp	406	TCP, UDP	Interactive Mail Support Protocol
timbuktu	407	TCP, UDP	Timbuktu
prm-sm	408	TCP, UDP	Prospero Resource Manager Sys. Man.
prm-nm	409	TCP, UDP	Prospero Resource Manager Node Man.
decladebug	410	TCP, UDP	DECLadebug Remote Debug Protocol
rmt	411	TCP, UDP	Remote MT Protocol
synoptics-trap	412	TCP, UDP	Trap Convention Port
smsp	413	TCP, UDP	SMSP
infoseek	414	TCP, UDP	InfoSeek
bnet	415	TCP, UDP	Bnet
silverplatter	416	TCP, UDP	Silverplatter
onmux	417	TCP, UDP	Onmux
hyper-g	418	TCP, UDP	Hyper-G
ariel1	419	TCP, UDP	Ariel
smpte	420	TCP, UDP	SMPTE
ariel2	421	TCP, UDP	Ariel
ariel3	422	TCP, UDP	Ariel
opc-job-start	423	TCP, UDP	IBM Operations Planning and Control Start
opc-job-track	424	TCP, UDP	IBM Operations Planning and Control Track
icad-el	425	TCP, UDP	ICAD
smartsdp	426	TCP, UDP	smartsdp
svrloc	427	TCP, UDP	Server Location

Keyword	Decimal	Protocol	Description
ocs_cmu	428	TCP, UDP	OCS_CMU
ocs_amu	429	TCP, UDP	OCS_AMU
utmpsd	430	TCP, UDP	UTMPSD
utmpcd	431	TCP, UDP	UTMPCD
iasd	432	TCP, UDP	IASD
nnsp	433	TCP, UDP	NNSP
mobileip-agent	434	TCP, UDP	MobileIP-Agent
mobilip-mn	435	TCP, UDP	MobilIP-MN
dna-cml	436	TCP, UDP	DNA-CML
comscm	437	TCP, UDP	comscm
dsfgw	438	TCP, UDP	dsfgw
dasp	439	TCP, UDP	dasp
sgcp	440	TCP, UDP	sgcp
decvms-sysmgt	441	TCP, UDP	decvms-sysmgt
cvc_hostd	442	TCP, UDP	cvc_hostd
https	443	TCP, UDP	https Mcom
snpp	444	TCP, UDP	Simple Network Paging Protocol
microsoft-ds	445	TCP, UDP	Microsoft-DS
ddm-rdb	446	TCP, UDP	DDM-RDB
ddm-dfm	447	TCP, UDP	DDM-RFM
ddm-byte	448	TCP, UDP	DDM-BYTE
as-servermap	449	TCP, UDP	AS Server Mapper
tserver	450	TCP, UDP	Tserver
#	451–511	TCP, UDP	Unassigned
exec	512	TCP	remote process execution; authentication via passwords and UNIX login names
biff	512	UDP	used by mail system to notify users of new mail received; currently receives messages only from processes on the same machine
login	513	TCP	remote login a la Telnet; automatic authentication performed based on priviledged port numbers and distributed databases which identify "authentication domains"

Keyword	Decimal	Protocol	Description
who	513	UDP	maintains data bases showing who's logged into machines on a local net and the load average of the machine
cmd	514	TCP	like exec, but automatic authentication is performed as for login server
syslog	514	UDP	syslog
printer	515	TCP, UDP	spooler
#	516	TCP, UDP	Unassigned
talk	517	TCP, UDP	like tenex link, but across machine—unfortunately, doesn't use link protocol (this is actually just a rendezvous port from which a tcp connection is established)
ntalk	518	TCP, UDP	
utime	519	TCP, UDP	unixtime
efs	520	TCP	extended file name server
router	520	UDP	local routing process (on site); uses variant of Xerox NS routing information protocol
#	521–524	TCP, UDP	Unassigned
timed	525	TCP, UDP	timeserver
tempo	526	TCP, UDP	newdate
#	527–529	TCP, UDP	Unassigned
courier	530	TCP, UDP	rpc
conference	531	TCP, UDP	chat
netnews	532	TCP, UDP	readnews
netwall	533	TCP, UDP	for emergency broadcasts
#	534–538	TCP, UDP	Unassigned
apertus-ldp	539	TCP, UDP	Apertus Technologies Load Determination
uucp	540	TCP, UDP	uucpd
uucp-rlogin	541	TCP, UDP	uucp-rlogin
#	542	TCP, UDP	Unassigned
klogin	543	TCP, UDP	
kshell	544	TCP, UDP	krcmd
#	545–549	TCP, UDP	Unassigned
new-rwho	550	TCP, UDP	new-who

Keyword	Decimal	Protocol	Description
#	551–555	TCP, UDP	Unassigned
dsf	555	TCP, UDP	
remotefs	556	TCP, UDP	rfs server
#	557–559	TCP, UDP	Unassigned
rmonitor	560	TCP, UDP	rmonitord
monitor	561	TCP, UDP	
chshell	562	TCP, UDP	chcmd
#	563	TCP, UDP	Unassigned
9pfs	564	TCP, UDP	plan 9 file service
whoami	565	TCP, UDP	whoami
#	566–569	TCP, UDP	Unassigned
meter	570	TCP, UDP	demon
meter	571	TCP, UDP	udemon
#	572–599	TCP, UDP	Unassigned
ipcserver	600	TCP, UDP	Sun IPC server
nqs	607	TCP, UDP	nqs
urm	606	TCP, UDP	Cray Unified Resource Manager
sift-uft	608	TCP, UDP	Sender-Initiated/Unsolicited File Transfer
npmp-trap	609	TCP, UDP	npmp-trap
npmp-local	610	TCP, UDP	npmp-local
npmp-gui	611	TCP, UDP	npmp-gui
ginad	634	TCP, UDP	ginad
mdqs	666	TCP, UDP	
doom	666	TCP, UDP	doom Id Software
elcsd	704	TCP, UDP	errlog copy/server daemon
entrustmanager	709	TCP, UDP	EntrustManager
netviewdm1	729	TCP, UDP	IBM NetView DM/6000 Server/Client
netviewdm2	730	TCP, UDP	IBM NetView DM/6000 send TCP
netviewdm3	731	TCP, UDP	IBM NetView DM/6000 receive TCP
netgw	741	TCP, UDP	netGW
netrcs	742	TCP, UDP	Network-based Rev. Cont. Sys.
flexlm	744	TCP, UDP	Flexible License Manager
fujitsu-dev	747	TCP, UDP	Fujitsu Device Control

Keyword	*Decimal*	*Protocol*	*Description*
ris-cm	748	TCP, UDP	Russell Info Sci Calendar Manager
kerberos-adm	749	TCP, UDP	kerberos administration
rfile	750	TCP	
loadav	750	UDP	
pump	751	TCP, UDP	
qrh	752	TCP, UDP	
rrh	753	TCP, UDP	
tell	754	TCP, UDP	send
nlogin	758	TCP, UDP	
con	759	TCP, UDP	
ns	760	TCP, UDP	
rxe	761	TCP, UDP	
quotad	762	TCP, UDP	
cycleserv	763	TCP, UDP	
omserv	764	TCP, UDP	
webster	765	TCP, UDP	
phonebook	767	TCP, UDP	phone
vid	769	TCP, UDP	
cadlock	770	TCP, UDP	
rtip	771	TCP, UDP	
cycleserv2	772	TCP, UDP	
submit	773	TCP	
notify	773	UDP	
rpasswd	774	TCP	
acmaint_dbd	774	UDP	
entomb	775	TCP	
acmaint_transd	775	UDP	
wpages	776	TCP, UDP	
wpgs	780	TCP, UDP	
concert	786	TCP, UDP	Concert
mdbs_daemon	800	TCP, UDP	
device	801	TCP, UDP	
xtreelic	996	TCP, UDP	Central Point Software

Keyword	Decimal	Protocol	Description
maitrd	997	TCP, UDP	
busboy	998	TCP	
puparp	998	UDP	
garcon	999	TCP	
applix	999	UDP	Applix ac
puprouter	999	TCP	
??????/			
cadlock	1000	TCP	
ock	1000	UDP	
	1023	TCP	Reserved
	1024	UDP	Reserved

D.2   Registered port numbers

The registered ports are in the range 1,024–65,535. These ports are not controlled by the IANA and on most systems can be used by ordinary user processes or programs executed by ordinary users. While the IANA cannot control use of these ports, it does register use of these ports as a convenience to the community.

Keyword	Decimal	Protocol	Description
	1024	TCP, UDP	Reserved
blackjack	1025	TCP, UDP	network blackjack
iad1	1030	TCP, UDP	BBN IAD
iad2	1031	TCP, UDP	BBN IAD
iad3	1032	TCP, UDP	BBN IAD
instl_boots	1067	TCP, UDP	Installation Bootstrap Proto. Serv.
instl_bootc	1068	TCP, UDP	Installation Bootstrap Proto. Cli.
socks	1080	TCP, UDP	Socks
ansoft-lm-1	1083	TCP, UDP	Anasoft License Manager
ansoft-lm-2	1084	TCP, UDP	Anasoft License Manager
nfa	1155	TCP, UDP	Network File Access
nerv	1222	TCP, UDP	SNI R&D network
hermes	1248	TCP, UDP	
alta-ana-lm	1346	TCP, UDP	Alta Analytics License Manager

Keyword	Decimal	Protocol	Description
bbn-mmc	1347	TCP, UDP	multimedia conferencing
bbn-mmx	1348	TCP, UDP	multimedia conferencing
sbook	1349	TCP, UDP	Registration Network Protocol
editbench	1350	TCP, UDP	Registration Network Protocol
equationbuilder	1351	TCP, UDP	Digital Tool Works (MIT)
lotusnote	1352	TCP, UDP	Lotus Note
relief	1353	TCP, UDP	Relief Consulting
rightbrain	1354	TCP, UDP	RightBrain Software
intuitive edge	1355	TCP, UDP	Intuitive Edge
cuillamartin	1356	TCP, UDP	CuillaMartin Company
pegboard	1357	TCP, UDP	Electronic PegBoard
connlcli	1358	TCP, UDP	CONNLCLI
ftsrv	1359	TCP, UDP	FTSRV
mimer	1360	TCP, UDP	MIMER
linx	1361	TCP, UDP	LinX
timeflies	1362	TCP, UDP	TimeFlies
ndm-requester	1363	TCP, UDP	Network DataMover Requester
ndm-server	1364	TCP, UDP	Network DataMover Server
adapt-sna	1365	TCP, UDP	Network Software Associates
netware-csp	1366	TCP, UDP	Novell NetWare Comm Service Platform
dcs	1367	TCP, UDP	DCS
screencast	1368	TCP, UDP	ScreenCast
gv-us	1369	TCP, UDP	GlobalView to Unix Shell
us-gv	1370	TCP, UDP	UNIX Shell to GlobalView
fc-cli	1371	TCP, UDP	Fujitsu Config Protocol
fc-ser	1372	TCP, UDP	Fujitsu Config Protocol
chromagrafx	1373	TCP, UDP	Chromagrafx
molly	1374	TCP, UDP	EPI Software Systems
bytex	1375	TCP, UDP	Bytex
ibm-pps	1376	TCP, UDP	IBM Person-to-Person Software
cichlid	1377	TCP, UDP	Cichlid License Manager
elan	1378	TCP, UDP	Elan License Manager

Keyword	Decimal	Protocol	Description
dbreporter	1379	TCP, UDP	Integrity Solutions
telesis-licman	1380	TCP, UDP	Telesis Network License Manager
apple-licman	1381	TCP, UDP	Apple Network License Manager
udt_os	1382	TCP, UDP	
gwha	1383	TCP, UDP	GW Hannaway Network License Manager
os-licman	1384	TCP, UDP	Objective Solutions License Manager
atex_elmd	1385	TCP, UDP	Atex Publishing License Manager
checksum	1386	TCP, UDP	CheckSum License Manager
cadsi-lm	1387	TCP, UDP	Computer Aided Design Software Inc LM
objective-dbc	1388	TCP, UDP	Objective Solutions DataBase Cache
iclpv-dm	1389	TCP, UDP	Document Manager
iclpv-sc	1390	TCP, UDP	Storage Controller
iclpv-sas	1391	TCP, UDP	Storage Access Server
iclpv-pm	1392	TCP, UDP	Print Manager
iclpv-nls	1393	TCP, UDP	Network Log Server
iclpv-nlc	1394	TCP, UDP	Network Log Client
iclpv-wsm	1395	TCP, UDP	PC Workstation Manager software
dvl-activemail	1396	TCP, UDP	DVL Active Mail
audio-activmail	1397	TCP, UDP	Audio Active Mail
video-activmail	1398	TCP, UDP	Video Active Mail
cadkey-licman	1399	TCP, UDP	Cadkey License Manager
cadkey-tablet	1400	TCP, UDP	Cadkey Tablet Daemon
goldleaf-licman	1401	TCP, UDP	Goldleaf License Manager
prm-sm-np	1402	TCP, UDP	Prospero Resource Manager
prm-nm-np	1403	TCP, UDP	Prospero Resource Manager
igi-lm	1404	TCP, UDP	Infinite Graphics License Manager
ibm-res	1405	TCP, UDP	IBM Remote Execution Starter
netlabs-lm	1406	TCP, UDP	NetLabs License Manager
dbsa-lm	1407	TCP, UDP	DBSA License Manager
sophia-lm	1408	TCP, UDP	Sophia License Manager
here-lm	1409	TCP, UDP	Here License Manager
hiq	1410	TCP, UDP	HiQ License Manager

Keyword	Decimal	Protocol	Description
af	1411	TCP, UDP	AudioFile
innosys	1412	TCP, UDP	InnoSys
innosys-acl	1413	TCP, UDP	Innosys-ACL
ibm-mqseries	1414	TCP, UDP	IBM MQSeries
dbstar	1415	TCP, UDP	DBStar
novell-lu6.2	1416	TCP, UDP	Novell LU6.2
timbuktu-srv1	1417	TCP, UDP	Timbuktu Service 1 Port
timbuktu-srv2	1418	TCP, UDP	Timbuktu Service 2 Port
timbuktu-srv3	1419	TCP, UDP	Timbuktu Service 3 Port
timbuktu-srv4	1420	TCP, UDP	Timbuktu Service 4 Port
gandalf-lm	1421	TCP, UDP	Gandalf License Manager
autodesk-lm	1422	TCP, UDP	Autodesk License Manager
essbase	1423	TCP, UDP	Essbase Arbor Software
hybrid	1424	TCP, UDP	Hybrid Encryption Protocol
zion-lm	1425	TCP, UDP	Zion Software License Manager
sas-1	1426	TCP, UDP	Satellite-data Acquisition System 1
mloadd	1427	TCP, UDP	mloadd monitoring tool
informatik-lm	1428	TCP, UDP	Informatik License Manager
nms	1429	TCP, UDP	Hypercom NMS
tpdu	1430	TCP, UDP	Hypercom TPDU
rgtp	1431	TCP, UDP	Reverse Gosip Transport
blueberry-lm	1432	TCP, UDP	Blueberry Software License Manager
ms-sql-s	1433	TCP, UDP	Microsoft-SQL-Server
ms-sql-m	1434	TCP, UDP	Microsoft-SQL-Monitor
ibm-cics	1435	TCP, UDP	IBM CISC
sas-2	1436	TCP, UDP	Satellite-data Acquisition System 2
tabula	1437	TCP, UDP	Tabula
eicon-server	1438	TCP, UDP	Eicon Security Agent/Server
eicon-x25	1439	TCP, UDP	Eicon X25/SNA Gateway
eicon-slp	1440	TCP, UDP	Eicon Service Location Protocol
cadis-1	1441	TCP, UDP	Cadis License Management
cadis-2	1442	TCP, UDP	Cadis License Management

Keyword	Decimal	Protocol	Description
ies-lm	1443	TCP, UDP	Integrated Engineering Software
marcam-lm	1444	TCP, UDP	Marcam License Management
proxima-lm	1445	TCP, UDP	Proxima License Manager
ora-lm	1446	TCP, UDP	Optical Research Associates License Manager
apri-lm	1447	TCP, UDP	Applied Parallel Research LM
oc-lm	1448	TCP, UDP	OpenConnect License Manager
peport	1449	TCP, UDP	Peport
dwf	1450	TCP, UDP	Tandem Distributed Workbench Facility
infoman	1451	TCP, UDP	IBM Information Management
gtegsc-lm	1452	TCP, UDP	GTE Government Systems License Man
genie-lm	1453	TCP, UDP	Genie License Manager
interhdl_elmd	1454	TCP, UDP	interHDL License Manager
esl-lm	1455	TCP, UDP	ESL License Manager
dca	1456	TCP, UDP	DCA
valisys-lm	1457	TCP, UDP	Valisys License Manager
nrcabq-lm	1458	TCP, UDP	Nichols Research Corp.
proshare1	1459	TCP, UDP	Proshare Notebook Application
proshare2	1460	TCP, UDP	Proshare Notebook Application
ibm_wrless_lan	1461	TCP, UDP	IBM Wireless LAN
world-lm	1462	TCP, UDP	World License Manager
nucleus	1463	TCP, UDP	Nucleus
msl_lmd	1464	TCP, UDP	MSL License Manager
pipes	1465	TCP, UDP	Pipes Platform
oceansoft-lm	1466	TCP, UDP	Ocean Software License Manager
csdmbase	1467	TCP, UDP	CSDMBASE
csdm	1468	TCP, UDP	CSDM
aal-lm	1469	TCP, UDP	Active Analysis Limited License Manager
uaiact	1470	TCP, UDP	Universal Analytics
csdmbase	1471	TCP, UDP	csdmbase
csdm	1472	TCP, UDP	csdm
openmath	1473	TCP, UDP	OpenMath
telefinder	1474	TCP, UDP	Telefinder

Keyword	Decimal	Protocol	Description
taligent-lm	1475	TCP, UDP	Taligent License Manager
clvm-cfg	1476	TCP, UDP	clvm-cfg
ms-sna-server	1477	TCP, UDP	ms-sna-server
ms-sna-base	1478	TCP, UDP	ms-sna-base
dberegister	1479	TCP, UDP	dberegister
pacerforum	1480	TCP, UDP	PacerForum
airs	1481	TCP, UDP	AIRS
miteksys-lm	1482	TCP, UDP	Miteksys License Manager
afs	1483	TCP, UDP	AFS License Manager
confluent	1484	TCP, UDP	Confluent License Manager
lansource	1485	TCP, UDP	LANSource
nms_topo_serv	1486	TCP, UDP	nms_topo_serv
localinfosrvr	1487	TCP, UDP	LocalInfoSrvr
docstor	1488	TCP, UDP	DocStor
dmdocbroker	1489	TCP, UDP	dmdocbroker
insitu-conf	1490	TCP, UDP	insitu-conf
anynetgateway	1491	TCP, UDP	anynetgateway
stone-design-1	1492	TCP, UDP	stone-design-1
netmap_lm	1493	TCP, UDP	netmap_lm
ica	1494	TCP, UDP	ica
cvc	1495	TCP, UDP	cvc
liberty-lm	1496	TCP, UDP	liberty-lm
rfx-lm	1497	TCP, UDP	rfx-lm
watcom-sql	1498	TCP, UDP	Watcom-SQL
fhc	1499	TCP, UDP	Federico Heinz Consultora
vlsi-lm	1500	TCP, UDP	VLSI License Manager
sas-3	1501	TCP, UDP	Satellite-data Acquisition System 3
shivadiscovery	1502	TCP, UDP	Shiva
imtc-mcs	1503	TCP, UDP	Databeam
evb-elm	1504	TCP, UDP	EVB Software Engineering License Manager
funkproxy	1505	TCP, UDP	Funk Software, Inc.
#	1506–1523	TCP, UDP	Unassigned

Keyword	Decimal	Protocol	Description
ingreslock	1524	TCP, UDP	ingres
orasrv	1525	TCP, UDP	oracle
prospero-np	1525	TCP, UDP	Prospero Directory Service non-priv
pdap-np	1526	TCP, UDP	Prospero Data Access Prot non-priv
tlisrv	1527	TCP, UDP	Oracle
coauthor	1529	TCP, UDP	Oracle
issd	1600	TCP, UDP	
nkd	1650	TCP, UDP	
proshareaudio	1651	TCP, UDP	proshare conf audio
prosharevideo	1652	TCP, UDP	proshare conf video
prosharedata	1653	TCP, UDP	proshare conf data
prosharerequest	1654	TCP, UDP	proshare conf request
prosharenotify	1655	TCP, UDP	proshare conf notify
netview-aix-1	1661	TCP, UDP	netview-aix-1
netview-aix-2	1662	TCP, UDP	netview-aix-2
netview-aix-3	1663	TCP, UDP	netview-aix-3
netview-aix-4	1664	TCP, UDP	netview-aix-4
netview-aix-5	1665	TCP, UDP	netview-aix-5
netview-aix-6	1666	TCP, UDP	netview-aix-6
licensedaemon	1986	TCP, UDP	Cisco license management
tr-rsrb-p1	1987	TCP, UDP	Cisco RSRB Priority 1 port
tr-rsrb-p2	1988	TCP, UDP	Cisco RSRB Priority 2 port
tr-rsrb-p3	1989	TCP, UDP	Cisco RSRB Priority 3 port
mshnet	1989	TCP, UDP	MHSnet system
stun-p1	1990	TCP, UDP	Cisco STUN Priority 1 port
stun-p2	1991	TCP, UDP	Cisco STUN Priority 2 port
stun-p3	1992	TCP, UDP	Cisco STUN Priority 3 port
ipsendmsg	1992	TCP, UDP	Ipsendmsg
snmp-TCP-port	1993	TCP	Cisco SNMP TCP, UDP port
snmp-UDP-port	1993	UDP	Cisco SNMP TCP, UDP port
stun-port	1994	TCP, UDP	Cisco serial tunnel port
perf-port	1995	TCP, UDP	Cisco perf port

Keyword	Decimal	Protocol	Description
tr-rsrb-port	1996	TCP, UDP	Cisco Remote SRB port
gdp-port	1997	TCP, UDP	Cisco Gateway Discovery Protocol
x25-svc-port	1998	TCP, UDP	Cisco X.25 service (XOT)
TCP-id-port	1999	TCP	Cisco identification port
UDP-id-port	1999	UDP	Cisco identification port
callbook	2000	TCP, UDP	
dc	2001	TCP	
wizard	2001	UDP	curry
globe	2002	TCP	
mailbox	2004	TCP	
emce	2004	UDP	CCWS mm conf
berknet	2005	TCP	
oracle	2005	UDP	
invokator	2006	TCP	
raid-cc	2006	UDP	raid
dectalk	2007	TCP	
raid-am	2007	UDP	
conf	2008	TCP	
terminaldb	2008	UDP	
news	2009	TCP	
whosockami	2009	UDP	
search	2010	TCP	
pipe_server	2010	UDP	
raid-cc	2011	TCP	raid
servserv	2011	UDP	
ttyinfo	2012	TCP	
raid-ac	2012	UDP	
raid-am	2013	TCP	
raid-cd	2013	UDP	
troff	2014	TCP	
raid-sf	2014	UDP	
cypress	2015	TCP	

Keyword	Decimal	Protocol	Description
raid-cs	2015	UDP	
bootserver	2016	TCP, UDP	
cypress-stat	2017	TCP	
bootclient	2017	UDP	
terminaldb	2018	TCP	
rellpack	2018	UDP	
whosockami	2019	TCP	
about	2019	UDP	
xinupageserver	2020	TCP, UDP	
servexec	2021	TCP	
xinuexpansion1	2021	UDP	
down	2022	TCP	
xinuexpansion2	2022	UDP	
xinuexpansion3	2023	TCP, UDP	
xinuexpansion4	2024	TCP, UDP	
ellpack	2025	TCP	
xribs	2025	UDP	
scrabble	2026	TCP, UDP	
shadowserver	2027	TCP, UDP	
submitserver	2028	TCP, UDP	
device2	2030	TCP, UDP	
blackboard	2032	TCP, UDP	
glogger	2033	TCP, UDP	
scoremgr	2034	TCP, UDP	
imsldoc	2035	TCP, UDP	
objectmanager	2038	TCP, UDP	
lam	2040	TCP, UDP	
interbase	2041	TCP, UDP	
isis	2042	TCP, UDP	
isis-bcast	2043	TCP, UDP	
rimsl	2044	TCP, UDP	
cdfunc	2045	TCP, UDP	

Keyword	Decimal	Protocol	Description
sdfunc	2046	TCP, UDP	
dls	2047	TCP, UDP	
dls-monitor	2048	TCP, UDP	
shilp	2049	TCP, UDP	
dlsrpn	2065	TCP, UDP	Data Link Switch Read Port Number
dlswpn	2067	TCP, UDP	Data Link Switch Write Port Number
ats	2201	TCP, UDP	Advanced Training System Program
rtsserv	2500	TCP, UDP	Resource Tracking system server
rtsclient	2501	TCP, UDP	Resource Tracking system client
hp-3000-telnet	2564	TCP	HP 3000 NS/VT block mode telnet
www-dev	2784	TCP, UDP	World Wide Web – development
NSWS	3049	TCP, UDP	
ccmail	3264	TCP, UDP	cc:mail/lotus
dec-notes	3333	TCP, UDP	DEC Notes
mapper-nodemgr	3984	TCP, UDP	MAPPER network node manager
mapper-mapethd	3985	TCP, UDP	MAPPER TCP, UDP/IP server
mapper-ws_ethd	3986	TCP, UDP	MAPPER workstation server
bmap	3421	TCP, UDP	Bull Apprise portmapper
udt_os	3900	TCP, UDP	Unidata UDT OS
nuts_dem	4132	TCP, UDP	NUTS Daemon
nuts_bootp	4133	TCP, UDP	NUTS Bootp Server
unicall	4343	TCP, UDP	UNICALL
krb524	4444	TCP, UDP	KRB524
rfa	4672	TCP, UDP	remote file access server
commplex-main	5000	TCP, UDP	
commplex-link	5001	TCP, UDP	
rfe	5002	TCP, UDP	radio free ethernet
telelpathstart	5010	TCP, UDP	TelepathStart
telelpathattack	5011	TCP, UDP	TelepathAttack
mmcc	5050	TCP, UDP	multimedia conference control tool
rmonitor_secure	5145	TCP, UDP	
aol	5190	TCP, UDP	America-Online

Keyword	Decimal	Protocol	Description
padl2sim	5236	TCP, UDP	
hacl-hb	5300	TCP, UDP	# HA cluster heartbeat
hacl-gs	5301	TCP, UDP	# HA cluster general services
hacl-cfg	5302	TCP, UDP	# HA cluster configuration
hacl-probe	5303	TCP, UDP	# HA cluster probing
hacl-local	5304	TCP, UDP	
hacl-test	5305	TCP, UDP	
x11	6000–6063	TCP, UDP	X Window System
sub-process	6111	TCP, UDP	HP SoftBench Sub-Process Control
meta-corp	6141	TCP, UDP	Meta Corporation License Manager
aspentec-lm	6142	TCP, UDP	Aspen Technology License Manager
watershed-lm	6143	TCP, UDP	Watershed License Manager
statsci1-lm	6144	TCP, UDP	StatSci License Manager – 1
statsci2-lm	6145	TCP, UDP	StatSci License Manager – 2
lonewolf-lm	6146	TCP, UDP	Lone Wolf Systems License Manager
montage-lm	6147	TCP, UDP	Montage License Manager
xdsxdm	6558	UDP	
afs3-fileserver	7000	TCP, UDP	file server itself
afs3-callback	7001	TCP, UDP	callbacks to cache managers
afs3-prserver	7002	TCP, UDP	users & groups database
afs3-vlserver	7003	TCP, UDP	volume location database
afs3-kaserver	7004	TCP, UDP	AFS/Kerberos authentication service
afs3-volser	7005	TCP, UDP	volume managment server
afs3-errors	7006	TCP, UDP	error interpretation service
afs3-bos	7007	TCP, UDP	basic overseer process
afs3-update	7008	TCP, UDP	server-to-server updater
afs3-rmtsys	7009	TCP, UDP	remote cache manager service
ups-onlinet	7010	TCP, UDP	onlinet uninterruptable power supplies
font-service	7100	TCP, UDP	X Font Service
fodms	7200	TCP, UDP	FODMS FLIP
man	9535	TCP, UDP	
isode-dual	17007	TCP, UDP	

D.3   Dynamic and/or private ports

These ports lie within the range 49,152 through 65,535 and are for private or on-demand use by applications and user-defined services.

Multicast and Broadcast Addresses

The following list of IP protocol identifiers comprises information from various sources, including RFC 1700 and some personal observations. Any errors or omissions are therefore my own. The list provided here is not exhaustive. For a complete up-to-date list of port assignments see the IANA URL below:

URL= ftp://ftp.isi.edu/in-notes/iana/assignments/multicast-addresses

E.1   IP multicast addresses

Host Extensions for IP Multicasting (RFC 1112) specifies the extensions required of a host implementation of IP to support multicasting. The multicast addresses are in the range 224.0.0.0 through 239.255.255.255. Current addresses are listed below. Note that the range of addresses between 224.0.0.0 and 224.0.0.255 is reserved for the use of routing protocols and other low-level topology discovery or maintenance protocols, such as gateway discovery and group membership reporting. Multicast routers should not forward any multicast datagram with destination addresses in this range, regardless of its TTL.

E.1.1   IP address usage

224.0.0.0	Base Address (Reserved)
224.0.0.1	All Systems on this Subnet
224.0.0.2	All Routers on this Subnet
224.0.0.3	Unassigned
224.0.0.4	DVMRP Routers
224.0.0.5	OSPFIGP All Routers

224.0.0.6	OSPFIGP Designated Routers
224.0.0.7	ST Routers
224.0.0.8	ST Hosts
224.0.0.9	RIP2 Routers
224.0.0.10	IGRP Routers
224.0.0.11	Mobile-Agents
224.0.0.12	DHCP Server/Relay Agent
224.0.0.13	All PIM Routers
224.0.0.14	RSVP-ENCAPSULATION
224.0.0.15	all-cbt-routers
224.0.0.16	designated-sbm
224.0.0.17	all-sbms
224.0.0.18	VRRP
224.0.0.19	IPAllL1ISs
224.0.0.20	IPAllL2ISs
224.0.0.21	IPAllIntermediate Systems
224.0.0.22	GMP
224.0.0.23	GLOBECAST-ID
224.0.0.24	Unassigned
224.0.0.25	router-to-switch
224.0.0.26	Unassigned
224.0.0.27	Al MPP Hello
224.0.0.28	ETC Control
224.0.0.29	GE-FANUC
224.0.0.30	indigo-vhdp
224.0.0.31	shinbroadband
224.0.0.32	digistar
224.0.0.33	ff-system-management
224.0.0.34	pt2-discover
224.0.0.35	DXCLUSTER
224.0.0.36	UDLR-DTCP
224.0.0.37– 224.0.0.250	Unassigned

224.0.0.251	mDNS
224.0.0.252– 224.0.0.255	Unassigned
224.0.1.0	VMTP Managers Group
224.0.1.1	NTPNetwork Time Protocol
224.0.1.2	SGI-Dogfight
224.0.1.3	Rwhod
224.0.1.4	VNP
224.0.1.5	Artificial Horizons - Aviator
224.0.1.6	NSS - Name Service Server
224.0.1.7	AUDIONEWS - Audio News Multicast
224.0.1.8	SUN NIS+ Information Service
224.0.1.9	MTP Multicast Transport Protocol
224.0.1.10	IETF-1-LOW-AUDIO
224.0.1.11	IETF-1-AUDIO
224.0.1.12	IETF-1-VIDEO
224.0.1.13	IETF-2-LOW-AUDIO
224.0.1.14	ETF-2-AUDIO
224.0.1.15	IETF-2-VIDEO
224.0.1.16	MUSIC-SERVICE
224.0.1.17	SEANET-TELEMETRY
224.0.1.18	SEANET-IMAGE
224.0.1.19	MLOADD
224.0.1.20	any private experiment
224.0.1.21	DVMRP on MOSPF
224.0.1.22	SVRLOC
224.0.1.23	XINGTV
224.0.1.24	microsoft-ds
224.0.1.25	nbc-pro
224.0.1.26	nbc-pfn
224.0.1.27	lmsc-calren-1
224.0.1.28	lmsc-calren-2
224.0.1.29	lmsc-calren-3

224.0.1.30	lmsc-calren-4
224.0.1.31	ampr-info
224.0.1.32	mtrace
224.0.1.33	RSVP-encap-1
224.0.1.34	RSVP-encap-2
224.0.1.35	SVRLOC-DA
224.0.1.36	rln-server
224.0.1.37	proshare-mc
224.0.1.38	dantz
224.0.1.39	cisco-rp-announce
224.0.1.40	cisco-rp-discovery
224.0.1.41	gatekeeper
224.0.1.42	iberiagames
224.0.1.43	nwn-discovery
224.0.1.44	nwn-adaptor
224.0.1.45	isma-1
224.0.1.46	isma-2
224.0.1.47	telerate
224.0.1.48	ciena
224.0.1.49	dcap-servers
224.0.1.50	dcap-clients
224.0.1.51	mcntp-directory
224.0.1.52	mbone-vcr-directory
224.0.1.53	heartbeat
224.0.1.54	sun-mc-grp
224.0.1.55	extended-sys
224.0.1.56	pdrncs
224.0.1.57	tns-adv-multi
224.0.1.58	vcals-dmu
224.0.1.59	zuba
224.0.1.60	hp-device-disc
224.0.1.61	tms-production
224.0.1.62	sunscalar

224.0.1.63	mmtp-poll
224.0.1.64	compaq-peer
224.0.1.65	iapp
224.0.1.66	multihasc-com
224.0.1.67	serv-discovery
224.0.1.68	mdhcpdisover
224.0.1.69	MMP-bundle-discovery1
224.0.1.70	MMP-bundle-discovery2
224.0.1.71	XYPOINT DGPS Data Feed
224.0.1.72	GilatSkySurfer
224.0.1.73	SharesLive
224.0.1.74	NorthernData
224.0.1.75	SIP
224.0.1.76	IAPP
224.0.1.77	AGENTVIEW
224.0.1.78	Tibco Multicast1
224.0.1.79	Tibco Multicast2
224.0.1.80	MSP
224.0.1.81	OTT (One-way Trip Time)
224.0.1.82	TRACKTICKER
224.0.1.83	dtn-mc
224.0.1.84	jini-announcement
224.0.1.85	jini-request
224.0.1.86	sde-discovery
224.0.1.87	DirecPC-SI
224.0.1.88	B1RMonitor
224.0.1.89	3Com-AMP3 dRMON
224.0.1.90	imFtmSvc
224.0.1.91	NQDS4
224.0.1.92	NQDS5
224.0.1.93	NQDS6
224.0.1.94	NLVL12
224.0.1.95	NTDS1

224.0.1.96	NTDS2
224.0.1.97	NODSA
224.0.1.98	NODSB
224.0.1.99	NODSC
224.0.1.100	NODSD
224.0.1.101	NQDS4R
224.0.1.102	NQDS5R
224.0.1.103	NQDS6R
224.0.1.104	LVL12R
224.0.1.105	NTDS1R
224.0.1.106	NTDS2R
224.0.1.107	NODSAR
224.0.1.108	NODSBR
224.0.1.109	NODSCR
224.0.1.110	NODSDR
224.0.1.111	MRM
224.0.1.112	TVE-FILE
224.0.1.113	TVE-ANNOUNCE
224.0.1.114	Mac Srv Loc
224.0.1.115	Simple Multicast
224.0.1.116	SpectraLinkGW
224.0.1.117	dieboldmcast
224.0.1.118	Tivoli Systems
224.0.1.119	pq-lic-mcast
224.0.1.120	HYPERFEED
224.0.1.121	Pipesplatform
224.0.1.122	LiebDevMgmg-DM
224.0.1.123	TRIBALVOICE
224.0.1.124	UDLR-DTCP
224.0.1.125	PolyCom Relay1
224.0.1.126	Infront Multi1
224.0.1.127	XRX DEVICE DISC
224.0.1.128	CNN

224.0.1.129	PTP-primary
224.0.1.130	PTP-alternate1
224.0.1.131	PTP-alternate2
224.0.1.132	PTP-alternate3
224.0.1.133	ProCast
224.0.1.134	3Com Discp
224.0.1.135	CS-Multicasting
224.0.1.136	TS-MC-1
224.0.1.137	Make Source
224.0.1.138	Teleborsa
224.0.1.139	SUMAConfig
224.0.1.140	Unassigned
224.0.1.141	DHCP-SERVERS
224.0.1.142	CN Router-LL
224.0.1.143	EMWIN
224.0.1.144	Alchemy Cluster
224.0.1.145	Satcast One
224.0.1.146	Satcast Two
224.0.1.147	Satcast Three
224.0.1.148	Intline
224.0.1.149	8x8 Multicast
224.0.1.150	Unassigned
224.0.1.151	Intline-1
224.0.1.152	Intline-2
224.0.1.153	Intline-3
224.0.1.154	Intline-4
224.0.1.155	Intline-5
224.0.1.156	Intline-6
224.0.1.157	Intline-7
224.0.1.158	Intline-8
224.0.1.159	Intline-9
224.0.1.160	Intline-10
224.0.1.161	Intline-11

224.0.1.162	Intline-12
224.0.1.163	Intline-13
224.0.1.164	Intline-14
224.0.1.165	Intline-15
224.0.1.166	marratech-cc
224.0.1.167	EMS-InterDev
224.0.1.168	itb301
224.0.1.169– 224.0.1.255	Unassigned
224.0.2.1	"rwho" Group (BSD) (unofficial)
224.0.2.2	SUN RPC PMAPPROC_CALLIT
224.0.2.064– 224.0.2.095	SIAC MDD Service
224.0.2.096– 224.0.2.127	CoolCast
224.0.2.128– 224.0.2.191	WOZ-Garage
224.0.2.192– 224.0.2.255	SIAC MDD Market Service
224.0.3.000– 224.0.3.255	RFE Generic Service
224.0.4.000– 224.0.4.255	RFE Individual Conferences
224.0.5.000– 224.0.5.127	CDPD Groups
224.0.5.128– 224.0.5.191	SIAC Market Service
224.0.5.192– 224.0.5.255	Unassigned
224.0.6.000– 224.0.6.127	Cornell ISIS Project
224.0.6.128– 224.0.6.255	Unassigned
224.0.7.000– 224.0.7.255	Where-Are-You

224.0.8.000– 224.0.8.255	INTV
224.0.9.000– 224.0.9.255	Invisible Worlds
224.0.10.000– 224.0.10.255	DLSw Groups
224.0.11.000– 224.0.11.255	NCC.NET Audio
224.0.12.000– 224.0.12.063	Microsoft and MSNBC
224.0.13.000– 224.0.13.255	UUNET PIPEXNet News
224.0.14.000– 224.0.14.255	NLANR
224.0.15.000– 224.0.15.255	Hewlett-Packard
224.0.16.000– 224.0.16.255	XingNet
224.0.17.000– 224.0.17.031	Mercantile & Commodity Exchange
224.0.17.032– 224.0.17.063	NDQMD1
224.0.17.064– 224.0.17.127	ODN-DTV
224.0.18.000– 224.0.18.255	Dow Jones
224.0.19.000– 224.0.19.063	Walt Disney Company
224.0.19.064– 224.0.19.095	Cal Multicast
224.0.19.096– 224.0.19.127	SIAC Market Service
224.0.19.128– 224.0.19.191	IIG Multicast
224.0.19.192– 224.0.19.207	Metropol

224.0.19.208– 224.0.19.239	Xenoscience, Inc.
224.0.19.240– 224.0.19.255	HYPERFEED
224.0.20.000– 224.0.20.063	MS-IP/TV
224.0.20.064– 224.0.20.127	Reliable Network Solutions
224.0.20.128– 224.0.20.143	TRACKTICKER Group
224.0.20.144– 224.0.20.207	CNR Rebroadcast MCA
224.0.21.000– 224.0.21.127	Talarian MCAST
224.0.22.000– 224.0.22.255	WORLD MCAST
224.0.252.000– 224.0.252.255	Domain Scoped Group
224.0.253.000– 224.0.253.255	Report Group
224.0.254.000– 224.0.254.255	Query Group
224.0.255.000– 224.0.255.255	Border Routers
224.1.0.0– 224.1.255.255	ST Multicast Groups
224.2.0.0– 224.2.127.253	Multimedia Conference Calls
224.2.127.254	SAPv1 Announcements
224.2.127.255	SAPv0 Announcements (deprecated)
224.2.128.0– 224.2.255.255	SAP Dynamic Assignments
224.252.0.0– 224.255.255.255	DIS transient groups
225.0.0.0– 225.255.255.255	MALLOC (temp – renew 1/01)

232.0.0.0–	VMTP transient groups
232.255.255.255	See single-source-multicast file
233.0.0.0–	Static Allocations (temp - renew 6/01)
233.255.255.255	
239.000.000.000–	Administratively Scoped
239.255.255.255	
239.000.000.000–	Reserved
239.063.255.255	
239.064.000.000–	Reserved
239.127.255.255	
239.128.000.000–	Reserved
239.191.255.255	
239.192.000.000–	Organization-Local Scope
239.251.255.255	
239.252.000.000–	Site-Local Scope (reserved)
239.252.255.255	
239.253.000.000–	Site-Local Scope (reserved)
239.253.255.255	
239.254.000.000–	Site-Local Scope (reserved)
239.254.255.255	
239.255.000.000–	Site-Local Scope
239.255.255.255	
239.255.002.002	rasadv

There is a concept of relative addresses to be used with the scoped multicast addresses. These relative addresses are listed here:

Relative	Description
0	SAP Session Announcement Protocol
1	MADCAP Protocol
2	SLPv2 Discovery
3	MZAP
4	Multicast Discovery of DNS Services
5	SSDP
6	DHCP v4

These addresses are listed in the Domain Name Service under MCAST.NET and 224.IN-ADDR.ARPA.

Note that when used on an Ethernet or IEEE 802 network, the 23 low-order bits of the IP Multicast address are placed in the low-order 23 bits of the Ethernet or IEEE 802 net multicast address 1.0.94.0.0.0.

E.I.2   Ethernet multicast addresses

An Ethernet multicast address consists of the multicast bit, the 23-bit vendor component, and the 24-bit group identifier assigned by the vendor. For example, DEC is assigned the vendor component 08-00-2B, so multicast addresses assigned by DEC have the first 24-bits 09-00-2B (since the multicast bit is the low-order bit of the first byte, which is in effect the first bit placed *on the wire*).

MAC Address	Type	Usage
01-00-5E-00-00-00- 01-00-5E-7F-FF-FF	0800	Internet Multicast
01-00-5E-80-00-00- 01-00-5E-FF-FF-FF	????	Internet reserved by IANA
01-80-C2-00-00-00	-802-	Spanning tree (for bridges)
09-00-02-04-00-01?	8080?	Vitalink printer
09-00-02-04-00-02?	8080?	Vitalink management
09-00-09-00-00-01	8005	HP Probe
09-00-09-00-00-01	-802-	HP Probe
09-00-09-00-00-04	8005?	HP DTC
09-00-1E-00-00-00	8019?	Apollo DOMAIN
09-00-2B-00-00-00	6009?	DEC MUMPS?
09-00-2B-00-00-01	8039?	DEC DSM/DTP?
09-00-2B-00-00-02	803B?	DEC VAXELN?
09-00-2B-00-00-03	8038	DEC Lanbridge Traffic Monitor (LTM)
09-00-2B-00-00-04	????	DEC MAP End System Hello
09-00-2B-00-00-05	????	DEC MAP Intermediate System Hello
09-00-2B-00-00-06	803D?	DEC CSMA/CD Encryption?
09-00-2B-00-00-07	8040?	DEC NetBios Emulator?
09-00-2B-00-00-0F	6004	DEC Local Area Transport (LAT)
09-00-2B-00-00-1x	????	DEC Experimental
09-00-2B-01-00-00	8038	DEC LanBridge Copy packets (All bridges)

MAC Address	Type	Usage
09-00-2B-01-00-01	8038	DEC LanBridge Hello packets (All local bridges) 1 packet per second, sent by the designated LanBridge
09-00-2B-02-00-00	????	DEC DNA Lev. 2 Routing Layer routers?
09-00-2B-02-01-00	803C?	DEC DNA Naming Service Advertisement?
09-00-2B-02-01-01	803C?	DEC DNA Naming Service Solicitation?
09-00-2B-02-01-02	803E?	DEC DNA Time Service?
09-00-2B-03-xx-xx	????	DEC default filtering by bridges?
09-00-2B-04-00-00	8041?	DEC Local Area Sys. Transport (LAST)?
09-00-2B-23-00-00	803A?	DEC Argonaut Console?
09-00-4E-00-00-02?	8137?	Novell IPX
09-00-56-00-00-00- 09-00-56-FE-FF-FF	????	Stanford reserved
09-00-56-FF-00-00- 09-00-56-FF-FF-FF	805C	Stanford V Kernel, version 6.0
09-00-77-00-00-01	????	Retix spanning tree bridges
09-00-7C-02-00-05	8080?	Vitalink diagnostics
09-00-7C-05-00-01	8080?	Vitalink gateway?
0D-1E-15-BA-DD-06	????	HP
AB-00-00-01-00-00	6001	DEC Maintenance Operation Protocol (MOP) Dump/Load Assistance
AB-00-00-02-00-00	6002	DEC Maintenance Operation Protocol (MOP) Remote Console 1 System ID packet every 8-10 minutes, by every: DEC LanBridge, DEC DEUNA interface, DEC DELUA interface, DEC DEQNA interface (in a certain mode)
AB-00-00-03-00-00	6003	DECNET Phase IV end node Hello packets.1 packet every 15 seconds, sent by each DECNET host
AB-00-00-04-00-00	6003	DECNET Phase IV Router Hello packets. 1 packet every 15 seconds, sent by the DECNET router
AB-00-00-05-00-00- AB-00-03-FF-FF-FF	????	Reserved DEC
AB-00-03-00-00-00	6004	DEC Local Area Transport (LAT) - old
AB-00-04-00-xx-xx	????	Reserved DEC customer private use

MAC Address	Type	Usage
AB-00-04-01-xx-yy	6007	DEC Local Area VAX Cluster groups Sys. Communication Architecture (SCA)
CF-00-00-00-00-00	9000	Ethernet Configuration Test protocol (Loopback)

E.1.3 Ethernet broadcast addresses

MAC Address	Type	Usage
FF-FF-FF-FF-FF-FF	0600	XNS packets, Hello or gateway search? 6 packets every 15 seconds, per XNS station
FF-FF-FF-FF-FF-FF	0800	IP (e.g. RWHOD via UDP) as needed
FF-FF-FF-FF-FF-FF	0804	CHAOS
FF-FF-FF-FF-FF-FF	0806	ARP (for IP and CHAOS) as needed
FF-FF-FF-FF-FF-FF	0BAD	Banyan
FF-FF-FF-FF-FF-FF	1600	VALID packets, Hello or gateway search? 1 packets every 30 seconds, per VALID station
FF-FF-FF-FF-FF-FF	8035	Reverse ARP
FF-FF-FF-FF-FF-FF	807C	Merit Internodal (INP)
FF-FF-FF-FF-FF-FF	809B	EtherTalk

EtherType Assignments

The following list of EtherTypes comprises information from various sources, including RFC 1700 and some personal observations. Any errors or omissions are therefore my own. For a complete up-to-date list of Ether-Types see the following IANA URL:

URL = ftp://ftp.isi.edu/in-notes/iana/assignments/ethernet-numbers

Note that within an Ethernet frame header, values greater than 0x05dc (decimal 1500) in the Type field indicate an LLC frame (in which case the value is interpreted as a length field, and the higher level protocol is identified by the LSAPs which follow).

EtherType (Hex)	*Description*
0000–05DC	IEEE802.3 Length Field
0101–01FF	Experimental
0200	XEROX PUP (see 0A00)
0201	PUP Addr Trans (see 0A01)
0400	Nixdorf
0600	XEROX NS IDP
0660–0661	DLOG
0800	Internet IP (IPv4)
0801	X.75 Internet
0802	NBS Internet
0803	ECMA Internet
0804	Chaosnet
0805	X.25 PLP (Level 3)
0806	ARP
0807	XNS Compatability

EtherType (Hex)	Description
081C	Symbolics Private
0888	Xyplex
0889	Xyplex XPSP Protocol
088A	Xyplex FDRB Protocol
0888–088A	Xyplex
0900	Ungermann-Bass net debugger
0A00	Xerox IEEE802.3 PUP
0A01	PUP Address Translation
0BAD	Banyan Systems
1000	Berkeley Trailer negotiation
1001–100F	Berkeley Trailer encap/IP
1600	Valid Systems
2F01	Cabletron
4242	PCS Basic Block Protocol
5208	BBN Simnet Private
6000	DEC Unassigned (Experimental)
6001	DEC MOP Dump/Load
6002	DEC MOP Remote Console
6003	DEC DECNET Phase IV Route
6004	DEC LAT
6005	DEC Diagnostic Protocol
6006	DEC Customer Protocol
6007	DEC LAVC, SCA
6008–6009	DEC Unassigned
6010–6014	3Com Corporation
7000	Ungermann-Bass download
7002	Ungermann-Bass dia/loop
7020–7029	LRT
7030	Proteon
7034	Cabletron
8003	Cronus VLN
8004	Cronus Direct
8005	HP Probe

EtherType (Hex)	Description
8006	Nestar
8008	AT&T
8010	Excelan
8013	SGI diagnostics
8014	SGI network games
8015	SGI reserved
8016	SGI bounce server
8019	Apollo Computers
802E	Tymshare
802F	Tigan, Inc.
8035	Reverse ARP (RARP)
8036	Aeonic Systems
8038	DEC LANBridge
8039–803C	DEC Unassigned
803D	DEC Ethernet Encryption
803E	DEC Unassigned
803F	DEC LAN Traffic Monitor
8040–8042	DEC Unassigned
8044	Planning Research Corp.
8046–8047	AT&T
8049	ExperData
805B	Stanford V Kernel exp.
805C	Stanford V Kernel prod.
805D	Evans & Sutherland
8060	Little Machines
8062	Counterpoint Computers
8065–8066	Univ. of Mass. @ Amherst
8067	Veeco Integrated Auto.
8068	General Dynamics
8069	Autophon
806C	ComDesign
806D	Computgraphic Corp.
806E–8077	Landmark Graphics Corp.

EtherType (Hex)	Description
807A	Matra
807B	Dansk Data Elektronik
807C	Merit Internodal
807D–807F	Vitalink Communications
8080	Vitalink TransLAN III
8081–8083	Counterpoint Computers
809B	Appletalk
809C–809E	Datability
809F	Spider Systems Ltd.
80A3	Nixdorf Computers
80A4–80B3	Siemens Gammasonics, Inc.
80C0–80C3	DCA Data Exchange Cluster
80C4–80C5	Banyan Systems
80C6	Pacer Software
80C7	Applitek Corporation
80C8–80CC	Intergraph Corporation
80CD–80CE	Harris Corporation
80CF–80D2	Taylor Instrument
80D3–80D4	Rosemount Corporation
80D5	IBM SNA Service on Ethernet
80DD	Varian Associates
80DE–80DF	Integrated Solutions TRFS
80E0–80E3	Allen-Bradley
80E4–80F0	Datability
80F2	Retix
80F3	AppleTalk AARP (Kinetics)
80F4–80F5	Kinetics
80F7	Apollo Computer
80FF–8103	Wellfleet Communications
8107–8109	Symbolics Private
8130	Hayes Microcomputers
8131	VG Laboratory Systems
8132–8136	Bridge Communications

EtherType (Hex)	Description
8137	Novell, Inc. (Old NetWare IPX)
8138	Novell, Inc.
8139–813D	KTI
8148	Logicraft
8149	Network Computing Devices
814A	Alpha Micro
814C	SNMP
814D–814E	BIIN
814F	Technically Elite Concept
8150	Rational Corp
8151–8153	Qualcomm
815C–815E	Computer Protocol Pty Ltd
8164–8166	Charles River Data System
817D–818C	Protocol Engines
818D	Motorola Computer
819A–81A3	Qualcomm
81A4	ARAI Bunkichi
81A5–81AE	RAD Network Devices
81B7–81B9	Xyplex
81CC–81D5	Apricot Computers
81D6–81DD	Artisoft
81E6–81EF	Polygon
81F0–81F2	Comsat Labs
81F3–81F5	SAIC
81F6–81F8	VG Analytical
8203–8205	Quantum Software
8221–8222	Ascom Banking Systems
823E–8240	Advanced Encryption Systems
827F–8282	Athena Programming
8263–826A	Charles River Data System
829A–829B	Inst Ind Info Tech
829C–82AB	Taurus Controls
82AC–8693	Walker Richer & Quinn

EtherType (Hex)	*Description*
8694–869D	Idea Courier
869E–86A1	Computer Network Tech
86A3–86AC	Gateway Communications
86DB	SECTRA
86DE	Delta Controls
86DF	ATOMIC
86E0–86EF	Landis & Gyr Powers
8700–8710	Motorola
8A96–8A97	Invisible Software
9000	Loopback
9001	3Com(Bridge) XNS Sys Mgmt
9002	3Com(Bridge) TCP-IP Sys
9003	3Com(Bridge) loop detect
c100	Cabletron Mgt
FF00	BBN VITAL-LanBridge cache
FF00–FF0F	ISC Bunker Ramo
FFFF	Broken Novell IPX encapsulation (followed by LSAPs)

G

Example MTTR Procedures

G.1 Mean Time to Repair (MTTR)—Rack-mounted PC chassis

The following examples are typical illustrations of the time to replace mechanical components in a 19-inch rack–mounted PC chassis. All times assume that fault isolation has taken place. Total times listed include boot time, estimated at 1 minute and 30 seconds (i.e., the time required for the unit and software to become fully operational after the repair is complete). All testing was done with a unit rack-mounted at approximately 5 ft.

G.1.1 Replace PCI Network Interface Card (NIC)

Procedure

- Open chassis (2 screws and slide chassis out)
- Remove brace (2 screws)
- Remove NIC (1 screw)
- Reboot system

  Total Time = 4 min 30 sec (3 min repair + 1 min 30 sec reboot)

G.1.2 Replace power supply

Procedure

- Power supply removes from rear of unit (2 screws)
- Reboot system

  Total Time = 2 min 30 sec (1 min repair + 1 min 30 sec reboot)

G.1.3   Replace CDROM or floppy drive

Note that the procedure and times were essentially the same for both the CDROM and the floppy drive.

Procedure

- Open chassis (2 screws and slide chassis out)
- Remove CDROM/floppy assembly (2 screws)
- Remove CDROM or floppy (4 screws)
- Reboot system

  Total Time = 7 min (5 min 30 sec repair + 1 min 30 sec reboot)

G.1.4   Replace FAN assembly

Procedure

- Open chassis (2 screws and slide chassis out)
- Remove FAN assembly (1 screw and slide up)
- Remove power cable to motherboard
- Reboot system

  Total Time = 4 min 30 sec (3 min repair + 1 min 30 sec reboot)

G.1.5   Replace hard disk drive and restore database

For this failure the time to reload software and restore a database was added to obtain the actual repair time.

Procedure

- Replace drive (7 min 45 sec)
- Reload OS software from CDROM (6 min 45 sec)
- Restore database from floppy and reboot (2 min 30 sec)

  Total Time = 16 min 20 sec

Index

100BaseVG, 594–95

AAA security services, 328–33
    accounting, 329
    authentication, 328–29
    authorization, 329
    biometrics, 331–32
    CHAP, 330–31
    defined, 328
    Kerberos, 333
    model, 328–30
    PAP, 330
    RADIUS, 332
    SKIP, 331
    static/aging passwords, 330
    TACACS, 332–33
    token cards, 331
    See also Security
Abstract Syntax Notation One (ASN.1), 665
Acceptance test, 14
Access control, 306
Access Control Lists (ACLs), 577
Access routers, 226
Accounting
    as AAA security service, 329
    defined, 329
    management, 636
Active Directory Services (ADS), 130
Adaptive Source Routing, 41
Addresses
    anycast, 77
    broadcast, 64–66

CIDR, 72
IPv4, 60–64
loopback, 77
MAC, 19, 31, 241, 443
mapping to Ethernet, 67–68
multicast, 77
multicast group, 66–68
NAT, 135
registered private, 73–74
unicast, 77
unspecified, 77
Addressing, 19–20
    design techniques, 131–50
    efficiency, 133
    hierarchical, 148–50
    IP, 59–82
    Layer 1, 19
    Layer 2, 20
    Layer 3, 20
    Layer 4, 20
    legal, 132
    meaning and consistency, 132–33
    model guidelines, 132–33
    private intranet, 73–74
    router, 219–22
    security, 133
Address mapping, 82–105
Address Resolution Protocol (ARP), 31, 83–88
    cache, 83–84, 87, 170
    defined, 83
    Gratuitous, 91
    header, 84

Address Resolution Protocol (ARP) *(cont'd.)*
  identification, 85
  implementation, 84, 87
  load sharing, 510
  load-sharing proxies, 454, 510
  on mixed-media LANs, 86–87
  on NBMAs, 87
  Proxy, 88–90
  request example, 85–86
  Reverse (RARP), 90–91
  synchronization, 87–88
  table size, 87
  VRRP and, 448
Adjacencies, 198–201
  on NBMA, 200–201
  packet distribution, 200
  states, 198–99
  trace of neighbors forming, 199
  See also OSPF
Admission control, 556, 596
  IEEE 802.1p and, 590
  IS, 599
  RSVP, 625
Advanced diagnostic tools, 694–98
  edit, playback, simulation, 697
  high-speed, real-time capture, 698
  protocol analyzers, 694–96
  real-time capture, 697–98
  trace format export/import, 698
  See also Troubleshooting tools
Aging passwords, 330
Alarm group, 660
American National Standards Institute
      (ANSI), 16
Annual Loss Expectancy (ALE), 406–7
  analysis, 407
  defined, 406
Anycast addresses, 77
AppleTalk
  broadcasts, 478
  Chooser, 478
  multicasts, 477–78
Application Layer
  OSI reference model, 17
  TCP/IP protocol suite, 27

Application models, 434–35
Application optimization, 519–35
  caching techniques, 522–35
  proxy services, 520–22
  use of multicasts, 519
  wide area tuning issues, 520
Applications, 20–24
  in client/server model, 22–23
  CMIP, 662–63
  computing models, 21–24
  in distributed model, 23–24
  IPSec, 376–77
  MBone, 286–87
  PKI, 326
  router, 224–26
  TCP/IP, 34–37
  types of, 20
  vulnerability, 308–12
Architectural model (internetwork), 156–57
Area Border Routers (ABRs), 195, 196
Areas, 195–96
  defined, 195
  nonstub, 196
  not so totally stubby, 195–96
  partitioning advantages, 196
  stub, 195
  totally stubby, 195
  See also OSPF
ASCII, 698
Asynchronous traffic, 594
ATM, 597–98
  IEEE 802.1p with, 626
  layer, 597
  service categories, 597
  SSCOP, 597
  switches, 42
ATM-like fabrics, 232
Attacks
  Christmas tree, 316
  classifying, 307
  Denial of Service (DOS), 307
  impersonation, 307
  IP spoofing, 314
  land, 315
  Man-In-The-Middle, 307

password/key guessing, 307
ping of death, 315
ping sweep, 315
Smurf, 315
SYN, 314–15
teardrop, 315–16
virus, 307
well-known, 313–16
WinNuke, 316
See also Security
Attack trees, 317
defined, 317
illustrated, 318
Authentication
in AAA security services model,
328–29
defined, 306
Authentication Header (AH), 362–65
defined, 362
header fields, 364–65
header format, 364–65
processing, 363
services, 362
See also IPSec
Authorization, 329
Autocratic model, 518
Autonomous System (AS), 157, 207
inter, routing, 210
intra, routing, 210
pass-through, routing, 210
Autonomous System Border Routers (ASBRs),
194, 197
Autonomous System Numbers (ASN), 81–82
administration, 81
defined, 81
possible, 81
representation, 82
requirement criteria, 82
Availability
analysis, 410–16
application models and, 434–36
component-level, 456–64
components, 412
for discrete systems, 413
for networked systems, 414–16

as percentage of uptime, 411
quantifying, 410–13, 414–16
values, 411

Backbone Routers (BRs), 194, 224–25
Backplane design, 457–58
Backup power, 431
Bandwidth, 53
choices, 51
as critical resource, 474
managers, 488
optimizing, 472–87
Berkeley Sockets Multicast API, 244
Biometrics, 331–32
Bit-wise subnets, 138
Blackouts, 461
BOOTP, 92–95
defined, 92
DHCP concurrent use, 102
field definitions, 92–94
issues, 95
message format, 92–94
operations, 94–95
uses, 95
Boot protocols, 475
Border Gateway Multicast Protocol (BGMP), 288
Border Gateway Protocol (BGP), 205–19
aggregation, 214
attributes, 212
backdoor routes, 215
BGP-4, 213
CIDR and aggregate addresses, 213–14
conceptual design, 209
decision algorithm, 211–12
default routes, 214–15
defined, 205
external (eBGP), 208, 209–10, 211
fields, 205–6
internal (iBGP), 208, 210–11
IRDP, 217
keep alive messages, 207
load balancing, 215–17
message types, 206–7
metrics, 212
Multicast (MBGP), 287

Border Gateway Protocol (BGP) *(cont'd.)*
    multihoming, 215–17
    notification messages, 207
    operation, 207–19
    packet formats, 205–6
    peering, 207–9
    protocol stack, 205
    route filtering/policy, 213
    router discovery protocol selection,
        217
    routers, 207
    routing session, 208
    scalability, 213
    symmetry, 215–17
    update messages, 206–7
Brainstorming, 13
Breath of Life (BOFL) features, 424
Bridges, 41–42, 520
    benefits, 47–48
    broadcast storms and, 48
    defined, 41
    filtering/forwarding capabilities, 42
    issues, 48–49
    price/performance, 47
    standards, 41
    topological control with, 427
    transparent, 48
    See also Hardware
Broadcast
    AppleTalk, 478
    forwarding, 65, 221
    relay, 221
    sources, 476–78
    storms, 48
    traffic, reducing, 476–78
Broadcast addresses, 64–66
    defined, 64
    directed, 64–65
    HostID, 65
    limited, 64
    performance issues, 66
    subnet, 65
    See also IP addressing
Brownouts, 460–61
Buffered repeaters, 39

Buffering, 232–33
    input queuing, 232
    output queuing, 233
    shared memory, 233
Building blocks, 15–53
    applications, 20–24
    framework, 15–20
    hardware, 37–50
    physical connectivity, 50–53
    protocols, 24–37
Building design, 466–67
Bump-in-the-Stack (BITS) implementation, 357
Bump-in-the-Wire (BITW) implementation, 357
Bus fabric, 230

Cable plans, 13
Cache servers
    access network concentrators, 532
    in default router, 530–31
    deployment, 528–29
    deployment location, 529–33
    deployment options, 530
    international gateway, 532
    in Layer 4 switches, 531
    nontransparent, 528–29
    perimeter gateways, 532
    satellite interfaces, 532
    semitransparent, 529
    transparent, 529
    WCCP, 531
    Web Hosting/Reverse Proxy Configuration,
        531–32
Caching
    applications benefiting from, 525–28
    basics, 523
    capacity planning, 533–35
    capacity/responsiveness and, 524
    content optimization and, 523–24
    defined, 523
    DNS, 117, 120
    hit ratio, 534
    in internetwork, 528–33
    management/control and, 524–25
    measurement techniques, 535
    performance metrics, 534–35

products, 535
reliability/availability and, 524
response time, 534
scalability and, 523, 525
synchronization and, 524
system design issues, 523–25
techniques, 522–35
Capacity planning, 533–35
Capture group, 660
Centralized model, 21–22
Certificate Authorities (CAs), 324–25
Certificate Repositories (CRs), 325
Certificate Revocation Lists (CRLs), 325–26
Challenge Handshake Authentication Protocol
(CHAP), 330–31
Channel Service Units (CSUs), 40–41
Christmas tree, 316
Circuit switching
defined, 52
packet switching vs., 52–53
Cisco Group Membership Protocol (CGMP), 249
Class-Based Queuing (CBQ), 497–99, 565
defined, 497–98
effects, 498
with RSVP, 498
strengths, 499
Classless InterDomain Routing (CIDR), 145–48
BGP-4 support, 213
defined, 145–46
implementation, 147–48
policies/guidelines, 146–47
process, 145
route summarization and, 222
service provider types, 147–48
Client/server model, 22–23
applications in, 22–23
defined, 22
workgroup productivity, 22
Clustering, 439–42
defined, 441, 442
software, 441–42
techniques, 441
VRRP, 442
with Web Cache Control Protocol (WCCP),
531

CMIP/CMIS, 637, 661–67, 707
advantages, 666
applications, 662–63
architecture, 662–64
ASN.1, 665
background, 661–62
COTS, 662, 664
defined, 661–62
design, 662
disadvantages, 666–67
implementations, 662
performance, 666
primitives, 664–65
protocols, 664
See also Network management
Command-Line Interface (CLI), 668
Comma Separated Value (CSV) format, 698
Common Management Information Protocol/
Common Management Information
Service. See CMIP/CMIS
Common Management Services and Protocol over
LAN (CMOL), 664
Common Management Services and Protocol over
TCP/IP (CMOT), 664
Common Object Request Broker Architecture
(CORBA), 23, 24
Common Open Policy Service (COPS) protocol,
705
Component-level availability, 456–64
backplane design, 457–58
boot/configuration data, 463
disk mirroring, 458–59
hot swap, 458
RAID, 459–60
reliable power, 460–63
standby modules and spares, 463–64
techniques, 456
Compression
design guidelines, 486–87
disk, 542–43
hardware, 486
ITU-T fax, 484
Lempel-Ziv (LZ), 483
MNP, 484
MRU and, 485, 486

Compression *(cont'd.)*
    in networking, 483–85
    proprietary header, 485
    ratio, 483
    RLE, 483–84
    software, 486
    Stac LZS, 485–86
    TCP header, 484
    techniques, 482–87
Computing models, 21–24
    centralized, 21–22
    client/server, 22–23
    decentralized, 22
    distributed, 22, 23–24
Confidentiality, 306
Configuration management, 667–70
    automation/integration need, 668–69
    defined, 635
    large-scale, 670
    operations, 667
    planning and administration, 667
    in practice, 667
    scalability and, 667
    Web-based, 669–70
    See also Network management
Configuration scripts, 14
Congestion
    control, 295
    defined, 523
Congestion avoidance, 499–502
    RED gateways, 500–502
    taildrop, 500
    techniques, 499–500
Connection-Oriented Transport Service (COTS),
        662, 664
Connectivity, 50–53
    methods, 50–51
    switching, 52–53
Conservation law, 487–88
Constraint-Based Routing (CBR), 578–82
    defined, 574, 578
    with DiffServ, 626
    implementation, 578, 581
    interoperability with, 626–27
    issues, 578

    with MPLS, 627
    route optimization, 580–82
    routing algorithms, 580
    routing granularity, 579
    routing table structure/size, 580
    with RSVP, 626–27
    Spanning Trees, 579
    summary, 628
    topological state information and, 579–80
    viable flow path, 581
Controlled load service, 602–3
Core-Based Trees (CBT), 281–82
    defined, 281
    design issues, 282
    example topology, 282
    interoperability, 283
    operation, 281–82
    See also Multicast routing
Cost(s)
    of downtime, 394–95, 396
    network, exploring, 9
    path, 474
    port, reducing, 226
Crossbar fabric, 230–31
Cryptography, 320–22
    asymmetric, 321
    Diffie-Helman (D-H) model, 321
    encryption algorithms, 321–22
    secret-key, 320
Custom queuing, 495–96
    defined, 495
    illustrated, 495
    uses, 496

Data collection models, 568
Data Collection Modules (DCMs), 655
Datagrams, 553
Data Link Layer (OSI reference model), 18
Data Link Layer (TCP/IP protocol suite), 28–29
    defined, 27
    LLC sublayer, 29
    Mac sublayer, 28–29
Data replication/disk mirroring, 399
Data Service Units (DSUs), 40–41
Dead host detection, 507

DECbit, 499
Decentralized model, 22
Dedicated VPNs, 352, 356
Default routes, 166
Demand circuits, 185–86
    acknowledgments/retransmissions, 185–86
    defined, 185
    flow control, 186
    presumption of reachability, 185
    triggered updates, 185
Demilitarized Zone (DMZ), 37
Democratic model, 518
Denial of Service (DOS), 307
Dense distribution model, 255
Dense-mode PIM (PIM-DM), 276–78
    conditions for use, 276–77
    defined, 276
    illustrated, 277
    operations, 277–78
    PIM-SM vs., 280
    See also PIM
Dense Wave Division Multiplexing (DWDM),
        400
Deployment, 14
Design. See Network design
Designated forwarder
    defined, 267
    DVMRP, 271
    OSPF, 201–2
Designated Router (DR), 201–2
    election of, 202
    LSA generation by, 275
    misconception, 201
    purpose, 201
Desktop management, 431–32
Detailed Requirements Specification, 7–8
Deterministic flow hashing, 515, 516
Dial on Demand Routing (DDR), 420
Dial VPNs, 351, 353–55
    client-initiated, 354–55
    defined, 351
    NAS-initiated, 355
    operation, 355
    service providers and, 354
    See also Virtual Private Networks (VPNs)

Differentiated Services (DS), 563–64, 617–23
    advantage, 618
    architecture, 619
    boundary nodes, 620–22
    byte format, 619
    CBR with, 626
    design considerations, 620–23
    domains, 620
    goal, 618
    interior nodes, 622–23
    with IPSec, 626
    PHB, 619–20
    RSVP with, 624–25
    service marking, 618–19
    source domains, 623
    specifications, 617
    summary, 629
    traffic conditioner, 621–22
Diffie-Helman (D-H) model, 321
Diffusing Update Algorithm (DUAL), 164–65
Dig, 693–94
Digital signatures, 324, 372–73
Directed broadcast, 64–65
Direct interface routing, 166
Directory-Enabled Network (DEN), 131
Directory Service Markup Language (DSML), 126
Directory services, 122–31
    benefits, 122
    client/server model, 124
    defined, 122
    DEN and, 131
    LDAP and, 126–31
    name services and, 123
    networked file systems and, 123
    RDBMSs and, 123–24
    relational databases and, 123
    uses, 123
    when not to use, 124–25
    X.500 standard, 125–26
Disaster recovery
    data replication/disk mirroring, 399
    defined, 394
    electronic vaulting, 398
    models, 398–401
    outsourced, 401

Disaster recovery *(cont'd.)*
    SANs/OSNs, 400
    server mirroring/clustering, 399
    tape/CD site backup, 398
Disaster Recovery (DR) plan
    approach, 397–98
    defined, 397
    development, 395–401
Disk compression, 542–43
Disk mirroring, 458–59
Distance-Vector Multicast Routing Protocol.
        See DVMRP
Distance-vector routing algorithms, 161–65
    convergence, 172
    defined, 161
    flooded updates, 163
    hybrid, 164–65
    link-state routing vs., 162–65
    RIP routing enhancements, 186–87
    See also Routing protocols
Distributed hashing techniques, 518–19
Distributed load-sharing algorithms, 505–6
Distributed model, 23–24
    CORBA, 23, 24
    defined, 22
    IIOP, 24
Documentation, 13–14
Domain names, 108–10
    format, 109–10
    FQDNs, 110
    hierarchy, 109
    registration, 110
    SLDs, 110
    TDLs, 108, 109, 110
Domain Name System (DNS), 107–21
    access, 107
    administrator, 113
    caching, 117, 120
    components, 110–14
    defined, 36, 107
    Domain Name Space, 111
    dynamic, 119
    extensions, 108
    implementing, 117–19
    inverse query operation, 116–17

ISP maintained primary and locally maintained
        secondary service, 118–19
ISP maintained primary/secondary service,
        117–18
load sharing, 507–9
load-sharing proxies, 454
locally maintained primary/secondary service,
        118
mapping names to addresses, 116
name resolvers, 113–14
name servers, 112–13
operations, 114–17
performance, 120–21
queries, 113
query operation, 114–15
resilience, 119
Resource Records (RR), 111–12
running over UDP or TCP, 110
SOHO configurations and, 121
split, 119
structure, 108
vulnerabilities, 310–11
Domains
    DS, 620
    source, 623
    tree hierarchy, 112
    zone relationship, 113
Downstream interfaces, 266
Downtime cost, 394–95
    example, 396
    financial models, 395
Dual-Modular Redundancy (DMR), 436
Dual port transceivers, 430–31
DVMRP, 264–72
    building multicast trees, 268–71
    defined, 264
    designated forwarder, 271
    design issues, 272
    field definitions, 265–66
    functioning of, 265
    grafting, 271
    interoperability, 283
    message format, 265–66
    multicast network running, 270
    operation, 266–72

pruning, 269–70
routers, 268, 371
routing process, 267–68
terminology, 266–67
timers, 267
tunneling, 271–72
versions, 272
See also Multicast routing
Dynamic Address Translation (DAT), 134
Dynamic DNS, 119
Dynamic Host Configuration Protocol (DHCP),
    95–102
    address allocation, 96
    allocating new network address, 97
    BOOTP concurrent use, 102
    client/server interaction, 98–100
    defined, 95
    features, 95
    field definitions, 97–98
    lease renewal, 100–101
    message format, 96–97
    operations, 97–101
    running over UDP, 101
    Safe Failover Protocol, 102
Dynamic router discovery, 174
Dynamic routing entries, 166

Education, 14
EIGRP, 175, 176–77
    defined, 176
    OSPF vs., 177
Electronic Industries Association (EIA), 16
Electronic vaulting, 398
Element management, 675
E-mail protection systems, 348
Embedded servers, 706
Encapsulating Security Payload (ESP), 366–69
    defined, 364
    header, 366
    header fields, 367–68
    packet format, 367–69
    trailer, 366
    transport mode, 369
    tunnel mode, 369
    See also IPSec

Encryption algorithms, 321–22
End-system routing, 172–74
    defined, 172
    dynamic router discovery, 174
    static gateway configuration, 173–74
End systems (ES)
    bridge transparency to, 47
    defined, 46
End System to Intermediate System (ES-IS)
    protocols, 159
Enterprise Java Beans (EJB), 23
Enterprise routers, 225
Ethernet, 86, 591
European Computer Manufacturers Association
    (ECMA), 16
Event group, 660–61
Expanding ring search, 253–54
    defined, 253–54
    exploitation, 254
Exterior Gateway Protocols (EGPs),
    157–58, 159
    choosing, 204
    weaknesses, 205
External BGP (eBGP), 208, 209–10, 211
    defined, 211
    neighbors, 210
    See also Border Gateway Protocol (BGP)

Failure
    analysis, 404
    defined, 493
    LAN, 425
    mitigation approaches, 409–10
    multiple points of, 393–94
    network design and, 392
    planning for, 393–416
    recovery times, 408
    scope, 402
    single point of, 393, 403–5
    terminology, 393–94
    types of, 392
Fault management, 636
Fault resilience, 416–32
    defined, 394
    systems, 433

Fault tolerance
  backbone design, 465
  defined, 394
  loading, 463
  star topology, 419–20
  topological, 417
Fault-tolerant systems
  defined, 433
  example application, 438–39
  features, 436–37
  HA clusters combined with, 455–56
  implementation, 435
  operating systems, 438
  resiliency, 437
  scalability, 435, 438
  server architecture, 433
FDDI, 86
Federal Information Processing Standards (FIPS),
      16
Feedback, design, 15
Fiber Distributed Data Interface (FDDI), 594
File Transfer Protocol (FTP), 34
  back connections, 510
  caching and, 526
  load sharing, 509–10
  load-sharing proxies, 454, 509
  vulnerabilities, 309
Filter group, 659
Filtering techniques, 478–82
Filterspec, 602
Firewalls, 338–46
  architectures, 339
  concepts, 339
  defined, 46, 338
  limitations, 346
  packet-filtering routers, 340–42
  personal, 345
  proxy servers/application gateways, 342–44
  stateful, 344–45
  types of, 339–40
  VPN interaction with, 382–84
'rst come, first served (FCFS), 235
    in, first out (FIFO), 235
    ˙nced queuing, 494
       ˙g, 493

Floor design, 467–68
Flows, 553–55
  classifiers, 556, 557
  defined, 553–54
  descriptors, 601–2
  handling, 555–57
  identification, 554–55
  for IP switching, 557–59
  IS, 601–2
  sessions, 601
Flowspec, 601–2
Forwarding
  algorithm, 169–71
  broadcast, 65, 221
  table, 171
Fragmentation, 537
Frame Relay, 596–97
  admission control, 596
  performance, 596
Frame size, 536
Full Qualified Domain Names (FQDNs), 110

GARP Multicast Registration Protocol (GMRP),
      248
Gateways, 45–46
  configuration, 173–74
  defined, 45, 46
  examples, 45
  international, 532
  perimeter, 532
  See also Hardware
Generic Router Encapsulation (GRE), 353, 356
Gratuitous ARP, 91
Group registration, 256–64
Guaranteed service, 598, 603–4

Hardware, 37–50
  bridges, 41–42
  compression, 486
  CSU/DSUs, 40–41
  end systems, 46
  firewalls, 46
  gateways, 45–46
  intermediate systems, 46–47
  line drivers, 40

location illustration, 38
MAUs, 38–39
modems, 40
repeaters, 39–40
routers, 42–45
switches, 42
Hashing
    deterministic flow, 516, 517
    distributed, 518–19
    techniques, 515–19
Hierarchical distributed database, 107
Hierarchical management, 675–77
Hierarchical routing
    benefits, 160–61
    defined, 148
    partitions, 148
    three-layer scheme illustration, 149
Hierarchical Storage Management (HSM), 543–44
    data classes and, 543–44
    defined, 543
    file tracking, 544
High-availability (HA) systems, 391–92
    clustering and, 439–42
    combined with fault-tolerant servers, 455–56
    defined, 433
    design features of, 440
    implementation, 435
    scalability, 435
    server architecture, 433
    server mirroring, 440–41
High-speed, real-time capture, 698
History group, 659
Host group, 659
HostIDs, 65
Hosts file, 106–7
Hot Standby Router Protocol (HSRP), 439, 452–54
    defined, 452
    support, 453
    terminology, 452–53
    VRRP vs., 453–54
Hot swap, 458
HP
    OpenView, 674
    SNMP++, 670

Hub resilience, 466
Hybrid media fabrics, 231
Hypertext Transfer Protocol (HTTP)
    caching and, 526
    load sharing, 509
    load-sharing proxies, 454, 509
    Secure (S-HTTP), 336
    Voyager interface, 669
    vulnerabilities, 310

IBM NetView, 637, 674
IEEE 802 service model, 587–91
IEEE 802.1p, 588–91
    admission control and, 590
    GMRP multicast filtering, 588
    interoperability and, 591
    issues, 590–91
    tag header, 588
    traffic class expediting, 588
IEEE 802.3, 591
IEEE 802.5, 591–93
IEEE 802.1Q, 588–90
IEEE 802.12, 594–95
    defined, 594
    frame format support, 595
    UPV mapping, 595
Impersonation, 307
In-band management, 677–78
Information
    collating, 11–12
    database, building, 11
    gathering, 10–12
    on existing site, 12
    on greenfield site, 11–12
Input queuing, 232
Institute of Electrical and Electronics Engineers (IEEE), 16
Integrated bridge router, 44–45
Integrated Services (IS), 562, 598–617, 629
    admission control, 599
    best-offer support, 617
    controlled load service, 602–3
    defined, 598
    design considerations, 616–17
    flows, 601–2

Integrated Services (IS) *(cont'd.)*
    guaranteed service, 598, 603–4
    implementation model, 598–601
    model, 555
    model illustration, 600
    packet classifier, 600
    packet scheduler, 600
    performance, 617
    predictive service, 598
    pricing model, 616
    real-time applications, 617
    RSVP, 598–99, 604–16
    scalability, 616
    service classes, 602–4
    traffic shaping, 602
Integrity, 306
Interception techniques, 454–55
Interdomain routing, 287–89
Interface modules, 229–30
Interior Gateway Protocols (IGPs), 157, 159, 572
    choosing, 174–77
    feature comparison, 174
    multiple, 222
    selection considerations, 175
    selection flowchart, 176
Intermediate systems (IS), 46–47
Internal BGP (iBGP), 208, 209, 210–11
    defined, 210
    routers, 209
    use of, 210
    See also Border Gateway Protocol (BGP)
Internal meshing, 423–24
Internal Router (IR), 195
International Organization for Standardization.
        See ISO
International Telecommunications Union,
        Telecommunications Sector (ITU-T), 16
Internet Advisory Board (IAB), 15–16
Internet Assigned Numbers Authority (IANA),
        66, 67
    allocation policies, 71
    authority, 68–69
    defined, 68
    hierarchy of assignment, 69
    responsibility, 71

Internet Control Message Protocol (ICMP),
        31–32, 102–5
    defined, 31, 102
    echo interaction, 447
    ICMPv4, 103–4
    ICMPv6, 104–5
    implementation, 102
    protocol packet exchanges, 104
    redirects, 105, 447
    Router Discovery Protocol (IRDP), 217
    use, 31
    vulnerabilities, 308
Internet Engineering Task Force (IETF), 239
Internet Group Management Protocol (IGMP),
        239
    building group membership tables, 260–61
    defined, 256
    field definitions, 256–57
    group registration with, 256–64
    IGMPv1 device compatibility, 263–64
    joining multicast group, 261
    leaving multicast group, 261–62
    local group database, 267
    message format, 257–58
    multicast distribution, 262–63
    multicast router running, 258
    operation, 258–64
    querier election process, 260
    snooping, 248–49
    timers, 258–59
Internet Inter-ORB Protocol (IIOP), 24
Internet Key Exchange Protocol (IKE),
        371–76
    automated negotiation of SAs, 371
    digital signatures, 372–73
    framework, 371
    initializing SAs with, 373–74
    ISAKMP vs., 371
    operation, 372–75
    performance issues, 375
    Phase 1, 373–74
    Phase 2, 375
    preshared keys, 372
    with remote access, 376
Internet Key Management Protocol (IKMP), 371

Internet Layer (TCP/IP protocol suite), 30–32
    Address Resolution Protocol (ARP), 31
    defined, 30
    Internet Control Message Protocol (ICMP),
        31–32
    Internet Protocol (IP), 30–31
Internet Protocol (IP), 30–31
    load balancers, 513
    MTU, 540
    vulnerabilities, 308
    See also IP addresses; IP addressing; IPv4; IPv6
Internetwork architecture, 156–61
    hierarchical model benefits, 160–61
    model, 156–57
    network hierarchy, 157–58
    router hierarchy, 158–60
Interoperability, 282–87
    ATM, 626
    CBR, 626–27
    CBT, 283
    DVMRP, 283
    IEEE 802.1p and, 591
    MOSPF, 282
    PIM, 282
    RSVP with, 625–26
Interprocess communication (IPC) facility, 23
Intrusion Detection Systems (IDSs), 348–49
    defined, 348
    deployment, 348–49
    examples, 349
    honeypots/burglar alarms, 349
    See also Security
Intrusive load-sharing algorithms, 506–7
IP addresses (official), 68–73
    allocation guidelines, 71–73
    depletion, 69–71
    obtaining, 68–69
    regional registries, 69
IP addressing, 59–82
    ASNs, 81–82
    broadcast classes, 64–66
    implementation, 59–60
    IPng, 74–81
    IPv4, 60–64
    multicast group addresses, 66–68

    official address space, 68–73
    private intranet addressing, 73–74
IP address space, 68
IP forward decision, 169–71
    forwarding algorithm, 169–71
    route lookup, 171
IP Next Generation (IPng). *See* IPv6
IP protocol suite. *See* TCP/IP protocol suite
IPSec, 326, 338, 356–80
    applications, 376–77
    Authentication Header (AH), 362–65
    automatic key management, 357
    concepts and terminology, 358–62
    databases, 360
    defined, 356
    design considerations, 376–80
    development strength, 357
    DS with, 626
    Encapsulating Security Payload (ESP),
        366–69
    end-to-end host security design, 377, 378
    end-to-end security with VPN support design,
        379, 380
    example designs, 377–80
    framework components, 358
    IKE, 371–76
    implementation formats, 357–58
    network administrator and, 257
    protocols, combining, 369–71
    remote access design, 379–80
    Security Association (SA), 358–59
    Security Association (SA) components, 359–60
    support, 356
    transforms, 367
    transport mode, 360–61
    tunnel mode, 361
    VPN support design, 377–79
    See also Security
IP spoofing, 314
IP switching
    defined, 557
    flows and, 557–59
    operation, 558
IPv4
    QoS-related fields, 561

IPv4 *(cont'd.)*
   Type of Service (ToS), 560
   See also Internet Protocol (IP)
IPv4 addresses, 59, 60–64
   Class A, 61, 63
   Class B, 61, 63, 70
   Class C, 61–62, 63, 70–71, 72
   Class D, 62
   Class E, 62
   classes, 60–64
   format, 61
   masks, 62–63
   prefixes, 62–63
   ranges, 63
   special and reserved, 64
IPv5, 74–75
IPv6, 74–81
   address format, 78
   addressing model, 76–80
   address type representation,
      78–80
   anycast addresses, 77
   Class of Service (CoS) model,
      561–62
   defined, 74
   design, 75
   field definitions, 76
   header, 75
   loopback address, 77
   message format, 75–76
   migration to, 80–81
   multicast addresses, 77
   performance, 80
   QoS-related fields, 561
   unicast address, 77
   unspecified address, 77
   See also Internet Protocol (IP)
IS-IS, 175, 176
ISO
   defined, 15
   OSI reference model, 17–19

Keep-alive spoofing, 521–22
Kerberos, 333

Label Distribution Protocol (LDP), 582
Label-Switched Paths (LSPs), 382, 383
   backup, 585
   full, calculating, 584
   partial, calculating, 585
Label switching, 560, 562
   examples, 562
   semantics, 562
   uses, 560
Label Switch Router (LSR), 582, 584
Land attack, 315
LAN QoS features, 587–95
   100BaseVG/IEEE 802.12, 594–95
   Ethernet/IEEE 802.3, 591
   FDDI, 594
   IEEE 802 service model, 587–91
   Token Ring/IEEE 802.5, 591–93
LANs
   failures, 425
   FDDI, 425
   multicast deployment on, 247–49
   resilient, 424–30
   switches, 42, 54
   Token Ring, 425
Large-scale configuration management, 670
Latency, 522
   monitoring, 570
   round-trip, 566
Layer 2 Forwarding (L2F), 353
Layer 2 Tunneling Protocol (L2TP), 353
Leaf network, 267
Least cost routing, 573
Legal addresses. *See* IP addresses (official)
Legal security issues, 319
Lempel-Ziv (LZ) compression, 483
Lightweight Directory Access Protocol (LDAP),
      59, 125, 126–31
   aliases, 130
   clients, 126
   commercial packages, 131
   Data Interchange Format (LDIF), 126
   as de facto standard, 127
   defined, 126
   directory information tree hierarchy, 128

implementations and APIs, 130–31
information model, 128
interaction phases, 126–27
LDAPv2, 127
LDAPv3, 127
naming model, 128–30
referrals, 130
replication, 128
security, 130
servers, 126
standalone, 127
URL, 129
Lightweight Presentation Protocol (LPP), 664
Limited broadcast, 64
Line drivers, 40
Link failure detection, 424
Link Layer Service Access Points (LSAPs), 20
Link Quality Monitoring (LQM), 424
Link-State Advertisements (LSAs), 190, 200
Link-state routing algorithms, 162–65
    convergence, 172
    defined, 162
    distance vector routing vs., 162–65
    drawbacks, 163
    network hierarchy support, 164
    OSPF as, 193
    scalability, 263
    See also Routing protocols
LLC sublayer, 29
Load balancers
    DNS, 507–8
    intelligent, 513
    IP, 513
    nonintelligent, 513
Load Share Network Address Translation
        (LSNAT), 511–12
Load sharing, 474, 503–12
    ARP, 510
    distributed algorithms, 505–6
    DNS, 507–9
    FTP, 509–10
    HTTP, 509
    intrusive algorithms, 506–7
    local algorithms, 504–5

NAT, 511–12
    proxies, 454
    VRRP with, 514–15
Local load-sharing algorithms, 504–5
Local proxy server algorithms, 503, 504
Logic bombs, 346–47
Loopback address, 77
Loss, quantifying, 402

MAC sublayer, 28–29
Maintenance service levels, 434
Management Information Services (MIS),
        633, 663
Manager-of-Manager (MoM) concepts, 678
Man-In-The-Middle attacks, 307
Matrix group, 659
MBone, 283–87
    access, 285
    defined, 283
    distribution threshold, 286
    example applications, 286–87
    modified tunnel topology, 286
    routers and links, 284
    routing, 285–86
    tunnel, 285
Mean Time Between Service Outages (MTBSO),
        412
Mean Time To Repair (MTTR), 412, 413
Media and Storage Extensions (MSE), 544
Media Attachment Units (MAUs), 38–39
    defined, 38
    types of, 39
    See also Hardware
Medium Access Control (MAC) addresses, 19, 31
    mapping multicasts onto, 241
    parts of, 19
    physical, 443
    virtual, 443
Meshing
    internal, 423–24
    point-to-point, 420–22
Metrics
    BGP, 212
    cache performance, 534–35

Metrics *(cont'd.)*
  OSPF, 191
  routing, 166–67
  SLA monitoring, 569–70
MIB, 640–44
  browsers, 670–71
  compiler, 644
  defined, 640
  MIB-I, 642, 643
  MIB-II, 642–43, 680
  RMON, 657–61
  tree hierarchy, 641
  See also SNMP
Microcom Network Protocol (MNP), 484
Microsoft LAN Manager, 674
Mid-Level Manager (MLM) model, 676–77
Midplane design, 457
Mixers, 291, 292
Modems
  access, 313
  defined, 40
  standards, 40
Multicast
  addresses, 77
  AppleTalk, 477–78
  in application optimization, 519–20
  border routers, 283
  deployment issues, 247–52
  distribution, 262–63
  with expanding ring search, 253–54
  group registration, 256–64
  groups, 240–41
  guaranteed delivery, 294
  internetwork topology requirement, 250
  interoperability, 282–87
  leaking in LAN environment, 248
  local area deployment issues, 247–49
  mapping, on MAC addresses, 241
  network design, 239–300
  packets, constraining scope of, 245–46
  with pruning and grafting, 253
  QoS, 294–95
  reliable, 295–98
  routing protocols, 254–56
  with RPF, 252–53

RSVP operations, 612–13
  service management, 298
  sources, 476–78
  spanning tree, 251
  summary, 299–300
  support, 240
  techniques, 252–54
  traffic engineering, 294
  wide area deployment issues, 249–52
Multicast applications
  Berkeley Sockets Multicast API, 244
  design and implementation issues, 245–47
  design guidelines, 243–47
  IP, 244–45
  legacy unicast, enabling, 245
  many-to-many model, 242
  models, 241–43
  one-to-many model, 242
  Open Transport API, 244
  reliable unicast model, 242
  scheduling, 246
  unreliable broadcast model, 242–43
  WinSock API, 244
Multicast BGP (MBGP), 287
Multicast group addresses, 66–68
  host groups, 66–67
  mapping, 68
  well-known, 67
  See also IP addressing
Multicast groups
  joining, 261
  leaving, 261–62
  membership tables, building, 260–61
  registration, 256–64
Multicast OSPF, 272–75
  defined, 272
  design issues, 275
  interoperability, 282
  message formats, 273
  multicast extensions, 272
  operation, 273–75
  routers, 272, 273
Multicast routing, 264–89
  with CBT, 281–82
  with DVMRP, 264–72

interdomain, 287–89
with MOSPF, 272–75
with PIM, 275–81
Multicast Source Discovery Protocol (MSDP), 288
Multicast support protocols, 289–94
RTCP, 292–93
RTP, 289–92
RTSP, 293–94
Multihoming, 215–17
Multi-Link PPP (MLPPP), 168
Multinetting, 220–21
applications, 221
defined, 220
Multipath backplane design, 457
Multiprotocol bridge router, 43–44
MultiProtocol Label Switching (MPLS), 386, 564, 582–87
benefits, 586–87
CBR with, 627
core, 586–87
defined, 573, 574, 582
efficiency, 582
Layer 3 routing, 582
operation, 583–84
performance considerations, 585–86
scalability, 582
summary, 628–29
target deployment, 583
traffic engineering with, 584–85
Murphy's Law, 393

Nagle algorithm, 538–39
Name resolvers, 113–14
Name servers, 112–13
Name-to-address mapping, 105–22
National Bureau of Standards (NBS), 16
NetBios Names Service (NBNS), 121
Netscape/iPlanet Directory Server, 130
Netstat, 690–91
defined, 690
MS-DOS option definitions, 690
using, 690–91
See also Software diagnostic tools
NetView, 637, 674
Network Access Point (NAP), 527, 533

Network addressing models, 14
Network Address Translation (NAT), 74, 133–37
addresses, 135
checksum fixes and, 136
concepts, 135
configuration illustration, 327
DAT, 134
defined, 133
embedded addresses and, 136
IP fragmentation and, 136
issues, 135–36
Load Share (LSNAT), 511–12
load-sharing proxies, 454
modes, 133–34
operation, 133
operations, 135
PAT, 134
performance issues, 136–37
preconfiguration, 327
SAT, 133–34
security issues, 137, 327–28
Network Attached Storage (NAS), 544–45
Network design, 1–2
cut-price, 8
as cyclic process, 3
defined, 1
elements, 2
feedback, 15
good, 1–2
illustrated, 4
implementation, 14–15
information gathering, 10–12
life cycle, 3–5
as living entities, 3
multicast, 239–300
planning, 12–14
process overview, 3–15
reliable, 391–469
requirements, 5–10
resilient, 464–69
secure, 305–87
sequence, 3–4
specifications, 13–14
suboptimal, 8

Networked system availability, 414–16
    in parallel, 415
    in parallel and in series, 416
    in series, 414–15
Network File System (NFS), 35–36, 520
Network Information Center (NIC), 106
Network Information Service (NIS), 117, 122
Network Interface Cards (NICs), 431, 589
Network Layer
    OSI reference model, 18
    TCP/IP protocol suite, 27
Network management, 633–708
    accounting management, 636
    categories, 635–36
    CMIS/CMIP, 661–67
    configuration management, 635, 667–70
    element, 675
    fault management, 636
    frameworks, 672–74
    hierarchical, 675–77
    implementation models, 675–78
    implementations, 670–75
    in-band, 677–78
    as key concern, 633
    NMS, 634–37
    out-of-band, 677–78
    performance management, 635–36
    platforms, 670–75
    policy-based, 699–707
    RMON, 655–61
    security management, 636
    SNMP, 636, 637–55
    station, 636
    summary, 707–8
    technologies, 634–78
    troubleshooting tools, 679–99
    vendor products, 672
Network management system (NMS), 36, 634–37
    defined, 634
    event logs, 679
    GUI, 634, 635
    monitoring, 679
    network map, 634, 679
    polling agents, 652
    using, 679–80

Network News Transport Protocol (NNTP), 526
Networks
    cost, 9
    high-availability (HA), 391–92
    LAN, 424–30
    leaf, 267
    NBMA, 66, 87, 200–201, 249
    nonleaf, 267
    optimization, 471–548
    OSN, 400
    OSPF, 193
    SAN, 400
    star, 418–20
    VPN, 349–56, 380–86
    WAN, 418–24
Network Service Access Points (NSAPs), 20
Noise, 461
NonBroadcast MultiAccess (NBMA) networks
    adjacencies on, 200–201
    ARP on, 87
    multicast deployment issues, 249
    scalability in, 66
Nonleaf network, 267
Nonrepudiation, 306
Non-volatile RAM (NVRAM), 463
Novell Directory Services (NDS), 130
Nslookup, 693–94

One-Time Passwords (OTPs), 330
Open Shortest Path First. See OSPF
Open Transport API, 244
Operating systems
    fault-tolerant systems, 438
    router, 235
    vulnerability, 312
Optical Service Providers (OSPs), 546
Optical Storage Networks (OSNs), 400, 546
    defined, 546
    DWDM technology, 546
Optimization, 471–548
    application, 519–35
    bandwidth, 472–87
    load-splitting/load-sharing, 502–19
    protocol, 536–41
    route, 580–82

routing, 473–74
storage, 542–46
summary, 547–48
system-level traffic, 487–502
OSI
Connection-Oriented Transport Service
(COTS), 662, 664
directory service standard, 125–26
Management Information Service (MIS), 663
management structure, 663
OSI reference model, 17–19
Application Layer, 17
Data Link Layer, 18
defined, 17
illustrated, 17
IP and, 26–28
Network Layer, 18
Physical Layer, 18
in practice, 19
Presentation Layer, 18
Session Layer, 18
Transport Layer, 18
OSPF, 175–76, 187–204
addressing model, 202–3
adjacencies, 198–200
adjacencies on NBMA, 200–201
areas, 195–96
backbone, 196–97
background, 187
characteristics, 187
convergence, 202
defined, 187
deployment, 176
designated router, 201–2
EGP choice, 204
EIGRP vs., 177
field definitions, 188–90
full-mesh peering, 201
header formats, 188
hello packet, 189
hierarchical internetwork, 194
hierarchy and route summarization, 203
as link-state protocol, 193
LSAs, 190
message authentication, 192–93

metrics, 191
Multicast, 272–75
neighbor acquisition, 198
networks, 193
operation, 193–204
packet formats, 187–93
protocol stack, 193
routing hierarchy, 194–95
routing information, 197–98
routing resources/bandwidth partitioning,
203
scalability, 202–3
timers, 191–92
variable-length packets, 189
virtual links, 197
VLSM support, 192
Out-of-band management, 677–78
Output queuing, 233
Overlay model, 380–81

Packet(s)
classifier, 556–57, 600
delay, 604
loss, 566
scheduler, 557, 600
size, 536
switch evolution, 227–28
Packet-filtering routers, 340–42
features, 340
information examined by, 340
problems, 341–42
rules, 341
Packet filters, 479–82
area and network, 481
capabilities, 479
defined, 479
examples, 479–81
issues, 481–82
lack of management, 481
Layer 2 type, 479–80
planning and transparency, 482
processing overhead, 481
security, 481
service type, 480–81
statelessness, 481

Packet switching, 52–53
  circuit switching vs., 52–53
  defined, 52
Passive backplane design, 457
Password Authentication Protocol (PAP), 330
Passwords
  aging, 330
  guessing attacks, 307
  one-time, 330
  static, 330
Path MTU Discovery (PMTUD), 540–41
Paths
  best, choosing, 168–69
  multipath, 167–68
  selection, 167–69
  single, 167–68
  See also Routing
Peer model, 381
Performance
  broadcast, 66
  characterizing, 3
  CMIP, 666
  DNS, 120–21
  IKE, 375
  Integrated Services (IS), 617
  IPv6, 80
  management, 635–36
  NAT, 136–37
  network, 2–3
  RIP, 185
  SNMP, 653–54
  VPN, 384–85
Per Hop Behavior (PHB), 619–20
  consistency, 620
  default, 620
  defined, 619
  standard, 620
  See also Differentiated Services (DS)
Peripheral switching, 460
Personal firewalls, 345
Phasing, requirements, 6–8
Physical Layer
  OSI reference model, 18
  TCP/IP protocol suite, 27
Pilot test, 14

PIM, 275–81
  defined, 275–76
  dense-mode, 276–78
  design issues, 280–81
  development, 276
  interoperability, 282
  mixed-mode, 280
  RP configuration, 280
  RP performance consideration, 280–81
  sparse-mode, 278–80
  See also Multicast routing
Ping, 682–87
  BSD UNIX option definitions, 684–85
  defined, 682
  MS-DOS option definitions, 683–84
  operations, 682–83
  options, 683–85
  potential problems, 686–87
  problems when using, 683
  uses, 682
  using, 685–86
  See also Software diagnostic tools
Ping of death, 315
Ping sweep, 315
Planning
  brainstorming and, 13
  design, 12–14
  documentation and, 13–14
  technology choices and, 12–13
Point-to-point meshing, 420–22
Point-to-Point Protocol (PPP), 326
Point-to-Point Tunneling Protocol (PPTP), 353
Policy
  clients, 704
  console, 702–3
  default QoS, 702
  default routing, 703
  default security, 702
  defined, 700–701
  distribution, 704–5
  peripherals, 702
  profiles, 706
  repository, 703
  security, 316–19
  servers, 703–4

Policy-based management, 699–707, 708
   benefits, 70, 700
   components, 702–5
   COPS, 705
   defined, 700
   deployment illustration, 701
   design and implementation issues, 706–7
   services, 701
   vendors, 707
   See also Network management
Policy-Based Routing (PBR), 576–78
   defined, 574, 576
   implementations, 577
   policies, 577
   router behavior and, 578
Port Address Translation (PAT), 134
Port hashing techniques, 515–19
Power
   faults, 460
   fault-tolerance approaches, 461–62
   multiple, supplies, 462–63
   reliability, 460–63
   sags, 460
   spikes, 461
   surges, 460
Presentation Layer (OSI reference model), 18
Pretty Good Privacy (PGP), 337
Priority queuing, 494–95
   defined, 494
   illustrated, 494
   uses, 495
Private intranet addressing, 73–74
   migration to public network access, 74
   registered private addresses, 73–74
Proprietary header compression, 485
Protocol analyzers, 694–96
   defined, 694
   examples, 694–95
   expert, 694
   illustrated example, 695
   performance parameters, 696
Protocol-based security services, 334–38
   IPSec, 338
   PGP, 337
   SET, 338

S-HTTP, 336
S-MIME, 337
SSH, 336–37
SSL, 334–36
See also Security
Protocol-Independent Multicast. *See* PIM
Protocol optimization, 536–41
   fragmentation, 537
   frame/packet size, 536
   TCP/IP tuning, 538–41
   window sizes, 537–38
Protocols, 24–37
   ARP, 83–91
   BGMP, 288
   BGP, 205–19
   boot, 475
   BOOTP, 92–95
   CHAP, 330–31
   CMOL, 664
   CMOT, 664
   COPS, 705
   DHCP, 95–102
   DVMRP, 264–72
   EIGRP, 175, 176–77
   GRE, 353, 356
   HSRP, 439, 452–54
   ICMP, 31, 102–5, 447
   IGMP, 239, 256–61
   IIOP, 24
   IKE, 371–76
   IKMP, 371
   IP protocol suite, 25–37
   IS-IS, 175, 176
   L2F, 353
   L2TP, 353
   LDAP, 59, 125, 126–31, 130–31
   LDP, 582
   LPP, 664
   MBGP, 287
   MSDP, 288
   OSPF, 175–76, 187–204
   PAP, 330
   PPP, 326
   PPTP, 353
   RAMP, 297

Protocols *(cont'd.)*
  RARP, 90–91
  RIP, 175, 177–87
  RSVP, 563, 604–16
  RTCP, 292–93
  RTP, 289–92
  RTSP, 293–94
  SCCP, 298
  SDAP, 298
  SIP, 298
  SKIP, 331
  SNMP, 636, 637–55
  SSL, 326, 334–36
  TFTP, 34–35, 310
  types of, 24
  unnecessary, disabling, 475–76
  VRRP, 439, 442–52
  vulnerability, 308–12
  WCCP, 531
Proxies, 342–43
Proxy ARP, 88–90
  applications, 88
  defined, 88
  illustrated example applications, 89
  issues, 90
  See also Address Resolution Protocol (ARP)
Proxy server techniques, 454–55
Proxy services, 520–22
  benefits, 520
  examples, 520–22
  keep-alive spoofing, 521–22
  routing announcements, 521
  service announcements, 520–21
Pruning and grafting, 253, 269–71
Public Key Infrastructure (PKI), 322–26
  applications, 326
  architectural model, 323
  caching and, 526
  Certificate Authorities (CAs), 324–25
  Certificate Repositories (CRs), 325
  Certificate Revocation Lists (CRLs),
    325–26
  defined, 322
  digital signatures, 324
  Registration Authorities (RAs), 325

  services, 322
  X.509 digital certificates, 323–24
Pulse Code Modulation (PCM), 52

QoS-Based Routing (QBR), 574, 575–76
  defined, 574, 575
  issues, 576
  models, 575
  objectives, 575–76
Quality of Service (QoS), 551–629
  features supported by leading network vendors,
    565
  importance, 551
  integrated, 623–27
  integrated services/RSVP model, 562–63
  label switching model, 562
  LAN features, 587–95
  models, 553–71
  multicast, 294–95
  policy, 702
  policy management, 627
  relative priority marking/differentiated services
    model, 563–64
  requirements, mapping, 552
  service marking model, 560–62
  SLAs, 565–71
  summary, 627–29
  traffic engineering and, 571–87
  from user perspective, 552
  vendor approaches, 564–65
  WAN features, 595–98
Queuing
  CBQ, 497–99
  custom, 495–96
  discipline classification, 492
  FIFO, 493–94
  priority, 494–95
  strategies, 491, 492
  WFQ, 496–97
  See also Scheduling

Random Early Detection (RED), 499, 500–502
  defined, 500
  gateway, 501
  implementation, 502

operation, 501–2
queue length thresholds, 501
variations, 502
Real-Time Control Protocol (RTCP), 292–93
defined, 292
functions, 292–93
Real-Time Protocol (RTP), 289–92
as best-effort protocol, 290
defined, 289
header, 290
implementations, 289
mixers, 291, 292
sessions, 290
simultaneous data transfer support, 289
translators, 291–92
Real-Time Streaming Protocol (RTSP), 293–94
caching and, 526
defined, 293
as framework, 293
RTP and, 293, 294
Received interface, 267
Recovery
disaster, 394, 398–401
times, determining, 408
Redistribution, route, 222–23
Redundant Array of Inexpensive Disks (RAID),
459–60
defined, 459
levels, 459
peripheral switching, 460
Redundant Link Management (RLM), 427–29
defined, 427
drawbacks, 429
illustrated, 429
implementation, 427
traffic, 428
Registered private addresses, 73–74
Registration Authorities (RAs), 325
Relational Database Management Systems
(RDBMSs)
directories and, 123–24
report-generation tools, 125
Relative priority-marking model, 563
Reliability, 413–14
defined, 413

improving, 432
power, 460–63
Reliable Adaptive Multicast Protocol
(RAMP), 297
Reliable multicast, 295–98
congestion control, 295
current status, 297–98
design issues, 296–97
framework (RMF), 297
requirements, 295–96
scalability, 295
security, 295–96
timely error detection, 296
Reliable Multicast Congestion Control (RMCC),
297
Reliable network design, 391–469
component-level availability, 456–64
failure planning, 393–416
fault-tolerance, 436–42
resilience, 416–32, 464–69
summary, 469
See also Network design
Remote Authentication Dial-In User Service
(RADIUS), 332
Remote Execution Protocol (REXEC), 35
Remote Network Monitoring (RMON), 655–61,
707
agents, 656
defined, 655
implementation costs, 656
MIB groups, 657–61
MIBs, 657
operation, 656–57
preemptive monitoring, 657
RMONv1, 656
RMONv2, 656
summary, 661
See also Network management
Remote Procedure Call (RPC), 35
Remote proxy server algorithms, 503, 504
Remote shell, 35
Repeaters, 39–40
buffered, 39
as commodity item, 39–40
defined, 39

Repeaters *(cont'd.)*
  examples, 39
  topological control with, 427–29
Request for Information (RFI), 7
Request for Proposals (RFP), 7
Requirements
  analysis, 10
  assessing, 9–10
  designing, 8–9
  desirable, 9
  end users and, 5–6
  establishing, 5–10
  highly desirable, 9
  mandatory, 9
  phasing, 6–8
  prioritizing, 9
  rolling process of, 5
  translating, 6
  See also Network design
Resilience, 416–32
  fault-tolerance architecture, 437
  features, 14
  hub, 466
  switched service, 423–24
  topological, 416–18
Resilient end-system topologies,
      430–32
  backup power and media, 431
  desktop management, 431–32
  dual NICs, 431
  dual port transceivers, 430–31
  multiple network points, 430
Resilient LANs, 424–30
  backbone design, 425–26
  with repeaters, 427–29
  with routers, 426–27
  segmentation, 429–30
  with switches and bridges, 427
  topological control, 426–29
Resilient network design, 464–69
  backbone, 465
  building, 466–67
  floor, 467–68
  testing, 468–69
  See also Network design

Resilient WANs, 418–24
  dial backup/top-up links, 420
  internal meshing, 423–24
  link failure detection, 424
  point-to-point meshing, 420–22
  point-to-point star network, 418–20
Resource Reservation Protocol (RSVP),
      563, 604–16
  admission control, 625
  Application Programming Interface (RAPI),
      615
  behavior with multicast flows, 614
  CBR with, 626–27
  common header, 606
  common header field definitions, 606–7
  defined, 604
  design, 604–5
  with DS, 614–15
  end-to-end support, 616
  field definitions, 607–9
  Fixed-Filter (FF), 614
  with IEEE 802.1p, 625–26
  IS use of, 598–99
  message format, 606–9
  multicast operations, 612–13
  object header, 606
  operation, 609–13
  path definition process, 610
  path setup, reservation, teardown,
      609–12
  process, 611
  requests, 605
  reservation style, 613–15
  rev message flow, 611
  router, 609, 610
  sender, 609
  sessions, 605
  Shared-Explicit (SE), 614
  summary, 629
  teardown messages, 612
  tearing down paths, 612
  Wildcard-Filter (WF), 614
Reverse ARP (RARP), 90–91
  Dynamic (DRARP), 90–91
  servers, 90

uses, 90
See also Address Resolution Protocol (ARP)
Reverse path forwarding (RPF), 252–53
RIP, 175, 177–87
    active, 184
    addressing, 182
    authentication, 181–82
    background, 177
    defined, 175, 177
    demand circuits, 185–86
    distance-vector routing enhancements, 186–87
    enhancements, 184
    handling new subnet mask information, 181
    issues, 184
    operation, 182–87
    packet formats, 178–82
    passive, 184
    performance, 185
    protocol stack, 177
    RIPv1 header format, 178
    RIPv1/RIPv2 compatibility, 186
    RIPv1 routing entries, 178, 179–80
    RIPv1 routing entry definitions, 178–79
    RIPv1 routing update message, 180
    RIPv2 authentication format, 182
    RIPv2 routing entry definitions, 180–81
    RIPv2 routing entry format, 181
    routing algorithm, 182–83
    routing tables, 183–84
    scalability, 185
    timers, 184
    uses, 175
Risk, quantifying, 405–8
Risk analysis, 317
    with ALE, 406–8
    defined, 401
    issues, 402–3
    weighted, 406
Risk management, 408–10
    approaches, 409–10
    as compromise, 408–9
    defined, 401
RMON MIB groups, 657–61
    alarm group, 660
    capture group, 660

    defined, 657–58
    event group, 660–61
    filter group, 659
    history group, 659
    host group, 659
    Host TopN group, 659
    matrix group, 659
    statistics group, 658–59
    See also Remote Network Monitoring (RMON)
Root-Addressed Multicast Architecture (RAMA), 288–89
Round-Trip Time (RTT), 520
Route lookup, 233–34
    avoiding, 234
    defined, 233
    performance, improving, 233–34
Router addressing, 219–22
    broadcast forwarding, 221
    multinetting, 220–21
    route summarization, 222
    unnumbered links, 219–20
Route redistribution, 222–23
Routers, 42–45, 54–55
    access, 226
    advantages, 49–50
    applications, 224–26
    architecture, 226–34
    backbone, 194, 224–25
    benefits, 49–50
    BGP, 207
    capabilities, 49
    defined, 42–43
    designated, 201–2
    DVMRP, 268, 271
    dynamic discovery, 174
    enterprise, 225
    hierarchy, 158–60
    hybrid multiprotocol, 54
    integrated bridge, 44–45
    interface modules, 229–30
    issues, 50
    MBone, 284
    misconfigurations, 160
    multicast border, 283
    Multicast OSPF, 272, 273

Routers *(cont'd.)*
  multiprotocol bridge, 43–44
  operating systems, 235
  operations, 223–24
  packet-filtering, 340–42
  packet switch evolution, 227–28
  routing processor, 228–29
  RSVP, 609, 610
  scheduling techniques, 235
  switch design issues, 232–34
  switching fabric, 230–32
  topological control with, 426–27
  troubleshooting features, 680–81
  upstream, 267
  virtual, 443
  VRRP, 443
Routing
  announcements, 521
  architecture, 156–57
  CBR, 574, 578–82
  CIDR, 145–48
  convergence, 172
  DDR, 420
  design issues, 165–77
  direct interface entries, 166
  dynamic entries, 166
  end-system, 172–74
  entry types, 166
  forwarding decision, 169–71
  granularity, 578, 579
  hierarchical, 148, 149, 160–61
  information maintenance, 223
  inter-AS, 210
  interdomain, 282–89
  intra-AS, 210
  Layer 3, 582
  least cost, 573
  levels, 158–59
  MBone, 285–86
  metrics, 166–67
  multicast, 264–89
  optimization, 474
  pass-through AS, 210
  path selection, 167–69
  PBR, 574, 576–78

policy, 703
  protocol classes, 159
  QBR, 574, 575–76
  static entries, 166
  strategy, choosing, 174–77
  technology, 155–236
  Type of Service (TOS)-based, 162
  VPN, 382
Routing Information Protocol. *See* RIP
Routing processors, 228–29
  configurations, 228
  coprocessors, 229
  multiprocessors, 229
  single, 228
  subsidiary, 228–29
Routing protocols, 161–65
  BGP, 205–19
  classification of, 165
  convergence, 172
  distance-vector, 161–65
  DUAL, 164–65
  legacy, 476
  link-state, 162–65
  multicast, 254–56
  OSPF, 175, 176, 187–204
  RIP, 175, 177–87
  selection, 473
Routing tables, 165
  creation of, 170
  RIP, 183–84
  size, 580
  structure, 580
Run-Length Encoding (RLE), 483–84

Scalability
  BGP, 213
  caching and, 523, 525
  configuration management and, 667
  fault-tolerant systems, 435, 438
  high-availability (HA) systems, 435
  Integrated Services (IS), 616
  for large-scale internetworks, 58
  link-state protocols, 163
  multicast, 295
  MultiProtocol Label Switching (MPLS), 582

in NonBroadcast MultiAccess (NBMA)
    networks, 66
OSPF, 202–3
PIM-SM, 281
RIP, 185
VPN, 385–86
VRRP, 451
Scheduling
    Class-Based Queuing (CBQ), 497–99
    custom queuing, 495–96
    FIFO queuing, 493–94
    priority queuing, 494–95
    techniques, 235, 491–99
    Weighted Fair Queuing (WFQ), 496–97
    Weighted Round Robin (WRR), 496
    See also Traffic engineering
Secure Electronic Transaction (SET), 326, 338
Secure HTTP (S-HTTP), 336
Secure Multipurpose Internet Mail Extensions
    (S/MIME), 326, 337
Secure Sockets Layer (SSL), 326, 334–36
    defined, 334
    operation, 334–35
    phases, 335–36
    security services, 334
    sessions, 335
Security, 305–87
    AAA services, 328–33
    access control, 306
    as addressing model guideline, 133
    attacks, 307
    authentication, 306
    confidentiality, 306
    cryptography, 320–22
    driving forces/issues, 306–16
    e-commerce, 377
    e-mail protection systems, 348
    feature documentation, 14
    firewalls, 338–46
    functions, 306
    integrity, 306
    Intrusion Detection Systems (IDSs), 348–49
    IPSec, 356–80
    LDAP, 130
    management, 636

multicast, 295–96
NAT, 137, 327–28
nonrepudiation, 306
PKI, 322–26
policy, 702
protocol-based services, 334–38
RIPv2, 181–82
as risk management, 305
SNMP, 650–52
solutions and features, 318
summary, 386–87
technology and solutions, 319–53
URL protection systems, 347–48
virus protection systems, 346–47
VPNs, 349–56, 380–86
Security Associations (SAs), 358–59
    automated negotiation of, 371
    bundles, 369–71
    components, 359–60
    defined, 358
    illustrated, 359
    initializing, for data transfer, 375
    initializing, with IKE, 373–74
    iterated tunneling, 370
    sequence, 369
    transport adjacency, 370
    transport mode, 360–61
    tunnel mode, 361
    See also IPSec
Security policy
    components, 316–17
    developing, 316–19
    implementation, 317–19
    legal issues, 319
    risk analysis, 317
Segmentation, 429–30
Server mirroring, 399, 440–41
Server Side Include (SSI), 311
Service announcements, 520–21
Service classes, 602–4
    controlled load service, 602–3
    guaranteed service, 603–4
Service-Level Agreements (SLAs), 551, 559,
    565–71, 627–28
    challenging, 571

Service-Level Agreements (SLAs) *(cont'd.)*
    defined, 565
    dynamic, 565
    end-to-end, 567
    guarantees, 566
    monitoring, 567–70
    packet loss, 566
    round-trip latency, 566
    static, 565
    vendors, 571
    See also Quality of Service (QoS)
Service marking, 560–62, 618–19
    field definitions, 618–19
    simple model, 560–61
Service-Specific Connection-Oriented Protocol
        (SSCOP), 597
Session Description Protocol (SIP), 298
Session Directory Announcement Protocol
        (SDAP), 298
Session Layer (OSI reference model), 18
Sessions, 601, 605
Shared memory, 233
Shared-memory fabric, 230
Shortest-distance path, 581
Shortest-widest path, 581
Simple Conference Control Protocol
        (SCCP), 298
Simple Gateway Management Protocol (SGMP),
        637
Simple Key Management Protocol for IP (SKIP),
        331
Simple Mail Transfer Protocol (SMTP)
    defined, 36
    vulnerabilities, 310
Simple Network Management Protocol.
        See SNMP
Single Loss Expectancy (SLE), 406, 407
Single Point of Failure (SPOF), 393, 403–5
SLA monitoring, 567–70
    circuit error rates, 570
    circuit stability, 570
    data capture/storage, 569
    data collection models, 568
    diagnostic features, 569
    external data feeds, 568

    metrics, 569–70
    network availability, 570
    network latency, 570
    predictive features, 568–69
    reporting features, 569
    throughput, 570
    tool features, 568–69
    traffic shaping, 569
    WAN interfaces, 568
    See also Service-Level Agreements (SLAs)
SMDS, 595–96
Smurf, 315
SNMP, 636, 637–55, 707
    advantages, 637, 654–55
    agent, 644
    application-wide type support, 639–40
    architecture, 638–44
    background, 637–38
    defined, 36, 637
    disadvantages, 655
    GetBulkRequests, 647
    GetNextRequests, 647, 648–50
    GetRequests, 647
    HP++ browser tool, 671
    Inform, 647
    message structure, 645–46
    MIB, 640–44
    over UDP, 653
    PDU, 646
    performance issues, 653–54
    porting, 644–45
    protocol stack, 645
    resilience, 652–55
    security, 650–52
    service primitives, 646–50
    SetRequests, 647
    SMI, 638–40
    SNMPv1, 648, 650
    SNMPv2, 650, 651–52
    SNMPv3, 652
    support, 638
    table traversal, 648–50
    transport independence, 644
    Trap PDUs, 646
    Traps, 647–48

version coexistence, 652
See also Network management
SOCKS, 343–44
   defined, 343
   operation, 343–44
   SOCKSv5, 344
Software compression, 486
Software diagnostic tools, 681–94
   dig, 693–94
   netstat, 690–91
   nslookup, 693–94
   ping, 682–87
   tcpdump, 691–93
   traceroute, 687–90
   types of, 681–82
   See also Troubleshooting tools
Source domains, 623
Spanning Trees, 579
Sparse distribution model, 255
Sparse-mode PIM (PIM-SM), 278–80
   conditions for use, 278
   defined, 278
   illustrated, 279
   operations, 278–80
   PM-DM vs., 280
   scalability, 281
   See also PIM
Split DNS, 119
SSH, 336–37
Stac LZS compression, 485–86
Standalone LDAP (SLDAP), 127
Standalone servers, 706
Standards organization, 15–16
   ANSI, 16
   ECMA, 16
   EIA, 16
   IAB, 15–16
   IEEE, 16
   ISO, 15, 17–19
   ITU-T, 16
   NBS, 16
Standby modules, 463–64
Star topology, 418–20
   fault tolerance improvement, 419–20
   illustrated, 419

Stateful firewalls, 344–45
Static Address Translation (SAT), 133–34
Static passwords, 330
Static routing entries, 166
Statistics group, 658–59
Storage Area Networks (SANs), 400
Storage Attached Networks (SANs), 545
Storage optimization, 542–46
   disk compression, 542–43
   HSM, 543–44
   NAS/SAN strategies, 544–46
   OSN, 546
Storage Service Providers (SSPs), 400, 546
Structure of Management Information (SMI),
      638–40
   Basic Encoding Rules (BER), 639
   defined, 638
   encoding rules, 638
   See also SNMP
Subnet broadcast, 65
Subnetting, 137–45
   bit-wise, 138
   class B example, 141
   class C example, 140
   defined, 137
   VLSM, 138
   VLSM with class B example, 141–45
Switches
   ATM, 42
   benefits, 429–30
   defined, 42
   LAN, 42, 54
   Layer 2, 429
   Layer 4, 531
   multicast-aware, 248
   topological control with, 427
Switching, 52–53
   circuit, 52
   IP, 557–59
   label, 560, 562
   packet, 52–53
   peripheral, 460
   tag, 559
Switching fabric, 230–32
   ATM-like, 232

Switching fabric *(cont'd.)*
  bus, 230
  crossbar, 230–31
  defined, 230
  hybrid media, 231
  shared-memory, 230
  See also Routers
SYN attack, 314–15
Synchronization, 524
Synchronous traffic, 594
Systems Management Application Entity (SMAE), 663

Tag switching, 559
Taildrop, 500
Tcpdump, 691–93
  defined, 691
  potential problems, 693
  using, 692–93
  See also Software diagnostic tools
TCP/IP applications, 34–37
  DNS, 36
  FTP, 34
  NFS, 35–36
  remote shell, 35
  REXEC, 35
  RPC, 35
  SMTP, 36
  SNMP, 36
  Telnet, 34
  TFTP, 34–35
  X Windows, 36
TCP/IP protocol suite, 25–37
  adoption of, 25
  Application Layer, 27
  Data Link layer, 27, 28–29
  defined, 26
  Internet Layer, 30–32
  IP MTU, 540
  Network Layer, 27
  performance factors, 538–39
  Physical Layer, 27
  PMTUD, 540–41
  TCP MSS, 540
  TCP window size, 541

Transport Layer, 27, 32–34
  tunable parameters, 539–41
  tuning, 538–41
Teardrop, 315–16
Technology
  choices, 12–13
  phased implementation, 14–15
Telnet, 34, 309
Terminal Access Controller Access Control System (TACACS), 332–33
  extended (XTACACS), 333
  TACACS+, 333
Third-party trust vulnerabilities, 312–13
Timers
  DVMRP, 267
  IGMP, 258–59
  OSPF, 191–92
  RIP, 184
Time to Live (TTL), 243, 263
Token bucket, 489–91
  defined, 489–90
  scheme illustration, 490
  system parameters, 490
  See also Traffic shaping
Token cards, 331
Token Ring, 86, 591–93
  capabilities, 593
  characteristics, 592
  defined, 591–92
  IEEE 802.5, 591–93
  station, 592
  user priority, 593
Topological resilience, 416–18
Traceroute, 687–90
  bottom line, 690
  defined, 687
  option definitions, 688–89
  options, 688–89
  potential problems, 689–90
  recording example, 688
  reporting syntax, 688
  See also Software diagnostic tools
Traffic
  asynchronous, 594
  broadcast, reducing, 476–78

differentiation, 553–60
matrix, 573
measurement on backbones, 572–73
synchronous, 594
unwanted, eliminating, 474–87
Traffic conditioner, 621–22
classifier, 621
illustrated, 621
marker, 621
meter, 621
shaper/dropper, 622
use of, 622
See also Differentiated Services (DS)
Traffic Conditioning Agreement (TCA), 622
Traffic engineering, 294, 487–502, 572–74
CBR, 574, 578–82
congestion avoidance, 499–502
conservation law, 487–88
defined, 487
least cost routing, 573
MPLS, 574, 582–87
on backbones, 572–73
PBR, 574, 576–78
with policy/QoS constraints, 571–87
QBR, 574, 575–76
scheduling techniques, 491–99
shaping techniques, 488–91
techniques, 574
Traffic shaping, 488–91
defined, 488
examples, 498
functionality, 489
IS, 602
SLA monitoring and, 569
techniques, 488–91
token bucket, 489–91
uses, 489
See also Traffic engineering
Transforms, 367
Transit Routing Domains (TRDs), 146
Translation Bridging, 41
Translators, 291–92
Transmission Control Protocol (TCP), 33–34
defined, 33
as end-to-end protocol, 34

header compression, 484
Maximum Segment Size (MSS), 540
message format, 33
Nagle algorithm, 538–39
packet loss and, 539
session use, 507
sliding window algorithm, 538
slow-start algorithm, 538
three-way handshake, 538
vulnerabilities, 308–9
window size, 541
See also TCP/IP protocol suite
Transport Layer (OSI reference model), 18
Transport Layer (TCP/IP protocol suite)
defined, 27
TCP, 33–34
UDP, 32–33
Transport Service Access Points (TSAPs), 20
Triple-Modular Redundancy (TMR), 436
Trivial File Transfer Protocol (TFTP),
    34–35
characteristics, 35
defined, 34
vulnerabilities, 310
Trojan Horses, 346
Troubleshooting tools, 679–99, 708
advanced diagnostic, 694–98
NMS, 679–80
router features, 680–81
selecting, 698–99
software diagnostic, 681–94
Tuning, 473
Tunneling, 224
DVMRP, 271–72
iterated, 370
MBone, 283–87
Type of Service (TOS)-based routing, 162

Unicast addresses, 77
Uninterruptible Power Supply (UPS), 462
Unnumbered links, 219–20
Unspecified address, 77
Upstream interface, 266
Upstream router, 267
URL protection systems, 347–48

User Datagram Protocol (UDP), 32–33
  defined, 32
  DHCP running over, 101
  DNS running over, 110
  header format, 32
  session use, 507
  SNMP running over, 36, 653
  vulnerabilities, 308
User Priority Value (UPV), 587

Variable-Length Subnet Masks (VLSM), 138
  with class B example, 141–45
  defined, 138
  OSPF support, 192
  routing protocols supporting, 150
Vendor management products, 672
Virtual links, 197
Virtual Private Networks (VPNs), 224, 313, 552
  address transparency and, 352
  architectures, 353–56
  connections, 350
  dedicated, 352, 356
  defined, 349
  deployment over Internet, 351
  designing, 380–86
  design models, 380–81
  dial, 351, 353–55
  firewall interaction, 382–84
  fragmentation, 385
  headers, 385
  illustrated, 350
  issues with, 352–53
  management/maintenance and, 353
  MPLS-based backbones, 386
  overlay model, 380–81
  peer model, 381
  performance, 384–85
  protocol encapsulation and, 352
  reliability and, 353
  routing, 382
  scalability and management, 385–86
  security and, 352–53
  types of, 351–52
Virtual router, 443

Virtual Router Redundancy Protocol (VRRP), 91,
        439, 442–52
  address seeding, 447
  advertisements, 446
  ARP interaction, 448
  backup routers, 446
  backward compatibility, 451–52
  clustering, 442
  configuration with LAN and WAN interfaces,
        451
  configuration with resilience for high-speed
        server form, 449
  convergence speed, 452
  defined, 442
  definitions, 442–43
  duplicate packets and, 452
  example design, 448–50
  field definitions, 444–45
  HSRP vs., 453–54
  ICMP echo interaction, 447
  ICMP redirects, 447
  issues, 450–52
  as LAN-based protocol, 443
  with load sharing, 514–15
  master election process, 445–46
  operation, 445–50
  packet format, 444–45
  routers, 443
  routing problems, 450
  scalability, 451
  topological knowledge, 450
  use of, 442
  virtual groups, 446
Viruses, 307
  defined, 307, 346
  protection systems, 346–47
  types, 346–47
Vulnerabilities
  application/protocol, 308–12
  DNS, 310–11
  FTP, 309
  HTTP, 310
  ICMP, 308
  IP, 308

operating system, 312
SMTP, 310
SSI, 311
TCP, 308–9
Telnet, 309
TFTP, 310
third-party trust, 312–13
UDP, 308

WAN QoS features, 595–98
ATM, 597–98
Frame Relay, 596–97
SMDS, 595–96
WANs
interfaces, 568
resilient, 418–24
Wavelength Division Multiplexing (WDM), 551
Web-based configuration management, 669–70

Weighted Fair Queuing (WFQ), 496–97, 565
algorithm, 497
defined, 496
goals, 496
response times and, 497
round-trip delay predication, 497
Weighted Random Early Discard (WRED), 502
Weighted Round Robin (WRR), 496
Well-known attacks, 313–16
Widest-shortest path, 581
Windows Internet Name Service (WINS), 121
Window sizes, 537–38
WinNuke, 316
WinSock API, 244, 615, 616
Worms, 346

X.509 digital certificates, 323–24
X Windows system, 36

Data Networks